x

th Finch
a
aphy, Inc.

tion, Inc.

Marcy P. Driscoll.—3rd ed.

index.

ive learning theory.   I. Title.

2004050373

rn; p. 190, Corbis-Bettmann; and p. 278,

Senior Editor: *Arnis Burvikovs*
Series Editorial Assistant: *Megan Smallidg*
Marketing Manager: *Tara Whorf*
Composition and Prepress Buyer: *Linda (*
Manufacturing Buyer: *Andrew Turso*
Cover Administrator: *Linda Knowles*
Editorial-Production Coordinator: *Mary*
Editorial-Production Service: *Barbara Gr*
Electronic Composition: *Omegatype Typo*

Library of Congress-in-Publication Data
Driscoll, Marcy Perkins.
   Psychology of learning for instruction
       p.   cm
   Includes bibliographical references an
   ISBN: 0-205-37519-7
   1. Learning, Psychology of.   2. Cogn

   LB 1060.D75 2005
   370.15'23—dc22

Printed in the United States of America

10   9   8   7   6   5   4   —   08   07   0

Photo Credits: pp. 33, 228, 246, Lyrl Ah
Martin M. Rotker/Photo Researchers.

To Robin
More than ever

Contents

Preface

Although this third edition of *Psychology of Learning for Instruction* is now written, the work on any book is never truly finished because there is always something that can still be updated, reshaped, or revised. I have struggled not only with finding enough time to write, but also with what changes are most important to incorporate into this edition. I sincerely hope that I have succeeded in this effort to bring you a text that is current and interesting.

As an instructor of advanced undergraduate and beginning graduate students in education, I have found most other books on learning theory to be unsatisfactory for my purposes. Many texts focus too much on psychology and not enough on education. Others include either too many theories, which are historically important but not especially relevant to instruction, or only one theory, usually the currently predominating one. Still others illustrate learning theory only as it can be applied in teaching, to the exclusion of other contexts in which learning and instruction routinely occur. Although many of my students *are* teachers (or are in training to become teachers), many are also instructional designers, media specialists, counselors, administrators, and adult educators. They typically do not have much background in psychology, and their concerns are largely applied. In writing this book, I took those things into consideration.

This is a book that focuses on learning *and* instruction. Specific implications and applications of learning theories are discussed. Examples are drawn from educational situations and educational problems. By education, I mean to include not just teachers of elementary and secondary schools, but also professionals working in higher education and environments outside of formal schooling. To the extent possible, then, I have attempted to illustrate theoretical concepts in concrete terms and with a wide variety of examples.

Along with its applied focus, the book embodies a theme of reflective practice. I do not believe that a single learning theory is the answer to all instructional problems. Nor do I believe that we have yet discovered or figured out all there is to know about learning. As a consequence, practitioners can do no more than make informed judgments about what theories have the most to offer them in the solution of their particular problems.

In reading reviews of the second edition and talking with instructors who were using the text, I learned that there are many points of view that I could consider in writing the third edition. Some instructors assign the chapters in order as written. Others assign a sequence that reflects an individual emphasis or interest, such as strategies for improving memory or shifting paradigms in psychological thought.

It is also clear that differences of opinion exist on how theories should be categorized. One reviewer suggested an organizational structure that would group the chapters into three parts. Another idea was to begin the book with a section showing the contrast among three fundamental approaches to instruction.

The point on which reviewers did agree concerned the pedagogy of the book. They requested more graphics, more examples, and more ways for students to summarize, contrast, and synthesize concepts across theories. I have attempted in this edition to meet those demands.

The chapters are outlined briefly below.

- Chapter 1, Introduction to Theories of Learning and Instruction, focuses on learning, learning theory, and the historic epistemological traditions and experimental approaches to learning. The section on epistemology focuses on three epistemological traditions that can be said to underlie the theories presented and discussed in this book. I have tried to clarify all the "isms" that make up the conceptual world of philosophy and which make it so difficult to understand.
- Chapter 2, Radical Behaviorism, focuses on the experimental analysis of behavior and the principles of behavior management. In the field of performance technology, behavioral theory has figured prominently in the identification and resolution of performance problems.
- Chapter 3, Cognitive Information Processing, presents cognitive information processing theory only. Alternative approaches to cognitive theory appear in Chapter 5.
- Chapter 4, Meaningful Learning and Schema Theory, includes the work of Ausubel on meaningful reception learning, which is still being explored and felt in education. The relation of his meaningful reception learning theory to schema theory makes it sensible to discuss them in the same chapter.
- Chapter 5, Situated Cognition, focuses on a shift in cognitive theory that has been embraced by learning psychologists and educators alike. This shift is characterized by the inclusion of community and culture as important determinants of knowledge acquisition and use.
- Chapter 6, Cognitive and Knowledge Development, compares Piaget's genetic epistemology—four stages of development and three developmental processes—with alternative information-processing approaches.

- Chapter 7, Interactional Theories of Cognitive Development, presents Bruner's three modes of representing understanding and Vygotsky's developmental method.
- Chapter 8, Biological Bases of Learning and Memory, focuses on the implications of evolution and the work of theorists such Cosmides and on neurophysiology and the work of theorists, Gazzaniga, Rosenzweig, and Schacter. Also reflected are the many new developments in the neurosciences.
- Chapter 9, Motivation and Self-Regulation in Learning, focuses on the role of self-regulation in motivation and learning. It includes Bandura's social learning and self-efficacy theories and Keller's ARCS: A model of motivational design.
- Chapter 10, Gagné's Theory of Instruction, presents the three components of Gagné's theory—a taxonomy of learning outcomes, conditions of learning, and nine events of instruction.
- Chapter 11, Constructivism, focuses on constructivism as a contrasting theory, which assumes knowledge is constructed. It presents learning goals, conditions for instruction, and methods of instruction.
- Chapter 12, Toward a Personal Theory of Learning and Instruction, encourages students to construct a personal theory of learning that will serve them as an improved guide to instructional practices.

New to this edition is a "Theory Matrix" at the end of each chapter that summarizes the theory in terms of its key aspects (prominent theorists, role of learner, role of instructor, learning outcome, inputs to learning, and process of learning). This matrix should help students make specific contrasts in perspective across theories.

In addition to the Theory Matrix, I have used a single scenario, "Kermit and the Keyboard" across chapters to better illustrate similarities and differences in what theories reveal and explain about learning. This scenario is true and drawn from my own experience. I hope that it is rich enough and universal enough to meet its intended purpose.

As with any new edition, there is updated content with references to research and literature that have been published since the last edition. A great deal of exciting research is being conducted on learning and instruction, and I know I have not captured it all.

My hope is that readers of *Psychology of Learning for Instruction* will develop a critical and reflective eye as they progress through this book, keeping in mind the full range of consequences that comes with the adoption of any particular approach. I also hope that they will take this book as a point of departure for continued study about learning and its implications for instruction.

I am grateful for the energy and diligence of my doctoral advisee, Youngmin Lee, who tracked down references, copied articles, and assembled folders on topics related to each chapter. He always brought me more than I asked.

To the reviewers who provided thoughtful critique and helpful suggestions, I owe a particular debt of gratitude. They are Ronald A. Beghetto, Indiana University; Andrew Katayama, West Virginia University; Ernescia M. Torbert Richardson, Cleveland State University, and Robert G. Winningham, Western Oregon University. I found myself referring back to their suggestions time and again. Even when I did not follow their counsel, their comments caused me to think deeply about what changes I would make.

I thank my editor, Arnie Burvikovs, for both his patience and impatience, and for reminding me that time was running out. I am also grateful to my husband and my good friend, Kathryn Ley, for their unwavering understanding and support. In Kathryn, I find a kindred spirit who listens to my ideas and helps me sort them out.

Finally, I am indebted to all the readers, especially students, who have communicated with me by e-mail over the years. Your questions and feedback help me to see areas of the book to be targeted for improvement. To engage with you in intellectual debate and conversation is also tremendously satisfying. So don't be a stranger; I'm only a click away!

M. P. D.

About the Author

Marcy P. Driscoll is the Leslie J. Briggs Professor of Educational Research in the Department of Educational Psychology and Learning Systems at the Florida State University. She is currently Associate Dean in the College of Education after serving seven years as chair of her department. She has won numerous awards, including the Outstanding Instructor Award in 1990–1991, 1991–1992, and 1994–1995 and a Teaching Incentive Program Award in 1995–96. She served as Editor of the Research Section of *Educational Technology* (1991–1997) and is in her third five-year term as an Editorial Board Member for *Contemporary Educational Psychology* (1990–1995, 1995–2000, 2000–2005). She has published numerous articles and chapters in books in the fields of learning, instructional design, and technology. She has co-authored with Robert M. Gagné, *Essentials of Learning for Instruction*, and with Rick R. McCown and Peter G. Roop, *Educational Psychology: A Learning-Centered Approach to Classroom Practice.* She received her masters and doctoral degrees in Educational Psychology from the University of Massachusetts.

Part I: Introduction

Introduction to Theories of Learning and Instruction

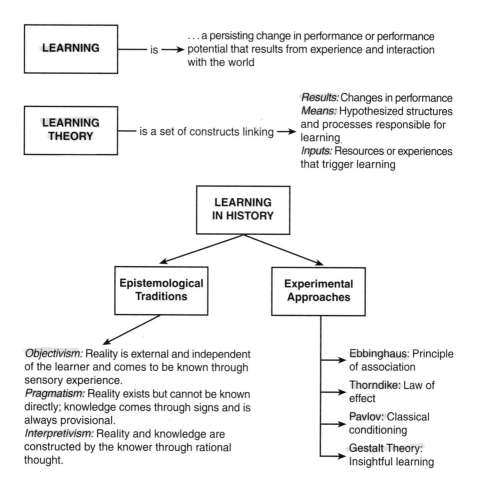

| LEARNING | — is → | . . . a persisting change in performance or performance potential that results from experience and interaction with the world |

| LEARNING THEORY | — is a set of constructs linking → | *Results:* Changes in performance
Means: Hypothesized structures and processes responsible for learning
Inputs: Resources or experiences that trigger learning |

LEARNING IN HISTORY

Epistemological Traditions

Experimental Approaches

Objectivism: Reality is external and independent of the learner and comes to be known through sensory experience.
Pragmatism: Reality exists but cannot be known directly; knowledge comes through signs and is always provisional.
Interpretivism: Reality and knowledge are constructed by the knower through rational thought.

Ebbinghaus: Principle of association

Thorndike: Law of effect

Pavlov: Classical conditioning

Gestalt Theory: Insightful learning

Children learn language in a remarkably brief period of time, but an athlete may take years to develop a powerhouse serve in tennis. Students in school learn how to solve complex problems in mathematics, and sales trainees learn how to mollify irate customers. Chess and bridge players learn tactical strategies; preloaders learn efficient strategies for packing milk crates. These are all examples of what we call learning. But what is learning and how does it occur?

Learning is a lifelong activity. Learning occurs intentionally in formal instructional settings and incidentally through experience. Learning encompasses a multitude of competencies, from knowledge of simple facts to great skill in complex and difficult procedures. Learning sometimes requires great effort and sometimes proceeds with relative ease. These are a few of the things we know about learning. But learning is a complex affair. The results of learning are often observable in human performance, but the process of learning is much less obvious. As a consequence, different theories have been developed to explain learning. These theories represent different perspectives, different assumptions, and different beliefs about learning. It is therefore worthwhile to consider both how learning theories develop and what historical roots underlie the specific theories discussed in this book.

What Is a Theory of Learning?

Most people have an intuitive answer to this question. A theory about learning is a set of laws or principles about learning. But what do these principles involve? What is their purpose? Where do they come from? Let's start with the last question first.

Theories about anything typically originate with questions. Why does the beach remain sunny when afternoon summer thunderstorms are widespread just 5 miles inland? What makes a person successful in reading? How much do adults know about world geography? How do effective teachers organize their instruction? Some of these questions are prompted by curiosity and a desire to understand the world around us. With the expansion of computers and other high-tech equipment in all educational settings, for example, what role will textbooks play? What role do they play now? Are they particularly useful for facilitating learning in certain subject matters? What, in fact, do people learn from reading textbooks?

Other questions may be motivated by problems that require the generation of new knowledge to effect their solutions. For example, should a school or company invest in the latest computer or internet technology? Is the cost of this equipment worth the learning gains that might be expected from its use in instruction? To make an informed decision about such a purchase, school or company officials might wish to know what impacts there are likely to be on learning, social processes, and the like.

Finally, many questions are provoked by events which somehow contradict our beliefs about the way things are. For example, consider the following story that I heard over National Public Radio. A teacher was describing what happened during a science experiment that his students were conducting, which involved putting empty or partially filled cans of soda into a tub of water and observing the degree to which they floated. To complete their experiment, the students added a couple of unopened cans, one of which happened to be diet soda. Lo and behold, the diet soda floated while the regular soda sank! Both were unopened 12-ounce cans. What could possibly account for the difference in their flotation capability? [The answer appears at the end of the chapter.]

Regardless of how questions arise, they generally lead researchers to conduct systematic observations on the basis of which plausible answers can be constructed. In some kinds of investigations, these observations are conducted without many advance, or a priori, expectations about what will be seen. Certainly, "inquiry demands the selection of a particular set of observations or facts from among the nearly infinite universe of conceivable observations" (Shulman, 1988, p. 5). But this selection may be quite broad and general. In a study examining textbook use and learning, for instance, the researchers might decide to look at grade level, subject matter, and teacher experience as possible variables in textbook use. Although these variables then help in the selection of classes to observe, they would not limit what the researchers observed in those classes.

By contrast, other kinds of investigations require the researchers to generate and test potential answers to the research question. The soda can story is illustrative. In this case, the students proposed a working hypothesis about one can containing slightly more liquid than the other (therefore, having more volume). A hypothesis, or one's suggested answer to a research question, determines what variables (in this example, amount of liquid) are thought to be important in understanding the event (sinking/floating). The hypothesis also specifies the presumed relationship between the variables and the observed event. That is, the can that sank should contain more liquid than the can that floated.

In order to examine the viability of hypotheses, a set of particular observations must now be conducted, which in this case consisted of the students pouring the contents of each can into a measuring cup and then comparing the amounts in the two cups. The results of these observations would then be compared with the prediction that was hypothesized. The extent to which results and prediction agree determines whether the hypothesis has been verified or refuted. If refuted, then other, alternative explanations must be considered.

The observations made in any investigation enable researchers to construct or verify propositions about what is going on. These propositions form the basis of theories. In the soda can example, the students can be said to have a theory of flotation in which the amount of liquid contained in the can determines whether it sinks or floats. Their subsequent observations, however, revealed that both the regular and diet soda cans contained the same volume of liquid. Therefore, the students were forced to abandon this variable as part of their theory and to consider alternative ones.

Likewise, consider how theory building might occur in an examination of textbook use and learning. Although the investigation would not proceed from specific hypotheses, it is likely that researchers would begin with a question such as, how do textbooks influence learning? In answering this question, they might first examine the degree to which students actually read or studied their textbooks, with the assumption that those who did so would learn more than those who never opened their books. Suppose that observations revealed a general tendency of this sort but that, even among the textbook users, there was considerable variability in performance. This would suggest that the relationship between textbook use and learning involves more than just time spent reading or studying the text. The original assumption must now be amended and might, for example, include the additional variable of what students do when they read or study their textbooks. Eventually, a complex picture, or theory, of textbook use would be drawn.

As can be seen in these two examples, the process of theory building is recursive. The results of each phase of inquiry influence subsequent phases, which eventually feed back to modify original assumptions or hypotheses. In this way, a theory constantly undergoes modifications as new results are accommodated. Figure 1.1 illustrates this process. In the figure we also see the essential purposes of a theory: to explain the occurrence of some phenomenon and to predict its occurrence in the future. A learning theory, then, should explain the results associated with learning and predict the conditions under which learning will occur again. It is obviously the goal of in-

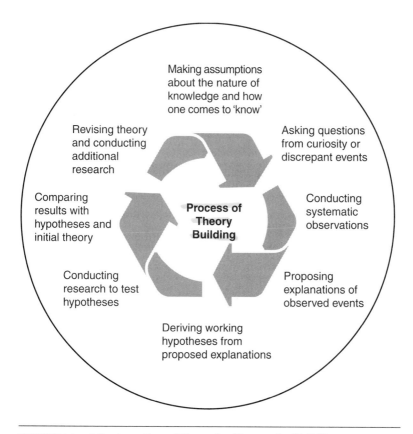

FIGURE 1.1 *A Systematic and Recursive Process for Building a Theory*

struction to apply this knowledge in the provision of appropriate conditions for facilitating effective learning.

Although theory building, as I have described it so far, seems orderly and objective, it is not necessarily either. Take, for instance, the problem of choosing what variables are important to investigate. If you assume that learning is a function of student characteristics, such as their motivation or preferred learning style, you could explain the effects of textbook use on performance in terms of how motivated students were to study the information or whether they possessed a verbal learning style. In other words, more motivated students would be expected to learn more than less motivated students, and those with a verbal learning style would be expected to learn more than their counterparts with a visual learning style. Adopting this perspective emphasizes the student and how he or she approaches the learning task. Finding support for this explanation would probably involve interviewing students, asking them to think aloud as they read through a text chapter, or administering an instrument to measure motivation and/or learning style. These results would then be correlated with performance.

Alternatively, you could assume that properties of the text itself are responsible for student learning. This might suggest that some textbooks (in the same subject matter) should facilitate learning more effectively than others because they contain objectives, chapter summaries, practice questions and feedback, or other features that influence how students read and study texts. Adopting this perspective emphasizes the textbook, and to find evidence of this explanation would require textbook analyses, with subsequent correlation of text features and student performance. How does one decide which perspective to adopt? Is one more true than the other? Or is there a third alternative that recognizes the importance of both perspectives in providing a more complete understanding of the phenomenon?

Research decisions such as these fundamentally stem from disciplinary assumptions, or beliefs, that investigators have about the phenomena they study. An anthropologist, for example, goes about the study of primitive cultures quite differently from how a psychologist would approach the same investigation.

> What distinguishes disciplines from one another is the manner in which they formulate their questions, how they define the content of their domains and organize that content conceptually, and the principles of discovery and verification that constitute the ground rules for creating and testing knowledge in their fields. These principles are different in the different disciplines. (Shulman, 1988, p. 5)

Because the study of learning is not itself a discipline, it has been approached by researchers representing a variety of disciplinary perspectives. You will see this in the resulting theories of learning that have been proposed. Behavioral psychologists, for example, argue that learning can be fully understood in terms of observable events, both environmental and behavioral. Cognitive psychologists, by contrast, believe that learning is mediated by thought processes inside the learner. A third perspective is offered by social psychologists, who contend that learning is a social enterprise, dependent upon interactions between the learner and his or her sociocultural environment. The point is, these beliefs dictate what questions about learning will be investigated and what theoretical constructs will be invented to provide explanations. This also means that two apparently competing theories may not be directed at even the same phenomena. What aspects of learning are obscured by one theory may be illuminated by another.

In the development of a particular theory, research tends to be cumulative, or what Kuhn (1970) called normal science. Investigators ask questions that are logical next steps based on previous findings. They aim to articulate theoretical principles that have already been devised, modifying those principles as necessary to account for unexpected or contradictory findings. Sometimes, however, the predictions that follow from a theory continue to fail, despite whatever modifications are made to the theory. The result is that anomalies are amassed that cannot be explained very easily. When this happens, one or more researchers will propose an alternative, truly competing theory. This is known as extraordinary science, and represents a real breakthrough in scientific progress and knowledge development.

To be a worthy competitor, any new theory must reinterpret all the previous findings as well as account for the anomalous ones that prompted its invention in the first place. This can occur on a limited scale within a particular theoretical orientation, as when cognitive psychologists propose new theories of long-term memory to accommodate research results not easily handled by the existing theory. It can also occur on a grand scale when researchers shift theoretical orientations altogether, adopting disciplinary assumptions that are incommensurate with the previous orientation. One cannot, for instance, simultaneously believe that learning is entirely understandable in terms of external, observable events and believe that learning depends on internal thought processes.

The ongoing fragmentation of knowledge caused by adherence to different disciplinary assumptions is, Wilson (1998) argues, more an artifact of scholarship than it is a reflection of the real world, and he makes a case for consilience. By consilience, he means "a 'jumping together' of knowledge by the linking of facts and fact-based theory across disciplines to create a common groundwork of explanation" (p. 8). Consider, for example, the four quadrants shown in the top half of Figure 1.2. Represented are four domains in which scholars conduct research on learning. Each domain has its own practitioners, assumptions, language, and standards of validation, and the problems in learning they choose to study vary markedly from one another.

Consider now a series of concentric circles superimposed on the four quadrants, as shown in the bottom half of Figure 1.2. According to Wilson (1998), the closer one gets to the innermost circle, the more likely one is to encounter important real-world problems. Yet it is in that innermost circle where the most confusion exists and where the perspectives of all four domains are essential for understanding the problem and constructing a potential solution. For example, think about the controversy over attention-deficit disorder. Is it caused by the delayed maturation of some part of the brain? What about evidence of adults who display attention-deficit symptoms? How can the disorder be treated effectively? What should teachers do who have students in their classes that are diagnosed with the disorder? Depending on the approach taken—whether biological, psychological, or educational—different answers are proffered to each of these questions. Yet none of the answers is truly satisfactory from someone's point of view.

As you study the theories presented and discussed in this book, keep in mind that, if we accept Figure 1.1 as a model of the theory building process,

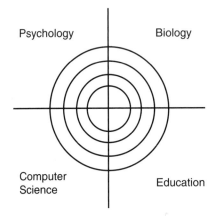

FIGURE 1.2 *An Appeal to Consilience in Developing Theories about Learning and Instruction*

Source: Adapted from Wilson, 1998.

then we must also accept the provisional character of theories. As much as we might like to think otherwise, theories do not give us the truth of the matter. They simply provide a conceptual framework for making sense of the data that have been collected so far. It is probably wise to adopt the attitude of a "disciplined eclectic" (Shulman, 1988) and view each theory critically for what it can contribute to solving important instructional problems. It is also useful, however, to contemplate how these theories might be synthesized to offer new insights on learning. According to Wilson (1998), "we are approaching a new age of synthesis, when the testing of consilience is the greatest of all intellectual challenges" (pp. 11–12). This is an exciting time for theory building about learning, with great potential for illuminating some of the difficult and challenging educational problems of our era.

A Definition of Learning

Despite the differences among the learning theories discussed in this book, they do share some basic, definitional assumptions about learning. First, they refer to learning as a persisting change in human performance or performance potential. This means that learners are capable of actions they could not perform before learning occurred and this is true whether or not they actually have an opportunity to exhibit the newly acquired performance. Typically, however, the only way a teacher, instructor, or researcher knows that learning has occurred is to ask the learners to demonstrate in some fashion what they have learned. Finding good indicators of learning is as important for designing instruction as it is for building theory.

Second, to be considered learning, a change in performance or performance potential must come about as a result of the learner's experience and interaction with the world. This statement has several implications. Some behavior changes, such as the acquisition of fine motor control, can be attributed to maturation and are therefore not considered learned. Other behavior changes, such as searching for food when hungry or becoming garrulous when drunk, are obviously explained on the basis of temporary states. These also do not imply learning. Learning requires experience, but just what experiences are essential and how these experiences are presumed to bring about learning constitute the focus of every learning theory.

A Definition of Learning Theory

A **learning theory**, therefore, comprises a set of constructs linking observed changes in performance with what is thought to bring about those changes. Constructs refer to the concepts theorists invent to identify psychological variables. Memory, for example, is a construct implicated in cognitive perspectives on learning. In other words, we look at the fact that people can demonstrate the same performance time after time and reason that they do so because they have remembered it. We have invented the concept of memory to explain this result.

To build a learning theory requires defining three basic components:

What?
- The results: What are these changes in performance to be explained by the theory?

how?
- The means: What are the processes by which the results are brought about (including any hypothesized structures that these processes are assumed to operate on)?

why?
- The inputs: What triggers the processes to occur? What are the resources or experiences that form the basis for learning?

The answers given to these questions, as well as how the answers themselves are determined, characterize the various perspectives taken on learning and the specific theories that have emerged. To help you keep these components in mind and to compare across theories, each chapter of this book will end with a "theory matrix" that displays the inputs, means, and results of learning explained by each theory. As theories are added to the matrix, their similarities and differences should become more evident, as should those aspects of learning that are not yet easily explained by existing theories.

Learning in History

How people learn is not a new question in psychology, having been established as a legitimate research pursuit in the late 1800s. But learning is also not the sole territory of psychologists; it has been a matter of deep concern to philosophers for many centuries. What is mind? How does the mind develop? What is knowledge, and how does the mind acquire knowledge? How does the mind come to know other minds? These are just a few of the questions that provide the intellectual and philosophical underpinnings to modern learning theory. It is not my intention to review comprehensively the history of learning theory, but it is useful to trace the major antecedents to today's theories in order to provide a framework for comprehending and evaluating them.

The study of learning derives from essentially two sources. Because learning involves the acquisition of knowledge, the first concerns the nature of knowledge and how we come to know things. What is knowledge? How is knowledge distinguished from opinion or falsehoods? What are legitimate ways of knowing? These are questions of epistemology. How they are answered reflects one's initial assumptions about how the mind acquires knowledge of the world, and these assumptions influence what research methodology is used to conduct investigations on learning.

For example, what does it mean to "know" that density affects an object's weight and therefore its ability to float? (This is a clue to the soda can problem described earlier.) Is it enough to state with conviction that very dense objects will sink while less dense objects will float? Or, does the knowledge lay in one's choice of a stryofoam block to be used for a buoy rather than a rock? Similarly, what counts as legitimate ways of coming to know the relationship between object density and flotation? Must one experience this relationship through actual manipulation of different objects in water, or can one simply be told about it with visual or verbal examples?

As you will soon see, theorists take opposing positions on these questions. Some believe that knowledge is a matter of internally representing the external world and is primarily acquired through experience, whereas others argue that knowledge is a matter of interpretations that learners actively construct by imposing organization on the world about them.

The second source in which modern learning theory is rooted concerns the nature and representation of mental life. When knowledge is acquired, how is it represented in the mind? What are the operations or rules that govern mental phenomena? Although these questions are not considered by behaviorists to be worth asking, their answers are part of any cognitive, developmental, or biological theory about learning. Mental phenomena have been conceptualized as associations among ideas, complex schemas of organized knowledge, and neurochemical changes in synapses, to name only a few. As you progress through this book, you will see that each of these levels of analysis provides a unique view of learning.

Let us now take a brief look at how these two sources have played out through history in the development of modern learning theory. In later chapters, these foundations will be recalled to help you trace arguments of particular theories.

The Epistemology of Learning

Any number of excellent texts present the history of psychology and provide accounts of how philosophers' views about knowledge and learning have changed over the centuries (e.g., Herrnstein & Boring, 1965; Leahey & Harris, 1997; Bower & Hilgard, 1981). It is not my purpose to repeat those accounts but instead to give you a sense of three epistemological traditions that can be said to underlie the theories presented in this book. In fact, criticisms leveled at one theory or another sometimes take an epistemological bent. That is, the critic appeals to epistemological assumptions of the theory under attack and argues that these assumptions are wrong. If the assumptions are wrong, then aspects of the theory must be open to question and implications drawn from it misleading at best and misguided at worst. Accepting alternative epistemological assumptions leads one to champion a competing theory that is assumed to provide a better explanation of learning and thus more valid guidelines for instruction.

Any discussion of these traditions, however, must be preceded by a vocabulary lesson on epistemological "isms," or as Wilson (1998) so irreverently called it, an introduction to the "hissing suffix." Table 1.1 presents a list of concepts representing various epistemological beliefs, each pertaining to either the nature of knowledge or how knowledge is acquired.

Empiricism, nativism, and *rationalism* (the concepts shown in the top block) concern what is permitted as a valid source of knowledge. Does knowledge come from experience (all learning theorists generally make this claim), or can it come from thinking and reasoning about things? Is some knowledge already present at birth and therefore inherited? There is interesting speculation, for example, that we are genetically predisposed for some fears because of our evolutionary history. Snakes and spiders were dangerous to the survival of prehistoric humans and still cause trepidations for many people today.

The concepts shown in the middle block—*skepticism, realism, idealism,* and *pragmatism*—refer to the content of knowledge, or what is presumed to

TABLE 1.1   *Concepts in Epistemology*

Concept	Definition
Source of Knowledge	
Empiricism	The belief that sensory experience is the only valid source of knowledge
Nativism	The belief that at least some knowledge is innate (i.e., present in some form at birth)
Rationalism	The belief that reason is the source of knowledge (i.e., the mind actively constructs knowledge)
Content of Knowledge	
Skepticism	The belief that the world may not be "knowable" at all (i.e., that our "knowledge" may never correspond to reality)
Realism	The belief that all things in the world can be known
Idealism	The belief that knowledge consists of only ideas or representations about reality
Pragmatism	1. The belief that reality exists but cannot be known directly. Knowledge is provisional, not absolute—sometimes it corresponds with reality and sometimes it doesn't—and it can be obtained through empirical or rational processes.
Knowledge Traditions	
Pragmatism	2. The epistomological orientation that corresponds to the beliefs described above.
Objectivism	The epistomological orientation in which reality is assumed to be external to and separate from the knower; empiricism and realism characterize this orientation.
Interpretivism	The epistomological orientation in which reality is assumed to be constructed by the knower; rationalism and idealism characterize this orientation.

be knowable. Skeptics question whether it is possible to know the world at all, whereas realists believe that all phenomena can be known, even that which is not directly perceptible to human senses. With the right instrument, they say, anything that is real can be detected. Opposite realists on the continuum are idealists who believe that knowledge consists only of ideas constructed about reality. In this view, all sensory data are unstructured and undifferentiated, to be interpreted by the mind with resulting knowledge constructed and organized. Finally, pragmatism occupies a middle ground where reality is acknowledged but not presumed to be known directly. Rather, it is assumed that knowledge can be ascertained by means of reason or experience, but it is always provisional. That is, sometimes our interpretations will reflect reality, but we must be prepared for when they do not.

The bottom block of Table 1.1 refers to three major epistemological orientations or traditions—*objectivism, pragmatism,* and *interpretivism*—that are still being debated in educational and psychological literature. Objectivists view reality as independent from and outside the knower, so that learning for them becomes a matter of transferring what exists in reality to what is known by the learner. Knowledge tends to be seen as absolute and becomes equated with truth. That is, we claim to know something when we can certify, or verify objectively, that it's true (Shank, 1992, 2002).

Interpretivists, by contrast, worry little about whether knowledge is true in an absolute sense, arguing instead that truth (and therefore, knowledge) depends on the knower's frame of reference. For example, I (who happens to be afraid of spiders) see a speck on the white wall of my bedroom and go in search of my husband to kill the spider. He discovers, however, that what looked like a spider to me was just a bit of dirt caught up in a cobweb. It didn't matter to me, then, whether the spider existed in reality or not; I behaved as if it did. Likewise, scientists behaved as though the sun revolved around the earth before it became an accepted fact that the sun is the center of our solar system. Changing one's frame of reference changes the nature of "facts" interpreted within it.

Objectivism and interpretivism are often discussed as polar opposites, with pragmatism somewhere between them on the continuum. However, pragmatism can also be viewed as a position that supercedes objectivism and interpretivism (cf. Shank, 1990), more like the diagram in Figure 1.3. For the most part, pragmatists hold absolute knowledge as a worthy, but probably unreachable, goal. Thus, they emphasize theories of meaning—of what works—with the understanding that what works may not reflect reality, but to the extent that it can, it should. Their theories are more like hypotheses, accepted and used for as long as evidence supports them.

As an example of the pragmatic epistemological orientation, consider the often inaccurate mental models we hold about the nature of the world and the things around us that nonetheless enable us to function quite effectively from day to day. How many times have you done something and heard, "That's not the way you're supposed to do it!" Your retort, of course, is "Well, it worked!" Examples of this come to mind every time I work on the computer. My knowledge of software programs such as Excel is adequate but not especially sophisticated. I have learned to use certain commands that work pretty faithfully. Only when they fail do I discover that I could be using a more accurate sequence of commands to do what I want to accomplish. My

Pragmatism

• reality is interpreted through signs, internal and external

• knowledge is negotiated from experience and reason

Objectivism
• reality is external, objective
• knowledge is acquired through experience

Interpretivism
• reality is internal, relative to a frame of reference
• knowledge is constructed

FIGURE 1.3   *A Conception of the Relations Among Three Epistemological Traditions*

mental model of Excel, therefore, is neither accurate nor complete, but it generally works. It is meaningful to me.

These three major epistemological traditions—objectivism, interpretivism, and pragmatism—are all evident in the learning theories discussed in this book. Although Leahey and Harris (1997) stated that pragmatism is the working philosophy of most psychologists, others (including myself) have argued that objectivism has been the dominant epistemology in psychology and education (cf. Phillips, 1983; Driscoll, 1984; Cunningham, 1992). Certainly, radical behaviorism (see Chapter 2) and cognitive information processing theory (see Chapter 3) rest on objectivist assumptions.

By contrast, the constructivist view of cognition (Chapters 5 and 11) is much more consistent with the interpretist perspective, as is Piaget's genetic epistemology (Chapter 6). Similarly related are the ideas of Bruner and Vygotsky (Chapter 7). Finally, biological theorists (Chapter 8) have raised the nature/nurture question again by proposing that learning is limited and influenced by the evolutionary history of humans. Summarized in Table 1.2 are assumptions and theoretical implications of the epistemological traditions described above, along with the learning theories most closely associated with them.

As you study the theories presented in this book, consider your own assumptions about the nature of knowledge and how they influence your views about learning. Interest in understanding personal epistemology has grown in recent years, because beliefs about knowledge and learning "appear to innervate almost every aspect of individuals' day-to-day lives"

TABLE 1.2 *Three Epistemological Traditions and Their Relation to the Study of Learning*

	Objectivism	Pragmatism	Interpretivism
Assumptions about reality	Reality is objective, singular, fragmentable	Reality is interpreted, negotiated, consensual	Reality is constructed, multiple, holistic
Nature of truth statements	Generalization, laws, focus on similarities	Working hypotheses, focus on similarities or differences	Working hypotheses, focus on differences
Source(s) of knowledge	Experience	Experience and reason	Reason
Types of research designs	Experimental, a priori	Any design may be useful for illuminating different aspects of reality	Naturalistic, emergent
Associated learning and instructional theories	Behaviorism, cognitive information processing, Gagné's instructional theory	Educational semiotics, Bruner's and Vygotsky's views of learning and development	Piaget's developmental theory, constructivism

(Schommer, 1994, p. 293). For instance, personal epistemological beliefs affect the extent to which students will actively engage in learning tasks, persist when the task becomes difficult, and cope with ill-defined problems or ill-structured subjects. It is likely that personal epistemological beliefs also affect how likely teachers are to use various sorts of instructional strategies. An instructor who believes that knowledge is constructed and relative to individual learners is more likely to select strategies such as discussion and group problem solving than one who believes knowledge is absolute and must be directly taught to learners.

Early Experimental Approaches to Learning

In addition to epistemological traditions, there is a legacy of experimental approaches to learning upon which modern learning investigators have drawn. Ebbinghaus's verbal learning experiments provided a foundation for later investigations in cognition, and the work of Pavlov and Thorndike laid the groundwork for B. F. Skinner's radical behaviorism. Finally, Gestalt theory established the basis for the cognitive process of perception that remains an integral part of cognitive learning theory today. Let us now turn to a brief consideration of these early approaches to the study of learning.

Ebbinghaus (1850–1909).   When psychology split off from philosophy to become the "science of mental life" (Bower & Hilgard, 1981), it was largely concerned with sensation and perception. But the research of Hermann Ebbinghaus ushered in a new era of interest in the study of learning. Herrnstein and Boring (1965) attributed the emergence of this interest to a growing faith in scientific research in general and scientific psychology in particular that encouraged researchers to experiment on learning.

By the time of Ebbinghaus, the classical doctrine of association, which was, in essence, a theory of learning, had already been established in psychology. This was the notion that ideas become connected, or associated, through experience. The more frequently a particular association is encountered, the stronger the associative bond is assumed to be. Association seemed to account well for learning. For example, the stimulus bread is likely to elicit the response butter more often and more rapidly than the response brown, because the association between bread and butter has been frequently experienced and thus has become well learned.

Ebbinghaus presumed, then, that if ideas are connected by the frequency of their associations, then learning should be predictable based on the number of times a given association is repeatedly experienced. This gave rise to the experimental paradigm used by Ebbinghaus and learning researchers after him. The independent variable was defined as the number of repetitions of a list of associated ideas. The dependent variable to measure learning was the subject's recall of the list.

Because Ebbinghaus wanted to investigate the learning of new associations, untainted by past experience, he invented nonsense syllables to simplify his investigations. These took the form of consonant-vowel-consonant trigrams (e.g., qap, jor, mol, kuw) and were assumed to be inherently meaningless. Then he arranged to present sequences of 16 syllables to himself (drawn from a pool of 2,300 syllables he had constructed; Ebbinghaus, [1885] 1913). With this method, Ebbinghaus had a quantifiable procedure for investigating various laws of association, as well as overall memory and forgetting. In conducting an experiment using six 16-syllable lists, for example, Ebbinghaus wrote,

> If I learn such a group, each series by itself, so that it can be repeated without error, and 24 hours later repeat it in the same sequence and to the same point of mastery, then the latter repetition is possible in about two thirds of the time necessary for the first. The resulting savings in work of one third clearly measures the strength of association formed during the first learning between one member and its immediate successor. (Ebbinghaus, [1885] 1913, 524)

By systematically varying such factors as the number of syllables in the list, the number of lists studied, and the amount of time spent studying each list, Ebbinghaus provided experimental verification of some obvious facts about memory. For instance, the more material there is to learn, the longer learning takes. The longer it has been since something was learned, the harder it is to remember. Ebbinghaus is also credited with establishing the now-classic forgetting curve (Figure 1.4), which shows that forgetting proceeds very rapidly at first and then more slowly as the time from initial learning increases. It pays us to remember, however, that Ebbinghaus' forgetting curve was derived from verbal learning experiments. The forgetting of other types of learned experiences (especially events that may have been personally traumatic) may reveal a quite different pattern (Bourne et al., 1986).

Finally, there can be little argument that Ebbinghaus' experiments established a verbal learning tradition that has carried through even to the present day. Although nonsense syllables have given way to meaningful concepts in memory experiments, the principle of association remains a driving force within many modern cognitive conceptions of learning.

Thorndike (1874–1949).   Like Ebbinghaus, Edward L. Thorndike was interested in the doctrine of association, but association between sensation and impulse rather than association between ideas. In other words, Thorndike investigated learning in terms of the associations related to action. For his studies, Thorndike preferred to use animals (mostly cats and chickens), which seemed reasonable at the time on the basis of Darwin's thesis of the continuity of species, and he formulated the first experimental procedures to

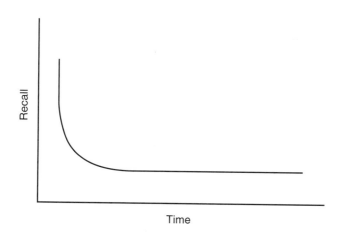

FIGURE 1.4   *The Classic Forgetting Curve (after Ebbinghaus, [1885] 1913)*

exp be used in the study of animal learning. These comprised repeatedly placing an animal in a "puzzle box" and recording, as a measure of learning, the decreasing amount of time it took the animal to operate the latch and escape.

Results The results of his experiments convinced Thorndike that an animal learned to associate a sensation and an impulse when its action had a satisfying consequence. In other words, the animal formed an association between the sense-impression of the interior of the box and the impulse leading to the successful escape action, because the action led to a satisfying result—namely, escape from the box. This principle Thorndike termed the **Law of Effect,** and it represented a modification of the classical principle of association that would have far-reaching implications for behaviorism.

Finally, Thorndike called into question the existence of mental associations in animals. He argued, albeit tentatively, that the associations which explain animal behavior do not necessarily mean animals feel or think while they act. Nor is it necessary to ascribe mental motives to their actions. Perhaps, said Thorndike, animals have no memories, no ideas to associate. This rather revolutionary notion stands as a second legacy to behaviorism, and behaviorists who followed Thorndike extended it quite boldly.

Pavlov (1849–1946).   A third experimental approach to the study of associations brought together associationism and reflexology. In his investigations of the digestive reflexes of dogs, Ivan Pavlov noticed that the dogs salivated not only to food, but often to a variety of other inappropriate stimuli (e.g., the sight of the trainer who brought the food). Whereas this phenomenon plagued other researchers, Pavlov saw it as an opportunity to experimentally study learning as well as innate reflexes. He called this salivation to the sight of the trainer a learned reflex that is established because of an association between the appropriate stimulus (food) and the inappropriate one (the trainer). In other words, something neutral is paired with something that causes a response until the neutral thing also causes the response. This proved to be the beginning of an extended research program in classical conditioning (or Pavlovian conditioning).

According to the **classical conditioning** paradigm, an unconditioned stimulus (UCS) biologically and involuntarily elicits an unconditioned response (UCR). The dog salivates when food is put in its mouth; you blink when a puff of air hits you in the eye; a child startles when a loud noise is made behind her. Theoretically, this is depicted as shown in stage 1 of Figure 1.5. Then, because it is paired with the UCS, a conditioned stimulus acquires the ability to elicit the same response. Because the response is now conditioned to the new stimulus, it becomes a conditioned response. So, for example, ringing a bell does not normally have any effect on salivation, but when it is repeatedly paired with the presentation of food, it can become a conditioned stimulus and will elicit salivation even in the absence of food. This might be depicted as shown in stages 2 and 3 of Figure 1.5.

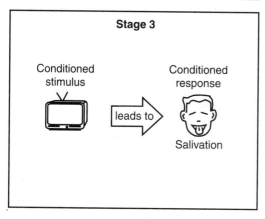

FIGURE 1.5 *The Three Stages of Classical Conditioning*

Pavlov

Examples of classical conditioning probably come readily to mind. My dog salivates at the sight of heartworm pills, because dog bones have customarily been given to him at the same time as the pill. A child cries (CR) at the sight of dogs (CS) after one growled (UCS) menacingly at him. Some years ago, I fell asleep in a church service because the minister turned the lights off. Since darkness had always been associated before with fatigue and going to sleep, it acted as a conditioned stimulus for sleep even though the service was in the morning and I was well rested.

Probably the most widely cited example of classical conditioning in humans is the study conducted by Watson and Rayner (1920) with a 9-month-old baby, Albert B. Interested in the conditioning of emotional responses, Watson and Rayner first sought an unconditioned stimulus that would reliably elicit the unconditioned response of crying in Albert. They eventually discovered that they could trigger the crying reflex with a loud noise, specifically a hammer being struck against a steel bar. Watson and Rayner then presented Albert with a large, tame white rat, and as Albert approached the animal, they hit the hammer against the steel bar. After seven pairings of the noise with the rat, Watson and Rayner presented the rat alone. Immediately, Albert began to cry; the rat was now a conditioned stimulus and crying the conditioned response.

In subsequent tests, Watson and Rayner reported that Albert also cried when exposed to a rabbit and a fur coat. Thus, he exhibited stimulus generalization, a phenomenon that Pavlov had already demonstrated with his dogs. In classical conditioning, stimuli that are highly similar to the CS will also elicit the CR in varying degrees. In addition, Pavlov showed that when a conditioned stimulus is paired with another neutral stimulus, the second stimulus can also become conditioned, resulting in the phenomenon known as higher-order conditioning. Finally, when a conditioned stimulus is presented over a sufficiently long period of time without the UCS, it will eventually lose its ability to elicit the conditioned response. In this way, extinction of the conditioned response to the conditioned stimulus occurs.

So what happened to Baby Albert? Watson and Rayner intended to cure him through extinction and counterconditioning (pairing a pleasant UCS with the rat CS), but they never had the chance, since Albert's mother moved, taking him with her. One can only hope that the conditioned response eventually weakened with time.

The principles of stimulus generalization and discrimination, extinction, and counterconditioning, originally established by Pavlov, became important elements of operant conditioning as well (see Chapter 2). Counterconditioning, now known as systematic desensitization (e.g., Wolpe, 1958, 1969), is also a standard therapeutic technique for treating various types of fears or anxieties. The question of whether humans truly condition in the Pavlovian sense, however, remains a debatable one. Brewer (1974) reviewed over 200 studies that purported to demonstrate conditioning and concluded that mental processes intervened in most cases. That is, only subjects who were told about UCS-CS pairings tended to acquire the conditioned response. Leahey and Harris (1997) commented that

> it is interesting to observe that the studies Brewer reviews, almost all of which support the cognitive position, go back as far early as 1919 and were produced in all the following decades up into the 1970s, right through the dominance of behavioral theories in the field of learning. This shows the power of tradition. If research programs are going well, then occasional challenging results are either quietly ignored, called interesting phenomena to be shelved for later study, or explained away. Only when an alternative view emerges, as cognitive theory emerged in the 1960s to rival behavior theory, do old problems appear significant. (p. 44)

Cognitive approaches to learning have dominated American psychology since about the 1970s, but they had a much longer-standing tradition in Europe with the Gestalt school. *"organization / gestalt = configuration"*

Gestalt Theory (Early 1900s).   While the doctrine of association was being articulated in the experiments of Ebbinghaus, Thorndike, and Pavlov, a countermovement developed among German theorists interested primarily in perception. Called the Gestalt school, it is thought to have started with the publication of Max Wertheimer's article on apparent motion in 1912 (Hergenhahn & Olson, 1997). Wertheimer noticed that two alternately blinking lights on a train appeared to be a single light moving back and forth. This illusion of motion, which he called the phi phenomenon, cannot be explained by analyzing the actual flashing of the lights. Rather, the psychological experience (i.e., perception of motion) appeared to be different from the sensory components (i.e., sensation of flashing lights) that composed it. Thus, consistent with the interpretivist tradition, Gestalt psychologists believed that knowledge comes from more than just experience; it also involves the knower actively imposing organization on sensory data. Indeed, the German word *Gestalt* means "configuration" or "organization."

Gestalt theory came to the attention of American psychologists by the publication in English of Wolfgang Kohler's *The Mentality of Apes* (1925) and Kurt Koffka's *The Growth of Mind* (1924) (Bower & Hilgard, 1981). Of particular interest are Kohler's experiments with apes, because it was on the basis of these that he struck a dissenting opinion to the associative view of memory. Instead of allowing that the mind learned simple connections between ideas or associations between stimuli and responses, Kohler argued that his apes learned relations among stimuli and could modify their behavior by perceiving stimuli in new ways.

The typical experiment conducted by Kohler involved placing food just out of reach of an ape in a cage. The food could be obtained, on different trials, by moving an obstructing box out of the way, pulling a cord in a particular direction, or putting two sticks together to make a lever long enough to reach the food. Although some of their attempts to reach the food failed, the apes did not behave in a random fashion, asserted Kohler. Nor did learning appear to occur in a regular, continuous way from a pattern of trial and error and a gradual buildup of correct associations. Instead, the apes exhibited what Kohler called **insight.** After a failed attempt or two and often a period of complete inactivity, the apes employed the correct solution and obtained the food.

According to Kohler, the behavior he observed could not be easily explained by the principle of association alone. Thus, he proposed a "class of inner processes" which enabled the apes to grasp the structure of a situation. That is, they acquired a relation between two things, an "interconnection based on the properties of the things themselves, not a mere 'frequent following of each other' or an 'occurring together'" (Kohler, 1917, p. 578; emphasis his).

For insightful learning to occur, Gestalt theorists argued that all the parts to a problem had to be exposed to the learner. They criticized Thorndike's experiments for keeping important elements of the problem hidden from the chickens, thus preventing insightful learning (Hergenhahn & Olson, 1997). Four features generally characterize insightful learning:

1. After a period of inactivity or trial and error, the learner suddenly and completely grasps the solution.
2. The learner performs the solution in a smooth and errorless fashion.
3. The learner retains the solution for a very long time.
4. The learner can easily apply a principle gained through insight to other, similar problems.

The fourth characteristic has important implications for instruction that differ radically from what might be suggested from the principle of association. Wertheimer (1959), for example, contended that memorizing rules or facts and applying them without thinking can lead to stupid mistakes, as when "a nurse, while making her rounds in the night shift, wakes up patients to give them their sleeping pills" (Michael Wertheimer, 1980, cited in Hergenhahn & Olson, 1997, p. 268). What is more important, according to Wertheimer, is coming to see the structure of problems, which leads to understanding how they can be solved. Although teachers can guide students toward understanding, in the end, the students themselves must experience the insight required for problem solution for it to be lasting.

Summary.   Most of the major issues for learning and the topics of this book have now been established. Ebbinghaus, Thorndike, and Pavlov shared the view that learning depends on associations and proceeded on the assumption that the complexity of thought and behavior can be reduced to simple connections among events. We see the same perspective underlying modern behavioral theory and cognitive information processing theory. In the former, the associations are between environmental stimuli and behavioral responses. In the latter, mental associations mediate between stimulus and response. In both, however, theorists fundamentally assume that they can account for complex behavior in terms of elemental associations.

By contrast, Kohler's view that learning is more than a collection of associations established the treatment of learning and perception associated with Gestalt psychology. This perspective is evident in constructivist conceptions of cognition which are finding voice in schema theory, situated cognition, and educational semiotics.

Largely ignored by both behavioral and cognitive information processing theorists have been issues of biology and development in learning. These were of prime concern to Piaget, whose theory has had a tremendous influence on the study of cognitive development, and Vygotsky, whose writings from the 1920s and 1930s are again exerting influence on learning and developmental theories. In addition, neuroscientists have now proposed their own theories of how learning and memory operate and suggested, once more, that evolution may impose constraints on learning.

Finally, motivation has met with a renewed interest in studies of learning. Originally investigated under the notion of "drive" in early behavioral theories, motivation has been reconceptualized as an affective variable mediating cognition and subsequent performance. Along with biological and developmental determinants of learning, motivation as well deserves our consideration.

Learning Theory and Instruction

Theories of learning focus on and describe the process of learning. For many learning theorists, this description is their primary goal and whatever applied knowledge may come from it is serendipitous. Cognitive psychologists, for example, concern themselves largely with the structure and processes of the mind and cognition. Development psychologists seek to understand human development from infancy to old age. Neuroscientists hope to discover the secrets of the brain. But some of these researchers, as well as educational and instructional psychologists, think about the implications of learning theories for instruction.

By **instruction** I mean any deliberate arrangement of events to facilitate a learner's acquisition of some goal. The goal can range from knowledge to skills to strategies to attitudes, and so on. The learners can be adults or children of any age, background, or prior experience. The setting in which learning takes place can be formal, school-based, on-the-job, or in the community—wherever programs for learning are being designed and implemented. Those in charge of instruction can include public and private school teachers, training instructors, or instructional designers. The basic assumption, no matter what the particulars of an instructional situation, is that effective instruction is informed by theories of learning.

Reigeluth (1983, 1999) distinguished between descriptive and prescriptive learning theory, as well as between learning and instructional theory. As indicated earlier, the very point of learning theory is descriptive—to describe the processes by which observed changes in performance are brought about. On the basis of descriptive theory, however, prescriptive principles can be derived and empirically tested. For example, the behaviorist principle of reinforcement, "pleasant consequences of any behavior increase the probability of the behavior's reoccurrence," can be rephrased in terms of a prescription: "To increase the occurrence of some desired behavior, reward it."

This prescription essentially indicates what conditions of instruction should facilitate learning, but it does not prescribe specific instructional methods. To do this, we might say, "To increase the occurrence of some desired behavior, begin instruction by modeling the behavior, then reward the learner with colored stickers for each succeeding attempt to perform the behavior. Then, when the behavior seems firmly established, reduce reinforcement to every third correct performance." Thus, according to Reigeluth (1983, 1999), a learning prescription is not exactly the same thing as an instructional prescription, as might be obtained from an instructional or instructional design theory. As a result, he argued, learning prescriptions may not be as easily applied by the classroom teacher or instructional designer as instructional prescriptions.

Although Reigeluth is undoubtedly right that learning theories are not as readily applied as instructional theories, there are few instructional theories as well developed as most learning theories. One of the few exceptions is Gagné's (1985) conditions of learning (see Chapter 10). But lest we become disheartened, there are instructional implications that can be drawn from the learning theories in this book, and many of these have been independently investigated and have amassed empirical support. To the extent possible, therefore, each chapter not only describes a given learning theory, but also presents instructional implications that either have been, or can be, derived from it. Moreover, questions are included with each chapter that are designed to help you compare and contrast theories and derive instructional implications of your own.

The General Plan and Approach of This Book

In Part II, the behaviorist perspective on learning is presented with the radical behaviorism of B. F. Skinner. Although traditional behavioral theorists who preceded Skinner are described briefly, they had relatively little to say about instruction, whereas Skinner had a great deal to say. The cognitive perspective on learning is the subject of Part III, which includes chapters on the information processing model of cognition, meaningful learning and schema theory, and situated cognition.

Developmental issues related to learning are raised in Part IV, beginning with Piaget's theory of cognitive development and information processing theories that have been proposed to cover areas where Piaget's theory seems to be in error. In addition, Bruner's concept formation and inquiry model of instruction and Vygotsky's social formation of mind are discussed.

Part V offers a chapter on learning and biology, in which the sociobiological and physiological bases of learning and memory are explored. Although these may seem rather far removed from instruction, researchers from a variety of fields have attempted an interdisciplinary discussion on the brain, cognition, and education.

Part VI focuses on motivation as a mediator of learning and performance. Albert Bandura's social learning theory is presented, along with John Keller's model of motivational design. Finally, in Part VII, learning and instruction are brought together in the contrasting instructional theories of Robert M. Gagné and modern-day constructivists.

Each chapter begins with a concept map and outline that provide both graphic and verbal organizers for the material discussed within. One or more scenarios follow that illustrate with concrete examples some of the theoretical concepts of the chapter; these are elaborated within the chapter so that you can get a sense of what each theory looks like in context. To help you make connections across chapters and discern similarities and differences among the different theories, a single story, "Kermit and the Keyboard," is presented at the end of this chapter that is discussed again in each succeeding chapter from a different theoretical perspective. This is essentially a true story, although some details have been altered or elaborated to make a particular point about one theory or another. By viewing the same situation from differing theoretical vantage points, you should begin to appreciate where theories converge on their explanations of learning and where they diverge.

As you read the story for the first time, try to identify what you think are the inputs, processes, and results of learning, as these concepts have been defined in this chapter. Try to do the same thing from the perspective of each new chapter that you study, before you read my interpretation of that theory as it relates to the story. If your interpretation differs from mine, what are the points of disagreement and why do you think they occurred? Consider as well your reaction to the explanation or view of learning that each theory appears to provide with respect to the story. What aspects of the explanation do you find compelling? Of what aspects are you skeptical, and why?

The book ends with a brief chapter entitled, "Toward a Personal Theory of Learning and Instruction." Any book on learning necessarily reflects its author's unique perspective and individual beliefs about the nature of knowledge and how we come to know things. My selection of theories to discuss, the sequence in which I have placed them, the examples I have used to illustrate them, and the conclusions I have drawn from them are all clues to my view of learning.

By the time you finish this book, however, you should have developed or fine-tuned your own informed view of learning. You should be ready to take a stand on the merits or faults of a particular theory as it might be applied to various instructional problems. You should be in a position to identify gaps in theory and to suggest where future research might profitably be conducted. In essence, if this book is effective, you will have become a "reflective practitioner," whether your practice is in the classroom, the training center, or the laboratory.

Kermit and the Keyboard

Three years ago, Kermit decided that he wanted to learn to play the keyboard. Many years ago, he studied music formally, and he enrolled as a music performance major at a local university. He became proficient at clarinet and saxophone and played in both the community symphony and a five-piece dance band. However, the repetitive nature of concerts— playing the same pieces time and again—eventually bored Kermit, and he dropped out of school before earning a degree.

Kermit became attracted to the keyboard because he liked the idea of a one-man band. The electronic capabilities of these instruments are truly amazing. One person at the controls can indeed sound like many instruments playing in harmony. The instrument Kermit bought had many built-in features (e.g., prerecorded backgrounds and accompaniments, different voices and rhythms, the ability to play and record multiple tracks, the ability to slow down or speed up the accompaniments). As one might imagine, the instrument also came with a lengthy manual illustrating and describing all its various features and how to use them.

Although Kermit learned to read a musical score when he was taking formal lessons, he has never played a keyboard before, so he spends time hunting and pecking on the keys to familiarize himself with the layout. He hauls out some old music instruction books with simple exercises in them, and he buys a couple of fake books that contain familiar popular songs. Fake books show what chords are to be played during each measure of a song. These chords correspond with shortcut keys on the keyboard, so the player has to play only one key instead of the entire chord. Kermit selects some exercises to practice and makes a list of a dozen or so songs that he would like to learn to play.

Every day, Kermit plays for about an hour. On some days, he plays for longer; on others, he might quit after 20 minutes. Some days, he plays more than once, perhaps 30 minutes in the morning and 20 minutes in the evening. The more mistakes he makes while playing, the more likely he is to quit after a short time. He plays a few songs frequently, but he makes so many mistakes on some songs that he stops playing them at all.

One of the songs that Kermit plays often is "House of the Rising Sun," and he tries many different voices and accompaniments to hear how different the song sounds using each one. He seems to enjoy coming up with unique arrangements by mixing voices and backgrounds. One day, toward the end of the song, Kermit makes a mistake and holds one note longer than the music score indicates, but it sounds fine with the rhythm of that particular accompaniment, so he doesn't seem aware that he has made a mistake. Every time he plays the song using that accompaniment again, he makes the same mistake. Playing the song with other backgrounds, though, he performs flawlessly. When he first started practicing this song, Kermit had to play it quite slowly to avoid making mistakes, but now he plays it at the recommended tempo.

About once a week, Kermit reads a section of the keyboard manual, usually pertaining to some feature with which he has been experimenting during his practice sessions. Occasionally, he seeks help understanding the text, asking questions of his wife or going on-line to participate in a chat session. He is considering joining a group that meets every other Sunday to play together. He has attended the jam session a couple of times, and it is mostly a social event. The group is very fluid; people attend as their schedules permit, and they play whatever pieces strike their fancy on a given evening. Some members of the group play by ear, but many share pieces of music that they practice individually before getting together. Kermit can't decide whether he would learn more by playing with others or whether the same boredom would set in that he remembers from his dance band and symphony days.

Initial Focus Questions about "Kermit and the Keyboard"

1. What is Kermit learning in this story?
2. What appear to be the inputs or preconditions to learning in this story?
3. What appear to be the processes of learning in this story?
4. What is Kermit's role during the learning process?
5. What instruction appears to be present in this story, and what is its role?
6. What are the implications of Ebbinghaus's forgetting curve for Kermit's practicing?
7. Do you see any examples of Thorndike's Law of Effect in this story?

Answer to the Soda Can Problem: Regular soda is much denser than diet soda because of the sugar it contains compared with the very small amount of artificial sweetener contained in diet soda.

Suggested Readings

Bower, G. H., & Hilgard, E. R. (1981). *Theories of learning* (5th ed.). Englewood Cliffs, NJ: Prentice-Hall.

Dills, C. R. & Romiszowski, A. J. (1997). *Instructional development paradigms.* Englewood Cliffs, NJ: Educational Technology Publications.

Leahey, T. H., & Harris, R. J. (1997). *Learning and cognition* (4th ed.). Upper Saddle River, NJ: Prentice-Hall.

Wilson, E. O. (1998). *Consilience: The unity of knowledge.* NY: Knopf.

Reflective Questions and Activities

1. Unger, Draper, and Pendergrass (1986) reported that students may have difficulty understanding epistemologies that clash with their own, tacit beliefs. They suggested, therefore, that students should examine their personal beliefs about knowledge and ways of knowing. Look up Unger et al.'s study, and complete the survey they provide (directions for self-scoring are included). How might your score be interpreted?

   REFERENCE: Unger, R. K., Draper, R. D., & Pendergrass, M. L. (1986). Personal epistemology and personal experience. *Journal of Social Issues, 42*(2), 67–79.

2. Unger et al. (1986) discuss a variety of reasons accounting for different epistemological beliefs among groups of individuals, including gender, for example. Ask your classmates to complete the survey, and then discuss the results. What are possible reasons for the differences in your scores?

   REFERENCE: same as above

3. According to Schommer (1990), the epistemological beliefs learners hold may influence the manner in which they approach a learning task and what they subsequently learn. Specifically, she examined such beliefs as "Knowledge is discrete and unambiguous," "Ability to learn is innate," "Learning is quick or not at all," and "Knowledge is certain." She found that students who believed in learning as a quick, all-or-none phenomenon generated simple, overly general conclusions from what they read and were overconfident in their own learning. What do Schommer's findings imply for instruction? Should teachers or instructional designers be concerned with their students' epistemological beliefs? How should instruction be modified based on these beliefs?

   REFERENCE: Schommer, M. (1990). Effects of beliefs about the nature of knowledge on comprehension. *Journal of Educational Psychology, 82*(3), 498–504.

Part II: Learning and Behavior

2

Radical Behaviorism

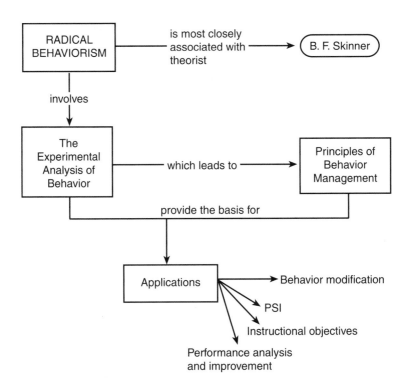

RADICAL BEHAVIORISM — is most closely associated with theorist → B. F. Skinner

involves

The Experimental Analysis of Behavior — which leads to → Principles of Behavior Management

provide the basis for

Applications → Behavior modification

PSI

Instructional objectives

Performance analysis and improvement

Consider these scenarios.

• Department X

As part of an organization-wide quality improvement effort, the head of a department sends her office manager and staff to training on the use of electronic mail. In addition to procedures such as logging on to the organization intranet to receive and send mail, the training included procedures for accessing the World Wide Web and locating and downloading information from the department's web page.

Within weeks after the training, the office manager routinely checks and reads her e-mail messages, but she continues to use paper memos and office mail to correspond and conduct business. The department is large, and some days the office manager puts as many as a half-dozen memos—each only a few lines long—in people's mailboxes.

• *Mr. Tanner's Class*

Mr. Tanner's fourth grade class reflects the ethnic diversity of his rural neighborhood—part Anglo American, Native American, Inuit, and African American. There are about as many boys as girls, and the range of their abilities is considerable. As in most classes, the students work at different rates, a few rarely participate in group assignments, and some seem to chronically misbehave.

Posted on the bulletin board in the class are these five rules (Evertson et al., 1994):

1. Be helpful and polite.
2. Respect the property of others.
3. Listen while others speak.
4. Respect all people.
5. Obey school rules.

At the beginning of each school year, Mr. Tanner discusses the rules with the students, and together he and the students determine what the consequences will be for failure to follow them.

• *Boot Camp*

Recruits are quick to learn at Boot Camp, USA. Besides doing assigned chores in their barracks, they get in shape with daily 5-mile runs and calisthenics. They learn to load, fire, dismantle, and clean their weapons. Performing their duties well can lead to privileges such as a day's pass to town, but breaking the rules inevitably leads to such consequences as extra push-ups, more miles to run, or forfeited time off.

It may not seem at first that these scenarios have much in common. Yet all of these situations illustrate (or will, with some fleshing out) the basic tenets of radical behaviorism.

The notion of behaviorism was introduced into American psychology by John B. Watson (1913). Watson promoted the view that psychology should be concerned only with the objective data of behavior. The study of consciousness or complex mental states, Watson argued, is hampered by the difficulty of devising objective and functional indicators of these phenomena. At some point, one is forced to consider the facts of behavior. These, at least, can be agreed upon because they are observable by anyone. To illustrate, suppose, in the scenario Boot Camp, that Private Johnson draws barracks duty one week, which consists of mopping and waxing the barracks floor each day. For completion of the task with no demerits (which means those floors were spotless!), she earns commendations every day and is awarded a pass to go off base Friday night. What can we conclude from this scenario? Did Private Johnson do such a good job because she looked forward to a fine meal at a local Italian restaurant instead of army food for one night? Or maybe she just takes pride in her work. The fact that any number of inferences are possible when we attempt to understand Private Johnson's mental state and the reasons for her behavior is precisely the problem Watson noted. Stick to the facts of behavior: She completed the assigned task, the results were spotless, she earned commendations, she was awarded a pass.

B. F. Skinner, a major proponent of radical behaviorism, followed Watson's lead in emphasizing behavior as the basic subject matter of psychology (Skinner, 1938, 1974). But Skinner's work differed in a fundamental way from Watson's and others' work contemporary with and immediately following Watson. In the early days of behaviorism, the concept of association permeated theories about learning. It was assumed that a response (R) came to be established, or learned, by its association with an environmental stimulus (S). Edwin R. Guthrie, for instance, believed that, "Stimuli which are acting at the time of a response tend on their reoccurrence to evoke that response" (1933, p. 365). This has been called one-trial learning because, according to Guthrie, it is the very last stimulus before a response occurs that becomes associated with that response.

Whereas Guthrie's ideas were never fully elaborated, Clark L. Hull's S-R theory of behavior became "fearsomely complex" (Leahey & Harris, 1997). Hull believed that responses become attached to controlling stimuli, but some of these stimuli must be internal because it was not always possible to observe an external stimulus for all responses. Thus, Hull proposed intervening variables such as habit strengths and argued that observed behavior was a function of these as well as environmental variables such as degree of hunger (drive), size of reward (stimulus-intensity dynamism), and so on.

Finally, E. C. Tolman believed that behavior was guided by purpose, which led to his being called a purposive behaviorist. According to Tolman (1948), organisms do not acquire S-R bonds simply by contiguity or reward; they selectively take in information from the environment and build up cognitive maps as they learn. This helped to account for latent learning, in which rats who explored a maze for several trials found the food on a subsequent trial as quickly as rats consistently reinforced in the maze.

Tolman's cognitive maps and Hull's habit strengths, however, smacked of mentalism to Skinner. One cannot directly observe cognitive maps in a rat's mind; they must be inferred from the rat's behavior. Likewise, one

radical behaviorism

B. F. Skinner

cannot directly observe habit strengths; they must be inferred from the rat's persistence in a learned behavior. Skinner argued that such inferences were neither necessary nor desirable.

B. F. Skinner's approach to the psychology of learning was to set out in search of functional relationships between environmental variables and behavior. In other words, he believed that behavior could be fully understood in terms of environmental cues and results. Cues serve as antecedents to behavior, setting the conditions for its occurrence. Results are the consequences of behavior which make it more or less likely to reoccur. What might go on in the mind during learning, then, is immaterial to understanding or describing it.

Skinner's approach to understanding learning and behavior is commonly described using the metaphor of a black box (Figure 2.1). That is, the learner is a black box and nothing is known about what goes on inside. However, knowing what's inside the black box is not essential for determining how behavior is governed by its environmental antecedents and consequences.

Consider Private Johnson again, for example. It may well be that she thought of Italian food while mopping floors, but explaining her behavior does not require making reference to those thoughts. Skinner went so far as to argue that theories of learning simply get in the way of collecting empirical data on behavior change (Skinner, 1950). He denied, in fact, that radical behaviorism should even be thought of as a theory; rather, it is an experimental analysis of behavior (Skinner, 1974).

black box metaphor

def kind of radical behaviorism

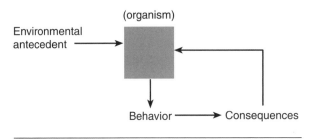

(organism)

Environmental antecedent ⟶

Behavior ⟶ Consequences

FIGURE 2.1   *The Black Box Metaphor of Behaviorism*

The Experimental Analysis of Behavior

def of learning

By systematically observing behavior and manipulating environmental variables surrounding it, Skinner set about to discover the laws that govern learning. He defined learning as a more or less permanent change in behavior that can be detected by observing an organism over a period of time. Suppose, for instance, that the office manager in Organization X is seen logging on to the office intranet once a day. Over time, her incidence of retrieving e-mail messages increases to once every half-hour or so. From observations of her behavior, it can be said that the office manager has learned to access e-mail on a regular and frequent basis.

Respondent and Operant Behavior

Skinner distinguished two classes of behavior, respondent and operant, and it is the latter that drew most of his attention. **Respondent behavior,** studied by Pavlov in his famous classical conditioning experiments, refers to *behavior that is elicited involuntarily in reaction to a stimulus*. Pavlov's dogs salivating to food is one example, as is a child's startled reaction to a loud noise. By contrast, **operant behavior** is simply *emitted by an organism*. Skinner contended that all organisms are inherently active, emitting responses that operate on their environment. Most behavior is of this type. Birds pecking at insects in the grass, circus animals performing tricks in the ring, and students raising their hands in class are all examples of operant behavior.

Contingencies of Reinforcement

To understand why some operants are expressed while others are not, Skinner argued that we must look at the behavior in relation to the environmental events surrounding it. That is, we should look at the antecedents and consequences of behavior. Although antecedents set the context for responding, the consequences of a response are critical in determining whether it ever occurs again. If a dog puts its nose in a bee's nest and gets stung, for example, you can be sure the dog will be wary of repeating the behavior. What Skinner proposed, then, was a basic S-R-S relationship, as shown below:

S	—	R	—	S
(discriminative stimulus)		(operant response)		(contingent stimulus)

This relationship provides the framework from which all operant learning laws are derived. Because the nature of the contingent stimulus determines what happens to the response, whether it is reinforced or lost, Skinner referred to learning principles as the contingencies of reinforcement (Skinner, 1969).

The concept of reinforcement, central to Skinner's behaviorism, was initially expressed by E. L. Thorndike as the Law of Effect:

> When a modifiable connection between a single situation and a response is made and is accompanied by a satisfying state of affairs, that connection's strength is increased. When made and accompanied by an annoying state of affairs, its strength is decreased. (1913, p. 4)

Put simply, behavior is more likely to reoccur if it has been rewarded, or reinforced. Similarly, a response is less likely to occur again if its consequence has been aversive. In order to understand learning, then, one must look for the change in behavior that occurred and determine what consequences of the behavior were responsible for the change. In the case of the dog, for example, the consequence of putting its nose in a bee's nest was aversive, and so it learned not to do that anymore. As for the office manager, she learned to retrieve e-mail messages frequently during the day. What could be the consequence responsible for strengthening that behavior? Suppose the manager received at least one message every time she logged on and the content of the messages was information important to her job. It is likely that both the receipt of the messages and their content comprised the stimulus that was reinforcing the office manager's behavior.

It is useful at this point to re-emphasize the functional nature of Skinner's contingencies of reinforcement. That is, reinforcement as a consequence of behavior functions to enhance the probability of that behavior reoccurring. But if this probability has not been enhanced, then reinforcement cannot be said to occur. In the same vein, anything that does enhance this probability functions as a reinforcer. To illustrate, consider the following two examples:

1. E-mail is sent to the office manager throughout the day, but she never logs on to retrieve any of the messages from the intranet.

2. The office manager checks e-mail with increasing frequency during the day, but she receives either no messages or ones that were directed to her by mistake.

In the first example, even though praise was contingent on the act of logging on and checking e-mail, the office manager does not increase her logging-on behavior. In this case, although receiving messages is presumed to be reinforcing, it does not function as a reinforcer. In example 2, on the other hand, the office manager's logging-on behavior does increase, but because of what consequence? In this example, it is likely that the reinforcing consequence (receiving pertinent messages) occurs at irregular times, so that the behavior of logging on is reinforced only some of the time. (The usefulness of intermittent reinforcement is discussed later in this chapter.)

Sometimes, what serves as a reinforcer is counterintuitive, as when a child keeps misbehaving despite the parent's disapproving actions. This happens because we tend to think of reinforcement as reward, and reward has generally positive connotations.

The point is, reinforcement is defined in terms of its function, its effect on behavior. Thus, we must be wary of everyday language usage of Skinner's principles, which may not precisely match his scientific meanings.

Principles of Behavior Management

Through systematic experimental manipulation of the contingencies of reinforcement, Skinner formulated learning principles to account for the strengthening or weakening of existing behaviors as well as the learning of altogether new ones. In addition, he studied reinforcement schedules to determine how learned behaviors are maintained over time. Although Skinner conducted most of his own research with animals, his principles of reinforcement have held equally well where human behavior is concerned. Since these principles are as often applied to the management of learning and behavior as to their understanding, it is perhaps easiest to discuss them in detail from that perspective.

Strengthening or Weakening Operant Behaviors

The basic principles of reinforcement describe the simple strengthening or weakening of a response already in the repertoire of the learner. That is, observation reveals whether the learner is not displaying some desired behavior often enough or is exhibiting some undesired behavior all too often. In the first instance, the desired behavior becomes a target for strengthening; in the second, the goal is to weaken the undesired behavior. As has already been discussed, the nature of the stimulus contingent on the response is an important factor in the behavior's occurrence.

But Skinner discovered a second factor that was also important. The contingent stimulus could be presented immediately after a response to influence the reoccurrence of that response, as in the receipt of e-mail causing the office manager to log on more frequently during the day. Or the contingent stimulus can be removed following a response, with a subsequent effect on the reoccurrence of the response. This would be the case, for example, if the office manager learned to delete messages regularly to avoid overloading her mailbox and causing her system to crash.

Crossing the presentation or removal of the contingent stimulus with the nature of that stimulus—whether satisfying or aversive—yields a set of basic principles for strengthening or weakening behavior, as shown in Figure 2.2. Let us consider, first, those principles that strengthen a response, followed by those that weaken it.

Strengthening a Response: Positive Reinforcement. **Positive reinforcement** refers to the *presentation of a reinforcer (satisfying stimulus) contingent upon a response that results in the strengthening of that response.* Several examples of positive reinforcement have already been discussed. Receiving e-mail reinforced the office manager's use of the intranet; commendations and an off-duty pass reinforced Private Johnson's completion of her daily floor-mopping task. Other examples of positive reinforcement can be readily observed in classrooms, at home, in social situations, or on the job. Dog trainers, for instance, reinforce "at attention" behavior with dog treats. Employers reinforce beyond

	Satisfying S	Aversive S
S *presented* contingent upon R	**Positive Reinforcement** Example: Worker earns bonus for ideas that improve company performance (R *strengthened*)	**Punishment** Example: Sailor earns night in the brig for fighting on duty (R *weakened*)
S *removed* contingent upon R	**Reinforcement Removal** Example: Driver must pay stiff fine for parking in a restricted area (R *weakened*)	**Negative Reinforcement** Example: Student exempts weekly quizzes by performing well on daily homework (R *strengthened*)

FIGURE 2.2 *Basic Principles of Reinforcement*

quota production on an assembly line with bonus pay. I reinforce my husband with chocolate bars for cleaning the bathtubs each week. One question that all these examples raise, however, is what precisely may serve as reinforcers? And how is one to determine which reinforcer to choose for a given situation?

Types of Reinforcers.   A **primary reinforcer** is *one whose reinforcement value is biologically determined* (Figure 2.3). Food, for example, is a biological requirement of all living organisms, and hungry animals will exhibit all sorts of behavior to obtain it. In the well-known Skinner box (Skinner, 1938), food-deprived rats learned to press levers in order to activate a food magazine which dispensed small food pellets. Although primary reinforcement does not function extensively in human learning, it has proven quite useful in some cases. Wolf, Risley, and Mees (1964) reported using bits of food to reinforce wearing his glasses by an autistic boy.

More important in accounting for human learning is the concept of conditioned reinforcers. **Conditioned reinforcers** are *those that acquire their reinforcement value through association with a primary reinforcer*. Thus, they have been conditioned to be reinforcing. Examples of conditioned reinforcers include gold stars, money, and praise. Praise is a special case of conditioned reinforcement, in that it is not a tangible item that can be saved up or used in trade, like money or baseball cards. For that reason, it has been termed a social reinforcer and shown to have powerful effects on human behavior. Ludwig and Maehr (1967), for example, demonstrated that making simple statements of approval regarding students' performance in a physical education class led to their making many more positive statements about themselves. Likewise, psychology students discovered that the incidence of seat belt use dramatically increased when grocery store checkers said to customers, "Be sure to buckle up. Remember, [store name] cares about your safety, too" (J. Bailey, personal communication).

Primary Reinforcer	Conditioned Reinforcer
...a stimulus whose reinforcement value is biologically determined	...a stimulus that acquires reinforcement value through association with a primary reinforcer
Examples:	Examples:
Food	Money
Sleep	Gold Stars

FIGURE 2.3   *Types of Reinforcers*

The Relativity of Reinforcers. In reviewing the conditions under which positive reinforcement influences behavior, David Premack (1959) demonstrated that behaviors in which learners already engage to a high degree may be used to reinforce low-frequency behaviors. *This procedure of making high-frequency behaviors contingent upon low-frequency behaviors in order to strengthen the low-frequency behavior* has come to be known as the **Premack principle**. It is simply a type of positive reinforcement, and one effectively exploited by parents everywhere. "You can watch TV (high-frequency behavior) as soon as you finish your homework (low-frequency behavior)."

Choosing a Reinforcer. The Premack principle illustrates well the need to observe learners in order to determine what reinforcer is likely to be most effective. In the case of the Premack principle, there is an empirical basis for selecting the reinforcer: The behavior serving as reinforcement is one the learner has been observed doing frequently. In other cases, it is often a matter of an educated guess on the basis of what is observed. Young children seem to like colored stickers and gold stars. Soldiers go off base when given the opportunity. Many adults appear to work hard, or take on additional tasks, in order to earn more money. These all have the potential, then, of serving as effective reinforcers. But only by selecting one—whatever seems most appropriate, given the learner and the behavior to be reinforced—and applying it, can one be absolutely sure of its effect. If it works, use it; if it does not, try another.

Cueing a Learned Behavior. Sometimes, a learned behavior is not exhibited, and therefore not available for reinforcement, until it is cued in some way. The case of the office manager offers a good example. Although she reads her e-mail, she doesn't send any, despite having learned how to do so during training. To evoke the appropriate response, the department chair sends the office manager, from another location, a message that requires an immediate reply. This is the discriminative stimulus. Unable to provide that reply in any way other than by e-mail, the office manager sends a return message supplying the requested information. Her response is promptly reinforced by the department chair's follow-up message, which says, "Thanks for the information. It was very helpful!"

Strengthening a Response: Negative Reinforcement. Refer to Figure 2.2. Note that in two cells, which are diagonal to one another, the behavioral principle results in the response being strengthened. Both principles are known as reinforcement, and reinforcement always results in behavior increases. In contrast to positive reinforcement, though, **negative reinforcement** *strengthens a response through the removal of an aversive stimulus contingent upon that response.* Remember that positive reinforcement was the presentation of a satisfying stimulus following a response.

The principle of negative reinforcement was initially discovered in experiments with rats in a Skinner box. The rats learned to press a lever, not for food this time, but to turn off a shock that was being delivered through bars on the floor of the cage. Thus, bar-pressing, a behavior that increased in frequency, was negatively reinforced by removal of the aversive stimulus, shock.

Examples of negative reinforcement are harder to find than examples of positive reinforcement. As a result, its applicability is not as easily evident. Consider, however, one of the principles behind seat belts. In most cars, a bell chimes or a buzzer sounds until the driver fastens the seat belt. Fastening the belt turns off the sound (which, in my car, is quite irritating). An increase in seat belt fastening, then, can be said to be negatively reinforced by the removal of the sound.

Other examples of negative reinforcement include the student who sits closer and closer to the front of the room in order to see the blackboard, and the child who finally starts brushing his teeth regularly so that his mother will stop nagging. In the first instance, sitting in front leads to the cessation of fuzzy vision. In the second, teeth-brushing brings an end to nagging.

Negative reinforcement is commonly confused with the behavioral principle of punishment, which is described next. The confusion appears to result from the connotations of the term *negative*. If something is negative, then it must be bad. If it's bad, then it must result in a decrease in behavior, rather than the increase that comes with true negative reinforcement. A typical example of this confusion occurred in an article about saving sea turtles that appeared in the *Tallahassee Democrat* on November 29, 2003. The article reports that conservationists were sprinkling habanero pepper powder around sea turtle nests to deter predators. "State sea-turtle protection officials said they are aware of the pepper strategy and that it didn't appear to interfere with turtle nests. They described it as 'negative reinforcement' for predators" (*Tallahassee Democrat*, p. 58). Rather than increasing a behavior, however, this strategy is aimed at reducing it, through the application of an aversive stimulus. This is a classic example of punishment for predators, *not* negative reinforcement for predators.

Weakening a Response: Punishment.   As illustrated in the sea turtle example, **punishment** is *the presentation of an aversive stimulus contingent upon a response that reduces the rate of that response*. No doubt other examples of punishment immediately spring to mind. A father spanks a child for taking something that did not belong to him. The drill sergeant hollers, "Twenty more push-ups! Let's go!" to the hapless recruit grousing in the back row of the formation. A teacher yells at the student who was talking with a neighbor instead of studying. In all instances, the individual administering punishment for some misbehavior does so with the expectation that the behavior will stop and not be repeated.

Although punishment has the effect of stopping behavior, and in fact is so-called because it has that effect, it also appears to have unfortunate side effects. First, its effectiveness tends to be short-lived. That is, the behavior being punished may come to an immediate halt at the time punishment is administered, but this does not mean it has been necessarily forgotten. The student may quit talking in class when yelled at, only to do it again at another time, perhaps more surreptitiously. A dog I once had provides another good example of this. Shadow was not permitted to jump on the furniture, and she was smacked with a rolled-up newspaper if she tried. My husband and I thought we had stopped this behavior altogether (and proud we were of our success in using behaviorist principles!). But one day when I was home alone, I walked into the living room, and although there was no dog in sight, the rocking chair was rocking furiously!

Azrin and Holz (1966) discussed other, more serious, problems with the use of punishment to reduce undesirable behavior. When punishment involves a particularly aversive stimulus or induces pain, it can lead to undesirable emotional responses being conditioned. If fear is elicited, then avoidance or escape behavior may be negatively reinforced inadvertently (Skinner, 1938). Running away and truancy are good examples. A child does poorly in school, is punished severely, and then manages to escape or avoid the punishment by leaving home or cutting class.

The emotional side effects of punishment that is painful are not limited to fear, however. Aggression and anger may result, particularly in individuals who are characteristically aggressive (Azrin, 1967). Moreover, punishment can serve as a model for aggression. In a series of studies examining aggressive behavior in children, Bandura, Ross, and Ross (1961, 1963) demonstrated that those who observed others being aggressive were more likely to be aggressive themselves. This is further supported by evidence from studies of abusive families; by and large, parents who are abusive were themselves abused as children (Steinmetz, 1977; Strauss, Gelles, & Steinmetz, 1980).

Finally, a long history of punishment may cause physical or psychological harm. Especially in situations where the aversive stimuli cannot be avoided or escaped from, the phenomenon of **learned helplessness** may result. This refers to *the passive acceptance of events seemingly beyond one's control*, a phenomenon first demonstrated in a now classic experiment conducted by Seligman and Maier (1967). In their study, conducted in two phases, unpredictable and painful shocks were administered to dogs. For some of the dogs, escape from the shock was possible through a panel in the cage. For the others, escape was not permitted, no matter what they did. In the second phase of the study, the dogs were placed in one of two compartments of a box. A tone sounded to warn of impending shock in that compartment, which the dog could escape by jumping the barrier into the second compartment. The dogs who had been allowed previously to escape the shock learned quickly to jump the barrier each time they heard the tone. The dogs who had previously been prevented from escaping the shock, however, made little attempt to escape under these new conditions.

When individuals perceive that their actions have little effect on aversive events, they, too, begin to exhibit symptoms of learned helplessness. In the context of learning, experiencing repeated failure or constant belittlement of their efforts can lead students to say, "I can't do this. I'm not a good reader" (or writer, or test-taker, or what have you).

With so many problems associated with punishment, under what conditions can it be useful? Azrin and Holz (1966) suggested that punishment has an advantage over other procedures when there is a need to stop a behavior quickly. For example, if a child is about to injure herself by picking up a hot iron, a fast slap on the wrist or loud "NO!" may be the most effective way to gain her attention and stop her in the act. Similarly, Corte, Wolf, and Locke (1971) found punishment to be the most effective procedure for eliminating self-injurious behavior in retarded children.

Finally, when used sparingly, punishment has the advantage of conveying information about what behaviors are considered appropriate or inappropriate in given situations (Azrin & Holz, 1966; Walters & Grusec, 1977). Sometimes, individuals simply are not aware that their behavior is unacceptable; it may be that the rules are different from what they have been accustomed to. This may happen particularly in multicultural situations, when, for example, ways of interacting that are socially acceptable at home or in one's neighborhood are not acceptable at school. It is for these situations that some behaviorists also recommend a warning precede punishment and reasons accompany it to explain why certain behaviors are not tolerated (Walters & Grusec, 1977).

Weakening a Response: Reinforcement Removal.   Whereas one way to reduce the frequency of behavior is to present an aversive consequence, another, perhaps more effective means is to take away reinforcement when the behavior occurs (see Figure 2.2). Removing reinforcement can be done with the principles of response cost and timeout. However, a special case of reinforcement removal, which involves the absence of reinforcement, is discussed first.

Extinction occurs when *previously existing contingencies of reinforcement are taken away, thereby causing a reduction in the frequency of a response.* In other words, reinforcement that has been maintaining some behavior is simply stopped. For example, a teacher stops paying attention to a student madly waving his arm in the air, and he eventually gives up. Or, a pet owner ignores a dog's whining and the dog eventually stops.

When extinction is used as a procedure for weakening some undesirable behavior, the key to its success is persistence. As most pet owners have undoubtedly experienced, the dog that is being ignored will redouble its efforts for attention at first. Woe to the owner who gives in at this point, however! Delaying attention simply serves as an intermittent schedule of reinforcement, which we see later in the chapter has the effect of greatly strengthening behavior. With extinction, it is important to consistently withhold reinforcement; eventually the behavior will lessen. As with punishment, it is also useful to reinforce some alternative, desirable response concurrent with extinguishing the undesirable behavior. In that way, learners are being rewarded for something even while they have lost reinforcement for something else.

Response cost, like extinction, involves *the removal of reinforcement contingent upon behavior.* But in the case of response cost, this is done by exacting a fine, requiring the offender to give back some previously earned reinforcer. It can have a strong and rapid effect on reducing certain behaviors for some people, depending on the history of the person and the value of the fine (Weiner, 1969). In society, for example, the fine for minor infractions of the law is usually monetary. To be effective, fine amounts should be set high enough to reduce the likelihood of repeat behavior, but it is certainly true that, no matter what the fee, it may have less effect on a rich person or one who has been successful at avoiding payment.

Response cost applied in a school setting can be seen in the following example. On a class field trip, Ms. Johnson was in charge of the six third grade boys most likely to cause trouble. The morning of the trip, she told them what rules of conduct they were to follow, that they would earn stickers for good behavior, but that they would have to give back a sticker every time they broke a rule. After warning one boy twice for the same behavior, Ms. Johnson said, upon the third occurrence, "You know what the rules are, right?" The little boy said yes and tearfully handed her the only sticker he had earned so far. The happy outcome to this story is that the boy behaved without incident the rest of the day and earned the big treat Ms. Johnson had been saving for last.

The final principle involved in reducing behavior, **timeout,** does so by *removing the learner, for a limited time, from the circumstances reinforcing the undesired behavior.* In some situations, it is very difficult to determine precisely what consequence is responsible for maintaining some behavior. It may be the case, moreover, that several events follow a behavior and all have some reinforcing effect. In a typical classroom, for example, a student's acting out, accompanied by "Watch me!," may cause the teacher to stop class and the other students to laugh, both of which may contribute to its reoccurrence. Stopping the behavior, then, may take more than simply ignoring it (extinction). Yet other conditions may not make response cost an appropriate alternative.

In cases such as these, individuals may be removed altogether from the sources of reinforcement. Wolf, Risley, and Mees (1964) used timeout to virtually eliminate temper tantrums thrown by an autistic boy. Every time a tantrum occurred, they isolated him in a room by himself for slightly longer than the tantrum had been. Solnick, Rincover, and Peterson (1977) added further evidence to the effectiveness of timeout, but noted that it can be reinforcing instead of punishing in some circumstances. Imagine, for example, a noisy classroom. The disruptive behavior of one student causes the teacher to put him out in the quiet hallway with his assignment. The next time the class is noisy, this student acts out again, with the same result. What appears to have happened is not timeout at all; rather, the disruptive behavior has been negatively reinforced by the student's escaping the noisy classroom for the quiet hallway.

Sulzer and Mayer (1972) suggested that for timeout to be most effective, the following conditions should be met. Timeout should not be used from an aversive situation (illustrated in the example above). It should provide for removal of all reinforcement, it should be consistently maintained, and the time period should be kept short (a general rule of thumb is one minute for each year of the learner's age). Finally, like extinction and punishment, time-out should be used with other procedures that reinforce alternative, desirable behaviors.

Depicted in Figure 2.4 is a concept tree for principles of behavior management. It illustrates in a visual way what attributes are shared by certain principles (e.g., those that strengthen behavior) and what attributes are unique to each one (e.g., high-frequency behavior as reinforcer is unique to the Premack principle). The tree also includes, for each principle, an example illustrating its use or occurrence.

Teaching New Behaviors

The principles discussed in the previous section concerned behaviors that were already present to some degree in the learner's repertoire. One might say that the learner already knew the behavior; what was learned seemed to be the frequency with which the behavior was to be performed. But how are behaviors learned that are not already present in the organism's repertoire? Bar-pressing, for example, is not a behavior that rats do in their natural environment. Similarly, one could watch a pigeon in a Skinner box for a long time without ever seeing it turn around in a complete circle. In Mr. Tanner's class, students are unlikely to spontaneously exhibit a complex behavior such as the foxtrot. If the students, the rat, and the pigeon never exhibit the behavior targeted for reinforcement, how does it come to be acquired? Behaviorists have defined three principles for teaching new, and in many cases, complex behaviors: shaping, chaining, and fading.

Shaping. **Shaping** refers to *the reinforcement of successive approximations to a goal behavior.* It involves positive reinforcement, in that a reinforcer is presented contingent upon desired behavior. But in the case of shaping, the desired

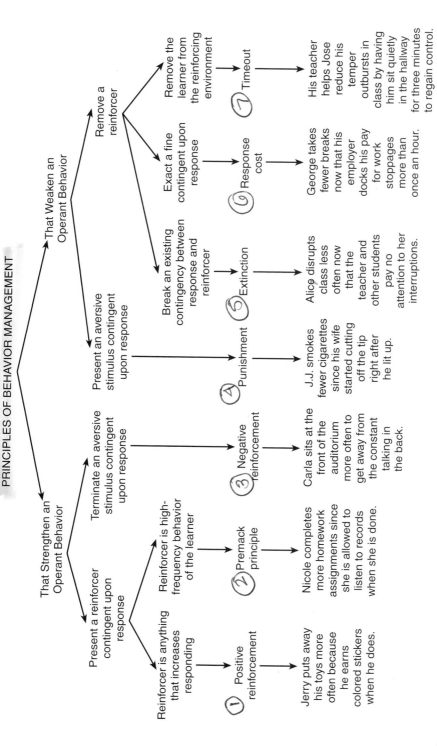

FIGURE 2.4 *A Concept Tree for Principles of Behavior Management*

45

behavior reinforced each time only approximates the target behavior. And successively closer approximations are required for the reinforcement to be presented (Reynolds, 1968). To teach a rat to press a bar, then, one might first reinforce proximity to the bar, then raising a paw, extending the paw toward the bar, touching the bar, and finally, pressing the bar. As soon as the rat has made the correct response—in this case, pressing the bar—then the principle of positive reinforcement is followed. That is, each bar press is reinforced until the desired frequency of behavior is exhibited.

Harris, Wolf, and Baer (1967) demonstrated the effectiveness of shaping to teach new behaviors to children. They selected climbing on the jungle gym for shaping in a little boy who spent no time on it. Teacher attention was the contingent reinforcer. Thus, teachers paid attention to the little boy first when he went near the jungle gym, then when he touched it, climbed on it, and finally, climbed on it extensively.

Shaping has also been found to be particularly effective in teaching autistic children. Wolf, Risley, and Mees (1964), for example, trained an autistic boy in speech acquisition, using bits of food to reinforce making eye contact, producing any sound, producing specific sounds, and finally saying complete words and sentences. In this example, however, as in the previous ones, it could still be argued that the learners were capable of producing the desired response; they just did not. Bar-pressing, in other words, is not a difficult response. Climbing on a jungle gym was well within the capabilities of the small boy. Even the autistic boy could produce sounds that were then shaped into language. Is shaping as effective with truly difficult responses, which are not initially within the capabilities of the learners?

That the answer is yes can be illustrated with the following example. A waiter at a Moroccan restaurant served tea with dessert by raising the teapot high above his head and pouring the tea into tall, narrow glasses on a very low table, where we diners were sitting on floor cushions. He spilled nary a drop, and so, of course, we marvelled at his skill and asked how he had learned to pour tea in such a manner. His reply went something like this. "Well, naturally, I couldn't do it at first without spilling tea all over the place. So, I tried holding the teapot only slightly above the glasses. When I could pour without spilling, I moved the teapot up a few inches. And I kept repeating this process until I could do it with the teapot over my head." Successive approximations had been reinforced until the goal behavior was achieved. In this case, the ability to make the response at one level of approximation served as the reinforcer to attempt the next approximation.

The above example also illustrates a factor critical to the success of shaping. The waiter did not attempt a more difficult approximation until he had mastered the easier one. Similarly, in shaping any new behavior, a closer approximation to the goal should not be reinforced until the previous one has been firmly established. If too large a step is expected of the learner at once, the behavior may break down and shaping may have to resume at the point where the learner has repeatedly demonstrated success. Finally, it is also important in shaping to ensure that reinforcement is delivered immediately contingent upon the desired response. Any delays can result in some random behavior being reinforced and becoming conditioned.

Skinner (1948) called this superstitious behavior and demonstrated its inducement by delivering noncontingent reinforcement to pigeons. That is, he offered food at random intervals, not dependent upon the animal's behavior. Whatever the pigeon happened to be doing at the moment reinforcement arrived, however, became more likely to reoccur because of the reinforcement. As a result, Skinner observed the inadvertent conditioning of all sorts of weird behavior, and he argued that the simple contiguity between response and stimulus could account for the learning of superstitious behavior in humans. For example, you buy a new pen with which to take a particular test, and you score well on the test. Scoring well rewards your use of that pen, and so you begin to attribute good performances to the causally irrelevant pen when, in fact, good performance was contingent upon your study behavior.

Chaining. Whereas shaping is used to teach new behaviors that are relatively simple and continuous in nature, **chaining** serves to *establish complex behaviors made up of discrete, simpler behaviors already known to the learner.* A typical example of chaining in human behavior is learning a new dance. Each dance step may be acquired through shaping, but then the steps are strung together in sequence through forward or backward chaining. In other words, one might begin by practicing the last step in the dance and then progressively add the steps that precede it (backward chaining). Or one could start with the first step and progressively add steps that follow until the entire dance can be performed (forward chaining).

Memorizing long passages of prose is another typical example of forward chaining. Sentences are added in succession until the entire passage can be repeated without error. Finally, reassembling their weapons after cleaning is a behavioral chain that is probably acquired through forward chaining by the soldiers in the scenario, Boot Camp.

Discrimination Learning and Fading. To this point very little has been said about the control the setting has over learning except in terms of the consequences of behavior. Behaviors are acquired and exhibited because they are reinforced; nonreinforced behaviors tend not to occur, at least in the setting where they have been ignored or punished. This is an important distinction. Individuals are clearly able to distinguish between settings in which certain behaviors will or will not be reinforced. A playful slap on the back may produce grins from the guys in the gym, but it is likely to have a quite different effect on one's commanding officer or teacher. Thus, something besides the behavior itself must be learned, and these are the cues, or discriminative stimuli (S^Ds), which signal to the learner when and where the behavior is to be performed.

Most learning in formal instructional situations is accompanied by cues. School bells signal the end of classes; getting up to leave before they ring is a behavior likely to be punished. Thus, staying in one's seat is reinforced before the bell rings; moving about the halls is reinforced after it rings. The bell simply acts as a cue to indicate what behavior is appropriate and will be reinforced (or conversely, what behavior is inappropriate and will be punished).

Discriminations are often learned, then, by a behavior being reinforced in the presence of one stimulus and being punished in the presence of another. Alternatively, a different behavior may be reinforced in the presence of the second stimulus. Motor vehicle drivers, for example, must learn to stop at a red light and go on the green light. Thus, the S^D for stopping is a red light, and the S^D for going is a green light. In either case, however, errors can sometimes be extremely costly, so that applying the simple principles of positive reinforcement and punishment may not be the most effective for establishing the discrimination.

In his studies with pigeons, Terrace (1963a, 1963b) demonstrated that almost errorless discrimination performance could be achieved with fading. He first taught the pigeons to peck a red key, so that red became a discriminative stimulus for pecking. Then he turned off the key, which caused the pigeons to stop pecking, and gradually lengthened the intervals during which the key was dark. The darkened key then became the discriminative stimulus for not pecking. Finally, Terrace slowly faded in a green light in place of the darkened key. Since the pigeons never pecked the dark key, and the fading was so gradual from darkened key to well-lit green key, the green key came to be established as the S^D for not pecking.

The concept of fading as it has been applied to human performance has come to refer to the fading out of discriminative stimuli used to initially establish a desired behavior (Sulzer & Mayer, 1972). In other words, the desired behavior continues to be reinforced as the discriminative cues are gradually withdrawn. A classic example of fading used in instruction can be seen in Skinner and Krakower's (1968) *Handwriting with Write and See* program. In this program, children trace letters in an instructional workbook. Gradually, portions of the letters, which serve as the discriminative stimuli for forming the right shapes, are faded, thus requiring the children to compose increasingly more of each letter. Reinforcement is accomplished through a special chemical reaction between the pens used by the children and the paper. They form a black line when their letters are correct, but the paper turns orange when the pen moves from the prescribed pattern.

Other examples of fading can be seen in the gradual reduction of verbal cues given by a laboratory instructor as students work through a set of procedures for staining slides or in the withdrawal of physical cues given by a golf pro showing a beginner how to hold and swing a golf club. Job aids in industrial settings are also good examples of fading. As employees become more proficient in their assigned duties, they rely less and less on the cues provided by the aid.

Maintaining Behavior

If we consider that the job of instruction is not only to bring about desired changes in behavior, but to maintain them as well, then we must determine what conditions will be most effective for behavior maintenance. A typical behaviorist approach to the question would be to find some high-frequency, persistent behavior occurring naturally and to study the consequences responsible for its maintenance. One good example is people playing the slot machines at Las Vegas or Reno. Some will stand there for hours, doing nothing but pumping coins or tokens into the machines and pulling the handle. Every so often, the player receives a payoff, accompanied by flashing lights and ringing bells. So what is going on here?

Skinner was apparently in search of a means to economize on the costs of feeding his experimental subjects when he made an interesting discovery (Leahey & Harris, 1997). When he reinforced only some of the bar-pressing responses made by his rats, rather than reinforcing every response, the behavior became much more resistant to extinction. In other words, continuous reinforcement, while necessary to establish a response in the first place, was not essential to maintaining that response. In fact, intermittent reinforcement worked much better for that purpose. By systematically investigating schedules of reinforcement, Ferster and Skinner (1957) were able to determine what pattern of reinforcement gave rise to what sort of behavior maintenance.

Although behaviorists have investigated reinforcement schedules and invented new ones since Ferster and Skinner's original experiments, four basic schedules remain. These are determined on the basis of whether reinforcement is contingent upon a given response (called a ratio schedule) or upon the passage of time (called an interval schedule). In addition, reinforcement can occur regularly, after a fixed amount of time or number of responses, or it can occur irregularly, after a variable amount of time or number of responses. Taking these characteristics together, we have four possible schedules, as shown in Figure 2.5: fixed ratio, fixed interval, variable ratio, and variable interval.

Fixed Ratio Schedules.   Continuous reinforcement, i.e., reinforcing every desired response, amounts to the same thing as a fixed ratio schedule of one (FR1). Ratio schedules of reinforcement are those in which the reinforcer is delivered contingent upon the response made by the learner. A fixed ratio schedule, therefore, requires the learner to make so many responses before

	Reinforcement is contingent upon:	
	Responses	*Time*
Reinforcement occurs *consistently*	**Fixed Ratio** Example: Students earn points for every skill mastered	**Fixed Interval** Example: Worker is paid every two weeks
Reinforcement occurs *intermittently*	**Variable Ratio** Example: Slot machines pay off after a randon number of pulls on the lever	**Variable Interval** Example: Drill sargeant makes spot-check inspections

FIGURE 2.5   *Types of Reinforcement Schedules*

reinforcement is delivered. Quota systems on factory assembly lines are examples of fixed ratio schedules. For every fifteen widgets produced (FR15) or for every 300 chickens inspected (FR300), employees earn a standard wage credited toward their pay. This type of reinforcement schedule tends to produce a response pattern like the one shown in Figure 2.6A. In other words, responding occurs at a high and steady rate, since the more employees produce, the quicker they earn more money. Animals responding on a fixed ratio schedule also show a tendency to pause immediately following reinforcement. While this phenomenon has not been demonstrated consistently with humans, studies have shown that it can occur. For example, I typically put myself on an FR15 schedule when grading undergraduate assignments, getting up for a snack or a short walk after each fifteen papers graded. Getting started again after the break, however, generally entails a pause before I am fully focused on the task once again.

Fixed Interval Schedules.   As indicated, time is the determining factor for an interval schedule of reinforcement. For a fixed interval schedule, then, reinforcement is delivered after some fixed period of time, such as 5 minutes (FI 5 min) or 10 days (FI 10 days). A commonly cited example of this type of schedule is the procedure by which many professors are tenured and promoted. Although tenure and promotion are ostensibly tied to performance, they are typically awarded, or become available for award, at particular times, such as after so many years in rank. As a result, performance over time may take on the characteristic "scallop" typically produced by a fixed interval schedule (Figure 2.6B). In other words, responding becomes more frequent as the time for reinforcement nears. Weekly quizzes can produce a

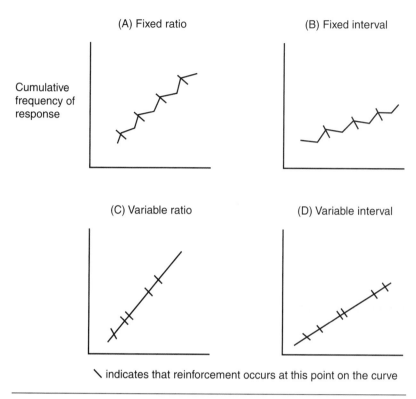

Cumulative frequency of response

(A) Fixed ratio

(B) Fixed interval

(C) Variable ratio

(D) Variable interval

＼ indicates that reinforcement occurs at this point on the curve

FIGURE 2.6 *Response Patterns Produced by Different Types of Reinforcement Schedules*

similar pattern, with students spending more time studying as the time for the quiz draws near.

Variable Ratio and Variable Interval Schedules. In variable schedules, the time or number of responses required for reinforcement is varied from reinforcement to reinforcement. Thus, a VR5 schedule means that, on the average, reinforcement is delivered for every five responses, but one time it may be given after the second response and the next time after the eighth response. Similarly, a variable interval schedule of 5 minutes (VI 5 min) means that reinforcement may be given after 3 minutes, then after 7 minutes, then after 4 minutes, and so on, creating an average interval of 5 minutes.

Variable schedules typically produce the highest and steadiest rates of responding, with variable ratio schedules producing the highest of all (Figure 2.6, C and D). The slot machine example provided earlier demonstrates the effect of a variable ratio schedule; typically, payoffs are scheduled to occur after some average number of pulls on the lever. (This average, by the way, is set high enough so that the money taken in is always more than the money paid out.) In a classroom setting, teachers can assure steadier rates of studying or homework completion by administering pop quizzes on the average of once a week (VI 5 days), or by collecting and spot-checking assignments (e.g., every third assignment, on the average, for a VR3 schedule).

Planning a Program of Behavior Change

To this point, principles have been discussed that relate the incidence of behavior to its environmental cues and consequences. Learning has been described as a relatively permanent change in behavior, and schedules of reinforcement have been presented that are useful for maintaining such changes. The question that remains is, How can these principles be systematically applied in order to bring about specific, desired changes in behavior? What follows are five essential steps in implementing a behavior change program (see Table 2.1 for a summary). Evaluating the success of such a program will be discussed last.

Step One: Set Behavioral Goals.   In order to go about changing behavior, one must determine what behavior is to be changed and what the change is. Questions to consider in this step are: What is desirable behavior? How often should the behavior occur? Does the change in behavior involve its being strengthened or reduced? Is some new behavior to be taught? What are the requirements for behavior maintenance? Also essential to setting behavioral goals is knowing to what extent the targeted behavior is being exhibited relative to its desired strength. In other words, is the learner not doing enough of something, or is some behavior being exhibited too often?

In order to have an accurate answer to the question of what learners are actually doing in any given situation, they must be observed. For example, suppose Charla is a student in Mr. Tanner's class who is "always acting out," which disrupts class and wastes valuable instructional time. Observation may reveal, however, that Charla acts out only three or four times a day. The results of her behavior are so severe in terms of lasting impact on the class that it just seems she is acting out more often.

Observation, therefore, provides a baseline of behavior, a measure of behavior incidence as it occurs before any intervention is implemented.

TABLE 2.1   *Implementing a Program of Behavior Management*

Step 1: Set behavioral goals.
Step 2: Determine appropriate reinforcers.
Step 3: Select procedures for changing behavior.
Step 4: Implement procedures and record results.
Step 5: Evaluate progress and revise as necessary.

From this baseline, goals for change can be determined. The teacher may still decide, for example, that Charla's acting-out behavior should be reduced because of its adverse impact on the class. A reasonable goal may be to reduce the incidence of acting out to no more than once a day. As we will also see, the baseline provides a basis against which the success of the intervention can be measured.

Although behavior management is typically implemented on an individual basis, it can be effective in group situations. Mr. Tanner, for example, has clearly set goals for appropriate behavior for all students with the rules he posts in his classroom. He and the students then jointly plan Steps Two and Three, which follow.

Step Two: Determine Appropriate Reinforcers. The choice of reinforcers for use in a behavioral change program depends on the learner, the instructor, the behavioral goals, and the practical circumstances surrounding the implementation of the program. Behavior in young children, for example, may be reinforced with colored stickers or gold stars, which would clearly not be appropriate or effective with older students or adults. Some teachers are opposed to the use of tangible rewards, preferring instead to use praise, attention, and other social reinforcers. A behavioral goal that involves reducing a behavior may call for a procedure such as response cost, which means that appropriate fines rather than reinforcers must be determined.

Finally, there will always be pragmatic considerations in choosing reinforcers. It is not always easy to determine what will be the most effective reinforcer for a particular individual, or, once a reinforcer is identified, it may not be within the control of the program designer. Peer approval, for example, can be a particularly potent source of reinforcement for teenagers (Sulzer & Mayer, 1972), but it is not something easily controlled by teachers or parents. Moreover, an ethical dilemma may arise in some situations as to whether the program professional has a right to control an effective reinforcer. In a community mental health facility, for example, money to buy cigarettes or candy has been found to have powerful reinforcing effects on the residents (Mulligan, Oglesby, & Perkins, 1980). But should the mental health professionals have control over the residents' money in order to use it as reinforcement?

Step Three: Select Procedures for Changing Behavior. The decision as to what procedure should be used obviously depends on what behavior change is desired. To strengthen an existing behavior, positive and negative reinforcement and the Premack principle are possibilities. To teach a new behavior, one might select from shaping, chaining, or fading. To maintain behavior, some schedule of reinforcement should be selected to produce the desirable pattern of performance. And finally, to reduce or weaken a behavior, punishment, response cost, timeout, or extinction could be implemented. To choose from among the options, where more than one procedure may be appropriate to a given goal, one should consider such questions as, How important is it that I effect this change in behavior quickly? How permanent is the result of this procedure likely to be? What other unintended effects might this procedure have that I would like to avoid? Are there any additional factors that should be taken into consideration?

Step Four: Implement Procedures and Record Results.   Once a plan for behavior change has been generated, it may be implemented and its results monitored. Observation again becomes important at this step, since only by looking at the behavior can any change from baseline be detected. Recording behavior incidence also helps to ensure that real, rather than imagined, changes are monitored. It is easy to engage in wishful thinking, hoping for changes or thinking that changes must have occurred by virtue of the program being in place.

Step Five: Evaluate Progress and Revise as Necessary.   Based on the records kept in Step Four, it should be easy to see whether, in fact, any change from baseline behavior has occurred. If the program was designed to reduce some behavior, it should have had that effect, or if it was designed to teach some new behavior, then that behavior should now be in evidence. Assuming that the desired behavior has been achieved, no change in the program may be warranted. However, after a new behavior is taught or a behavior is established at a desirable rate, some alteration in the reinforcement schedule may be required to sufficiently maintain the behavior.

What if, on the other hand, the program has not produced the intended results? Any number of possibilities could be the problem, but according to Skinner, simple observation and systematic alteration of the program should enable you to find out which one is the culprit. It may be that another procedure would be more effective, or that a different reinforcer should be selected. Perhaps a combination of procedures should be tried, as in reducing one behavior while at the same time reinforcing an alternative to take its place. Whatever the problem, the program should be modified appropriately and implemented again. This process of monitoring results and revising as necessary should be repeated until success has been achieved.

Since radical behaviorism is the experimental analysis of behavior, and behavior is assumed to be reliably, functionally related to environmental events, a behaviorist would not necessarily be content with showing that a behavior change had occurred following the implementation of some program. It would also be necessary to reverse the procedure, or remove the implementation, to see whether the behavior reverted to baseline levels. Only in this way can we be sure that it was the program, and not some confounding, random set of variables, that was responsible for the change in behavior.

To take an example, suppose that Mr. Tanner decides to implement timeout in order to reduce Charla's acting-out behavior. During baseline, conducted over a week's period, observations revealed that Charla acted out about four times each day, for an average duration of 5 minutes each. The typical results of the acting out included the teacher stopping class, paying attention to Charla to get her under control, and then spending some minutes trying to regain the attention of the rest of the students. At the beginning of week 2, Mr. Tanner implements the timeout procedure, isolating Charla for 8 minutes each time she acts out. He does this by taking Charla by the hand without saying a word and putting her in a chair just outside the classroom door. At this point, he says, "When you can be quiet, you can return." Mr. Tanner continues class and after 8 minutes allows Charla to return to her seat.

Suppose that timeout appeared to be effective, and Charla's acting out dropped to once a day by the end of the week. To be sure that it was timeout, and not something else going on in class having the desired effect, the teacher would institute a reversal in procedure and stop using timeout during week 3. Thus, he would go back to his original reaction to Charla's behavior, which should have the effect of increasing its incidence. Finally, at week 4, timeout would again be reinstituted and its results monitored. If timeout is indeed an effective procedure for reducing the undesired behavior of acting out, then the record of results should resemble that displayed in Figure 2.7.

Although this reversal process has the advantage of demonstrating the functional relationship between any behavioral procedure and behavior, it also has several disadvantages in a practical, rather than experimental, context. First, it is time-consuming to establish a reasonable estimate of baseline and to carry out each phase long enough to demonstrate a procedure's effectiveness. More importantly, however, once a behavior change has been effected, it may be extremely counterproductive, or even unethical, to return that behavior to its original rate. For example, performing tasks without demerits is desirable behavior in boot camp whether or not earning off-base passes is the only factor responsible for its occurrence. As such, most applications of behaviorist principles are considered to be successful when the goals for behavior change have been met.

Contributions of Behaviorism to Instruction

Few would argue that radical behaviorism has had a profound impact not only in psychology but on instruction as well. And its influence continues to be felt in fields ranging from clinical therapy to instructional design. Although many applications and new developments in behaviorism go beyond the scope and purpose of this book (e.g., biofeedback, treatment of clinical depression), others bear examining. The ones I have chosen to discuss pertain to

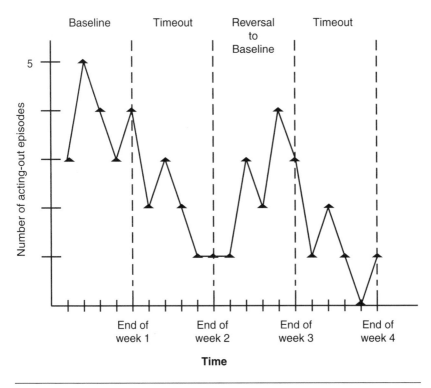

FIGURE 2.7   *Occurrences of Acting-Out Behavior in Relation to Timeout: A Hypothetical Case*

changing personal behaviors, managing learning and behavior in instructional systems, and improving performance in organizational systems.

Changing Behavior Through Behavior Modification

Application of behavioral principles in the way described so far in this chapter is essentially the same as behavior modification (also known as behavior therapy or contingency management). Typically, behavior modification is used to treat problem behaviors in social, personal, or school situations. Clinical applications include treatments for phobias, or obsessions, or eating disorders, to name a few (Bower & Hilgard, 1981). Instructional applications involve treatment of school-related problems, such as inattention, hyperactivity, temper tantrums, or any behavior that interferes with learning and the normal conduct of classroom activities. Special education teachers are typically well trained in the use of behavior modification, since they regularly deal with children who have special problems and special needs. As part of the individual education plans for individual students, teachers may target problem behaviors, devise and implement interventions, and keep records to monitor student progress and inform changes to the original plan.

In recent developments, behavior modification methods are taught to individuals, who then use them to change their own behavior. This is an application of behavior modification known as self-control, and it has been successfully demonstrated with people who wish to lose weight, quit smoking, or improve their social skills, study habits, or concentration. Bower (Bower & Hilgard, 1981) reported that he taught a college seminar in which students teamed up with a cooperative friend in order to change some aspect of their own behavior. One of my own favorite examples of self-control came from a friend whose husband enlisted her help to quit smoking. Given his propensity toward saving money, they decided an appropriate punishment would be sending money to fly-by-night charities. Therefore, the husband wrote a series of $25 checks and handed them to his wife with instructions to mail one every time she saw him smoking. Three checks later, he had quit smoking altogether and, to my knowledge, has never smoked since.

Managing Learning and Behavior in Instructional Systems

Whereas behavioral therapists and special education teachers generally focus on the needs of individuals, teachers in regular classrooms may have twenty to thirty students or more to manage at one time. Likewise, instructional designers may be developing instruction with goals to be achieved by individuals or groups. For teachers and designers, behavioral principles are useful for managing learning and behavior within instructional settings such as classrooms, individualized instruction, and on-the-job training.

Classroom Management. To a limited extent, teachers may apply behavior modification to change the problem behaviors of one or another student. More often, like Mr. Tanner, they set up group contingencies, i.e., a standard reinforcement given to individuals or the group as a whole for following certain rules of conduct.

One means of applying group contingencies in the classroom that some teachers find useful is the token economy (Ayllon & Azrin, 1968). In this system, tokens serve as conditioned reinforcers that can later be exchanged for objects or privileges. Tokens are earned for good conduct—whatever behaviors have been identified by the teacher for strengthening. But since tokens operate much like money, students may be fined for breaking the rules or engaging in behavior the teacher has deemed undesirable.

In one of the first formal uses of a token system for reinforcing and maintaining desired behaviors, patients at a mental hospital earned tokens for appropriate behaviors in the ward (Ayllon & Azrin, 1968). With their tokens, patients could buy candy, soda, trips to town, movies, and the like. Bushell,

Wrobel, and Michaelis (1968) demonstrated the effective use of a token system with preschool children to strengthen school-related behaviors. The study took place in a regular classroom setting, and children earned tokens for such behaviors as attending to assigned tasks, being quiet, asking questions, and so forth.

When tokens can be exchanged for objects, such as books or toys, keeping a steady supply of such things can become rather expensive. Sulzer and Mayer (1972) therefore recommended that teachers consider using a variety of activities for which students can exchange tokens.

Instructional Objectives. According to the behavioral perspective, just as we can set goals for appropriate behavior, so can we express in behavioral terms the instructional outcomes we desire students to achieve. In fact, behaviorists would argue the only evidence we have of learning comes from the students' behavior; they can do something after instruction that they could not do before. It is important, therefore, to specify desired instructional outcomes in terms of clear, observable behavior. These goal statements are variously called behavioral objectives, instructional objectives, or performance objectives.

Mager (1962) made popular the three-component objective, which states the behavior to be acquired, the conditions under which the behavior is to be demonstrated, and the criteria governing how well the behavior is to be performed. Typical Mager-type objectives, for example, would include the following:

1. Given the values of two sides of a right triangle, students will be able to correctly solve for the value of the third side.
2. Handed the pieces of an unassembled M-16, the soldier will be able to assemble the weapon in no more than 2 minutes.

Although other objective formats are used (for example, the five-component formats used in the instructional design models of Merrill [1983] and Gagné, Briggs, & Wager [1992]), all specify essentially the same information.

The effectiveness of instructional objectives for enhancing academic performance has been debated since the 1960s, primarily because research studies have yielded mixed results. Gagné (1985) argued for informing learners of objectives, since doing so readies them for learning. Objectives also provide a framework for studying what will eventually be tested. In a meta-analysis of research on objectives, Klauer (1984) provided evidence of a small, positive effect of objectives on learning, but also noted that objectives tend to focus learners' attention on certain information and away from other information. This would suggest that, to enhance learning, objectives must be written for all information considered important to learn.

As will be discussed again in Chapter 10, many educational and training programs today are based on objectives. However, they probably do not include objectives for each and every skill or piece of information that students might expect to learn. Rather, objectives are written for critical skills or the minimum information deemed acceptable for a graduate of the program to know. In addition, some educators (e.g., Popham, 1988; Reiser & Dick, 1996) suggest that students be given simpler, perhaps more general, statements of objectives to guide their learning, since these are easier to understand and yet still keep students and teachers alike on the same track toward particular goals.

Contingency Contracts. *An instructional application that may make use of both behavior modification and instructional objectives* is the **contingency contract.** Used with individual students, the contract sets out the terminal behavior the student is to achieve, along with any conditions for achievement and the consequences for completion (or noncompletion) of the assigned task(s). The contract is negotiated between teacher and student, and both agree to its terms.

Contingency contracts are particularly useful in open educational systems, where students from several grade levels participate together in learning activities. Since students are not all at the same achievement levels, they negotiate individual contracts each week indicating their expected progress in accomplishing objectives in subject areas such as math or reading, for example. Instructors at all levels of schooling have also found contingency contracts to be a useful means of managing independent study projects. Instead of simply giving an assignment such as, "write a 10-page research paper on a topic related to behavioral psychology," instructors may negotiate with individual students on what should be included in the paper and how well it should be written.

Personalized System of Instruction (PSI). In 1968, Fred Keller proposed a whole new approach to college instruction that was based on behavioral principles (Keller, 1968). Keller noted problems with typical group instruction in the classroom—delays in reinforcing achievement, students progressing to more difficult instruction when they have not mastered basic material—that he believed could be solved with the personalized system of instruction (PSI), also known as the Keller Plan. PSI calls for course material to be broken up into units, or modules, each with a set of behavioral objectives specifying what is to be learned in that unit. Units generally correspond with chapters in a textbook, so that they are taken up in sequence. What makes PSI unique are the following characteristic features:

1. *Emphasis on individual study.* Students tackle course material on their own, often aided by study guides which provide practice on unit objectives (e.g., Johnson & Perkins, 1976). The teacher and any course aides serve as resources to students when they encounter difficulty understanding information or answering questions in the textbook or study guide.

2. *Self-pacing.* Students work at their own pace, and report to class only when they are ready to take a unit quiz. As a result, some students work quickly, finishing the course in half the semester or less, while other students, who require more time to master concepts, take the entire semester to finish.

3. *Unit mastery requirement.* Students are required to meet a prespecified mastery level on each unit. When they take a unit quiz, they receive feedback immediately, and if unit mastery has not been achieved, they may take the quiz again with no penalty. Typically, three or four versions of a unit quiz are available to students, and individual records are kept, noting which version a student took at a given time.

4. *Use of proctors.* The requirement to provide immediate feedback to students regarding their quiz performance obviously means considerable work for the teacher. To alleviate this problem, proctors are used to score quizzes and provide feedback. Proctors may be advanced students who have already taken the course, or they may be students in the class who have mastered the unit they are now proctoring. Advantages to the latter arrangement include students solidifying their own knowledge of the material as well as getting to know their fellow students better.

5. *Supplementary instructional techniques.* Since the primary mode of instruction in a PSI course is self-study, lectures, demonstrations, and other modes of delivery may be used in a supplementary way to enhance motivation and transfer. Students may be motivated to reach a particular unit, for example, because mastery of the unit is their ticket to attend a special demonstration related to the next unit.

In the decade following Keller's proposal, PSI was tried in literally thousands of college courses. Kulik, Kulik, and Cohen (1979) reported that students generally liked PSI better than traditional courses, course grades were higher in PSI than in traditional courses, and student achievement on course final examinations was higher in PSI than traditional courses. There are several reasons, however, why PSI is not more popular currently.

Offsetting its effectiveness are the costs of PSI in time and resources. Preparation time is likely to be great initially, because study materials must be generated and multiple versions of quizzes written. Some arrangement for quiz-taking and proctoring must be made, and in the days before computers, this often meant scheduling two rooms for a significant number of hours each week (which is not looked upon kindly by college administrators). Record-keeping can also be burdensome, since individual records must be kept on the progress of all students, and copies of all quizzes and keys must be accounted for.

Although problems of record-keeping and quiz-taking may be ultimately solved through the use of computers, other disadvantages of PSI are not so easily counteracted. Some students, for example, are simply unable to meet the mastery criterion set for passing quizzes, despite repeated testing (e.g., Sussman, 1981). It may be that more moderate levels of mastery should be set (cf. Reiser, Driscoll, & Vergara, 1987), or that some students would better profit from alternative instructional presentations. Finally, self-pacing permits procrastination, which means that some students will not finish the requirements of a PSI course within the designated semester-long period. After several semesters of experience with a PSI course that I taught, I learned to reduce procrastination by limiting self-pacing. That is, quizzes were made available for a 3-week window, which essentially forced students to maintain a reasonable rate of progress.

Teaching Machines to Computer-Based Instruction. "Educational toys with feedback are to be found in patent files reaching back at least a hundred years," said Sydney Pressey in 1964 (Pressey, 1964, p. 354). So perhaps it is not entirely accurate to attribute teaching machines and programmed instruction solely to the influence of behaviorism, but certainly automation has been viewed as the solution to the problem of providing immediate reinforcement for correct responses in instruction. Although contingency contracts allow for reinforcement at task completion and PSI provides for immediate feedback on quiz performance, neither provides for sufficient reinforcement during learning. An automated teaching machine, however, has this capability.

After the early teaching machines of Pressey (1926, 1927), Skinner (1958) proposed applying behavioral principles to teaching academic skills through programmed instruction. In an instructional program, content is arranged in small steps, called frames, which progress from simple to complex and require a response from the learner to go on. Since the steps are small and increase gradually in difficulty, learners respond correctly most of the time, which means their responses are reinforced frequently. What this amounts to is shaping of complex academic skills.

A typical example of a programmed text can be found in Holland and Skinner's (1961), *The Analysis of Behavior,* an excerpt of which is shown in Figure 2.8. It should be obvious from this excerpt that early programmed instruction, despite providing immediate and frequent reinforcement, suffered from one serious flaw: It was boring. The small steps, for some students, were too small. Furthermore, all students had to work through the frames in the same order.

To improve on this linear style of program, Crowder (1960) introduced the notion of branching. In branching programs, frames are larger and are typically followed by questions with several possible answer options. Depending on how students answer a given question, they are branched to another segment of the program. In this way, students who know the material already may skip quickly ahead to new material. Likewise, students having

FIGURE 2.8 *A Typical Example of Programmed Text*

Source: Holland & Skinner, 1961, pp. 42–45.

difficulty with the instruction may be branched to remedial segments, which provide additional information and practice.

Computer-based instruction, as originally conceived, is simply programmed instruction presented via computer. The computer provides obvious advantages over text-based programmed instruction, which can be very cumbersome for both the writer of the program and the student. The computer allows for complex branching sequences and can automatically record a student's responses (corrects, errors, even the particular sequence followed through the instruction). Increased computer technology has also enabled program designers to include complex graphics and synthesized speech along with text. As a result, instructional software is increasingly available that provides drill and practice on various academic skills, simulations to enhance problem-solving, or tutorials in various subject matters.

Improving Performance in Organizational Systems

A focus on performance improvement in organizations is the professional orientation of a fast-growing field known as performance technology (Stolovich & Keeps, 1992; Kaufman, Thiagarajan, & MacGillis, 1997). Behaviorism is commonly acknowledged as one of the primary origins of this hybrid field, contributing an emphasis on observable performance and the importance of incentives in shaping behavior.

In much the same way that behavior therapists have sought to manage individual behavior, performance technologists attempt to manage performance, usually within a team setting. "Managing performance (rather than judging or appraising it) is the key way in which managers can be successful through delegating effectively, gaining support, and building synergy with their team members" (Bell & Forbes, 1997). And several behavioral principles comprise the key to effective performance management. These include, for example, well-defined objectives for employee performance that are linked to the organization's business plan and regular feedback, consisting of knowledge of results and knowledge of progress (Spence & Hively, 1993).

In the traditional behavioral paradigm, feedback is the consequence of a response, typically reinforcement for an appropriate behavior. From decades of research on feedback, however, we have learned the importance of the information value of feedback. That is, feedback not only reinforces a response, it also provides information to the learner as to how performance can be improved. Knowledge of results provides feedback as to the quality of a particular performance, and knowledge of progress provides feedback of performance over time.

In studies of performance improvement within organizations, feedback as an intervention appears to have a profound effect. For example, consultants to a senior center used public feedback to increase contributions to the center (Jackson & Matthews, 1995). Volunteers clipped coupons, stamped the name of the senior center on the back, and then put them on products in local grocery stores. When store patrons bought these products, they could choose to redeem the coupon or donate its value to the senior center. While this procedure alone brought in some donations, both the value and frequency of donations increased substantially when the stores began posting signs indicating the progress each week of the dollars donated through the "Coupons for Caring" program.

According to Dean, Dean, and Rebalsky (1996), feedback is one of several environmental factors that support or hinder exemplary performance in an organization. In a study examining perceptions about performance blocks, they found that two-thirds of employees and managers identified environmental factors such as feedback, clear guides to expected performance, resources, and appropriate incentives as their biggest performance blocks. In contrast, only one-third identified individual factors such as sufficient knowledge and motivation to do assigned tasks. Interestingly, when teachers were asked to identify performance blocks of their students, individual factors were cited more often than environmental ones (Dean, Dean, & Rebalsky, 1996). The researchers concluded that analysis of the work environment is critical for managing performance improvement.

Planning for performance improvement is a process analogous to planning for behavior management or modification (Table 2.2) Once the desired performance has been determined and the gap is identified between what it

TABLE 2.2 *Planning for Performance Improvement*

Step 1: Determine desired performance and the gap between what is and what should be.

Step 2: Identify appropriate rewards and incentives for performance.

Step 3: Generate a plan for communicating performance goals and implementing incentives.

Step 4: Carry out the plan.

Step 5: Evaluate results and revise as necessary.

is and what it should be, appropriate rewards and incentives for performance can be selected (Zigon, 1997). Then a plan is generated, implemented, evaluated, and revised as necessary.

The Behaviorist Perspective on Learning: Issues and Criticisms

Behaviorism has contributed to a number of instructional innovations, and behavioral principles continue to be useful to professionals in a number of disciplines. But what of behaviorism's shortcomings? What aspects of learning does it fail to account for readily? What problems can be seen in the behavioral paradigm that suggest alternative theories should be explored? This chapter concludes with examination of these questions.

Verbal Behavior

The astute reader may have noticed that nowhere in this chapter has the learning of language been mentioned. Skinner maintained a long-standing interest in language, publishing an extensive operant analysis of language learning in 1957 with *Verbal Behavior* (Skinner, 1957). Skinner treated language as he did any other set of complex operant responses. He proposed that the verbal behavior of children is shaped, with appropriate verbal labels for objects and events being maintained through reinforcement as inappropriate ones are extinguished.

Skinner's position on language learning met with heavy criticism (e.g., Chomsky, 1959), and, indeed, accounting for certain kinds of utterances is difficult. Although a child's learning to call only cows by that label may hold up under operant analysis, consider a sentence such as, "I am looking for my glasses" (Leahey & Harris, 1997). Our immediate reaction to such a statement is to explain it in terms of what the person is thinking. He has an image of his glasses, which he has misplaced and is now trying to find. But Skinner, not permitting references to thought or mind, would argue that the stimulus in control of the verbal statement is the person's observation of his own searching behavior. That is, searching behavior in the past has resulted in the person finding his glasses and stopping the behavior; so he has learned to say, "I am searching for my glasses" as a response to this stimulus situation (Leahey & Harris, 1997).

This account of language learning seems a bit weird (Malcolm, 1964), and not all modern behaviorists adhere to it. Schoenfeld (1993) argued that behaviorists and nonbehaviorists alike must agree on the objective physicality of verbal behavior and the fact that language is learned within one's sociocultural environment. What differs between them, he claims, is their explanation for how each culture does its teaching.

Reinforcement and Human Behavior

While Skinner was interested in deriving functional laws of learning, i.e., the probability of behavior is increased when it is followed by reinforcement, some researchers wondered why reinforcement operates as it does. Why are some consequences of behavior reinforcing when others are not? Shedding light on this question are results summarized by Leahey and Harris (1997) on the use of different sorts of reinforcement schedules with humans. In order for human learners to exhibit the response patterns characteristic of certain reinforcement schedules, they had to be instructed as to the schedule in effect. Moreover, when given false information about what schedule would be in effect, human subjects responded according to what they believed was going on and not according to the actual manipulation (cf. Brewer, 1974).

In attempting to explain why reinforcement works, Estes (1972) provided an important link between behaviorism and later cognitive conceptions of motivation. Estes reviewed studies indicating that humans must have an expectation of being rewarded in order for reinforcement to work, and they must value the reward. As we will see in later chapters, the concepts of expectancy and value will play major roles in social learning theory (e.g., Bandura, 1986) and motivation (e.g., Keller, 1983).

Intrinsic Motivation

Finally, problems cropping up with the behaviorist conception of reinforcement were only further exacerbated by investigations into the notion of intrinsic motivation. It seems obvious to the casual observer that learners sometimes do things without ostensibly being reinforced. Some children spend hours reading, for example, because they "like to read." Others will spend days putting together jigsaw puzzles "just for the fun of it." Skinner would explain this behavior by referring to the reinforcement history of the individual. Some time ago, he would argue, the sources of reinforcement for that behavior were undoubtedly external (e.g., the child's parents praised her for reading and spent time reading with her). Over time, however, internal referents became associated with the behavior and became conditioned reinforcers to sustain it.

Skinner's account of motivation, like his ideas about language, met with criticism. Bates (1979) reviewed studies which demonstrated how intrinsic satisfaction can even be undermined by extrinsic reinforcement. When rewards were given to learners for behavior in which they had already engaged on their own (e.g., puzzle solving or creating artwork), their response rate went down. This supports the notion that reinforcement is not necessarily a straightforward affair. In Chapter 9, the topic of motivation is taken up in greater detail.

Conclusion

Perceived problems and limitations with radical behaviorism as an explanatory paradigm for learning have led many investigators to propose cognitive, neurological, developmental, and other theoretical constructs as alternative ways of understanding learning. To Skinner, reliance on internal mechanisms of learning has led psychology away from a science of behavior to "questions that should never have been asked" (Skinner, 1987, p. 785). And he argued for a return to consideration of behavior "as a subject matter in its own right" (Skinner, 1987, p. 780).

Yet, "all psychological research is essentially behavioral," claimed Bornstein (1988), "in that psychological data inevitably take the form of observable, measurable behaviors, whether those are conditioned responses, responses to questionnaire items, or descriptions of inkblots" (pp. 819–820). In a commemorative issue of *Psychological Review,* Kimble (1994) and Thompson (1994) agreed, citing modern behaviorism as a "sophisticated statement of the scientific method applied to the study of behaving organisms. From Watson to the present day, the emphasis has been on measurement" (Thompson, 1994, p. 263).

"Because behavioral data must ultimately serve as the dependent variable in all psychological research, however, it does not necessarily follow that internal states, causes, and motivations are inappropriate or misleading constructs" (Bornstein, 1988, p. 820). In the chapters that follow, these constructs will be examined, as behaviorism was in this chapter, for their explanatory value in understanding learning and their usefulness for planning effective instruction.

A Behaviorist Perspective on "Kermit and the Keyboard"

How might a behaviorist explain learning in the story of Kermit and the keyboard? If learning amounts to behavior change, then the first step is to look for what behaviors are being exhibited and how they have changed. Two behaviors that are easy to spot are that Kermit selects songs and then plays them. Let's examine those behaviors in detail. Are they increasing or decreasing in frequency? What is the consequence of each that might reveal the contingencies of reinforcement that are operating?

Selecting Songs

Behavior change: Increasing for some, decreasing for others

Consequence: Kermit plays some songs that he selects with ease, whereas he makes a lot of mistakes on other songs.

Contingencies of reinforcement: Kermit selects more often those songs that he can play easily and less often those on which he makes mistakes. Thus, particular song selection appears to be positively reinforced by playing well and punished by making mistakes.

Playing Songs

Behavior change: Here we see that the time Kermit spends playing appears to vary.

Consequence: As with song selection, the consequence of time spent playing is either performing well or making mistakes.

Contingencies of reinforcement: Kermit plays longer when he is playing well (positive reinforcement) but stops when he makes a lot of mistakes (punishment).

There is also evidence of shaping in this story, in that Kermit first practiced "House of the Rising Sun" very slowly and gradually increased the tempo until he could perform the song as it written without making any mistakes. The mistake that he continues to make while using the one accompaniment was reinforced by this arrangement but not by other arrangements he has tried. It is likely as well that chaining has taken place. Chaining would occur if he practiced a portion of each song individually and then put the sections together to successfully play a complete song.

Some aspects of this story are hard to explain by using behaviorist theory. Why, for instance, did Kermit choose to learn the keyboard in the first place? Motivation is usually explained in terms of reinforcement history. However, Kermit has had no prior experience with either the keyboard or a one-man band, so it is hard to see how he could have been reinforced previously to make this choice. When you read subsequent theories in this book, consider what aspects of this story they explain or fail to explain and how those explanations compare to these.

Theory Matrix

Theory	Radical Behaviorism
Prominent Theorists	B. F. Skinner; J. B. Watson
Learning Outcome(s)	Observable behavior
Role of the Learner	Active in the environment, consequences that follow behavior determine whether it is repeated.
Role of the Instructor	Identify learning goals
	Determine contingencies of reinforcements
	Implement program of behavior change
	Negotiate all of these with the learner's input
Inputs or Preconditions to Learning	Environmental conditions serve as discriminative stimuli, cueing which behavior is appropriate to perform.
Process of Learning	Not specifically addressed in this theory. All learning is assumed to be explained in terms of observable behavior and environmental events surrounding its occurrence.

Suggested Readings

Bijou, S. W., & Ruiz, R. (Eds.) 1981. *Behavior modification: Contributions to education.* Hillsdale, NJ: Erlbaum.

Sulzer, B., & Mayer, G. R. (1972). *Behavior modification procedures for school personnel.* New York: Holt, Rinehart and Winston.

Educational Technology, Special Issue: *Behaviorism Today, (1993) 33,* 10.

In addition, two journals—*Journal of Applied Behavior Analysis* and *Journal of Experimental Analysis of Behavior*—routinely publish articles dealing with some aspect of radical behaviorism.

Reflective Questions and Activities _____

1. Consider the principles of behaviorism in light of the epistemological traditions described in Chapter 1. To what view of knowledge is behaviorism most closely aligned? What evidence supports your choice?

2. View the movie, *A Clockwork Orange,* which was produced by Stanley Kubrick in the 1970s. Analyze the procedures used in terms of classical and operant conditioning.

   a. What image, or metaphor, of conditioning is presented in this movie?

   b. How do you think B. F. Skinner would have reacted to the procedures used in the movie?

   c. What alternative procedures might Skinner have proposed for altering Alex's violent behavior?

   d. What events were occurring in the 1970s that might have influenced Kubrick's decision to portray conditioning in this light?

3. Read B. F. Skinner's *Beyond Freedom and Dignity* or *Walden Two.* Consider the following questions.

   a. What is Skinner's vision of a "perfect" society?

   b. Do you think such a society could ever be realized? Why or why not?

   c. Do you think such a society is desirable? Why or why not?

4. Describe a learning situation in which you (or someone of your acquaintance) had (or are currently having) difficulty achieving some desired performance. Analyze the event in terms of the principles of behavior modification. Then, develop a plan to overcome the difficulty. Finally, describe how implementation of the plan should be monitored, including what you would do if it seemed to be ineffective.

5. As you will see in the following chapters, many theorists have rejected the concepts of behaviorism, believing that an understanding of learning is better served by other concepts. Take an initial position on the usefulness of behavioral principles, both for practitioners and for researchers.

Part III: Learning and Cognition

3

Cognitive Information Processing

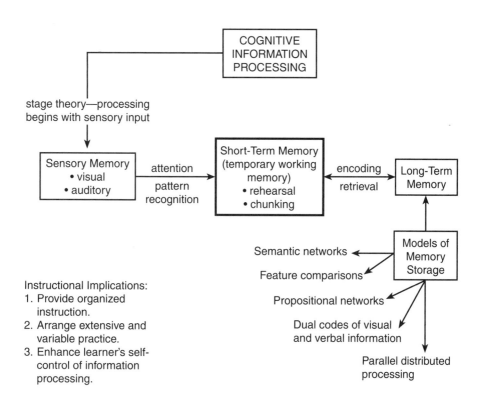

COGNITIVE INFORMATION PROCESSING

stage theory—processing begins with sensory input

Sensory Memory
• visual
• auditory

attention

pattern recognition

Short-Term Memory (temporary working memory)
• rehearsal
• chunking

encoding

retrieval

Long-Term Memory

Models of Memory Storage

Semantic networks

Feature comparisons

Propositional networks

Dual codes of visual and verbal information

Parallel distributed processing

Instructional Implications:
1. Provide organized instruction.
2. Arrange extensive and variable practice.
3. Enhance learner's self-control of information processing.

Consider these scenarios.

• *A Tale of Two Readers*

Sarah lives in a small rural community and participates nightly in the county's adult literacy program. She reads haltingly, sounding out unfamiliar words. The selection she has chosen to work on this week is a simple tale about village life, and she is able to comprehend the gist of the text quite easily.

Rosemary decided to go back to graduate school when the last of her three children graduated from high school and left home for college. Although her children had used their home desktop computer regularly for school assignments, Rosemary had never bothered to learn. Now, some of her courses required access to the Internet, so she was forced to purchase a modem. The salesperson (and her classmates) assured her that hooking it up and using it was a simple matter. Unfortunately, an operating problem sent Rosemary to the manual about the modem, where she attempted to make sense of sentences such as, "The primary application for the local digital loopback is to permit a modem that is not CCITT V.54 compatible to engage in a remote digital loopback test with your modem."

• *The Mechanic and the Web Surfer*

Marcy arrived to pick up her car, which had been in for service, and her mechanic, Wes, explained the repairs that had been made in addition to the routine oil service. One of the reasons Marcy liked this particular shop was that Wes never talked down to her but took the time to explain what was wrong with the car when it needed to be fixed. In this case, Wes said, the steering damper and center link had to be adjusted, and the noise she had reported was coming from worn bushings around the tie rod ends in the suspension. Marcy nodded in understanding. As she prepared to leave, she and Wes chatted about an incident reported in the paper concerning a hacker who had shut down the local Freenet. Wes mentioned that his wife enjoyed using her account to e-mail friends and relatives all around the United States. He, on the other hand, didn't quite understand how the Internet worked and had become concerned after the hacker incident. Marcy, who enjoyed Web surfing herself, stayed a few moments longer to give Wes a basic lesson on the Internet.

Arriving at their respective homes that evening, Marcy and Wes had remarkably similar conversations with their spouses. In response to his question about her car, Marcy told her husband, "Oh, they fixed something on the steering, and that squeak is being caused by some rod rubbing against something or other. Nothing to worry about." Her husband shook his head; why did he even ask? To his wife, Wes said, "One of my customers today told me all about computers and e-mail and that stuff." "What about it?" his wife wanted to know, but unfortunately, Wes couldn't remember anything more specific.

Before proceeding further, reflect momentarily on the behaviorist perspective discussed in the previous chapter. How might a behaviorist account for the behaviors exhibited in these two scenarios? How is a complex behavior such as reading acquired? Why did Marcy and Wes experience such difficulty in recalling to their spouses what they had been told earlier in the day? Questions similar to these pose problems for behaviorism. And although behaviorism had dominated American psychology for half a century, it was to be supplanted by cognitive challenges.

Remember that the study of cognition was not new to psychology. Before radical behaviorism had gained such a stronghold on psychological research and theory, Tolman used cognitive maps to explain purposive behavior in rats, and Hull relied on a number of cognitive mediators between stimulus and response. Pavlov, as well, had introduced the concept of the "second signal system" to account for language learning. Vygotsky had launched his theory of how inner speech functions as a cognitive mediator explicitly in reaction to American behaviorism. Moreover, Gestalt psychologists in Germany had proposed that organizational processes in cognition were important to perception, learning, and problem solving. What was new in American psychology was the computer metaphor adopted for conceptualizing cognition.

The birth of computers after World War II provided a concrete way of thinking about learning and a consistent framework for interpreting early work on memory, perception, and learning. Stimuli became inputs; behavior became outputs. And what happened in between was conceived of as information processing. Today, what is known as cognitive information processing (CIP) is in reality an integration of views developed from a variety of perspectives.

> Like the traditional cognitive view, the CIP model portrays the mind possessing a structure consisting of components for processing (storing, retrieving, transforming, using) information and procedures for using the components. Like the behavioral view, the CIP model holds that learning consists partially of the formation of associations. (Andre & Phye, 1986, p. 3)

Overview of the Information-Processing System

According to the cognitive information processing view, the human learner is conceived to be a processor of information in much the same way a computer is. When learning occurs, information is input from the environment, processed and stored in memory, and output in the form of some learned capability. Adherents of the CIP model, like behaviorists, seek to explain how the environment modifies human behavior. But unlike behaviorists, they assume an intervening variable between environment and behavior. That variable is the information processing system of the learner.

Most models of information processing can be traced to Atkinson and Shiffrin (1968), who proposed a multistore, multistage theory of memory. That is, from the time information is received by the processing system, it undergoes a series of transformations until it can be permanently stored in memory. This flow of information, as it is generally conceived, is shown in Figure 3.1. Displayed in the figure are the three basic stages of the proposed memory system—sensory memory, short-term memory, and long-term memory—along with the processes assumed to be responsible for transferring information from one stage to the next. Let us briefly consider what these stages are and how they are believed to function.

The Stages of Information Processing

Sensory memory represents the first stage of information processing. Associated with the senses (vision, hearing, etc.), it functions to hold information in memory very briefly, just long enough for the information to be processed further. For example, imagine yourself in a dark, unfamiliar room. You strike a

FIGURE 3.1 *The Flow of Information as Generally Conceptualized in Information-Processing Theory*

match, which flares briefly and then goes out. In the split second after the match has gone out, you retain a visual after-image of the room, which stays with you just long enough for you to determine where the door or light switch is located. There is a separate sensory memory corresponding with each of the five senses, but all are assumed to operate in essentially the same way.

Working memory, also called short-term memory or short-term store (Atkinson & Shiffrin, 1968, 1971), is the stage at which further processing is carried out to make information ready for long-term storage or a response. Originally a unitary construct, working memory is generally thought to have independent processors for individual sensory modes (Baddeley, 1992). Working memory has been likened to consciousness. When you are actively thinking about ideas and are therefore conscious of them, they are in working memory.

Working memory not only holds information for a limited amount of time, but also holds a limited amount of information. In other words, you can think about only a few ideas at one time or read and understand relatively few phrases at once. With very long and complex sentences, for example, the reader has typically forgotten the beginning of the sentence by the time the end of it is reached. You can well imagine the effect on comprehension and recall that this limited capacity for keeping things in mind will have.

The **long-term memory** represents a permanent storehouse of information. Anything that is to be remembered for a long time must be transferred from short-term to long-term memory. Although forgetting is a phenomenon we have all experienced (and will be discussed in detail later in the chapter), it is assumed that once information has been processed into long-term memory, it is never truly lost. As for capacity, despite the protests of many children, long-term memory cannot be filled up. As far as we know, long-term memory is capable of retaining an unlimited amount and variety of information.

Table 3.1 displays a summary of the three stages of information processing that may help you keep their properties in mind as you progress through this chapter.

The Flow of Information During Learning

As indicated earlier, information is transformed—or processed—as it passes from one stage of memory to the next. What are the processes assumed to be responsible for these transformations? Let's examine a particular example from A Tale of Two Readers to trace what may happen during learning. Suppose Sarah comes to this sentence in the story she is reading: "Visitors to the town are always struck by the beauty of its wide, azalea-lined avenues." The letters on the page stimulate Sarah's visual sensory register, which receives and briefly records a representation of the information as it originally occurred. Then, familiar shapes of letters and words are perceived as pattern recognition takes place. It is at this point that the process of attention also exerts an effect. An unfamiliar word may cause processing to slow, because added attention must be paid to individual letters rather than whole words.

Upon entering working memory, the information is coded conceptually, i.e., takes on meaning. Meanings of the individual words are retrieved from long-term memory to assist Sarah in constructing a representation of the whole sentence. Since the sentence is more than a few words, internal rehearsal may also occur to preserve the first few words in memory while the end of the sentence is being perceived.

Finally, in order for the information to be processed into long-term memory, Sarah must encode its meaning. This means that the representation

TABLE 3.1 *Summary of Memory Stages*

	Stages		
Properties	*Sensory Register*	*Short-Term Store*	*Long-Term Store*
Capacity	Large	Small	Large
Code	Literal copy of physical stimulus	Dual code —verbal —visual	Episodic/semantic
Permanence	0.5 seconds	20–30 seconds	Permanent
Source	Environment	Environment and prior knowledge	Effective encodings from STS
Loss	Decay	Displacement or decay	Irretrievability

Source: From McCown, R. R., Driscoll, M. P., & Roop, P., *Educational psychology: A learning-centered approach to classroom practice.* Boston: Allyn & Bacon, 1996. Reprinted with permission.

she constructs of the sentence must be meaningful and make connections with related knowledge already in long-term memory. For example, her previous experience with azaleas and wide streets may allow her to construct an image of what this sentence describes. Her image then becomes a useful retrieval cue when she is asked to recall what she has read.

It may be evident from this example that processing does not truly occur in the unidirectional, linear way in which it is often depicted (e.g., in Figure 3.1). Instead, the representation Sarah constructs of the sentence is determined both by the information itself (data-driven, bottom-up processing) and by her prior knowledge (conceptually driven, top-down processing). The degree to which either type of processing dominates seems to depend on the nature of the learning task itself and the amount of prior knowledge the learner brings to it.

Little has yet been said about the control processes influencing information flow. Whether these are thought of as comprising a system component (e.g., Gagné, 1985; Andre & Phye, 1986) or as processes modifying information flow within and between components (e.g., Atkinson & Shiffrin, 1971), they have the same effect. In some way, an executive monitor keeps track of the information flow and makes decisions about processing priorities. This may occur in a conscious, strategic fashion or in an unconscious, automatic way. For example, Sarah may have very deliberately chosen to associate an image with the sentence she read, because she has found imagery to be a very effective study strategy. On the other hand, suppose the story had previously described only camellias adorning villagers' lawns. Sarah may then have developed an expectation that could cause her to mistakenly perceive "camellias" instead of "azaleas" in the target sentence. In either case, a control process has modified the information flow and what was ultimately understood and learned.

The sections that follow focus on each of the major stages and processes of the human processing system. As you read them, keep in mind two things. First, the computer provided a concrete metaphor for human information processing and, thus, a language for describing and integrating a variety of learning phenomena. Second, for instruction to be meaningful and relevant, it must build upon learners' prior knowledge and help learners to construct cognitive connections between what they already know and what they are being asked to learn.

Sensory Memory

The existence of some sort of perceptual store in the information-processing system that registers information and holds it very briefly was demonstrated in a series of experiments conducted by Sperling (1960). Sperling presented subjects with a visual array of twelve letters (arranged in three rows of four letters each), such as the one shown in Figure 3.2. He flashed the array on a screen for 50 milliseconds (one-twentieth of a second) and then asked subjects to report what letters they had seen. Even with such a brief exposure, subjects could consistently report three or four letters accurately.

Although this result seemed to indicate a limited processing capacity, Sperling was able to show that, in fact, all of the letters had entered sensory memory. He did this by using a partial report technique. That is, he used a high, medium, or low tone to signal to subjects which row of the array they were to report. Instead of a relatively poor performance (three or four of twelve letters), subjects showed remarkably good performance, reliably reporting three or four letters in the row (so, three or four of four) no matter which row was signaled. It appears, then, that sensory memory is temporally, rather than visually, limited. In other words, a great deal of visual information registers, but it decays very rapidly without further processing, within a quarter of a second, according to Sperling's experiments.

Relatively little is known about the sensory memories corresponding to the other senses, but they are presumed to function in a similar way. Darwin, Turvey, and Crowder (1972) replicated Sperling's results with the auditory system. They found, however, that the auditory sensory memory (or echo) lasted longer than the visual sensory memory (or icon), typically up to 4 seconds under partial report conditions. An explanation for this difference is thought to lie in the requirements for speech perception. In other words, sounds must remain in sensory memory long enough for them to be combined with other sounds so that speech may be understood.

Sperling's use of the partial report technique also illustrates the effect that attention has on information processing. The tone served as a cue to focus attention on a particular part of the display so that it could be processed further and recalled. Attention is a process that has been conceptualized in a variety of ways. Instructors admonish students to pay attention in class, but they also adopt measures to focus students' attention on particular features of instruction. Either way, a student who is not attentive misses some of the information to be learned.

Cognitive psychologists, noting that some information always seems to be lost in processing, initially thought that attention acted as a bottleneck or

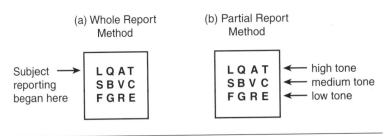

FIGURE 3.2 *Visual Displays Similar to Those Used by Sperling (1960)*

filter preventing information from entering the system (e.g., Broadbent, 1957). Treisman (1960) showed, however, that attention is not an all-or-none proposition and suggested that it serves to attenuate, or tune out, stimulation. Her ideas are easily illustrated by thinking about what happens at parties. You may be attending to one conversation, ostensibly unaware of what else is being said around you. But when you hear your name spoken or someone else talking about a topic that interests you, your attention shifts. Apparently enough information was being processed to prompt you to react and pay closer attention to the secondary source.

Researchers have come to view attention as a resource with limited capacity to be allocated and shared among competing goals (cf. Kahneman, 1973; Grabe, 1986). This suggests that learners have some control over the process and may selectively focus attention to meet certain ends. It is also true, however, that some tasks require relatively little attention and may be accomplished effortlessly and automatically. The concepts of selectivity and automaticity are important aspects of attention that hold implications for instruction. Let us consider each in turn.

Selective Attention

Selective attention refers to the learner's *ability to select and process certain information while simultaneously ignoring other information.* The extent to which individuals can spread their attention across two or more tasks (or sources of information) or focus on selected information within a single task depends upon a number of factors. The most obvious, perhaps, is the meaning that the task or information holds for an individual. Your name spoken in a crowded room catches your attention because it is highly meaningful to you.

Second, similarity between competing tasks or sources of information makes a difference. It is hard to listen to two conversations at the same time when both speakers are the same sex and are speaking in a similar tone and volume. Imagine the poor student, for example, who is trying to listen to the teacher at the same time a classmate talks in her ear. Similarly, a learner may enjoy studying to classical music but find her concentration slipping when vocal music is played.

Task complexity or difficulty is a third factor that influences attention. Simple tasks, such as winding yarn into a ball, require relatively little attention and are easily done at the same time as other things. Watching a light-hearted TV comedy, putting together a jigsaw puzzle, and talking to your family about tomorrow's schedule are probably all tasks that can be accomplished simultaneously. But reading a medical history for purposes of diagnosis or assembling an intricate set of electrical circuits demands more complete and focused attention. A task may also demand more attention when it is something about which the learner has little prior knowledge. For example, a post-baccalaureate student taking his first course in learning theory is likely to find it necessary to pay close attention to both his instructor and the textbook.

Finally, the ability to control attention, in both a general and specific sense, appears to differ with age, hyperactivity, intelligence, and learning disabilities (Grabe, 1986, p. 66). For example, attention deficit disorder is a condition afflicting a small proportion of preadolescent children. They seem to be unable to focus attention or to turn off irrelevant stimulation. As a result, their school performance typically suffers.

How, then, is attention best managed in instructional situations? To influence attention or alertness of students during the course of a classroom lesson, Good and Brophy (1984) recommended that instructors employ standard signals (e.g., "Let's begin," "Back on task!," turning the lights on or off). A third grade teacher of my acquaintance uses a maraca to gain the attention of all students when they are working in pairs or small groups. Because he has used that signal from the first day of class, students know when they hear it that they are to stop whatever they are doing and look at him for direction.

When it is important to focus students' attention on certain aspects of the instructional materials, stimulus features can be highlighted through the use of color or type of print (in textual materials), voice inflections or gestures (in classroom presentations), and novelty. To emphasize the different sorts of roles that computer consultants often play, for example, a community college teacher wears different hats during his lecture, each one representing a different role.

Finally, Grabe (1986) reviewed ways in which learners themselves may be taught to stay on task and selectively attend to important features of instruction. He indicated that two things appear to be important: (1) Learners should be taught to take more time in responding to a learning task (to reduce impulsiveness), and (2) they should be given a strategy for focusing attention and allowed to practice that strategy (p. 74). Certain games that require attention, e.g., *Concentration* or *Simon Says,* can be used to help students develop better attending skills.

Automaticity

When tasks are overlearned or sources of information become habitual, to the extent that their attention requirements are minimal, **automaticity** has occurred. Driving a car provides a good example of the distinction Shiffrin and Schneider (1977) made between automatic and controlled processing. For the most part, the driving task is automatic, enabling the driver to listen attentively to a radio program, for example. But when traffic is heavy or something unusual occurs to demand the driver's attention, driving shifts to a controlled process. The driver then must pay much closer attention to driving and fails to hear what is being said on the radio.

LaBerge and Samuels (1974) have developed a theory to account for automatic processing in reading. They believe decoding words should be so automatic for readers that they can concentrate their attention on comprehending the meaning of what is read. In A Tale of Two Readers, for example, Sarah has learned to decode but has not yet learned the skill to the point where it is automatic. As a result, her reading is slow and fraught with difficulty. Rosemary, on the other hand, may decode automatically most of the time, but here faces unfamiliar information that makes her comprehension of the meaning difficult. As a result, she, like the driver in traffic, must shift from automatic to controlled processing in order to decode the unfamiliar words.

To develop automatic decoding skills in readers, researchers have explored a number of possibilities, including extended word identification practice as part of the regular text-reading curriculum (e.g., Beck, 1981, 1983). More recently, researchers have become encouraged by the potential of the computer for providing many different types of word tasks in an engaging environment (Perfetti & Curtis, 1986). It may also be useful for teachers to include read-aloud activities (such as reading and answering questions) after learners have read silently. Readers' sensitivity to different kinds of scripts can impair their comprehension, but such impairment seems to be obviated by reading aloud during rereading (Jacoby, Levy, & Steinbach, 1992).

Once reading is automatic, however, what readers will comprehend and remember from text depends upon how they allocate their attention as they read. Readers will generally allocate greater attention to important elements in a text (Anderson, 1982). They determine importance based on the purpose for which they are reading as well as features of the text that signal something is important.

As noted in the previous section, the reader's attention can be directed by typographical cues in the text (e.g., boldface print, capitalization [Glynn & Divesta, 1979]), as well as the presence of titles (Kozminsky, 1977), specific phrases (e.g., "an important cause of…" [Armbruster, 1986]), and idea unit structure (Kintsch & van Dijk, 1978). Idea unit structure refers to the placement of main ideas and supporting details within a paragraph. Ideas that appear high in the structure are more likely to be attended to and remembered than details buried deep within a paragraph. Writers of instructional texts, then, are well advised to employ these features to direct learner attention to the important, to-be-learned information.

Readers, on their own, also differentially allocate attention according to the purpose for which they are reading. Reading a novel, for example, typically involves reading for the gist of a story, and readers may be hard pressed to recount very specific details when they are finished. Reading a textbook or technical manual, on the other hand, is done with a specific purpose in mind—to locate and learn important information. Assigning instructional objectives (Klauer, 1984) or inserting questions in the text (Andre, 1979) has

idea unit structure (handwritten marginal note)

proven effective for helping students focus their attention on specific text information.

Automatization of other basic skills besides reading (such as the rules of arithmetic operations and grammar) is considered to be a desirable educational goal for the primary grades (Gagné, 1983; Bloom, 1986). By extension, one can also see the usefulness of learning certain tasks as adults to automaticity. Pilots must react automatically to a variety of information sources in the cockpit. Astronomers automatically process patterns of stars in the search for anomalies that might be signs of new stars or other astral phenomena. And detection of signs of abuse is probably automatic for skilled therapists.

Pattern Recognition and Perception

Just attending to information is not enough to ensure its further processing, however. One might say that attention is necessary but not sufficient; information must also be analyzed and familiar patterns identified to provide a basis for further processing. **Pattern recognition** refers to the process whereby *environmental stimuli are recognized as exemplars of concepts and principles already in memory.* This recognition is preconceptual, something like finding a shape that matches a stencil without identifying what the shape or stencil pattern actually represents.

Pattern recognition is a particularly difficult process to model in the human information-processing system, and, consequently, several different models have been proposed. Each carries particular implications for how the process operates and for what form information is represented in memory. Briefly, template matching assumes that mental copies of environmental stimuli, or templates, are stored in memory. Pattern recognition, then, consists of simply matching the incoming information to the appropriate template in memory. Although this seems intuitively appealing, look at Figure 3.3 and consider what this means for a template-matching model of pattern recognition. In order for you to recognize all of those figures as representations of the letter *A*, you would have to have templates in memory to match each one. For obvious reasons, this model fails as a reasonable account of human pattern recognition.

According to an alternative, prototype model, what is stored in memory is not an exact copy of a stimulus, but rather an abstracted, general

template matching (no!)

A a A **A** *a* a A a

FIGURE 3.3   *Variations of the Letter A*

Prototype model

prototype. Pattern recognition in this case involves comparing the incoming information with the prototype. If a close enough match is found, then the incoming stimulus is recognized as an example of the class of objects or events represented by the prototype. Thus, all of the letters in Figure 3.3, for example, are similar enough to the assumed prototype to be recognized as *As*.

The prototype model has become popular for explaining pattern recognition, primarily because of evidence that suggests we tend to store prototypic concepts in memory (see, in particular, Eleanor Rosch's work [1973, 1975]). For example, asked to indicate what color comes to mind in response to the verbal stimulus *red*, you are likely to choose a color that is close to fire-engine red. Similarly, reading about Olympic athletes or shore birds tends to evoke general ideas about these concepts rather than specific, previously encountered examples.

A third model of pattern recognition, called feature analysis, presumes that specific, distinctive features are stored in memory. Incoming information is then analyzed for the presence of these features. To consider the letter *A* one more time, its defining features might include the two sides, the angle at which they are joined, and the horizontal connecting line. All stimulus letters would be analyzed for these features and, if found, would be identified as *As*.

Feature analysis, like the prototype model, is supported by experimental evidence and together, the two models have influenced pedagogical recommendations for concept learning. Tennyson and Cocchiarella (1986) proposed a model for teaching concepts that calls for presenting, first, a best or prototypic concept example followed by a variety of examples that differ from the prototype in systematic ways. The examples help learners to abstract the meaningful dimensions of the concept and determine which features are critical and invariant and which are nonessential and variable across examples.

To see how this model might work, consider one of the concepts from the previous chapter: positive reinforcement. A best or prototypic example might be one in which positive reinforcement is shown with animals and the use of a primary reinforcer. Then, additional examples could be explored in which positive reinforcement is demonstrated with children in school or adults at work and the use of secondary or social reinforcers. Or consider how a medical student might learn to distinguish diseased from normal cells. With stained slides showing clear examples of each for comparison, the student could examine other slides bearing cells that show a range of what is considered normal characteristics and a range of what is identified as diseased.

Although the feature comparison and prototype models account well for most instances of pattern recognition, they also are unable to account for why certain patterns are recognized even though all the features are not

feature analysis

the letter "A"

3 sets of 3
not 9

black "X"

Closure	Proximity	Similarity

FIGURE 3.4   *Gestalt Principles of Organization*

Gestalt theory

present or they fail to resemble their prototype. For example, a degraded copy of the letter *A,* as might be seen on a badly eroded tombstone or a poorly produced overhead transparency, is still recognized as an *A.*

To explain this and other perceptual phenomena not easily handled with the prototype or feature analysis models, we rely on principles of organization, context, and past experience. Gestalt psychologists, in studies dating from the early twentieth century, demonstrated that human perception tends to involve "going beyond the information given" in order to construct a meaningful interpretation. That is, the way in which stimuli are organized will prompt the viewer to see them in certain ways, apart from what is actually there. For example, look at the pictures displayed in Figure 3.4. What do you see? Chances are, you did not say, "Just a bunch of dots." The principle of closure prompts us to close up the spaces between the dots in Figure 3.4 (left) and to perceive the figure as an "*A*". Due to proximity, we view the dots in Figure 3.4 (center), not as *nine dots,* but as *three sets of three dots.* Finally, similarity dictates that similar units will be perceived as one, so that we do not see black and white dots in Figure 3.4 (right), we see a black *X.*

The effect of context on pattern recognition can be illustrated by reference to the tombstone and overhead transparency mentioned earlier. In those instances, why is it likely for the degraded letter to be perceived as an *A*? Presumably, the reason is that clues to its identity exist in the context that surrounds it. Other, more easily perceived letters suggest what words are on the tombstone and transparency. Once the word containing the degraded letter has been determined, the identity of the letter is obvious. Figure 3.5 illustrates how context is used to resolve some perceptual ambiguity. The figure in the center could be either the letter *B* or the number *13.* Which will be perceived depends on whether the other letters in the row or the figures in the column are used to provide contextual clues.

Past experience, or prior learning, is the last factor to be considered for its effect on pattern recognition. This refers to the simple fact that what has been learned or experienced previously will have some impact on what is perceived in later situations. A good illustration of this can be seen in the

I2

A I3 C

I4   FIGURE 3.5 *Context Effects on Perception*

Stroop effect. An individual is shown a series of color words (e.g., blue, green, or red) that are printed in different colors and is asked to "name the colors as quickly as you can." What happens is that the person has great difficul ty in identifying the colors of the words, tending instead to read the words themselves. Knowledge of color words, coupled with reading skill, interferes with one's ability to perceive the colors. The same would hold true for proofreading; one has a tendency to read the words as they should be typed rather than as they actually are.

Solving problems can also require overcoming the effects of past experience on perception. In other words, some problem situations must be perceived in a new way in order for a solution to be reached. In Kohler's (1925) experiments with a chimpanzee, for example, bananas were placed just out of the chimpanzee's reach with a stick near at hand. In order to get at the bananas, the chimpanzee had to perceive the properties of the stick as affording its use as a tool to knock the bananas within reach. Similarly, solving an insight problem such as "If the lily pads on a pond double every day, and the pond is completely covered on the 100th day, on which day is it half-covered?" requires thinking of the problem in terms of logic rather than math.

Although little is known about how people come to be proficient at casting problems in a new light in order to solve them, there is evidence to suggest that practice on many different kinds of problems may help (Sternberg & Davidson, 1983). Practice with a variety of problems can make learners more aware of the role of context in problem solution and thus more open to the consideration of alternate assumptions.

The influences of past experience and context on perception can also come together in expectations about students. It has been well documented that teachers' expectations of students may affect their evaluations of student achievement, as well as their own behavior toward students (e.g., Good, 1987). In other words, expecting a student to be a problem in class can predispose the instructor to perceiving more problem behaviors. Similarly, a student with a reputation for high achievement is more likely to be perceived in that light.

The expectations themselves may develop from previous experiences of the teacher, from the immediate context, or both. For example, the teacher has learned to associate, and therefore comes to expect, certain behaviors with high- and low-achieving students, males and females, or well- and poorly behaved children. But context also plays a part. Teachers may expect less of the same individual in a generally high-achieving class than in a class that performs less well overall.

Although the self-fulfilling prophecy (Rosenthal and Jacobson, 1968) has had a considerable influence in schools over the past 20 years, recent evidence has shown that what teachers do (or fail to do) matters more than what teachers expect with regard to student achievement. Goldenberg (1992) described two cases of paradoxical expectancy in which the children's first grade, year-end achievements were in marked contrast to what the teacher had expected. He concluded in one case that "The teacher had failed to take corrective action when she should have *because she had expected* [the student] to do well on her own" (Goldenberg, 1992, p. 539). In the other case, "*in spite of the teacher's low expectations* for [the student's] success, the teacher took actions that appear to have influenced [her] eventual first-grade reading achievement.... Low expectations were clearly evident, but they were irrelevant in determining the teacher's actions" (p. 539). Although expectations can have an influence on teacher behavior, then, they do not always matter. What appears to be more important is whether the instructor monitors student achievements and takes corrective action as necessary.

Sensory memory, attention, and pattern recognition, while important, obviously tell only part of the story. When learners have paid sufficient attention and pattern recognition of selected portions of the stimulus has occurred, a great deal more processing is still required for the information to become a meaningful and permanent part of memory. The next stage of activity occurs in working memory.

Working Memory

Information selected for further processing comes to the working memory. At this stage, concepts from long-term memory will be activated for use in making sense of the incoming information. But, as indicated earlier in the chapter, there are limits to how much information can be held in working memory at one time and for how long information may be retained there, unless, of course, something is done to increase capacity or duration in some way.

In a now classic study of short-term memory, George Miller (1956) demonstrated that about 7 ± 2 numbers could be recalled in a digit-span test. This test consisted of reading subjects a list of numbers and asking them to immediately repeat what they had heard. With seven items being the typical memory span, is it any surprise that local phone numbers are exactly seven digits? Miller also whimsically wondered whether there are magical qualities to the number 7; after all, there are "the seven wonders of the world, the seven seas, the seven deadly sins, the seven daughters of Atlas in the Pleiades, the seven ages of man, the seven levels of hell, the seven primary colors, the seven notes of the musical scale, and the seven days of the week" (Miller, 1967, pp. 42–43).

Despite Miller's whimsy, seven bits of information have been shown to constitute the memory span for a great variety of materials. Moreover, each bit of information can vary tremendously in size. A ten-letter word, for example, may be one bit, along with a six-word sentence. Discovery of this fact has led to the notion that *working memory capacity may be increased through creating larger bits*, known as the process of **chunking.** Take, for example, the span of letters shown below.

JFKFBIAIDSNASAMIT

As individual letters, they more than exceed working memory capacity. But as five chunks—JFK, FBI, AIDS, NASA, and MIT—they are easily processed.

What this has been taken to mean for instruction is that learning tasks should be organized so that they can be easily chunked by the learner. This may be as simple as breaking complex tasks into manageable steps, as in a science experiment, or presenting discrete bits of information to be studied and practiced, as in the frames of a computer-based tutorial lesson. In addition, issues in political science that involve very complex arguments, for example, will be better understood if the arguments are broken down and examined bit by bit.

How chunks of information are actually stored in working memory has been likened to a series of slots, with each chunk taking up one slot. As new chunks come into memory, they push out those that were previously occupying the available spaces. This is now the accepted explanation for the serial position effect known as recency. In the serial position task, subjects are given a list of words or nonsense syllables to learn. Typically, fifteen or twenty items are presented at a rapid rate, and immediately following the last item, subjects recall as many as they can. You can guess which ones they recall best—the items at the end of the list or those seen most recently. It was assumed, then, that later items on the list pushed out of memory those that had been seen first. There was simply not enough room for them all.

To determine the duration of working memory, Brown (1958) and Peterson and Peterson (1959) presented subjects with sets of three letters they were to recall after brief intervals. What seems like an easy task becomes much more difficult when rehearsal is prevented during the retention interval. That is, subjects had to count backwards by threes from a given number until the retention interval was up. Results indicated that memory for the letters was still good after only 3 seconds, but after 18 seconds, decay was nearly complete. Given individual differences, it is generally accepted that unrehearsed information will be lost from working memory in about 15 to 30 seconds. In the days of the rotary dial, this is about the same amount of time it took to dial a number and get a busy signal!

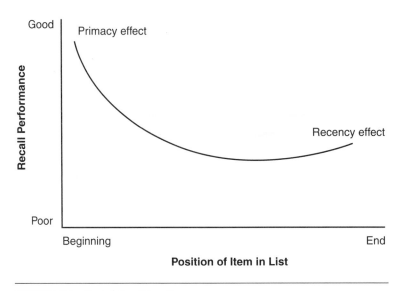

FIGURE 3.6   *Serial Position Curve*

In order to prevent the loss of information from working memory, and to ensure its being transferred to long-term storage, two processes are necessary: rehearsal and encoding.

Rehearsal   *Pౡactice ... CX: phone #*

When you repeat a phone number to yourself over and over while waiting to use the phone, you are engaged in rehearsal. Some would call this maintenance rehearsal because the repetition serves to maintain the information in the working memory for some designated period of time. Once you have made the call and reached your party, you no longer have the need to maintain the phone number in the short-term store.

Rehearsal has been used to explain the primacy effect of the serial position curve. When items are presented as described earlier, but at a slower rate, subjects remember not only the last items on the list, but the first ones as well (Figure 3.6). You can imagine why. With only a few items in memory at the beginning of the list, subjects have time between items to rehearse all the items they have seen. As more items crowd in, however, the rehearsal task becomes more difficult, so that items in the middle of the list receive less practice. As before, items at the end are recalled well because they are still in working memory at the time of recall.

Whereas recency and primacy effects are ostensibly associated with short-term memory, there are anecdotal data to suggest that something similar goes on even after information should be in long-term memory. For example, if a pop quiz is given after a typical 50-minute lecture, chances are students will remember best what was discussed in the first 10 minutes of class and in the last 10 minutes before the quiz. Likewise, most journalists adhere to the maxim that important information should go at the beginning and end of their articles, because these are the paragraphs best remembered by readers. These phenomena have led some researchers to question the dual-stage nature of memory and to propose instead some sort of intermediate memory or a continuum from short-term to long-term memory.

Finally, for information to reach a relatively permanent state in long-term memory, maintenance rehearsal is not enough. Learners will argue that simple repetition is an effective means for them to remember something for a long time. In the case of highly overlearned material, such as arithmetic facts, spelling words, or a memorized script, they are probably right. But repetition of more complex and meaningful information will not ensure its being fully processed into long-term memory. Elaborative rehearsal, or encoding, will.

Encoding *elaborative rehearsal*

Encoding refers to the process of relating incoming information to concepts and ideas already in memory in such a way that the new material is more memorable. Left to their natural inclinations, humans will always try to make things meaningful, to fit some new experience into the fabric of what they already know. We have already seen the evidence of this in perception and attention. Encoding serves to make permanent what these processes have initiated.

Studies demonstrating the various ways in which encoding may take place are too numerous to review in any comprehensive fashion here. But it is useful to consider briefly the major types of encoding schemes that have been investigated. The concept of organization, to begin with, has long been of interest to psychologists and educators alike. Bousfield (1953) found that people will group related pieces of information into categories in order to learn and remember them better. Even when information is seemingly unrelated, learners will impose their own, subjective organization on the material in order to learn it (Tulving, 1962). To assist learners in organizing material meaningfully, outlines (Glynn & Divesta, 1977), hierarchies (Bower et al., 1969), and concept trees (see the examples provided in Chapter 2 and later in this chapter [Tessmer & Driscoll, 1986]) have all proven effective.

Mnemonics and mediation (Matlin, 1983) provide other effective means for encoding. Learning a list of unrelated words, for example, is facilitated by linking the words together in the form of a story (Bower and Clark, 1969). The story then serves as a mediator to make the words on the list, which are meaningless by themselves, more memorable. This can be a helpful strategy for young children to use while learning to read. By themselves, single words

ex. mnemonics ; mediation

may not have much meaning at first. But when children write stories incorporating certain words, they often find it easier to read and recognize these words later. Similarly, mnemonics such as ROY G BIV or "My Very Earnest Mother Just Showed Us Nine Planets" serve to aid in the learning and recall of the colors in the spectrum and the planets in our solar system (see reviews of mnemonic strategies by Higbee [1979] and Bellezza [1981]).

imagery

Finally, imagery can be a very effective means of encoding information. Studies have shown that pictures suggesting visual images (Levin & Kaplan, 1972) or simply instructions to form images related to text material (Kulhavy & Swenson, 1975) are effective in facilitating learning. Some teachers now find that combining this method with story creation, as described, can be a very powerful means for facilitating not only learning but motivation (D. Cooper, personal communication, September, 1992). Children "publish" their stories by drawing illustrations to accompany them. In so doing, they strengthen their understanding of words in a very personal, meaningful way.

Before leaving this topic, it is perhaps wise to point out that nearly any method of elaborative encoding is better for learning than is mere repetition of information. But which approach is best depends upon the learners and the material to be learned. Moreover, learners who have developed idiosyncratic but effective encoding strategies will not necessarily benefit from some strategy imposed by the instruction. For this reason, there has been considerable interest in determining how learners may be taught to develop and use their own strategies effectively (cf. Pressley & Levin, 1983; Levin & Pressley, 1986; Segal, Chipman, & Glaser, 1985).

Learners may be encouraged to invent their own mnemonics, for example. Instructors in a driving-under-the-influence program who attended a workshop I presented invented the acronym VOMIT to remind themselves of the effects of drinking on the driving task. (I no longer recall what the individual letters stand for, but no doubt they do! This just illustrates how individually effective mnemonics can be; what works for one learner may not for another.)

Self-questioning has also been investigated as a means for learners to encode information they hear in lectures or read in printed instructional materials. Sometimes learners ask themselves questions to aid in comprehending material, such as, "How does the meaning of this concept differ from what was discussed on the previous page?" Other questions, which call for drawing inferences, should help learners to integrate new information with what they have already learned.

In reviewing research on self-questioning as an encoding strategy, Snowman (1986) pointed out that some learners must be taught how to frame good questions if the strategy is to be effective. Some teachers do this as early as the second grade by asking their students, "What could you ask yourself to be sure you understand ___?," and then providing feedback on the students' responses (S. Briggs, personal communication, October, 1992).

But Ormrod (1990) speculated that it might be just a matter of students asking fact-based, low-level questions because they have learned to expect such questions on class examinations. Perhaps requiring learners to demonstrate inferential thinking in class and on assessments will prompt them to generate more inferential self-questions at encoding.

It may seem, in this discussion of working memory, that some aspects of permanent memory have already been touched upon, and indeed they have. It is virtually impossible to divorce the processes of working memory from those of long-term memory completely, because they are intimately related. Encoding, for example, by virtue of its role in transforming information as it passes from working to long-term memory, could be as easily discussed under the framework of the latter as the former. Encoding will continue to play an important role as we now consider what happens to information when it reaches long-term memory.

Long-Term Memory

Do you remember what you had for dinner last night? Or what you did on your birthday last year? Perhaps you recall a visit to another country where the most memorable events were your donkey ride down a steep embankment, the shopkeeper who offered you ouzo at nine o'clock in the morning, and the hotel manager who kept repeating, "So sorry. No reservation." Now consider how these memories differ from your knowledge that Albany, not New York City, is the capital of New York and that reading a weather map will tell you whether to expect rain in the next few days. Although these are all examples of information you retain in long-term memory, they differ in whether they represent specific experiences unique to you or general knowledge of the world that is shared by others.

Tulving (1972) was the first to make the distinction between episodic and semantic memory. He conceived of these as two information processing systems, each selectively receiving information, retaining certain aspects of that information, and retrieving the information as required. Episodic memory is memory for specific events, as when you remember the circumstances surrounding how you learned to read a weather map. Semantic memory, on the other hand, refers to all the general information stored in memory that can be recalled independently of how it was learned. For example, perhaps you cannot remember how you learned to read a weather map, because the circumstances surrounding the event were not particularly memorable. But you do remember the skill.

Although the two systems are related, it is semantic memory that most concerns educators. Generally, what is supposed to be learned in school, or indeed in any instructional situation, is semantic in nature. Before 1972, Tulving argued, most memory research concerned episodic learning. Since

episodic and semantic

then, however, researchers have focused primarily on semantic memory, devising theories for how semantic information is represented in memory, how it is retrieved for use, and how it is forgotten. These questions provide the basis for discussion in the next several sections.

Representation and Storage of Information

How information is represented and stored in semantic memory is a central issue in the study of long-term memory (LTM) and one that has concerned researchers for centuries. Consider the difficulty of the task. Questions must be answered such as, What is the nature of the knowledge unit that is stored in memory? How are relations among these units represented? How can we account for individual differences in memory? Is there only one kind of knowledge unit, or are visual images substantively different from verbal propositions? Try to keep these questions in mind as some of the proposed answers are presented.

Network Models of LTM.   One way to conceive of long-term memory is to think of it as a sort of mental dictionary (Klatzky, 1980), but instead of words being represented alphabetically, concepts are represented according to their associations to one another. For example, if I say "black," what comes to mind? I expect you said "white," which is closely associated with *black* by virtue of being its opposite. Other kinds of associations are obviously possible. A *canary* is a kind of bird, while *has gills* is a property of fish.

Network models assume the existence of nodes in memory, which correspond to concepts, i.e., things and properties. These nodes are thought to be interconnected in a vast network structure that represents learned relationships among concepts (e.g., Collins and Quillian, 1969).

Network models have the advantage of representing individual differences among learners, because individual learning histories presumably lead to different memory networks. These models also enable predictions, which can be easily verified by the performance of learners on certain memory tasks. For example, look at the partial network shown in Figure 3.7. That memory might be structured this way can be ascertained by asking subjects to respond to sentences such as, "A bird has wings," or "A blue heron is a fish." Since the concept *bird* points to the property *has wings* (assuming this was a learned relationship), the subject should say the first sentence is true. In the case of the second sentence, however, *blue heron* and *fish* cannot be directly connected, because the search process can only proceed in the direction indicated by the arrow. Thus, this sentence must be false.

In a similar fashion, predictions can be made about the speed at which subjects should be able to verify sentences as true. For example, learners should be faster in recognizing the truth of "A blue heron has long legs" than "A blue heron is an animal." In the first case, search had to proceed across

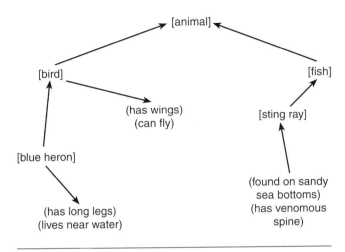

FIGURE 3.7 *A Partial Network Representing Concepts Associated with Animal, in the Tradition of Collins and Quillian (1969)*

only one pointer; in the second case, two pointers, or levels of memory, are searched.

Predictions such as these were, in fact, confirmed by Collins and Quillian (1969), providing experimental support for the network models. But they also encountered some troubling findings. Subjects more quickly recognized a canary as a bird, for example, than a penguin as a bird, yet recognition times should be equal since the distance in both cases is the same. Typicality of concepts, then, presented a real difficulty for network models, which was to be overcome by feature comparison models of long-term memory.

Feature Comparison Models of LTM. Smith, Shoben, and Rips (1974) proposed that concepts in memory were not stored in interconnected hierarchies, as suggested by network models, but with sets of defining features. Association to other concepts is then accomplished through a comparison of overlapping features, hence, the label feature comparison models. For example, to verify "A blue heron is a bird," an individual would search all the characteristics of *blue heron* and all those of *bird*, and finding a sufficient overlap, would say the sentence is true.

Feature comparison models nicely explained the typicality effects so troubling to network models. Some concepts simply do not have clearly defined members; they are "fuzzy sets" in which some members are better examples of the concept than others. Thus, feature comparison models distinguished between defining and characteristic features. Defining features are those that a bird, for example, must have in order to be classified in that category. Characteristic features, on the other hand, are those that are usually associated with typical members of the category. That most birds fly is an example. Thus, canaries are more quickly recognized as birds than are penguins because they are more typical than penguins, which swim instead of fly. In a similar way, it takes longer to say that a bat is not a bird, because bats share features characteristic of birds even while the match on defining characteristics is poor.

Since there are a great many real world concepts of the fuzzy type (Kintsch, 1974), feature comparison models can seem very attractive. But they are not particularly economical, i.e., large collections of features would be required for learning, and the models make no claims about how such collections would be organized. Finally, semantic comparison models have been criticized for their failure to account for semantic flexibility. That is, context can cause certain aspects of a concept's meaning to be more or less prominent. If you hear, "Help me move the piano," you will probably think of it as a heavy piece of furniture, but the sentence, "You play the piano beautifully" emphasizes its musical aspect (Barclay et al., 1974).

Propositional Models of LTM. How different from one another are network and feature comparison models? In posing this question, Klatzky (1980) cited evidence that feature comparison models may in fact be rewritten as enhanced network models. Perhaps for this reason, the network has remained the primary metaphor for long-term memory. Propositional models, however, offered a new twist to the network idea. Instead of concept nodes comprising the basic unit of knowledge that is stored in memory, propositional models take this basic unit to be the proposition (Anderson & Bower, 1973). A proposition is a combination of concepts that has a subject and predicate. So, for example, instead of the concept *bird* representing a node in memory, the propositions "A bird has wings," "A bird flies," and "A bird has feathers" are stored.

There appears to be some psychological reality to the notion of propositions, because subjects will take longer to read sentences containing many propositions than those containing few, even when the number of actual words is the same (Kintsch, 1974). In addition, recall tends to reflect propositional structure rather than sentence structure. For example, suppose you read the following sentence as part of a passage on shorebirds: "The blue heron, a tall bird with a long neck and long legs, can usually be found in the marshy areas near water." Asked to recall later what you had read, you would be unlikely to reproduce this sentence. Instead, you might recall some of the ideas, or propositions, expressed in it, such as: "The blue heron is a tall bird. It has long legs and a long neck. It lives near water." For this reason, propositions have been used as a measure of recall in some memory experiments (e.g., Royer & Cable, 1975; Royer & Perkins, 1977).

John R. Anderson has developed perhaps the most comprehensive network model of memory that emphasizes propositional structure. Known initially as ACT (adaptive control of thought) (Anderson, 1976), the model evolved to ACT* as Anderson (1983) distinguished between procedural and declarative knowledge and added a system for modeling the long-term store of procedural knowledge. He has revised the model again (Anderson, 1996; Schooler & Anderson, 1997) to make it more consistent with research on the neural structure of the brain and to more strongly emphasize the adaptive nature of cognition. Now known as ACT-R, Anderson's model is so global that Leahey and Harris (1997) fear it may be too complex to definitively test or falsify.

Parallel Distributed Processing (PDP) Models of LTM. Parallel processing is distinguished from serial processing in that multiple cognitive operations occur simultaneously as opposed to sequentially. In a sentence verification task such as "A blue heron is an animal," for example, serial processing dictates that the search would start at *blue heron* and proceed along the pathways connected to the concept, one pathway at a time. In parallel processing, however, the search task is distributed, so that all possible pathways would be searched at the same time.

As they evolved, network models such as Anderson's came to include the assumption of parallel processing, but this assumption is at the very core of PDP, or connectionist, models of long-term memory. With connectionist models, researchers seek to describe cognition at a behavioral level in terms of what is known about actual neural patterns in the brain.

The PDP Research Group pioneered the development of these models (McClelland, Rumelhart, and the PDP Research Group, 1986; McClelland, 1988, 1994; Rumelhart, 1995), which propose that the building blocks of memory are connections. These connections are subsymbolic in nature, which means that they do not correspond to meaningful bits of information like concept nodes or propositions do. Instead, the units are simple processing devices, and connections describe how the units interact with each other. They form a vast network across which processing is assumed to be distributed. When learning occurs, environmental input (or input from within the network) activates the connections among units, strengthening some connections while weakening others. It is these patterns of activation that represent concepts and principles or knowledge as we think of it. This means that knowledge is stored in the connections among processing units.

Bereiter (1991) offered a "rough physical analogy" for understanding how a connectionist network might operate:

> Imagine that in the middle of a bare room you have a pile of a hundred or more frisbees, which are connected among themselves by means of elastic bands that vary in thickness and length. On each wall is a clamp to which you fasten a

frisbee. Take any four frisbees and clamp one to each wall. There will be an oscillation set up as those four frisbees pull on the other ones, and those pull on
each other. In time, the oscillations will cease, and the frisbee population will
settle into a pattern that reflects an equilibrium among the tensions exerted by
the elastic bands. (p. 12)

If one were to change which frisbees are clamped to the wall or the lengths or
thicknesses of the bands connecting the frisbees, oscillation would reoccur
and a new pattern would settle out.

Because connections among units are assumed to carry different
weights of association, learning occurs in the continual adjustment of the
weights. Moreover, since processing occurs in parallel, many different adjustments can take place simultaneously, and there can be continuous error
adjustments as a function of new information.

Consider how a PDP model might account for the experiences of Wes
and Marcy in The Mechanic and the Web Surfer. In Marcy's case, the units and
connections representing her knowledge of car mechanics are likely to be neither extensive nor strong, but some are already stronger than others. It is probably safe to assume, for example, that connections related to steering are
stronger than those related to tie rods. Marcy's conversation with Wes serves
to activate and strengthen further some of those connections and perhaps in-
troduces new connections (e.g., steering damper may be a new concept to her,
although both "steering" and "damper" are familiar). When it comes to recalling the conversation later, then, the stronger connection weights associated
with "steering" enable Marcy to remember that as the gist of what was said.
Likewise, the very weak connection weights associated with "steering
damper" are not enough to prompt its specific recall. A similar analysis could
be applied to Wes and what he remembers about the Internet.

PDP models offer a number of advantages over the other models in
terms of what they explain about human information processing. First, they
seem to account well for the incremental nature of human learning. With
constant readjustment of connection weights, they provide a more dynamic
picture of human learning than has been suggested heretofore (Estes, 1988).
PDP models also offer "for the first time a convenient way of incorporating
goals into the dynamics of information processing systems" (Estes, 1988,
p. 207). That is, connection weights in most PDP systems are adjusted to
reduce disparity between their output and some target output, which may
be viewed as a goal.

Finally, there is potential in PDP models to explain cognitive development (McClelland, 1988, 1995). Some knowledge, in terms of prewired connection weights, can be built into the network. Exploring different
configurations of initial memory architecture may lead to breakthroughs in
determining just how much of human memory is "hard-wired."

Estes (1988) sounded some cautionary notes, however, concerning the
conclusions over the long term to which PDP models may lead. He cited the

lack of forthcoming evidence to support PDP models as a mirror of neural processes in the brain. He reminded us that there is little reason to believe a single processor model will be sufficient to model brain functions. After all, "the evolution of the brain has not yielded a machine of uniform design like a digital computer but rather a melange of systems and subsystems of different evolutionary ages" (Estes, 1988, p. 206). He concluded that the final test of any theory will come in the record of extended research that follows from it.

Table 3.2 presents a summary of the models that have been proposed to account for how learned information is represented in memory. To this point, however, only verbal and procedural information have been addressed. What about memory for information of a visual or olfactory nature?

TABLE 3.2 *Summary of Models Proposed to Account for the Storage of Information in Long-Term Memory*

Proposed Model	Characteristics	Data the Model Explains	Difficulties Faced by the Model
Network model	Memory represented as a web of nodes (concepts) connected by relations between concepts	Individual differences in memory Swift recognition of class and property relationships (e.g., bird has wings)	Cannot explain typicality of concepts (e.g., faster to recognize canary than penguin as birds)
Feature comparison model	Memory represented as sets of concept features	Typicality of concepts and "fuzzy sets"	Unwieldy and fails to account for semantic flexibility
Propositional model	Memory represented as network of propositions	Memory for gist Procedural as well as declarative knowledge	May be too complex to definitively test or falsify
Connectionist or PDP model	Memory represented as connections among subsymbolic units of processing	Incremental, dynamic nature of learning Possibility of hardwiring of memory in the brain	A single model may be insufficient to represent brain functions

Dual-Code Models of LTM.   Ask anyone what imagery is, and the response is likely to be, "pictures in my mind." Does this mean that imaginal information is represented in some way different from verbal information? How do we account for the variety of imaginal information, especially since there is more to imagery than just visual representations? We can imagine the tune of a favorite song, or the feel of a kitten's fur against our skin—examples of auditory and tactile imagery, respectively. In the same way, it is possible to generate examples of olfactory imagery ("Is that a hot apple pie I smell?") as well as kinesthetic imagery, which is often used in relaxation training.

Despite our subjective impressions of imagery, not all psychologists have been convinced of its existence as a separate form of information storage (e.g., Pylyshyn, 1973). Some investigations of visual imagery, for example, have shown that people remember a picture's meaning, rather than its visual attributes (e.g., Bower, Karlin, & Dueck, 1975; Light & Berger, 1976). This supports a unitary view of visual and verbal coding, which means that information about pictures is assumed to be represented in the same way as verbal information.

Other research, however, has challenged the unitary view. In a series of experiments conducted by Shepard and his associates (reviewed in Shepard, 1978), subjects appeared to mentally rotate images of three-dimensional figures in order to find their match among sets of distractors. That is, the amount of time it took to find a match was directly related to the number of turns required to rotate the test figure to the position of its match. This result held true even when subjects were given verbal instructions so that they had to rely on information in memory to generate the images.

The superiority of memory for concrete words over abstract words also poses problems for a unitary view of memory representation. People find it much easier to remember words like *sailboat, apple,* and *zebra* when they appear on a list than words such as *liberty* and *justice* (see, for example, Paivio, Yuille, & Rogers, 1969). If a dual-code or dual-systems approach is taken, however, these results are easy to explain. According to the dual-systems view (Paivio, 1971, 1986, 1991), there are two systems of memory representation, one for verbal information and the other for nonverbal information. Thus, for input such as concrete words, two codes are possible. The meaning of the words can be represented by the verbal system, but images of the words can also be represented by the imaginal system. With two memories available at recall, as opposed to one for abstract words, subjects should remember concrete words better.

Exactly how the imaginal system operates to store visual or other imaginal information is not known, although dual-code theorists agree that mental images are not exact copies of visual displays. Images tend to be imprecise representations, with many details omitted, incomplete, or, in some cases, inaccurately recorded. They also require effort to maintain and have parts that fade in and out (Kosslyn, 1980). Think of someone you know well, for example, and try to visualize that person's face. Does he or she wear eyeglasses, and can you remember what they look like? Chances are you may remember verbally whether your friend wears glasses and then try to reconstruct visually what he/she looks like.

Researchers assume a strong connection between the verbal and imaginal systems, and for this reason, directions to form images and visual aids to instruction are both likely to enhance learning of some verbal material. Kosslyn (1980) suggested that images may be important to learning in enabling learners to represent what is not depicted in the instruction and then to transform these representations to facilitate comprehension and problem solving. Visual aids can function in the same way, particularly for learners with poor verbal skills (cf. Levin, 1983).

Retrieval of Learned Information

Once information has been stored in long-term memory, no matter in what form, it can be retrieved for use, retained over time, or forgotten. The process of **retrieval** from long-term memory is relatively simple to understand. Previously learned information is brought back to mind, either for the purpose of understanding some new input or for making a response. Using previous knowledge to understand and learn new material has already been discussed as encoding. But making a response based on previous knowledge raises the question, What kind of response? Consider the two questions below. Which question is likely to be more difficult to answer?

1. What does the word *esoteric* mean?
2. Which of the following words is the best synonym for *esoteric*?
   a. essential
   b. mystical
   c. terrific
   d. evident

Clearly, the first question is harder than the second because it provides fewer clues as to what the answer might be. This distinction between cued and noncued retrieval is the same as the difference between recall and recognition. To recall information, learners must both generate an answer and then determine whether it correctly answers the question. In recognition, however, potential answers are already generated, and the learner must only recognize which one is correct.

Recall.   In free recall situations, learners must retrieve previously stored information with no cues or hints to help them remember. Subjects in many memory experiments, for example, are exposed to target information and then told to "write down everything you can remember about what you just read." Similarly, instructors ask such recall questions on tests as, "Write an essay about America's involvement in World War II," or "Describe the connectionist view of human memory." Because there are no cues present to potentially bias retrieval, the output of free recall is assumed to represent accurately what is in memory. However, researchers have found that the amount subjects recall under these conditions tends to be low. Providing them with cues raises the overall amount subjects are able to remember.

Cued recall tasks, then, are those in which a hint or cue is provided to help learners remember the desired information. This happens, for example, when teachers add qualifiers to their essay questions, such as "Be sure to discuss the role Pearl Harbor played in changing America's war policies." Leahey and Harris (1997) also cited the example of an actor learning lines as a cued recall task. Each line serves as a cue for remembering the next line.

Recognition.   Recognition, in contrast to recall, involves a set of pregenerated stimuli presented to learners for a decision or judgment. In some cases, learners are asked to determine whether the stimulus information has been seen before, as in old-new recognition tasks. Tasks of this nature are common in memory experiments, but are becoming increasingly popular for assessing reading comprehension (e.g., Royer et al., 1984; Royer, 1990, 1995). For example, students read a target passage and then complete a sentence verification test. On the sentence verification test are test sentences of four types: (1) an original sentence from the passage; (2) a paraphrase of the original sentence in which the words are changed but the meaning is retained; (3) a meaning-change sentence in which one or two words in the original sentence are replaced to alter its meaning; and (4) a distractor sentence, which is consistent with the gist of the passage but unrelated to the original sentence. Students who comprehended the passage should be able to recognize the original and paraphrase sentences as old and classify the meaning-change and distractor sentences as new. Those who fail to comprehend the meaning of the passage, on the other hand, are likely to think that the meaning-change and distractor sentences are old on the basis of their similarity to sentences in the passage.

Two factors appear to influence old-new recognition. The most obvious is the strength of the memory trace, in that stronger memories will be more accurately recognized than weaker memories. But regardless of the strength of a memory trace, a decision must still be made about its match to the test stimulus. Imagine, for example, that you are choosing drapes to match the color of your living room carpet. You must make a decision concerning a particular set of drapes from your memory of the carpet's color. Now consider two possible scenarios: (1) the drapes are inexpensive, and besides, you can return them if the color is a poor match, (2) the drapes are expensive, must be paid for in advance, and cannot be returned. In which scenario are you more likely to make a yes decision?

The second factor influencing yes-no or old-new recognition is a decision criterion based on the context surrounding the recognition task. High-risk conditions lead to a more stringent criterion than do low-risk conditions, even though the memory trace in both situations is equivalent in strength and match to the test stimulus.

Besides yes-no recognition, there is also forced-choice recognition as exemplified in multiple-choice tests. As before, memory strength plays a role in the decision to choose a particular answer. The decision criterion, however, is determined not only by risk conditions surrounding the overall task, but by the distractors in each test item. That is, a severe penalty for wrong answers will decrease guessing overall, even though, in a four-distractor item, the chances of getting an item right by pure guessing is 25 percent. But suppose, in question 2, you could eliminate two of the distractors immediately. This increases to 50 percent the chances of getting the answer right, high enough odds, perhaps, to offset the penalty. An obvious implication of this for test construction is to write distractors that have equal probability of being chosen if the learner is forced to guess.

Encoding Specificity.   Regardless of expected response type, the process of retrieval can be greatly influenced by the cues available to learners at test time. Two different principles have been investigated by researchers that suggest a relationship between conditions at encoding and conditions at recall.

The **encoding specificity** principle states, in essence, that *whatever cues are used by a learner to facilitate encoding will also serve as the best retrieval cues* for that information at test time (Thomson & Tulving, 1970; Tulving & Thomson, 1973). To illustrate, Anderson and Ortony (1975) gave subjects the sentences, "The container held the apples" and "The container held the cola." What images come to mind when you read those sentences? Most likely, you encoded an apple basket and a cola bottle. In fact, Anderson and Ortony found that *basket* served as an effective retrieval cue for the first sentence but not the second, while *bottle* served as a good cue for the second sentence but not the first.

Retrieval, then, is very much influenced by the context of encoding. This suggests for instruction that many different contexts or examples may be important to discuss during the presentation of new concepts. In this way, students will have many cues available to assist in encoding that may later be used for recall. If new information is presented in only one context, students may not find sufficient cues in test questions to support retrieval of information that is actually in memory.

Related to encoding specificity is the concept of state-dependent learning. Some years ago, a study was conducted in which subjects learned lists of paired words in one situation and recalled the lists in a different situation (Bilodeau & Schlosberg, 1951). The situations differed in the rooms in which the sessions (whether learning or testing) took place, whether the subjects were standing or sitting, and the method of list presentation. Results indicated that recall was best for those who were instructed and tested in the same situation. When the instructional situation differed from the testing situation, recall suffered. More recent studies on the effects of drugs have suggested that these recall differences can be explained in terms of the subjects' state of mind during learning and testing. Information learned in a particular state of mind (e.g., free from the influence of alcohol or other drugs) will be remembered best in the same state of mind (Goodwin et al., 1969).

Bower (1981) has demonstrated a similar phenomenon with moods. Words learned under a happy mood were better recalled under a happy mood than a sad mood, and words learned under a sad mood were best recalled in that state. Bower argued that emotions, just like information, are coded in memory. And indeed it seems likely that chemical changes in the brain induced by drugs, strong emotions, and learning may all be similarly explained.

Forgetting

At some point, all theories of memory must address the phenomenon of forgetting. We all forget things, but we may do so for many different possible reasons. The most common explanations for forgetting are failure to encode, failure to retrieve, and interference.

Failure to encode simply means that *the information sought during retrieval was never learned in the first place.* Learners often have the illusion of knowing. Poor readers, for example, typically do not monitor their reading very well and so believe they have read and understood something when they have not done so. Learners with ineffective study strategies face the same problem. They tend to equate effort with learning rather than monitor the actual effects of their learning strategies. A student in one of my classes, for example, could not understand why she had achieved such a low score on one of the examinations. "But I studied for hours!" she wailed. When I asked how she had studied, she looked back at me blankly—by rereading her notes and the book, of course. Repetition can only go so far. Elaboration may have helped to ensure that course material was solidly encoded in memory.

The concept of encoding failure emphasizes once again the importance of having and activating relevant prior knowledge in learning. In The Mechanic and the Web Surfer scenario, consider what relevant knowledge either Wes or Marcy could bring to bear in their discussions of car mechanics and Internet browsing. It is possible that each could retrieve enough to comprehend the other and respond appropriately during the conversation but not enough to encode details of the conversation for retrieval at a later time.

Failure to retrieve information that has been encoded in memory is a second cause of forgetting and refers to *the inability to access previously learned information.* This is something like losing the directory to your computer's hard drive. The files are still there, but without the appropriate cues (i.e., file names), they cannot be accessed and retrieved. Issues of encoding specificity and state-dependent learning have obvious relevance here. The more cues that are used in encoding, the more likely one or another of them will be available to facilitate retrieval. In addition, assuming the validity of the dual-code theory, the more often encoding cues are generated in both the verbal and imaginal systems, the more likely retrieval will be facilitated.

A common strategy for enhancing retrieval is note-taking (Gagné & Driscoll, 1988). This is sometimes known as an external retrieval strategy (Kiewra, 1985; Kiewra & Frank, 1988; Kiewra et al., 1991) because its product—notes—serves as memory storage external to the learner. Students who elaborate on their notes also tend to perform better than those who simply reread them (Peper & Mayer, 1978), in essence optimizing the effects of encoding together with external retrieval.

Finally, long before the development of information-processing theory, **interference** was proposed as a cause of forgetting, which meant that *other events or information got in the way of effective retrieval.* McGeoch (1932) described forgetting of verbal materials in terms of two major laws. According to the first, forgetting was considered to be a function of the similarity between the circumstances of learning and testing, much as encoding specificity accounts for retrieval and forgetting now. The second set forth the conditions of interference, i.e., that numerous events and competing information can interfere with the retrieval of target information. Moreover, interference can occur from information learned either before or after the to-be-remembered information is learned. For example, retroactive interference has occurred when you read this chapter, read the next chapter, and then have difficulty recalling information from this chapter. Later learning interferes with the recall of earlier learned material, particularly as practice on the later material increases. This makes sense when we consider that information learned later is more recent and thus probably yields stronger memory traces than information learned earlier.

It is also possible, however, for previous learning to interfere with later learning. This is known as proactive interference, and the degree of interference is related to the amount of practice on the original task. Take, for example, the case of a long-time tennis player trying to learn racquetball. Since both are racket sports, it seems reasonable to believe that knowing one would facilitate learning the other. Instead, the well-learned skill of swinging a tennis racket interferes with the recently learned response of swinging a racquetball racket. Many players will find themselves swinging with the entire arm, as in tennis, rather than with just the wrist.

Proactive interference of a kind has also been demonstrated in the learning and memory of verbal materials by aging adults. Rice and Meyer (1985) investigated so-called memory deficits among older adults. Results of some studies had indicated that older adults remember less from a prose passage than do younger adults. In the series of experiments Rice and Meyer conducted, however, they found no evidence to support a memory deficit. Instead, they found that older adults, because they had so much more experience and prior knowledge, tended to get caught up in the details of the passage (which prompted reminiscing) and lose sight of the main ideas they were to recall. In other words, proactive interference had occurred. When main ideas were signaled, however, the effects of the interference were averted, and older adults remembered just as much as younger readers.

In a review of studies conducted with aging adults, Fry (1992) reached similar conclusions, and he suggested several concrete ways in which practitioners can help older adults learn and remember. For instance, visual displays of how the subject matter is structured and concepts related can provide useful encoding and retrieval cues. Similarly, because problems in the learning and remembering of adults seem to be a function of declining speed rather than declining mental powers, allowing adults to work at their own pace is a desirable instructional strategy. Finally, like children, adults can be taught more effective strategies for encoding and retrieval (Fry, 1992).

There is no denying that memory failure can also be caused by other conditions, such as amnesia or Alzheimer's disease. These causes, however, have relatively little relevance to instruction and are therefore beyond the scope of this chapter.

Implications of CIP for Instruction

Take a moment to reflect on the stages and processes of cognitive information processing that have been discussed in this chapter. What might they imply for instructional strategies? Some suggestions have already been made, and an integrated model of instruction based on CIP is presented in Chapter 10. Nonetheless, three general recommendations are worth exploring here. These are:

- Providing organized instruction
- Arranging extensive and variable practice
- Enhancing learners' encoding and memory
- Enhancing learners' self-control of information processing

Providing Organized Instruction

The organization of instruction has long been of interest to researchers because people will try to impose some meaningful structure or organization on any new information in order to make sense of it. So if learners are supposed to understand new information in particular ways, then the instruction must be organized to help them do this. As discussed earlier in the chapter, instructional tactics such as signaling what information is important and drawing learners' attention to specific features of that information can facilitate selective attention and appropriate pattern recognition. To enhance encoding and retrieval, as well as counteract the effects of interference, other tactics are appropriate, such as using imagery and representing information in multiple ways.

Graphic representations have been particularly effective in facilitating encoding and memory storage of information. Beissner, Jonassen, and Grabowski (1994; see also Jonassen, Beissner, & Yacci, 1993) reviewed the use of graphic techniques in acquiring structural knowledge, which represents relationships between concepts in a content domain. They concluded that graphic techniques (such as semantic maps, concept maps, networking) analyze, elaborate, and integrate subject matter content, as well as illustrate concept relations. The result is enhanced structural knowledge on the part of the learner. The concept maps that introduce each chapter of this book are a good example of graphic representations. If designed well, they should assist you in organizing and understanding the concepts discussed.

Arranging Extensive and Variable Practice

"Practice makes perfect" is a dictum well known to most learners, and in fact, there is some truth to the saying. As noted earlier in the chapter, automaticity of basic skills is a desirable educational goal, and extensive practice is one of the ways to help achieve it. Behavioral theorists referred to overlearning, or practicing a skill until it is so habitual as to require very little conscious attention. As will be seen in the discussion of learning motor skills (see Chapter 10), the amount of practice is not the only important variable. The kind of practice also matters. (As motor learning theorists are apt to say, "Perfect practice makes perfect!")

As noted from the evidence on encoding specificity, if the context changes substantially from encoding to retrieval, learners' performance may be impaired. Providing a great deal of varied practice helps learners to attach multiple cues to what they are learning, so they are more likely to recall it at test time in a range of appropriate contexts.

Enhancing Learners' Encoding and Memory

Many students come to college lacking study skills that will help them be successful as learners in the post–high school environment. Often, the goals they are asked to achieve are sufficiently more difficult than what they experienced in high school to put them at risk for failing. To help these students become better learners, community colleges and universities offer a variety of courses and experiences aimed at enhancing learners' encoding and memory. The strategies that are taught in these courses come directly from research on CIP that has been discussed in this chapter, and although they are aimed at college students, they are by no means limited to this population. Elementary and secondary school teachers, as well as instructional designers and trainers, can help the learners with whom they work to improve their encoding skills and memory.

Table 3.3 displays some suggested strategies for helping learners to enhance encoding and memory, along with the CIP process or principle with which they are most related. Think of how you might have used these strategies effectively in your own learning or how you might employ them with learners.

Enhancing Learners' Self-Control of Information Processing

When we shift the focus from instruction to learners, different aspects of information processing become prominent, suggesting different sorts of instructional implications. Earlier in the chapter, executive control processes were mentioned that enable the learner to modify information flow within and between components of the memory system. These processes have been investigated under the rubric of metacognition (Flavell, 1979; Brown, 1980;

TABLE 3.3   *Some Strategies for Enhancing Encoding and Memory*

Suggested Strategy	*Corresponding CIP Process*
Listen actively and pay attention to cues signaling what is important.	Selective attention
Encode information in more than one way and more than one mode. Use acronyms and imagery.	Dual code, multiple memory connections
Break down complex information into manageable parts.	Chunking
Elaborate on new information with examples that are meaningful to you.	Elaboration in encoding
Read actively. Make the information personal by relating it to your own life.	Elaboration in encoding
Take notes in your own words; don't just write it down verbatim.	Elaboration in encoding
Overlearn the material. Keep practicing even after you got them all right.	Rehearsal, automaticity
Review your class notes the same day that you take them.	Forgetting curve (Ebbinghaus)
Learn information in a similar way to what it needs to be recalled.	Encoding specificity
Avoid alcohol, caffeine, nicotine, or medications that might cause drowsiness during learning.	State dependent learning

Duell, 1986). **Metacognition** refers to *one's awareness of thinking and the self-regulatory behavior* (also known as conditional knowledge [cf. Prawatt, 1989]) *that accompanies this awareness.* "thinking about thinking"

> In the course of learning and problem solving, representative kinds of regulatory performance include: knowing when or what one knows or does not know; predicting the correctness or outcome of one's performance; planning ahead and efficiently apportioning the outcomes of one's cognitive resources and one's time; and checking and monitoring the outcomes of one's solution or attempt to learn. (Gagné & Glaser, 1987, p. 75)

What is currently known about metacognitive skills and their acquisition goes well beyond the scope of this chapter, and the interested reader is referred to Derry and Murphy (1986) and Duell (1986) for their excellent reviews on the topic. Research results generally indicate, however, that metacognitive ability depends on person variables, task variables, strategy variables, and the interaction among all three (Duell, 1986).

With respect to person variables, older learners seem to have a better understanding of their memory abilities and limitations than do younger learners. Although students of all ages appear capable of learning various memory strategies, older learners are more planful and purposeful in their use of these strategies. Additionally, there is evidence that learning-disabled children are less efficient and less planful than normal children (Torgeson, 1977). This suggests that instructors should frequently remind younger and less planful learners when and how to use memory strategies.

Task variables refer to differences in instructional content that influence use of metacognitive strategies. For example, information that is new to learners will be approached with quite general learning strategies. As learners become more proficient in a subject or if the material they are to learn relates to a subject they know quite well already, they employ more domain-specific strategies (Gagné & Driscoll, 1988). For instructors to use or suggest the use of particular strategies, then, they should have some idea as to how much their students already know about the material to be learned.

Finally, strategy variables have to do with the metacognitive strategies themselves, the various ways in which learners may go about encoding, storing, and retrieving information. Some strategies are so simple that learners can acquire them easily by being told what to do. Breaking a complex or long learning task into manageable segments is one example. Other strategies, however, require extensive practice before they can be used easily and effectively. Taking notes or self-questioning with inferential questions may be examples of this type.

Educators generally agree on the importance of self-regulatory skills in learning, as will be especially evident in Chapter 9. Successful learners seem to acquire and refine these skills throughout their school and learning history. But what about the less successful and less proficient learners? Teaching learners to assume an active and purposeful role in their own learning has been a growing concern among instructors and researchers alike. Programs now exist to train students in metacognitive or study skills (e.g., Weinstein, 1982; Feuerstein et al., 1980; Dansereau et al., 1979; De Bono, 1985; Wang & Palincsar, 1989). Some are aimed at college students, others at younger learners. Some concentrate on domain-specific skills pertaining to a particular subject, such as reading comprehension; others train more general strategies that may be useful across a broad range of tasks. And some programs are embedded within school curricula, while others exist as separate, study skills courses.

Despite the variety among these programs, those that are effective seem to have at least two criteria in common. First, students must have a base of prior knowledge that may be related to the strategies they are learning. Domain-specific strategies, in particular, are virtually useless when students know little about the subject to which they pertain. Second, students must know when and why various self-regulatory strategies may be effectively employed (e.g., Pressley, Borkowski, & O'Sullivan, 1984; Prawatt, 1989; Sawyer, Graham, & Harris, 1992). Knowing how to be planful is not enough to guarantee that one will be planful. Having such conditional knowledge does not guarantee that one will always use it. But realizing when and why such behavior will be useful in furthering learning goals helps to motivate students to engage in metacognitive, self-regulatory ways.

Conclusion

As noted in the previous chapter, B. F. Skinner continued to argue against the necessity for inventing mental fictions to account for learning. At first, Roediger (1980) seemed to side with Skinner when he pointed out the proliferation of mental entities in current models of human memory and questioned what we have really learned from them. His conclusion, however, was not that mental constructs are useless, but that we should be cautious in what we take them to mean about learning and memory.

> Advances in theories of human memory parallel, and perhaps depend on, advances in technology.... The information processing approach has been an important source of models and ideas, but the fate of its predecessors should serve to keep us humble concerning its eventual success.... Unless today's technology has somehow reached its ultimate development, and we can be certain it has not, then we have not reached the ultimate metaphor for the human mind either. (Roediger, 1980, p. 244)

Cognitive information-processing theorists have not been the only ones interested in learning and memory from a cognitive perspective. In Chapter 4, the ideas of educational psychologist David P. Ausubel will be presented, along with the similar ideas of schema theory and mental models. In Chapter 5, situated cognition, with its emphasis on the integration of declarative and procedural knowledge, will be explored.

A CIP Look at "Kermit and the Keyboard"

Let us consider some cognitive information-processing concepts that might be relevant in understanding and explaining Kermit's learning in this story. An information-processing analysis of the act of performing a song at the keyboard might go something like this.

Kermit must first attend to the printed page of a musical score (the input). To process its contents requires recognition of the symbols (reading music is a process similar to reading text) and relating this to what he already knows. For instance, he notes the signature, which tells him how many beats per measure, and the key, which indicates how many sharps or flats. This information is retrieved to assist him in organizing a response, which is pressing down each key as it corresponds to that indicated in the score.

Frequent rehearsal helps Kermit's playing to become more automatic and less fraught with mistakes. Using different voices and backgrounds enables Kermit to vary the encoding cues so that he learns to play the same song in different contexts. One might explain his persistent error in "House of the Rising Sun" as a consequence of encoding specificity. He makes this mistake only when a particular background is used, the same background with which he made the mistake in the first place.

Reading the keyboard manual could be, for Kermit, very much like Rosemary's experience of reading the computer manual in the scenario "A Tale of Two Readers." Highly unfamiliar and complex and difficult content can cause comprehension problems, which Kermit encounters.

CIP offers a useful perspective on the continuing development of Kermit's keyboarding skills, but behaviorism provides a better explanation of why Kermit spends 20 minutes practicing some days and an hour other days. However, like behaviorism, CIP offers no particular insights into Kermit's motivation to study the keyboard to begin with.

Theory Matrix

Theory	Cognitive Information Processing
Prominent Theorists	Includes: J. R. Anderson; R. C. Atkinson; A. M. Collins; G. A. Miller; A. Paivio; M. R. Quillian; R. M. Shiffrin
Learning Outcome(s)	Declarative knowledge, procedural knowledge, memory
Role of the Learner	Attend to and process incoming information, relating it to what is already in memory
Role of the Instructor	Organize information, direct attention, enhance encoding and retrieval, provide practice opportunities, and help learners monitor their learning
Inputs or Preconditions to Learning	Sensory information in the environment
Process of Learning	Processing information and storing it in memory (including processes of attention, pattern recognition, encoding, chunking, rehearsal, and retrieval)

Suggested Readings

Dillon, R. F., & Sternberg, R. J. (1986). *Cognition and instruction.* Orlando: Academic Press.
Gagné, E. D. (1985). *The cognitive psychology of school learning.* Boston: Little, Brown.
Phye, G. D., & Andre, T. (1986). *Cognitive classroom learning.* Orlando: Academic Press.

Reflective Questions and Activities

1. Consider cognitive information-processing theory in light of the epistemological traditions described in Chapter 1. To what tradition do CIP theorists seem most closely aligned? What evidence supports your choice?

2. Look for examples of the computer metaphor for learning and memory in popular culture and literature. Early episodes of *Star Trek* are likely sources. Analyze the characters' actions in terms of the information processing model. Are any of the model's assumptions or characteristics violated in the name of science fiction? If so, consider the implications for learning and instruction if those violations were indeed true.

3. Using the same learning episode you described in Question 4 of Chapter 2, generate a plan for improving performance that is based on cognitive information-processing theory. How does this plan differ from your behavioral plan? What aspects of learning are highlighted by each plan? Are they mutually exclusive, or might a combined plan be more effective than either alone?

4

Meaningful Learning and Schema Theory

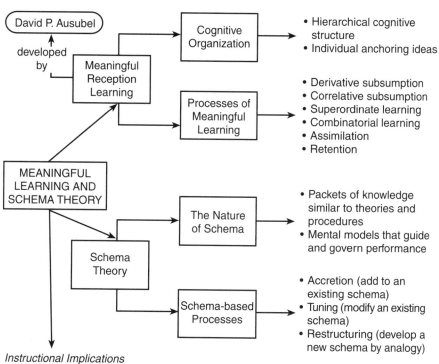

David P. Ausubel

developed by

Meaningful Reception Learning

Cognitive Organization
- Hierarchical cognitive structure
- Individual anchoring ideas

Processes of Meaningful Learning
- Derivative subsumption
- Correlative subsumption
- Superordinate learning
- Combinatorial learning
- Assimilation
- Retention

MEANINGFUL LEARNING AND SCHEMA THEORY

The Nature of Schema
- Packets of knowledge similar to theories and procedures
- Mental models that guide and govern performance

Schema Theory

Schema-based Processes
- Accretion (add to an existing schema)
- Tuning (modify an existing schema)
- Restructuring (develop a new schema by analogy)

Instructional Implications
1. Activate prior knowledge using advance organizers and schema signals. Manage cognitive load.
2. Make instructional materials meaningful with comparative organizers and elaboration.
3. Use thought-demanding activities to promote skillful use of mental models.
4. Provide new contexts and examples to apply prior knowledge.

Consider these scenarios.

• *A Lesson on Democracy*

   The place is a public school seventh grade social studies classroom. A lesson on democracy with a focus on American history has begun. The students have brainstormed a list of characteristics describing their understanding of government, and from their answers, their teacher Mr. Amaya has written a simplified definition of the term on the board. With this, the students prepare to discuss different forms of government (including oligarchy, democracy, fascism, etc.), following which they will focus on democracy and all its related concepts. Mr. Amaya presents a conceptual model to help students organize their growing knowledge about different forms and functions of government, and he tests their understanding with questions such as, "Does a vice-president or governor (member of the executive branch) have the right to keep secret who attended energy meetings and what was discussed when the results of these meeting may influence policy development by the legislature (legislative branch)? Does the Supreme Court (judicial branch) have the right to force this information to be made public?"

• *Making Mayonnaise*[1]

The study of cooking provides a useful example of the difficulty of learning complex subjects. To a noncook, the combination of ingredients in mayonnaise is not at all an obvious one. It is for this reason that it is interesting to ask naive subjects just what they expect mayonnaise to be made of:

Protocol of the experimenter (DAN) and CN, an 8-year-old girl

Dan: How do you make mayonnaise?

CN: How you make mayonnaise is you look at a cookbook.

Dan: OK, but without looking at a cookbook, can you guess what it is that's inside mayonnaise?

CN: Uh.

Dan: How would you make it?

CN: Uh, Butter—uh, let me think (5-second pause), hmmm (10-second pause), whipped cream very, very, very finely whipped so it's smooth. That's probably how you make it, just with whipped cream, very, very, very, very fine and smooth.

Dan: Anything else?

CN: You might add a little taste to it.

Dan: Taste of what?

CN: (10-second pause) Sort of a vanilla taste.

Dan: Suppose I said that mayonnaise is made from egg yolk—and oil. What would you say?

CN: I would say it's very, very wrong.

Dan: Why?

CN: You can't make mayonnaise out of eggs and water—I mean oil.

Dan: Why not?

CN: Because of taste and smoothness and stuff like that.

Protocol of the experimenter (DAN) and GB, an adult male psychology professor

Dan: How would you make something like mayonnaise?

GB: Mayonnaise? How do you make mayonnaise? You can't make mayonnaise; it has to be bought in jars. Mayonnaise. Um. You mix whipped cream with, ummm, some mustard.

---

[1]From Norman, Gentner, & Stevens, 1976, p. 185

Learning to make mayonnaise and learning about democracy probably seem as though they have little in common. However, both involve learning and making use of information, information that may not always be meaningful to learners, even when, as in the case of mayonnaise, the result is highly familiar.

Learning information meaningfully has roots as a field of study in the verbal learning tradition begun by Ebbinghaus (1885; see Chapter 1). Whereas Ebbinghaus believed that human learning and memory should be uncontaminated by old associations or meaning, others, such as David P. Ausubel, thought that meaning was at the very core of cognitive experience. It made no sense to Ausubel, an educational psychologist, to study learning with materials so bereft of meaning as the nonsense syllables invented by Ebbinghaus and adopted by many cognitive psychologists. Ausubel preferred to use prose, or textual materials of some length, because text passages more closely approximate the kinds of learning materials students encounter in actual classrooms.

Ausubel developed a theory of meaningful learning on a course parallel with and essentially unaffected by the cognitive information-processing theory discussed in the previous chapter. Although he regarded the human nervous system as a "data-processing and storage mechanism" (Ausubel, 1965, p. 8), Ausubel did not consider as cognitive theory the computer models of cognition being developed at the time by Newell, Simon, and Shaw (1958).

Ausubel also considered his work, at least initially, to be fundamentally different from the thrust of schema theory, which began to draw the attention of cognitive scientists at about the same time Ausubel was publishing. As the concept of schema has developed in the cognitive literature, however, it is similar to Ausubel's position, and in 1977, Richard Mayer proposed a synthesis of verbal learning research from a variety of perspectives that included schema theory and Ausubel's meaningful learning theory.

Today, Ausubel's theory is not considered particularly current, whereas the concept of schema has retained an active position in learning research and theory. Nonetheless, there are several aspects of Ausubel's meaningful learning theory that have become a standard part of educational practice. Moreover, the emphasis on understanding that characterizes Ausubel's work is gaining ground in other approaches to instruction, although with a slightly different twist. "Understanding...is knowledge in thoughtful action. This would be no more than a philosophical point if it could be taken for granted that the acquisition of knowledge brought about understanding like the caboose of a train" (Perkins & Unger, 1999, p. 95). Ausubel wrote as though he did take it for granted that understanding automatically followed knowledge. For him, that is what meaningful learning was all about. However, subsequent research has shown that transfer, or use of prior learning in new or related contexts, is by no means as assured as Ausubel might have believed.

This chapter therefore begins with Ausubel, proceeds to schema theory, and concludes with practical implications of both, with particular emphasis on teaching for understanding. This juxtaposition should help you better judge their competing claims as well as determine what these theories explain that theories presented in prior chapters do not.

Ausubel's Meaningful Reception Learning

Meaning, according to Ausubel, is not something that resides "in the text" and outside the learner. He considered textual materials, like anything else learners might experience, to be "potentially meaningful." Meaning occurs when learners actively interpret their experiences using certain internal, cognitive operations. To account for these cognitive operations and how they interact with experience to give rise to learning, Ausubel proposed a theory of meaningful, reception learning (Ausubel, 1962, 1963a, 1968; Ausubel, Novak, & Hanesian, 1978).

As a means of differentiating the types of learning that go on in typical classrooms, Ausubel (1961, 1963b) made two important distinctions. First, he distinguished between reception and discovery learning, a distinction he considered important because he contended that most school learning is of the reception type. In reception learning, Ausubel (1961) stated, "the entire content of what is to be learned is presented to the learner in its final form" (p. 16). The learner is therefore required to internalize the information in a form that will be available for later use. In discovery learning, on the other hand, learners are required to "rearrange a given array of information, integrate it with existing cognitive structure, and reorganize or transform the integrated combination in such a way as to create a desired end product or discover a missing means-end relationship. After this phase is completed, the discovered content is internalized just as in reception learning" (Ausubel, 1961, p. 17).

Reception learning, then, is essentially the same as what commonly occurs in expository instruction, where learners are told information rather than discovering it for themselves. Science textbooks, for example, state principles (often with a description of the research conducted to arrive at these principles) and provide examples of their application. From the principle's definition and examples, along with practice in its application, students are expected to understand what it means. By contrast, science teachers often facilitate discovery learning by having students conduct experiments from which they derive their understanding of scientific principles.

Although discovery learning methods certainly have a place in instruction (e.g., in laboratories or everyday problem solving) (see also discussions in Chapter 7 and Chapter 11), Ausubel believed that such methods "hardly constitute an efficient *primary* means of transmitting the *content* of an academic discipline" (Ausubel et al., 1978, p. 26, emphases theirs).

The second distinction made by Ausubel (1961, 1963b) and Ausubel et al. (1978) is between rote and meaningful learning. Rote learning is the same as verbatim memorization, and to Ausubel, that means the learner has made no real connection between what was already known and what was memorized. What was memorized stands as an arbitrary piece of information in isolation from the rest of cognitive structure. Children frequently memorize the Pledge of Allegiance, for example, and cannot tell you what the pledge means. By contrast, meaningful learning refers to the process of relating potentially meaningful information to what the learner already knows in a nonarbitrary and substantive way. This means that, in the previous example, the children would have some notion as to what the flag means as a symbol of the United States. With this prior knowledge, they can construct an understanding of what is entailed by pledging allegiance.

It is important to realize, said Ausubel, that either rote or meaningful learning can occur in reception and discovery learning situations. Students may attempt to memorize the results of a science experiment, for example, instead of understanding what the results suggest about the principle under study. Likewise, in reception learning, just because the learner is in a position of receiving information does not mean the learner must be passive. Quite the contrary, meaningful reception learning implies that the learner is cognitively active.

Three conditions are essential to meaningful learning. One is that the learner must employ a meaningful learning set to any learning task. If the learner intends to memorize, then meaningful learning will not result, no matter whether learning is by reception or by discovery. A second essential condition is that the material to be learned must be potentially meaningful. This suggests that learning tasks and materials should be organized, readable, and relevant, so that learners do not fail to learn because they can make no sense of the learning task. Finally, the third and most important condition for meaningful learning is what learners already know and how that knowledge relates to what they are asked to learn. According to Ausubel (1963b), "existing cognitive structure, that is, an individual's organization, stability, and clarity of knowledge is the principal factor influencing the learning and retention of meaningful new material" (p. 217). Given the importance Ausubel placed on prior knowledge in learning, how did he conceive of memory structure?

Cognitive Organization in the Learner

"The model of cognitive organization proposed for the learning and retention of meaningful materials assumes the existence of a cognitive structure that is hierarchically organized..." (Ausubel, 1963b, p. 217). As indicated earlier, Ausubel acknowledged the existence of neurophysiological events underlying learning, but he expressed his theory in terms of hypothetical constructs of memory structure and learning processes. He proposed **cognitive structure** as the learner's *overall memorial structure or integrated body of knowledge.* This cognitive structure is made up of sets of ideas that are organized hierarchically and by theme. Moreover, within any given hierarchy, the most inclusive ideas are the strongest and most stable. Except for its emphasis on a hierarchy of ideas, this structure is similar to those proposed by the propositional model of memory that was discussed in the previous chapter.

For an example of cognitive structure, consider what you know about cooking that might be relevant if you were learning how to make mayonnaise. You know that cooking involves mixing together ingredients that might be known by heart or listed in a recipe. Generally, the ingredients must be mixed in a particular order, and certain types of mixing might be used, such as "stir until moistened," "beat until firm," and "whip until smooth." Mixing might also require different types of implements, such as a spoon, fork, whisk, or electric mixer. Figure 4.1 displays a partial hierarchy that might represent this knowledge about cooking. According to Ausubel, the general ideas high in the hierarchy (e.g., "cooking involves preparation") would be more stable and therefore more easily remembered than specific ideas low in the hierarchy (such as the type of implement best used for beating).

The cognitive structure provides an overall framework into which new knowledge will be incorporated, but to describe how specific linkages occur, Ausubel proposed the notion of anchoring ideas. **Anchoring ideas** are the *specific, relevant ideas in the learner's cognitive structure that provide the entry points for new information to be connected.* They are what enable the learner to construct meaning from new information and experiences that are only potentially meaningful.

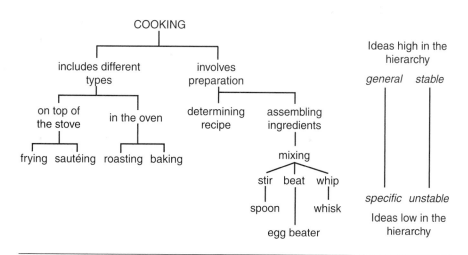

FIGURE 4.1   *A Partial Hierarchy of Knowledge about Cooking*

For example, the most relevant anchor GB can think of in the Making Mayonnaise scenario is the jar of mayonnaise that he has probably taken out of the refrigerator countless times. Like GB, CN doesn't know the ingredients of mayonnaise or how to make it, and the most relevant anchor that came to her mind was "cookbook." Even when she is told the ingredients, however, her reaction is disbelief, most likely because she has no anchor that is specifically relevant to making mayonnaise. After all, how many ingredients might she have direct experience with that take on completely different perceptual characteristics when they are mixed together?

Cognitive structure and specific anchoring ideas within the cognitive structure, then, are prerequisites to meaningful learning. They describe the memory structure within which new knowledge will be integrated. But we have yet to see how the processes of learning occur, i.e., how the new knowledge is actually connected with and incorporated into the learner's existing knowledge.

Processes of Meaningful Learning

If memory is actually organized in the fashion that Ausubel proposed, then how is new information likely to be added to an existing structure? There are three possible ways: New information can be subordinate to (lower in the structure), superordinate to (higher in the structure), or coordinate with (at the same level in the structure) an existing idea. Consistent with each of these ways, Ausubel proposed a process of learning.

Derivative and Correlative Subsumption.   The principal way of adding information to cognitive structure, in Ausubel's view, is to attach new ideas and details in a subordinate fashion to the anchoring ideas already present. This is the process Ausubel called subsumption (Ausubel, 1962, 1963a, 1968; Ausubel et al., 1978). That is, *new, incoming ideas are* **subsumed** *under more general and inclusive anchoring ideas already in memory.* Another way to think of subsumption is to consider the anchoring ideas as hooks that snag those incoming details and modifiers pertaining to them.

Because incoming details can relate to anchoring ideas in two possible ways (both still subordinate), subsumption is said to occur in two ways. **Derivative subsumption** refers to the *learning of new examples or cases that are illustrative of an established concept or previously learned proposition.* If we consider A in Figure 4.2 to be the anchoring idea in a learner's cognitive structure, with examples a1, a2, and a3 associated in a subordinate fashion, then new example a4 will be derivatively subsumed under A.

For example, if A is the general concept, dog, and collies, cocker spaniels, and poodles are known as examples, then it is relatively easy to learn the example, whippet, and subsume that information under the general con-

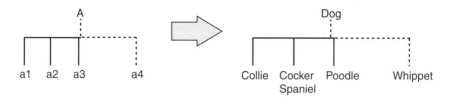

FIGURE 4.2 *An Example of Derivative Subsumption*

cept. The criterial attributes of the concept A remain unchanged; simply, new examples are recognized as relevant (see Figure 4.2).

Other instances of derivative subsumption include learning in geography that Texas and India are both places where rice is grown. Or in law, cases may be found that were all decided based on the same legal precedent. Finally, a teacher or instructional designer might encounter numerous examples where a particular principle of learning has been employed.

More typical of the way most learning occurs, according to Ausubel, is **correlative subsumption.** This process refers to the *elaboration, extension, or modification of the previously learned concept or proposition by the subsumption of the incoming idea.* Instead of simply adding a new example, then, the new information adds a new characteristic or feature to the existing idea. In so doing, it interacts with the existing idea to change the learner's understanding of it in some way. The original A becomes A' as shown in Figure 4.3.

For example, suppose A represents the concept positive reinforcement in an education student's cognitive structure of behavioral management. The student knows that positive reinforcement increases behavior (attribute u) through the presentation of a reinforcer (attribute v) that is contingent upon the desired response (attribute w). When the student now learns that the reinforcer can be a high-frequency behavior (new attribute x), his or her understanding of positive reinforcement has now been extended to include the special circumstances surrounding the Premack principle. The criterial attributes of the concept have been modified. As indicated above, A has also

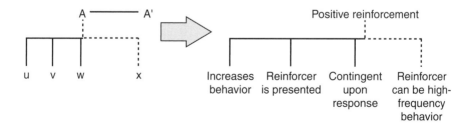

FIGURE 4.3 *An Example of Correlative Subsumption*

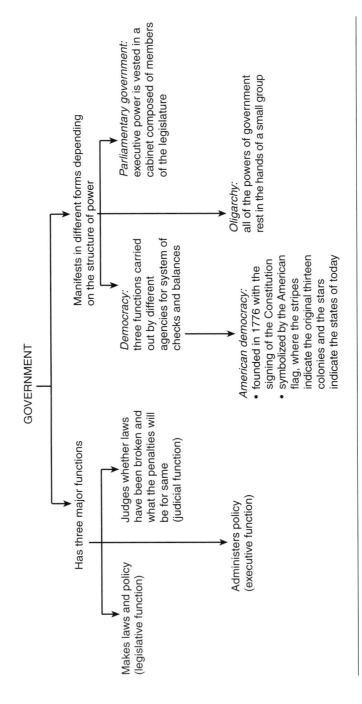

FIGURE 4.4 *A Cognitive Structure about Democracy Learned through Subsumption*

been replaced by A', because the student's understanding of the positive reinforcement principle is no longer the same as it was.

Examples of correlative subsumption can also be readily seen in the content being taught by Mr. Amaya in his social studies class. As the students learn about different aspects of government, they correlatively subsume these characteristics under the inclusive concept, government. (They may also derivatively subsume the labels, democracy and oligarchy, for example, under the label, government.) Then when discussion turns to expressions of patriotism, for example, such as displaying the American flag to commemorate the founding of America's democracy, students correlatively subsume this information under the anchoring idea of democracy (Figure 4.4).

Superordinate and Combinatorial Learning. Not all learning can be explained through the processes of derivative and correlative subsumption, because not all learning occurs in a subordinate fashion. In discovery learning, for instance, students may be working with examples to discover the more general concept or proposition. Thus, learning must be occurring in a superordinate, rather than subordinate, way. Similarly, what about instances in which students learn about similar concepts at the same level in the hierarchy as the anchoring idea? Learning in that case must be neither subordinate nor superordinate, but coordinate, or lateral. To account for learning that is not subordinate in nature, Ausubel, et al. (1978) proposed the processes of superordinate and combinatorial learning.

Superordinate learning occurs through a synthesis of established ideas. That is, a *new, inclusive proposition or concept is learned under which already established ideas can be subsumed.* If ideas x, y, and z are already established in the learner's cognitive structure and their association is discovered, then new idea A is learned under which they are all subsequently subsumed, as shown in Figure 4.5.

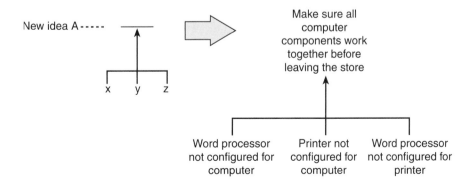

FIGURE 4.5 *An Example of Superordinate Learning*

FIGURE 4.6 *An Example of Combinatorial Learning*

An example of subordinate learning is evident in my experience with purchasing my first home computer. At the time, I knew virtually nothing about microcomputers except that I wanted one with which to do word processing. A slick salesman sold me a computer with monitor, word-processing package, and dot matrix printer. I took it all home, hooked it all up, and nothing worked. To make a long story short, the word processor was not configured for the computer (event x); it was adjusted. The printer did not work with the computer (event y); a different printer card solved the problem. The word processor was not compatible with the printer (event z); the designers of the word processor never could figure this one out, so I sold the printer. What did I learn (new idea, A) from these events? Make sure all components of the system work together before leaving the store!

When new concepts or propositions are neither more inclusive of nor subordinate to relevant anchoring ideas in the cognitive structure, they are meaningfully learned in a combinatorial way. In other words, **combinatorial learning** occurs when *the new idea is not relatable in a specific sense to an existing anchor but is generally relevant to a broad background of information,* which may contain a number of similar ideas sharing criterial attributes, as shown in Figure 4.6.

An example of combinatorial learning can be seen in the relationship between the flow of heat and the conducting of electricity through metals. Heat flow and electrical conductivity are not specifically related, in a subordinate or superordinate sense. Yet to understand each, a learner must have some previous knowledge of how metals are structured. Moreover, since the processes are analogous, having already learned about how heat flows through metals can facilitate understanding how electricity is conducted and vice versa (cf. Royer & Cable, 1975; Royer & Perkins, 1977; Driscoll, 1985).

Concepts exist in most subject matter disciplines that are coordinate to one another. And even though many coordinate concepts are also subordinate to some inclusive idea, their relationships to one another must be learned as well as their relationships to the subsuming idea. To take the government example again, democracy, oligarchy, and fascism all bear a coordinate relationship to one another. Thus, learning about one can provide a general background of information, which may be useful in learning the others. Ausubel and Fitzgerald (1961) found, for example, that knowing a lot about Christianity aided learners in acquiring new knowledge about Buddhism. Like the types of government in the previous example, these types of religion bear a coordinate relationship to each other, appropriate to combinatorial learning. According to Ausubel et al. (1978), "Most of the *new* generalizations that students learn in science, mathematics, social studies, and the humanities are examples of combinatorial learnings, for example, relationships between mass and energy, heat and volume, genic structure and variability, demand and price" (p. 59).

Assimilation Theory. By 1978, Ausubel had adopted the label assimilation theory to describe the meaningful learning processes of subsumption, superordinate learning, and combinatorial learning. In earlier versions of the theory (Ausubel, 1963a, 1968), assimilation referred primarily to the process of retention, whereby new information tends to be reduced to (or assimilated by) the meaning of the stable, more established anchoring idea. Although Ausubel's notions of what happens in retention changed little, which will be discussed in the next section, he came to use the concept of assimilation more broadly. Taking together learning and retention, "The result of the interaction that takes place between the new material to be learned and the existing cognitive structure is an *assimilation* of old and new meanings to form a more highly differentiated cognitive structure" (Ausubel et al., 1978, pp. 67–68).

Retention of Meaningful Learning

As indicated earlier, retention involves maintaining the availability of acquired information so that it may be accessed for use at a later time. Immediately following initial meaningful learning, new information is easily accessible, its stability enhanced by virtue of its anchorage to relevant concepts in the cognitive structure (Ausubel, 1963b). Over time, because it is more economical to remember a single inclusive concept than a large number of specific details, subsumed ideas become less and less distinguishable, or dissociable, from the inclusive anchor. When they can no longer be retrieved as entities separate and distinct from the anchoring idea, they are said to be forgotten.

Ausubel believed the consequences of forgetting are far more serious for correlative, superordinate, and combinatorial learning than for derivative learning (Ausubel et al., 1978). It is probably immaterial, for instance, if a particular example of dog or rice-growing place learned through derivative subsumption cannot be remembered. But suppose not enough about standard deviation is recalled to enable the learner to reconstruct the formula for its calculation. Since correlatively subsumed details should have modified the learner's overall understanding of the concept, forgetting them to this degree would be a true loss of knowledge.

Finally, it is important to note the difference between forgetting after rote learning and forgetting after meaningful learning. Despite the fact that information in both cases becomes irretrievable, there is still a net gain in the cognitive structure following meaningful learning. The concept or proposition that provided anchorage for meaningful learning is generally more differentiated than it was previously. Thus, as Ausubel (1963b) put it, there is "memorial residue of ideational experience," which enables the concept or proposition to be "more functional for future learning and problem-solving occasions" (p. 218).

Readiness for Learning

In the generally accepted sense of the term, learning readiness refers to a learner's developmental level of cognitive functioning. It is this cognitive maturity that is assumed to determine the extent to which learners are capable of learning at various levels of abstraction within a subject matter discipline. While not discounting the impact this type of readiness may have on learning, Ausubel (1963b) and Ausubel et al. (1978) emphasized readiness as a function of previously acquired subject matter knowledge. "If [Ausubel] had to reduce all of educational psychology to just one principle, [he] would say this: The most important single factor influencing learning is what the learner already knows. Ascertain this and teach him accordingly" (Ausubel et al., 1978, p. 163).

Readiness in this sense, then, depends upon both the substantive content in the learner's cognitive structure and its organizational properties. In the first place, experts in a subject matter simply have a lot more extant knowledge than do novices in the subject. The idea that extensive background knowledge facilitates subsequent learning has been consistently demonstrated (e.g., Ausubel & Fitzgerald, 1961, 1962; Tobias, 1976; Glaser, 1984). But the organization of knowledge also influences subsequent learning.

> If cognitive structure is clear, stable, and suitably organized, accurate and unambiguous meanings emerge and tend to retain their dissociability strength or availability. If, on the other hand, cognitive structure is unstable, ambiguous, disorganized, or chaotically organized, it tends to inhibit meaningful learning and retention. (Ausubel et al., 1978, p. 164)

It follows from the previous argument that learners with poorly organized cognitive structures in a subject matter should be aided in learning by materials that make clear similarities and differences among concepts to be learned. In fact, early studies conducted by Ausubel and his associates (e.g., Ausubel & Fitzgerald, 1961; Ausubel & Youssef, 1963) provided evidence that this was true. When learners already possessed organized and stable cognitive structures, however, such materials made no difference in what else they learned (Ausubel & Fitzgerald, 1961).

Royer, Perkins, and Konold (1978) provided evidence of a different sort to support Ausubel's claim that cognitive organization influences learning. They gave students passages to read, labeled with either the name of a fictitious person or the name of a famous person (e.g., Adolf Hitler). After studying the information, students rated sentences as to whether the sentences were old (i.e., from the passage) or new (i.e., never seen before). Subjects' judgments were quite accurate when the passage they read was ostensibly about a fictitious person. Having no anchoring information into which to meaningfully subsume the new information, students essentially learned the new ideas by rote. When they thought the information was about Adolf Hitler, however, learners typically had prior knowledge about Hitler to which they could attach the new ideas. As a result, they tended to misidentify as "old" sentences that were new but were thematically related to Hitler, such as, "He hated and persecuted the Jews."

To be ready for learning new material, then, learners of all sorts must possess a relevant, stable, and organized cognitive structure. Ausubel acknowledged, however, two additional influences on readiness that are important to mention. The first has to do with age differences among learners, and the second concerns culturally diverse learners.

According to Ausubel et al. (1978), "the cognitive organization of children differs mainly from that of adults in containing fewer abstract concepts, fewer higher order abstractions, and more intuitive-nonverbal than abstract-verbal understandings of many propositions" (p. 140). This simply means that children have a greater reliance during learning on concrete-empirical experience. Perhaps more so than adults, then, children should be taught in concrete ways. By extension, adults should be taught concretely when they know very little about the subject matter.

Accounting for the effects of culture on learning, Ausubel claimed, can be done within the same theoretical framework established for learning in general. That is, children who are culturally diverse relative to their classmates have different cognitive structures owing to the differences in their life experiences and prior learnings. This means that some learning tasks are likely to exceed the cognitive readiness of these children (Ausubel et al., 1978). What should be done about it? According to Ausubel, the basic principles underlying appropriate teaching strategies are essentially the same, regardless of who the learners are. To repeat the principle he considers most important: Ascertain the cognitive structures of your learners and teach accordingly. How one might do this most effectively is discussed next.

Meaningful Learning as Assimilation to Schema

Although "Ausubel's thinking about the role of abstract knowledge structures in learning from text generally was on the right track," Anderson, Spiro, and Anderson (1978, p. 439) found the theory of meaningful learning vague and inconclusive. They claimed that schema theory could bring precision to Ausubel's ideas.

Most modern cognitive conceptions of schema harken back to Bartlett (1932). In a study investigating the nature of remembering over a long period of time, Bartlett used the term *schema* to mean an organizing and orienting attitude that involves active organization of past experiences. Bartlett found that his subjects' recall of "War of the Ghosts" contained inaccuracies that could be directly related to their own interests and attitudes. He theorized that they invoked a relevant schema for understanding the story, and then, at recall, reconstructed in accord with the schema details about the story that they had forgotten.

Ausubel et al. (1978) acknowledged a similarity between anchoring ideas and Bartlett's notions of schema, but then they dismissed Bartlett's position as being fundamentally different from Ausubel's. Schemata are perceptually based, they argued, whereas anchoring ideas are cognitive. Bartlett theorized about the reconstructive nature of retention; Ausubel was interested in the constructive nature of learning. Ausubel et al. (1978) suggested that recall is really not reconstructing original meanings, it is reproducing information that has undergone memorial reduction.

When Anderson et al. (1978) suggested that the concept of schema might clarify Ausubel's theory, they took a fundamentally cognitive approach, conceiving of schema as a generic characterization of things and events. Thus, "to interpret a particular situation in terms of a schema is to match the elements in the situation with the generic characterizations in the schematic knowledge structure. Another way to express this is to say that schemata contain *slots* or placeholders that can be *instantiated*...with certain particular cases" (Anderson et al., 1978, p. 434; emphasis in original).

As an example, consider how CN's and GB's knowledge about cooking in the Making Mayonnaise scenario can be reinterpreted in terms of a schema. A "cooking" schema is likely to have slots for details about cooking, such as what utensils are used, what types of mixing could be employed, and so forth. To the extent that individuals have had experience cooking different things, these slots may be filled, or instantiated, with particular information. CN's and GB's responses to the question of how to make mayonnaise are evidence that they have not experienced beating eggs and oil together. Because of this, their schema about mayonnaise itself is based on perceptual features such as taste and consistency. This incomplete schema leads them to incorrect expectations about what mayonnaise is made of and how it is made.

A Lesson on Democracy can also be interpreted in terms of schema theory. That is, the seventh graders in Mr. Amaya's class are acquiring a government schema that will eventually enable them to instantiate details about different types of governments. According to Anderson et al. (1978), schema theory enables one to predict learning from textual materials, because "the schemata a person already possesses are a principal determiner of what will be learned from a text" (p. 438).

Efforts Toward an Understanding of Schema

Notions about the nature and function of the schema developed from several lines of research that were all focused on the impact of prior knowledge on comprehension and memory. Many studies demonstrated that what is remembered is largely a function of what was understood to begin with. But studies also revealed that both comprehension and memory are driven by meaning, or gist. Consider the following sentences, for example:

> The house was in the valley.
> The house was little.
> The valley was green.
> The house burned down.

If asked to read and later recall these sentences from memory, you are likely to produce the following response: "The little house in the green valley burned down" (Bransford & Franks, 1971). Rather than store sentences separately in memory, it appears that learners construct and store the gist of the sentences together.

Likewise, learners comprehend and remember information better when they can relate it to a familiar theme. For example, read the following passage:

> The procedure is actually quite simple. First you arrange items into different groups. Of course one pile may be sufficient depending on how much there is to do. If you have to go somewhere else due to lack of facilities that is the next step; otherwise you are pretty well set. It is important not to overdo things. That is, it is better to do too few things at once than too many. In the short run this may not seem important but complications can easily arise. A mistake can be expensive as well. At first, the whole procedure will seem complicated. Soon, however, it will become just another facet of life. It is difficult to foresee any end to the necessity for this task in the immediate future, but then, one never can tell. After the procedure is completed one arranges the materials into different groups again. Then they can be put into their appropriate places.

Eventually they will be used once more and the whole cycle will then have to be repeated. However, that is part of life. (Bransford, 1979, pp. 134–135)

None of the sentences in the above paragraph seems particularly difficult to understand, but together they do not make much sense. Bransford and Johnson (1972, 1973) and Dooling and Lachman (1971) found that without benefit of the theme, "washing clothes," subjects had difficulty comprehending and remembering the passage. Similar effects also have been demonstrated with pictures providing the theme (Bransford & Johnson, 1972), and Bransford (1979) argued that appropriate verbal knowledge can support the understanding of physical features of stimuli as well. For example, the flat blades of a dressmaker's shears might go unnoticed without the knowledge that they enable cutting on a flat surface. Finally, new, thematically consistent information is often falsely recognized as having been previously presented (Sulin & Dooling, 1974; Royer, Perkins, & Konold, 1978). This phenomenon was discussed earlier in the chapter as providing evidence for meaningful learning. Recall that learners are assumed to integrate new information within a related cognitive structure. "Remembering" information that was inferred rather than actually experienced has also been taken as evidence of active brain processes (National Research Council, 2000) and suggests a link to research discussed in Chapter 8.

In addition to gist and theme, the amount of prior knowledge possessed by learners and their interests can affect their interpretation and recall of information as well as their ability to solve problems. Chiesi and co-workers (Chiesi, Spilich, & Voss, 1979; Spilich et al., 1979) demonstrated that subjects who knew a lot about baseball were able to remember much more from a summary of a baseball inning than were subjects who knew little about the game. Similarly, Chi (1978) replicated the results of Chase and Simon (1973a, 1973b) with findings that expert chess players outperformed novices at recalling the positions of chessmen on the board. Finally, Anderson (1977) reported a study in which an ambiguous passage that could be interpreted in terms of playing cards or playing music was read to music students. As might be expected, students with an interest in music interpreted the passage to be about music and were unaware that the passage could be interpreted any other way.

This effect of perspective on learning and memory was also demonstrated by Pichert and Anderson (1977) and Anderson and Pichert (1978). In their studies, individuals were asked to read a passage describing two boys playing in front of a house. Half the subjects were told to read the story from the perspective of a real estate agent, while the other half were to adopt the perspective of a burglar. As predicted, perspective affected recall. That is, the real estate agent subjects remembered details about the number of rooms and condition of the house, whereas the burglar subjects remembered details about valuable objects and the isolation of the house from surrounding neighbors. But there was an unexpected finding as well. When asked to adopt the alternate perspective, without rereading the story, subjects remembered information that they did not report the first time! How was this notion of perspective to be explained in theories of memory? The answer to this, and indeed the way to incorporate the results of all these studies of prior knowledge, was found in schema theory.

The Nature of Schema

A schema is "a data structure for representing the generic concepts stored in memory" (Rumelhart, 1980, p. 34). Schemata are packets of knowledge, and schema theory is a theory of how these packets are represented and how that representation facilitates the use of the knowledge in particular ways. Thus, there are schemata "representing our knowledge about all concepts: those underlying objects, situations, events, sequences of events, actions, and sequences of actions" (Rumelhart, 1980, p. 34). To illustrate these various aspects of schemata, Rumelhart presented four different analogies.

First, schemata are like plays, in that a schema has variables that can be associated with different aspects of the environment, just as a play has characters, settings, actions, and so forth. Suppose, for example, that a playwright has written a very simple play about beating egg yolks in order to make mayonnaise. There must be a person to do the beating, an implement that person will use, a container for the eggs, and an overall setting in which the action will occur. Rumelhart would argue that our schema for egg-beating is very much like this description. And when the playwright specifies who will do the beating, what implement will be used, and where the action will take place, this amounts to the same process as schema instantiation. In other words, the schema variables take on specific values. Moreover, these values are typically constrained. Only certain tools are used to beat eggs, for example, and egg-beating generally takes place only in kitchens.

Schemata are like theories. Theories enable us to interpret events and phenomena surrounding us. To the extent that our theories work, they also allow us to make predictions about unobserved events. So it is with schemata. "The total set of schemata instantiated at a particular moment in time constitutes our internal model of the situation we face at that moment in time" (Rumelhart, 1980, p. 37). In addition, schemata provide the basis for making inferences about unobserved events. Consider the egg-beating event, for example. If you read a description of someone beating eggs that never mentioned what tool was being used, your egg-beating schema would fill in that gap with the default value (cf. Minsky, 1975) for egg-beating implement. Asked later what tool was used to beat the eggs, you are likely to reply, "Oh, an egg beater, hand mixer, something like that...." Default values are our initial guesses for variables whose values have not yet been observed.

While plays and theories are passive, schemata are active, so that schemata are like procedures, such as computer programs. They actively evaluate incoming information for the quality of fit, and they may involve a network of subprocedures. For example, the egg-beating schema undoubtedly has a subschema for how hard and how long to beat for given purposes. Schemata such as these that direct one's actions in a given situation have come to be called scripts. Finally, schemata are like parsers, in that they break down and organize incoming information to fit appropriate schema structures.

Because schemata are active in influencing how people interpret events and solve problems, they have also been conceived as mental models. Mental models are schemata that not only represent one's knowledge about specific subject matter, but also include perceptions of task demands and task performances. Thus, mental models are schemata that guide and govern performance as one undertakes some task or attempts to solve some problem.

Norman (1983) made the following observations about mental models (p. 8):

1. Mental models are incomplete.
2. People's ability to control their models is limited.
3. Mental models are unstable.
4. Mental models do not have firm boundaries.
5. Mental models are unscientific.
6. Mental models are parsimonious.

What this means is that people bring to tasks imprecise, partial, and idiosyncratic understandings that evolve with experience. Additionally, these understandings are utilitarian for the most part, rather than necessarily accurate.

As an illustration of a mental model in action, consider this brief description provided by Norman (1983). He observed people using handheld versions of several types of calculators and questioned them about their methods and understanding of the calculator.

> One of the subjects I studied (on a four-function calculator) was quite cautious. Her mental model seemed to contain information about her own limitations and the classes of errors that she could make. She commented, "I always take extra steps. I never take short cuts." She was always careful to clear the calculator before starting the problem, hitting the clear button several times. She wrote down partial results even when they could have been stored in the machine memory. (Norman, 1983, p. 8)

In trying to describe subjects' mental models of calculators, Norman speculated that most develop a rule to hit the clear button excessively because the action is functional across all kinds of calculators. The rule enables generalization to occur and thus makes the mental model work in a variety of situations. Note that the model is not accurate for all calculators, since some require only one press of the clear button to clear all registers.

Schema-Based Processing

How do schemata or mental models function to influence information processing? At the least, schema theory must deal with how schemata and mental models are acquired in the first place, how they are elaborated and modified through experience, and how they are selected and used in a processing task. Let us first consider selecting and using schemata in the face of various tasks.

Comprehending Text. Rumelhart (1980) described how readers construct interpretations of the following brief passage:

> Business had been slow since the oil crisis. Nobody seemed to want anything really elegant anymore. Suddenly the door opened and a well-dressed man entered the showroom floor. John put on his friendliest and most sincere expression and walked toward the man. (p. 43)

Sentence by sentence readers appear to invoke and evaluate schemata for their relevance to the story and ability to account for the available facts. So, for example, a business schema is selected with the first sentence, which suggests hypotheses about what is being sold. Encountering the word *elegant* in the second sentence causes readers to modify their interpretation; perhaps people do not want to buy large, elegant cars. *Showroom* is consistent with the car-selling schema, so that *well-dressed* signals money and buyer schemata, and so on. You can see the interaction between bottom-up and top-down processing that occurs in schema theory accounts of processing. An incoming stimulus activates a schema (bottom-up), which, by virtue of its variables, sets up expectations (top-down) for additional information as to the values of these variables. To the extent these expectations are met, that schema is instantiated. Information contrary to expectation, however, leads to alternate schema activation or modification of the current schema.

Comprehending lengthy texts is likely to involve not only activating and instantiating specific schemata, but also organizing those schemata into complex mental models. Johnson-Laird (1983) used the following illustration to demonstrate. Excerpted from Arthur Conan Doyle's (1905) story, "The Adventure of Charles Augustus Milverton," is this account of how Sherlock Holmes and Dr. Watson set out to burgle the house of a blackmailer, "the worst man in London."

> With our black silk face-coverings, which turned us into two of the most truculent figures in London, we stole up to the silent, gloomy house. A sort of tiled veranda extended along one side of it, lined by several windows and two doors.

"That's his bedroom," Holmes whispered. "This door opens straight into the study. It would suit us best, but it is bolted as well as locked, and we should make too much noise getting in. Come round here. There's a greenhouse which opens into the drawing room."

The place was locked, but Holmes removed a circle of glass and turned the key from the inside. An instant afterwards he had closed the door behind us, and we had become felons in the eyes of the law. The thick, warm air of the conservatory and the rich, choking fragrance of exotic plants took us by the throat. He seized my hand in the darkness and led me swiftly past banks of shrubs which brushed against our faces. Holmes had remarkable powers, carefully cultivated, of seeing in the dark. Still holding my hand in one of his, he opened a door, and I was vaguely conscious that we had entered a large room in which a cigar had been smoked not long before. He felt his way among the furniture, opened another door, and closed it behind us. Putting out my hand I felt several coats hanging from the wall, and I understood that I was in a passage. We passed along it, and Holmes very gently opened a door upon the right-hand side. Something rushed out at us and my heart sprang into my mouth, but I could have laughed when I realized that it was the cat. A fire was burning in this new room, and again the air was heavy with tobacco smoke. Holmes entered on tiptoe, waited for me to follow, and then very gently closed the door. We were in Milverton's study, and a portiere at the farther side showed the entrance to his bedroom.

It was a good fire, and the room was illuminated by it. Near the door I saw the gleam of an electric switch, but it was unnecessary, even if it had been safe, to turn it on. At one side of the fireplace was a heavy curtain which covered the bay window we had seen from the outside. On the other side was the door which communicated with the veranda. A desk stood in the centre, with a turning-chair of shining red leather. Opposite was a large bookcase, with a marble bust of Athene on the top. In the corner, between the bookcase and the wall, there stood a tall, green safe, the firelight flashing back from the polished brass knobs upon its face.

Below is a simple plan of the house with the veranda running down one side of it. Which way did Holmes and Watson make their way along the veranda—from right to left, or from left to right?

According to Johnson-Laird (1983), about one in a hundred people can spontaneously give the right answer to this question. Upon rereading the passage with the question in mind, most people can answer it correctly. This suggests two conclusions. (1) There appear to be different levels of comprehension, perhaps governed by task requirements. Reading for pleasure may result in only partial representations of passage information. (2) In order to make the required inference about Holmes' and Watson's direction, one must construct a mental model of the spatial layout. (The solution, by the way, can be found at the end of the chapter.)

Understanding Events and Guiding Actions.   Schemata also guide human actions as people find themselves in situations in which they must interpret what is going on and respond appropriately. Schank and Abelson (1975, 1977) investigated what they termed the "restaurant script," or what people know about restaurants and how to behave in them.

The restaurant script contains information about what it is like to go to a restaurant. There are roles to be filled (customer, waiter/waitress, cashier), certain props (such as table, menu, food, check, or tip), and certain activities (sitting down, ordering, paying the bill, tipping, and so on). This general script is also likely to vary depending upon the type and location of the restaurant. For example, fast-food restaurants differ in predictable ways from five-star restaurants, and restaurant customs in the West are likely to differ from those of other cultures.

Several studies (e.g., Anderson, Spiro, & Anderson, 1978; Bower, Black, & Turner, 1979) demonstrated that such a restaurant script served as the context for understanding and remembering information from stories taking place in restaurants. Subjects used their general knowledge about restaurants to comprehend particular events described in the stories. But now consider a story such as the following:

> Jim went to the restaurant and asked to be seated in the gallery. He was told that there would be a one-half hour wait. Forty minutes later, the applause for his song indicated that he could proceed with the preparation. Twenty guests had ordered his favorite, a cheese souffle. (Bransford, 1979, p. 184)

Because this story violates your general restaurant script, there seems to be something wrong with it. Bransford (1979) made two points with this illustration. First, the fact that schema violations impede comprehension and memory argues for the very existence of knowledge structures like schemata. Second, suppose you subsequently learn that Jim went to a very special type of restaurant, where customers who can cook are allowed to compete for the honor of preparing their specialties for other customers. The competition involves the customer entertaining the crowd, by singing, dancing, or whatever. Now, the target passage probably makes more sense when you reread it. But Bransford contended that you must have a general restaurant schema in the first place in order to construct a modified one in which to incorporate this story.

Evidence for schema-based processing comes from another source as well. Elizabeth Loftus and her colleagues conducted a series of studies examining eyewitness memory (see Loftus, 1979, for a review). The typical procedure followed in these studies was to show subjects a videotape of a crime or automobile accident and then to ask them questions about what they remembered seeing. The type of question had significant implications for recall. In one study (Loftus & Palmer, 1974), for example, students viewed a film of an auto accident and were asked either, "About how fast were the cars going when they smashed into each other?" or "About how fast were the cars going when they hit each other?" Subjects' memory for the speed of the cars differed significantly depending on which question they were asked. Moreover, subjects asked the question with the word *smashed* reported having seen broken glass significantly more often than subjects asked the question with the word *hit.* These results suggest the possibility of a smash schema being activated and used to reconstruct memory for the auto accident event; a hit schema activates slightly different knowledge.

Although the results of Loftus' research provide support for schema theory, they should be viewed with caution when considered for their application to eyewitness testimony in a court of law. The biasing effects of questions that have been produced in the laboratory do not necessarily hold when witnesses are actively involved in a real crime or accident. Yuille and Cutshall (1986) interviewed witnesses to an actual shooting in which one person was killed and another seriously injured. Subjects showed highly accurate memory for the event over a period of 5 months, and they resisted attempts to mislead them through the wording of questions.

Solving Problems.   Finally, there is evidence that schema-based processing occurs as people solve problems. Many studies have shown that experts in a domain structure their knowledge in ways different from novices (e.g., Chase & Simon, 1973a, 1973b; Chi, Glaser, & Rees, 1982; Larken et al., 1980). When attempting to solve problems, then, experts and novices build different mental models to guide their efforts.

> Our research suggests that the knowledge of novices is organized around the literal objects explicitly given in a problem statement. Experts' knowledge, on the other hand, is organized around principles and abstractions that subsume these objects. These principles are not apparent in the problem statement but derive from the knowledge of the subject matter. (Glaser, 1984, pp. 98–99)

An important aspect of mental models is that they provide a basis for reasoning. Because of their greater subject matter knowledge, experts in a domain tend to reason using specific, domain-based strategies. In a sense, their approach to problem solving is a matter of recognizing patterns that they have experienced before and matching these patterns to corresponding aspects of the problem at hand (Margolis, 1987). Novices, on the other hand, do not possess sufficiently elaborated mental models of the subject matter to permit such inferences. They are consequently forced to apply more general problem-solving strategies (such as, "Break the problem into its component parts") that lack both efficiency and power in solving specific problems.

The impact of schemata on problem solving can be quite dramatic. In a series of investigations on a logical problem known as the "four-card selection task," researchers repeatedly demonstrated that few people could solve the problem when it was presented in an abstract fashion. For instance, only 4 percent of subjects correctly determined which cards to turn over when presented with the rule, "If a label has a vowel on one side, then it has an odd number on the other" (Wason, 1968). However, when the same logical problem was put into a familiar context (e.g., "Every time I go to Manchester, I travel by train"), more than 60 percent of the subjects selected the correct cards (Wason & Shapiro, 1971).

D'Andrade (cited in Rumelhart, 1980; Rumelhart & Norman, 1981; D'Andrade, 1995) suggested that the familiar context enabled subjects to access an appropriate mental model for solving the problem. He told participants they were to imagine themselves as quality control experts in a label-making factory, and their task was to determine whether labels were incorrectly constructed. A label was correctly constructed if, when there was a vowel on one side of the label, there was an odd number on the other side. Only 13 percent of the subjects were able to appropriately apply this rule. But then D'Andrade had subjects imagine themselves as store managers inspecting store receipts with the rule, if any purchase exceeds $30, the signature of the store manager must be on the back of the receipt.

Most people have probably experienced situations such as that described in the store scenario, so that they would have developed schemata related to the checking of receipts by store managers. Checking labels at a factory, on the other hand, is probably unfamiliar to most people, which means they would have to rely upon general problem-solving logic to come up with the correct solution.

Schema Acquisition and Modification

What about learning, then? How does experience contribute to the permanent modification of schemata? Three different processes have been proposed to account for changes in existing schemata and the acquisition of new schemata due to learning. They are accretion, tuning, and restructuring (Rumelhart & Norman, 1978; Rumelhart, 1980; Vosniadou & Brewer, 1987). **Accretion** is roughly equivalent to fact learning in that *information is remembered that was instantiated within a schema as a result of text comprehension* or understanding of some event. For example, remembering from the description of mayonnaise making that a blender was used to beat the eggs is indicative of accretion. The egg-beating schema remains unchanged, but the variable for implement has been filled with blender.

When existing schemata evolve to become more consistent with experience, then **tuning** has occurred. Rumelhart and Norman (1978) suggested that this process accounts for the minor schema modifications that come with new exemplars of concepts and principles. Adding to one's egg-beating schema, the information about how long to beat for mayonnaise versus omelets is an example of tuning.

Finally, **restructuring** involves the creation of entirely new schemata which replace or incorporate old ones. This may occur through schema induction (Rumelhart, 1980), in which a new schema is configured from repeated consistencies of experience. Or, as Rumelhart and Norman (1981) argued, restructuring occurs most of the time through learning by analogy. In this case, a new schema is created by modeling it on an existing schema and then tuning it to fit the new situation. What typically occurs, according to Rumelhart and Norman, is that learners will try to use an existing schema to interpret the new situation, as did the child who initially applied her understanding of whipped cream to the mayonnaise problem. Areas of mismatch suggest ways in which the new schema must differ from the old, while areas that were not contradicted are carried over into the new schema.

Schema Automation and Cognitive Load

The notion of cognitive economy surfaced in Ausubel's thinking when he wrote about retention and forgetting. Recall that it is easier—more economical—to remember an inclusive concept or anchoring idea than to remember all of the details associated with it. Because schemata are conceived as packets of knowledge with slots to be filled with relevant, associated details, they are, by definition, an economical means of storing information. When schemata also become automated, processing capacity is freed so that more working memory can be devoted to tasks such as comprehending text or solving problems. This integration of concepts from information-processing theory and schema theory is the basis of cognitive load theory (Kirschner, 2002; Paas, Renkl, & Sweller, 2003; Sweller, van Merrienboer, & Paas, 1998).

Cognitive load refers to the strain that is put on working memory by the processing requirements of a learning task. When learners encounter a task for which they do not have an appropriate or automated schema, they must hold in mind all elements of the task individually and simultaneously. Think back to the examples given earlier in the chapter of readers constructing interpretations of text. If a schema to aid comprehension is not called to mind immediately, then the reader must struggle to remember each sentence in the paragraph as he or she attempts to construct a schema. However, comprehension proceeds with ease when an appropriate schema is automatically activated and brought to bear on the reading task. Similarly, in problem solving, learners who already possess an automated schema or mental model have more processing capacity in working memory to apply that schema toward solving more sophisticated problems. An important question, then, is how to facilitate the construction and automation of schemata that are useful for solving problems of interest (Sweller, van Merrienboer, & Paas, 1998).

Sweller, van Merrienboer, and Paas contend that the general strategies most learners use to solve problems when they cannot activate an appropriate schema put heavy demands on working memory. Furthermore, these strategies (such as breaking the goal into component parts) are only peripherally related to learning. The desired learning goal is for learners to construct and automate the appropriate schema or mental model that pertains to the particular class of problems to be solved. Therefore, instructional strategies should be sought that reduce extraneous cognitive load but increase germane cognitive load (Sweller, van Merrienboer, & Paas, 1998). Germane cognitive load has to do with making sure that learners engage in the cognitive processes required to construct an appropriate schema. How instruction might facilitate meaningful learning and schema construction is discussed next.

Meaningful Learning, Schema Theory, and Instruction

What do meaningful reception learning and schema theory have in common when it comes to implications for instruction? Clearly, prior knowledge plays an enormous role in both theories. What learners bring to the learning situation dictates to a large extent what they will take away from it in terms of new knowledge—concepts added to their cognitive structure or details elaborating schemata. But the content and organization of instructional materials are also important in both perspectives. Materials must be potentially meaningful to learners, organized so that connections are easily made between new information and that which is already known. To conclude this chapter, then, let us consider implications of meaningful reception learning and schema theory for activating prior knowledge, using prior knowledge in new situations, and making instructional materials meaningful.

Activating Prior Knowledge

Most learners already know something about any new topic they are asked to study, or they can make meaningful connections between what they know and what they are being asked to learn. However, possessing relevant prior knowledge is no guarantee that learners will activate and use it appropriately. It has been found in many conventional memory experiments, for example, that participants tend to view information they are asked to learn as separate and distinct from their prior knowledge (Spiro, 1977). They adopt an experiment set, which means that they approach the learning material in a rote fashion and fail to assimilate the information into related prior knowledge. Unfortunately, all too often learners tend to approach learning tasks in much the same way, regardless of whether they have prior knowledge to apply to the task. I have seen this happen in my graduate courses in which former teachers fail to use what they know about teaching to help them in learning about formal theories of learning and instruction.

In an instructional situation, then, the activation of prior knowledge should not be left to chance. To assure that meaningful learning takes place, instructors and designers can employ a variety of strategies to help learners relate their prior knowledge to new information they are to acquire. Making these connections is what Ausubel referred to as the first function of instruction, and he proposed the advance organizer as a means of accomplishing it (Ausubel, 1963a, 1968; Ausubel et al., 1978).

Advance Organizers.   Advance organizers are relevant and inclusive introductory materials, provided in advance of the learning materials, that serve to "bridge the gap between what the learner already knows and what he needs to know before he can meaningfully learn the task at hand" (Ausubel et al., 1978, pp. 171–172). Ausubel et al. (1978) also stated, "organizers are presented at a higher level of abstraction, generality and inclusiveness than the new material to be learned" (p. 171). Consider why this might be so. For one thing, learners are likely to have somewhat idiosyncratic cognitive structures, and while it might be desirable to construct advance organizers for each and every learner to meet their unique needs, that is not a very practical strategy. Thus, organizers should be sufficiently general to function for a variety of learners. In addition, remember Ausubel's call for using the most inclusive and relatable concepts of a discipline to guide learning. Constructing organizers more abstract and inclusive than the learning materials is one way of doing this.

The effectiveness of advance organizers for enhancing learning and retention of verbal materials was a subject of great debate in the research literature, but in spite of contradictory findings, the concept has persisted. Some studies (e.g., Ausubel, 1960; Ausubel & Fitzgerald, 1961; Ausubel & Youssef, 1963; Kuhn & Novak, 1971; West & Fensham, 1976) confirmed the positive effects of advance organizers on learning. Others suggested that the facilitating effect might be limited to learners with low verbal or analytic ability (e.g., Ausubel & Fitzgerald, 1962). But research reviews conducted by Bames and Clawson (1975) and Hartley and Davies (1976) pointed to even more equivocal findings.

Some of the problems cited in the research concerned methodological flaws in conducting the studies. For example, researchers may have failed to ascertain whether the organizers in their studies contained relevant concepts that would activate existing subsumers. In the absence of analyses of the learners' cognitive structures and the concepts to be learned, Ausubel et al. (1978) argued, it is unlikely that an appropriate organizer could be constructed. Moreover, if criterion tests are either too easy or too hard, or if they are designed to measure verbatim recall, then no organizer effects should be expected.

A more serious criticism of advance organizers is that their definition is vague (Hartley & Davies, 1976). If researchers operationalize the concept of advance organizers in different ways, then it should come as no surprise that their results do not agree. Ausubel et al. (1978) countered this criticism by pointing to the volume of space in an earlier work (Ausubel, 1968) devoted to the "nature and definition of an organizer and how it affects information processing" (p. 175).

Focusing on the conditions under which advance organizers might be expected to facilitate learning, Mayer (1979) reported the results of a set of experiments he conducted to test the claims and criticisms regarding advance organizers. From his results, Mayer suggested that advance organizers should exhibit the following characteristics:

1. Have a short set of verbal or visual information,
2. Be presented prior to learning of a larger body of to-be-learned information,
3. Contain no specific content from the to-be-learned information,
4. Provide a means of generating the logical relationships among the elements in the to-be-learned information, and
5. Influence the learner's encoding process. The manner in which an organizer influences encoding may serve either of two functions: to provide a new general organization as an assimilative context that would not have normally been present or to activate a general organization from the learner's existing knowledge that would not have normally been used to assimilate the new material. (Mayer, 1979, p. 382)

Mayer (1979) went on to suggest that further research is required to determine what analogies, images, and examples in various subject matters may best serve as effective advance organizers. In order for advance organizers to work with particular students as well, they should probably be constructed by the teacher or instructional designer who has specific knowledge about what the learners already know. Mayer concluded with the following checklist for producing organizers to be used in research, suggesting that organizers that generate a yes for each question should be explored further:

1. Does the organizer allow one to generate all or some of the logical relationships in the to-be-learned material?

2. Does the organizer provide a means of relating unfamiliar material to familiar, existing knowledge?
3. Is the organizer learnable, i.e., is it easy for the particular learner to acquire and use?
4. Would the learner fail to normally use an organizing assimilative set for this material, e.g., due to stress or inexperience? (Mayer, 1979, p. 382)

Research on the advance organizer since Mayer's recommendations were published has resulted in greater emphasis on the learners' prior knowledge (e.g., Sui, 1986; Mannes & Kintsch, 1987). Learners must have necessary prior knowledge for the organizer to activate, and the organizer must draw explicit connections between old and new topics (West, Farmer, & Wolff, 1991). Synthesizing Ausubel's ideas with the results of more recent research, West et al. (1991) suggested the following procedures for constructing advance organizers:

1. Examine the new lesson or unit to discover necessary prerequisite knowledge. List.
2. Reteach if necessary.
3. Find out if students know this prerequisite material.
4. List or summarize the major general principles or ideas in the new lesson or unit (could be done first).
5. Write a paragraph (the advance organizer) emphasizing the major general principles, similarities across old and new topics. Examine examples in this text. Use them as models.
6. The main subtopics of the unit or lesson should be covered in the same sequence as they are presented in the advance organizer. (p. 125)

As can be seen in Step 5 and in the example provided in Box 4.1, West et al. have also emphasized the verbal (as opposed to visual) nature of advance organizers. Box 4.2, however, illustrates how visual material may serve effectively as an advance organizer. In this example are two diagrams I have successfully used to introduce different learning theories. These two metaphors tap what individuals know about black boxes and computers and map these onto the major concepts of behaviorism and cognitive information processing. In the former, for example, no reference is made to events or processes inside the learner. In the latter, by contrast, specific hypotheses are made to suggest that such processes are akin to what computers do with information.

Schema Signals.   Like Ausubel, schema theorists recognized the importance of activating prior knowledge in learners as they engage in new learning. In reading, for example, comprehension and memory for what is read are facilitated when learners know and can access a relevant schema. This appears to

BOX 4.1 • *Advance Organizer for a Lesson on the*
Government of the United Kingdom

Assume that Mr. Amaya's class from the Lesson on Democracy scenario has now completed their lesson on the democratic government of the United States. As a part of that unit, they eventually discussed the three branches of government—executive, legislative, and judicial. In the following advance organizer, these branches are mentioned as a bridge to the next unit on the government of the United Kingdom.

In our unit on the U.S. government we learned that there are three branches in the federal government: the executive, the legislative and the judicial. The primary function of the legislative branch, the Congress, is the passage of laws, whereas the major task of the judicial branch is the protection of citizens' rights under the national Constitution. In this next unit on the United Kingdom, we will learn that there are also these three branches: executive, legislative, and judicial, with similar functions.

(From West, Farmer, & Wolff, 1991, p. 116.)

be true not only for subject matter content but for the structure of the text as well. Many stories in Western culture, for example, share a common abstract structure, which includes an initial setting, adventures of a main character, and resolution of some problem that faces the main character. This story grammar or narrative schema guides both comprehension and later recall of story events (Kintsch, 1976, 1977; van Dijk & Kintsch, 1983; Rumelhart, 1975; Mandler, Johnson, & Deforest, 1976).

People may also develop schemata to guide their understanding of scientific or technical articles (Bransford, 1979; cf. Brooks & Dansereau, 1983). Most of the research articles cited in this book follow a standard schema: introduction to the problem under study, method used to conduct the investigation, results, and discussion. Other basic text structures can include simple listing, comparison/contrast, temporal sequence, cause/effect, and problem/solution (Armbruster, 1986, p. 255). Finally, different schemata may be developed for various literature genre—newspaper stories, detective fiction, etc.

In Chapter 3, the recommendation was made to signal a text's organization to readers. Not only should this help readers pay more attention to important information, but it also provides a foundation for more effective encoding. On the basis of schema theory, this recommendation must be both qualified and expanded. Instructors should alert students to the schematic structures of text materials in order to facilitate their learning, especially when the subject matter is unfamiliar. Poor readers, in particular, can comprehend more of what they read if they are taught to focus on the structure of the text (Varnhagen & Goldman, 1986).

BOX 4.2 • *An Advance Organizer for Theories of Learning*

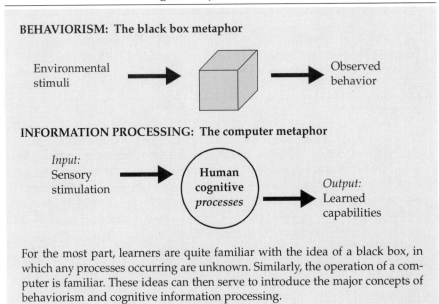

BEHAVIORISM: The black box metaphor

Environmental stimuli → [black box] → Observed behavior

INFORMATION PROCESSING: The computer metaphor

Input: Sensory stimulation → Human cognitive *processes* → *Output:* Learned capabilities

For the most part, learners are quite familiar with the idea of a black box, in which any processes occurring are unknown. Similarly, the operation of a computer is familiar. These ideas can then serve to introduce the major concepts of behaviorism and cognitive information processing.

In addition, "Authors can help readers access the appropriate textual schemas by (a) organizing the textbook using conventional text structures—the basic text structures and/or more genre- or content-specific text structures and when these are known and appropriate, and (b) clearly signaling the text organization" (Armbruster, 1986, p. 258).

Armbruster reviewed research in which certain types of signals appeared to be effective in emphasizing certain types of text structures. For example, additive conjunctions (e.g., also, likewise) can be useful in signaling compare/contrast text structures, whereas causal conjunctions (e.g., consequently, as a result) are likely to be effective with cause/effect text structures. To help readers access or construct relevant content schemata, Armbruster (1986) concluded that current research suggests (1) the "judicious use of analogies or comparisons" (p. 261), and (2) the presentation of "well-developed concepts and thorough explanations that make explicit the important relationships among ideas" (p. 264).

Signaling the appropriate schema for word problems can also be a factor in learning arithmetic (e.g., Greeno, 1980; Sweller, Mawer, & Ward, 1983; Cooper & Sweller, 1987; Derry, Hawkes, & Tsai, 1987). Sweller (1989) asserted that a schema, if available, provides for rapid and relatively effortless problem solving. In the absence of an appropriate schema or in the case of incorrect classification of a problem, however, an inappropriate schema will be used instead.

This suggests that students should be taught and provided practice in recognizing and representing problem types. Lewis (1989), for example, taught students a diagramming method for representing compare problems in arithmetic. Fuson and Willis (1989) demonstrated that classroom teachers could successfully teach children to use schematic drawings to represent the structure of addition and subtraction problems. In both instances, the representational strategy benefited students in conceptualizing and solving a variety of problems.

An issue in problem-solving instruction as well is to manage cognitive load. That is, learners will be better able to construct and automate an appropriate schema or mental model for a particular class of problems when the instruction minimizes extraneous cognitive load but increases germane cognitive load. For example, goal-free problems focus learners on relevant problem states rather than the gap between the current state and the desired state. A goal-free problem asks learners to approach solving a problem by "calculating as many variables as you can" rather than "finding the value of *x*," which is the ultimate solution to the problem. Other strategies for managing cognitive load in problem-solving tasks include providing worked examples and partially completed problems that learners must elaborate or finish solving (Sweller, van Merrienboer, & Paas, 1998).

Finally, because social behavior and cultural knowledge can be framed in terms of schemata (e.g., Harris, Schoen, & Lee, 1986), it makes sense to consider how schema signals cue appropriate (or inappropriate) behavior in instructional situations. One of my doctoral graduates from Taiwan, for example, found his schema for multiple-choice tests to be inappropriate for taking tests in the United States. He was accustomed to selecting more than one response on multiple-choice items and did not realize, on his first test in graduate school in the United States, that only one answer would be considered correct. Needless to say, he quickly modified that schema. Given our increasingly multicultural society and the increased demands for training in international settings, it is probably wise to keep in mind the cultural schemata learners may bring to instruction.

Making Instructional Materials Meaningful

When learners encounter instruction that makes no sense to them, it becomes an impossible task to call upon prior knowledge, because there is no way to judge what knowledge will be relevant. According to Ausubel, *potentially* meaningful information must be made understandable to learners or they will approach it in a rote fashion. He claimed that the second function of instruction was to improve the discriminability among concepts. Likewise, schema theorists looked for ways to represent the content and structure of information so that learners could more easily develop appropriate schemata and mental models.

Comparative Organizers and Elaboration.   Ausubel (1963) deplored the common practice of textbook writers to compartmentalize ideas or topics into separate chapters without exploring their relationships. The result, he claimed, is "incalculable cognitive strain and confusion" on the part of the learner. Students may not see, for example, how new propositions differ in substance from what they already know, causing them to dismiss the new information as unimportant. Or, they may fail to see inherent similarities or differences among concepts in the learning material itself. In this case, misconceptions are likely to result.

Consider, for example, the principles of behavior management that you studied in Chapter 2. Because there are similarities among principles that result in behavior increase (e.g., positive reinforcement, Premack principle), and among those that result in behavior decrease (e.g., punishment, extinction), these principles can be easily confused. Moreover, many learners experience confusion with negative reinforcement, which sounds like an oxymoron. The concept negative is closely associated in everyday life with aversive events, which seems to connote punishment, whereas reinforcement positively influences behavior.

To help make similar concepts more easily discriminable, Ausubel suggested the comparative organizer, which provides a means for systematically comparing and contrasting concepts. The concept tree and rational set generator depicted in Chapter 3 are examples of comparative organizers. Providing organizers to learners is one means of facilitating learning of unfamiliar, and potentially confusable, information (e.g., Ausubel & Fitzgerald, 1961; Ausubel & Youssef, 1963), but so is having learners generate them using frames such as that shown in Figure 4.7 (West et al., 1991). Mr. Amaya might find the technique especially useful in his lesson on democracy.

To enhance the stability and clarity of anchoring ideas in cognitive structure, and thus facilitate learning of information related to those ideas, Ausubel recommended starting instruction with the most general and inclusive ideas and progressively elaborating them. Ausubel called this process progressive differentiation, but Reigeluth adopted it as elaboration in his Elaboration Theory (Reigeluth, 1979, 1999; Reigeluth & Stein, 1983). According to Elaboration Theory, progressively more detail is to be elaborated in each level of instruction (from the most general, inclusive content to the most specific) until the desired level of detail is reached. The specific sequence chosen for instruction depends on which type of domain expertise is desired. Reigeluth (1999) distinguished between conceptual expertise (understanding what) and theoretical expertise (understanding why) and suggested that the general-to-detailed sequence is different for each (p. 437). In Mr. Amaya's class, for instance, it is likely that conceptual understanding is being stressed; students are learning what the different functions of government are and what differences there are among types of governments. By contrast, learning principles of cooking might involve theoretical understanding, for example, why beating eggs and oil together results in a creamy consistency. Elaboration theory provides specific guidelines for making instructional decisions about scope and sequence.

Conceptual and Pedagogical Models. According to schema theorists, the provision of conceptual and pedagogical models is a means of making instructional materials meaningful and helping learners access and refine relevant schemata and mental models.

> As designers, it is our duty to develop systems and instructional materials that aid users to develop more coherent, useable mental models. As teachers, it is our duty to develop conceptual models that will aid the learner to develop adequate and appropriate mental models. (Norman, 1982, p. 14)

Conceptual models are any of the models invented by teachers, designers, scientists, or engineers to help make some target system understandable.

Before instruction even takes place, however, teachers and designers should identify the mental models that learners bring to the instructional situation (Glaser, 1984; Gagné & Glaser, 1987). Studies in physics, for example, have shown that many learners have naive theories of physical phenomena (e.g., Lewis, Stern, & Linn, 1993; Champagne, Klopfer, & Anderson, 1980; McCloskey, Caramazza, & Green, 1980). Such naive theories may contain

	Executive	Legislative	Judicial
Description of function			
United States			
Great Britain			

FIGURE 4.7 *A Comparative Organizer, or Frame, for a Unit on Government*

contradictory, erroneous, or unnecessary concepts, with the result that learning and problem solving become difficult and ineffective.

Tracking the development of learners' mental models through the transition from novice to expert can be a means for determining what next steps in instruction should be taken (Gagné & Glaser, 1987). In a developmental study, Carey (1985a) documented changes in children's concept of alive as they gained domain-specific knowledge about biological functions. Likewise, Siegler and co-workers (Siegler & Klahr, 1982; Siegler & Richards, 1982) found that children's reasoning about balance-scale problems was greatly influenced by experience with new information. Using a task analysis procedure to determine what theory guided children's performance, Siegler was able to match their current knowledge state with learning events that helped them move to a new level of reasoning.

Teachers' knowledge of students' problem-solving knowledge has also been associated with problem-solving achievement. Peterson, Carpenter, and Fennema (1989) concluded that more knowledgeable teachers appeared to pose problems to students, question their problem-solving processes, and listen to their solutions. These actions were related to problem-solving achievement. Less knowledgeable teachers, by contrast, tended to explain problem-solving processes to students, "thereby also doing the thinking for students" (Peterson et al., 1989, p. 568).

How can teachers ascertain the mental models of their students? There are at least four possible ways to do it: (1) Observe them; (2) ask them for an explanation; (3) ask them to make predictions; and (4) ask them to teach another student (Jih & Reeves, 1992). A mathematician who does research on math instruction, Schoenfeld (1985) often asks his students without warning to explain their reasoning on a problem or to justify the approach they are taking to solve it. Not only does this enable him to judge their mental models, but also the tactic encourages students to monitor their own mental models. "By the end of the term, I don't need to ask questions anymore. Students have gotten into the habit of analyzing where they are" (Schoenfeld, quoted in *A Mathematician's Research on Math Instruction*, 1987).

By understanding what models learners are currently using to guide their performance, teachers and designers can build upon them by specifying what Glaser (1984) called pedagogical models. These may be the same as conceptual models that have been invented to make some system understandable, or they may be a series of approximations that may be thought about and debugged in the course of instruction. diSessa (1982) referred to a kind of task analysis for identifying components of preexisting theories that can be involved in developing more sophisticated theories. Collins and Stevens (1982, 1983) offered a model of inquiry instruction that provides strategies for helping learners make predictions from and debug their current models of understanding (see Chapter 7 for more discussion of this model). For example, Anderson (cited in Collins & Stevens, 1983) assisted learners in formulating models of what geographic factors affect average temperature by getting them to form and test hypotheses about the locations and temperatures of specific places. In addition, diSessa (1982), Champagne et al. (1982), and Lewis et al. (1993) have designed computer simulations that allow physics students to explore the implications of their own theories and compare these results to the predictions of other theories.

Finally, mental models may be explicitly taught to facilitate performance (Gagné & Glaser, 1987). These conceptual models provide an important supplement to teaching strategies. "We have found that students make up their own conceptualizations anyway, and if we don't give them guidance, their models can be bizarre and difficult to overcome" (Norman, 1982, p. 108). Choosing an appropriate conceptual model to use in instruction, however, can be a difficult task. In studies of how computer-ignorant students learned to use a text editor, Norman and his colleagues faced a choice between providing an incomplete model or spending a great deal of time conveying a complete model. They found their way out of this dilemma by providing different conceptual models at different points in the instruction, each designed to elucidate a different aspect of the editor (Norman, 1982).

For pedagogical or conceptual models to effectively facilitate learning, they should meet three basic criteria: learnability, functionality, and usability (Norman, 1983). A good model is easy to learn, most likely drawing upon information that is highly familiar to learners. A good model is functional, in that it corresponds to important aspects of the target system it is designed to clarify. For example, the components making up a system might be identified as well as how these components function together to enable the system to operate (Mayer & Gallini, 1990). A good pedagogical model may not necessarily be a complete model, in the sense of representing all important aspects of the target. If this is the case, then several models may be required to fully conceptualize the desired information, and learners should be told that each one is not a perfect representation of the system being learned (Jones, 1988). Finally, a good model is easily used, given the limitations of the human information-processing system. Again, this argues for a series of incomplete models over a complete one that taxes learners' processing capabilities.

Acquisition of a mental model might not be enough for true understanding, however. "To plan, predict, invent, or otherwise make good use of a mental representation, one must not just have it, but operate with and through it" (Perkins & Unger, 1999, p. 97). For instance, the students in Mr. Amaya's class in "A Lesson on Democracy" might learn to define and explain various functions of government as well as recognize and provide pertinent examples. But can they offer and defend an interpretation of a Supreme Court ruling or elaborate connections of the case to events in their own lives?

To help learners develop the ability to understand or think flexibly about a topic, Perkins and Unger (1999) suggested what they called thought-demanding activities or *performances of understanding.* "An understanding performance both displays the learner's current understanding-so-far and, by asking the learner to solve problems, make decisions, and adapt old ideas to new situations, expands that understanding further" (p. 97). So by engaging his students in generative topics such as a Supreme Court case, Mr. Amaya may promote not only the construction of a mental model of government, but also students' ability to use that model personally and productively.

Using Prior Knowledge in New Contexts

Transfer, or the use of prior knowledge in new contexts, is routinely taken to be one of the most important instructional goals. Teachers want students to transfer the arithmetic skills they learn in school to everyday activities such as balancing a checkbook and judging good buys at the supermarket. Or, they hope learners will use their knowledge of science to make wise choices about the use of energy and other environmental resources. Bank executives want manager-trainees to transfer to the job the knowledge and skills they acquire in training programs. And fighter pilots must be able to solve problems in the air similar to those they have encountered in simulators or printed instructional manuals.

Both Ausubel's meaningful reception learning and schema theory can be conceived as theories about transfer, because they are concerned with the effect that prior knowledge has on the learning of new information. Schema theory is more comprehensive than meaningful reception learning in being able to account for how learners bring to bear what they know on solving problems. But neither theory is focused particularly on how people learn when to use their knowledge. Although transfer may be a matter of invoking a relevant schema, determining when a schema is relevant turns out to be no easy task.

Recall the study by D'Andrade in which subjects were given the rule, "If a label has a vowel on one side, it should have an even number on the other." They performed poorly unless problems were couched in the context of a familiar schema (i.e., store receipts in amounts greater than $30 must have the manager's signature on the reverse side). In a similar study, individuals trained in the logic of the conditional were expected to perform well on problems involving this rule (Cheng et al., 1986). Results indicated, however, that knowledge of logic did not transfer. Like D'Andrade's subjects, the individuals in the study of Cheng et al. (1986) performed much better when the rule was phrased in more familiar terms (e.g., "if a person is drinking alcohol, then he must be over 21" or "If a person enters this country, she must have had a cholera shot"). Cheng et al. (1986) explained their findings in terms of a permission schema, which has a limited range of transfer.

Price and Driscoll (1997) concluded, however, that schema theory may be more limited in its ability to account for such results than Cheng et al. (1986) believed. They replicated D'Andrade's study with two modifications. Some subjects had practice in solving the problem in the familiar scenario before encountering the same problem in an unfamiliar scenario, and some subjects were provided feedback after the first problem to help them abstract the problem schema. Although feedback eliminated one of the errors subjects commonly make, neither intervention improved problem-solving performance.

Results such as these contribute to the ongoing debate as to whether transfer is highly limited in scope or whether it is broad and ranges across diverse domains. Whichever is the case, it should not be left to chance (Price & Driscoll, 1997). Rather, it is probably worth the effort of a teacher or designer to consider just what sort of transfer is desired and take steps to include instructional conditions that will effectively support it. In Chapter 5, situated cognition theory is explored as a promising approach to facilitating knowledge transfer.

Conclusion

The question of how knowledge is acquired, represented, accessed, and used is a complex one, for which there are no easy answers. This chapter has presented several contemporary approaches to knowledge representation for learning, thinking, and problem solving that provide insights beyond those of cognitive information-processing theory. But they, along with this chapter, have only scratched the surface.

> The solution to the riddle of Holmes and Watson is that they must have walked along the veranda from right to left. After they broke into the house round the corner from one end of the veranda, they passed through various rooms and along a corridor, and then they turned right into Milverton's study and saw a door that communicated with the veranda. (Johnson-Laird, 1983, p. 166)

Schema and Meaningful Reception Learning in "Kermit and the Keyboard"

Ausubel had little to say about learning of motor skills, so his theory does not account well for aspects of Kermit's learning that involve actually playing the keys to produce a sound. However, the conceptual knowledge about music that goes along with the ability to play is subject to analysis from the

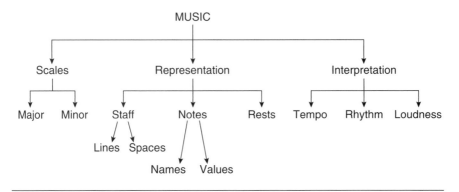

FIGURE 4.8

perspective of Ausubel's theory. For instance, Kermit might have developed a cognitive structure like the one in Figure 4.8 (please keep in mind that this is not my area of expertise!).

As he learns particular notes, particular rhythms, and so on, Kermit's cognitive structure would become progressively more elaborated. How might we account for the mistake that Kermit makes in playing "House of the Rising Sun"? Let's assume that under the anchoring idea "rhythm," Kermit subsumes different types of the 4/4 time signature, such as ballad, march, and beguine. These also correspond to different backgrounds on the keyboard, and it is only when Kermit selects beguine that he plays one note too long. That version of the song is now derivatively subsumed as an example of beguine, whereas the correct version of the song is subsumed under ballad.

From the standpoint of schema theory, Kermit may have developed a schema for "symphony" in which was instantiated for "music played in concert" the detail of "a small set of music pieces repeated over time." His schemas for types of music such as ballads and marches would also include the tempos and styles in which they are played (at least the schemas would come to include these attributes as Kermit learned them and instantiated their unique characteristics; both ballad and march would be instantiated as examples of the larger schema related to time signature). Because of this, the background he selected to play with "House of the Rising Sun" could activate a schema that might cause him to misinterpret how long the offending note should be played. Thus, he expected to see something different than what was actually written, and this expectation guided his action. Because the result still sounded fine, there was nothing to correct Kermit's mistake.

Theory Matrix

Theory	Meaningful Reception Learning	Schema Theory
Prominent Theorists	D. P. Ausubel; R. E. Mayer	D. A. Norman; D. E. Rumelhart; J. Sweller; J. van Merrienboer
Learning Outcome(s)	Organized conceptual knowledge that involves understanding	Organized conceptual knowledge and mental models that can be used to interpret events and solve problems
Role of the Learner	Make connections between prior knowledge and to-be-learned information that results in an elaborated cognitive structure	Construct schemata and mental models Use, modify, and automate schemata in solving problems
Role of the Instructor	Make materials meaningful to the learner Activate learners' prior knowledge, and organize instruction to help them make meaningful connections to what they already know	Activate learners' existing schemata Help learners develop and refine appropriate mental models, manage cognitive load. Use thought-demanding activities to facilitate understanding
Inputs or Preconditions to Learning	Potentially meaningful materials, an orientation toward meaningful (as opposed to rote) learning, relevant prior knowledge	Preexisting schemata that can be modified or reconstructed by analogy to account for new knowledge Materials and problems that do not overload working memory.
Process of Learning	Incorporating new information into cognitive structure by attaching it to anchoring ideas through processes of subsumption, superordinate and combinatorial learning	Accretion, tuning, and restructuring of schemata Automation of schemata

Suggested Readings _____

Ausubel, D. P., Novak, J. D., & Hanesian, H. (1978). *Educational psychology: A cognitive view.* New York: Holt, Rinehart and Winston.

Anderson, R. C., Spiro, R. J., & Anderson, M. C. (1978). Schemata as scaffolding for the representation of information in connected discourse. *American Educational Research Journal, 15*(3), 433–440.

Educational Psychologist. (1988). Special Issue: Learning mathematics from instruction, *23*(2).

Johnson-Laird, P. N. (1983). *Mental models.* Cambridge, MA: Harvard University Press.

Sweller, J., van Merrienboer, J., & Paas, F. (1998). Cognitive architecture and instructional design. *Educational Psychology Review, 10*(3), 251–296.

Reflective Questions and Activities _____

1. Consider the tacit assumptions about knowledge and knowing that theorists make in this chapter. To what epistemological tradition do they seem to fit most appropriately? What evidence supports your position?

2. How is Ausubel's conception of cognitive structure similar to or different from the models of long-term memory presented in Chapter 3? To illustrate your answer, select a concept (or set of concepts) that might be the focus of instruction. Indicate how, once learned, it would be represented in memory, according to Ausubel versus information-processing theorists.

3. How do notions about schemata and mental models differ from the models of memory proposed by information-processing theorists? What kinds of learning performances are accounted for by each?

4. Describe a possible study that investigates the differential effects of instruction designed from the perspectives of meaningful reception learning versus information processing. What variables might be important to examine? What differences might you expect between the two perspectives on those variables?

5. How would a schema theorist analyze a situation in which learners are experiencing difficulty achieving some instructional goal? What recommendations might be suggested for ameliorating the situation?

6. Select an instructional goal that involves the learner developing a mental model. Describe what instruction you would design to ensure that learners acquired the desired model.

7. Many current textbooks on learning mention Ausubel's work only briefly. Take a position on the probable impact of his ideas on educational theory and practice. In your opinion, does his theory of meaningful reception learning provide new or additional insights into learning and/or instruction?

5

Situated Cognition

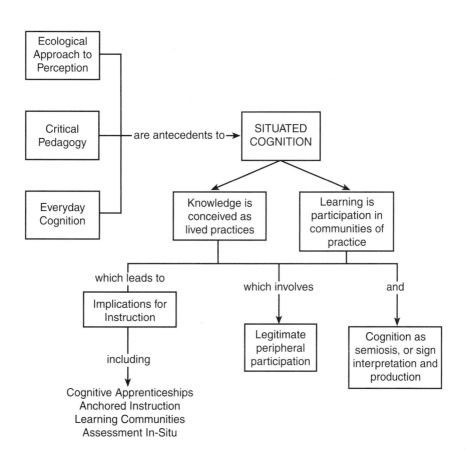

Consider these scenarios.

• *The Weight Watcher*[1]

As a new member of a dieting program, the Weight Watcher must learn how to measure and calculate food portions as he prepares meals. At one point, he is asked to fix a serving of cottage cheese, and the amount allotted for the meal is three-quarters of the two-thirds cup the diet program allows.

> The [Weight Watcher]…began by muttering that he had taken a calculus course in college…. Then after a pause he suddenly announced that he had "got it!"… He filled a measuring cup two-thirds full of cottage cheese, dumped it on a cutting board, patted it into a circle, marked a cross on it, scooped away one quadrant, and served the rest…. At no time did the Weight Watcher check his procedure against a paper and pencil algorithm, which would have produced $3/4$ cup $\times$ $2/3$ cup $= 1/2$ cup. (Lave, 1988, p. 165)

• *The Research Assistant*[2]

Carlo is a graduate student in educational psychology at a major research university. In his first year as a doctoral student, he hasn't yet decided

---

[1]This scenario is based on de la Rocha's (1986) study of Weight Watchers as described by Lave (1988).

[2]"The Research Assistant" is dedicated to my former major advisor, Professor James M. Royer, who was the "master teacher" with whom I apprenticed in my doctoral program. My experience epitomizes the essence of situated cognition theory, and it is one I try to recreate with each doctoral student who chooses to study under my tutelage.

on a direction for his career, so he takes the required courses and participates in whatever interesting study opportunities come his way. He hires on to a project as a research assistant for his major advisor, helping to conduct and report studies on the cognitive processes involved in reading and learning from text materials. Carlo's first assignment is to locate published articles related to the research and write abstracts of them to be shared with the rest of the research team. As the year progresses, Carlo is asked to draft a portion of the article reporting on the first completed study. After that, he presents the results of the study at a regional conference. By the end of the year, he is fully engaged in the research, suggesting variables to be investigated and research designs to carry out the investigations.

Recall from Chapter 4 that context plays an important role in learning. In familiar contexts, learners can relate new information and skills more easily to what they already know than if the learning context is unfamiliar. Similarly, when an appropriate schema fails to be activated, learners experience difficulty making sense of the learning materials and are forced to memorize or otherwise learn by rote. Finally, it was noted that when context changes from learning to application or practice, learners often fail to transfer the knowledge they acquired in one context to the other, related context.

How does context, then, relate to the two scenarios with which this chapter opens? One would assume, in the first scenario, that the Weight Watcher learned simple calculations of fractions in school. Yet faced with a calculation problem in determining the correct portion of cottage cheese, he resorts to a very practical strategy: Measure two-thirds of a cup, apportion the resulting amount into four parts, and discard one of the parts. Is this an "inventive resolution" of the problem (Brown, Collins, & Duguid, 1989) or "an act of desperation, born of ignorance" (Palincsar, 1989)?

In the scenario, The Research Assistant, context plays a different sort of role in learning. Here we see Carlo learning the skills of an academician by working as a kind of apprentice to a "master academician," his major advisor who wrote the grant that funds him and who directs the research project. As he acquires competence and is able to contribute more and more to the project, he is given increasingly more responsibility. This is known as learning-in-practice (Lave, 1990/1997), and it represents an approach to learning that is fundamentally different from the theories discussed so far.

In Chapter 3, the distinction was made between declarative knowledge ("knowing that") and procedural knowledge ("knowing how"). In situated cognition theory, or situated learning, declarative and procedural knowledge are integrated within a single framework. As Brown et al. (1989) put it,

> Many methods of didactic education assume a separation between knowing and doing, treating knowledge as an integral, self-sufficient substance, theoretically independent of the situations in which it is learned and used. The

primary concern of schools often seems to be the transfer of this substance, which comprises abstract, decentralized formal concepts. The activity and context in which learning takes place are thus regarded as merely ancillary to learning—pedagogically useful, of course, but fundamentally distinct and even neutral with respect to what is learned. Recent investigations of learning, however, challenge this separating of what is learned from how it is learned and used. (p. 32)

In other words, cognition is assumed to be social and situated activity (Kirshner & Whitson, 1997); one learns a subject matter by doing what experts in that subject matter do (Lave, 1990/1997). Proponents of situated learning argue that knowledge remains inert and unused if taught in contexts that separate knowing from doing. As an illustration, consider the following problem cited by Schoenfeld (1988). It is an example of students mastering computational skills in mathematics without understanding their use in mathematical practice. "An army bus holds 36 soldiers. If 1,128 soldiers are being bused to their training site, how many buses are needed?" Although 70 percent of 13-year-olds nationwide correctly performed the long division that is required to answer this question, only 23 percent actually gave the correct answer. Almost a third said "31 remainder 12" (Schoenfeld, 1988, p. 150). "That [students] failed to connect their formal symbol manipulation procedures with the 'real-world' objects represented by the symbols constitutes a dramatic failure of instruction" (Schoenfeld, 1988, p. 150).

What is situated cognition theory, then, and what implications does it have for instruction? These are the topics taken up in this chapter. It is important to note that one of the research traditions contributing to situated cognition theory as it is evolving is Vygotsky's sociocultural theory, which is presented in Chapter 7. Given the continuing influence of Vygotskyian theory on the thinking of situated cognition theorists, I vacillated over the placement of this chapter. Interestingly, there is little consensus yet on the positioning of situated cognition in modern learning theory. Some authors link it closely to constructivism in education (Bruning, Schraw, Norby, & Ronning, 2004; Schunk, 2004), whereas others discuss it in the context of transfer of problem-solving skill and contrast it to other perspectives such as cognitive information processing (Ormrod, 2004). None of these authors consider the theory in much depth or breadth, nor do they make connections to the growing body of literature on semiotic theory, some of which is also discussed in this chapter.

Yet situated learning has drawn the attention of prominent cognitive psychologists, such as John Anderson and Herbert Simon, who have considered its relation to information processing theory. Simon argued that situated cognition is compatible with modern CIP theory (Vera & Simon, 1993), whereas Anderson took issue particularly with the claim of context dependence in learning (Anderson, Reder, & Simon, 2000). He concluded that evidence for information-processing approaches to instruction is stronger and better validated than evidence for approaches based on situated cognition.

Researchers within the situated learning perspective tend to contrast their views with information-processing theory, even while they draw upon theories such as Vygotsky's. For this reason, I have placed the chapter in the section on learning and cognition while recognizing its connections to other sections of the book (especially Chapters 7 and 11). Moreover, there is no requirement that the chapters of the book be read in sequence; the interested reader might wish to read the portion of Chapter 7 that is devoted to Vygotsky's theory while studying the ideas contained in the present chapter. Finally, it is also important to keep in mind that situated cognition theory is considered by its proponents to be "a work in progress" (Kirshner & Whitson, 1997). As such, it has yielded promising implications for education but not yet educational models that are "sufficiently robust" in the eyes of situated cognition theorists. Thus, it should come as no surprise that evidence for instructional approaches based on the more mature theory of CIP might be stronger and letter validated.

The Nature of Situated Cognition

"The theory of situated cognition…claims that every human thought is adapted to the environment, that is, *situated*, because what people *perceive*, how they *conceive of their activity*, and what they *physically do* develop together" (Clancey, 1997, pp. 1–2; italics in original). Moreover, what people perceive, think, and do develops in a fundamentally social context. To make such statements requires a reformulation of individual psychology, an individual psychology that is implicit throughout most of this book.

Think back to Chapter 1, in which learning theory was defined as comprising a set of constructs linking changes in performance or the capability to perform with what is thought to bring about those changes. That is, the results of learning are to be explained through inputs (largely external to the learner) and means (largely internal to the learner). The learning process is implied to be an individual one, unique to each learner. This individual psychology is implicit in behavioral theory (recall Figure 2.1) as well as in the cognitive theories presented thus far. In Figure 5.1, you can see how the cognitive perspective differs from the behavioral one primarily in the assumptions one makes about processes occurring within the learner. Moreover, knowledge is presumed to be something that resides within the learner.

To the extent that social and cultural influences are considered at all in these theories (see Chapter 4, as well as Piaget's developmental theory coming up in Chapter 6), they are treated as decomposable "into discrete facts or rules that can be entered into the individual's cognitive system" (Kirshner & Whitson, 1997, pp. 5–6). They provide a context for learning, but learning continues to be viewed as "a process by which a learner internalizes knowledge, whether 'discovered', 'transmitted' from others, or 'experienced in interaction' with others" (Lave & Wenger, 1991, p. 47).

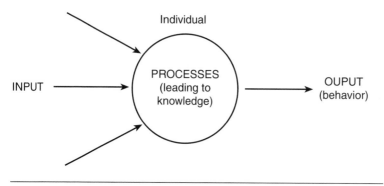

FIGURE 5.1 *Learning as Internalization in the Cognitive Perspective*

Knowledge as Lived Practices

Situated cognition theory, by contrast, shifts the focus from the individual to the sociocultural setting and the activities of the people within that setting. Knowledge accrues through the lived practices of the people in a society. These practices are "meaningful actions, actions that have relations of meaning to one another in terms of some cultural system" (Lemke, 1997, p. 43).

Knowledge as lived practices must be understood in its relation to the social aspect as well as the individual aspect that is generally stressed in other theories of learning. According to Lemke (1997),

> [Psychological] individuality can only be properly identified and analyzed after the levels of community have been factored out. You cannot define how someone's reading of a text or affective reaction to a math problem is uniquely individual until you understand which aspects of their participation are typical of their social subject-positioning, of the use of the resources and common patterns of a particular culture or subculture, or a function of how brains and material environments couple together generally in processes of self-organization. (p. 49)

To fully understand the Weight Watcher's solution to the cottage cheese dilemma, for example, we would have to know more about the sociocultural communities—the communities of practice—in which he participates. Computational algorithms or the recognition of quantitative relationships may not be a part of his ordinary, day-to-day existence, despite the fact that he probably learned those things in school. By contrast, someone who packs milk crates or egg cartons for a living is likely to recognize immediately that $3/4$ of $2/3$ is the same as $2/3$ of $3/4$, or simply $1/2$ (Whitson, 1997).

A good example of this concept of lived practices can be seen in a study investigating teaching and learning in a physical therapy program. Rose (1999), interested in the cognitive processes involved in skilled work, spent time observing and interviewing the instructors and students of Orthopedic Management II, a 14-week course. The primary instructor described the wide range of instructional approaches she used in the course, which included lecturing, demonstration, modeling, telling stories about clinical practice, collaborative learning, guided practice, and more. As the researcher attempted to understand the instructor's range of pedagogical strategies, he concluded that "some of these methods and orientations are part of the educational tradition of Australian manual physical therapy, developed and modified over time and place, used to help Nicole [the instructor who earned her graduate degree in Australia] learn....The methods and their purposive interplay provide one way to assist the transmission of the manual techniques, their connection to concepts, and the philosophy of their use in service of clinical reasoning" (Rose, 1999, p. 149).

Learning as Participation in Communities of Practice

In the situative perspective, learning is conceived as increasing participation in communities of practice. Learning as participation "focuses attention on ways in which it is an evolving, continuously renewed set of relations... [among] persons, their actions, and the world" (Lave & Wenger, 1991, p. 50). In this perspective, learning is a co-constitutive process in which all participants change and are transformed through their actions and relations in the world (Figure 5.2). Think about Carlo in The Research Assistant, for example. As a sort of apprentice, he is perhaps the most dramatically changed through what he learns as a research assistant, moving from a peripheral role in looking up literature to a more central one in determining new directions the research project might take. However, he has also acted upon his environment, and others, including his research advisor, have learned in their interactions with him.

This dialectic of individual and context has prompted some researchers to avoid the labels of situated cognition or situated learning as syntactically misleading. As Greeno (1997) put it,

FIGURE 5.2 *Learning as Increasing Participation in Communities of Practice: The Mutually Co-constitutive Nature of Persons-Actions-World in the Situated Learning Perspective*

> I use the term "situative" to designate a theoretical perspective…because those other terms suggest that some learning or cognition is situated but other learning or cognition is not situated. In the situative perspective, all learning and cognition is situated by assumption. (p. 16)

Learning as participation in communities of practice also implies that individuals participate in more than one community and that they achieve their identity in each community through their personal trajectories of participation (Wenger, 1998). A good example of overlapping communities of practice can be seen in my recent experience planning a section of a conference for a professional association to which I belong. I invited a doctoral student of mine to co-chair the planning process with me, and my invitation alone illustrates the dialectic of our relationship. On one hand, I wanted him to have a professional experience that would serve him well as he embarks on his own academic career. Through planning this conference, he would interact with other professionals in the field and see the range of research topics and ideas they were writing about. This part of the experience is consistent with a community of practice in which we were both very comfortable in our respective roles, he as student and I as professor and mentor.

On the other hand, I knew my student had computer expertise far beyond my own competence. (He had worked as a computer analyst and instructor prior to entering the doctoral program.) Given the intent of the association to try electronic submission and reviewing of proposals, I thought the technical assistance my student could provide would be invaluable. As we embarked on the conference planning process, then, we entered a community of practice in which our roles reversed themselves. I became the student and he the instructor when it came to technical aspects of the planning process. In other ways, we were equal partners, sharing the load of correspondence with proposers and reviewers and selecting the proposals that would ultimately compose the conference program. There is no question but that our interaction and our participation in this particular community of practice changed both of us in many ways. Learning as participation "shapes not only what we do, but also who we are and how we interpret what we do" (Wenger, 1998, p. 4).

Before delving into the specifics of situated cognition theory, its promises as well as its failings, let's examine briefly some of the scientific traditions from which it is evolving.

Antecedents to Situated Cognition Theory

McLellan (1993, 1994) prefaced two special issues of *Educational Technology* on situated learning by stating that "situated learning was introduced in a 1989 article" by Brown, Collins, and Duguid. Indeed, that article, "Situated Cognition and the Culture of Schooling," had an impact at my own university that, in retrospect, seems almost unprecedented. Brown et al. argued that many traditional teaching practices result in inert knowledge, or the inability of students to use what they know in relevant situations. They contrasted novices, or students, with experts and "just plain folks" (JPFs). Novices have difficulty solving complex, real-world problems because they tend to memorize rules and algorithms in school in a decontextualized way. Experts and JPFs, on the other hand, are similar in their ability to use situational cues to solve emergent and complex problems, JPFs through causal stories and experts through causal models. The problem-solving success of JPFs and experts is attributed to the situated nature of knowledge, and Brown et al. proposed a model of cognitive apprenticeship as a means to enculturate students into authentic practices of a discipline.

Brown et al. (1989) were met immediately with criticism for their failure to discuss other scientific traditions that are consistent with (and very likely contributed to) their notions about situated learning. According to Clancey (1997), the notion of situatedness that was prevalent in sociological studies was brought to the cognitive science community by Suchman (1987). Greeno (1997) reminded us that

> The idea of analyzing systems in which individuals participate as the basic level of analysis is not new, of course.... Dewey (1896) argued for this in a classic paper that is just over 100 years old this year, as well as in his other writings (e.g., Dewey, 1929/1958). Other proponents of this interactionist perspective, in various forms, have included Bartlett (1932), Bateson (1979), Gibson (1979/ 1986), Kantor (1945), Lewin (1936, 1946), Mead (1934), and Vygotsky (1934/ 1987). (p. 7)

This interactionist perspective has also been called contextualism, "an American philosophical position...[that] has its roots in William James, C. S. Peirce, and John Dewey" (Jenkins, 1974, p. 786). Finally, the writings of political philosopher Michael Oakeshott (1962) have been cited as a more eloquent rendition of the epistemology "popularized by situated cognition theorists" (Tripp, 1993, p. 71).

It seems clear that scientific work from a variety of traditions has contributed to current conceptions of situated learning, and it is not my purpose to review all of it here. Instead, I offer brief discussion on several of what I conceive to be the major influences on the situated cognition movement as it appears to be evolving: the ecological psychology of perception, critical pedagogy, and everyday cognition. Although I would also include Vygotsky's sociocultural theory in this list, it is discussed at length in Chapter 7.

The Ecological Psychology of Perception

The ideas of J. J. Gibson, a psychologist studying perception, are at the heart of ecological psychology, which is an attempt by researchers to analyze behavior of organisms in relation to their environments. That is, the environment for an organism can be described in terms of both where the organism lives and how it lives (Clancey, 1997; Turvey & Shaw, 1995). Gibson coined the term *affordance* to characterize the impact of the environment on an organism's behavior, or how it lives in its environment. Gibson argued that an organism's direct perception of these affordances controls its behavior.

To take a simple example, imagine the environment that an upright piano provides for a palmetto bug (a kind of large cockroach that is ubiquitous in Florida). As it is rarely moved, the piano affords a stable, dark, warm home for nesting and breeding, and these characteristics would be perceived as such by the bug, leading to its taking up residence there. But what might the piano afford to other organisms? To the student learning music, it affords an instrument with which to make music, and to the person vacuuming the living room floor, it affords a place to pile newspapers and magazines. The various characteristics of the piano are thus perceived and acted upon differently depending on whose environment is the focus.

The idea of affordances suggests an interactive and reciprocal relation between an organism and its environment. "Facts," as such, "are not properties of the world in some independent sense, but the product of interaction" (Clancey, 1997, p. 262). Or, as Gibson (1966) put it, "The stick's invitation to be used as a rake does not emerge in the perception of a primate until he has differentiated the physical properties of a stick, but they exist independently of his perceiving them" (p. 274). Thus, affordance emerges with the action of an organism.

When the complexity of people as organisms is considered, perception of affordances must go beyond a physical state of affairs to a conceptual state of affairs (Clancey, 1997). That is, people interact not only with the physical properties of their environments, but also with concepts that they have constructed. Take, for example, the concept of cooperative learning. What does cooperative learning afford the individual student who is placed in a group with peers and given a learning task to complete? Research on this learning structure has repeatedly demonstrated that it can facilitate learning and motivation if done well, but it can also afford an opportunity for "free-loading" if individual accountability is not included.

"People move within a physical and conceptual space…[that] is so overwhelmingly more complex and ordered than the natural scale out of which it is constructed that *our world* of buildings, lawns, chairs, tools, and documents is the *recognizable* structure of our culture's making" (Clancey, 1997, p. 265; emphasis in original). As a consequence, any theory of learning must start with the culture in which the learner resides, one of the hallmarks of situated cognition theory.

Critical Pedagogy

With a shift in thinking about psychological factors involved in learning to sociological factors comes an interest in cross-cultural comparisons and a question about "whose knowledge is of interest to the designers of educational systems" (Damarin, 1993, p. 27). If knowledge is co-produced by the learner and the situation in the context of a culture or society, then the position of the learner within the culture can become an important variable.

For example, consider the learning environment that is afforded girls versus boys in many classrooms where a computer or two are used primarily to reward performance. Students who complete their work before their classmates are permitted to play computer games. In Western culture, many computer games embody action-oriented, shoot-em-up scenarios that are typically enjoyed more by boys than by girls. If these are the only games available on the classroom computer, then boys are far more likely to be found playing them. With their greater time on the computer, they are gaining technological skill and expertise that is, in a sense, denied to the girls.

Damarin (1993, p. 28) writes,

> The proletarian standpoint of Marxism, the feminist standpoints elaborated by Nancy Hartsock (1983), Sandra Harding (1986, 1991) and others, the Black Woman's standpoint described by Patricia Hill Collins (1990), and the Africanist "optimal psychology" described by Linda James Myers (1988) are among the theories of knowledge as situated by and constructed in diverse communities and under various forms of subjugation.

Damarin points to the importance of respecting the knowledge communities from which learners come and helping them to become comfortable in multiple worlds. For her, this means a sharing of language, norms, and histories, not the imposition of one worldview on another. She also cautions us about the potential uses of technology in instruction (see also Streibel, 1993, 1994). Hypertext, for example, offers a multiplicity of directions and sites that students can explore, but it "tends to suppress and make invisible both the exigencies of travel from one knowledge world to another and the situational power of local languages, norms, and histories" (Damarin, 1993, p. 31).

Everyday Cognition

The situational power of local and familiar conditions is dramatically revealed in comparisons between activities in the laboratory and everyday activities. People who perform poorly in test situations show great skill on similar problems in their everyday lives (Rogoff, 1984). For example, Micronesian navigators scored low on standard tests of intellectual functioning, but they navigated with ease from island to island, demonstrating the use of memory, inference, and calculation skills (Gladwin, 1970). Likewise, developmental theorists observed young children having difficulty with referential communications tasks in the laboratory but adjusting their communication to their listeners in everyday situations (e.g., Gleason, 1973).

These differences in performance have led researchers to theorize that cognition is socially defined, interpreted, and supported (Rogoff, 1984).

Moreover, by studying cognition in everyday situations, researchers hoped to determine the generality of cognitive skills and articulate the role of culture in the development of these skills. One outcome of this research is a clearer understanding of how social contexts constrain and aid cognition. For example, supermarket shoppers were found to use the ordered arrangement of items in the supermarket to help them remember what they wanted to buy, rather than generate a written shopping list to take with them (Lave, Murtaugh, & de la Rocha, 1984). In a similar vein, dairy workers' use of arithmetic was influenced by the sheets they used to fill orders and the way they packed cases. They found very practical and efficient ways of solving complex mathematical problems that did not involve using the general computational algorithms learned in school (Scribner, 1984).

Rogoff (1984) concluded that everyday thinking "is not illogical and sloppy but instead is sensible and effective in handling the practical problem" (p. 7). In other words, "rather than employing formal approaches to solving problems, people devise satisfactory opportunistic solutions" (p. 7). Does this suggest that formal procedures are never used, or that cognitive skills are entirely context-specific? Hardly. What it does suggest is the adaptivity of successful reasoning and the need to examine learning as participation in interactions that succeed over a broad range of situations (Greeno, 1997).

Summary: Toward a Theory of Situated Cognition

The cultural context, the co-constitutive nature of individual-action-environment, and multiple knowledge communities have all become elements of situated cognition theory. Wenger (1998) succinctly summarized the basic premises of situated cognition theory as follows:

1. We are social beings. Far from being trivially true, this fact is a central aspect of learning.
2. Knowledge is a matter of competence with respect to valued enterprises, such as singing in tune, discovering scientific facts, fixing machines, writing poetry, being convivial, growing up as a boy or a girl, and so forth.
3. Knowing is a matter of participating in the pursuit of such enterprises, that is, of active engagement in the world.
4. Meaning—our ability to experience the world and our engagement with it as meaningful—is ultimately what learning is to produce. (p. 4)

With respect to a specific knowledge community, or community of practice, Wenger (1998) defined three interacting dimensions: mutual engagement, a joint enterprise, and a shared repertoire (Figure 5.3). That is, "people are engaged in actions whose meanings they negotiate with one another" (p. 73). The actions are in service of a mutually negotiated goal which defines the enterprise in which they are engaged and which "creates among participants relations of mutual accountability" (p. 78). Finally, over time, the activity of the individuals engaged in the enterprise gives rise to specific practices, symbols, and artifacts that are shared by all members of the community.

With these premises and dimensions in mind, let us turn now to the processes of situated cognition as they are presently constituted. This chapter closes with a discussion of potential implications of situated cognition theory for instruction.

Processes of Situated Cognition

"Learning viewed as situated activity has as its central defining characteristic a process [called] *legitimate peripheral participation*" (Lave & Wenger, 1991, p. 29; emphasis in original). This process accounts for the way a newcomer to a community of practice develops into a full participant, or from the viewpoint of a learner, how a learner engages in the activity of a sociocultural practice and becomes increasingly competent in this practice. This process describes, for example, how Carlo and other graduate students like him learn to become scientists in the academy.

Legitimate Peripheral Participation

According to Lave and Wenger (1991), **legitimate peripheral participation** should be understood as *defining ways of belonging to a community of practice.*

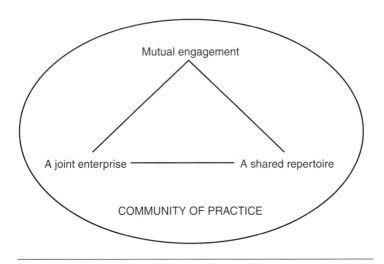

FIGURE 5.3 *Dimensions of a Community of Practice*

In other words, there is no such thing as an "illegitimate peripheral participant." Rather, the concept of legitimate refers to the social organization of and control over resources. Someone who is not a legitimate participant would not be allowed access to the resources of the practice. For example, casual Web surfers who happen upon a university Web site cannot gain access to the information resources that are provided as a matter of course to the university's enrolled students. Furthermore, it takes time and experience in the community of practice for newcomers to gain full access to the community's resources. To continue the example of a university, students often fail to recognize the resources available to them, or they fail to take full advantage of these resources until they have learned how to negotiate within the system.

The notion of peripheral is used to distinguish those who are newcomers to a practice from the oldtimers, who are considered "full" participants. Thus, if Carlo is a legitimate peripheral participant in the academic discipline of psychology, then his professors and other professionals in the field would be the full participants. Likewise, a senior would be a full participant and oldtimer in comparison to a freshman in the university community of practice.

Peripherality encompasses the "multiple, varied, more- or less-engaged and -inclusive ways of being located in the fields of participation defined by a community" (Lave & Wenger, 1991, p. 36). An undergraduate student in psychology who is hired to work on the research project, for example, would be less engaged in the project than would someone like Carlo. The nature of that student's participation in the project would also be quite different. Peripherality also accounts for the sort of participation Carlo might have in the discipline of psychology if he chose, upon graduation, to take a position at a company that designs computer-based training. He would enter a new community of practice, but without having left the previous one entirely. He may still read the psychological journals to stay current on theories of learning to inform his work, but his engagement with and participation in the field of psychology would not be as full as it once was.

There is another aspect of legitimate peripheral participation that deserves mention, and that is the changing forms of participation and identity of individuals who participate in a community of practice over a long time (Lave & Wenger, 1991). They enter as newcomers, progress to the point of seeming to be oldtimers with respect to new newcomers, and eventually become the oldtimers themselves. With respect to teaching and learning, "this points to a richly diverse field of essential actors and, with it, other forms of relationships of participation" (Lave & Wenger, 1991, p. 56). As Carlo's participation in the research project makes him less a newcomer and more an oldtimer, for example, he may become a mentor and teacher to the newcomers after him.

Wenger (1998) suggested that learning as participation be conceived on three broad levels:

1. For individuals
2. For communities
3. For organizations

As already discussed, individual learning means participating in the practices of the communities of which the learner is a member. Community learning is a matter of refining practice of the community and ensuring new members (so that new newcomers enter as the original newcomers become oldtimers). As a graduate student of psychology myself many years ago, I sometimes resisted engaging in some of the practices of my discipline. My rationale was that I never intended to enter the academy myself; I wanted to be a practitioner, a designer of instruction. However, years later I understood the importance of educating new generations of members to assure the continuation and growth of the community.

Finally, learning at the level of organizations "is an issue of sustaining the interconnected communities of practice through which an organization knows what it knows and thus becomes effective and valuable as an organization" (Wenger, 1998, p. 8). Colleges of education as professional schools provide an illustrative case-in-point. Education as a professional discipline draws on many core academic disciplines, including psychology, and it remains a vital enterprise to the extent that it stays connected to those other communities of practice. The same holds true for the connection between colleges of education and the communities of practice into which they place their graduates.

For the most part, the focus of this book is on the learning of individuals. Therefore, the remainder of the chapter focuses on individual learning in reference to the community of practice, rather than on community or organizational learning.

Apprenticeship.   To explore the concept of legitimate peripheral participation, Lave and Wenger (1991) studied actual cases of apprenticeship. Forms of apprenticeship appear all over the world and throughout history to the present day. As Lave and Wenger pointed out, "In the United States today much learning occurs in the form of some sort of apprenticeship, especially wherever high levels of knowledge and skill are in demand (e.g., medicine, law, the academy, professional sports, and the arts)" (p. 63). They also cautioned, however, that "conditions [placing] newcomers in deeply adversarial relations with masters, bosses, or managers; in exhausting overinvolvement in work; or in involuntary servitude rather than participation distort, partially or completely, the prospects of learning in practice" (p. 64).

So what do effective apprenticeships appear to have in common? For one thing, a specific master-apprentice relationship is *not* a uniform characteristic of apprenticeship learning. Yucatec midwives, for example, learn midwifery in the course of everyday life, where a young girl might begin her participation by running errands for her mother or grandmother and eventually take on more and more of the workload (Jordan, 1989, as cited in Lave & Wenger, 1991). Where specific masters are involved, little intentional teaching appears to go on. Rather, the master confers legitimacy on the apprentice and makes resources of the community available when the apprentice is "ready" for them. This certainly characterizes Carlo's experience. He is assigned limited and well-defined tasks at first and then given more responsibility as he shows himself ready to accept such responsibility.

As apprentices, learners have strong goals and motivation, and through engagement in practice, they develop a view of what the enterprise is all about (Lave & Wenger, 1991). In apprenticeship learning, there also tends to be communication among peers and near-peers to the extent that relevant information is spread rapidly and effectively. As I often tell newly admitted students, if you want to know what *really* goes on in the department, ask another student, not a faculty member.

Other Forms of Legitimate Peripheral Participation.   While apprenticeship learning serves as an exemplary case of legitimate peripheral participation, it is not the only means for learning in practice to occur. Learners belong to many different communities of practice, and their participation in those communities can take many forms, including nonparticipation as a consequence of being excluded from participation. The concept of a **learning trajectory** helps to *describe a learner's participation over time.* Wenger (1998) defined five types of learning trajectories:

1. Peripheral
2. Inbound
3. Insider
4. Boundary
5. Outbound

Each suggests a different form of participation in the community of practice.

Learners on a peripheral trajectory never, for one reason or another, engage in full participation. They may choose not to seek full participation, as in the case, for example, of a student who takes music lessons through high school but then fails to continue them in college. Or they may be excluded from participation, implicitly or explicitly. The example given earlier in the chapter about girls and computer games shows the impact of implicit exclusion from participation. Game designers may not have intended to exclude girls from learning and using technology, but the features of the products they designed have had that unfortunate consequence. Explicit exclusion from participation can be seen in communities of practice that establish criteria for full acceptance into the community. Music again provides a reasonable example. Only the most accomplished players will secure seats in world-class orchestras and make their living as professional musicians.

Peripheral participation may occur because there are no "explicit pedagogical mechanisms to encourage, guide, and sustain involvement" in the community of practice. Rose (1999) observed an automotive class where, as expected, the more skilled students participated more fully in the activities of car repair. Some of the less skilled students became more involved as their skills grew, but others simply hung back, apparently marking time. Rose suggested that "to move into authentic practice does not rule out along the way a host of traditional teacherly devices, from the pep talk, to direct instruction, to the quick quiz. In fact, for some, full participation may require it; otherwise one gets a shadowy involvement never leading to true participation and competence" (1999, p. 152).

An inbound trajectory suggests that a newcomer has invested in the community of practice and is headed toward full participation. This would be the case for apprentices who remain in the profession in which they are apprenticed. Full participation does not mean an end to learning, however, so the concept of an insider trajectory suggests a means for continued evolution of practices within the community. For example, when I came to the university as a new faculty member nearly 20 years ago, it was rare to see instructors using any sort of technology in their teaching beyond a chalkboard. Now, my colleagues are exploring innovative ways of supporting learning through the use of Web technologies. The practices of teaching at the university, therefore, have continuously evolved, with oldtimers seeking new ways to define their practice.

Boundary trajectories occur when learners sustain membership and participation in related communities of practice and, in essence, "broker" interactions between them. For example, consider the case of an instructional designer who participated in the development of a concept plan for an interactive science museum. As a member of the planning team, he worked together with scientists, educators, child development experts, and museum specialists, all with the belief systems and practices of their primary communities of practice. It was his role to find a common ground among the participants that enabled each to contribute his or her own unique expertise.

Finally, learners on outbound trajectories are in the process of leaving a community. "Being on the way out of such a community...involves developing new relationships, finding a different position with respect to the community, and seeing the world and oneself in new ways" (Wenger, 1998, p. 155).

To this point, we have examined situated learning from a mostly macro or global perspective, what it means to learn by participating in communities of practice. But how does one come to understand, at a micro level, what is involved in such participation? How does one apprehend what it means to think and act like an oldtimer in the community of practice? It is this process that we turn to next.

Cognition as Semiosis

Inherent in all the models of cognition and memory that were presented and discussed in Chapters 3 and 4 is the basic assumption that knowledge is an internal representation of some kind of external reality. Information is out there, to be received and stored by the human processing system, whether as memory networks, cognitive structure, or schemata. Fundamental to situated cognition theory, however, is the assumption that learning involves social participation, such that cognition "takes place within the world and not in 'minds' construed as somehow separate from or outside the world" (Whitson, 1997, p. 98). Put another way,

> If human knowledge doesn't consist of stored descriptions, what then is the relation of what we say to what we do? Speaking must be seen not as bringing out what is already inside, but as a way of changing what is inside. Speaking is not restating what has already been posted subconsciously inside the brain, but is itself *an activity of representing*. Our names for things and what they mean, our theories, and our conceptions *develop in our behavior* as we interact with and reperceive what we and others have previously said and done. (Clancey, 1997, p. 3; emphasis in original)

Cognition from a situated perspective, then, is a matter of sign activity, or semiosis (Cunningham, 1987, 1992; Whitson, 1997).

According to the Peircean tradition of semiotic theory (Peirce, 1955; Houser & Kloesel, 1992), **semiosis** is *"the continuously dynamic and productive activity of signs"* (Whitson, 1997, p. 99). A sign is anything that stands for something else, such as the word *dog* or a drawing of a dog standing for the animal we experience as a dog. Semiotic theory makes the claim that all knowledge of the world is mediated through signs, which are jointly determined by the physical world and the cognizing organism (Cunningham, 1987, 1992). Humans are unique in our ability to create and use signs that go beyond our immediate experience. So how does something come to be a sign?

The simplest answer can be found in the quote above—through our actions and interpretation of those actions in the world. Take, for example, the drawing of a dog. In an ancient society, a cave dweller might have produced a drawing such as the one shown in Figure 5.4 and through gestures and sounds conveyed to the rest of the tribe that the drawing represented the tribal dog. The drawing becomes a sign when the cave dweller claims it to stand for the dog and the rest of the tribe interprets it as such. In other

FIGURE 5.4   *A Hypothetical Cave Dweller's Depiction of a Dog*

words, the sign (drawing) represents an object (a dog) by virtue of the fact that it produced an interpretant (the common understanding that the drawing portrays a dog). See Figure 5.5.

A sign represents its object in one of three ways,

- As an index (e.g., the rising mercury in a thermometer is a sign of rising temperature)
- As an icon (e.g., the cave drawing is a picture of a dog)
- As a symbol (e.g., the English language word dog represents the actual animal)

Signs are productive in the sense that they can yield chains of signs from a single object, where the first sign stands for an object and a related sign comes to stand for the first sign, and so on. This productivity of signs can be seen in the example of taking the temperature of a sickly person. An increase over normal temperature (accepted as 98.6° Fahrenheit) would indicate fever, but the further interpretation is possible that the fever is a sign of some infectious disease. And if it's a disease I could get by being exposed to this person, then I should increase my vitamin intake to fortify my system in an attempt to ward off the disease. You can see the potential for a chain of signs and interpretants (Figure 5.6).

You should also begin to see the potential for increasing abstraction, where the sign and its object become so far removed that their relation is

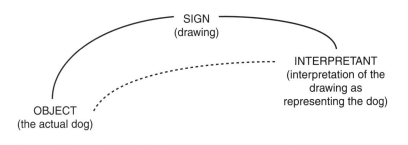

FIGURE 5.5   *Peirce's Triadic Sign Relations*

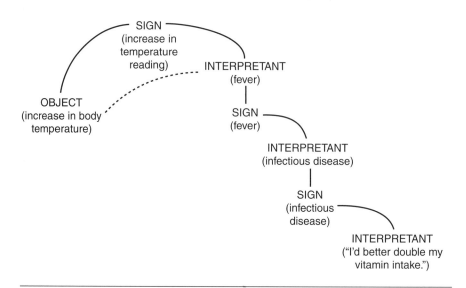

FIGURE 5.6   *An Example of the Productivity of Signs*

apparently arbitrary. Walkerdine (1997) illustrated this with an example of a mother getting her young daughter to name people for whom they were pouring drinks and to hold up one finger for each person named. A name stands for a particular person, but the raised finger stands for any person to be given a drink or the drink to be given to one of the persons in the crowd. When the mother starts counting fingers by verbally stating numerals, it becomes apparent that the numerals and fingers can be made to stand for anything. They can also be manipulated independently of their original referent. So, for example, simple problems can be worked out, such as "five and one more is…" (p. 67).

The apparent arbitrariness of signs can also be seen in situations in which a sign stands for an object on the basis of an analogy or metaphor. My favorite example comes from a former student's experience in evaluating the effectiveness of a hypermedia program. One of the icons used in the program was a parachute, which was intended to stand for the QUIT function in the program. I could not fathom why the software designer would have chosen that particular icon for that particular function until it was explained that the parachute meant "bail out" (see Driscoll & Rowley, 1997, for a complete semiotic analysis of this example). In this case, however, the designer ultimately had to replace the parachute icon because too few users understood what it meant without clicking on it to see.

As people interact with each other and the things in their material world, they create systems of signs, such as language and mathematics, to help them represent knowledge and their understanding of the world. These sign systems develop in ways that are unique to a community of practice and become part of the language and culture that a newcomer must learn upon joining that community. Most people become aware of their own sign systems when they are suddenly confronted with those of an unfamiliar culture, such as when traveling to another country. I can recall, for example, my first few weeks in Iran, where I lived for almost 2 years following graduate school. I did not own a car there, because public transportation was efficient and inexpensive. To flag down a public cab (we called them orange cabs because they were all painted a distinctive orange or orange and white), you stood by the side of the road and held out your hand, much like a hitchhiker would do in the United States. When a cab slowed or swerved your direction, you called out where you wanted to go, and if the cabbie was going that direction and had room in the cab, he would stop. Sometimes, however, the cabbie would dip his head in a nod and speed away! At first I was mystified by this behavior; here the cabbie was signalling yes and then driving off. I soon came to understand, however, that the signal—the head nod—did not mean yes, as it does in my culture. It meant, "No, I am not going there."

The productivity of signs and the fact that they incompletely represent their objects (e.g., the dog's picture represents what it looks like but provides no information about what it feels like when touched) make sign interpretation a process like detecting. This is particularly true when artifacts of a culture or community remain long after the community itself has ceased to exist. At least in a present, albeit unfamiliar culture, I can test my interpretations of a particular sign by using the sign myself and observing its effects or verifying it with a member of the culture I am in.

However, consider once again the drawing produced by our hypothetical cave dweller. Imagine that the drawing is unearthed by a group of anthropologists. What might they take the drawing to depict? It could stand for potentially many animals—badger, fox, wolf, horse—depending on the size and scale of the drawing. How might the researchers decipher its meaning? They could look for other drawings nearby to help determine scale and thus the size of the animal represented. They could look for bones in the cave and compare them with modern-day animals. In essence, these researchers would be looking for other artifacts of the long ago community that would provide clues to the meaning of the drawing in that society.

As a final note, "one virtue of the Peircean approach is that it reveals a basis, in the fundamental constitution of signs and sign activity, for a critical realism (both in cognition and the study of cognition)" (Whitson, 1997, p. 143). This means that signs and interpretations are not just relative in nature; they relate in meaningful ways to ultimate causes. For example, whether the anthropologists are able to construe the actual meaning of the dog drawing, the fact is that it had a particular meaning in the culture that produced it. In addition, "a sign represents not only its object; it also represents itself to be sufficient to its office, and any insufficiency can be reflectively responded to in modifications of the habits or practices in which the object is signified through the production of further interpretants" (Whitson, 1997, p. 144). In other words, the parachute was not sufficient as a sign for QUIT in the hypermedia program because not enough users understood what it meant. Likewise, the thermometer reading is sufficient as a sign of body temperature because it produces other interpretants that follow logically from the first one.

It is time to consider now the implications for instruction of legitimate peripheral participation and cognition as semiosis.

Implications of Situated Cognition for Instruction

Proponents of situated cognition believe that it represents a shift in thinking about learning and instruction that is "at least as profound, philosophically and methodologically, as was the shift to cognitivism from behaviorism" (Kirshner & Whitson, 1997, p. vii). Most are also motivated by practical concerns for education, although education is conceived as more than what takes place in schools. Wenger (1998) argued that education should be addressed in terms of identities and modes of belonging (p. 263). "From this perspective," he stated, "we need to think of education not merely in terms of an initial period of socialization into a culture, but more fundamentally in terms of rhythms by which communities and individuals continually renew themselves" (p. 263).

For the most part, however, situated cognition theorists have occupied themselves with designs for education of children. As I describe these efforts in the remaining sections, I try also to illustrate potential implications for the continuing education of adults.

Cognitive Apprenticeships

According to Brown et al. (1989), one means by which students can participate in a community of practice is through cognitive apprenticeships. As an example, they described how apprentice tailors learn about cutting and sewing first by ironing finished garments. By implication, school children could acquire the knowledge and skills of historians, mathematicians, or scientists by becoming apprentices in those disciplines.

Certainly in higher education, the concept of apprenticeships has long been a part of instructional programs, typically taking the form of an internship in the student's final semester of study. The usual purpose of internships is to provide students with an opportunity to practice the skills and knowledge they have spent (in some cases) years studying. Advantages accrue from the authentic environment in which the student is placed and from the transitional nature of the assignment. In other words, students do the same work as regular employees, but are not yet expected to bear the same responsibilities.

Although school children and learners in other situations cannot become apprentices in quite the same way as interns, they may experience some of the same advantages through projects in which the instructor models desired skills and coaches learners as they attempt to follow suit. Honebein et al. (1993) described an educational research class, for example, designed to engage students in the authentic activities of educational research such as generating researchable ideas, formulating research problems, and designing studies to investigate those problems. The instructor assumed a role similar to that of a research center director—meeting with students individually and collectively throughout each phase of the projects they planned, providing feedback on their decisions, and helping them to refine the process. In this example, we see an emphasis on both authenticity and complexity of experience, which, in the absence of true internships, can be provided to some degree through lengthy, multifaceted projects.

Along with the potential advantages of cognitive apprenticeships—authentic activity, sharing of culture—there may also be disadvantages. Wineburg (1989) commented that, unless well-planned and monitored, apprenticeships can be "tedious, inefficient, repressive, servile, tradition-bound, and in some cases downright mean" (p. 9). The same could be true for lengthy projects.

Tripp (1993) also pointed out the potential for "fossilization" that can occur with learning on the job. In discussing how people have been shown to acquire language in everyday conditions, he states:

> Fossilization refers to the learning of incorrect, but understandable, syntax and pronunciation which suffices for communication. Since this interlanguage allows satisfactory social interaction, the learner does not progress to a higher degree of mastery. (p. 72)

A similar situation arises when students leave the academy and discover that the practices of the community in which they are apprenticed are different from what they were taught. In this case, I have observed two types of consequences. The first is similar to fossilization in that the intern or apprentice simply adopts the practices of the organization and fails to develop more competent or sophisticated skills. The second consequence occurs when the intern or apprentice tries to reshape the practices of the organization to make them resemble more closely those taught in the professional program at school. Unfortunately, this can lead to continuing difficulties for the apprentice in terms of feeling a part of the organization and doing the work expected of him or her.

According to Kirshner and Whitson (1997), outcomes such as these in cognitive apprenticeships stem from literal apprenticeships that "[sacrifice] the opportunities that schools provide for abstractive and reflective activity [and expose] certain insufficiencies in the...traditions that currently underpin situated cognition theory" (p. viii). In other words, cognitive apprenticeships should not be exactly the same as trade apprenticeships. Rather, there should be continual interaction between the two communities of practice such that the intern or apprentice is afforded opportunities to critically reflect on what he or she is learning. In that way the intern or apprentice can explore patterns of participation as unique to a given community of practice or successfully used in other communities of practice.

Coteaching, for example, was designed to help preservice teachers make connections between their university preparation and their student teaching experience (Eick, Ware, & Williams, 2003). In a study examining the impact of coteaching, education students worked with a classroom teacher for two successive class periods each school day. In the first period, the students assisted the teacher in teaching the lesson, and in the second period, the roles reversed so that the student was the primary instructor. While the teachers modeled good practice during the first period, they coached and assisted during the second, prompting critical reflection on what occurred in both periods. Results of the study showed positive outcomes for both the students and the teachers.

Anchored Instruction

In 1990, the Cognition and Technology Group at Vanderbilt (CTGV) introduced the idea of anchored instruction as a means of implementing the conditions of situated learning. They proposed that an information-rich videodisk environment could provide a situated context for solving complex and realistic problems. In the program *The Jasper Woodbury Problem Solving Series,* for example, a boy named Jasper is shown in a variety of situations in which he must solve mathematical problems. To rescue a stranded eagle in one episode, he must figure out how much fuel is needed to fly an ultralight aircraft into a remote and wooded area. In a companion episode, Jasper must determine whether he has enough fuel on a boat trip to make it home before dark without running out of gas.

The CTGV believed that showing such adventures to students would involve them in the stories and motivate them to seek possible solutions to the problems Jasper faces and to compare their solutions with Jasper's. Instructional materials accompanying the videodisk series provide links to other aspects of the curriculum, such as history, literature, and science (CTGV, 1993, p. 53). Thus, teachers can use the series in many ways to support curriculum goals.

Anchored instruction has had its share of critics (e.g., Tripp, 1993) who have argued that the video adventures put students in the role of observers rather than participants. The result is that the instruction provides only a simulation of communities of practice. In response to this criticism, the CTGV point out the activities that the video anchors afford, which include

(a) noticing aspects of the video that suggest issues for further inquiry; (b) identifying sources of information relevant to those issues (usually through library or database searches); (c) reading the relevant information and taking it back to one's work group; and (d) communicating the results of the work groups to other members of the class. (1993, p. 56)

The problem-solving process described in these activities is very similar to that promoted by problem-based learning, which is discussed in Chapter 11.

The impact and effectiveness of anchored instruction have been widely demonstrated by the CTGV, which has shown that students become better able to solve problems analogous to the video-anchored problems as well as those that are partially analogous. Recently, the CTGV (1994; Lin et al. & the CTGV, 1996) have begun to explore the advantages of networking, via distance technologies, classrooms of students who are working on video-anchored problems. They aim to create a kind of learning community, which, as an implication of situated cognition, has seen great popularity in recent years.

Learning Communities

When the situative concept of communities of practice is applied to a classroom context, it becomes apparent that the culture of the classroom has to change. The traditional social structure of schools is one in which teachers dispense knowledge to students through classroom activities, textbooks, and possibly other media (Brown, 1992). Within such a structure, teachers are typically in charge; they set not only the learning agenda and goals, but also the means by which these goals are pursued and achieved. When a classroom becomes a learning community, however, the social structure transforms into one in which teacher and learners work collaboratively to achieve important goals, goals that may well have been established jointly. Learning communities typically emphasize distributed expertise (e.g., Brown, et al., 1993; Pea, 1993b), which refers to the idea that students come to the learning task with different interests and experiences and are provided the opportunity within the community to learn different things. Or, as Bereiter (1997) expressed it, "The situated learning that [occurs] is learning how to function in a community of practice whose work is work with knowledge" (p. 298).

A learning community application with over 10 years of research and development behind it is CSILE, or Computer-Supported Intentional Learning Environment (Scardamalia et al., 1989; Scardamalia & Bereiter, 1994, 1996; Bereiter & Scardamalia, 1996). CSILE provides a means for students to engage in knowledge-building within a learning community. That is, students focus on a problem of interest and begin to build a communal database of information about the problem. They pose questions, make hypotheses, suggest solutions, and contribute information obtained from outside sources and "experts," either in text or in graphics. All of these activities occur online as students add information to the database.

Students are thus engaging in the discourse of a subject matter discipline in a scholarly manner. There is opportunity for reflection and peer review, and as Scardamalia and Bereiter (1994) put it, "Conversation tends to favor the ideas of the most vocal... and most intentional students. In CSILE, each student is responsible for contributing to the discourse" (p. 279). Scardamalia and Bereiter (1996) stated further, "When students are at work on knowledge problems in CSILE, questions that push against the limits of current knowledge assume a natural importance" (p. 156). There is also a natural self-correction when students post things in CSILE that others in the class know to be inaccurate.

How might the concept of learning community be extended to adult students or trainees, and what will be the impact on learning when it is? These are questions driving research currently underway at my university (e.g., Gilbert & Driscoll, 1998; Wager & Driscoll, 1999), where we have been developing and testing technological tools and strategies for developing communities of learners in graduate and undergraduate courses. In one course, for example, a collective course goal was emphasized within the context of the subject domain. Students worked in collaborative groups on problems that related to each other and contributed to the course goal. Like students working in CSILE, these learners published all their work on-line, and, in fact, to accomplish the goals and learning tasks of their group, students had to rely on work being done by other groups.

A result of this planned interdependence among groups was that students became conscious of their own roles in contributing to the knowledge-building efforts of the class, and they assumed responsibility for doing work in a timely way. When one student got behind because of a personal problem, for example, he sent an e-mail to the entire class apologizing for his delay and promising to catch up. He knew others in the class were depending on his part of the course goal, and he wanted them to know he would carry through with his responsibilities (Gilbert & Driscoll, 1998).

Assessment In-Situ

Adopting the situative perspective changes the way researchers and educators view learning and instruction in very fundamental ways. So, too, does it change the way assessment of learning is viewed. In fact, Greeno (1997) contended that the problem of assessment from a situative perspective is much harder. "When students take tests they show how well they can participate in the kind of interaction that the tests afford" (p. 8), but test performance does not show very well how students have learned to participate in the social practices of a community. It is in assessment that the learning process so heavily emphasized by situated cognition theory conflicts with the products of learning. What products will serve as valid evidence of students' learning to participate appropriately in a community of practice?

In discussing reading or doing mathematics as examples of desired learning goals, Greeno (1997) suggested that assessment "requires that the way in which we characterize the person's performance captures the various kinds of situation types in which the person's reading or mathematical activity is significant" (p. 8). It may be possible for paper-and-pencil tests to do this, but other forms of assessment are touted as more appropriate ways to measure situated learning (e.g., Collins, 1990; McLellan, 1993).

McLellan (1993) recommended that a three-part model originally proposed by Collins (1990) be adopted as an approach to assessing situated learning. The three parts provide three different kinds of assessment measures:

1. Diagnosis
2. Summary statistics
3. Portfolios

With diagnosis, teachers "must at every moment analyze the progress of learners and adapt or customize the methods, sequencing, and other conditions of learning to meet the emergent needs of the learners in real time" (McLellan, 1993, p. 39). McLellan noted that this type of assessment requires great skill on the part of the teacher, not to mention the time it might take to keep up with thirty or more learners in a class.

With current technologies, however, diagnosis need not be as burdensome as it seems. A technique that I call confidential reports serves to provide diagnostic information about learners in a systematic way throughout the semester. Three times during the term, learners send me a confidential e-mail message that addresses four topics:

1. *Their own, individual learning* (What are their personal goals for learning? Are they learning what they hoped? Are they having any problems that I might assist them in remedying?)

2. *The learning of their collaborative group* (How is the group functioning? Are there problems that I might help the group to solve?)

3. *The learning of the class as a community* (How is the class functioning overall? Are there any adjustments that should be made in the collective goal that the class is seeking to achieve?)

4. *Suggestions for improvement* (What can be implemented immediately that will improve the learning of the individual, group, or class?)

With the information provided in these reports, I am able to make midcourse adjustments that help to meet the emergent needs of learners. Sometimes, learners request that their confidential reports be shared with the rest of the class. In these cases, they may have a question or suggestion that they would like the class to discuss and resolve as a group. The result is nearly always an improvement that I would not have conceived on my own.

The second kind of assessment measure in Collins's (1990) model is summary statistics. These are usually kept via computer and show patterns and trends in learners' performance over time. With instruction that is already computer-based, such as hypermedia programs, summary statistics are easy to collect. Data can be kept on a learner's path through the program—what information has been visited and how much time the learner has interacted with that information. Such data can also show when learners have achieved certain benchmarks and whether they are progressing at an adequate pace. For instance, the Web site designed for the course in which I am attempting to implement a learning community keeps track of every assignment that every student publishes on-line. On a week-to-week basis, I can see immediately who is doing what. If I notice no activity for a particular student, I can contact that student individually to determine whether he or she needs help, or perhaps just an encouraging word.

Finally, the third form of assessment in Collins's (1990) model is portfolios. Portfolio assessment has a long history independent of situated cognition, but it seems particularly well suited for assessing situated learning because of its emphasis on process as well as product. Portfolios also engage students in assessment, because they are responsible for selecting the works that will comprise the portfolio. Typically, following guidelines outlined by the teacher, students select works that illustrate their progress and achievements over time. In addition, "portfolios can be amplified by logs or journals that students write and to which teachers react. These reflections aid learners in the process of evaluating their own work" (Reeves & Okey, 1996, p. 195).

Conclusion

Whether situated cognition theory revolutionizes thinking about learning or yields the robust educational models that its proponents hope remains to be seen. Anderson, Reder, and Simon (1996, 1997, 2000) have questioned already what the situative perspective contributes that is new or different from the cognitive perspective (as discussed in Chapters 3 and 4). They presented four claims of the situative perspective and then proceeded to show how these claims are handled from a cognitive perspective. They concluded that the situative and cognitive perspectives are in agreement on many important educational issues so that little is to be gained by adopting the "fuzzy language" of situated cognition.

Greeno (1997) responded to criticisms of Anderson et al. (1996) by identifying the presuppositions of their arguments and illustrating how these presuppositions differ from those of the situative perspective. In essence, he described how the cognitive and situative perspectives differ in their most basic, grounding assumptions about the nature of knowledge. Greeno contended that Anderson et al. interpreted the claims they discussed in terms of cognitive presuppositions and therefore did not accurately represent the propositions of situated cognition theory. They counterargued that Greeno was, in effect, linguistically hair-splitting (Anderson et al., 1997).

So what now? Greeno (1997) offers this:

> The issue between the cognitive and situative perspectives at this point is how to proceed next. As I hope is clear from this discussion, the approach I will take is to try to develop analyses of information structures of socially organized activity, using concepts and methods developed in cognitive science, as well as ecological psychology. At the same time, I believe that the field should have people working in both the situative and cognitive perspectives, informing and challenging each other's ways of formulating questions as well as their conclusions and arguments. It will be enjoyable and interesting to see how we can develop more comprehensive and coherent theories of fundamental processes of learning and contribute more productively to discussions of educational practice. (p. 15)

Another perspective is offered by Rose (1999), who supported Greeno's call for parallel developments from the situative and cognitive perspectives:

> It seems to me that if we are to assert the rich and nuanced character of activity and of real-world practice that belies, at every turn, attempts to easily categorize it, and if we are to honor the diversity of actors, the wide variability in the histories of participants, then how can we advocate a single conceptualization of how people become proficient? (p. 154)

A Situative Perspective on "Kermit and the Keyboard"

Knowledge as lived practices, learning as participation in communities of practice—How do these concepts help us to understand Kermit's experience as he goes about learning to play the keyboard? To begin with, we might consider the communities of practice that Kermit is or has been a part of and how they might have shaped his understanding of the task that confronts him. We know from the story that he was at one time a music major in college and played in a community symphony and dance band. It is likely that Kermit participated in both systematic practice and recitals as a member of these communities. The concerts were in fact one of the reasons that Kermit chose to leave those communities, but we see that the systematic practice and use of instructional materials (the old music instruction books) still affect his approach to the learning task.

If Kermit chooses to join the Sunday jam sessions, then he could be on an inbound trajectory wherein he would begin working on some of the pieces regularly played by the group. As he moves toward full participation, he would suggest pieces that he has already been practicing and ultimately have a say in how the group functions. Until that point, Kermit is probably guided most by participation in the community of his family and the norms of general society. He chooses songs to play that are familiar to him and his wife. He goes online to seek information and assistance when he runs into a problem. And then there are the affordances of the keyboard instrument itself.

Kermit first became attracted to the keyboard because of its extensive features in enabling him to create music in many different ways. No other instrument makes as many different sounds as the keyboard or enables the performer to sound like many players at once. In addition, it is possible to accompany oneself by making a recording and then playing along with it. Thus, the possibilities for music making are nearly endless, but they were not available before the growth of computer technologies and so would not have been available to Kermit when he first studied music.

Theory Matrix

Theory	Situated Cognition
Prominent Theorists	Among others: C. Bereiter; A. L. Brown; J. G. Greeno; J. Lave; J. L. Lemke; M. Scardamalia; E. Wenger
Learning Outcome(s)	Ability to use the concepts and tools of a community of practice
	Contribute to invention of new tools and practices within the community
Role of the Learner	Participate increasingly in the activities of a community of practice
Role of the Instructor	Model appropriate practices as a "senior partner" in the learning enterprise
	Nurture semiosis and promote reflexivity in learning
	Help learners value participation in a community of practice
Inputs or Preconditions to Learning	Materials and activities of the culture or community of practice
Process of Learning	Semiosis, or sign activity (the process of interpreting and creating signs and sign systems); legitimate peripheral participation

Suggested Readings

Kirshner, D., & Whitson, J. A. (Eds.). (1997). *Situated cognition: Social, semiotic, and psychological perspectives.* Mahweh, NJ: Erlbaum.

Lave, J., & Wenger, E. (1991). *Situated learning: Legitimate peripheral participation.* New York: Cambridge University Press.

Wenger, E. (1998). *Communities of practice: Learning, meaning, and identity.* New York: Cambridge University Press.

Reflective Questions and Activities

1. Read the debate between Anderson et al. (1996, 1997) and Greeno (1997) about the situative versus cognitive perspectives, and consider their arguments in light of the epistemological perspectives discussed in Chapter 1. With which position do you agree most? Why?

2. Prepare a list of metaphors that have been or could be used to describe and understand learning (e.g., learning is information processing [a computer metaphor]; learning is growing [an organismic metaphor]; learning is making progress toward a goal [a travel metaphor]; learning is participating in a community of practice [a situative metaphor]). For each metaphor, describe the implied roles of the learner, instructor, and instructional materials. For each metaphor, consider what assumptions are being made about the nature of knowledge and ways of knowing. Add to your list as you complete the chapters of this book.

3. List all the communities of practice to which you belong. Describe the nature of your participation in these communities. How would you characterize your learning trajectory within each of these communities?

4. Explore how a community of learning might be implemented in your professional discipline.

Part IV: Learning and Development

6

Cognitive and Knowledge Development

Four Stages of Development
- Sensorimotor
- Preoperational
- Concrete operational
- Formal operational

Three Developmental Processes
- Assimilation
- Accommodation
- Equilibration

Jean Piaget's Genetic Epistemology

Evidence Countering Piaget's Claims

1. Not all cultures reach formal operations.
2. Reasoning is not always consistent within a stage.
3. Children learn more in a stage than Piaget thought.
4. Reasoning is domain specific.

most established theory

THEORIES OF COGNITIVE DEVELOPMENT

more recent, less global views

Alternative Information-Processing Approaches

A Neo-Piagetian View

Biological maturation affects STM operational capacity.

A Computational Model

Generalization is primary mechanism of development.

A Componential Analysis

Development is the process of a novice becoming an expert.

A Framework Theory Approach

Intuitive theories develop with experience in specific domains.

A New Agenda

Children's thinking is endlessly variable and endlessly changing.

Consider these scenarios.

• *Conserving Numbers*

In the Piagetian assessment for number conservation, the experimenter begins by aligning two rows of blocks (or pennies, or some other object familiar to young children) as shown below:

❏ ❏ ❏ ❏ ❏ ❏ ❏ ❏

❏ ❏ ❏ ❏ ❏ ❏ ❏ ❏

Then the experimenter questions the child, in this case, Aaron, a preconserver.

> *E:* Do both these rows have the same number of blocks, or does one have more than the other?
>
> *Aaron:* They're the same.
>
> *E:* How do you know?
>
> *Aaron:* Because I counted them. (Pointing first to one row and then the other) One, two, three, four, five, six, seven, eight. One, two, three, four, five, six, seven, eight.

The experimenter rearranges the blocks as follows:

❑ ❑ ❑ ❑ ❑ ❑ ❑ ❑

❑ ❑ ❑ ❑ ❑ ❑ ❑ ❑

> *E:* (Repeating the original question) Do these rows now have the same number of blocks, or does one have more than the other?
>
> *Aaron:* (Pointing to the top row) This one has more.
>
> *E:* How do you know?
>
> *Aaron:* Because it sticks out more.
>
> *E:* Count the blocks for me, would you please?
>
> *Aaron:* (Counting) One, two, three, four, five, six, seven, eight. One, two, three, four, five, six, seven, eight.
>
> *E:* So, are there the same number of blocks in each row?
>
> *Aaron:* No, that one (pointing to the top row) has more.

The experimenter later questions Shauna, who conserves numbers. Regardless of how the lines of blocks are arranged, she insists that each has the same number of blocks: "I counted them, and you haven't added any or taken any away!"

• *Discovering Relations*

Nan, a 6-year-old, is participating in a study of children's logical reasoning. The experimenter presents her with a matrix completion task, which is a 2×2 matrix with one empty square. Her task is to choose the object that will result in the bottom two objects being related in the same way as the top two objects. The objects can differ in shape (bird, mouse), color (light gray, dark gray), size (large, small), and orientation (facing left, facing right).

At the beginning of the study, Nan made errors like this:

 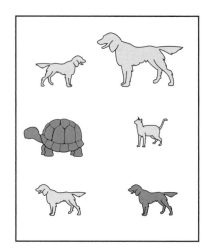

Experimenter: "There are three animals here [pointing to the objects in the matrix]. Here [pointing to the empty cell], one is missing—one of these. Which one is missing?"

Nan (selecting small, light gray cat, facing left):   "This one."

Experimenter: "Why do you think so?"

Nan: "Because it's the same as this one (pointing to the light gray cat facing left in the group of three)."

Experimenter: "Ok."

In the training sessions that followed, the experimenter responded to each correct answer Nan gave by saying, "Ok, that's correct. Why was it correct?" After each incorrect answer, the experimenter said, "No, I would pick this one [pointing to the correct object]. Why do you think I would pick that one?" Regardless of what Nan said then, the experimenter replied, "Ok." At first, Nan made a lot of mistakes, consistently picking a duplicate object to one in the matrix. Then, her mistakes shifted and it appeared that she was choosing randomly. A few trials later, she consistently chose the correct answer. When she did make a mistake, she chose the right animal of the right color, but tended to miss its orientation or size.

By the end of the study, Nan performed much better than other 6-year-olds who had not been trained and about as well as 8-year-olds, who could solve matrix problems reliably from the beginning of the study.

How can we account for the behavior seen in the children described in these scenarios? Take Aaron in "Conserving Numbers," for example. He knows how to count, and the evidence of his senses (he sees eight blocks in each row; he counted eight blocks in each row) should be enough to convince him that there are the same number of blocks in each row. Yet he steadfastly maintains they are different when one appears longer than the other. He seems unable to overcome his focus on the single salient dimension of line length. By contrast, even at a young age, Nan in "Discovering Relations" learns to consider multiple dimensions simultaneously and successfully solve reasoning problems that older children can do easily. What accounts for the differences in these children's behavior? Is it a matter of age, as appears to be so in "Conserving Numbers"? If that is the case, why does Nan in "Discovering Relations" demonstrate an ability similar to that of older children?

Evidence of this nature presents problems for many learning theories, which do not always distinguish between the learning of children and the learning of adults. That distinction, in itself, is an open question. Do children learn in a manner significantly different from that of adults? Or can whatever differences are observed be attributed to the greater experience of adults rather than a qualitative difference in the process of learning between adults and children? Issues related to these questions will be examined in this chapter and the next.

If something more than learning as it has so far been described is responsible for behavioral and conceptual differences across the life span, then just what is it? And precisely what role does learning play? For many psychologists, cognitive development provides the answers. "The idea of development entails the existence of an endpoint: the child moves, steadily or erratically, toward a goal" (Kaplan, 1967, cited in Kessen, 1984). Werner (1957) saw this goal as the result of differentiation, articulation, and integration whereby a nonspecialized cell gradually becomes an efficient, fully functioning organism. Werner also distinguished development from both change and growth, since change can be regressive and growth can mean quantitative improvement without necessarily involving qualitative improvement. For humans, then, cognitive development is the transformation of the child's undifferentiated, unspecialized cognitive abilities into the adult's conceptual competence and problem-solving skill.

For development to be understood, Sternberg (1984a) suggested that two fundamental questions must be answered. One, What are the psychological states that children pass through at different points in their development? And two, What are the mechanisms by which they pass from one state to another? Siegler (1996), on the other hand, offered this question as the inherent core of cognitive development: How do changes in children's thinking occur?

Jean Piaget's theory of cognitive development remains unmistakably the most complete and widely accepted view. However, developmental theorists recognize now that the Piagetian account is wrong in some aspects and incomplete in others. Recent efforts stemming from an information-processing

Jean Piaget

perspective are aimed therefore at reformulating basic assumptions about children's thinking. The Piagetian view is the primary focus of the chapter. However, alternative perspectives are introduced to provide a sense of recent areas of investigation in the developmental literature. The chapter concludes with their combined implications for instruction.

Jean Piaget's Genetic Epistemology

Jean Piaget (1896–1980) has been variously characterized as a biologist, philosopher, and child psychologist. In fact, he was all of these. But while spanning all three fields, Piaget's work was directed at elaborating a theory of knowledge, of how the child comes to know his or her world (Gruber & Voneche, 1995). This study of the origins (genesis) of knowledge (epistemology) led to Piaget's calling his view genetic epistemology.

If you recall from Chapter 1, empiricists argue that knowledge results from an accumulation of experience, whereas nativists believe that the organism is born with an innate set of ideas that form the basis for knowledge. Interpretists, some of whom are also nativists, assume that all knowledge is actively constructed within the organism, rather than being received passively from the environment. Piaget was highly critical of empiricism, but he was not particularly comfortable in presuming that knowledge is entirely innate (the nativist position). Instead, he evolved a view, consistent with interpretivism, that suggested a compromise between nativism and empiricism. He sometimes labeled his view interactionism, since cognition was assumed to be an interaction between heredity and environment.

Piaget also called his view constructivism, because he firmly believed that knowledge acquisition is a process of continuous self-construction. That is, knowledge is not out there, external to the child and waiting to be discovered. But neither is it wholly preformed within the child, ready to emerge as the child develops. Instead, knowledge is invented and reinvented as the child develops and interacts with the world surrounding her. This point cannot be overemphasized. Piaget believed that children actively approach their environments and acquire knowledge through their actions. Moreover, such actions are neither random nor aimless. Very young infants, for example, immediately suck upon any object placed in their mouths. And they mouth objects as a way to learn about their worlds. Piaget called these goal-directed behaviors schemes and contended that schemes evolve as children develop.

Finally, Gruber and Voneche (1995) apply the label logical determinism to Piaget's theory. This label captures Piaget's emphasis on the functioning of logic in each stage of development. He proposed, in other words, that certain logical structures develop at each stage, and how these structures operate during a particular stage determines the structure of the stage to follow. This is something like the unfolding of a logical argument (Leahey & Harris, 1997). At any stage, the child's cognitive structures are like the premises of the argument. Experience provides information on which to base deductions from these premises, deductions which then yield a new set of premises or cognitive structures. At any point in the process, however, whatever logical structures currently exist will dictate the schemes children will employ to find out more about the world. The sucking scheme, for example, rapidly gives way to other actions, and when children acquire the ability to mentally represent symbols, imitation becomes a widely initiated scheme.

Types of Knowledge

Piaget distinguished among three types of knowledge that children acquire: physical, logical-mathematical, and social knowledge (Piaget, 1969; Wadsworth, 1996). **Physical knowledge,** also called empirical knowledge, has to do with *knowledge about objects in the world, which can be gained through their perceptual properties.* Aaron and Shauna in Conserving Numbers, for example, undoubtedly know that blocks are solid and cube-shaped and come in different colors and sizes. These are inherent properties of blocks, and children acquire knowledge of these properties by seeing and handling the blocks. Objects themselves and a child's physical actions on objects are therefore the source of physical knowledge.

The acquisition of physical knowledge has sometimes been equated with learning in Piaget's theory (Gruber & Voneche, 1995). That is, thought is fit directly to experience. The child experiences the hardness of blocks and learns, for example, that blocks cannot be easily crushed themselves but can crush softer or more brittle objects. Internally representing these experiences results in cognitive schemas, or concepts, which stand as organized collections of properties of objects. Schemas are essentially passive modes of organization (Brainerd, 1978), and learning occurs when new information is added to them.

It is useful at this point to mention the differences in meaning associated with Piaget's (and others') use of the terms *scheme, schema,* and *schemata.* In an edited collection of Piaget's writings, Gruber and Voneche (1995) consistently used the term *scheme* to refer to units of generalized behavior (or actions) that provide the basis for mental operations. Piaget (1969) clearly intended the same meaning when he spoke of the "schema of an action" being the generalizable quality in the action.

Brainerd (1978), however, distinguished between schema (as a passive mode of organization) and scheme (as an active organizational principle). In justification, Brainerd cited Piaget (in Piaget & Inhelder, 1969), who noted that schema was often a mistranslation for scheme, the preferred term. Finally, Siegler (1986, 1996) and Wadsworth (1996) avoided the issue altogether, Siegler by referring only to mental structures and Wadsworth by using the plural *schemata* to represent the totality of children's logical structures. Both, however, consistently emphasized the active nature of children's thinking.

What can we conclude from this discussion? It is apparent that Piaget strongly believed in the active role of the child during development. Cognition is rooted in action, and actions (I will use the term *schemes*) evolve to become increasingly internal as children acquire rudimentary physical knowledge.

The second type of knowledge, logical-mathematical, goes beyond simple physical knowledge and is therefore not available from the perceptual properties of objects. **Logical-mathematical knowledge** *is abstract and must be invented,* but through actions on objects that are fundamentally different from those actions enabling physical knowledge. For example, to acquire physical knowledge of blocks, a child may pick one up, feel it, taste it, hit another object with it, or throw it. But to understand how two rows of blocks are in some way the same when they look physically different requires a different kind of action scheme. To acquire what Piaget called conservation of number, children must experience many different arrangements of blocks and other objects, with the number of objects remaining invariant. Such actions make possible, claimed Piaget, a new construction of thought which is evidence of development. Thus Shauna, because she reasons beyond her perceptual information, is thought to be at a later point in development than is Aaron.

The abstract character of logical-mathematical knowledge gives it an advantage over physical knowledge in its greater range of application. Physical knowledge of blocks, for instance, can be extended only to other blocks, but conservation of number applies to blocks, pennies, people, or what have you. The cognitive result, therefore, of schemes enabling the invention of logical-mathematical knowledge is a coherent set of mental operations. These operations exist within relational structures or networks of operations that are considered to be the highest order mental organizations (also called schemata; Wadsworth, 1978, 1996).

Finally, much of Piaget's own work, and the work of others his theory has stimulated, concentrates on the development of logical-mathematical knowledge. But in acknowledging the social aspect of children's development, he distinguished a third type of knowledge. **Social knowledge** is *culture-specific and can be learned only from other people within one's cultural group.* Actions again hold the key to the acquisition of this kind of knowledge—that is, actions on, or interactions with, other people. Presented in Table 6.1 is a summary of the types of knowledge proposed by Piaget.

TABLE 6.1 *Three Types of Knowledge*

	Physical Knowledge	*Logical-Mathematical Knowledge*	*Social Knowledge*
Defined	Knowledge about the physical properties of objects	Abstract knowledge	Knowledge made by people
How Acquired	Discovered by actions on objects; *objects* are the source	Invented from actions on objects; *actions* are the source	Obtained from actions on and interactions with others; *people* are the source
Reinforcer	Objects	Objects	People
Examples of Areas of Knowledge	Size, color, texture, thickness, taste, sound, flexibility, density	Number, mass, area, volume, length, class, order, time, speed, weight	Language, moral rules, values, culture, history, symbol systems

Source: Adapted from *Piaget for the Classroom Teacher* by Barry J. Wadsworth. Copyright © 1978. By Longman Publishing Group. Reprinted by permission of Longman Publishing Group.

The Stages of Development

The concept of stage has already been implicated in the discussion of physical versus logical-mathematical knowledge. Knowledge about blocks as physical objects, for example, precedes a child's ability to reason or solve problems using blocks. Thus, reasoning is evidence of a later stage in development. Piaget believed that children progress through an invariant sequence of four stages. These stages are not arbitrary, but are assumed to reflect qualitative differences in children's cognitive abilities. Piaget's criteria for defining true developmental stages can be summarized as follows:

1. Each stage must represent a qualitative change in children's cognition. Significant quantitative improvements in intelligence with age are not enough to satisfy this first criterion. Children must demonstrate qualitative leaps as well, which imply that changes have occurred in the underlying logical structures of cognition. Conservation of number, for example, seems to represent such a change; preconservers behave very differently from conservers.

2. Children progress through the stages in a culturally invariant sequence. This means that every child passes through the stages in exactly the same order of necessity, not just on the average. Moreover, once a higher stage has been entered, regression to a lower stage is not possible, and all normal children reach the last stage. Now that Shauna demonstrates number conservation, she will never again act as a nonconserver.

3. Each stage includes the cognitive structures and abilities of the preceding stage. This is known as the hierarchization requirement and is closely related to the second criterion. The more primitive structures of early stages are not lost as a child progresses to a later stage. Rather, they form the foundation for more sophisticated abilities, becoming integrated and coordinated with the more complex structures of the later stage. This also means that each stage is more adaptive, more adequate, than the one preceding it.

4. At each stage, the child's schemes and operations form an integrated whole. As mentioned earlier, what schemes a child employs to explore her world depend upon her stage of development. These, in turn, provide information to be integrated within the existing logical structures of the present stage. If Shauna and Aaron are in different stages, for example, they would each employ different schemes and exhibit different cognitive capabilities. But their behavior would be logically consistent with the cognitive structures presumed to exist at their respective stages.

Before turning to a description of Piaget's four stages, it is important to remember that some variability is apparent in the ages at which children attain each stage. That is, Shauna and Aaron might be the same age but appear to be in different stages. But whether she is precocious for her age or he is slow does not invalidate the stage concept. Both will ultimately be expected to exhibit the characteristics of every stage at some point and to reach the last stage.

What are Piaget's stages of development? In order of appearance, they are: the sensorimotor period (birth to approximately age 2), the preoperational period (roughly age 2 to age 6 or 7), the concrete operational period (age 6 or 7 to age 11 or 12), and the formal operational period (age 11 or 12 through adulthood). Table 6.2 presents a summary of the characteristics typical at each stage, and Figure 6.1 displays the timeline of developmental stages.

The Sensorimotor Period (Birth to 2 Years). Siegler (1986) wrote of his questioning students in a developmental psychology class about aspects of intelligence in infancy. "A number of students commented that they found it odd to describe infants as having intelligence at all. By far the most frequently named characteristics of infants' intelligence were physical coordination,

TABLE 6.2   *Piaget's Stages of Cognitive Development*

Stages of Development	Typical Characteristics
Sensorimotor (birth to approximately age 2)	Modifies reflexes to make them more adaptive
	Becomes goal-directed in behavior, with goals moving from concrete to abstract
	Begins to mentally represent objects and events
Preoperational (2 to 7 years)	Acquires the semiotic function; engages in symbolic play and language games
	Has difficulty seeing another person's point of view; thought and communication are egocentric
	Reasons from a focus on one perceptual dimension of problems
Concrete Operational (7 to 11 years)	Performs true mental operations (conservation, reversibility) and solves concrete problems in a logical fashion
	Has difficulty thinking hypothetically and systematically considering all aspects of a problem
Formal Operational (11 years onward)	Solves abstract problems in systematic and logical fashion
	Reasons hypothetically and often develops concerns over social issues

alertness, and ability to recognize people and objects. It was evidence of Piaget's genius that he perceived much more than this" (Siegler, 1986, p. 30). In fact, immense cognitive changes occur from immediately after birth to approximately age 2.

Newborns come into the world with a variety of innate reflexes (e.g., sucking, reacting to noises, focusing on objects within their view). Within a short time, they begin to modify these reflexes to make them more adaptive (e.g., sucking a finger becomes a different action from sucking a nipple). Initially, infants' actions are directed primarily at their own bodies, but they increasingly center on the external world. In addition, infants' behavior begins to reflect clear goals, and these goals progress from concrete to abstract. Piaget (1951) described his son deliberately dropping objects (a concrete goal) and then varying the heights from which he dropped them (an abstract goal).

Toward the end of the sensorimotor period, children begin to mentally represent objects and events. To that point, they can only act, and during the transition to mental representation, they may use simple motor indicators as symbols for other events. Piaget (1951) described his daughter Lucienne, for example, playing with a partly open matchbox in which a watch chain had been placed. Apparently aware of what the opening represented and wanting it to become wider, Lucienne opened her mouth wider and wider!

FIGURE 6.1   *Timeline of Cognitive Development*

Years from Birth	Developmental Stages
One year	*Sensorimotor*
Two years	(form basic schemes; become goal-directed)
Three years	*Preoperational*
Four years	(object permanence; early problem solving; egocentric)
Five years	
Six years	
Seven years	*Concrete operational*
	(conservation, reversibility; concrete logical reasoning)
Eleven years	*Formal operational*
	(abstract logical reasoning, able to hypothesize, develops concern over social issues)

The Preoperational Period (2 to 7 Years).   Early in the preoperational period, children acquire what Piaget called the semiotic function. This means they are able to mentally represent objects and events, as evidenced in their imitation of some activity long after it occurred. Pretending, or symbolic play, is highly characteristic of this stage, and language acquisition proceeds rapidly.

Also characteristic of preoperational intelligence are children's egocentrism and centration, which are thought to place limits on their thinking. First, preoperational children have difficulty in seeing points of view other than their own. A conversation between two preschoolers, for example, sounds less like a conversation than like two monologues; children typically talk past one another rather than to one another. This egocentrism is also evident in children's inability to mentally rotate spatial arrangements in order to identify a different perspective. As for centration, preoperational children focus solely on one dimension of a problem, as Aaron focused on the length of the two rows of blocks. He was unable to reconcile the dimension of number with the dimension of length, thus failing to conserve number.

The Concrete Operational Period (7 to 11 Years).   Children overcome the limitations of egocentrism and centration when they enter the stage of concrete operations. It is at this stage that they demonstrate logically integrated thought. In other words, through actions that have become increasingly internalized, they invent logical-mathematical knowledge resulting in operations. Operations are reversible and maintain some invariant property through a series of transformations. In the number conservation task, for example, the rows are rearranged, but the number in each row stays the same. Moreover, any new arrangement can be reversed so that the rows again look the same. Solving number conservation tasks, then, is evidence that a child has acquired these operations.

Despite their ability to solve many different kinds of problems, concrete operational children still cannot think hypothetically. In other words, they would have difficulty thinking about and discussing possible answers to the question, "If people could know the future, would they be happier than they are now?" (Siegler, 1986).

The Formal Operational Period (11 Years Onward).   Propositional logic is the hallmark of formal operations. That is, operations become more abstract so that the individual can reason, not just with objects, but with formally stated premises or propositions. This enables children not only to think hypothetically, but to plan a systematic approach to solving problems. Inhelder and Piaget (1958) presented children and adolescents with a chemistry problem, in which they were to mix clear liquid chemicals from four beakers until they achieved a yellow color. Concrete operational children were rather random in their approach to the problem, sometimes repeating combinations of chemicals they had tried before. In addition, they typically combined only two chemicals at a time, or all four, without considering combinations of three. By contrast, formal operational adolescents generated a systematic plan of testing chemical combinations until they found the solution. Moreover, they kept records of their tests and generated appropriate hypotheses concerning their results.

Finally, the ability to imagine possibilities above and beyond current reality is characteristic of formal operational reasoners. "This leads at least some of them to think about alternative organizations of the world and about deep questions concerning the nature of existence, truth, justice, and morality" (Siegler, 1986, p. 41).

The Processes of Development

If Piaget's description of stages answers the question of psychological states children pass through in development, what mechanism did he propose as responsible for children's progression from one stage to the next? In essence, he considered three processes as being critical to development: assimilation, accommodation, and equilibration.

Assimilation.   Assimilation occurs when a child perceives new objects or events in terms of existing schemes or operations. Consider once again the infant who puts things in his mouth. This scheme, and others such as grasping, throwing, or shaking, are means of assimilating information about the objects. Because these schemes are also relatively broad and undifferentiated, they are used without regard to whether an object is appropriate for throwing or putting in one's mouth.

It is important to note that Piaget emphasized the functional quality of assimilation (Siegler, 1986). That is, children and adults alike tend to apply any mental structure that is available to assimilate a new event, and they will actively seek to use a newly acquired structure. Children learning to talk, for example, have been observed to talk endlessly to themselves, whether or not anyone else is there to listen. Even adults who have learned a new skill (such as how to use a word processor) will seek to apply their knowledge in as many situations as possible thereafter. Piaget has compared this apparent self-motivation with the external reinforcers for behavior that behaviorists such as Skinner emphasize.

Accommodation.   When existing schemes or operations must be modified to account for a new experience, accommodation has occurred. It is likely, for example, that Nan in Discovering Relations and Shauna in Conserving Numbers have experienced shifts in their thinking for all salient aspects of their respective tasks to be accommodated.

Obviously, accommodation influences assimilation and vice versa. An inadequate attempt to assimilate some new event into existing schemes or operations may result in some adjustment of those schemes or operations (thus accommodating the event). Such accommodation, however, affects subsequent assimilation, which will now proceed in accord with the new structure.

Equilibration.   According to Piaget, equilibration is the master developmental process, encompassing both assimilation and accommodation. Equilibration particularly characterizes the child's transition from one stage of development to the next. Within each stage, children operate from a set of logical structures that, for their purposes, work quite well. But toward the end of a stage, they may become aware of shortcomings in their way of thinking. Anomalies of experience create a state of disequilibrium which can only be resolved when a more adaptive, more sophisticated mode of thought is adopted. At some point, for instance, the counting strategy that Aaron uses in Conserving Numbers is likely to create disequilibrium because it causes a discrepancy with his perception of the rows. When this happens, his thinking will shift, and he will be able to accommodate the dimension of number as well as the dimension of length in his conception of this problem,

Criticisms of Genetic Epistemology

Piaget's genetic epistemology has been widely influential, attracting both devoted adherents and outspoken critics. There can be no argument regarding Piaget's contribution to the field of cognitive development. His theory is notable first for its exceptional breadth, covering a broad age span and bringing together a large variety of children's achievements at any given age. Piaget also offers a wealth of observations, and the stages he describes "appeal to our intuitions and to our memories of childhood" (Siegler, 1986, p. 22). Finally, Piaget's theory addresses in an integrated fashion issues of interest to scientists and philosophers, parents, and teachers.

Despite its virtues, Piaget's theory has faced serious challenges, especially in recent years. The question we must consider, then, is: How well have the theory's specific claims about children's thinking held up in the face of contemporary research? Table 6.3 presents a summary of the evidence challenging the fundamental claims of Piaget's theory.

Claim 1: The Sequence of Stages Is Invariant.   Piaget believed that all children, regardless of culture, progress through the four stages of sensorimotor to formal operations. Moreover, once a particular stage is reached, regression to an earlier stage cannot occur, and all children are expected to eventually reach formal operations. These comprise an easily testable claim, and many replications of Piaget's experiments have been conducted. For the most part, results have shown that children in different cultures do pass through the same types of reasoning as did Piaget's children (Dasen, 1972). However, the

TABLE 6.3   *A Summary of Evidence Challenging the Fundamental Claims of Piaget's Theory*

Piaget's Claim	*Counterevidence*
1. The sequence of stages is culturally invariant, with formal operations inevitably reached.	• Not all cultures show evidence of formal operations. • Even in Western culture, people fail to reason at the formal operational level much of the time.
2. There is a qualitative change in cognition from stage to stage and consistency of reasoning within a stage.	• Children actually learn more at given stages than Piaget thought, and they do not always reason consistently within a stage.
3. Children exhibit the characteristics of each stage, and each stage includes all the competence of the previous stage (hierarchization).	• Children are sometimes egocentric beyond the preoperational stage. • Preoperational children are not egocentric all the time.
4. Global restructuring characterizes stage shifting.	• Reasoning appears to be more domain-specific than global.

ages at which children reached certain stages varied from culture to culture, and reaching formal operations was by no means assured. Even in advanced societies, only a minority of adolescents exhibited formal operational reasoning (Siegler, 1986), and Leahey and Harris (1997) go so far as to argue that scientists do not routinely reason at that level.

Imagine, for example, pouring the liquid from a partly filled bottle into a glass (Figure 6.2). On a separate sheet of paper, draw what you think the

FIGURE 6.2   *An Exercise in Formal Operational Thinking: Imagine Pouring the Liquid from the Bottle into the Glass. What would it look like? (Answer shown at the end of the chapter in Figure 6.4.)*

bottle would look like being held over the glass. If your picture matches that shown at the end of the chapter, you have exhibited formal operational reasoning. If not, you have performed much like the adults who participated in Piaget's study (reported in Piaget & Inhelder, 1967), whose results are taken as evidence for the fact that, most of the time, people operate at concrete, rather than formal operational thinking.

As for the question of regression, Inhelder, Sinclair, and Bovet (1974) observed temporary regression in the reasoning of early concrete operational children. Inhelder and Piaget (1964) also reported a non-monotonic path of change in children's development of competence in solving matrix completion problems like the one described in Discovering Relations. Matrix completion tasks are much like conservation tasks in that children's ability to solve them appears to develop with age, and children's performance tends to change very rapidly with competence. Their results showed that although 8-year-olds performed best of all, 7-year-olds actually performed less well than 6-year-olds (Inhelder & Piaget, 1964). These results may mean that cognitive restructuring occurring at stage transitions is not particularly stable for a brief time. Or, they may be evidence against the stage concept altogether. In other words, perhaps cognitive development occurs in steady, incremental changes rather than discontinuous stages. This suggestion brings us to the next claim of Piaget's theory.

Claim 2: The Stages Represent Qualitative Changes in Cognition. This claim carries two implications: (1) that development is discontinuous, and (2) that reasoning on different problems is consistent within a given stage. Whether the cognitive changes that occur during development are continuous or discontinuous is difficult to judge. Siegler (1986) offered the analogy of a bridge collapsing to suggest that development might be reasonably viewed as either continuous or discontinuous. The forces that cause a bridge to give way, for example, build up over a long period of time. But the collapse itself is sudden. Perhaps, then, what appear to be sudden changes in children's thinking are actually part of a gradual progression.

The question of continuity/discontinuity raises the related issue of whether development can be accelerated, which Piaget has called the "American question" (Gruber & Voneche, 1995). A discontinuity in stages suggests that such acceleration would be difficult to achieve. Teaching a nonconserver to conserve number, for example, should be virtually impossible while the child is squarely within the preoperational stage. Success at this training task, however, would undermine the concept of discontinuous stages.

Studies attempting to train children on Piagetian tasks have shown that children can learn more than Piaget thought they could. A number of studies provide convincing demonstrations of children benefiting from a variety of instructional techniques (Siegler, 1986). For example, the procedure used by Siegler and Svetina (2002) included three training components: (1) experience solving matrix completion problems, (2) correct answer feedback, and (3) attempts by the child to explain the correct answer. Like Nan in Discovering Relations, the children in the experimental condition improved significantly in their ability to solve this type problem. "This finding adds matrix completion to the increasing set of tasks on which this procedure has been shown to produce positive effects: number conservation (Siegler, 1995), balance scales (Pine & Messer, 2000),…biology (Chi, de Leeuw, Chiu, & LaVancher, 1994), and computer programming (Bielaczyc, Pirolli, & Brown, 1995)" (Siegler & Svetina, 2002, p. 814).

The changes in reasoning that children demonstrate through training appear to parallel those that occur naturally as children mature, suggesting that the training provided a "denser presentation of the types of experiences that are the sources of change in the everyday environment" (Siegler & Svetina, 2002, p. 815). It is encouraging that the positive effect appears robust of asking children questions to encourage them to adopt new reasoning strategies, but it remains to be seen from more longitudinal research whether the observed changes will persist over the long term.

Finally, with respect to unity of reasoning within a given stage, children should learn to solve, at the same time, a variety of problems that share a dependence on the logical structures developed during that stage. However, "it is increasingly apparent that this view does not accurately characterize children's thinking" (Siegler, 1986, p. 54). In other words, conservation tasks that require similar reasoning are not all mastered at the same time. "Differing amounts of experience with the problems, differences in the ease of drawing analogies to other, better-understood problems, and differences in the complexity of the most advanced solution formulas contribute to [the differences in children's reasoning within a stage]" (Siegler, 1986, p. 55).

To confound the issue, researchers using non-Piagetian tasks have discovered that children sometimes demonstrate unsuspected cognitive strengths. Very young children, for example, seem to have at least some sense of number conservation, even though they may fail the Piagetian task for number conservation. In her experiments, Gelman (1972) discovered that children knew when a penny was secretly removed from a small pile of coins if it caused them to lose a game with the experimenter. Likewise, most parents and many early childhood education teachers will attest to children's sense of number when they are asked to share cookies or crackers with a sibling or peer. In her research, Gelman (1978, 1983) also found similar effects for other Piagetian concepts, suggesting that Piaget's discrete stages might be an artifact of the particular tasks used in Piagetian experiments (cf. Donaldson, 1978).

Claim 3: Children Exhibit the Characteristics of Each Stage.   Whether Piaget's stages form a hierarchy of structured wholes that integrate all characteristics of a previous stage (criteria 3 and 4) is difficult to test. But one can examine the traits purported to characterize children's thinking at each stage and ask whether these traits are an adequate description. Do children consistently behave in these ways? Here again, the answer is somewhat mixed. The evidence of unexpected cognitive strengths and the inability of children to master, at the same time, a variety of tasks based on the same underlying reasoning both suggest problems with Piaget's stage descriptions. The problem, however, lies not so much with Piaget's observations of children's behavior, but in his account of stages and their constraints.

With respect to egocentrism in preoperational children, for example, "Piaget's work…records a deep insight: for every task where point of view is an issue, one can find an age such that children younger than that age usually err by failing to see the other person's viewpoint" (Carey, 1985a, pp. 13–14). This suggests that children are egocentric, but the nature of the task rather than the stage of development appears to be the critical factor determining when they are egocentric.

There is ample support in the research literature for this conclusion. Flavell (1985) argued that children well beyond the preoperational period continue to be at risk for egocentrism in particular types of tasks. For example, Siegler (1986) cited the classic demonstration in which children are to describe selected pictures from a set in such a way that another child can determine which picture is being described. Although older children are better at this task than are younger children, they still cannot overcome their own perspective sufficiently well to generate a description that will allow another child to select the right picture.

Finally, preoperational children are not egocentric all the time. In some situations, they will communicate nonegocentrically. "If you ask 3-year-olds to show you their drawings, they hold the side with the artwork toward you. If they were completely egocentric, they would do the opposite, since they would assume that what they see is what you see" (Siegler, 1986, p. 57).

Claim 4: Global Restructuring Characterizes the Shift from Stage to Stage. In part, this claim results from Piaget's requirement that stages represent qualitative changes in children's cognition. But more than that, for children to make the transition between stages, cognitive restructuring (i.e., accommodation in response to disequilibrium) must occur. Carey (1985b) called this global restructuring since it is assumed, in Piaget's theory, to constrain children's ability to acquire knowledge in all domains. In other words, the logical structures available to the child are dependent upon his or her stage of development, and these set limits to thinking within any given domain.

As with other aspects of Piaget's theory, global restructuring has come into question as an adequate mechanism for explaining conceptual changes in children's thinking (Carey 1985a, 1985b; Gelman & Baillargeon, 1983). "In much of their research, Piaget and his colleagues confounded the child's problems with domain-specific scientific concepts…and domain-general inferential abilities" (Carey, 1985a, p. 191). Like Piaget's children, the children in Carey's studies had similar ideas about the concept of alive and shifted their concepts at similar ages. But rather than appeal to changes in overall logical abilities to account for these conceptual changes, Carey (1985a) presented a convincing case for children's increased knowledge of biology being the cause. Thus, Carey's results showed that children knew considerably more about basic biological functions and bodily processes shared by animals than did younger children.

Piaget's theory of cognitive development was certainly groundbreaking in its recognition that children are not just mini-adults. Radical behaviorism, by virtue of its emphasis on behavior, presumed no special principles of development. Children, like adults, were thought to acquire behaviors through their reinforcement contingencies. But Piaget's observations established that children do not see the world quite like adults do. Piaget also raised the right questions: What mental processes lead children to think differently from adults, and how do they represent what they see?

An increasing body of empirical evidence exists now, however, to suggest that Piaget's answers to these questions were not always correct. With this evidence has come a variety of theories to explain how and why children think the way they do. Neo-Piagetian views attempt to extend Piaget's theory while accepting many of its basic assumptions. Views focusing on the apparently limitless variability in children's thinking, however, challenge the very foundations of Piaget's theory.

Beyond Piaget: Alternative Perspectives on Cognitive Development

One advantage to stage theories is that the assumption of general shifts in development brings order to a multitude of "bewilderingly diverse developments" (Carey, 1985a). Giving up stages means giving up some of this order. The result is a proliferation of more limited theories to account for these diverse observations. For the most part, however, these theories are consistent with two basic assumptions of Piaget's views:

1. Children think about any particular topic in only one way at most points in development.

2. A major goal of developmental theory should be identifying *the* way of thinking used by children at particular ages (Siegler, 1996, p. 219).

What makes the alternative theories different from Piaget's is an additional assumption that thinking is information processing (see Chapter 3 for a review of information-processing theories of cognition). Thus, researchers from this perspective focus on "the information that children represent, the processes they use to transform the information, and the memory limits that constrain the amount of information they can represent and process" (Siegler, 1986, p. 63).

One theory is emerging among current conceptions of development that retains an information-processing perspective but rejects any assumption that children reason in only one way at various points in development. The implications of all these alternative views are discussed next.

A Neo-Piagetian View

Robbie Case (1984, 1992, 1995) has described his view as consistent with Piaget's in the assumption of developmental stages and increasingly sophisticated mental structures within each stage. Unlike Piaget, however, he believes that "children's mental structures can best be modeled by using the sorts of concepts developed in the field of information processing and computer simulation, rather than those developed in the field of symbolic logic" (Case, 1984, p. 20). Accordingly, Case has examined children's problem solving in terms of short-term memory capacity and the proportion of that capacity devoted to operating space or storage space. He has argued that developmental shifts can be explained by the automatization of problem-solving operations. That is, as processing becomes more automatic, the requirements for operating space diminish, allowing for more storage space. This means that older children can solve problems containing more operations, since the others can be held in storage while one is being performed. Younger children, on the other hand, must devote all their memory capacity to performing a single operation. See Figure 6.3 for a visual representation of Case's model.

What contributes to increases in operational efficiency? What happens to decrease a 6-year-old's requirements for operational space and increase available storage space? One answer, clearly, is that massive practice in basic

FIGURE 6.3 *Case's Model of Memory Capacity and Use in Two Stages of Development*

operations enables them to become automatic, and automatic processes require less memory capacity (see Chapter 3 for a more extensive discussion of automaticity). Although Case accepts automaticity as one factor determining increases in operational capacity, he doubts that automaticity is the only factor. Research on the biology of the brain has led Case to speculate that biological maturation will be an important contributor to operational efficiency. In particular, myelinization of nervous tissue apparently proceeds unevenly in neurological development.

> Since there is an approximate correspondence between the myelinization that takes place in different areas of the brain at different ages, on the one hand, and the changes in the efficiency of the types of operations that these areas control, on the other, the possibility exists that the degree of myelinization may be the factor that sets the developmental ceiling on operational efficiency at any age. (Case, 1984, p. 40; see Chapter 8 for a more extensive discussion of the biological bases of learning)

Case (1993; Case & Okamoto, 1996) also elaborated on an aspect of Piaget's theory that he believes was abandoned prematurely by information-processing developmentalists, namely, the notion of a general logical-mathematical structure. In a second-order analysis of data on local conceptual developments, Case found evidence for greater generality of children's thinking than had been commonly accepted before. To account for this, he proposed the construct of central conceptual structures in children's thinking. These are not thought to be systemwide, as Piaget suggested, but are assumed to be broadly applicable within and across culturally defined disciplines or content areas. For example, Case and Okamoto (1996) presented analyses showing commonalities shared among spatial, social, and mathematical understandings in children. It remains to be seen, of course, just what domains of understanding exist and what conceptual structures are central to each domain.

A Computational Model

In the early 1970s, Klahr and Wallace undertook a research program aimed at uniting Piaget's theory of development with techniques for simulating human cognition. They faced a difficult challenge: to construct a program that would adequately describe children's behavior at a particular stage and to build one that would modify itself to account for children's transitions among stages. Undaunted, Klahr and Wallace (1976) maintained that "Piaget's steadfast insistence on the characterization of the child as an organism functioning under the control of a developing set of central processes" kept them searching for an appropriate computer language by which to simulate those processes. In addition, recognizing the enormity of simulating all aspects of Piaget's theory, Klahr and Wallace concentrated on building a model of one aspect, quantitative development.

In order to model conservation of number, Klahr and Wallace (1973, 1976) began with the proposal that humans mentally represent quantity through one of three quantifiers. These are subitizing, counting, and estimating. Subitizing refers to the rapid recognition of collections of four or fewer objects. That is, shown an array of four objects, most people can immediately and accurately report how many are there and do so in less time than it would take to count the items. When more than four items are present, people resort to counting. Then, when the collection grows large enough that counting is impractical, estimating enables a quantity to be represented.

Along with the quantifiers, Klahr and Wallace assumed basic processes of self-modification and generalization. In other words, over time children experience regularities in quantification. For example, they may subitize three cookies, then three dolls, or three pennies. Repeated experiences of this sort enable generalization across episodes, so that a rule is formed representing subitizing three items. With additional experience, the cognitive system modifies itself to reflect increasingly abstract rules. Thus, conservation can be explained by reference to what rules have been acquired. According to Klahr (1984), nonconservers can count (i.e., produce and order quantitative symbols) and therefore know that five comes after four. But they have not yet acquired the rule that a collection of five things is more than a collection of four things. Hence, nonconservers like Aaron in the Conserving Numbers scenario continue to assert that the longer row has more blocks.

Critics of computer simulations such as Klahr's and Wallace's contend that they may account for learning but do not capture the essence of development. Yet perhaps the very success of these systems argues for a different conception of development. Klahr (1984) noted, for example, that the distinction between global and local restructuring is blurred in his system. Klahr (1995; also Simon & Klahr, 1995) argued, for example, that computational models help to explain change in cognitive development. "From local changes come global effects, and from incremental modifications come structural reorganizations" (Klahr, 1984, p. 131). He also noted,

> Assimilation and accommodation have been with us so long that it is easy to forget that they are not empirical regularities demanding theoretical account. Instead, they are obscure theoretical constructs, imported by Piaget as analogies from the biology of the digestive process.
>
> ...I believe we should abandon the criterion of how well computational models can account for assimilation and accommodation.... (Klahr, 1995, p. 372)

A Componential Analysis

Sternberg (1984b, 1985, 1997) differs from the other theorists discussed so far in his almost total lack of reference to Piaget's theory. Instead, Sternberg grounded his research squarely within information-processing theory and proposed to account for intellectual development in terms of "changes in the availability, accessibility, and ease of execution of a variety of kinds of information-processing components" (1984b, p. 164). Moreover, Sternberg's work is distinguished by his interest in the measurement of intelligence; he relates his findings to those yielded by traditional intelligence tests.

According to Sternberg, intelligence is made up of three types of information-processing components: metacomponents, performance components, and knowledge-acquisition components. "Metacomponents are executive processes used in planning and decision making in task performance" (Sternberg, 1984b, p. 165). So, for example, determining just what problem is to be solved and deciding upon a particular strategy for solving it are types of metacomponents. Performance components are those processes involved in the actual completion of a problem-solving task. Encoding relevant features of the task or comparing possible answer options are examples of performance components. Finally, knowledge-acquisition components are those used for learning new information required to solve a problem at hand. Selectively encoding relevant information, meaningfully interpreting this information, and integrating it with previous knowledge compose the set of knowledge-acquisition components.

To this point, Sternberg's analysis is no different for children's thinking than the thinking of adults. To account for developmental changes, Sternberg proposed several mechanisms on which intellectual change is thought to be based. First is a feedback mechanism stemming from the knowledge-acquisition components. These components lead to increased knowledge, which leads to more effective use of the components, which again increases the knowledge base, and so on. Second, in a similar fashion, self-monitoring provided by the metacomponents enables a self-correcting feedback loop. One can learn from mistakes in using metacomponents and become more efficient in resource allocation.

Finally, besides feedback, automatization within a component set can give rise to improved intellectual performance. In this aspect, Sternberg's approach resembles Case's. As some processes become automatic, processing resources can be directed toward what is new in a problem-solving situation.

To a large extent, Sternberg conceived of the developing child as similar to a novice becoming an expert. A novice has limited knowledge of not only a subject matter domain, but also processes that are not automatic within that domain. Both characteristics serve to limit temporarily the novice's, or child's, intellectual performance within that domain.

A Framework Theory Approach

Piaget believed that the logical structures associated with each stage of development provide the basis for thinking and reasoning across domains. However, this claim has been undermined by evidence that children are not consistent in their thinking across subject matter domains. Although Case has argued for a return to general conceptual structures, other developmentalists posit commonalities of reasoning only within specific subject matters.

This framework theory approach (Carey, 1996; also called a theory-theory approach [Siegler, 1996]) evolved from several lines of research focused on conceptual change. Novice-expert studies (e.g., Chase & Simon, 1973; Chi, Glaser, & Rees, 1982) drew attention to qualitative differences in how experts and novices represent information and solve problems. Mental models researchers (see Chapter 4), investigating how knowledge within a domain is represented, noted that learners typically have preconceived (and often inaccurate) conceptions of scientific phenomena. Studies such as those of Posner et al. (1982) exemplified the concern of science educators for how students' "central, organizing concepts change from one set of concepts to another set, incompatible with the first" (p. 211). Initial mental models, that is, are potentially inaccurate and most certainly inadequate. Therefore, they must change over time to become more adequate representations of scientific ideas. The question is, Does this change characterize development, and if so, how does it come about?

Based on the results of her extensive case studies, Carey (1985a) suggested that children begin with a very few conceptual structures: "perhaps only a naive mechanics and a naive psychology" (Carey, 1985a, p. 201). These intuitive theories constitute cognitive domains that specify the kinds of things there are in the world and provide explanations for the phenomena involving those things. Intuitive theories that have been explored in the literature include the 4-year-old's theory of mind (Perner, 1991), the 10-year-old's theory of matter (Carey, 1991), an infant's theory of physical bodies (Baillargeon, Kotovsky, & Needham, 1995), and the intuitive cosmology of elementary school children (Vosniadou, 1992). Some researchers have also proposed that these cognitive domains may be innate modules that govern young children's perception and reasoning (e.g., Sperber, 1994; Leslie, 1994).

Regardless of whether intuitive theories are believed to be innate, the problem for developmentalists is what causes them to change as children grow up. That is, what is the engine of cognitive development? Carey (1996; also Carey & Spelke, 1994) suggested that evidence is strong for the role of two heuristic processes in conceptual change:

1. Construct mapping across domains, including physical analogies
2. Thought experiments, including limited case analyses

Construct mapping occurs, for example, when scientists map physical phenomena to mathematics and reason about them without the constraints imposed by the core principles of physics. Thought experiments involve mental model simulations, such as when Galileo imagined a light object and a heavy object in free fall and concluded that they would fall at the same speed in a vacuum.

Construct mapping and thought experiments are both reflective and deliberate strategies for understanding and so are probably not the only mechanisms stimulating conceptual change. It is likely that framework theories change and are replaced with new theories as children learn causal facts that become interrelated and mutually constraining. Carey (1996) cited the example of preschool children who were told two facts: Babies grow in their mommy's tummies, and when inside, are not subject to any external influences. "Just learning these two facts lead children to perform better on a range of tasks that diagnose an understanding of biological inheritance" (Carey, 1996, p. 210). Learning, it appears, plays a critical role in a framework theory approach to cognitive development.

A New Agenda Based on Variability, Choice, and Change

Siegler (1996) challenged researchers in cognitive development to adopt a new agenda, which, in his view, will require reformulation of basic assumptions about children's thinking. Like Case, Klahr and Wallace, and Sternberg, Siegler (1983, 1984, 1986) took an aspect of Piaget's theory as a starting point and began to develop a theory utilizing information-processing concepts and analyses. He focused on how children encode features of a problem and select rules to solve it. His results showed that performance was related to age on a problem requiring the use and combination of multiple rules to solve. That is, older children were able to attend to critical features of the problem, select appropriate dimensions of rules related to those features, and then combine them to successfully solve the problem. Younger children experienced difficulty at several points in the problem-solving process. With tutoring, however, young children learned to encode, monitor, and use features of a problem that they previously ignored. But what caused the changes in children's thinking to occur?

Siegler's research led him to question the assumption that children think or reason about a problem in only one way at a particular point in development. Although framework theory researchers established that children's thinking is more domain-specific than global, Siegler questioned how consistent it is even within a domain. According to his observations, "Thinking is not monolithic within a given domain, nor within a given task, nor within a given item. Even when the same child is presented the identical problem on two successive days, the child quite often uses different approaches on the two occasions" (Siegler, 1996, p. 220). In other words, in Siegler's view, variability is a basic property of human thought.

With variability comes the need to choose among strategies available to solve a given problem. Siegler noted that children tend to choose adaptively, using a backup strategy when a problem gets hard, switching strategies that were incorrect or involved little effort, and matching strategies to task demands. Moreover, it appeared to Siegler that children's thinking is constantly changing, with undergeneralization of new ways of thinking the typical pattern (Siegler, 1996). Siegler concluded that the time may be ripe for a new metaphor of cognitive development. Instead of a staircase (thinking at a certain level for prolonged periods followed by moving rapidly upward for a brief period), Siegler (1996) proposed overlapping waves as a more accurate picture of development: "Endlessly variable, endlessly changing—a wave, like children's thinking, never stands still" (p. 239).

Characterizing the changes and variability in children's thinking, Siegler has proposed a framework of five dimensions of cognitive growth: its path, rate, breadth, source, and variability (Siegler & Svetina, 2002). With respect to the path of change, children become more variable in their strategy use just before they discover a new, more effective approach. Rate of change tends to be gradual, and children continue to use old approaches long after new, more sophisticated approaches become part of their repertoire. New strategies, when they first emerge, are also applied rather narrowly, not generalized widely across other problems or contexts, and children continue to use a variety of strategies. Finally, the source of change concerns what causes change to be set in motion. As noted earlier in the critique of Piaget's theory, instruction can facilitate cognitive change when it encourages children to explain their observations and reasoning.

Conclusion: Comparisons Among Theories

Think back for a moment to the two basic questions with which this chapter began: What are the psychological states children pass through? What develops? What are the mechanisms responsible for development? How does development occur? For the most part, information-processing theorists have disagreed minimally with Piaget on what develops (see Table 6.4 for comparisons). Clearly, children acquire knowledge and the ability to act upon that knowledge. Whereas Piaget believed knowledge is represented in logical, operational structures, information-processing theorists presume that children's knowledge is most likely represented by the same sorts of semantic networks and memory connections as adults' knowledge. But they also "presuppose, in the Piagetian spirit, that children are active, self-directing cognitive entrepreneurs who develop their minds through a great many spontaneously generated information-processing activities" (Flavell, 1984, pp. 198–199).

Where information-processing theorists appear to differ most from Piaget is in their conceptions of the mechanisms of development. Only Case retains the Piagetian notion of developmental stages, but he proposes that overcoming short-term memory limits, rather than equilibration, accounts for progress from stage to stage. Moreover, none of the information-processing theorists retain Piaget's sense of the biological organism "that has evolved the

TABLE 6.4 *Comparison Among Theories of Cognitive Development*

Genetic Epistemology (Piaget)	*Neo-Piagetian (Case)*	*Computational Model (Klahr)*	*Componential Analysis (Sternberg)*	*Framework Theory (Carey)*	*Variability, Choice, and Change (Siegler)*
Features of Theory					
Four stages of development • Sensory-motor • Preoperational • Concrete-Operational • Formal-operational	Stages similar to those of Piaget Increasingly sophisticated logical structures at each stage Biological maturation assumed	Computer simulations of Piaget's theory	Development more or less equivalent to novice becoming expert Based on information-processing theory exclusively	Qualitative differences in knowledge states Domain-specific development	Variability is characteristic of thinking Strategy choice is adaptive Children's thinking is always changing
Developmental Processes					
• Accommodation • Assimilation • Equilibration	Automatization (to reduce operating space in STM)	Generalization global restructuring (brought on by local, domain-specific restructuring)	Feedback (to provide a self-correcting function)	Knowledge restructuring in specific domains	Encoding, monitoring of task demands, trial and error, learning

capability and disposition to acquire some things differently, and with more naive talent or special aptitude, than other things" (Flavell, 1984, p. 192). Again, only Case raises the possibility of a biological factor setting age-dependent limits to cognitive development, and he does so only speculatively.

Flavell (1984) lamented this loss and criticizes information-processing theories for their failure to distinguish different mechanisms involved in child and adult cognition. After all, most theorists implicitly agree that development does not continue past young adulthood. Yet, if no biological mechanism operates to set the limits of development, then it should go on throughout life.

Finally, information-processing theorists have demonstrated that learning plays a more significant role in development than Piaget supposed. Specifically, "a good deal of human cognitive development can be profitably conceptualized in terms of the acquisition of domain-specific expertise and of the high-quality cognitive functioning that expertise brings with it" (Flavell, 1984, p. 195). Expertise, however, is not to be conceived as simply an accumulation of knowledge. Rather, it implies a process of building rich, conceptual structures—mental models that restructure with experience.

Implications for Instruction of Developmental Theory

Piagetian-Inspired Instruction

Brainerd (1978) wrote of an experience he once had at a school for gifted children. He noted that one of the students there seemed particularly bright compared with the rest, and he asked the teacher how she went about teaching this prodigy. "Surprised that I should ask a question whose answer was so obvious," wrote Brainerd, "she replied, 'I water him and he grows'" (1978, pp. 285–286). This horticultural metaphor is singularly descriptive of most Piagetian-inspired curricula, because it emphasizes a child-centered educational philosophy. "The basic assumption seems to be that children's minds, if planted in fertile soil, will grow quite naturally on their own" (Brainerd, 1978, p. 286).

Consider the implications of this horticultural metaphor for specific instructional techniques. What can teachers and designers of instruction do to ensure fertile soil? According to Wadsworth (1996) and Gruber and Voneche (1995), both of whom make this point rather emphatically, there is no Piagetian dogma about education. There is no set of teaching practices that constitutes a Piagetian approach to instruction. Rather, educators have interpreted Piaget's theory to suggest broad instructional principles. Beyond these, any specific methods depend upon the teacher's understanding of children's thinking. "Piaget has devoted his efforts to changing our understanding of the child; for some this is only a prelude to the development of new educational means, for others it is the new means" (Gruber & Voneche, 1977, p. 691).

There are perhaps three basic instructional principles on which Piagetian theorists generally agree. Each is discussed below.

Principle 1: The Learning Environment Should Support the Activity of the Child.   According to Piaget, activity is of paramount importance in the growth of intelligence. Children acquire knowledge through their actions, and thinking is considered to be action-based. Thus, a learning environment should be created that encourages children to initiate and complete their own activities.

> Good pedagogy must involve presenting the child with situations in which he himself experiments, in the broadest sense of the term—trying things out to see what happens, manipulating symbols, posing questions and seeking his own answers, reconciling what he finds one time with what he finds at another, comparing his findings with those of other children.... (Duckworth, 1964, p. 2)

An active, discovery-oriented environment consistent with Piaget's theory does not mean that children discover what the teacher wants them to discover (Brainerd, 1978). Bruner (e.g., Bruner, Goodnow, & Austin, 1956; see Chapter 7) has advocated a form of inquiry teaching in which children are presented with specific examples and carefully questioned in such a way that they discover a general concept or rule. For Piagetian educators, such an approach is fundamentally flawed because it brings children to the teacher's conception instead of allowing them to construct their own conceptions.

Inherent in Piaget's emphasis on activity is the fact that children receive feedback from their own actions. In acquiring physical knowledge, for example, the child learns what characteristics are true about an object by her actions with it. She does not have to be told that blocks can crush softer or more brittle objects; the evidence is there in the thousands of cracker crumbs that resulted from her blow. In the same way, feedback regarding logical-mathematical knowledge is available from the child's actions. Only arbitrary knowledge depends upon feedback from other people, who reinforce cultural values and socially appropriate behaviors. To supply feedback for anything but social knowledge is to potentially persuade the child to disregard her natural disequilibrium (Wadsworth, 1996).

Since feedback comes from objects and actions upon objects, concrete, manipulable materials play an important role in a Piagetian-based classroom. To the extent possible, children should be permitted to manipulate materials for themselves. Thus, an experiment to illustrate some scientific principle is likely to mean more when the child conducts it than when the teacher demonstrates it. Although Wadsworth (1978) maintained that pictures are still abstract, Brainerd (1978) argued that their inclusion in textbooks can help to bring some level of concreteness to otherwise exclusively abstract material.

Finally, Piagetian educators encourage play as a pedagogic strategy for active self-discovery (Brainerd, 1978; Gruber & Voneche, 1995). Play effectively represents all of the requisite characteristics of Piagetian-inspired instruction that have been discussed so far. In play, children initiate and control their own activities. They employ concrete objects, either referentially (the object stands for itself) or symbolically (the object represents something other than itself). And they learn from the feedback that is inherent in the play situation. Most of all, they are self-motivated and will persist until the activity has been carried to completion (cf. Wadsworth, 1996).

Principle 2: Children's Interactions with Their Peers Are an Important Source of Cognitive Development.   As noted earlier in the chapter, preoperational children are characteristically egocentric in their thinking and language. Piaget believed that peer interactions are essential in helping children move beyond egocentric thought. Other children, thought Piaget, are more likely than adults to have cognitive structures similar to the egocentric child (Piaget, 1951). Therefore, they will be more effective in providing information or feedback to that child about the validity of his or her logical constructions. Thus, instructional strategies are favored that encourage peer teaching and social negotiation during problem solving.

Principle 3: Adopt Instructional Strategies That Make Children Aware of Conflicts and Inconsistencies in Their Thinking.   This principle derives largely from Piaget's master developmental process, equilibration. Recall that children must experience disequilibrium, or an imbalance between their current cognitive structures and new information to be assimilated, in order for them to move to a new stage of development. Training studies involving conservation tasks demonstrated that, when confronted with the inadequacy of their reasoning, children learned to adopt more complex and adequate rules. Brainerd (1978) called this confrontation conflict teaching and argued that it serves to induce disequilibrium. Gruber and Voneche (1995) noted that a Socratic dialogue serves much the same function, since the teacher asks questions of the learner that bring out misconceptions and faulty reasoning.

Two important points should be made about this third Piagetian principle. The first is the criticality of diagnosing what children already know and how they think. Obviously, what questions are posed to create conflict or illustrate inconsistency in thinking depend on the teacher's knowing the current state of the child's knowledge. In this way, content is not introduced until the child is cognitively ready to understand it. Piagetian educators also caution that attempts to accelerate learning should be avoided, and this can be ensured through careful diagnosis of existing logical structures.

The second is taking into account the order in which concepts spontaneously emerge in cognitive development for conflict instruction. From a Piagetian perspective, concepts are acquired as a function of the logical structures that underlie them. Thus, questions or experiences designed to induce conflict will only be effective when the logical structures on which they depend have been or are being developed. We will see shortly that this same recommendation will emanate from the information-processing perspective, but with a different explanation.

Instructional Implications of an Information-Processing View

Even though Brainerd (1978) was less than optimistic about the promise of Piagetian-based principles for instruction, these principles may yet endure. Despite their different perspectives on development, information-processing theorists have suggested implications for instruction that, in a general way, resemble Piaget's. In a sense, information-processing theorists have attempted to articulate, in more detail than did Piaget, just what activity is beneficial for intellectual growth and how cognitive conflict can be most effectively induced. So far, however, the developmental theorists discussed in this chapter have had little to say about strategies for peer interaction (although researchers from various other learning traditions have provided ample evidence concerning the instructional value of collaborative learning structures).

The Role of Rules in Children's Thinking.   Taken together, the work of Case, Klahr and Wallace, Siegler, and Sternberg suggests that rules are a useful means for characterizing children's thinking. Viewing children's thinking in terms of rules yields specific recommendations for instruction.

Case, for example, believes that children's short-term memory places limits on the number of operations (or rules) they can manage at one time. He suggests that these limits lead children to oversimplify problems and ignore important information (Case, 1978). To help children overcome memory limits, Case (1980) recommended that teachers follow a three-step procedure. First, the ways in which children are oversimplifying a given type of problem must be identified. Then students should be shown why their strategy will not work to solve the problem and what information they are ignoring. Finally, they should be taught and given many opportunities to practice a better strategy incorporating all the rules necessary to solve the problem. Throughout this process, Case (1980) cautioned, every means should be taken to reduce overall memory load, including use of familiar terms or objects, small steps, and lots of practice at each step.

While Sternberg (1984b) shares Case's emphasis on rule automatization, Siegler (1983) shares his concern for determining the rules children are currently using to solve problems. Rather than appeal to short-term memory limits to explain children's failure to use certain rules, Siegler argues that children adopt rules based on predictive accuracy. In other words, they will stick with the simplest rule possible that, based on their experience, is most likely to work in a given situation. This implies, however, a corrective procedure similar to that proposed by Case when the rule used by a child is inadequate.

Siegler differs from Case mostly in his emphasis on encoding processes once children have become aware that their rules are faulty. In order to identify the focus of encoding strategies, for example, Siegler recommends analyzing the task for requisite rules along with analyzing the child for the sequence of rule using. In this way, instruction can be effectively designed to facilitate the child's acquisition of new rules.

Promoting Conceptual Change.   Like Piaget, theorists from an information-processing perspective firmly believe that conceptual change is an integral part of cognitive development. Unlike Piaget, however, they explain this change in terms of domain-specific expertise and changing mental models, as opposed to general logical structures. As a result, they agree with the general Piagetian recommendation that children will learn best from experiences that induce cognitive conflict and indicate inadequacies in their thinking. But what are these experiences and how are they to be arranged?

Posner et al. (1982) contended that useful guidelines for instruction can be found in the metaphor of conceptual change as scientific paradigm shift. New scientific conceptions emerge when (1) there is existing dissatisfaction with the old conception, (2) a new conception can be grasped, (3) the new conception appears plausible, and (4) the new conception opens up new areas of inquiry (Posner et al., 1982, p. 214). Let us examine the implications of these four conditions.

Creating dissatisfaction with an existing conception is partly accomplished through the existence of anomalies (Posner et al., 1982). These consist of experiences or information that cannot be easily assimilated to the existing conception. Vosniadou (1988) gave the example of children hearing an adult say that the earth is "round like a ball" when their mental model is of a flat and stationary earth. But Vosniadou argued that the anomaly alone will not necessarily cause dissatisfaction with the existing conception. Rather, children are apt to be confused or assume that they misunderstood the contradictory statement. After all, the adult could not be wrong, but the experience of a flat earth cannot be reconciled to an earth that is round like a ball. As a consequence, Vosniadou discovered children either remain confused or construct an assimilatory model that in some way makes sense of the new information.

In order to prepare students for conceptual change, then, claimed Vosniadou (1988), teachers must be aware of children's experiential beliefs, point out the contradictions between those beliefs and adult scientific conceptions, and provide persuasive reasons to children for questioning their beliefs.

According to Posner et al. (1982), these persuasive reasons, at least among older students, may have already been established as a commitment to consistency between one's beliefs about the world and empirical evidence. Both authors point out, however, that questioning one's beliefs can be threatening and lead to defensive moves for which the teacher should be prepared.

Ensuring the intelligibility of a new conception can be accomplished through analogies, metaphors, and physical models (Vosniadou & Brewer, 1987; Posner et al., 1982). Scientists often notice an analogy to something known when they attempt to make sense of the unknown (e.g., Oppenheimer, 1956). Although such spontaneous reference to analogies does not come easily to students, they can benefit from analogies explicitly taught to establish a new schema or restructure an existing one. The explanatory potential of analogies and metaphors has already been discussed in relation to schema theory and mental models (see Chapter 4).

Physical models, too, have been discussed as useful for helping students structure appropriate mental models of concepts (see Chapter 4). For example, "physical models are particularly appropriate in a domain like that of planetary mechanics in which the structure of a solar system and its operation can be easily captured in a physical representation" (Vosniadou & Brewer, 1987, p. 62). It should be noted, however, that we still know relatively little about what models are best for what content domains, how these models might best be presented in instruction, and how misrepresentations of models can be most effectively avoided (Vosniadou & Brewer, 1987). This is an area in which more empirical investigation is certainly warranted.

The plausibility of a new conception hinges on its relation to the learner's experiential beliefs and its ability to account for anomalies. Clearly, any new model or theory must account for all previous data as well as the anomalous data that caused its creation in the first place. This consistency with past and present findings should therefore be an area of focus in instruction. But more than that, students' own experiences should be examined relative to the phenomena under study. As discussed earlier, their experiential beliefs can lead them to resist a new conception or to adopt a model that is somewhere between their beliefs and the new conception.

Referring to the earlier example of a round versus flat earth, a teacher might initiate a discussion about the difficulties Christopher Columbus had in finding men willing to sail with him. Since they, like the students, conceived of the earth as flat, they believed ships could fall off the earth if they sailed too far in one direction. Then the teacher could present a physical model of the earth in the solar system and discuss findings and experiences consistent with the representation of the earth as round. Socratic dialogues may also be useful in making students aware of inconsistencies in their current schema relative to the new conception to be acquired (Vosnaidou & Brewer, 1987).

Fruitfulness of a new conception is perhaps best illustrated in the applications to which the new conception may be put. The model of a round earth, for example, led to revolutionary changes in map-making and the planning of explorations. Discussing and illustrating implications of this sort, as well as having students create inventions stemming from a new conception, are ways teachers have found to enhance understanding of the new idea.

Finally, researchers studying conceptual change make two additional pedagogical recommendations. First, interdependencies among concepts within a domain can determine to a great extent the order of acquisition of these concepts (Vosniadou, 1988). Therefore, "instruction that utilizes the information about the order of acquisition of the concepts that comprise a given domain will be much more effective than instruction that does not" (Vosniadou, 1988, p. 10). Yet, when Vosniadou examined the astronomy units of four science text series, she found problems with their organization of concepts. For example, "a unit on the moon at grade one…takes the children from a description of the size and shape of the moon to an explanation of the moon's phases (which most of our adult subjects cannot explain),…before providing any instruction on the relative size and location of the earth, the sun and the moon in the solar system" (Vosniadou, 1988, p. 10).

Second, teachers should spend a substantial portion of their time diagnosing student misconceptions and guiding them to mental models more consistent with scientific findings (Vosniadou & Brewer, 1987; Roth, Anderson, & Smith, 1986; Posner et al., 1982). This recommendation should sound familiar since it is precisely the same as that proposed by schema theorists and mental models researchers, who investigated learning rather than development. What we might conclude, then, is that the learning and development of children in some ways closely resembles the learning of adults.

This conclusion will receive additional support in the next chapter, where the developmental theories of Bruner and Vygotsky are examined. Although both theorists set out to study cognitive development, many of their ideas appear to apply equally well to adult learning. In addition, what makes Bruner and Vygotsky stand apart from the theorists discussed in this chapter is their emphasis on learning and development within a cultural context.

A Piagetian Perspective on "Kermit and the Keyboard"

Because Kermit is an adult, he would be expected according to Piaget's theory to have reached the formal operational stage of development. As such, Piaget's theory would have relatively little to contribute to our understanding of Kermit's learning in this story. However, children clearly learn some of the same knowledge and skills. In fact, my 12-year-old niece has been taking lessons in piano and violin for several years, so her learning has spanned the concrete operational stage (she should be entering formal operations about now). What insights might therefore be gained through a Piagetian perspective?

To begin with, we might consider what type of knowledge is being acquired from Piaget's viewpoint (see Table 6.1). Certainly, there is physical knowledge of the keyboard itself—what the keys feel like, how much pressure it takes to depress them, what sounds they make and under what settings. According to Piaget, this type of knowledge is acquired through actions on objects, so Kermit and my niece must actually experiment with the instrument to discover these properties. Learning to read music involves learning a symbol system, which Piaget defined as social knowledge, or knowledge made by people. And according to Piaget, acquiring social knowledge requires actions on and interactions with people. This is an interesting point. For the most part, Kermit is learning by himself in this story, although he has already acquired the basic skills of reading a musical score. What about my niece? This would suggest that for her to be successful in learning music, she must interact with others. Certainly, she is doing that by taking music lessons and playing in the school orchestra. In addition, there is a great deal of social support at her home for learning music, as most of the family either plays an instrument or sings in a choir. These experiences would be considered critical for learning, according to Piagetian theory.

It is hard to see how Piaget's stages of development might apply to this story, even if we consider my niece's experience rather than Kermit's. The reason is likely to be that most of the research surrounding cognitive development (whether Piaget's or information-processing theorists') has focused on logical-mathematical knowledge rather than either physical or social knowledge. This shows, perhaps, the privileged position occupied by logical-mathematical knowledge in traditional school learning.

FIGURE 6.4 *An Exercise in Formal Operational Thinking: The Level of the Liquid Should Appear Parallel with the Table Surface and Floor*

Theory Matrix

Theory	Genetic Epistemology
Prominent Theorist	J. Piaget
Learning Outcome(s)	Physical knowledge, logical-mathematical knowledge, social knowledge
Role of the Learner	Actively manipulate objects and ideas
	Experience cognitive conflict
	Invent and reinvent knowledge through interaction with the world and people surrounding him or her
Role of the Instructor	Provide a rich learning environment that supports activity of the learner and encourages interactions with peers
	Ask probing questions to make children aware of conflicts and inconsistencies in their thinking
Inputs or Preconditions to Learning	Concrete materials to manipulate, cognitive conflicts to stimulate disequilibrium
Process of Development	Development of cognitive structuring progresses through 4 stages involving processes of assimilation, accommodation, and equilibration
	Global restructuring occurs through cognitive conflict

Suggested Readings

Siegler, R. S. (1996). *Emerging minds.* New York: Oxford University Press.
Gruber, H. E., and Voneche, J. J. (1995). *The essential Piaget.* New York: Basic Books.
Wadsworth, B. J. (1996). *Piaget's theory of cognitive and affective development* (5th ed.). White Plains, NY: Longman.

Reflective Questions and Activities

1. Summarize your understanding of Jean Piaget's genetic epistemology. How does his view of knowledge and knowledge development fit with the epistemological traditions described in Chapter 1?

2. As a class project, debate the merits of Piaget's stage theory for explaining cognitive development. What evidence can be amassed to support the theory? What evidence calls it into question?

3. Consider the difference between learning and development. Take a preliminary position on which influences which. That is, must a child be at a certain point in development in order for learning to occur effectively? Or, does learning prompt movement from one stage of development to the next? What evidence would support one position or the other?

4. Researchers who focus on learning through the life span have sometimes criticized Piaget's theory because it seems to imply that development is essentially complete once learners enter the formal operational stage. Review literature on lifelong learning or educational gerontology and indicate what evidence there is to suggest that development continues from birth to death. Suppose a new manuscript is discovered in which Piaget proposes a fifth stage of development, beyond formal operations. Speculate on the possible characteristics of this stage and its implications for adult learning.

5. Select a topic that could represent new information to groups of children and adults (one example might be how to operate a personal computer). From what you have studied of learning theory so far, would you design different instruction for the children than you would for the adults? Why or why not? If you would create different instruction for the two groups, what would these differences entail? Why would you make those instructional decisions?

7

Interactional Theories of Cognitive Development

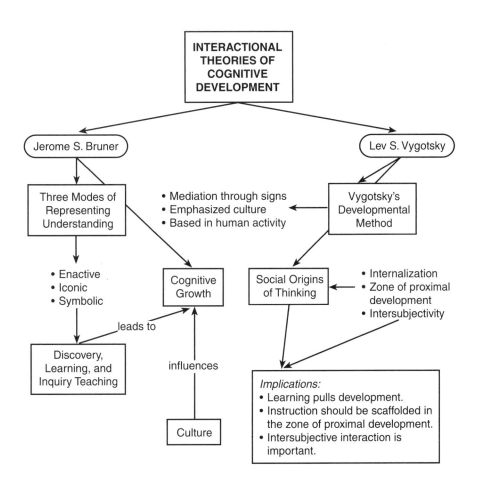

Consider the following scenarios.

• *Pet Monkey*[1]

Mrs. Bell teaches kindergarten in a school district zoned to increase integration of underrepresented minority children into its predominantly white schools. She has a class of nineteen and begins a lesson with eight students on the concepts of animals with four legs and pets. She draws two overlapping circles on the chalkboard, and says, "The blue circle is for all animals that have four legs. The red circle is for pets. Now I want you to think of some animals and what circle they belong in."

As the children clamor to make suggestions, Mrs. Bell questions them about where the animals belong (in the blue circle, in the red circle, or in both, and thus in their intersection). She also asks the children to justify their selection. Then, with each correct classification, Mrs. Bell hands her chalk to someone, who comes to the board and makes a mark in one of the circles or in the intersection. During the course of the lesson, the following scene takes place.

---

[1]This scenario was inspired by Emihovich (1981), who studied interaction patterns among kindergarten children as a function of their race and gender.

Mrs. B: Shannon, have you thought of another animal? (She calls on a petite girl, who has been waving her hand madly.)

Shannon: Yes, a monkey.

Mrs. B: And where does your monkey belong?

Shannon: (Softly) In the red circle.

Mrs. B: In the red circle? Why does it belong there? Is a monkey a pet?

Darren: (A boy who has been clowning around, paying no apparent attention to the lesson) I know someone who had a monkey for a pet!

Mrs. B: (Ignores Darren, paces in front of the board holding the chalk close to her chest) But where do you find monkeys?

Chorus: In the circus!

Mrs. B: So, is a monkey a pet if it's in the circus? Shannon?

Shannon: (Softly) Maybe.

Mrs. B: (Tries again) But don't people usually keep pets in their homes? (Shannon nods) Monkeys aren't usually kept at home, because they don't make very good pets. So where does your monkey belong?

Shannon: In the blue circle. (Mrs. B hands Shannon the chalk to put a mark in the blue circle.)

• *Beginning Spanish*[2]

Pete and Richard are high school students in a third-year Spanish class. The teacher has put students in pairs for an "information gap" activity in which the two participants sit opposite one another with a wooden barrier between them. Both have a diagram of puzzle pieces, and the task is to work together in Spanish to find out and draw what each other one has in front of him. When finished, the partners should have a representation of the same diagram.

Pete begins the activity.

Pete: Oh, un momento. El semicircula *faire*…um…no, not *faire*, that's French (general laughter)…um…el semicircula derecha de el…um …de el botóm…which way does it face? Down, right?

Richard: Arriba.

Pete: ¿Arriba?

Richard: Sí.

---

[2]The conversation in this scenario is taken from Brooks and Donato (1994), who argued for a Vygotskian approach to understanding the discourse of foreign language learners.

Pete: Oh, we're all screwed up!

Richard: Okay, hold it…um…no dere—no arriba.

What is going on in these scenarios? How might we explain the events described in terms of the learning theories discussed so far? From a behaviorist perspective, we might say that Mrs. Bell in Pet Monkey rewards correct responses with the chalk and opportunity to write on the chalkboard. Thus, Shannon is rewarded only when she acknowledges that a monkey is not a pet and so belongs in the blue circle instead of the red circle. Darren, on the other hand, is ignored by the teacher. This prompts a logical hypothesis that Mrs. Bell considers his behavior disruptive and hopes to extinguish it.

An information-processing perspective on Beginning Spanish would suggest that Pete and Richard are engaged in decoding and encoding messages about the task at hand. Pete experiences interference when he retrieves the French word *faire* from memory instead of the Spanish word he is trying to remember.

But have we now understood all the events related to learning in the two scenarios? Some researchers have argued that current theories of learning and development overlook the social and cultural context within which cognitive development and learning occur. In other words, the events in Pet Monkey and Beginning Spanish do not take place in a vacuum, and so they must be infused with expectations and patterns of interaction that are culturally based.

In Pet Monkey, for example, the teacher might be viewed as perpetuating a metaphor of teacher as authority figure. She, after all, has knowledge and power, and it is her agenda that prevails in the classroom. Children soon learn, as Shannon appears to in Pet Monkey, that there *are* right answers and it is the teacher who has them, not other students. In Beginning Spanish, Pete and Richard use English (their first language, or L1) to help them control the problem-solving task. This metatalk, once seen by second language researchers as nonrelevant task talk, plays an important role in the participants' establishing mutual goals and control over the learning task.

In this chapter, the cultural context of cognitive development and learning is examined. Of central importance is viewing education as more than curriculum and instructional strategies. Rather, one must consider the broader context in how culture shapes the mind and provides the toolkit by which individuals construct worlds and their conceptions of themselves and their powers (Bruner, 1996a). It is important to note that social and cultural factors have not been entirely ignored by the theorists discussed in other chapters.

Piaget, in particular, included social knowledge as a kind of knowledge that children acquire, and he placed great store on the actions of a child in developing all knowledge. But, Bruner and Bornstein (1989) contended,

It is our view that developmental psychology [has] been dominated for a decade or two by theories that [seek] primarily to formulate explanations of growth and development in terms of intra-individual factors: processes of accommodation and assimilation, of impulse control, of learning, of genetic predisposition, of cognitive representation, and so forth. When issues of interaction [are] treated in these theoretical accounts, it [is] usually in the spirit of taming them by showing how they [are] simply sources of variance that affect such processes as those just mentioned. (p. 1)

Interaction is therefore important to consider in its own right (Bruner & Bornstein, 1989), and it is this focus on interaction that distinguishes the theories discussed in this chapter.

The work of Jerome S. Bruner is presented first. Although his approach to cognition has changed over the years, Bruner retains a belief that a theory of development should go hand in hand with a theory of instruction. He reflected recently about his career. "I never felt I was going into education. If you didn't take into account this most powerful institution—schooling—how could you talk about cognitive development?" [conversation with Jerome Bruner, October, 2000, as cited in (Lutkehaus & Greenfield, 2003, p. 409)]. Therefore, implications of his views for instruction will be discussed as his theory of development unfolds.

In the second half of the chapter, the ideas of Lev Semenovich Vygotsky (1896–1934) are examined. There has been a resurgence of interest in the theories of Vygotsky, a Russian psychologist whose writings were originally published in the late 1920s and early 1930s. Wertsch (1985) described Vygotsky as a brilliant scholar whose interdisciplinary ideas preclude one from considering him only a psychologist. Today, these ideas provide information for theory development in both developmental and educational psychology.

Bruner: Going Beyond the Information Given

Recall from Chapter 6 that one of the hallmarks of developmental theory is the idea of an endpoint to which all children are assumed to develop. In order to explain how this endpoint is reached, developmental theory must account for the states through which children pass as they develop and the mechanisms by which transition occurs from state to state. Like the theorists discussed in the previous chapter, Bruner proposed answers to these questions.

First and foremost, the outcome of cognitive development, for Bruner, is thinking. That is, the well-developed mind, the intelligent mind, creates from experience "generic coding systems that permit one to go beyond the data to new and possibly fruitful predictions" (Bruner, 1957/1973, p. 234). Moreover, the aim of education is to make the learner "as autonomous and self-propelled a thinker" as possible (Bruner, 1961, p. 23).

Jerome Bruner

The attempt to understand both what it means to know and how one comes to know led Bruner through several phases in his early empirical and conceptual work. When Bruner was a student in psychology during the 1930s (he did his undergraduate work at Duke University and his graduate study at Harvard), "the mainstream world of psychology…was dominated by sensationalism, empiricism, objectivism, and physicalism. But…my heroes and mentors were almost to a man swimming against that mainstream" (Bruner, 1983, p. 59). He was interested in the work of Gestalt psychologists and cultural anthropologists, and cultural factors later came to play a significant role in his theory of cognitive development.

Taking together the bulk of Bruner's work reveals two major themes. The first concerns the sequence of representational systems children acquire through which they understand their worlds. The second pertains to the role of culture in the course of cognitive growth and of schooling as an instrument of culture in the "amplification of human intellectual powers" (Bruner, 1964, p. 13). Let us consider each in some detail.

Three Modes of Representation

"Children, as they grow, must acquire ways of representing the recurrent regularities in their environment" (Bruner, 1964, p. 13). This involves, according to Bruner, an interaction between basic human capabilities that have evolved over a long period of years and culturally invented technologies that serve as amplifiers of these capabilities. "Cognitive growth, then, is in a major way from the outside in as well as from the inside out" (Bruner, 1964, p. 1). Although it is almost impossible to entirely separate discussion of these two aspects of cognitive development, this section focuses on the inside out and the next section discusses the outside in.

Based on his study of human evolution, Bruner proposed three systems by which people structure their understanding of the world. In particular, he suggested that humans respond to their environment through action or patterned motor acts, through conventionalized imagery and perception, and through language and reason. These capabilities formed the basis for the modes of representation that Bruner called enactive representation, iconic representation, and symbolic representation.

Enactive representation refers to *"a mode of representing past events through appropriate motor responses"* (Bruner, 1964, p. 2). Young children, for example, may not be able to tell you directions to the store from their house, but they can take you there by way of a route previously traveled. Similarly, many adults may not be able to adequately describe or picture the layout of their office complex, but they negotiate its corridors with ease every day. Likewise, pianists have described the need to play a chord on an imaginary piano in order to know how it will sound; their fingers seem to carry the meaning of the chord. Some types of understanding, then, appear to be represented solely within our muscles.

Iconic representation enables the perceiver to *"summarize events by the selective organization of percepts and of images,* by the spatial, temporal, and qualitative structures of the perceptual field and their transformed images" (Bruner, 1964, p. 2). A child who can draw a map depicting the route from her house to the store now represents her experience and understanding of that route in an iconic mode. Likewise, a person who has experienced a fire might represent his understanding of the experience in images of red-hot flames, black smoke, and charred remains.

Finally, **symbolic representation** comes about with the acquisition of *"a symbol system [which] represents things by design features that include remoteness and arbitrariness"* (Bruner, 1964, p. 2). Language, for example, is the primary symbol system by which humans can encode and represent experience. Not only do words stand as arbitrary designates for objects, events, and ideas, they can be combined to produce "far beyond what can be done with images or acts" (Bruner, 1964, p. 2). The same is true, of course, for other symbol systems, such as the numeric codes used by mathematicians. Table 7.1 provides a summary of Bruner's three modes of representation.

The Sequence of Representational Stages. Although Bruner believed that "the usual course of intellectual development moves from enactive through iconic to symbolic representation of the world" (1966, p. 49), he is also famous for the statement that "any subject can be taught effectively in some

TABLE 7.1   *Bruner's Three Modes of Cognitive Representation*

Mode	Definition	Implication for Instruction
Enactive	Representing one's understanding through motor responses	Use manipulables and tactile instructional strategies with young children to teach concepts with which learners have no prior experience.
Iconic	Using images to represent understanding	Accompany instruction with diagrams and other strategies that appeal to the imagination.
Symbolic	Using symbol systems such as language, musical notation, and mathematical notation to represent understanding	Use familiar symbol systems when teaching new concepts in a subject with the learner already has prior experience.

intellectually honest form to any child at any stage of development" (Bruner, 1960, p. 33). How do we reconcile the two?

Stage theories like Piaget's (see Chapter 6) hold that developmental stages proceed in a fixed sequence, transitions among stages occur at certain approximate ages, and certain logical operations develop at each stage. In addition, the operations of each stage are both more complex and adaptive than those of the preceding stage. A Piagetian would consider it futile, therefore, to teach any subject requiring logical operations to a child in a stage where these operations had not yet developed.

Bruner, in contrast to Piaget, believed in the invariant sequence of stages through which children pass but not in their age dependency. He argued instead that influences from the environment play a significant role in amplifying the internal capabilities that learners possess. In other words, the fact that children acquire enactive, iconic, and symbolic modes of representation, in that order, supplies the inside out part of the developmental story. The outside in aspect of development is explained through an examination of how the environment specifically influences the acquisition of these modes. These influences are discussed more fully in the next section.

There are at least two important implications of this distinction in theory between Bruner and Piaget. First is that it redefines what is meant by readiness for learning. Whereas Piaget might speak of the cognitive readiness of the learner to understand the logical operations inherent in a subject matter, Bruner would ask whether the subject matter is ready for the learner to which it is to be taught. In other words, has the subject matter been structured so as to match the internal, cognitive structure of the learner (Lutkehaus &

Greenfield, 2003)? "Any idea can be represented honestly and usefully in the thought forms of children of school age" (Bruner, 1960, p. 33). The task, in Bruner's view, is one of translation, and the challenge is to provide problems in instruction that both fit the manner of children's thinking and tempt them into more powerful modes.

Bruner (1960) described an experienced teacher of elementary mathematics, for example, who recognized the need for presenting material to students in terms they can understand. In the words of the teacher,

> Given particular subject matter or a particular concept, it is easy to ask trivial questions or to lead the child to ask trivial questions. It is also easy to ask impossibly difficult questions. The trick is to find the medium questions that can be answered and that take you somewhere. This is the big job of teachers and textbooks. (Bruner, 1960, p. 40)

Consider how this view of readiness compares with that of Ausubel (see Chapter 4). Like Bruner, Ausubel believed that instructional materials should be appropriate for the child. But Ausubel defined appropriateness in terms of the child's prior knowledge—i.e., what she knows and how she structures that knowledge in memory—whereas Bruner considers the child's dominant mode of thinking as the basis for appropriateness. As we have seen, the two are certainly related in that more knowledge of a subject correlates with the ability to think symbolically about that subject.

Assuming an invariant sequence of developmental stages and considering learning difficulty to be a function of the interaction between child and subject matter together raise a second important implication. Might not adults, as well as children, pass through the same sequence of enactive to symbolic representation when they learn a subject for which they have no prior experience? "We know little about the conditions necessary for the growth of imagery and iconic representation," wrote Bruner (1964, p. 3). He noted, however, that adults typically require a certain amount of motoric skill and practice before they are able to develop an image representing their actions.

In other cases, as well, adults may require practice with iconic forms before they can understand and use a symbolic mode of representation. For example, in a course taught by a colleague of mine, adults were being introduced for the first time to how a computer works. They became frustrated when they experienced difficulty in comprehending what the instructor thought were simple operations. Even diagrams of a computer's functions proved difficult for the class to understand. Finally, the instructor built a board with slots representing addresses in computer memory and removable cards representing bits of information. Actually moving the cards through input, storage, and output met the students' requirement for learning—they understood through action. Whereas symbolic representation is likely to be used for learning something new in a familiar topic, then, learners of all ages may resort to enactive or iconic representation when they encounter unfamiliar material. Indeed, Bruner (1985) recognized this possibility when he called his theory a "bogus stage theory"; a true stage theory assumes a relationship between age and stage of development.

Sequence and Instruction.   The enactive through iconic to symbolic representational sequence of intellectual development implies an optimum sequence for instruction, namely, one that progresses in the same direction (Bruner, 1966). Any domain of knowledge, Bruner contended, can be represented in each of those three modes. "When the learner has a well-developed symbolic system, it may be possible to by-pass the first two stages. But one does so with the risk that the learner may not possess the imagery to fall back on when his symbolic transformations fail to achieve a goal in problem solving" (Bruner, 1966, p. 49). This seems to be precisely what occurred in the computer class described above. Although adults presumably have well-developed symbolic systems (i.e., they read and understand language, and they undoubtedly have had the rudiments of mathematics), these systems failed when the instruction was entirely symbolic in nature. Because the students also failed to have corresponding imagery to fall back on, the instructor was forced to begin instruction in the enactive mode.

To determine what mode of representation will be optimal for instruction, then, requires knowing something about the learners' prior knowledge and dominant modes of thinking. Are they capable of symbolically representing the to-be-learned material? Or should the conservative course be followed and instruction developed that follows an enactive to iconic to symbolic sequence?

A second factor should also be considered when this decision is made. Bruner (1966) argued that "optimal sequences…cannot be specified independently of the criterion in terms of which final learning is to be judged" (p. 50). In other words, whether speed of learning or transfer of learning is the desirable goal may dictate what representation modes should be included in the instruction. And these, he noted, are sometimes antithetical goals. The ability to transfer what has been learned to new situations may require considerable time to achieve and may depend upon symbolic representation. Conversely, if learning time is short, of necessity, and the to-be-learned material relatively complex, learners may only be able to achieve iconic representation of what they understand.

Let us consider two hypothetical examples. In the learning of mathematics, desirable goals frequently include that learners can apply mathematical concepts to solve a variety of problems. Transferability of knowledge is important and depends upon a true understanding of the concepts. So, for example, suppose the skill of multiplying fractions is being taught. Students are asked to solve word problems such as:

By the end of the day, Mr. Green had sold 2/3 of the onions he brought to market. He exchanges half of his remaining 1/3 for some corn from the merchant in the stall next to his. What proportion of the onions he brought to sell does he take home?

This problem can certainly be represented symbolically (i.e., $1/2 \times 1/3 = ?$; the correct answer is 1/6), and students can be taught the procedures for solving this type of problem (multiply the numerators to get the numerator of the answer, multiply the denominators to get the denominator of the answer, then reduce if necessary). However, learning the mathematical procedures does not alone guarantee students an understanding of the concept of fraction. If a computational mistake is made, students may not immediately recognize the error or be able to correct it. Suppose, for example, a student decodes the problem to mean he should divide by 1/2, instead of multiplying, and arrives at an answer of 2/3 by following the procedure invert and multiply. Without understanding that taking 1/2 of something means the result will be smaller than the original amount, he will simply not realize he has made a mistake.

Instead of teaching only mathematical procedures in a symbolic mode, Bruner would recommend that instruction include activities in the enactive and iconic modes for establishing the concept of fractions. These might take the form of games in which students act the part of grocers and customers, buying and selling portions of their wares. Actually making exchanges, such as "I'll take 3/8 of your layer cake," facilitates enactive representation. Similarly, using pie charts and other diagrams to picture fractions will serve to facilitate iconic representation. Although it is time consuming, having students solve many such problems, from enactive to symbolic modes, will ensure a deep understanding of the concept and the ability to apply it appropriately in many contexts.

Now consider an alternative situation in which speed of learning, rather than transfer, is a goal of instruction. Students in a vocational center are learning skills that will enable them to acquire jobs as automobile mechanics. Initially at least, it is more important for them to be able to successfully carry out such procedures as replace spark plugs than to understand the physics underlying what a spark plug does. In this case, then, instruction may never progress beyond the enactive or iconic modes. And the criterion for judging learning may be exclusively enactive, i.e., can the student successfully change a spark plug on an actual engine?

Finally, Bruner (1960) proposed the spiral curriculum as a strategy for translating material into children's modes of thought. It is in this proposal that we see Bruner's beliefs concerning the relations among the three representational modes. Not only can ideas be honestly represented in any mode, but also "these first representations can later be made more powerful and precise the more easily by virtue of this early learning" (Bruner, 1960, p. 33). It makes good instructional sense, then, claimed Bruner, to introduce students "at an early age to the ideas and styles that in later life make an educated man" (1960, p. 52). To accomplish this requires presenting topics consistent with children's forms of thought at an early age and then reintroducing those topics again later in a different form.

The Course of Cognitive Growth

Except to acknowledge the influence of environment on children's acquisition of the three representational systems, little has yet been said about how the transition occurs from stage to stage. In other words, what enables learners to develop the capacity for symbolic thinking when they have been thinking in iconic modes?

It is in answer to this question that we see Bruner's increasing emphasis on interaction. There is interaction between genetic predispositions and experience. Learners may be predisposed, for example, to representing their experience in iconic modes, but with appropriate medium-level questions from a tutor, be brought to a symbolic understanding of some idea. There is also interpersonal interaction; learning is a social enterprise. And there is interaction of the individual with the cultural. Indeed, culture provides the backdrop against which all forms of interaction play (Bruner & Bornstein, 1989). "The growth of intellect," then, "...moves forward in spurts as innovations are adopted. Most of the innovations are transmitted to the child in some prototypic form by agents of the culture: ways of responding, ways of looking and imaging, and most important, ways of translating what one has encountered into language" (Bruner, 1964, p. 13).

Just what interactions best transmit innovations that will promote cognitive development? Here we will see how Bruner's proposals for development are interwoven with his ideas about education and schooling.

Learning by Discovery. Bruner defined *discovery* as "all forms of obtaining knowledge for oneself by the use of one's own mind" (1961, p. 22). In essence, this is a matter of "rearranging or transforming evidence in such a way that one is enabled to go beyond the evidence so assembled to additional new insights" (1961, p. 22). Bruner believed that the process of discovery contributes significantly to intellectual development and that the heuristics of discovery can only be learned through the exercise of problem solving. That being so, he proposed discovery learning as a pedagogic strategy with such important human implications that it must be tested in schools. Before we examine the results of such testing, however, it is important to understand what Bruner had in mind when he proposed discovery learning.

A true act of discovery, Bruner contended, is not a random event. It involves an expectation of finding regularities and relationships in the environment. With this expectation, learners devise strategies for searching and finding out what the regularities and relationships are. Characterizing this searching and finding, however, should also be an attitude of construction-ism. In other words, it is not enough to seek information and generate hy-potheses without regard to constraints. Bruner (1961) described children who did this (i.e., generated random hypotheses for what information to seek) as "potshotters." Their information gathering lacked connectivity and organization and, as a result, their ability to solve problems was deficient. By contrast, those who demonstrated a connectionist approach were systematic and organized in collecting information that would help solve the problem.

What conditions, then, promote true discovery? For one thing, "dis-covery, like surprise, favors the well prepared mind" (Bruner, 1961, p. 22). In order to solve any problem, learners must determine what variables are rele-vant, what information should be sought about those variables, and, when the information is obtained, what should be done with it. In large measure, doing this easily depends on prior knowledge of a range of phenomena, or in Bruner's words, sheer "knowing the stuff"! Learners without such prior knowledge will undoubtedly face frustration and failure in a discovery learning environment.

A second, equally important, condition for discovery concerns the pro-vision of models to help guide discovery. After the publication of "The Act of Discovery" in 1961, the concept of discovery became the basis of a "school of pedagogy" by some educators. Bruner (1973a) wrote,

> As so frequently happens, the concept of discovery, originally formulated to highlight the importance of self-direction and intentionality, had become de-tached from its context and made into an end in itself. Discovery was being treated by some educators as if it were valuable in and of itself, no matter what it was a discovery of or in whose service. (p. xv)

In response to this pedagogical movement, Bruner attempted to clarify "some elements of discovery" in a convention address and later published essay. In particular, he reemphasized that discovery is not haphazard; it pro-ceeds systematically toward a model which is there all the time. "The con-stant provision of a model, the constant response to the individual's response after response, back and forth between two people, constitute 'in-vention' learning guided by an accessible model" (Bruner, 1973b, p. 70). Moreover, "Discovery teaching generally involves not so much the process of leading students to discover what is 'out there', but rather, their discover-ing what is in their own heads" (Bruner, 1973b, p. 72).

Bruner, Goodnow, and Austin (1956) proposed a concept attainment model that exemplifies this notion of discovery teaching. Concepts, in es-sence, are rules for organizing the regularities of experience, and as such, stand as models of the world to be constructed and internalized. In Bruner's view, learners acquire concepts by setting forth tentative hypotheses about the attributes that seem to define a concept and then testing specific instances against these hypotheses (Bruner et al., 1956). Discovery of a concept, then, proceeds from a systematic comparison of instances for what distinguishes examples from nonexamples. To promote concept discovery, the teacher presents the set of instances that will best help learners to develop an appropriate model of the concept.

Note the similarity between the concept attainment model and the discovery teaching demonstrated by Mrs. Bell in the scenario, Pet Monkey. In asking for examples and questioning students about those they suggest, Mrs. Bell systematically guides them toward discovery of relationships between animals (a concrete concept) and pets (an abstract concept). She herself is guided by her own mental models of the relationships she hopes they will discover. That is, some four-legged animals are pets, some pets have four legs, and some animals are neither pets nor have four legs. Specific examples also raise issues regarding category definition and who is doing the defining. Mrs. Bell obviously excludes monkeys from her concept of pet, yet people have been known to keep monkeys as pets. Instead of leading Shannon to accept her concept of pet, Mrs. Bell might better have used the opportunity to explore how concepts come to be known. For example, only through the experience of living with the 10-foot Burmese python owned by my husband did my concept of pet come to include snakes.

The provision of models is important for discovery in another aspect. By asking certain kinds of questions or by prompting certain hypotheses during problem solving, the teacher also models the conduct of inquiry. It is necessary, according to Bruner, to teach children how to cut their losses, to pose good testable guesses, to persist in seeking appropriate evidence, and to be concise. In regard to the latter, for example, he described a fifth grader who, when asked what a particular movie was about, responded with a blow-by-blow account instead of giving a synopsis of it. Similarly, Duffield (1990) observed children play a computer game designed to teach problem solving. They were to locate an animal hidden behind "magic squares" by opening one square at a time and posing hypotheses based on the information presented behind each square. Instead of posing guesses that would minimize the number of squares they opened, some children systematically opened every square until they found the animal. The twin goals of hypothesis testing and conciseness were clearly not met in this instance.

Guided practice in inquiry and sufficient prior knowledge, then, constitute minimum conditions for discovery learning to be successful. To these, Bruner later added reflection and contrast (1966, 1973b). The need for reflection occurs when children can accomplish some task but are not able to represent to themselves what they did. In other words, they may successfully solve a problem but have little clue as to why they were successful. Reflecting back on the problem and recasting what occurred in a mode of thought understood by learners may help them to figure it out, to make the knowledge their own.

Finally, contrasts that lead to cognitive conflicts can set the stage for discovery. That is, "readiness to explore contrasts provides a choice among the alternatives that might be relevant" in a discovery learning situation (Bruner, 1973b, p. 81). In science lessons, for example, surprising events can provide an effective venue for discovery. As part of a unit on space science, seventh grade science teachers conducted the following demonstration. As shown in Figure 7.1, two funnels connected together at their wide openings are placed in the middle of a sloped, triangular ramp. The ramp has been constructed of two wires such that one end is higher and wider than the other end. Students are asked to predict which direction the funnels will roll. Without question, they all indicate that the funnels will roll downhill, toward the narrow end. When the funnels instead appear to roll uphill, the students are mystified and ask to see the demonstration done several more times. To the question of whether this might be an antigravity machine, most of the students are even willing to say yes.

Eventually, they discover that they have overlooked two important factors: The incline of the funnels is greater than the slope of the ramp, and the

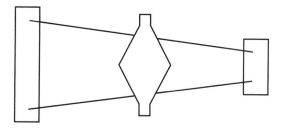

(a) A top view of the funnels as they are set upon the ramp

(b) The funnels appear to roll uphill when they sink toward the wider end of the ramp

FIGURE 7.1 *The "Anti-Gravity" Demonstration: A Surprising Event for Seventh Grade Students in Science Class*

ramp is wider at one end. Taken together, these cause the funnels to sink downward into the opening of the ramp. They in fact go downhill, but they appear to go uphill (S. Edwards and R. Driscoll, personal communication, March, 1992; Friedl, 1991, p. 169).

Bruner's recommendation for contrasts that cause cognitive conflict parallels that made by Piaget and other developmental theorists who have focused on restructuring as the major developmental process. Although they have all offered different explanations for why the strategy works, the important point is that it does and can be reliably used in instruction.

Bruner noted in 1973 that by the mid-1960s, educational pedagogy based on discovery learning seemed to have moved far from his intended course. During this time, discovery teaching came to imply providing a rich environment for learning with an accompanying freedom for learners to set their own learning agenda, and there was a surge of popularity for open, unstructured classrooms. The 1970s, however, brought criticism to this pedagogic movement, a new wave of back-to-basics adherents, and a second look at what inquiry teaching was really about.

Out of this arose a model of inquiry teaching that Collins and Stevens (1982, 1983; see also Collins, Warnock, & Passafiume, 1975; Stevens & Collins, 1980) inductively derived from their observations of effective inquiry teachers. Although no claim is made regarding this model and its relation to Bruner's discovery learning, it nevertheless represents a means by which his ideas may be systematically carried out. According to Collins and Stevens (1983), inquiry teachers pursue two basic goals. The most common is for their students to derive a particular concept, rule, or principle that the teacher has in mind. The second, no less important, is for students to derive general rules or theories, or in other words, learn the conduct of inquiry.

In their model, Collins and Stevens (1983) presented ten of what they considered to be the most important instructional strategies used by inquiry teachers in service of their goals. These strategies are thought to be useful for concept learning and problem solving in any subject matter with any age learner, and numerous and diverse examples are offered to support this claim. For the most part, the examples come from teacher-student dialogues collected by Collins and Stevens during the course of their research. However, other researchers have also conducted studies that demonstrate the effectiveness of these strategies. Moreover, it is important to note that students' more advanced peers, or a well-designed computer-based tutor, may serve in the role of inquiry teacher as effectively as an adult instructor. Listed in Table 7.2, then, are the ten strategies together with examples of how each might be implemented in instruction.

In addition to the strategies themselves, teachers must have some means for making decisions about which ones to employ and at what point in the instructional dialogue to employ them. Indeed, "the control structure that the teacher uses to allocate time between different goals and subgoals

TABLE 7.2 *Collins and Stevens's (1983) Model of Inquiry Teaching: Instructional Strategies Used by Inquiry Teachers*

Strategy	Example in Use
1. Selecting positive and negative exemplars	A teacher presents dog (example), whale (example), and shark (non-example) in a dialogue about mammals.
2. Varying cases systematically	To consider factors that influence average temperature, the teacher offers places that vary in latitude (e.g., Amazon jungle, North Dakota) but not in other factors, such as distance from the ocean.
3. Selecting counterexamples	In a discussion on birds, ostrich is suggested as a counterexample for the attribute "flying."
4. Generating hypothetical cases	To illustrate the unfairness of boys dominating the classroom computer, a teacher asks, "How about a rule that boys can use anything in class except the computer? Would you like that?" (hypothetical case)
5. Forming hypotheses	After considering places where rice is grown, the teacher asks students to suggest what factors influence rice-growing.
6. Testing hypotheses	Students have generated a rule for how sets of 3 numbers (e.g., 2–4–6) relate to one another (e.g., all even numbers, or $a + b = c$). They are asked for sets to be used to test the rule.
7. Considering alternative predictions	In criminology, students piece together evidence to determine what must have happened at a crime scene. The instructor suggests an alternate explanation that could account for the available evidence.
8. Entrapping students	Students have suggested that a critical feature of fish is that they live in water. The instructor leads them to an incorrect prediction by suggesting that a whale must be a fish.
9. Tracing consequences to a contradiction	In a math lesson, a student suggests doubling the length of a side to double the area of a square. The teacher does what the student suggests, with the result being 4 times the square's area.
10. Questioning authority	An instructor refuses to accept examples of learning theory applications that came from the students' textbooks. She asks students for their own examples, and questions, "Do these principles ever work in practice?"

may be the most crucial aspect for effective teaching" (Collins & Stevens, 1983, p. 274).

Based on their analyses, Collins and Stevens proposed four basic parts to this control structure. First is a set of strategies for systematically selecting cases that will facilitate student achievement of a particular, top-level goal. These strategies help to determine the beginning of an instructional dialogue. As it proceeds, however, teachers adjust their questioning according to their model of the student. Students continually reveal errors in reasoning or misconceptions when they respond to the teacher's questions. As teachers identify specific problems, then, they add subgoals to their instructional agenda, using a set of priority rules. Summarized in Table 7.3 are the four parts of an inquiry dialogue control structure. Figure 7.2 provides a visual representation of the strategies involved in inquiry teaching.

"By turning learning into problem solving…, teachers challenge the students more than by any other teaching method. The students come out of the experience able to attack novel problems by applying these strategies themselves" (Collins & Stevens, 1983, p. 276). Bruner could hardly have said it better.

Culture and Cognitive Growth. "What does it mean, intellectually, to grow up in one cultural milieu and not another?" (Bruner, 1973c, p. 20). Developmental theorists discussed in the previous chapter of this book might reply,

TABLE 7.3   *Collins and Stevens's (1983) Model of Inquiry Teaching: A Dialogue Control Structure*

1. Strategies for selecting cases	Select cases to illustrate more important factors before less important ones.
	Select cases to move from concrete to abstract factors.
	Select more frequent cases over less frequent ones.
2. A student model	Ask questions to reveal both what students know as well as what gaps exist in their knowledge or reasoning.
3. A teacher's agenda	Begin inquiry according to a top-level goal. Add subgoals as necessary.
4. Priority rules for adding subgoals	Correct errors before omissions.
	Correct prior steps before later steps.
	Implement shorter fixes before longer ones.
	Deal with more important factors than less important factors in correcting errors.

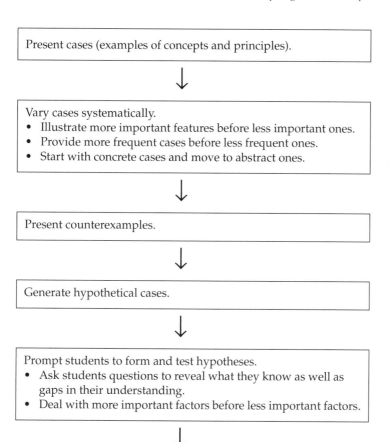

FIGURE 7.2 *Strategies for Inquiry Teaching*

"Not much." Their focus has been largely on the search for universal structures of the mind that are presumably unaffected by cultural differences. Bruner, however, found "intrinsic anticulturalism" to be a weakness of context-free approaches to cognitive development. He alluded to the Geneva dilemma (in reference to Piaget): "If the child only takes in what he is 'ready to assimilate,' why bother to teach before he is ready, and since he takes it in naturally when he is ready, why bother afterwards?" (Bruner, 1973d, pp. 153–154). The reason to bother, for Bruner, comes from understanding how culture interacts with human development and biology to define the human condition.

"Intelligence is to a great extent the internalization of 'tools' provided by a given culture" (Bruner, 1973c, p. 22). Members of different cultures, because of the specific and unique demands of living in their societies, make sense of their experiences in different ways. This is similar to the concepts as tools view promulgated by the situated learning theorists discussed in Chapter 5. But what determines the particular use or application of concepts is the cultural environment of the user.

Eskimos, for example, depend upon group cooperation to hunt seal or fish in order to subsist. Their children, as an apparent consequence, do not exhibit the egocentrism that is characteristic of American and European children (Bruner, Olver, & Greenfield, 1966). Recall that Piaget proposed egocentrism as a universal characteristic of all preoperational children, but he based this proposal on observations of mostly European and American children. Other observations of schooled versus unschooled children in a region of Africa also showed differences in cognitive development that suggested Piaget's descriptions may be "neither 'natural' nor universal" (Lutkehaus & Greenfield, 2003, p. 417). A student of Bruner's, Patricia Greenfield, found that unschooled children had no awareness of their thoughts as separate from what they were thinking about. Thus, they did not understand questions such as "Why do you *think* X is the case?" whereas they had no difficulty answering questions phrased as "Why *is* X the case?" (Greenfield, 1966, cited in Lutkehaus & Greenfield, 2003).

Cole and Bruner (1971) cited another example in which the ability to make estimates of volume or distance was compared between nonliterate rice farmers from Central Africa and Yale University sophomores. Whereas the Yale students were superior in judging distance, the rice farmers were far more accurate in estimating how much rice was contained in different sized bowls. What these results suggest, Cole and Bruner believed, is a cultural influence on the manifestation of inherent competence. Inherently, there must be no difference between the two groups in their ability to make estimates. But demands of their respective cultures have made it more likely for them to develop different manifestations of this ability.

The same argument can be seen in studies of children selling candy in northeastern Brazil (Saxe, 1990). Although all the children studied were from the same culture (in the sense of all being Brazilian), the candy sellers developed different mathematical understandings from their non-candy-selling agemates. Whereas the non-candy sellers learned standard number orthography for manipulating numbers on paper, the candy sellers developed alternative procedures linked to currency exchanges. The candy sellers' understandings were "interwoven with the mathematical and economic problems linked to the practice" of candy selling (Saxe, 1990, p. 99). As in the research discussed in Chapter 5, culture here begins to take on a broader meaning.

So what does this influence of culture mean for instruction? For one thing, Bruner sees schooling as an instrument of culture. What goes on in schools should equip students with the cognitive skills required for control and utilization of the resources of the culture (Cole & Bruner, 1971; Bruner, 1992, 1996a). This implies further that

> To instruct someone in [the] disciplines is not a matter of getting him to commit results to mind. Rather, it is to teach him to participate in the process that makes possible the establishment of knowledge. We teach a subject not to produce living libraries on that subject, but rather to get a student to think mathematically for himself, to consider matters as an historian does, to take part in the process of knowledge-getting. Knowing is a process, not a product. (Bruner, 1966, p. 72)

Moreover, children should be accepted as members and participants in the culture and provided opportunities to make and remake the culture in each generation (Bruner, 1996b). This suggests that thinking like a mathematician or historian also means working on problems relevant to the student's own particular culture.

Bruner also called for a change in the way in which competence and performance are viewed. If performance is treated only as a shallow expression of underlying competence, then achievement differences between, for example, black ghetto children and white middle class children become evidence of underlying capability differences. The black child is then seen as having a deficit in learning caused by cultural deprivation.

Instead, Bruner argued, performance differences evident in the classroom should be viewed in the context of situational differences in how the children have learned to apply their skills outside of school. Surviving in the ghetto, for example, may require verbal negotiation and a show of bravado, but these same skills may be seen by a middle class white teacher as disruptive and counterproductive to learning in the classroom. By understanding how skills are influenced by culture, however, teachers will be in a better position to capitalize on the performances students do exhibit. In other words, teaching new intellectual structures may not be required so much as getting students to transfer skills they already possess to other situations relevant to the school context (Cole & Bruner, 1971).

Cross-cultural differences also appear to manifest themselves in what Bruner refers to as two cognitive cultures—logical scientific thinking and narrative thinking. Narrative thinking is the use of story telling to affirm connections with family members, and it is often a dominant mode of interaction in immigrant families. When children of these families express their understanding using stories at school, however, they are ignored in favor of children who express themselves in the more customary and privileged logical scientific ways (Lutkehaus & Greenfield, 2003). A teacher training project called Bridging Cultures is designed to help teachers learn to value the stories of immigrant and minority children and to use them effectively in the educational process.

Summary: Toward a Theory of Instruction

As mentioned earlier, Bruner believed that theories of development and instruction should go hand in hand. Cognitive growth, in his view, is a matter of growing from the outside in as much as from the inside out. Whereas inherent biological predispositions provide direction to the inside out aspect of cognitive development, the outside in depends upon the mastering of techniques and cognitive tools passed on by agents of the learner's culture. As such, cognitive development can be facilitated and even accelerated through effective instruction. Cross-cultural studies provide evidence that "some environments 'push' cognitive growth better, earlier, and longer than others" (Bruner, 1973c, p. 50). To hold as a goal then, in Bruner's words, "an intellectually more evolved man" is ultimately a question of values.

Assuming that one's curriculum goals stem from a desire to develop self-propelled thinking in learners, Bruner suggested that an adequate theory of instruction must bring together the nature of knowledge, the nature of the knower, and the nature of the knowledge-getting process (Bruner, 1966). Interaction of the first two components influences decisions about what mode of representation should be emphasized in instruction. These decisions affect whether learning proceeds economically or whether learners experience cognitive strain.

Economy relates to how much information must be kept in mind at one time in order to achieve comprehension (Bruner, 1966). It is a function of both the content structure of the material to be learned and the preferred processing mode of the learner. Characterizing the Allied Forces' war against Iraq, for example, as a "battle over oil" is an economical means of representing the conflict. But it also overlooks many other factors that are equally important for understanding the event, such as the long history of strife in the Middle East, Iraq's invasion and occupation of Kuwait, and Saddam Hussein's aim to acquire nuclear weapons. Summarizing the conflict in a long sentence which alludes to all these factors, however, is likely to overload a learner's processing capacity, causing cognitive strain. The aim for effective instruction, therefore, is to tread the fine line between economy of representation and power of representation to convey important meanings.

An example where meaning has been sacrificed for economy can be seen in some corporate logos. In the effort to be concise, images or abbreviations are used that fail to convey appropriate or enough information about the organization for which they stand.

The knowledge-getting process dictates the types of instructional strategies that should be employed for instruction to be optimally effective. For reasons already discussed, Bruner recommended strategies that promote discovery in the exercise of problem solving. The activity of problem solving, furthermore, is influenced by the culture in which it is embedded. Because of this, instructors should foster cognitive strategies that will have the greatest likelihood of solving the particular problems faced by the culture.

An illustration of this principle might be seen in a third grade class where students are working in teams to produce instructional videos designed to teach various science concepts to their classmates (G. Stier, personal communication, October, 1992). The teams are multiculturally diverse, as is the overall class (which includes whites, blacks, Native Americans, and Hispanics). The students, with help from their teacher, have selected concepts to investigate such as air pollution (which is a significant problem in this urban area). They must research the concept/problem and then determine how their results might be conveyed most effectively through video in order for their classmates to learn what they have discovered.

To accomplish all this, the students must engage in multifaceted problem solving. They must work out differences among team members in order to work collaboratively. They must acquire research skills in order to locate and make use of information related to their topic. They must learn specific roles involved in video production. And they must decide how to illustrate what they have learned in ways to help others learn it as well. All of these are important aspects of learning within a cultural context.

Finally, Bruner spoke to the instructional issues of reinforcement and motivation (1961, 1966, 1973b). Although feedback which can be used for correction is obviously important, Bruner contended that it must be provided in a mode that is both meaningful and within the information-processing capacity of the learner. In the example above, for instance, the students can find satisfaction not only in the product of their videotapes but in how well their tapes promote learning in their classmates. Extrinsic reinforcement, on the other hand, can develop a pattern in which children look for cues to the right answer or right way of doing things. Exposing children to discovery learning can therefore promote a sense of self-reward in which students become motivated to learn because of the intrinsic pleasure of discovery.

Vygotsky: The Social Formation of Mind

"If life illustrates science, Vygotsky's own life can best be understood with reference to the very things that he came to argue were essential to understanding development: the interrelations of the individual, the interpersonal, and the cultural-historical" (Tudge & Scrimsher, 2003, p. 208). Lev S. Vygotsky was born in 1896 into a Jewish family in Russia. He attended Moscow University and graduated with a degree in law just before the start

Lev S. Vygotsky

of the Russian revolution in 1917, having studied also philosophy, linguistics, sociology, psychology, and the arts. At the end of the German occupation and after the small town in which he lived came under Soviet control, Vygotsky began a career teaching literature and psychology, founding a psychological laboratory at a regional teacher training institute.

On delivering a paper at the Second All-Russian Psychoneurological Congress in 1924, however, Vygotsky's life changed. His brilliant performance led to an invitation to join the Psychological Institute of Moscow University, where he completed a dissertation, "The Psychology of Art," in 1925. Thereafter, he helped to found an institute for studying handicapped children and became its director in 1929.

In this postrevolutionary era, there was a "zeal to create new ways of doing things, transform ideas on education, and develop a 'new' psychology that would be based on Marxist-Leninist dialectical materialism" (Tudge & Scrimsher, 2003, p. 209). Vygotsky participated in this movement and published a book about psychology in 1926 that was "the most ideology-related of his writings, seen not simply in the frequent citations of Marx, but in the apparent acceptance of the Marxist-Leninist perspective" (p. 210). Heavily influenced at first by Pavlov's ideas about reflexology and conditioning, Vygotsky moved away from these ideas in the late 1920s and began developing his cultural-historical theory. By the time he died in 1934 of tuberculosis, Vygotsky had written extensively of "pedology," or the "science of child development" (van der Veer & Valsiner, 1991, as cited in Tudge & Scrimsher, 2003). His writings were attacked on political grounds even before his death; afterward, Vygotsky's theory was banned in the Soviet Union and not published again until 1956—a wide-ranging impact on psychological theory (Cole & Scribner, 1978; Wertsch, 1985).

Bruner (1962) wrote in an introduction to Vygotsky's *Thought and Language* that "Vygotsky is an original" (p. vi). He "represents still another step forward in the growing effort to understand cognitive processes" (Bruner, 1962, of Vygotsky, p. ix). Like Bruner, Vygotsky attempted to understand the formation of intellect by focusing on its process of development. Also like Bruner, he believed that individual development could not be understood without reference to the social and cultural context within which such development is embedded. But unlike Bruner or Piaget, Vygotsky focused on the mechanisms of development to the exclusion of specific, distinguishable developmental stages. He rejected the idea that a single principle, such as Piaget's equilibration, could account for development. Instead, he suggested that development is much more complex, its very nature changing as it unfolds.

In criticizing developmental stage theories, Vygotsky (1962) wrote,

> These schemes do not take into account the reorganization of the process of development itself, by virtue of which the importance and significance of any characteristic is continually changing in the transition from one age to another. This excludes the possibility of breaking childhood down into separate epochs by using a single criterion for all ages. Child development is a very complex process which cannot be fully defined in any of its stages solely on the basis of one characteristic. (p. 115)

Bruner (1997), discussing differences in Vygotsky's and Piaget's theories, suggested that their views are probably incommensurate. He noted that the incommensurability highlights two ways human beings can make sense of their world: by means of logical necessity (Piaget) or by means of interpretive reconstruction of circumstances (Vygotsky).

So how does Vygotsky's notions about "interpretive reconstruction of circumstances" function as an explanation of intellectual development? And what implications does his theory suggest for learning and instruction? These questions provide the focus for the remainder of this chapter. Wertsch (1985; see also Wertsch & Tulviste, 1992; and Wertsch & Sohmer, 1995) described three themes which appear to form the core of Vygotsky's theoretical framework: "(1) a reliance on a genetic or developmental method; (2) the claim that higher mental processes in the individual have their origin in social processes; and (3) the claim that mental processes can be understood only if we understand the tools and signs that mediate them" (pp. 14–15). Let us begin by examining the first of these three themes. This will provide a foundation for considering the social origins of mental processes, together with the function of signs in mediating their development.

Vygotsky's Developmental Method

Vygotsky took a fundamentally different approach toward development than is typical of other developmental theorists. As we have seen in Chapter 6, most researchers interested in cognitive development assume the existence of some endpoint toward which the developmental process is aimed. They frame investigatory questions such as, "By what mechanism does a child become an adult?" or "How are the cognitive abilities of the child transformed into those of the adult?" Vygotsky, on the other hand, maintained a broader perspective. He posed research questions about the process of intellectual development "in all its phases and changes—from birth to death" (Vygotsky, 1978, p. 65). Thus, "by a developmental study of a problem, [Vygotsky meant] the disclosure of its genesis, its causal dynamic basis" (1978, p. 62).

The larger question for Vygotsky, then, had to do with how human beings came to develop higher psychological processes in the first place. A part of this question concerns how individuals, through childhood, come to possess the cognitive functions they exhibit later in life. The answers to either question, in Vygotsky's view, must emanate from a triangulation of multiple sources. He believed it important to study the natural development of cognitive skills in humans, to make cross-species comparisons, and to consider sociohistorical factors that mediate development.

The Natural Process of Development.   In order to examine the origin of intellectual skills and their changes through the course of learning and development, Vygotsky believed that experiments should be conducted which provide "maximum opportunity for the subject to engage in a variety of activities that can be observed, not just rigidly controlled" (Cole & Scribner, 1978, p. 12). To achieve this, Vygotsky employed three techniques in his experiments with children. The first involves introducing obstacles that will disrupt normal problem solving. In studying egocentric speech, for example, Vygotsky asked children who spoke different languages to complete a cooperative activity. A second technique is to provide external aids to problem solving that can be used in various ways. Under varying task conditions, children of different ages would be expected to use the materials in systematically different ways. Finally, children may be asked to solve problems that exceed their current knowledge and skills. In this way, Vygotsky sought to discover the rudimentary beginnings of new abilities (Cole & Scribner, 1978).

What all three techniques have in common is their emphasis on illuminating process, rather than product. In other words, the question of interest is not how well did the children perform, but rather, what did they do under varying task conditions? How did they seek to meet task demands? The findings from his experiments utilizing these techniques provided Vygotsky with evidence supporting a mediational view of development. By **mediation,** Vygotsky meant that "in higher forms of human behavior, *the individual* *actively modifies the stimulus situation as a part of the process of responding to it"* (Cole & Scribner, 1978, p. 14). The implications of this view will be explored shortly.

Phylogenetic Comparisons. According to Wertsch (1985), Vygotsky drew heavily from Kohler's research on insight (see Chapter 1) to propose the use of tools as a prerequisite for the evolution of human cognitive functioning. Recall that Kohler's chimpanzees were observed to use a stick as a tool to reach bananas dangled out of arm's reach. Vygotsky also believed, however, that tool invention and use, although prerequisites to human cognition, were not sufficient conditions. To account for the differences in mental functioning between humans and other animals, then, Vygotsky adopted the Marxian position that socially organized labor activity, which is founded on the use of technical tools, is the basic condition of human existence. In other words, the structure and practices of socially organized labor provide the context for how people act, and subsequently, how they think. But Vygotsky also went beyond this position to consider the emergence of speech to be equally important in distinguishing humans from other animals.

From these phylogenetic comparisons, then, Vygotsky derived a belief very similar to Bruner's, discussed earlier. That is, biological and cultural development do not occur in isolation. It is therefore important to consider social and cultural factors as they mediate the development of human intellectual capabilities.

Sociocultural History. Like Bruner, Vygotsky considered the development of intelligence to be the internalization of the tools of one's culture. But tools emerge and change as cultures develop and change. This suggested to Vygotsky that an historical perspective is as important as a cultural perspective in understanding human mental functions. As an example, witness how the concepts that we use to represent and understand the mind have changed through history. Among the tools of Aristotle's day were wax tablets, and he likened memories in the mind to impressions made in the wax on these tablets. Today, however, computers function in many aspects of our lives, and the increasing sophistication of their technology is reflected in increasingly complex computer models of the mind (see Chapter 3).

To Vygotsky, cultural and historical perspectives are almost one and the same, because different cultures can be viewed along a continuum of social evolution. For example, Wertsch (1985) wrote of research conducted by Vygotsky and a colleague in which they investigated subjects' performance on several reasoning tasks. The subjects who participated came from societies in Soviet Central Asia that differed in the degree to which they were literate. Vygotsky argued, in other words, that the literate society represented a later point in social evolution than the nonliterate society, and therefore, should have evolved higher psychological functions.

The results of the research were interesting. On a task requiring them to group familiar objects, nonliterate subjects tended to categorize on the basis of how the objects might go together in a concrete setting. So, for example, *hammer, saw, hatchet,* and *log* were thought to be related. Literate subjects, by contrast, tended to categorize objects by their relationship independent of context. Thus, *hammer, saw,* and *hatchet* were grouped as *tools* (Wertsch, 1985).

Analogous results can be seen in research reported by Lakoff (1987) concerning the categorization schemes of Dyirbal-speaking aborigines in Australia. Glance at the concepts listed in Box 7.1. How would you categorize them? Now examine the categories shown in Box 7.2. The categories of the aborigines reflect their society—what things go together in their world. Your categories, by contrast, are less likely to be context-bound and more likely to reflect abstract concepts, such as things related to romance, for example, males, females, moon, wine, figs (S. Aljabari, personal communication, November 1992). The degree to which thinking is context-bound came to represent, for Vygotsky, an important indicator of intellectual development.

In the section that follows, then, we will see how Vygotsky's developmental method led him to a theory of the social formation of mind.

The Social Origins of Higher Mental Processes

One of the important characteristics distinguishing Vygotsky's theory from the theories of other developmentalists is his premise that "individual development cannot be understood without reference to the social milieu...in which the child is embedded" (Tudge & Rogoff, 1989). Social milieu, however, is not just another variable to be explained in the equation of human development (Bruner & Bornstein, 1989). Rather, it causes a shift in how that explanation is derived. The cognitive theorists of Chapter 6, for example, focused on the individual as the unit of analysis, but Vygotsky contended that a more appropriate focus is social activity. Development "does not proceed toward socialization"; it is "the conversion of social relations into mental functions" (Vygotsky, 1981, p. 165).

BOX 7.1 • *Sociocultural Influence on Cognition*

Sort the following words into whatever categories make sense to you, and provide a label or rationale for each category.

males, females, figs, kangaroo, mean, dogs, honey, bees, the moon, cigarettes, water, sun, spear, wine, wind, fish, mud, fire, birds, rainbow.

Now compare your categories to those shown in Box 7.2.

BOX 7.2 • *Classification of Concepts Made by Aboriginal Dyirbal Speakers in Australia*

Research reported in Lakoff (1987) reveals that Dyirbal aborigines possess four basic concept classifications. They are listed below, along with the words presented in Box 7.1.

> Bayi: *males, kangaroo, the moon, rainbow, fish, spear*
> Balan: *females, dogs, birds, fire, water, sun*
> Balam: *figs, honey, wine, cigarettes*
> Bala: *meat, bees, wind, mud*

Proposed explanations for these classifications include (1) domain of experience (e.g., wine is made from fruit; water extinguishes fire); (2) myths and beliefs (e.g., rainbows are believed to be mythical men; birds are believed to be female spirits); and (3) dangerous and exceptional things are marked by special classification, that is, put in minimally contrasting category (e.g., dogs are considered to be exceptional animals and so they appear in the second class instead of with men). Consider how different these classifications are from typical Western thinking.

This perspective "highlights the *bi*directional nature of individual and context.... Neither organism nor context constitutes the unit of analysis, but rather their interaction does" (Bruner & Bornstein, 1989, p. 9). This refers again to the essentially Marxist-based dialectical nature of Vygotsky's theory (Tudge & Scrimsher, 2003, p. 216). Bruner and Bornstein go on to suggest that such a view of development is not readily grasped nor easily investigated, but is "decisive to the next step in comprehending human development" (p. 13).

From this interactional perspective, how does the child convert social relations into psychological functions? The answer lies in mediation. We already know that mediation means changing a stimulus situation in the process of responding to it. What this implies is that the conversion from the social to the psychological is not direct. Instead, it is accomplished through some kind of link—a tool, or "sign," as Vygotsky terms it. This can be understood by thinking of what is meant by tool and sign. A tool, for example, is something that can be used in the service of something else; a sign is something that stands for something else. In order to solve the problem of the bananas being out of reach, then, the chimpanzee had to change the situation by using the stick, not as a stick, but as a banana-reaching implement. It used the stick as a tool. Similarly, students learn that an economical way to solve complex word problems is to "let x stand for the unknown quantity which is to be found." They transform the problem into mathematical signs in order to find its solution.

Recall from Chapter 5 that the science of signs, or semiotics, concerns how people develop signs and systems of signs (or codes) to interpret and explain their experience. Three types of signs are possible. Indexical signs are those that bear a cause-effect relationship to the objects for which they stand. For example, smoke is a sign of fire; it is caused by fire. Likewise, the reading on a thermometer is an index of temperature, because heat causes it to rise whereas cold causes it to fall.

Iconic signs are images or pictures of the objects for which they stand. Examples of icons can be seen in many computer applications. The trash can on the Macintosh screen, for example, stands for its function; it is used for throwing out or deleting files. Finally, signs that are symbolic in nature bear an abstract relationship with the objects or events for which they stand. Language and mathematics are two examples of symbolic sign systems. (Notice the similarity between these three types of signs and the modes of cognitive representation proposed by Bruner.)

So how do children learn to use signs in the first place? Vygotsky (1978) argued that sign use arises from something that was originally not a sign operation. He gave the example of a child stretching out her hand for an object she cannot quite reach. An adult interprets the gesture as pointing and responds accordingly. Gradually, as the child apprehends the same meaning as the adult, she will deliberately use the gesture as a sign for pointing.

It is also possible to apprehend different meanings from signs than those they are intended to convey. It is unlikely that Mrs. Bell in Pet Monkey, for example, thought about what her possession and use of the chalk might come to mean for her students other than "writing on the board during an activity." Yet the gesture of holding the piece of chalk close to her chest and giving it up only when the student said the "right" answer could easily become a symbol (sign) of her authority in the classroom.

Higher mental processes are created, then, when mediation becomes increasingly internal and symbolic. Two concepts proposed by Vygotsky for understanding this process are internalization and the zone of proximal development.

Internalization.   "Any higher mental function necessarily goes through an external stage in its development because it is initially a social function" (Vygotsky, 1981, p. 162). The gesture of pointing, for example, could not have been established as a sign without the reaction of the other person. Until the adult responds, the child is simply grasping, on her own volition, for an object out of reach. With the adult's response, however, the situation has changed to one of social exchange, and it is in that exchange that the act of grasping takes on a shared meaning of pointing. When the child internalizes this meaning and subsequently uses the gesture as pointing, the interpersonal activity has been transformed into an intrapersonal one.

Vygotsky (1962) argued that internalization provides a good explanation for the egocentric speech observed by Piaget in preoperational children. In Piaget's theory, egocentric speech reflects the egocentric thought and reasoning patterns of the preoperational child. It disappears when the logical operations of the next stage are acquired. Vygotsky believed, however, that egocentric speech evolves into inner speech and denotes "a developing abstraction from sound, the child's new faculty to 'think words' instead of pronouncing them" (1962, p. 135). "From the child's own point of view," Vygotsky (1962) argued further, "egocentric speech is not yet separated from social speech" (p. 136). He conducted experiments to test this belief and concluded that when children have made the transition of isolating their own consciousness from the social world around them, their egocentric speech will be entirely subvocal and inner-directed.

Similar logic has been applied to second language learning in characterizing the role that the first language (L1) plays as the second language (L2) is being learned. Just as egocentric speech helps the child to regulate his or her thinking, so metatalk in L1 can help learners regulate and structure their responses to task demands in L2 (cf. Brooks & Donato, 1994; Donato, 1994). This can readily be seen in the scenario, Beginning Spanish, in which Pete and Richard are clearly focused on the task, which they are supposed to conduct entirely in Spanish. Because Spanish is not yet entirely internalized, however, they rely on English to help orient themselves as they attempt to solve the problem.

The Zone of Proximal Development.   Consistent with his emphasis on the process of development, Vygotsky sought to understand the beginnings of skill development. As such, he looked for a means to examine "those functions that have not yet matured but are in the process of maturation, functions that will mature tomorrow but are currently in an embryonic state. These functions could be termed the 'buds' or 'flowers' of development rather than the 'fruits' of development" (Vygotsky, 1978, p. 86). The means he discovered consisted of assigning tasks to children that went beyond their current capabilities. This technique enabled Vygotsky to reveal a gap between a child's *"actual developmental level as determined by independent problem solving"* and the higher level of *"potential development as determined through problem solving under adult guidance or in collaboration with more capable peers"* (1978, p. 86). This gap he called the **zone of proximal development** (see Figure 7.3).

Vygotsky argued that the standard way of assessing a child's mental age reveals only what abilities have developed and provides no information about what will yet develop. To illustrate, he described a hypothetical example:

> Suppose I investigate two children upon entrance into school, both of whom are ten years old chronologically and eight years old in terms of mental development. Can I say that they are the same age mentally? Of course. What does

this mean? It means that they can independently deal with tasks up to the degree of difficulty that has been standardized for the eight-year-old level. If I stop at this point, people would imagine that the subsequent course of mental development and of school learning for these children will be the same, because it depends on their intellect.... Now imagine that I do not terminate my study at this point, but only begin it. These children seem to be capable of handling problems up to an eight-year-old's level, but not beyond that. Suppose that I show them various ways of dealing with the problem. Different experimenters might employ different modes of demonstration in different cases: some might run through an entire demonstration and ask the children to repeat it, others might initiate the solution and ask the children to finish it, or offer leading questions. In short, in some way or another I propose that the children solve the problem with my assistance. Under these circumstances it turns out that the first child can deal with problems up to a twelve-year-old's level, the second up to a nine-year-old's. Now, are these children mentally the same? (Vygotsky, 1978, pp. 85–86)

According to Vygotsky (1978), "the zone of proximal development defines those functions that have not yet matured but are in the process of maturation" (p. 86). In this hypothetical example, then, the first child shows evidence of skills that will develop beyond those of which the second child will be capable.

The zone of proximal development, in separating actual development from potential development, suggests rather revolutionary implications for assessment of children's intellectual abilities. It is likely, for example, that children's learning potential is masked by standard IQ or problem-solving tests that measure only independent, or intrapsychological, performance. To test this possibility, A. Brown and her colleagues (e.g., Brown & Ferrara, 1985; Campi-

Developed capabilities	Developing capabilities	Undeveloped capabilities
	Zone of Proximal Development	
What the child can do unassisted	What the child can do with assistance	What the child cannot do yet

With appropriate instruction in the Zone of Proximal Development, the boundaries of the zone shift.

	ZPD	

FIGURE 7.3 *A Conceptualization of Vygotsky's Zone of Proximal Development*

one et al., 1984) developed a measure of interpsychological performance. Specifically, they observed the number of standardized prompts children required in order to reach a preset performance criterion on a letter sequencing task.

This index of learning potential, while correlated with IQ and grade level, provided information about students' cognitive levels that went beyond what could be explained by IQ or grade level. For instance, Brown and Ferrara (1985) reported:

> Overall, the IQ of almost 50 percent of the children did not predict learning speed and/or degree of transfer. Thus, from this wide range of "normal"-ability children (IQ range 88–150) a number of different learning profiles have emerged, including (1) slow learners, narrow transferrers, low IQ (slow); (2) fast learners, wide transferrers, high IQ (fast); (3) fast learners, narrow transferrers (context-bound); (4) slow learners, wide transferrers (reflective); and (5) fast learners, wide transferrers, low IQ (somewhat analogous to Budof's high scorers). All of these profiles are hidden when one considers only the child's initial unaided performance. (p. 293)

A second, equally important, implication of the zone of proximal development concerns the role of social interaction in determining its precise boundaries. Its lower limit is obviously fixed by the actual level of development that a child demonstrates. But what about its upper limit? This, Vygotsky believed, is set by processes of instruction that can occur in play, in formal instruction, or in work (Vygotsky, 1978; Wertsch, 1985). What is essential, regardless of the setting, is that "the child is interacting with people in his environment and in cooperation with his peers" (Vygotsky, 1978, p. 90). When we consider the nature of this interaction, we encounter Vygotsky's views on learning and instruction.

Learning, Instruction, and Development

"The only good kind of instruction is that which marches ahead of development and leads it" (Vygotsky, 1962, p. 104). "The only 'good learning' is that which is in advance of development" (Vygotsky, 1978, p. 89). From these statements, it is clear that Vygotsky viewed the processes of learning and development to be separate, in that learning is not the same thing as development, but linked, in that learning can set developmental processes in motion. The lagging behind of development from learning is what results in zones of proximal development. Moreover, "each school subject has its own specific relation to the course of child development, a relation that varies as the child goes from one stage to another" (Vygotsky, 1978, p. 91). When we also take into consideration the impact of social interaction on zones of proximal development, a rather complex picture emerges of just what "good instruction" should be. Let us examine some possibilities.

Teaching Thinking Versus Content-Specific Skills.   Vygotsky (1978) considered and rejected three views of how development and learning may interact. The first, that development is a precondition for learning, he attributed primarily to Piaget. The logical implication for instruction based on this view is that concepts or problems in any subject should not be taught until children have developed the necessary logical operations to understand them. Furthermore, since logical operations cut across subject matter areas, "instruction in certain subjects [should] develop[s] the mental faculties in general" (Vygotsky, 1962, p. 96). This is the basic idea behind instruction in formal disciplines and amounts to instruction in how to think.

The second perspective, that development is learning, is more characteristic of behaviorist and cognitive information-processing theories. In describing this view, Vygotsky wrote, "Learning is more than the acquisition of the ability to think; it is the acquisition of many specialized abilities for thinking about a variety of things" (1978, p. 83). For the design of instruction, this suggests attention to specific prerequisites within content domains. And only to the extent that content domains have skills and knowledge in common should we expect a transfer of abilities developed in one to problems in the other.

A third view merely combines the first two, and Vygotsky found it equally unsatisfactory. Instead, he proposed a more complex view of the interaction between learning and development, which Wertsch (1985) criticized as being unclear in its implications for instruction. On the one hand, learning—and therefore, instruction—precedes development and, in fact, draws it along. As such, demonstrated ability within a subject area must necessarily depend upon organized instruction within that area. On the other hand, development must also occur in part because of its own internal dynamic. How else can we explain differences among children's zones of proximal development when their learning histories are similar? How else can we account for the changing relation that Vygotsky proposed between the subject and the child during development? Unfortunately, it is not entirely clear what this means for instruction.

Perhaps we may draw a parallel between Vygotsky's views of learning and development and Bruner's. Acquiring specific prerequisite skills and knowledge within a content discipline is obviously important. But so is solving problems that require learners to go beyond their current skill and knowledge levels. As Vygotsky noted, "Learning which is oriented toward developmental levels that have already been reached is ineffective from the viewpoint of the child's overall development. It does not aim for a new stage of the developmental process but rather lags behind this process" (1978, p. 89). We may conclude from his statement that Vygotsky agrees with Bruner about the need for those "medium-level questions" in instruction, the ones that will "take you somewhere."

Vygotsky's acceptance of Marxian philosophy offers another clue to what he regarded as effective instruction. If socially organized labor activity provides the context for how people act and think, it also provides an appropriate context for learning. That is, "cognition is constituted in dialectical relations among people acting, the contexts of their activity, and the activity itself" (Lave, 1988, p. 148; cf. Leontiev, 1981). And learning involves solving problems that arise out of conflict-generating dilemmas in everyday situations. Shoppers learn certain arithmetic practices, for example, because living within a limited budget requires that they calculate the best buys. This suggests that instruction should supply similarly relevant situations in which students are called upon to resolve dilemmas. We have seen the same argument expressed in Chapter 5, and it will come up again as a driving force in constructivist learning environments (Chapter 11).

Interaction in the Zone of Proximal Development. For instruction to precede development implies that certain types of interaction will be more effective than others in the child's zone of proximal development. In other words, "children learn to use the tools and skills they practice with their social partners" (Tudge & Rogoff, 1989, p. 25). This means that the social interactions they encounter could lead to developmental delays or abnormal development as well as to normal or accelerated development. Contrast this position to Piaget's, whose theory assumes that development is unidirectional, with all normal children expected to reach the last stage at approximately the same time.

Given that the role of a child's social partner is critical to the zone of proximal development, what can be said about it? For one thing, Vygotsky's theory "requires not only a difference in level of expertise but an understanding on the part of the more advanced partner of the requirements of the less advanced child, for information presented at a level too far in advance of the child would not be helpful" (Tudge & Rogoff, 1989, p. 24). Ideal partners in an instructional enterprise, then, should not be equal in terms of their present level of knowledge and skill. The more advanced partner, whether adult or peer, will function to bring about cognitive development in the less advanced partner.

This is consistent with the notion of scaffolding, where the instructor or more advanced peer operates as a supportive tool for learners as they construct knowledge (Greenfield, 1984; Wood, Bruner, & Ross, 1976). "The scaffold, as it is known in building construction, has five characteristics: It provides a support; it functions as a tool; it extends the range of the worker; it allows the worker to accomplish a task not otherwise possible; and it is used selectively to aid the worker where needed...a scaffold would not be used, for example, when a carpenter is working five feet from the ground" (Greenfield, 1984, p. 118).

The characteristics of a scaffold define the characteristics of an ideal instructor. An instructor should neither present information in a one-sided way nor shape successive approximations to some goal behavior. Rather, an instructor should provide the guidance required for learners to bridge the gap between their current skill levels and a desired skill level. As learners become more proficient, able to complete tasks on their own that they could not initially do without assistance, the guidance can be withdrawn (Greenfield, 1984).

A second requirement of the social interaction between partners is that their relationship be one of intersubjectivity. By this, Vygotsky meant that partners must come to some degree of joint understanding about the task at hand (Wertsch, 1984). It is not enough, in other words, for the partners to simply work together or for one partner to dominate and demonstrate solutions to the other. They must co-construct the solution to a problem or share in joint decision making about the activities to be coordinated in solving the problem. It should be apparent that the requirement of intersubjectivity denotes a different relationship between social partners in instruction than is typical between a teacher and student or between a tutor and tutee. Intersubjectivity implies shared power and shared authority, where inequality between partners resides only in their respective levels of understanding.

Think back to the two scenarios with which this chapter began, Pet Monkey and Beginning Spanish, and consider the extent to which scaffolding or intersubjectivity has been established. In Pet Monkey, there are clear signs that the teacher and students are *not* partners in the instruction. She is evidently standing near the board, the children are seated, and they can come to the board only when she gives them permission by handing them her piece of chalk. By contrast, Pete and Richard are partners in the instructional enterprise by design of the teacher who instigated the activity. Between them, they must construct a shared understanding of the task and of the means to accomplish it.

Social interaction among partners during instruction (whether the partners are peers or one is an adult or teacher) has been investigated for its effect on learning, and several conclusions have resulted. First, it is useful to distinguish between the learning of skills and adopting new perspectives as the goal of instruction (Tudge & Rogoff, 1989).

In the learning of skills, adults were more effective as partners than children's peers. They tended to promote more advanced planning strategies (e.g., Radziszewska & Rogoff, 1988), provide more verbal instruction, and elicit greater participation (e.g., Ellis & Rogoff, 1982) than did the child partners. By contrast, "the child teachers appeared relatively unskilled at guiding instruction within the learner's region of sensitivity to instruction" (Ellis & Rogoff, 1982, p. 323).

In learning to consider another's perspective, however, child partners were more effective than were adult partners, provided there was a free and active exchange of ideas without one child dominating the conversation. It is likely that peer interaction may provide for a more open forum for discussing issues than is available in adult-child interaction (Tudge & Rogoff, 1989).

Finally, research findings seem to converge in support of the requirement for intersubjectivity between social partners during instruction. Advances in development occurred when partners collaborated to arrive at a solution to a problem (e.g., Forman, 1987). But interaction was less successful when one partner dominated, or when partners argued or engaged in off-task behavior (e.g., Glachan & Light, 1982; Russell, 1982).

An instructional strategy in which intersubjectivity comes together with scaffolding is reciprocal teaching. Developed for reading instruction by Palincsar and Brown (1984; see also Brown & Palincsar, 1982; Palincsar, 1986), reciprocal teaching is designed to improve comprehension of poor readers. In this program, poor readers engage in dialogue among themselves and with the teacher, during which they jointly construct meaning from whatever text they are reading. The dialogue is structured to emphasize four comprehension strategies: questioning about the main points in the passage, clarifying to resolve difficulties in understanding, summarizing to capture the gist of the text, and predicting to forecast what might happen next.

Initially, the teacher leads and sustains the discussion, modeling the four comprehension strategies. But as the instruction proceeds, the teacher transfers more and more control of the dialogue to students, who assume the role of instructor. Evaluations of this program have consistently shown significant gains in students' reading comprehension. In addition, they appear to use their newly acquired skills in reading texts in content domains, such as science and social studies.

The Role of Language and Other Sign Systems.   A consequence of internalization is the ability to use signs in increasingly elaborative ways that extend the boundaries of children's understanding. In play, for example, young children use whatever resources are available to them to "project themselves into the adult activities of their culture and rehearse their future roles and values" (John-Steiner & Souberman, 1978, p. 129). Although the tools at hand may include sophisticated, prefabricated toys, children are equally successful at creating imaginary situations with sticks and other common objects in their environment. In play, Vygotsky argued, children stretch their conceptual abilities and begin to develop a capacity for abstract thought. The signs they establish in their imaginations, in other words, can make up a very complex symbol system, which they communicate through verbal and nonverbal gestures.

The development of language, however, was thought by Vygotsky to have the greatest impact on children's acquisition of higher psychological processes. Vygotsky believed that language constitutes the most important sign-using behavior to occur during cognitive development, because it frees children from the constraints of their immediate environment. It provides for decontextualization, wherein signs (or words, in this case) become more and more removed from a concrete context (Wertsch, 1985; Wertsch & Sohmer,

1995). In learning concepts, for example, children initially associate the concept name, such as horse, with a specific animal they have encountered. With experience, however, they learn to abstract the concept from a particular concrete context and so generalize it to other situations and instances of horses.

This process of decontextualization must occur with any symbol system if it is to serve higher mental functions such as reasoning. To illustrate, Wertsch (1985) described the results of Saxe (1977, 1982), who investigated children's understanding of numeration (counting) systems. The children Saxe studied came from New Guinea and counted by employing their body parts in a particular order. Young children, he discovered, focused on the physical characteristics of the body parts, rather than their role in the counting process. Imagine, for example, counting up to four on your fingers, by starting either from the right or left of your hand. The fact that a different finger is reached would mean to the young children of this study that two different numbers must have been counted. Older children, however, were able to abstract the body part from its role in numeration and so would respond that four had been counted in each case.

Although Vygotsky did not address specific implications for instruction of language and other sign systems, other than to suggest that play is important for learning in young children (Vygotsky, 1978), other researchers have begun to pick up the slack. Lemke (1985, 1988) suggested that mastery of a subject entails mastery of its specialized language structures. In one study of a high school class in earth science, for example, Lemke (1988) illustrated how a teacher and his students, with different understandings of what light and heat mean, talked at cross-purposes. He concluded that "meaning relations, in particular, need to be frequently glossed, paraphrased, and made explicit, and students need to be explicitly alerted to the genres of paraphrase and semantic clarification, so that they can use them actively in asking questions, posing problems, and refining their mastery of the thematics of a subject" (Lemke, 1988, p. 97).

Similarly, Emihovich (1981) has demonstrated gender and race differences in discourse structure, not only in teacher-student interactions, but in student-student interactions as well. This reinforces the need for teachers to realize that children's misbehavior may simply stem from misunderstanding rather than willful disobedience. In addition, misunderstanding may be a problem of translation, or differences in language structure, rather than a problem of misconception.

Conclusion

In this chapter and the preceding one, the concept of human cognitive development has been explored as it relates to learning and instruction. In some respects, the theorists discussed in Chapter 6 represent opposing positions.

Despite an apparent common focus on interaction between children's native capabilities and their environment to explain development, Piagetian and cognitive information-processing theorists diverged in their explanatory emphases. With its proposal of age-based stages and a single developmental mechanism (equilibration), Piaget's theory is more nativistic. By contrast, information-processing theorists put more emphasis on environmental factors in development.

In this chapter, Bruner and Vygotsky might be said to offer intermediary positions, with their explicit focus on the role of interaction in development. As John-Steiner and Souberman (1978) suggested, Vygotsky "offers a model for new psychological thought and research to those who are dissatisfied with the tension between traditional behaviorists and nativists" (p. 121). Finally, perhaps recent cognitive developmentalists, and most certainly Bruner and Vygotsky, now recognize a complexity in human development that belies the sufficiency of a single model or theory of development. "The age of global claims appears to be at an end" (Bruner & Bornstein, 1989, p. 13). Instead, many theories may each provide insight into some aspect of learning and development. As we have seen throughout this book, what one theory conceals, another illuminates.

"Kermit and the Keyboard" from the Perspective of Interactional Theories of Cognitive Development

Like Piaget's theory, the interactional theories of Bruner and Vygotsky are focused on cognitive development as it relates to learning, not on learning itself per se. Because Kermit is an adult learner, we would expect these theories to have relatively little to contribute toward understanding what and how he is learning in this story. However, Bruner himself pointed out that his "bogus stage theory" did not put age limits on the modes of understanding that children develop, and I suggested in the chapter that adults might well exhibit the same progression through the three modes of understanding as they are learning subject matter that is new and unfamiliar.

Because Kermit had prior training in music, the task of learning to play the keyboard is not entirely new or unfamiliar. Reading music is a skill that is already in his repertoire, and we can see that he easily understands the music symbol system involved in being able to do this. Thus, he may be learning specific songs at the symbolic level. Enactive understanding can perhaps be seen in Kermit's trial-and-error playing, as he attempts to connect particular notes on the keyboard with the notes represented on the musical score.

Vygotsky's ideas about the interaction of an individual with his cultural milieu might be implicated in Kermit's decision to study the keyboard in the first place. After all, why not take up the instruments that he learned to play years ago? Surely, it would be easier to become proficient on those a second time than to become as well skilled on the keyboard. However, the computer is ubiquitous in the modern age, and today's computer-based keyboard is truly an incredible tool for making music. It enables the performer to sound like almost any instrument, to play with many different accompaniments, and to compose and record his or her own arrangements. The versatility of this tool is a powerful incentive because the player can sound nearly professional on simple compositions in a relatively short period of time.

Theory Matrix

Theory	Interactional Theories of Cognitive Development
Prominent Theorists	J. S. Bruner; L. S. Vygotsky
Learning Outcome(s)	Thinking, conceptual knowledge, ability to use the tools of one's culture, awareness of one's own thinking
Role of the Learner	Interact with the instructor, peers, and sociocultural environment to solve problems
Role of the Instructor	Involve learners in a process of inquiry and problem-solving
	Ask medium-level questions to provoke cognitive conflict
	Engage learners in socially organized labor activities relevant to their culture with learning partners appropriate for the desired goals of instruction.
Inputs or Preconditions to Learning	A "well-prepared mind", culturally relevant tools, and prior knowledge
Process of Development/ Learning	For Bruner, a progression through successively more sophisticated modes of thinking (enactive to iconic to symbolic)
	For Vygotsky, mediation to apprehend tools of the culture, internalization of socially-mediated understanding to become personal knowledge
	For both, learning serves to pull development along

Suggested Readings

Bruner, J. S. (1986). *Actual minds, possible worlds.* Cambridge, MA: Harvard University Press.

Bruner, J. S. (1996). *The culture of education.* Cambridge, MA: Harvard University Press.

Wertsch, J. V. (1998). *Mind as action.* New York: Oxford University Press.

Wertsch, J. V., del Rio, P., and Alvarez, A., Eds. (1995). *Sociocultural studies of mind.* New York: Cambridge University Press.

Zimmerman, B. J. & Schunk, D. H. (2003). *Educational Psychology: A century of contributions.* Mahwah, NJ: Erlbaum.

Reflective Questions and Activities

1. Consider the underlying assumptions that Bruner and Vygotsky appear to make about knowledge and its development. With what epistemological position would they most closely align? How are their assumptions similar to or different from those of Piaget or the cognitive information-processing theorists?

2. At the end of the last chapter, you took a preliminary position on which comes first, learning or development. Reflect upon your answer and decide whether your opinion has changed or remained the same. In either case, indicate why.

3. Describe an instructional program (hypothetical or actual) that makes use of Vygotsky's "zone of proximal development." What is being taught and learned? By whom? And utilizing what instructional strategies?

4. Although Bruner and Vygotsky concerned themselves with the development of knowledge among children, their ideas have been used to apply to adults. What, in your opinion, might be the most likely concepts from their theories to apply to adult learning? Why? Illustrate your answer with specific examples.

Part V: Learning and Biology

8

Biological Bases of Learning and Memory

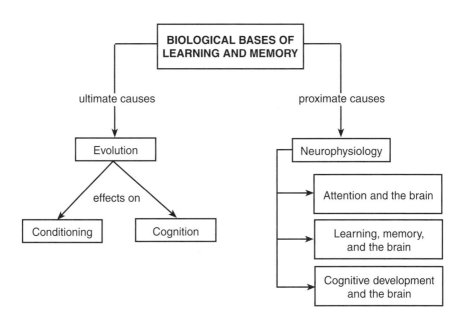

Implications of Evolution
1. Humans may be predisposed to certain fears.
2. Behaviors for which there is no predisposition to learn may be difficult to establish.
3. Previously adaptive behavior may be difficult to overcome.
4. Actions associated with decreased fitness in ancestral populations may be difficult to establish.

Implications of Neurophysiology
1. Cognitive functions are differentiated.
2. The brain is relatively plastic in nature.
3. Language may be biologically pre-programmed.
4. Learning disabilities may have a neurological basis.

Consider the following scenarios.

• *Twins*

Miriam and Mercedes, twins separated at birth, grew up in communities that were different on many counts. Miriam lived with her adoptive family in a small apartment on the east side of a large metropolitan area. She attended a nearby, crowded urban school that, except for math class, she was glad to leave upon graduating. Mercedes, by contrast, made her home in a rambling farmhouse located far from the nearest neighbors. She rose early on a daily basis to do chores before the school bus picked her up at 7 A.M. She, like her sister, excelled in math at the rural school she attended.

As adults, the twins chose engineering careers, married men named Bob, and enrolled, at the sponsorship of their respective companies, in a management training seminar, where they met for the first time.

• *Brain Damage*

Mario was about 4 years old when a severe viral infection irreparably damaged part of his brain. Doctors were unsure whether he would ever recover his speech, much less learn to any normal extent. However, within months, he had begun talking again, and by first grade, appeared to be like every other first grader in his class.

What do these scenarios have in common? On the surface, perhaps not much. But they raise similar questions about learning that have not yet been accounted for in detail by any learning theory. That is, to what extent is learning governed by biological factors? Is it just coincidence that Mercedes and Miriam excelled in the same academic subject, chose the same career, and enrolled in the same job-related training program? Can their behavior be satisfactorily explained by reference to contingencies of reinforcement in their respective learning histories? Can similar conditions be found in their environments that would account for particularly well-learned mental models in mathematics? Or is their genetic inheritance responsible to some degree for the way their lives play out?

Similarly, most of us carry an intuitive belief that the brain is somehow implicated in learning. Children with Down syndrome, for example, rarely attain the mental functioning of normal children. At the other end of the age continuum, Alzheimer's disease, associated with a severe reduction of a particular neurotransmitter in the brain cortex, can cause extensive memory loss and mental impairment. Yet Mario, in the Brain Damage scenario, appears to fully overcome the impairment caused by brain injury. (Although this scenario is fictional, it is consistent with the results of neurophysiological studies to be discussed in this chapter.) The question remains, then, What role does the brain play in learning, cognitive development, and memory retention?

Genetic inheritance and brain physiology are the focal points for two basic lines of biological research related to learning. Together with individual development and the adaptive significance of species characteristics, they correspond to the types of causes biologists seek as explanations for behavior (cf. Dewsbury, 1991). Consider, for example, the characteristic of binocular vision in humans. Depth perception can be explained in terms of the structure and placement of human eyes. Our eyes are set relatively close together in our heads, and their anatomical structure permits them to work together in creating the sensation of depth. When biologists provide such physiological explanations of phenomena, they assign proximate causes to behavior. In Mario's case, then, his return to normalcy might be attributed to proximate causes in that other parts of his brain assumed the functions of the damaged part.

Searching for environmental factors thought to influence behavior is also a matter of assigning proximate causes. So, for example, a teenage boy's preference for looking at pictures of nubile young women may be attributed to liking the pictures or to peer approval of this behavior. Both are proximate causes. In the Twins scenario, a reasonable explanation for the girls' mathematical talent might be found in their families' emphasis on and support for learning in math. These, too, would be proximate causes.

Explaining binocular vision only in terms of human anatomy and physiology, however, still leaves open the question of why humans developed the anatomical structures and processes that they have. In other words, why are our eyes set close together in our heads? Asking questions such as this are evolutionary psychologists in search of ultimate causes of human behavior. They look to evolution to provide the answers. With regard to binocular vision, for example, those ancestors who could distinguish depth were undoubtedly more successful at hunting prey and finding their way through a variety of terrains. These behaviors, in turn, proved to be adaptive in the overall struggle for survival. As a result, the genes governing close eye placement gradually dominated through a process of natural selection.

Understanding teenage boys' viewing preferences might also be enlightened by reference to ultimate causes. That is, sexual behavior in general is related to reproductive fitness in ancestral populations. In the Pleistocene environment, during which 99 percent of human evolution occurred (Cosmides, Tooby, & Barkow, 1992), the physical correlates of female nubility probably indicated a young woman of 15 to 18 years of age. Although the perception of a woman's sexual attractiveness in modern times is less dependent on age than it was in ancestral times, younger women are still likely to be seen as more sexually attractive than are older women (Symons, 1992). It stands to reason, then, that adolescent boys are attracted to pictures of nubile young women.

From two branches of biology, then, we see separate and distinct contributions to an overall understanding of the biological bases of human learning and behavior (Figure 8.1). Both are examined further in this chapter. In addition, however, the question is addressed as to what, if any, practical implications for instruction may be drawn from these two fields of study.

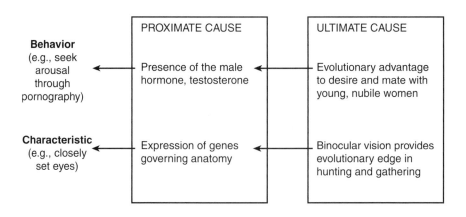

FIGURE 8.1   *Examples of Two Types of Biological Causes*

Chipman (1986) noted with concern that educators often adopt uncritically and inappropriately results from neuroscience research. She argued for more multilevel theorizing that will situate neurological interventions within an overall educational enterprise, since, "pills do not, after all, teach reading" (Chipman, 1986, p. 226). Bruer (1997) expressed a similar sentiment when he concluded that it was a bridge too far to suggest that particular educational activities will lead to specific changes in the brain. In light of these concerns, the intersection between biology and instruction is examined.

Ultimate Causes: Evolution and Behavior

It goes without saying that Charles Darwin's concept of natural selection in evolution lies at the very heart of sociobiology. The idea of evolution—that present living forms are descendents of long-extinct ancestors—had already been established prior to the publication in 1859 of Darwin's most famous work, *Origin of Species.* What Darwin contributed was a reasonable theory for how evolutionary changes come about. That is, he proposed a process of natural selection. In the struggle for existence, organisms that are perfectly adapted to their environments will survive unchanged. In conditions of less than perfect adaptation, however, those organisms that have traits enabling them to struggle more effectively than other organisms will pass on these genes to more offspring. Over many generations, some traits will be naturally selected over others, with these changes manifested in the genetic makeup and behavior of the organisms.

Evolutionary psychology rests on the assumption that the psychology of behavior is well informed by evolutionary biology. That is, "understanding the process that designed the human mind [is expected to] advance the discovery of its architecture"—neural, cognitive, and behavioral (Cosmides et al., 1992, p. 3). Evolutionary psychologists focus on evolved psychological mechanisms (Tooby & Cosmides, 1992), which are adaptations constructed by natural selection to serve some specific function associated with survival.

Two points are important to remember here. First, human history as we tend to think of it does not comprise much time from an evolutionary perspective—about one thousand years compared to the two million years humans spent as hunter-gatherers in the Pleistocene environment (Cosmides et al., 1992). As a consequence, evolved psychological mechanisms of the human mind are adapted to an ancient way of life, not to conditions present in the modern world. Indeed, evolutionary psychologists refer to today's world as an "evolutionary novel environment" and point out the risk in making inferences about evolution from observations of behavior that is adaptive in present conditions.

Second, evolutionary adaptations are both functional and specific. This means that a given structure, organ, or process was designed by selection to serve a specific function and thus solve a specific problem or natural selection pressure (Symons, 1992). There is no general function or mechanism for promoting gene survival. The goal of evolutionary psychology, then, becomes one of understanding the many domain-specific specialized functions of the mind, how these arose to solve the problems of survival, and what they might mean for human behavior.

Let us now take a closer look at some of the possible insights an evolutionary perspective might offer for theories of learning and behavior.

Evolution and Conditioning

Reflect back, for a moment, on the discussions in Chapters 1 and 2 of classical and operant conditioning. No hint was ever given that the laws of conditioning might be species-specific. Skinner, in fact, held just the opposite view. He believed strongly that learning proceeded in much the same way for all species. Whatever biological constraints could be identified (e.g., animals can hear only certain frequencies of sound and see only certain spectra of light) were assumed to be peripheral to learning.

Despite Skinner's assumption of, and belief in, general learning laws, others have not been so convinced. Students in my learning classes, for example, pose questions every semester about the limits of conditioning principles. Even before we discuss biological factors in learning, they wonder why pigeons learn to peck circles much faster than rats learn to press levers (both undergoing shaping in a Skinner box). Could the differences in performance be attributed to species-specific evolutionary differences—differences that predispose organisms to learning certain things? An evolutionary view of learning and behavior in effect integrates common notions of instinctive versus learned behavior. Some researchers have gone so far as to say that "this distinction [between learned and instinctive behavior] is completely spurious; you cannot have one without the other.... Learning itself may be the primary instinct" (Garcia, Brett, & Rusiniak, 1989, p. 200).

There is evidence now to suggest that both classical and operant conditioning are subject to biological influences. With respect to the former, results of studies on taste aversion indicate that animals are prepared to associate some conditioned stimuli with some unconditioned stimuli, but are not prepared to associate other conditioned stimuli with those unconditioned stimuli (Mowrer and Klein, 1989). Garcia and Koelling (1966) conducted the now-classic study in which this phenomenon was discovered.

In a 2 × 2 factorial design, Garcia and Koelling (1966) paired two conditioned stimuli (flavor and noise) with two unconditioned stimuli (a drug producing illness and a shock producing pain). Under the standard classical conditioning paradigm, the researchers expected the subjects (rats in this case) to avoid any conditioned stimulus that was associated with the consequences of illness or pain. What they found instead is summarized in Figure 8.2. The rats developed a strong aversion to saccharine-flavored water only when it co-incided with illness. They continued to drink it when pain was the consequence. Likewise, rats who were shocked attempted to avoid the associated noise, but rats who were sickened paid no attention to it.

Varied replications of this study (e.g., Domjon, 1980; Garcia, Clarke, & Hankins, 1973) strengthened the conclusions that rats are genetically predisposed to these associations. Upon becoming sick, the rat is likely to attribute the cause of its distress to the most recent, novel substance ingested. In other words, "It must be something I ate," but since familiar foods had not previously caused illness, that something must be the most recent, unfamiliar food. Pet owners may recognize this same phenomenon in their animals. Shortly after eating a new kind of dog food I had purchased, my dog became ill. Although a kind of viral infection was later diagnosed, he thereafter refused to eat that brand of dog food.

Clearly, developing taste aversions to foods that cause illness and avoiding external cues associated with pain are adaptive mechanisms that increase an animal's fitness for survival. Based on the same logic, associations involved in phobias may also be both selective and adaptive (Lohordo & Droungas, 1989). Snakes and spiders were dangerous to pretechnological man. As a result, we may now be predisposed to fear them.

Like classically conditioned associations, operant behaviors appear to be influenced by biological factors. Breland and Breland (1961) coined the term *instinctive drift* after witnessing a deterioration of operant behavior in trained animals over an extended period of training. As part of an advertising gimmick, they trained pigs and raccoons to deposit coins in a piggy bank. They followed typical shaping and chaining procedures, using food as the

Unconditioned Stimulus

		Drug (producing illness)	Shock (producing pain)
Conditioned Stimulus	Flavor	**Strong Association**	No Results
	Noise	No Results	**Strong Association**

FIGURE 8.2   *Results of Pairing Two Types of Conditioned Stimuli with Two Types of Unconditioned Stimuli*

Source: Modified from Garcia and Koelling (1996).

reinforcer. At first, the pigs and raccoons demonstrated flawless performance—picking up, on cue, a coin or two and depositing it in the receptacle that served as the piggy bank. With repeated trials, however, the pigs began to root at the coins. The raccoons, after initiating the procedure properly, would not release the coins into the bin, instead rubbing them together and dipping them in and out of the bin.

The Brelands hypothesized that the food reward elicited species-specific feeding patterns which ultimately interfered with the operant response being conditioned. With the notion of instinctive drift, they suggested that instinctive behaviors may eventually dominate operant behavior in many circumstances. Their results have been supported by studies investigating neural substrates of reinforcement (e.g., Vaccarino, Schiff, & Glickman, 1989). That is, significant correlations have been found between stimuli that serve as reinforcers and stimuli that elicit species-characteristic feeding patterns.

Evolution and Cognition

"Even simple organisms, such as scorpionflies and bluegill sunfish, must process information from their environment and make decisions on the basis of it if their interactions with…physical aspects of their environment are to be adaptive" (Crawford & Anderson, 1989). This suggests that human information-processing mechanisms may have evolved to reflect the types of problems faced by early humans in their ancestral environment.

As a means of studying evolutionary influences on cognition, Cosmides and her colleagues (Cosmides, 1989; Cosmides & Tooby, 1989, 1994, 1995; Tooby & Cosmides, 1989, 1992; Cosmides et al., 1992) conceptualized specialized learning mechanisms called Darwinian algorithms. Darwinian algorithms are presumed to be in the neural architecture (Crawford, 1993), and they constitute the psychological adaptations that have occurred in cognition over evolutionary time.

For example, recall from Chapter 4 the reasoning task that cognitive researchers have used to investigate context dependency in logical reasoning. Subjects are asked to reason from such rules as, "If there is a vowel on one side of the card, there should be an even number on the other side." While performance is poor on problems using the rule as stated, it improves dramatically when the rule is put into a familiar context (e.g., "If a purchase is greater than $30, the store manager's signature must be on the back of the receipt").

Schema theorists interpreted such results to support the context dependency of reasoning, but Cosmides has argued (cf. Cosmides & Tooby, 1989) that the results provide evidence of Darwinian algorithms. That is, ancestral humans must have evolved some cognitive mechanism that enabled them to rapidly and accurately detect cheaters on social contracts. This "detection of cheaters" mechanism is then assumed to account for the comparative ease with which problems can be solved using the store manager rule.

A focus on invariant cognitive mechanisms, rather than invariant behavior, highlights two important points made earlier in the chapter. First, not all behavior is assumed to be adaptive under current environmental conditions. Second, numerous, task-specific mental mechanisms are assumed to account for learning rather than a single, general mechanism. Remember from Chapter 3 that Estes (1988) has already cautioned cognitive scientists to expect their models of memory to be proved inadequate, because such models are currently based on a uniform, parallel processing computer metaphor. However, "organisms have not evolved general mechanisms for digestion; they have evolved particular devices for dealing with the particular foods encountered in their ancestral environment. Similarly, from an evolutionary perspective, the human brain/mind can be expected to comprise numerous, specific, complex mechanisms that evolved in response to ancestral environmental conditions, rather than simple, general processes of association and symbol manipulation" (Crawford & Anderson, 1989, p. 1454). By attempting to understand ancestral environmental conditions, then, we may gain clues to the nature of human cognitive mechanisms.

Evolutionary biology has also influenced theories of cognitive development, as we have seen with Piaget's theory in Chapter 6. Piaget believed that children's transitions from stage to stage in development resulted in ever more adaptive modes of thinking and reasoning. In this way, he conceived of cognitive development as a process paralleling evolutionary change. Evolutionary concepts, then, served for Piaget as a framework for understanding cognitive development.

Others have suggested that Piaget's genetic epistemology may inform evolutionary biology. For example, the reasons for organisms developing the particular forms they do cannot be attributed solely to genetic factors adapting to particular environments. Certainly that does occur, just as children develop operative schemes adapted to their environments. But children also "spontaneously create new schemes of behavior for which appropriate environments are then realized if possible" (Goodwin, 1985, p. 53). In Chapter 6, the example was given of children actively seeking conditions under which to apply some new understanding. Translated into biological terms, this suggests that "spontaneous reorganization within the hereditary constraints can occur, producing organisms with new morphologies and behavior patterns which must then either discover or create appropriate environments" (Goodwin, 1985, p. 54).

This view of evolution has been hailed as insightful but also limited. It draws attention to an overlap in developmental and biological theories in that both attempt to explain the capacity of organisms to internalize aspects of their environment. But the disregard for the impact of social structures on human development is considered a serious oversight (Scaife, 1985), a sentiment in obvious agreement with the theoretical positions of Bruner and Vygotsky that were discussed in Chapter 7.

Implications of Evolutionary Psychology for Learning and Instruction

What conclusions can we draw from sociobiology that might inform our study of learning? One, undoubtedly, is that our genetic, evolutionary heritage imposes certain constraints on learning, or determines predispositions to learn certain things in certain ways. Another, however, is that "predispositions and constraints are outcomes, not causes" (Timberlake & Lucas, 1989, p. 260). In other words, what is actually learned and exhibited depends as much on particular environmental stimuli as it does on genetic history. Let us examine these two conclusions more closely.

The role of evolutionary factors in conditioning suggests a more careful analysis of current behavior, desired behavior, and possible reinforcers in light of potential learning predispositions. For example, if humans are predisposed to fear snakes and spiders, such phobias, once acquired, may be extremely resistant to extinction (Lohordo & Droungas, 1989). A program designed to teach people to overcome their fears may therefore be ineffective if it relies solely on cognitive, informational factors (e.g., "Spiders are good because they eat other insects"). A learner might agree with such statements intellectually, but find that instinctive reactions prevail when a spider is encountered. Systematic desensitization programs, on the other hand, provide continued and increasing exposure to the feared object in such a way that instinctive reactions can be overcome.

In behavioral interventions, the type of reinforcer chosen may influence the degree to which desired behavior is learned. Breland and Breland (1961) hypothesized that their food reward elicited species-specific feeding patterns that interfered with the animals' acquisition of the desired operant behavior. It is possible that the overuse of primary reinforcers with humans would have a similar effect. Finally, behaviors that are most similar to what proved adaptive in ancestral populations are likely to be the easiest to condition (Timberlake & Lucas, 1989). Likewise, behaviors for which no predisposition to learn has developed are likely to be more difficult to establish. As an example, these might include reactions to people who are different from ourselves. In early human societies, strangers were commonly feared and excluded from participation within the group. However, today's global and multicultural society requires that different races learn to live in harmony. For this to occur, cooperative behaviors must be strengthened with sufficient practice and training to become dominant over more instinctual behaviors (Garcia, Brett, & Rusiniak, 1989).

That current environmental conditions are important to the expression of evolutionary predispositions is the primary thesis of Crawford and Anderson (1989). They argued against the notion that traits with evolutionary significance must necessarily appear in all individuals. Similarly, they argued against the idea that all current behavior must be adaptive. Instead, they suggested that evolutionary traits and ecological conditions interact to produce behavior. Moreover, environmental conditions can exert an influence either at the time a behavior is exhibited or during the individual's development.

To understand how these interactions may operate, consider the following examples described by Crawford and Anderson (1989). Three mating tactics can be observed in male scorpionflies: (1) presenting a dead insect to the female as a nuptial gift, (2) generating a salivary mass to offer as a nuptial gift, or (3) forcing copulation without a nuptial gift. Which tactic is followed depends solely on current environmental conditions, namely, how many males are competing for the limited number of females and how abundant are the insects offered as nuptial gifts. When there are few females and many males, for example, forced copulation is the observed tactic. When the numbers are reversed, however, and plenty of insects are available, the male scorpionfly is most likely to offer an insect as a nuptial gift.

Looking at the reproductive tactics of humans reveals an analogous example, except that the tactic pursued later in life appears to depend upon circumstances experienced in childhood. That is,

> The child whose father is not involved in the family is 'being prepared' for life in a society where males frequently compete for access to a number of females and do not form enduring bonds or provide much investment in their offspring. The child whose father is deeply involved in the family, on the other hand, is developing attributes enabling it to maximize its reproductive success in a society where males form long-lasting relationships with a single female and provide a high level of investment in their offspring. (Crawford & Anderson, 1989, p. 1452)

Thus, whereas genes may control the mechanisms that produce behavioral differences (e.g., three, and only these three, mating patterns are passed on through generations of scorpionflies), environmental and developmental interactions determine which behavior is learned and manifested.

Unraveling the relationship between genetic histories and environmental contingencies is no easy task, especially in humans. For obvious reasons, the study of twins, particularly those reared apart, offers the best hope. Crawford and Anderson (1989) suggested that groups of identical twin pairs be studied on the basis of known genetic differences. Moreover, they recommended a focus on behaviors closely related to reproductive function and sensitive to environmental conditions in a way that would have contributed to fitness in an ancestral population. Similarly, examination of dominance hierarchies and social organizations of groups may prove fruitful for understanding sociobiological influences (Bernhard, 1988). From a single pair of twins, then, as described in the Twins scenario, we can reach no firm conclusions about the relative impact of genetic history versus environmental conditions on learning. Yet, the striking similarities seen among twins reared apart perhaps precludes an extreme environmentalist interpretation.

Finally, it is important to realize that the human environment has changed dramatically in recent years. This leads to the possibility that previously adaptive behavior may be no longer adaptive or socially acceptable (Crawford & Anderson, 1989). Behaviors related to sexual competition among men for women, for example, probably correlated highly with reproductive fitness in ancestral populations. Today, however, they are more likely to be viewed as sexist. Similarly, behaviors that could have reduced fitness thousands of generations ago may now be culturally accepted or even desirable. The adoption of unrelated children is a possible example. In either case, such behaviors may present problems for learning. No matter what our training, we may occasionally respond negatively to situations once associated with reduced fitness. In the same way, we may find it difficult to eliminate completely ways of thinking, speaking, or acting that have been favored by natural selection in the distant past.

In schools, one impact of a rapidly changing environment has been the neglect of children's biologically based needs for belonging to and working within a group (Bernhard, 1988). Even in cooperative learning structures, individual achievement and individual accountability are stressed (Slavin, 1991). Yet, in early human societies, "effective defense against predators and the hunting of game were both necessarily cooperative ventures" (Sagan, 1977, p. 104). And "reciprocity in a foraging band [was] ensured by a variety of relationships and conventions that tie[d] individuals together and motivate[d] cooperation. No such relations or traditions exist in the school, except in the most attenuated and abstracted forms" (Bernhard, 1988, pp. 121–122).

What this view suggests for instruction, then, is a greater emphasis on cooperation in learning, which supports the views of Bruner and Vygotsky that were discussed in the previous chapter. Perhaps what a sociobiological perspective adds to the picture thus far created is an emphasis on extended experiences in groups, where students work within the same group for a long time. In that way, children must work out their social differences and develop cooperative behaviors that enable them to reach their goal. Bernhard (1988) argued for multi-age groups, as well, because mixed-age groupings occurred naturally in foraging societies and occur naturally in today's adult society. Younger children can learn much from observing and imitating their older peers, and older children gain valuable information about parenting when they interact with younger children (Bernhard, 1988).

Summarized in Table 8.1 are principles for learning that may be derived from an evolutionary perspective and their potential implications for instruction.

TABLE 8.1 *Implications of Sociobiology for Learning and Instruction*

Principle	Implication for Instruction
1. Humans may be predisposed to certain fears.	Programs designed to teach people to overcome their fears are likely to be most effective when they include systematic desensitization.
2. Behaviors for which there is no predisposition to learn (e.g., that were either not required or not adaptive for ancestral populations) may be difficult to establish.	Extensive time and practice should be built into teaching programs for these behaviors. For example, computers are an artifact of current culture, so that humans may require extensive practice to become skilled in their use.
3. Previously adaptive behavior, which is no longer useful in today's society, may be difficult to overcome.	Time and practice are again key variables for effective instruction when these behaviors are inadvertently triggered. For example, learners in cooperative learning groups may initially experience difficulty working together, because they must work out their differences and establish appropriate social bonds.
4. Actions once associated with decreased fitness in ancestral populations may be difficult to establish.	Attitude learning is at issue here, because learners must be convinced that these actions are now desirable in the context of today's society. For example, learning to work cooperatively with other races may be a matter of perceiving and valuing a common goal.

Proximate Causes: Neurophysiology of Learning

"One of the great scientific questions of our day is: How is information acquired and stored in the brain?" (Martinez & Kesner, 1991, p. xv). As in sociobiology, no easy answers to this question are forthcoming. Consider the very difficulty of the task. The human brain has some 12 billion neurons and 5000 synapses, all linked together in incredible complexity (Bower & Hilgard, 1981). Moreover, most studies of the brain are aimed at understanding what enables information storage. This means that the physiology of receptors (i.e., our sensory systems for vision, hearing, smell, taste, and feeling) and the physiology of effectors (i.e., different muscle systems) are not considered relevant to study. Even without taking these systems into account, understanding the neurobiology of the brain and its relation to memory and cognition is a formidable enterprise.

Despite the difficulties inherent in studying the brain, neuroscientists have made remarkable progress in understanding its structures and functions. From early beliefs that specific memories and cognitive functions must be located in particular regions of the brain, views about information storage have evolved to implicate brain systems regulating storage and the capacity for storage. In addition, most neuroscience evidence is used together with cognitive analyses in drawing conclusions about the brain and learning (cf. Schacter, 1992). Let us look further at how these views have evolved, as well as the evidence for prevailing views. In addition, brain systems as they relate to processes of attention, cognitive development, and knowledge representation are discussed.

An Overview of Neural Architecture Implicated in Learning

Perhaps the best way to begin is with a review of the neural architecture of learning and memory as we currently know it. Pictured in Figure 8.3 is a right side view of the human brain, showing the lobes of the cerebral cortex, the cerebellum, and part of the brain stem. The line labeled *hippocampus* points from the general location of the organ. Since it is found on the medial area (or inside) of the temporal lobe, it would not actually be seen from this view.

Which structures in the brain have been specifically implicated in learning? First, the frontal lobe appears to be associated primarily with attention, specifically, the ability to pay attention on cue. The left frontal lobe is also the site of what is known as Broca's area, which seems to be responsible for our ability to speak. The parietal lobe has been associated with the organizing aspects of attention, that is, the ability to attend to specific differences in stimulation, such as different letters in reading. The parietal lobe also

FIGURE 8.3   *A Right Side View of the Human Brain*

seems to be involved in procedural memory, or being able to carry out procedural tasks.

The hippocampus plays perhaps the largest role in learning and memory. On one hand, it appears to be involved in our ability to selectively allocate attention and orient us to sudden events which demand attention. In this role, the hippocampus appears to be aided by subcortical mechanisms, probably from the thalamus (in the brain stem structure). A second function of the hippocampus, however, seems to be as mediator of declarative learning, or knowledge of facts and concepts. It is also likely that this role involves organizing memory traces made up of cell assemblies in many areas of the brain. Finally, the left hemisphere (the unseen side of Figure 8.3) is implicated in language and analytic functions, whereas the right hemisphere (shown in Figure 8.3) is implicated in visual-spatial functions.

What is not obvious in the diagram, of course, is that each brain structure is made up of millions of neurons and thousands of synapses. Strong evidence suggests that number alone, however, cannot fully explain human intelligence (Gazzaniga, 1995). Development causes a differentiation of neurons and synaptic changes. But learning, as well, appears to result in new dendrites and many new temporary synapses (at least in the hippocampus [Rosenzweig, 1986]), some of which remain as stable modifications to the neural architecture. Finally, hormones and neurotransmitters (substances that permit communication between neurons) are certainly involved in memory formation and modulation, but their roles are far from being fully understood.

Let us now consider the evidence for how the brain is involved in learning and memory.

Cerebral Localization and the Search for the Engram

Our intuitive beliefs about the brain as the seat of memory and mind have a long and distinguished history. Early Greek philosophers, including Pythagoras and Plato, subscribed to this view. Medieval physicians, long influenced by the medical pronouncements of Galen in the second century A.D., believed that different parts of the brain were each responsible for different psychological functions. Even Descartes, the father of mind-body dualism, located memories in the brain and not the soul. With the work of Franz Joseph Gall (1758–1828), however, came extended efforts to locate mental faculties in the specific areas of the brain thought to be responsible for them.

Gall was a neuroanatomist who located more than thirty psychological functions in distinct organs of the brain. He assumed that the degree to which certain cerebral parts were developed would be manifested not only in behavior but in the form of the head. Thus, the propensity to steal, for example, corresponded with a well-developed "organ of cunning," which was apparent in a long prominence on the skull of thieves (Gall, cited in Herrnstein & Boring, 1968).

Although Gall's phrenology captured the imagination of the populace at the time, it was not held in high regard by his scientific colleagues. One of his harshest critics, an experimental physiologist named Jean Marie Flourens (1794–1867), conducted studies to prove that the brain's functions are distributed throughout rather than localized to a specific region. Flourens removed (ablated) or destroyed (lesioned) parts of animals' brains and observed the behavior changes that resulted. Instead of losing specific abilities or cognitive functions, as phrenology predicted, animals simply became more stupid overall as more of their brain was removed.

Despite Flourens's evidence for a distributionist view of brain function, scientists continued to find appealing the idea of localized centers for brain activity. In 1861, Paul Broca published the clinical findings of a patient who suffered from loss of articulate speech. After the patient's death, an autopsy of his brain revealed lesions in the left front neocortex. Broca argued that this region of the brain, subsequently known as Broca's area, must be responsible for the observed aphasia. A few years later, two German physiologists, Fritsch and Hitzig, conducted a series of studies in which they were able to produce eye movements in a patient by stimulating certain areas of the cerebral cortex (Herrnstein & Boring, 1968). Their findings, together with those of Broca, suggested that the brain does possess some specialized areas for certain functions. Whether specific memories could be traced to regions of the brain, however, was still an open question.

In the early 1900s, while still a graduate student working with John B. Watson, Karl Lashley began the search for the engram, or trace in the brain storing a particular memory. "One has the feeling that then and throughout his life, Lashley wanted to believe in localization of the memory trace, but his own results kept confounding his belief" (Donegan & Thompson, 1991, p. 8). In a series of investigations, Lashley and Franz (1917) had rats learn mazes and systematically ablated or lesioned varying amounts of their frontal cortex before or after learning. Their results forced Lashley to conclude, in his classic 1929 monograph, that memory traces are stored in the cerebral cortex but that they are not localized.

In Lashley's studies, the rats appeared to gradually lose their ability to learn or remember a maze as more and more of their brains was removed or destroyed. But loss in learning ability or memory did not occur as a function of the site of brain tissue destruction. Lashley's results, then, were consistent with those of Flourens, providing additional evidence to support a distributionist view of the brain.

If we accept the proposal that learning and memory are activities of the whole brain, then how are we to account for the findings of Broca, Fritsch, and Hitzig mentioned earlier? At least one answer can be found in the lesion approach to localization adopted by Flourens, Lashley, and others. Given the delicate and complex nature of the brain, it is likely that the destruction of one part will have widespread effects, not confined to a single memory. "It is, in the words of Pavlov, as if one struck a delicate machine with a sledge hammer and then studied the results" (Brogden & Gantt, 1942; cited in Donegan & Thompson, 1991, p. 9).

More modern approaches to localization now include electrical stimulation to parts of the brain, as well as intracranial injections of drugs to block or activate particular neurotransmitter-receptor systems. Although these techniques are admittedly less invasive than removal or destruction of brain tissue, they, too, typically affect more than a single cell or anatomical location in the brain. As a result, for progress to be made in understanding the neural substrates of learning and memory, the problem of localization had to be conceptualized with alternate assumptions. Donald Hebb, a former student of Lashley's, provided the insight when he proposed the concept of cell assembly (Donegan & Thompson, 1991).

According to Hebb, memories are not represented by a single neuron, but by a network of neurons—the cell assembly—in the cerebral cortex. Moreover, these neurons are thought to be distributed and able to participate in more than one memory. This means that a given memory is localized in the sense of it being represented by a particular cell assembly, but it cannot be anatomically located since the neurons making up the assembly are distributed throughout the cortex. Notice the similarity between the cell assembly and the model of memory proposed by the parallel distributed processing theorists (see Chapter 3). They, too, argued that networks of sub-symbolic units participated in processing and memory. Hebb's theory not only had the effect of renewing interest on the part of researchers in analyzing neurological substrates of learning and memory in the brain, but also demonstrated that understanding how memories are represented in the brain is no easy or simple matter.

Hebb's concept of the cell assembly remains "the best currently accepted idea about how information is stored in the nervous system" (White & Salinas, 1998). However, questions about localization of memory have changed, to the point where researchers are even questioning the value of attempting to correlate structure with function in the brain (Sarter, Berntson, & Cacioppo, 1996).

In the past few years, advances in the technology of brain imaging have offered researchers an entirely noninvasive means of studying cognitive processing. In most imaging studies, subjects are presented two tasks that are presumed to differ only in the cognitive operations they require. The brain images from the control task are subtracted from those of the experimental task, and the resulting image is assumed to reflect the portion of the brain that was uniquely stimulated by the experimental task. According to Sarter et al. (1996), "Imaging studies have become a major force in national neuroscience policy and have emerged as a basis for the definition of programmatic research goals" (p. 14) despite "the [questionable] manner in which many inferences are drawn about the cognitive significance of localized brain activity" (p. 17). They provided analyses illustrating that areas activated in a brain image may or may not contribute meaningfully to a cognitive process. Likewise, they argued that a brain area should not be excluded as potentially relevant simply because it was not activated in a brain image.

It appears that complex and distributed systems of neurons are implicated in learning, with some systems centrally involved with the development and representation of a memory trace and others peripherally involved in the expression of a learned behavior (cf. Donegan & Thompson, 1991). Questions that remain to be answered concern just what neuronal systems change with certain types of learning and by what mechanisms they change. These are general questions that can now be examined more closely in the context of learning processes that concern educators.

Attention and the Brain

Cognitive researchers have long recognized the importance of attention in learning. For information to be processed for permanent storage in memory, it must first be noticed. Moreover, learners selectively attend to certain aspects of stimulation that pertain to their learning goals, that are novel and require additional processing resources, or that are distinctive and unconsciously attract notice. Finally, skills that are well learned and practiced typically require less attention of learners, freeing them to allocate attentional capacity to related, higher-level tasks. In reading, for example, decoding of letters and words is more or less automatic as learners concentrate their attention on comprehending the meaning of what is read. (See Chapter 3 for an extended discussion of attention.)

Given the importance of attention, what unique contributions may a neurological perspective offer to our overall understanding of the phenomenon? What brain systems underlie attention? What investigations of these systems have been conducted and to what new insights have the investigations led? Many different aspects of attention have been studied, and myriad results make difficult any theoretical synthesis. Moreover, many scholars include attention as one of many mechanisms to be accounted for in a systems view of memory (e.g., Johnson & Chalfonte, 1994). Nonetheless, they do agree that attention, however investigated or conceptualized, involves selectivity.

Characterizing attention as a state, a resource, or a process provides a useful framework for discussing and evaluating results of studies on attention. All three concepts involve selectivity. Attention as a state occurs when a learner maintains an attitude of expectation, alert to information and heedless of distractions. This is characteristic of learners who are interested in what they study. By contrast, learners who are bored or suffer from an attention deficit disorder are easily distracted from a learning task.

Attention as a resource refers to a learner's capability of selectively allocating more attention to one of several simultaneously occurring events. Although this is often done quite unconsciously, as in driving a car while attending to a program on the radio, it may also occur quite deliberately, as in listening to one conversation at a party while ignoring all others.

Finally, attention as a process involves selecting particular information for further analysis and interpretation over other, available information. For example, a high school clarinetist who attends a local symphony performance is likely to selectively process the overall sound of the orchestra for the specific notes of the clarinet. More than the average person, the clarinetist may hear any sour notes this section of the orchestra plays during the performance.

These three aspects of selective attention have been investigated for their neurological substrates in the brain. Studies have typically focused on identifying what parts of the brain and what mechanisms within the brain are responsible for attention. In some studies, the effects of lesions are investigated. In others, electrical signals from the brain, as well as eye movements, are recorded and monitored as attention is systematically varied. Let us now look at the specific evidence related to the state, resource, and process aspects of attention.

Controlling Attentional States.   The ability to sustain attention and adapt attention to changing task demands has been extensively studied in patients with varying degrees of brain damage. Lack of attentional control and inattention have been observed frequently among patients with frontal lobe damage (Picton, Stuss, & Marshall, 1986). In one case, for example, a man with damage to the left frontal lobe had difficulty concentrating on various counting tasks. He was able to count by 3s, but "on subtracting serial 7s, which was completed after counting by 3s, he was unable to stop himself from subtracting (correctly) by 3s. He verbalized that he should subtract by 7s, and yet said, 'Here I go with 3s again'" (Picton et al., 1986, p. 24). This patient simply could not control his attention when multiple tasks required a shift in attention from one task to another.

The syndrome of inattention refers to the failure of a patient to respond to stimuli when such stimuli are presented on the side opposite a cerebral lesion. Thus, individuals fail to attend at all to a task rather than experience difficulty controlling their attention between tasks. This apparently occurs most often with lesions in the right parietal lobe, but has also been reported with lesions to the frontal lobe and elsewhere (Damasio, Damasio, & Chang Chui, 1980; Picton et al., 1986). Recent evidence continues to support the dominance of the right hemisphere in maintaining alertness (e.g., Ladavas et al., 1994).

Two attentional disorders for which no specific pathological findings have been identified are schizophrenia and hyperactivity. In both disorders, behavioral symptoms resemble those of patients with frontal lobe damage, causing researchers to speculate that the frontal lobe is in some way involved. One reasonable hypothesis is that, for hyperactive children, maturation of the frontal lobe has been delayed (Stamm & Kreder, 1979). Equally probable, however, is the possibility that attention problems in hyperactive children and schizophrenics are caused by disruptions in catecholamine metabolism.

Catecholamines are neurotransmitters, substances that influence or modulate the electrical activity of neurons. Increased or decreased levels of the cerebral catecholamines appear to result in attentional disorders. In hyperactivity, a depletion of catecholamines is assumed, because the attention deficit symptoms can be successfully treated with amphetamines or amphetamine-like drugs, which increase the release of catecholamines (cf. Margolin, 1978). Take note, however, that people whose catecholamine levels are normal should experience increased attentional problems with administration of amphetamines, because of abnormally increased catecholamine levels. Similarly, an excess of catecholamines in schizophrenics is assumed, because drugs that block the reception of catecholamines by cerebral neurons are effectively used for treatment (Carlsson, 1978).

Unfortunately, not enough is known about the long-term effects of drug treatments to reach firm conclusions about the role of catecholamines in attention. "The prolonged changes in transmitter concentration brought about by chronic drug administration may alter the sensitivity of the receptors and the metabolism of the transmitter" (Picton et al., 1986, p. 38). In other words, over time drugs may significantly change brain metabolism in ways that we cannot yet predict. It is for this reason that other means besides drugs are often chosen in the treatment of hyperactive children.

Finally, results of studies using electroencephalograms to record electrical activity in the brain support the general conclusion that both the frontal lobe and cerebral catecholamines are involved in controlling attention. In typical electroencephalographic studies, brain waves are recorded over a period of time in which subjects selectively attend to different stimuli. One measure of attention is the difference in wave amplitude between what is evoked by a stimulus when it is ignored and when it is attended to. This has been termed *processing negativity* (Hansen & Hillyard, 1980).

When the brain wave patterns of patients with frontal lobe damage are compared with those of normal subjects for selective attention tasks, their processing negativities are smaller. The same is true for children with hyperactivity, who also show a decreased amplitude of a particular wave known as P3. Drug treatment has been shown to increase the P3 amplitude in hyperactive children, as well as their processing negativities (Picton et al., 1986). From these results, then, it seems likely that the frontal lobe and cerebral neurotransmitters play a critical role in an individual's ability to control his or her attentional state.

Selectively Allocating Attentional Resources. Attention as a matter of allocating resources obviously depends upon the concept of capacity. As we have seen from Chapter 3, conceiving of attention in terms of capacity is perhaps the predominant approach currently taken by cognitive theorists. But there is support for this conception from the biological perspective as well. On the one hand, our apparently limited capacity for attention may be viewed as an evolutionary adaptation (Simon, 1986). That is, without some kind of limitation, we would be disposed to processing so many irrelevancies from the wealth of stimulation surrounding us that goal-directed behavior might be impossible. This was the case for a Russian man whose photographic memory produced a flood of remembrances with every interaction, rendering him incapable of living a normal life (Heminway & Tegriti, 1984).

On the other hand, discovering just what biological mechanisms govern attentional limitations may assist us in determining how to make the most of the capacity we have. Until recently, it has been difficult to separate attentional capacity from processing strategy, because both influence overall processing efficiency (Gazzaniga, 1984). However, neurological evidence now points to a subcortical mechanism governing the allocation of attention, rather than the cortical mechanisms already implicated in the control of attentional states.

In one study, Holtzman and Gazzaniga (cited in Gazzaniga, 1984) presented subjects with 3 × 3 matrices and the task to detect the location of several *x*s. These matrices, sometimes the same and sometimes different, were simultaneously presented to both sides of the visual field while subjects fixated on a point between them. Subjects with normal brains could not do the task, but patients whose brains were hemispherically disconnected could do it easily, in effect processing more stimuli at once than is possible for a normal person. Normal brains, then, are limited in attentional capacity that can be allocated to processing stimuli.

Additional studies revealed interactions between the hemispheres in attentional allocation, which suggests a subcortical rather than cortical mechanism at work. That is, if attentional resources are allocated cortically, the hemispheres should operate independently of one another. What Holtzman and Gazzaniga (1982) found, however, was that working on a hard problem in one hemisphere diminished the attention by the other hemisphere on a concurrent task. Similarly, subjects with separated hemispheres could scan bilateral arrays twice as fast as unilateral arrays, indicating that the hemispheres scanned independently. Normal subjects, on the other hand, performed the same on both arrays, indicating that the intact corpus callosum was responsible for maintaining a focused attention (Luck et al., 1994; see also Kingstone et al., 1995).

Finally, there is evidence that cortical processes, in particular the hippocampus, also influence attention allocation. Animals with hippocampal lesions fail to orient as quickly to novel stimuli introduced into their environments. The orienting response is thought to be a critical means of adapting to the environment, because it enables an organism to suppress ongoing behavioral activity in order to respond to a sudden change in real-time requirements. As Simon (1986) put it, "Because bricks do fly through the air sometimes, it is good to be able to notice and dodge a brick even if you are not scanning the horizon for missiles when it comes flying" (p. 106).

Selectively Organizing Attention.   When learners not only allocate attentional resources to a particular task, but also then direct those resources to selectively process certain information, they are organizing their attention. This is an important concept for learning, because readers must attend to differences among letters to competently decode words. Orchestral performers must attend to differences among sounds to be sure they are playing in tune. Wine tasters must attend to subtle differences in flavor and bouquet to rate quality of wines. Attentional differences of this sort have been studied primarily in terms of evoked potentials in human brain wave activity, eye movements, and a variety of cognitive measures (such as response times to pattern-recognition tasks).

To begin with, promising results have emerged from studies evaluating event-related potentials of children with learning disabilities. Typically, certain types of learning problems, which relate in some way to attention patterns, are diagnosed in children through behavioral techniques. Dyslexic children, for example, may experience difficulty attending differentially to similar letters, such as *b* and *d*. The brain wave patterns of these children are then compared with those of normal children to discover systematic differences that might distinguish between the two groups (cf. Duffy, Burchfiel, & Lombroso, 1979). In addition, children with diagnosed differences in learning abilities may be given specific cognitive tasks and their brain patterns observed while they complete the tasks.

Brain activity mapping has been shown to discriminate between normal and dyslexic children (Duffy, Denckla, Bartels, & Sandini, 1980; Duffy, Denckla, Bartels, Sandini, & Kiessling, 1980; Torello & Duffy, 1985), and among gifted learning disabled, gifted normal, normally achieving, and learning disabled students (Languis, Bireley, & Williamson, 1990; Languis, Miller, & Bertolone, 1990). In the latter study, gifted learning disabled learners were defined as those who score very high on measures of intelligence, such as the Wechsler Intelligence Scale for Children, Revised (WISC-R), but who display a discrepancy between their verbal and performance IQ subscores. In general, gifted children demonstrated greater overall activity in brain patterns than their nongifted counterparts, but the gifted learning disabled students also showed some of the same specific patterns as nongifted learning disabled students.

Despite the apparent success of brain mapping in detecting neurological differences between learning disabled and normal children, caution is recommended in the use and interpretation of the technique (cf. Picton et al., 1986). Although the brain patterns of dyslexic children, for example, may indicate abnormalities in the area of the brain important for speech and language, they may also be symptomatic of boredom or drowsiness. Overall, the results of brain mapping studies can be very difficult to interpret. Sometimes, anomalous patterns appear on electroencephalograms that have no clinical significance. Additionally, similar brain patterns may be observed among individuals that cannot be interpreted along a meaningful dimension. In spite of these difficulties, researchers are hopeful that brain patterns may prove useful both in diagnosing learning problems and in finding appropriate interventions for those problems.

Along with brain mapping, researchers have used eye movements to study the organization of attention. This work stems from a basic assumption that orienting of attention plays a critical role in visual processing. It seems obvious that items are more likely to be recognized and processed appropriately within the focus of attention than outside it. Moreover, this focus is extremely limited because only the fovea is capable of detailed pattern vision. In reading, for example, learners can perceive about ten items to the right and three to four items to the left of their fixation point (Rayner, Well, & Pollatsek, 1980). Thus, eye movements represent an important indicator of attentional orienting and subsequent processing.

There is also evidence, however, that a covert attentional mechanism, linked to neural systems in the parietal lobe, operates independently of the eye movement system. Posner and Friedrich (1986) described a study by Chang (1981) that most clearly illustrates this mechanism. Chang presented stories in such a way that subjects could read the words while maintaining a point of fixation. This procedure should eliminate any right-left asymmetry in reading if such asymmetry is a function of the eye-movement system. Chang found instead that bias in the visual field remained, and it reflected the internal scan of the words. That is, when words were presented normally, subjects had a larger visual field to the right of fixation. When words were presented upside down, subjects had a larger visual field to the left of fixation. Posner and Friedrich (1986) took these results to mean that attention was covertly driven by some internal semantic operation.

The influence of semantic codes on attention has also been documented by so-called priming studies. When learners are presented with a word from a particular category, their recognition of other words from the same category is facilitated. This effect occurs regardless of the modalities in which the words are presented. That is, both spoken and written words facilitated subjects' recognition of other spoken or written words. Posner and his colleagues contend, therefore, that learners represent meaning in a single semantic code which can be accessed through different sensory pathways (cf. Posner, 1984; Posner & Friedrich, 1986; Sen & Posner, 1979). Assuming this to be true, an important question arises. That is, to what extent do specific intentional strategies influence the ability to shift attention from one kind of code to another in order to accomplish a specific task?

It appears that learners commonly shift attention among different sensory codes, depending upon the nature of the task in which they are engaged, as well as their own abilities and preferences. Beginning spellers, for example, typically rely on phonological codes whereas beginning readers make use of mostly visual codes. With experience, able learners become efficient in coordinating information from several codes and flexible in shifting attention among codes to suit task demands. It is also true, however, that some learners prefer particular codes and may rely on one kind of information when they might better focus on an alternate kind. Good proofreading, for example, probably depends on the ability to isolate and use visual information, to the exclusion of phonological information.

So what should we make of this evidence regarding the organization of attention? As with other aspects of attention, the cerebral cortex is implicated as the neurological basis, but precisely what systems operate and how they operate in attentional organization are not yet fully known. Simon (1986) noted that Posner's discovery of covert attention should call into question the use of eye movements as a primary indicator of attention. Posner (and Friedrich, 1986) suggested that it is too early to make firm prescriptions for instruction from the current neurological evidence on attention. Employing multiple codes during instruction is likely to facilitate learning. But it is not yet clear whether curricula should emphasize one type of code over another or attempt to match learner coding preferences to materials relying upon those preferences. A third alternative is to provide learners with experiences in many types of codes in order to develop their skills in nonpreferred modes. This latter suggestion is consistent with implications of dual-code theory as well as educational semiotics (see Chapters 3 and 5).

The fact that attention is not a unitary construct offers an additional implication for instruction. One should probably not assume that a particular instructional technique "commands students' attention" and is therefore sufficient to assure learning (Schunk, 2004). Rather, it is likely that multiple techniques are necessary to alert learners, help them allocate their attention appropriately during learning, and focus their attention on relevant aspects of the task so as to optimize processing.

Learning, Memory, and the Brain

In the search for the engram, early biological researchers primarily examined one aspect of learning and memory, namely, information storage. To some degree, these researchers also tackled the twofold question of how memories are acquired in the first place and how acquired knowledge is used. Donegan and Thompson (1991), for example, suggested two separate systems as responsible for one, acquisition and storage, and two, performance (or use). More recently, interest in multiple memory systems has expanded rapidly, with a "growing number of cognitive and behavioral neuroscientists [advancing] increasingly detailed hypotheses concerning the nature of and relations among different memory systems" (Schacter & Tulving, 1994).

Efforts to understand the biology of learning and memory have proceeded simultaneously on many fronts, from studies with invertebrate animals to studies with both normal and brain-damaged humans (Martinez & Kesner, 1998). Various approaches to the problem have also been undertaken, including cognitive, neuropsychological, neurobiological, and computational (Schacter & Tulving, 1994). It is an exciting time for researchers in this field, and only an overview of current developments can be presented here. The nature and variety of memory systems that have been proposed is considered first. Then, because "language is a paradigm case for understanding how humans represent, acquire, and use a complex cognitive system" (Gleitman, 1986, p. 119), the biological substrates of language acquisition are discussed.

Types of Memory Systems. The impetus for distinguishing types of memory came initially from attempts to explain global anterograde amnesia (Mishkin, Malamut, & Bachevalier, 1984). With this type of amnesia, patients suffer memory loss but can retain new experiences of a certain type. They can, for instance, acquire the skills necessary to trace mirror images of words but then cannot later recall what the words were that they traced. Characterizing the lost versus spared abilities of these patients, researchers have used the labels "recognition versus associative memory...episodic versus semantic memory ...working versus reference memory...vertical versus horizontal associative memory...declarative versus procedural knowledge...elaborative versus integrative processing..., and automatic versus effortful encoding" (Mishkin et al., 1984, p. 65).

The plethora of concepts proposed to distinguish a multiple-memory-systems view from a unitary-memory view led to enough confusion in the literature that Schacter and Tulving (1994) proposed criteria for defining memory systems. They wrote, "Memory systems are not forms of memory or memory processes or memory tasks or expressions of memory" (p. 11). Rather, "a memory system is defined in terms of its brain mechanisms, the kind of information it processes, and the principles of its operation" (p. 13).

Reviewing current research on human learning and memory also led Schacter and Tulving to suggest a classification of memory systems, depicted in Table 8.2. (Note the similarities in this classification with the types of memory proposed and investigated by cognitive information-processing researchers in Chapter 3.) Subsystems may also be distinguished from systems by the different kinds of information they are presumed to process. For

TABLE 8.2 *Major Systems of Human Learning and Memory*

System	Other Terms	Subsystems	Retrieval
Procedural	Nondeclarative	Motor skills Cognitive skills Simple conditioning Simple associative learning	Implicit
Perceptual representation (PRS)	Nondeclarative	Visual word form Auditory word form Structural description	Implicit
Semantic	Generic Factual Knowledge	Spatial Relational	Implicit
Primary	Working	Visual Auditory	Explicit
Episodic	Personal Autobiographical Event memory		Explicit

Source: From "What are the memory systems of 1994?" by D. L. Schacter & E. Tulving. In D. L. Schacter & E. Tulving (Eds.), *Memory Systems 1994,* Cambridge, MA: MIT Press, 1994.

example, procedural memory has been characterized as a performance system, and it is thought to be involved in learning both motor skills and cognitive skills (its subsystems).

The argument for a nondeclarative procedural system comes from studies conducted with amnesic patients, of which perhaps the most well known and extensively studied is H.M. In 1953, at the age of 27, H.M. underwent an operation to relieve epileptic seizures that had become uncontrollable. Although the operation successfully eliminated the seizures, it also unfortunately caused total anterograde amnesia. Thus, although his short-term memory is intact, H.M. can form no new memories (Squire, 1987).

What is interesting about H.M.'s abilities is that he, like other amnesiacs, could perform the mirror drawing task but never remember that he had done it or what the words were. Moreover, he was able to acquire the skills necessary to solve the Tower of Hanoi puzzle (Figure 8.4), but he could not remember any specific facts or experiences related to his performance.

H.M. displays impairment in declarative or cognitively oriented memory systems while his procedural system remains intact (Cohen & Squire, 1981; Cohen, 1984; Squire, 1983, 1986, 1994). It logically follows that the kind of brain damage sustained in amnesiacs—namely, to the medial temporal lobe—must mediate declarative but not procedural memory. Interestingly, research conducted with monkeys demonstrated the same sort of

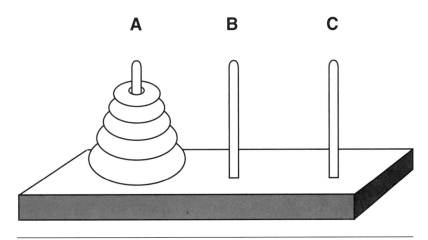

FIGURE 8.4 *The Tower of Hanoi Puzzle. The goal is to transfer the rings from A to C without ever placing a larger ring on top of a smaller ring.*

performance pattern as observed in amnesic humans (e.g., Mishkin & Petri, 1984), providing additional evidence for the existence of a procedural memory system.

The other memory systems included in Table 8.2 relate to cognitive representation and storage, with working memory distinctive in the brevity with which it is able to retain information. Evidence of these systems comes from a variety of sources, and the neuroanatomical basis for some distinctions is still uncertain (Schacter & Tulving, 1994). Based upon their review of current findings, Squire and Knowlton (1995) proposed a taxonomy of memory systems that is shown in Figure 8.5. You can see that they distinguish primarily between declarative and nondeclarative systems but include most of the same subsystems as Schacter and Tulving (1994). Is one scheme more right than the other? Only time will tell. As Kesner (1998) put it, "Even though there are many similarities among the different neurobiological views of memory in terms of the proposed memory systems, there are important differences that should stimulate the development of new paradigms and further experimentation" (p. 405). It seems clear at least that the entire brain participates in learning and memory, but different brain systems contribute in different ways (Gershberg & Shimamura, 1998).

A Biological Basis for Language Learning. One approach to the neurophysiology of learning, as we have seen, is to study the capabilities of brain-damaged individuals, whether humans or other animals. The nature and location of the physical damage are then related to the types of impairments observed. Another approach, however, is to study a human capability that has an obvious and unquestioned biological component to it. Language

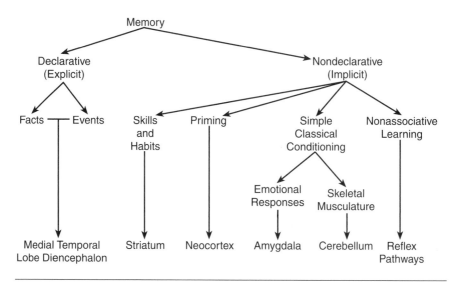

FIGURE 8.5   *A Taxonomy of Memory and Associated Brain Structures*

Source: From "Memory, hippocampus, and brain systems" by L. R. Squire and B. J. Knowlton. In M. S. Gazzaniga (Ed.), *The Cognitive Neurosciences 1995,* Cambridge, MA: MIT Press, 1994.

provides such a test case, because "to believe that special biological adaptations are a requirement, it is enough to notice that all children but none of the dogs and cats in the house acquire language" (Gleitman, 1986, p. 119).

The idea that language may be innate is not a new one. Leahey and Harris (1997) observed that Descartes assigned a special role to language as a vehicle for the expression of thought. In more modern times, however, Noam Chomsky (1965, 1972) has been largely responsible for promoting the view that language is an evolved, species-specific organ. Recall from Chapter 2 that behaviorists attempted to explain language as just another complex behavior, acquired through processes of operant conditioning. Chomsky was extremely critical of the behaviorist position and argued convincingly for a universal language faculty in humans. At the same time, Eric Lenneberg (1964, 1967) articulated a biological view of language acquisition. He pointed to clinical evidence that language functions are located in the left hemisphere, that language can neither be suppressed (e.g., deaf children will spontaneously invent sign language in the absence of verbal capabilities) nor language learning speeded up, and that certain forms of speech disorders are inheritable.

In the traditions of Chomsky and Lenneberg, Gleitman (1986) proffered three arguments as essential to a case for language being biologically preprogrammed. First is the fact that language learning proceeds uniformly within a linguistic community despite tremendous differences in individuals' experiences. "Isolated words appear at about age 1 year, followed by two-word utterances at about age 2 years. Thereafter, sometime during the third year of life, there is a sudden spurt of vocabulary growth accompanied, coincidentally or not, by elaboration of the sentence structures. By about 4 years of age, the speaker sounds essentially adult" (Gleitman, 1986, pp. 121–122; cf. Lenneberg, 1967).

Second, children do not simply copy what they hear. They make systematic errors that suggest the use of an emerging grammar, of which the rules are never explicitly taught. For example, young speakers will systematically misplace auxiliary verbs in wh-questions, such as "What can I eat?" They will say instead, "What I can eat?"—a form that is never produced by older speakers or adults (cf. Bellugi, 1967; cited in Gleitman, 1986). Similar evidence comes from the order in which children acquire lexical categories. A child's first words are overwhelmingly nouns. Verbs appear slightly later, with adjectives and adverbs appearing still later (Gentner, 1982). These examples are difficult, perhaps impossible, to explain without reference to some sort of innate basis.

Finally, a third argument for the biological preprogramming of language lies in the mistakes that children do not make as they learn to speak. Gleitman provided an illustration with the following two sentences:

1. The man who is a fool is amusing.
2. The man is a fool who is amusing.

Now consider how these are transformed to yield yes/no questions:

1. Is the man who is a fool amusing?
2. Is the man a fool who is amusing?

Children apparently recognize that which *is* moves depends on the structure of the sentence, not the serial position of the word *is*. They never make the mistake of saying, "Is the man who a fool is amusing?" or "Is the man is a fool who amusing?" Yet it is extremely unlikely that children are ever taught the rather abstract rule, "It's the *is* in the higher clause that moves."

If we accept the premise, therefore, that biology plays a significant role in language learning, then we may proceed to the question of just what role it plays. From the studies conducted by Gleitman and others (cf. Feldman, Goldin-Meadow, & Gleitman, 1978; Newport, Gleitman, & Gleitman, 1977; also Fowler, 1986), she reaches the conclusion, first suggested by Lenneberg, that language acquisition is maturationally driven. The progress of normal children was better predicted by their age than by the speech patterns of their mothers. Deaf children learned a gestural language in the same developmental increments that hearing children learned spoken language. Language onset and structural development were the same for blind as for sighted children. Finally, although the onset of language was late for Down syndrome children, its rate and nature of development paralleled that of normal children until a point when learning simply stopped. These results consistently point to the child's neurological age as a critical factor in his or her language learning.

Neurological age may also set limits on language learning in a manner different from what has already been discussed. Anecdotal evidence supports the hypothesis that children are better language learners than are adults. They easily manage two languages at a time while adults struggle through second language classes with great difficulty (Gleitman, 1986; cf. Miller, 1981). In addition, findings from studies investigating deaf individuals learning American sign language indicate that final knowledge of the language is best predicted by the age of the learner at first exposure (Newport & Supalla, cited in Gleitman, 1986). Late learners, in other words, failed to acquire all the linguistic structures of American sign language, despite years of subsequent exposure and use. This suggests the possibility of a critical period in language learning, akin to chick imprinting or bird song-learning.

Reflect back, for a moment, on the case of Mario, described at the beginning of this chapter. Although the scenario did not state which part of his brain sustained damage, we might assume that the left cerebral hemisphere was involved because his speech was affected. That Mario regained his speech may be taken as evidence for critical periods in language development. Lenneberg (1967) reported normal language development following damage to the left hemisphere at an early age but loss of linguistic ability when damage occurred after puberty. Recent studies may call Lenneberg's results into question, because more sophisticated psycholinguistic testing has revealed specific competence failures in the language of brain-damaged individuals. "Nevertheless, the clinical impression is that such persons are linguistically normal. The classical conclusion that the young brain is quite flexible in reallocating functions seems to remain valid" (Chipman, 1986, p. 212).

Finally, just as individuals exhibit differences in their preference for processing in certain modes, they also exhibit differences in the areas of the brain that subserve language functions. Females appear different from males, and left-handed persons appear different from right-handed persons. These differences do not, however, result in language deficiencies, which means there is much more to the story of language learning than we currently know.

Cognitive Development and the Brain

In at least one respect, studying cognitive development from a neurophysiological perspective is no different from studying it from a cognitive perspective. The primary question of interest is: To what extent is cognitive development biologically or environmentally determined? Obviously, behaviorists put little stock in biological factors, arguing that development can be fully understood in environmental terms. But cognitive developmentalists have been more open to the possibility of biological determinants in cognitive development. Piaget appealed to a biological model for understanding development, although his ideas never extended to investigations of actual biological processes or substrates of development. And Case suggested that maturation of certain brain systems may be responsible for limitations to children's working memory compared to adults (see Chapter 6).

To characterize the diversity of neuroscience research related to development, four conceptual models are suggested: fixed circuitry, critical periods, plasticity, and modularity (Chall & Peterson, 1986). To some degree, these models integrate much of the research already discussed concerning the neurophysiology of learning. They provide a useful working framework for a look at cognitive development and the brain.

Fixed Circuitry and Critical Periods. In normal prenatal development, what eventually becomes the brain begins as a single layer of cells lining the wall of the neural tube. Cell mitosis results in the genesis of waves of neurons which migrate to destinations in various parts of the developing brain. Elaboration of neuronal dendrites and synapses follows, with the establishment of connections between neurons the ultimate achievement of development (Goldman-Rakic, 1986). What is noteworthy about this process (highly oversimplified here) is the very orchestrated plan it requires. Brain cell generation and migration is virtually complete in humans by the sixteenth week after gestation. Neurons by then have assumed specific functions in specific regions of the brain. Although dendritic development and synapse formation take longer, generally continuing well into the postnatal period, they form particular patterns of connections that depend upon their location.

What do these fixed circuits and their pattern of development mean for learning and complex cognitive functioning? For one thing, the developing brain will be more or less sensitive to different types of injuries at different times. Dividing cells are now known to be selectively vulnerable to radiation; during the period of cell division, then, subsequent development of the brain can be irreparably harmed if it is exposed to radiation. This helps to explain why many women who survived Hiroshima, and who were 8 to 16 weeks pregnant at the time the atom bomb was dropped, gave birth to mentally retarded children. For children whose gestational age was outside this critical period, however, mental retardation was not common. As Goldman-Rakic (1986) put it, "Toxins, injuries, and stress-induced maternal influences can certainly alter the number of cells generated, their patterns of migration and ultimate synaptic connections" (p. 253). What effects there will be depends upon the critical periods during which the influences are felt.

Critical periods apparently occur not only before birth, but after as well. There is now evidence to believe that the brain may not be fully mature until individuals reach at least 8 to 10 years of age (Heminway & Tegriti, 1984), and a few researchers believe that figure is closer to 18 to 20 (Epstein, 1990). Moreover, data from electroencephalograms show evidence of growth spurts in the brain that some have attempted to correlate with Piaget's stages of cognitive development. This would suggest critical periods for learning that occur around the ages at which children make transitions among stages.

At this point, however, the correlations between brain maturation and Piaget's stages of development are at best weak. For one thing, very global measures of cognitive performance have been used, which are likely to have been insensitive to small increments in brain growth. For another, it has been difficult to reconcile the continuous rate of regional brain maturation with the discrete stage changes that Piaget's theory proposes (Hudspeth & Pribham, 1990). As a consequence, although it may be tempting to draw curricular implications from these data, McCall (1990) has argued that they would be premature.

Eventually, the more that is known about how and when circuits are fixed in the brain, the more likely we will be able to determine neurological causes of certain learning problems. Chall and Peterson (1986) expressed the hope, for example, that reading disabilities may be more accurately detected and treated with knowledge of their neurological origins and potential critical periods. Bruer (1999) also argued the need for developing and testing interventions to help learners who, for whatever reason, may have missed critical experiences during development. Thus, even though a critical period may have been passed, there is evidence that children can make up some of the lost ground.

Plasticity.   On the other side of the coin from fixed circuitry is the cortical plasticity of the developing brain. It has already been mentioned that dendritic branching and synaptic formation continue after birth. In fact, although subject to critical periods, "anatomical plasticity during development of the nervous system...is the rule rather than the exception" (Crutcher, 1991, pp. 107–108). Yet, there is now ample evidence to suggest that cortical plasticity is characteristic of the brain throughout life. Rosenzweig (1984, 1986, 1998) described studies he and others conducted with rodents, investigating brain changes induced by experience. He compared the brain development of rats, mice, ground squirrels, and gerbils raised in standard, enriched, or impoverished environments. The standard environment consisted of a small laboratory cage for three rodents, furnished with food and water. The enriched environment was a larger cage for ten to twelve animals, with food, water, and a variety of objects changed daily (such as shelves and slides). The impoverished environment meant that each animal was raised alone in a small private cage.

Rosenzweig's results were rather astounding. The brains of animals raised in the enriched environment showed increases in weight, dendritic branching, and the size of synaptic contacts relative to the comparison groups. Moreover, the brains of adult rats showed a continued ability to change in response to experience, with these changes related to improvements in learning.

Studying neurological changes in the brain in response to experience is obviously more difficult when it concerns humans rather than rodents. Nonetheless, there is compelling evidence to believe that human brains are also characterized by plasticity. Studies analogous to those of Rosenzwieg have been conducted in which researchers compared the cognitive abilities (as measured by IQ tests) of children raised in different types of environments (Friedman & Cocking, 1986). In general, results suggested the same conclusion. An enriched environment can significantly enhance cognitive development, especially when the enrichment comes at an early age.

Additional evidence of neuronal plasticity, this time in mature brains, is provided by studies of stroke victims who regained functions incapacitated by the stroke (Bach-y-Rita, 1980, 1982) and split-brain patients who regained the ability to produce speech years after a callosotomy (Gazzaniga et al., 1996). Despite these findings, however, there is also evidence that neuronal plasticity declines with age in many species, including humans (Crutcher, 1991; see also Barnes, 1998). This is thought to be a function of mature individuals committing increasing portions of their nervous system to memory storage. And memory storage, of necessity, must be relatively stable in order for information to be later recalled. It seems likely, then, that older learners are capable of learning new things throughout their lives, but doing so in a flexible manner is somewhat more difficult than it is for younger learners.

Modularity. Conceptualizing memory in terms of modules offers a means for understanding the differences between memories that are lost or retained with brain damage (Chall & Peterson, 1986). This is similar to the declarative-procedural distinction that has already been discussed. Modularity can also refer to differences of another sort. Gardner (1983, 1986) proposed that cognitive development proceeds independently in at least seven relatively autonomous domains, or modules—language, music, logical-mathematical reasoning, spatial processing, bodily-kinesthetic activity, interpersonal knowledge, and intrapersonal knowledge. These make up the sum of one's intelligence.

Evidence for brain modularity comes first from investigations of fixed circuits referred to earlier. Cortical connections associated with visual perception have been found to be arrayed in cellular columns (Hubel & Wiesel, 1962), but so have connections in the frontal cortex that are unrelated to sensory perception. "Modular organization seems to be a universal rule for disposition of connections in the cerebral cortex" (Goldman-Rakic, 1986, p. 249).

As for the different types of intelligences proposed by Gardner, language seems to be predominantly associated with the left cerebral hemisphere, visual-spatial abilities with the right hemisphere, music perception and production with the right anterior lobe, and emotional difficulties with the right temporal lobe (Gardner, 1986). These conclusions have been drawn from observations of mostly brain-damaged patients, but Gardner (1982, 1983) has also examined individuals from what he calls "unusual populations." These included idiot-savants, prodigies in single domains, and retarded individuals who may have a single spared organ of development. From his analyses, Gardner believes that normal individuals possess independent capacities to develop in the seven separate domains mentioned previously. Each domain is subserved by separate neural mechanisms, which can therefore be differentially affected by biological and environmental factors.

Finally, cognitive development in any domain is activated, according to Gardner (1986), within a cultural context. He argued that humans evolved as cultural members just as they evolved as biological creatures. Thus, biological potential is constrained to some extent by cultural factors within the environment. This argument is certainly consistent with the views of evolutionary psychologists and helps to provide a link between the neurophysiology of learning and the sociobiology of learning.

Implications of Neurophysiology for Learning and Instruction

There is likely to be unanimous agreement by this point that the neurophysiology of learning is a complex affair. Is it even possible to integrate the various perspectives described in order to draw sensible and useful implications for instruction? There appear to be at least five areas in which implications emerge, related to (1) modularity, (2) enriched environments, (3) plasticity, (4) language learning, and (5) learning problems. These are explained in the following discussion and summarized in Table 8.3.

Modularity and "Brain-Based" Curricula.   Whether humans possess seven distinguishable cognitive capacities, as Gardner proposes, they undoubtedly possess some differentiation of cognitive function that is neurologically based. Both cognitive (see Chapter 3) and neurological findings point to differences between general (or procedural) and specific data-based (or declarative) memory. The same is true for different sensory codes that may be activated by attention to establish and access a single semantic memory. These findings, coupled with brain modularity and hemisphere differences that have been observed, suggest two implications.

First, learners are likely to demonstrate considerable variation in their processing preferences and cognitive abilities. If we agree that cognitive competence depends partly upon biological capacity and partly upon experience, then normal variation in both factors should produce extensive observed variability. This certainly comes as no surprise, but Gardner (1986) reminded us that education has routinely placed more emphasis on some types of cognition over others. This means that some learners may be disadvantaged compared to others if their cognitive strengths fall into areas generally over-

TABLE 8.3 *Implications of Neurophysiology for Learning and Instruction*

Principle	Implication for Instruction
1. Cognitive functions are differentiated.	Learners are likely to have preferred modes of processing as well as different capabilities in various modes. This suggests a multimodal approach to instruction: Include activities that draw upon different sensory modes.
	For example, Ms. Lilly teaches geography locations using maps and songs. Students learn the locations of countries by singing the names as they locate and touch the countries on the map (November, 1992).
2. The brain is relatively plastic in nature.	Enriched, active environments are likely to facilitate learning in developing children. As for adults, although plasticity seems to decrease with age, learning can remain flexible if a variety of instructional strategies are offered.
	For example, children's literature can serve as an effective means to teach reading, and historic literature may be used effectively in social studies instruction.
3. Language may be biologically preprogrammed.	Children have implicit knowledge about language, which should be made explicit during language instruction. In addition, instructors should be aware that language problems could interfere with subject matter learning.
	For example, arithmetic problems should be phrased in language understood by the students.
4. Learning disorders may have a neurobiological basis.	Neurological testing may assist in diagnosing, treating, and evaluating the effectiveness of programs designed to ameliorate various learning problems.

looked by educators. The challenge to educators, then, is to discover each learner's cognitive profile, so that "we can make more informed decisions about which program of education to follow if we want to play from strength or if we want to shore up weaknesses" (Gardner, 1986, p. 278).

Gardner's statement leads directly to a second implication of modularity for curriculum and instruction. That is, how can educators use this knowledge of differences in memory and processing modes to provide learners with instruction most appropriate to their needs? For one thing, the existence of different memory types and cognitive capabilities implies different instructional strategies suitable for each type. In other words, acquiring a procedural skill in music is likely to demand different learning experiences than acquiring facts about logic. Once we better understand the nature of various cognitive capabilities, we will be in a better position to devise tasks appropriate to help learners progress in a particular domain.

This argument is similar to that which underlies Gagné's (1985) theory of instruction (see Chapter 10), as well as many models of instructional design (cf. Reigeluth, 1983). The difference among views appears to concern not whether learners acquire different capabilities but just what these capabilities are. It is hoped that future neurological research may help to sort out the possibilities.

Although domain differences suggest specific instructional strategies, learner differences may do so as well. There may be a problem, however, in the premature application of neuroscience findings to instruction. Educational programs that are designed to exercise both sides of the brain have been popular (Chipman, 1986; Rosenzweig, 1986). Other programs have used appeals to brain research to justify their emphasis on educating the right side of the brain or meeting the needs of predominantly "right-brained" learners. Such programs, however, "are certainly premature and probably misguided" (Rosenzweig, 1986, p. 352). Brain researchers stress the cooperative interaction between the two cerebral hemispheres and argue that their functional roles are only just beginning to be characterized. It would be simplistic to describe hemispheric differences as "analytic-holistic, verbal-spatial, or any others of the popular polar pairs that are often used for this purpose" (Bertelson, 1982, quoted in Rosenzweig, 1986, p. 352).

Although brain-based curricula are not well justified, instructional strategies that appeal to multiple sensory modes and cognitive capabilities probably are. Learners having difficulty understanding an instructional presentation in one mode may benefit from the same presentation in an alternate mode. Exploring how meaning can be conveyed differently in different modes can also be valuable for learning (cf. Tessmer, Wilson, & Driscoll, 1990) and constitutes a central tenet of semiotic (see Chapter 5) and constructivist (see Chapter 11) approaches to instruction. Not only may different pathways be established to the same memory, but that memory may be enhanced and broadened by unique contributions of different codes.

Use It or Lose It: Enriched Environments, Critical Periods, and Plasticity. During the postnatal period of the developing animal, synapses proliferate. Many more are produced by the young brain than are commonly seen in mature or adult brains. This initial overproduction of synapses is then followed by a period of consolidation, in which some synapses will be retracted until adult levels are reached (Goldman-Rakic, 1986). Although behavioral indicators of this sprouting and pruning period are still being determined, many researchers believe that it correlates with critical periods in cognitive development. This may help to explain, for example, why "certain precocious behaviors (like neonatal swimming or imitation) drop out" and why flexibility declines after a certain period (Gardner, 1986, p. 270).

Critical periods for the development of visual perception (cf. Hubel & Wiesel, 1962) are well established, and they are presumed to account for some observed differences in language learning, discussed earlier. There may also be critical periods in each of the seven domains of competence that Gardner has proposed. Whether or not Gardner's proposal is confirmed, what do critical periods in general suggest for instruction? At the least, they imply an important role for environmental events during the period of development deemed critical. Just what this role should be is the question.

In Piaget's view (see Chapter 6), equilibration is the major developmental process, implying that whereas environment provides the necessary raw material, the main impetus for development comes from within the learner. Consistent with this view was Piaget's opposition to speeding up development through instructional interventions. Most educators in the Piagetian tradition, then, would consider enriched environments to be those that provide a variety of resources promoting child activity.

By contrast, Bruner and Vygotsky (see Chapter 7) accorded the environment a more extensive role, believing that instruction can precede and contribute to development. Similarly, biological evidence from studies of enriched versus impoverished environments supports the influence of environment on development (Friedman & Cocking, 1986). Enrichment can take the form of guided learning or formal, planned instruction. Guided learning includes such tactics as parents, siblings, or peers helping children solve problems, prepare for school tests, or read challenging books. In fact, more challenging textbooks have been associated with higher Scholastic Aptitude Test (SAT) scores, and more difficult books appear to promote language and reading achievement (Chall & Peterson, 1986).

Because critical periods typically occur early in development, with both brain and behavior exhibiting less flexibility over time, a common assumption has been that cortical plasticity may be restricted to early development. However, Rosenzweig's findings effectively debunked this notion. "While acknowledging the importance of the developmental processes that set the stage before birth for later cognitive development and accomplishments, it seems to me that it is equally if not more vital for educators and cognitive scientists to know about the capacity of the nervous system, even in adults, to undergo plastic changes in response to experience" (Rosenzweig, 1986, p. 365).

In clear agreement with Rosenzweig are Friedman and Cocking (1986), who extended their notion of guided learning to include experts helping novices complete a task or generate important questions and therapists helping patients recover functions lost through accident or illness. Their point is that instruction of all sorts can facilitate changes in brain processes. What needs to be better understood, however, are the separate roles of learner motivation and maturity, family support, experience, and patience (Friedman & Cocking, 1986).

Language Learning.   What help to educators is offered by knowledge that language may be biologically preprogrammed? Perhaps it comes down to one simple maxim:

> ...much of what is taught—and should be taught—about language to children is already known to the children implicitly.... I believe that the best teaching methods will be those that specifically take advantage of this prior knowledge, that call the child's attention to what she or he knows, and build as directly as possible from that knowledge. (Gleitman, 1986, pp. 144–145)

This maxim, it seems to me, suggests two related implications for instruction.

First, teachers of multicultural classrooms would be well advised to consider nonstandard English as a language or languages other than English. In other words, children from predominantly black or other ethnic neighborhoods typically speak English in a way that sounds wrong to most teachers. It is certainly wrong in the sense that it does not conform to the rules of standard English. But neither do other, so-called foreign languages; they have their own internal structure and grammatical rules. The same appears to be true for black English and other forms of nonstandard English. Thus, children of all backgrounds probably speak quite grammatically in the language of their surroundings. Knowing this may help teachers to determine what implicit knowledge children have of their language and to use this to best advantage in teaching standard English.

Second, differential patterns of language development are likely to be reflected in the differential difficulty of various language tasks. For example, "children are able to think about and manipulate word- and syllable-level representations of language much earlier in life than they can do the same for phoneme-segment representations of language" (Gleitman, 1986, p. 145). Thus, to be most effective, language instruction should proceed in the same sequence, helping to draw out and call attention to students' implicit knowledge about language.

This relation between language knowledge and task difficulty is also important to remember in other areas of instruction besides language itself. Recent studies in arithmetic problem solving have shown that the linguistic structure of a word problem can greatly influence its difficulty. For example, consider the two simple problems below.

> *Problem A:* John has 5 apples. Mary has 8 apples. How many more apples does Mary have than John?
>
> *Problem B:* John has 5 apples. Mary has 8 apples. If Mary gives Sally the same number of apples as John, how many will she have left?

Ostensibly, these two problems are the same, in that they are both solved by subtracting 5 from 8. If subtraction is the skill to be assessed, then either problem presumably should suffice. However, the problems are not linguistically the same, and, in fact, one is more difficult to answer than the other. You are right if you guessed Problem A to be the more difficult one. Concepts of more than and less than appear later in language use than concepts of adding to or taking away. Thus, word problems of this sort can assess linguistic competence and, indeed, mask arithmetic competence. Recall, as well, the influence of schemata on arithmetic problem solving that was discussed in Chapter 4 and the conception of language as a sign system that was discussed in Chapter 7. It seems likely that different linguistic structures will trigger different problem schemata or sign understandings, which may either enhance or interfere with solving the problem at hand.

Learning Disabilities and Their Treatment. There is great hope that neurological testing will some day be sophisticated enough to detect and diagnose a variety of learning problems. However, better diagnosis does not make the problem go away. Rather, the challenge lies in designing effective educational programs to overcome the learning difficulty. The solutions to that challenge are as apt to come from elsewhere as from advances in the neurophysiology of learning (Chipman, 1986).

Perhaps two additional points are salient here. The first concerns how we characterize what neurological causes are discovered for various learning problems. Calling such causes "defects in cerebral architecture" may signify to some people that they are immutable, impossible to alter or fix. Such an assumption might lead to the unwarranted abandonment of efforts to remediate the learning problem. On the other hand, finding neurological bases of cognitive functions does not have to imply that some functioning is normal and some defective. Rather, one might expect the brains of two individuals to be different, with one possessing some skill that the other lacks. Neural indicators of this sort might be helpful as an additional source of information used to evaluate the effectiveness of educational programs (Chipman, 1986).

Finally, it pays us to remember the neurological evidence of brain plasticity. Chall and Peterson (1986) suggested that we adopt the view of the learner as "an active constructor of knowledge, and the brain as a structure that changes physically as well as behaviorally with learning" (p. 314). Learners do overcome disabilities, albeit sometimes with great difficulty and prolonged effort.

A Biological Understanding of "Kermit and the Keyboard"

A reasonable assumption to make about Kermit in this story is that he is a normal adult male who has not yet faced the potential ravages of old age such as strokes or Alzheimer's disease. We know that he studied music formally "many years ago," but we do not know whether this occurred while he was a small child or whether music lessons began for him as it does for many children—at the age of 7 or 8 (or later). Therefore, it is impossible to speculate on the role critical periods may have played in his early music learning or whether his parents sought to enrich his environment with experiences that might have enhanced this learning. Likewise, there is no evidence to suggest that Kermit suffers from any sort of attentional problem. Quite the opposite—he demonstrates that he can focus his attention appropriately in coordinating his reading the music and playing the corresponding notes.

The biological concepts that are perhaps most clearly illustrated in this story are those pertaining to different memory systems. Using Schacter and Tulving's classification system, we can see that several memory systems appear to be involved in Kermit's learning. The motor skill of playing the keyboard invokes the procedural system, whereas reading the music invokes the primary, semantic, and perceptual systems. The conditioning of the mistake that becomes part of Kermit's repertoire also appears to involve the procedural system. Similarly, this could be understood as a kind of priming, which in Squire's taxonomy (Figure 8.5) would be an example of nondeclarative, or implicit, memory. That is, because of the association Kermit has made between playing that note a particular way and the background that accompanies his playing, the background serves to prime, or cue, Kermit to play the note wrong. The implicit nature of the memory means that he is unlikely to become aware of the mistake until someone points it out, or makes it explicit.

According to neuropsychology, all of the experiences that Kermit has with his keyboard cause modifications in his brain that organize and encode his learning. As long as he continues to practice and experience new things, these modifications will continue to occur and reorganize with his growing proficiency.

Theory Matrix

Theory	Biological Bases of Learning
Prominent Theorists	L. Cosmides (evolution); M. S. Gazzaniga; M. R. Rosenzweig; D. L. Schacter (neuropsychology)
Learning Outcome(s)	Thoughts, behaviors, emotions, physical changes in the brain
Role of the Learner	Interact with a hierarchy of environments
Role of the Instructor	Understand the interactive relation between nature and nurture
	Attempt to determine what things in learning are tied to critical periods for development
	Provide rich, complex, and engaging learning environments and allow for practice
Inputs or Preconditions to Learning	Maturation, different kinds of experiences
Process of Learning	Synaptic formation and pruning; organizing and reorganizing brain structures

Suggested Readings

Barkow, J. H., Cosmides, L., & Tooby, J. (Eds.). (1992). *The adapted mind: Evolutionary psychology and the generation of culture.* New York: Oxford University Press.

Friedman, S. L., Klivington, K. A., & Peterson, R. W. (1986). *The brain, cognition, and education.* Orlando: Academic Press.

Gazzaniga, M S. (1998). *The mind's past.* Berkeley, CA: University of California Press.

Gazzaniga, M. S. (Ed.). (2000). *The new cognitive neurosciences.* Cambridge, MA: MIT Press.

Martinez, J., & Kesner, R. (Eds.). (1998). *Neurobiology of learning and memory.* San Diego: Academic Press.

Squire, L. R. & Schactor, D. L. (2002). *Neuropsychology of memory* (3rd ed.). NY: Guilford Press.

Reflective Questions and Activities

1. What underlying assumptions about knowledge and knowing can be detected in the research presented in this chapter? Are they different among researchers interested in ultimate causes versus those interested in proximal causes of learning? With what epistemological tradition do these views seem most closely related?

2. Revisit once more your thoughts about learning and development. What do biological theorists add to the discussion? Does the evidence they present better support one position or the other concerning whether development influences learning or the other way around? Is there any evidence to suggest that learning and development might be mutually interactive? What implications would this third position have for instruction?

3. View the movie *Blade Runner*, which was produced in the 1980s, and/or an episode of *Star Trek: The Next Generation*, produced in the 1990s. In the former, replicants are being engineered that are "more human than human itself," whereas in the latter, Data is an android with a "positronic" brain. Discuss the view of the brain that these films present in relation to the neurophysiological research summarized in this chapter. How is learning characterized, and how would these characteristics affect the design of instruction?

4. Review literature on the "nature versus nurture" controversy in education. Using your findings and the research summarized in this chapter to support your arguments, discuss your conclusions with respect to which side of the controversy has the weight of evidence on its side. In particular, consider what implications are suggested for education of ethnic minorities and other special populations.

5. Seek out research and literature describing the effects of various drugs on the brain (including caffeine, alcohol, antihistamines, and herbs such as gingkobiloba). What implications might there be of this research for learning and memory?

6. Select an instructional goal that has proven difficult to achieve by some learners. Analyze the goal for the major concepts that must be understood in order for the goal to be attained. Then, brainstorm ways in which these concepts could be presented to or practiced by learners that appeal to different learning modalities. Speculate on what aspects of the goal would be highlighted or obscured in each modality.

Motivation and Self-Regulation in Learning

Consider the following scenarios.

• *Workshop Worries*

Sean is a former teacher who has been appointed to the post of field education officer in a developing country because of his record as an outstanding instructor. His assignment is to work with teachers in a particular region of the country to help them improve the quality of instruction in their classrooms. In addition, however, he is expected to conduct research in those same classrooms to help determine the impact of methods and techniques he recommends. Because he does not have the research skills with which to do this part of the job effectively, he attends a 1-week training workshop on action research. Although he wants to learn these skills quickly, he worries that his current lack of knowledge will put him at a disadvantage in the class. Moreover, despite difficulty in understanding the concepts being presented, Sean asks no questions for fear of looking stupid and holding up the rest of the group.

• *Camouflage Training*

Rob is the drill instructor responsible for training soldiers in the art of camouflage. Time after time, he faces men and women whose military assignments (as clerk, radio operator, or band member) seem only remotely related to the need for combat readiness. As a result, the soldiers don't understand why they should have to learn camouflage techniques, and they are convinced they will never be in a position to apply what they are being told to learn. With each group he confronts for the first time, Rob remembers what a hard sell this training is. He has, however, discovered tactics that draw the soldiers in and pique their interest.

Rob begins the first day of class with a challenge. He asks for a volunteer to come to the front of the room where he has put a number of coins on a table. He holds up a quarter and tells the volunteer to stack the coins until the height of the stack is equal to the diameter of the quarter in his hand. By now, every person in the room is paying close attention, and a few are offering words of advice to the volunteer.

"One more!" shouts out a person from the back of the room.

"No, that's too high," offers another.

When the volunteer is satisfied that the stack is the right size, Rob hands over the quarter and says to compare it with the stack of coins on the table. Groans can be heard around the room; the stack is several coins too high. Another volunteer offers to try, so Rob rearranges the coins. Again the volunteer builds a stack with a different combination of coins, and again the stack is too high. At this point, Rob turns to the group and asks what can be learned from this simple demonstration that might be relevant to camouflage.

The second volunteer, still standing near the table, says, "It's a lot easier to fool the eye than I realized."

On the surface, the problems presented in Workshop Worries and Camouflage Training do not seem to have much in common. Sean wants to learn the skills and knowledge being covered in the workshop, but his anxiety about his performance prevents him from seeking the help that will enable him to comprehend and learn from the instruction. The soldiers, on the other hand, are indifferent to the instruction until Rob does something to capture their attention. In both situations, however, some aspect of motivation is at issue.

"Motivation," according to Schunk (1990), "refer[s] to the process whereby goal-directed behavior is instigated and sustained" (p. 3). Motivation is also "a work-related rather than a play-related concept" (Weiner, 1990, p. 621). Teachers say students are not motivated, for example, when they study halfheartedly, complete a task only for the external reward it assures, or spend time on things antithetical to the learning task (e.g., daydreaming about ballet instead of working on fractions). Lack of motivation is also cited when students plainly refuse to become engaged in a learning task or fail to take actions that will assist them in successfully completing it.

The questions of what underlies motivation and how teachers can effectively motivate their students have been the subject of investigation for many years. Although the theories that have emerged from this research cannot strictly be called learning theories, the study of motivation for educators is certainly confounded with the study of learning. As Weiner (1990) put it, "Motivation is often inferred from learning, and learning usually is an indicator of motivation for the educational psychologist" (p. 618). A central issue, then, is: How do we motivate people to engage in new learning?

Of equal importance for many in today's complex and information-rich society is: How do we help learners develop self-regulatory skills to set their own goals and manage their own learning and performance? Schunk and Zimmerman (1994) considered self-regulation to be the reciprocal of motivation and defined it as "the process whereby students activate and sustain cognitions, behaviors, and affects, which are systematically oriented toward the attainment of their goals" (p. 309; see also Zimmerman, 1989, and Pintrich, 2000).

In this chapter, issues related to motivation and self-regulation are explored. After a brief look at the history of research on these twin constructs, origins and determinants of motivation are presented and discussed in some detail. These are factors influencing whether learners initiate and persist in goal-directed learning tasks. As a consequence of these factors and the learners' engagement (successful or not) in learning tasks, they may or may not demonstrate continuing motivation to learn. Continuing motivation and self-regulation are therefore discussed next. Finally, instructional strategies related to motivation and self-regulation are reviewed with two goals in mind:

1. To design instruction so as to be appealing to the intended learners
2. To design instruction that will facilitate the development of learners' self-regulatory knowledge and skills

A Brief History

"At one time, motivation was the dominant field of study [in psychology]" (Weiner, 1990, p. 616). This was true primarily because psychologists in the 1930s and 1940s conceived of motivation as "what moved a resting organism to a state of activity" (Weiner, 1990, p. 617). You may see already the relationship this concept bears to learning as it was studied in those days. Hull (see Chapter 2), for example, developed a theory of learning in which behavior was presumed to come about as a result of drives toward anticipated goals.

That is, behavior was motivated toward a goal by the existence of some (usually biological) need—e.g., a need for food, sex, or shelter. Learning occurred when the response was reinforced and the drive that motivated the behavior in the first place was reduced.

Tolman's research on latent learning (see Chapter 2), however, had the effect of separating concerns about motivation from concerns about learning (Weiner, 1990). If you recall, Tolman demonstrated that animals appeared to learn a maze simply by exploring it, in the absence of a goal or incentives for drive reduction. Since learning seemed to occur without a clear motivation for it, psychologists began to argue that motivation relates to the use of knowledge, not the development of it.

In the 1960s and 1970s, the shift from a behavioral to cognitive perspective in American psychology (see Chapter 3) brought a reintegration of motivation with learning. Psychologists began to examine in new ways the effects of rewards on behavior. Although it had been widely accepted that rewarding a response automatically increased the probability of its reoccurrence, new findings called this into question. In some cases, rewards had little effect on subsequent behavior unless learners generated an expectancy for, or anticipation of, the reward (Estes, 1972). Moreover, some rewards, if perceived by the learners as controlling, tended to reduce their natural interest in the learning task (Deci, 1975). Similarly, rewards for the completion of an easy task tended to signal to learners that they were low in ability. For humans, then, reward can mean a variety of different things, and each meaning can have different motivational—and learning—consequences.

With researchers now concentrating on human behavior, motivational research became dominated by investigations into humans' need for achievement (Weiner, 1990). Also called incentive motivation, effectance, and the urge for mastery, achievement motivation is thought to be a fundamental tendency of humans to manipulate, dominate, or otherwise master their environment (White, 1959). Among the most prominent researchers in achievement motivation were David McClelland and John Atkinson. They sought to understand why some people appear to strive for excellence simply for the sake of achieving while others do not (McClelland et al., 1953). It was assumed that a high need for achievement developed in children whose parents stressed achievement and competitiveness at home. But achievement motivation can also be situationally affected. Individuals will work harder under certain conditions, such as particular test instructions, competitive environments, and failure (Atkinson, 1964).

Atkinson's work was paralleled by investigations into other individual difference variables related to motivation. For example, besides having high or low achievement motivation, people can have high or low anxiety (Spielberger, 1966), or high or low internal control (Rotter, 1966). Excessive anxiety can interfere with learning and performance, leading to a reduction in continuing motivation to learn. Conversely, students show greater motivation when they have an internal, as opposed to external, orientation. This means that they tend to perceive learning tasks as skill determined and thus subject to personal control. Externally oriented students tend to believe that their success at a learning task will be determined by chance rather than by means within their control. These students are therefore less likely to be motivated to engage in the learning task.

These trends in motivation research have continued (Weiner, 1990), with an even greater focus on human behavior, particularly the self and learners' attempts to manage their own achievements (Schunk & Zimmerman, 1994; Pintrich, 2000; Zimmerman, 2000). Paris and Paris (2001) noted that over 30 articles have been published on self-regulation since 1990 in a single journal, *Educational Psychologist*. This is in addition to articles published in the same journal that touched on related issues, such as academic studying, motivational influences on education, and social influences on school adjustment (Paris & Paris, 2001, p. 90).

As we shall see in the next section, significant attention is being paid to personal goal setting, ways to enhance self-perceptions of control in learning, and strategies to maintain personal beliefs in high ability. Weiner called for more motivational investigations that are not linked with learning, and indeed, there is a growing body of literature demonstrating effects of motivation on variables such as self-esteem, emotions, and so on (Weiner, 1990). However, for educators, the interaction between motivation and learning is what is most important, so that is the specific focus of this chapter. Therefore, the ensuing discussion is limited to sources and strategies of motivation as they affect and promote learning.

Origins and Determinants of Motivation

Whereas drive theorists clearly demonstrated that physiological needs (e.g., hunger) motivate organisms to engage in certain behavior (e.g., seek food), cognitive theorists have increasingly shown that cognitive processes are important mediators of motivation. Staying with the food example momentarily, when humans seek food to satisfy hunger, not just any food will do. You might, for example, forego a stop at the nearest hamburger joint to go home and fix a nutritious vegetable salad for lunch. Why might you do this? Perhaps because you value a healthy lifestyle, to which low-fat, nutritious meals can contribute. Your values, then, have mediated between the drive (hunger) and your response (eating). Likewise, deciding to engage in a learning task and persisting in that task are no simple matters. As we have already seen, motivation can be influenced by one's need for achievement or locus of control (internal versus external orientation). Motivation is also a function of one's cognitions about the task at hand, about the consequences of task completion, and about one's ability to do the task. Each of these sources of motivation is elaborated further in the sections that follow.

Curiosity and Interest

When Alice entered the Looking Glass, she remarked at how "curiously [the path] twists," always coming back to the house no matter which route she followed away from it. This made her all the more determined to figure out how to reach the nearby hill so that she could continue her adventures (Carroll, 1946, p. 22). Curiosity, in children and adults alike, is a strong motivator of learning. One type of curiosity, perceptual arousal, is initially stimulated by novel, complex, or incongruous patterns in the environment (Berlyne, 1965), much like what Alice encountered in the Looking Glass and Wonderland. Not only do learners pay greater attention to these unexpected events, but they are also moved to try new ways of perceiving what they are looking at (Gagné & Driscoll, 1988). Alice, for example, puzzled over the many curious things that happened to her, sometimes venturing hypotheses about what they meant.

Teachers, too, can make good use of interesting events to stimulate curiosity in learners. Rob's opening demonstration with the coins in Camouflage Training is a good example. To begin with, the soldiers weren't certain what he was about to do with the coins on the table, which activated their attention, and then the result of the demonstration was intriguing. Because people adapt rather quickly to surprising events, curiosity must be sustained for it to be a continuing source of motivation. Rob attempts to do this by having the soldiers make a conscious link between the demonstration and its relevance for what they are about to learn. If the tactic is successful, the students will maintain their interest and pay attention as the instruction continues.

Maintaining attention on a perceptual level can also be achieved by varying the instructional approaches used in a class period or training session (Keller, 1983, 1987a).

Most of you have undoubtedly been bored, at one time or another, by an instructor who did nothing but lecture monotonously and unendingly. To keep learners alert, instructors can employ such strategies as varying their tone of voice, using relevant humor occasionally, and interspersing demonstrations and group activities with lecture.

Another means of sustaining curiosity involves fantasy. "The use of fantasy in learning entails providing learners with a meaningful context for learning that is easy to augment with their imaginations. The context is meaningful to the learner in the sense that it offers a very personal degree of fascination and intrigue" (Rieber, 1991a, p. 320; cf. Malone, 1981). So, for example, learning about longitude and latitude occurs in context and maintains students' attention when a concurrent goal is to locate a "pirate's sunken treasure."

Finally, "a deeper level of curiosity may be activated by creating a problem situation which can be resolved only by knowledge-seeking behavior" (Keller, 1987a, p. 2). Keller (1983) called this inquiry arousal, and it is a factor that researchers in the Cognition and Technology Group at Vanderbilt (CTGV) contend is brought about by the problem complexity inherent in their instructional videos (cf. CTGV, 1990, 1991a, 1991b). They intentionally pose very complex and realistic problems for students to solve, and then provide throughout each video numerous clues and information necessary to solve the problems. The result, they say, is enhanced motivation on the part of learners, who experience the complexity of problems that is characteristic of real life.

Goals and Goal Orientation

Actively setting goals can be an important source of motivation (Bandura, 1977). When individuals set goals, they determine an external standard to which they will internally evaluate their present level of performance. To the extent that this standard is not met and their goals are not yet achieved, learners will persist in their efforts. Undoubtedly, most of us have had the experience of "sticking with it" until a goal we have set for ourselves has been achieved. This was certainly true some years ago when I decided to take up windsurfing. I already knew how to sail and so thought learning to windsurf would be a snap. Instead, it took teeth-gritting patience and persistence over the better part of one summer.

Not all goals, however, will prompt this persistence in learning. Certain properties of goals appear to be important to the goal-setting process (Locke et al., 1981):

- The generality of the goal
- Time it may take to achieve the goal
- The orientation of the goal

Setting specific goals (e.g., "I will be able to connect a circuit to light a lamp") is better than setting general goals (e.g., "I will learn about electricity") for motivating persistent behavior. And as long as the learner is capable of performing the goal, setting more difficult goals tends to lead to greater persistence and better performance than setting easy goals (Locke et al., 1981).

There are also differences between setting proximal versus distal goals (Schunk & Gaa, 1981). Proximal goals are those that are close at hand and achievable quickly (e.g., "I will learn to distinguish between negative reinforcement and punishment"), whereas distal goals are ones that set criteria to be met in the distant future (e.g., "I will learn to be a behavior analyst by the time I graduate from school"). Not surprisingly, results indicate that setting proximal goals improves self-motivation and performance to a greater extent than setting distal goals. This result may be especially important in the teaching of young children, since they may not be capable of representing distal goals in thought (Schunk & Gaa, 1981).

Finally, the types of achievement goals set by learners influence their task persistence and problem-solving efforts (Dweck, 1986; Dweck & Elliot, 1983; Dweck & Leggett, 1988; Elliot & Dweck, 1988; Meece, 1994), as well as their study behaviors and what they remember (Graham & Golan, 1991; Nolen, 1988; Nolen & Haladyna, 1990). When learners set performance goals, they "seek to gain favorable judgments of their competence or avoid negative judgments of their competence" (Dweck, 1986, p. 1040). When they set learning goals, on the other hand, learners "seek to increase their competence, to understand or master something new" (Dweck, 1986, p. 1040). The difference between these two types of goals can be seen in statements such as, "I want to get an A on this test" (performance goal) versus "I want to understand why the United States was one of the last countries to enter World War II" (learning goal).

Faced with a performance goal, students who have little confidence in their abilities display helplessness. They avoid challenge and, given the chance, will quit rather than persist in the task. In the same situation, learners who have high confidence in their abilities will seek a challenge and tend to demonstrate high persistence toward the task. Where learning goals are concerned, on the other hand, students' assessment of their present ability is irrelevant. They all display what Dweck and Leggett (1988) called a "mastery-oriented" pattern of motivation. That is, they select challenging tasks, which are believed to benefit learning, and they demonstrate persistence in those tasks (Elliott & Dweck, 1988; Dweck & Leggett, 1988).

The reason for these differences appears to lie in how individuals interpret their failures within the two goal orientations. Performance goals foster the implicit belief that intelligence is fixed. Under this goal orientation, then, learners ask whether their abilities are adequate to the task, and failing is taken to mean that the answer is "no." By contrast, learning goals are associated with the belief that intelligence is malleable and can be developed. Under a learning goal orientation, strategies for task mastery are emphasized, and learners ask themselves how their abilities might best be applied and increased to achieve the goal. Failure in this case signals a problem with the current strategy and the necessity to revise that strategy. An obvious result is that learners will expend more effort to learn in this situation than when they believe they do not have the ability to achieve the goal (Dweck & Leggett, 1988).

The recommendation to foster a learning goal orientation runs counter to much current educational practice, which attempts to instill learner confidence within a performance goal orientation (Dweck, 1986). Strategies of this sort are, in fact, discussed later in the chapter. It is likely that the behavioral perspective on learning (specifically, positive reinforcement) contributed to this situation. Recall, for example, the effect of positive reinforcement on learning. How does this relate to motivation? Presumably, behavior that can be described as motivated comes about through its consistent reinforcement. However, "a deeper understanding of the principles of reinforcement would not lead one to expect that frequent praise for short, easy tasks would create a desire for long, challenging ones or promote persistence in the face of failure" (Dweck, 1986, p. 1045).

What conclusions may we draw for instruction from this research on goals? It is apparent that setting challenging, proximal goals contributes to motivation and can lead to enhanced performance. But this is most likely to occur when the goals are oriented toward learning, as opposed to performance.

Self-Efficacy Beliefs

To this point, the roles in motivation of curiosity and students' cognitions about learning tasks have been explored. But another strong source of motivation comes from learners' beliefs about themselves in relation to task difficulty and task outcome. According to Bandura (1997), "Perceived self-efficacy refers to beliefs in one's capabilities to organize and execute the courses of action required to produce given attainments" (p. 3). Self-efficacy beliefs

> influence the courses of action people choose to pursue, how much effort they put forth in given endeavors, how long they will persevere in the face of obstacles and failures, their resilience to adversity, whether their thought patterns are self-hindering or self-aiding, how much stress and depression they experience in coping with taxing environmental demands, and the level of accomplishments they realize. (Bandura, 1997, p. 3)

Bandura (1977, 1982, 1997) proposed self-efficacy as a belief system that is causally related to behavior and outcomes. That is, people make judgments about their ability to perform certain actions required to achieve a desirable outcome (Figure 9.1). Then, based on their judgments, they proceed or not to engage in those actions. In the Workshop Worries scenario, for example, Sean doubts his ability to learn the research skills being taught in the workshop because he has no prior knowledge of the subject matter. As a consequence, he does not seek the help that could enable him to learn successfully in this situation.

In addition to self-efficacy beliefs, people have expectations about what actions will produce the desirable outcomes. Sean fully expects, for instance, that learning the research skills being taught in the workshop would enable him to perform a job function that he cannot do now. Bandura called these outcome expectations and defined them as the judgments people make

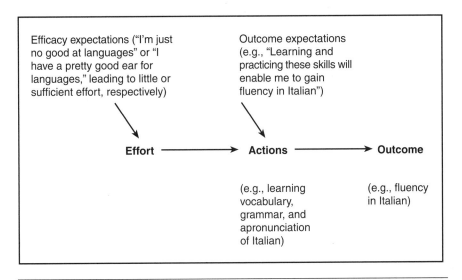

FIGURE 9.1 *Bandura's Theory of Self-Efficacy as a Mediator of Performance and Achievement*

about the consequences of performance. Positive expectations serve as incentives (i.e., Sean was motivated to sign up for the workshop), and negative expectations serve as disincentives (i.e., Sean would have looked elsewhere for training if he thought the workshop was not oriented toward the skills he wants to learn).

Outcome expectations comprise three major types (Bandura, 1986, 1997):

1. Physical effects that accompany an action (e.g., pleasure or pain)
2. Social effects (including approval, social recognition, and monetary compensation on the positive side and disapproval, rejection, and penalties on the negative side)
3. Self-evaluative reactions to one's own behavior

In addition to Sean's outcome expectation that the workshop will lead to desirable research skills, therefore, he may well have outcome expectations that his success in the workshop could lead to a promotion or the commendation of his supervisor.

Performance clearly determines whether outcome expectations are satisfied, and self-efficacy beliefs control performance. People can harbor beliefs about their capabilities (or lack thereof) that bear no relation to their actual ability to perform some task. But making good use of the capabilities they possess depends upon the self-assurance with which they approach and manage difficult tasks (Bandura, 1997).

Self-efficacy is thought to be a generative capability, not a fixed trait (Bandura, 1997). That is, people develop self-efficacy beliefs in different areas and to different degrees, and these differences help to explain why people with similar skill levels may perform differently or why an individual may perform differently under different circumstances without a change in skill level. Moreover, Bandura (1997) argued that optimistic self-efficacy appraisals benefit the individual whereas realistic appraisals can be self-limiting. If Sean in Workshop Worries, for example, went into the workshop believing he could achieve the goals no matter how little prior knowledge he possessed, his behavior would probably have been quite different. Clearly, though, there is a limit to how much optimism in efficacy beliefs is a good thing. As long as self-beliefs are grounded in past mastery experiences (as opposed to wishful thinking), people will "motivate themselves and construct efficacious courses of action in an anticipatory, proactive way" (Bandura, 1997, p. 77).

How do learners acquire self-efficacy beliefs initially, and how might these beliefs be changed when they prevent learners from undertaking tasks that they have the capability to do? Bandura (1982, 1997) suggested four principal sources by which people gain information to influence their self-efficacy beliefs:

1. Enactive mastery experiences that provide feedback on learners' own capabilities
2. Vicarious experiences that provide comparative information about the attainments of others
3. Verbal persuasion, which provides the learner with information about what others believe he or she is capable of doing
4. Physiological states, internal feelings by which learners judge their ability to engage in the task at hand

Let us consider each of these in turn.

Enactive Mastery Experiences. **Enactive mastery experiences** refer to *a learner's own previous success at a task.* They are the most influential source of self-efficacy beliefs because they provide the most authentic information to learners on their ability to do what it takes to succeed.

An example of how success begets success (and the increased self-beliefs about being successful) can be seen in the following case. Bill was an older student who took a class from me some years ago. I had structured the course so that students had to master a unit quiz before going on to the next unit. They could take each quiz as many as three times in order to achieve an A on it, or they could settle for grades as low as C. One day, early in the semester, Bill took a unit quiz, on which he achieved a B. I asked him, "Bill, do you want to take this quiz over for an A?" He replied, "Oh no, ma'am. I'm not an 'A' kind of guy." Later that day, in proctoring another student's quiz, Bill came back to me and said he thought a mistake might have been made in the scoring of his paper. I checked, and sure enough, one item had been marked wrong that was, in fact, correct. That raised his grade to an A, which I pointed out to him, "You see, Bill, you are an 'A' kind of guy after all." From that day on, Bill nearly always attempted a second try when he achieved less than A on a unit quiz, and on the whole, performed far better than he had ever expected.

According to Bandura (1997), one's interpretation of success or failure on a task, along with perceptions about the difficulty of the task and the amount of effort expended, mediate the effect of enactive experience on self-efficacy beliefs. For example, suppose Sean in Workshop Worries perceives an assignment to be particularly difficult, but he persists and earns praise for his efforts. He is likely to reassess and raise his self-efficacy beliefs as a consequence of this mastery experience. However, suppose Sean views an assignment as something he already knows how to do and so has to exert little effort to be successful. In this case, his self-efficacy beliefs are likely to remain unchanged; he will remain convinced that the workshop is beyond his capabilities and this one assignment is not representative of what he will be asked to do eventually.

Vicarious Experiences.   A second source of information that affects self-efficacy beliefs comes from **vicarious experiences,** or *the learner's observation of a role model attaining success at a task.* I frequently witness examples of vicarious experience influencing self-efficacy among the graduate students at my university. Many are convinced that the papers they write, or the research they conduct, will not be good enough for publication or presentation at a conference. This expectation then leads to their failure to complete the work, or their failure to submit it once completed. However, these same students change their self-expectations after attending a conference at which they hear a fellow student present a paper or witness a senior researcher present a boring or flawed paper. Generally, their thoughts run something like, "Gee, I can do at least as well as him (or her)!"

Implied in the story above is the fact that who the role model is affects the extent to which the observer's self-efficacy is enhanced. For example, a graduate student who attends a conference at which he or she is overawed by the presentations is unlikely to modify expectations of not being capable of the same performance. A review of studies on the effects of modeling as a function of the model's attributes revealed a number of conclusions (Schunk, 1987). First, the role model's age appears to have little effect on whether a learner's self-efficacy is enhanced through his or her observation of the model. The one exception to this general statement occurred in a study by

Schunk and Hanson (1985). In their study, elementary school students who had trouble subtracting observed a peer, the teacher, or no model demonstrate regrouping. Observing their peers led to students' reporting greater self-efficacy and achieving greater subtraction skill during the instructional program than observing the teacher, but a teacher model was better than no model.

Second, children are more likely to follow the behavior of those they perceive to be competent in the skill being learned than those they see as less competent. Moreover, when they are fearful about the learning situation, they responded more positively to coping models than mastery models. That is, learners gained confidence and were likely to improve their performance when they observed models who initially showed the same fears but who gradually reached a mastery performance.

Finally, more is better, and peer models can contribute to the self-efficacy of remedial and handicapped students. Presumably, multiple models are superior to one, because chances are greater for the learners to see themselves as similar to at least one of the models. Remedial and handicapped students are among those who have had difficulty learning academic material or coping with stressful situations, both conditions under which peer models can help raise observers' self-efficacy (cf. Bandura, 1986; Schunk, 1987).

Learning from modeled performances involves more than just the learner's perceptions about the model. In his social cognitive theory, Bandura (1986, 1997) proposed four sets of psychological processes that govern what people learn through vicarious experience (Figure 9.2).

The first set of processes refers to what information the learner pays attention to in the modeled events. This depends on attributes of the learner (observer) as well as aspects of the modeled events themselves. Then, the learners constructs a cognitive representation by which to remember the modeled events. The third set of processes enables the learner to transform remembered information into appropriate courses of action. Whether the learner actually performs these actions depends on the fourth set of processes. Learners are more likely to perform modeled events themselves when

- their actions lead to positive consequences,
- they observe benefits experienced by others for similar actions, or
- they find the activities self-satisfying.

Verbal Persuasion.   **Verbal persuasion** is a third means by which self-efficacy can be modified, one that is probably most familiar to parents. This refers to *others persuading a learner that he or she is capable of succeeding at a particular task.* "C'mon, you can do it!" is a common exhortation of someone persuading another to attempt a task. This occurred to me when my husband and I decided to restain our cedar home, which stands on stilts approximately

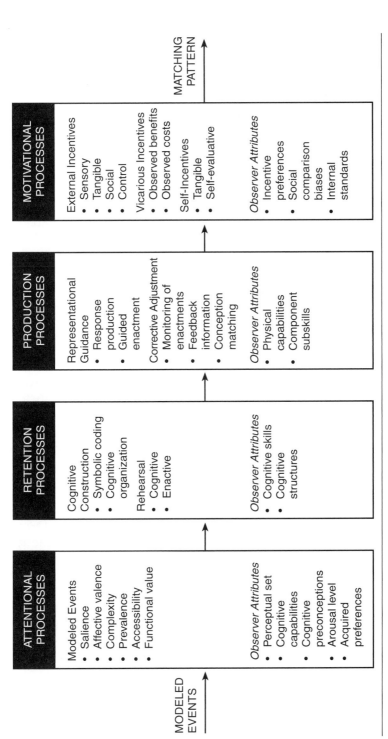

FIGURE 9.2 *Four Subprocesses Governing Observational Learning*

Source: SOCIAL FOUNDATIONS OF THOUGHT AND ACTION by BANDURA, © 1986.

Reprinted by permission of Prentice-Hall, Inc., Upper Saddle River, NJ.

321

20 feet in the air. My self-efficacy for painting from an unstable scaffold that high up was decidedly low, so my husband tried verbal persuasion. "It's easy," he said. "You can do it. Just follow my lead" (vicarious experience). I managed to get to where he was standing before the fourth source of self-efficacy information took over. At that point, out of sheer terror, I froze—unable to look up or down or let go of my tight-fisted grip on the bars of the scaffold.

The way in which persuasory information is framed to learners makes a difference in how it will be perceived and whether it will have a positive effect on self-beliefs. For instance, when teachers praise a student for succeeding at an easy task or make statements such as, "You're making good progress," they may unknowingly reinforce low self-efficacy beliefs. Students who have failed previously are particularly sensitive to this kind of feedback, and their self-beliefs will suffer as a consequence (Graham & Barker, 1990). On the other hand, evaluative feedback that communicates how a learner's work demonstrates competence will produce a higher sense of self-efficacy (Bandura, 1997).

Bandura (1997) also noted that persuasory influences work best when they are only moderately beyond peoples' judgments of their own capabilities. This is probably the reason my husband's exhortations were not effective in persuading me to paint from the scaffold. It wasn't just the height of the scaffold, or its instability, or the narrowness of the platform. All three, plus the painting task itself, contributed to my self-beliefs in my inability to successfully perform this task.

Physiological States.   Finally, individuals monitor feelings of self-efficacy on the basis of their **physiological states** (Bandura, 1982). That is, their *"gut feeling" convinces them of probable success or failure.* In my case, my "gut feeling" convinced me that I was about to die! (Obviously, I didn't, but my husband finished the job with me assisting from the ground.)

Identifying internal arousal states is something that Bandura (1986) contended is learned from social labeling coordinated with experienced events. In other words, my identification of fear as the sensation I was feeling in the pit of my stomach probably arose from having experienced events in which that sensation was called "fear" by someone else. Under different circumstances, that same sensation might be labeled "nervous anticipation" and the arousal could have a positive influence on performance. Consider, for example, the arousal felt by an actor waiting in the wings to go on or a teacher preparing to meet a class for the first time. Whether the arousal is debilitating depends on how the person identifies it and the extent to which he or she dwells upon it. There is probably little a teacher can do to alter a student's physiological state, other than to suggest relaxation exercises or desensitization training (see Chapter 2) to overcome fears and anxiety.

Integration of Efficacy Information. With information about self-efficacy coming from so many different sources in so many different ways, an important question is how people integrate all of it to inform their efficacy judgments. Bandura (1997) described the process as complex and indicated that people are generally poor at weighting and integrating multidimensional information. Rather, they tend to pay attention to only some of the information, that which springs more readily to mind or appears most salient. Bandura argued further that "the development of self-appraisal skills...relies on growth of self-reflective metacognitive skills to evaluate the adequacy of one's self-assessments" (1997, p. 115). As we will see later in the chapter, these self-reflective metacognitive skills are also critical to the development of self-regulated behavior as learning proceeds.

Summary

In this section, factors have been considered that influence whether learners will initiate and persist in learning tasks. These have to do with individuals' motivation to learn before the learning has actually begun, and while it is taking place. Most theories of motivation that attempt to account for and explain these factors are classified as expectancy-value theories. As we have seen, for motivation to occur, certain expectancies—about one's abilities, about the task, and about the value of task achievement—must be satisfied.

In the next section, factors are examined that contribute to the overall context of motivation and to continuing motivation. At the end of a learning episode, for example, learners may decide not to continue in further study. This is often caused by expectations that are not met in the original learning situation.

Continuing Motivation

What happens as a result of past learning determines to a large degree whether students will engage in new learning at some time in the future. At least two factors are important to consider in understanding the continuing motivation to learn:

1. Whether learners' expectations about learning and its consequences are being met
2. What attributions learners are making about their failures and successes in learning

Satisfying Expectancies

Imagine that you have just accomplished a challenging goal that you set for yourself. It was a struggle at times, but you remained confident that you would eventually succeed, and so you persisted (this describes me and my windsurfing experience). Now that you have done it, how do you feel? For me, there was an immediate sense of euphoria (I guess I had entertained some doubts that I would not succeed), followed by a feeling of satisfaction and the thought, "I knew I could do it!"

Chances are your reactions were not unlike mine. When learners succeed at a task, two expectations have typically been met. There is the satisfaction of the outcome expectation. That is, I expected that the outcome of my efforts to learn windsurfing would be mastery of the skills involved. Or, similarly, a student may have expected her efforts to result in a course grade of A; when that occurs, her expectation is satisfied.

There is also, however, the satisfaction of efficacy expectations. Recall that a source of information about self-efficacy is one's previous success at the task. Thus, once success is attained, self-efficacy is increased. Having succeeded once in sailing the windsurfer from one end of the bay to the other without falling down, I am more confident in being successful a second time. Moreover, my self-efficacy for learning, in general, has also been increased.

One of the most rewarding (and subsequently, motivating) results of learning is to use the newly acquired skills or knowledge. Keller (1983, 1987a) referred to this as the natural consequences of learning. Natural consequences occur most often when students see the relevance in what they are learning and have the opportunity to apply newly acquired information. Natural consequences are likely, for example, in the Workshop Worries scenario, in which Sean is learning skills that are immediately useful to him in his job. Natural consequences may be a little harder to identify at first for Rob's students in the Camouflage Training scenario. They do not see the benefits initially of learning camouflage skills, but Rob's hope is to engage their interest long enough that participation in some of the activities he has planned will demonstrate the relevance of the skills.

In the event that new knowledge cannot be made useful immediately, outcome expectations may still be satisfied through positive consequences of completing the task (Keller, 1983, 1987a; Bandura, 1997).

Despite Dweck's concern that extrinsic reinforcement may fail to influence (or may even undermine [Deci, 1975]) intrinsic motivation, there are situations when it is appropriate. It might be useful first, however, to consider when extrinsic rewards are not appropriate for stimulating motivation.

Providing rewards only for participation in an activity has generally led to decreased interest in that activity (Bates, 1979). This is especially true when the activity is itself entertaining or stimulating. So, for example, it would probably be unwise to reward learners for engaging in some task that already interests them. Bates (1979) also concluded that providing rewards may adversely affect motivation when the rewards are not normally regarded as intrinsic to task performance. For example, earning extra wages for more work is salient to tasks performed on an assembly line and therefore might contribute to enhanced motivation. But earning tokens for completed school tasks is not especially intrinsic to performance and may have an effect opposite to that intended. Consider how this relates to the token systems discussed in Chapter 2.

Positive consequences can be especially useful, on the other hand, when learning tasks are inherently boring or their relevance is not perceived by the learner. Learning to spell might be a good example of this case. Many students find spelling assignments to be sheer drudgery; moreover, they often fail to understand why they should learn to spell in the first place. After all, isn't that what spell checkers in word-processing programs are for? In this case, students may find no particular satisfaction in spelling words correctly, but may be satisfied by the attainment of some reward attached to spelling achievement. A fifth grade teacher of my acquaintance gives surprise prizes to students when they achieve certain spelling goals. Although this practice might not interest them in spelling over the long term, it does keep them on task with their spelling assignments by temporarily raising their interest in the subject (cf. Calder & Staw, 1975).

Keller (1987a) also pointed out that "even when people are intrinsically motivated to learn the material, there are likely to be benefits from extrinsic forms of recognition. For example, public acknowledgment of achievement, privileges, student presentations of products, and enthusiastically positive comments are welcome" (p. 6). This is consistent with Bandura's (1997) notion of social effects.

In summary, continuing motivation to learn is facilitated through the satisfaction of expectancies in the current learning episode. When learners succeed at a learning goal, their self-efficacy increases and they experience the natural consequences of learning success. Where natural consequences are less likely to occur, positive consequences can serve in some situations to satisfy an outcome expectation.

Making Attributions

Consider, for a moment, what you think when turning in a test paper on which you know you performed poorly. Do you think, "I didn't study the right things," or "I'm just not feeling up to par today," or "I'm not a good student anyway," or "It's my roommate's fault; he (she) kept me out late so I couldn't study." All of these statements reflect ways in which learners attempt to understand their own performances. Whereas those above pertained to an experience of failure, learners make similar judgments about their successes. For example, "I studied really hard"; "Today is just my lucky day"; "The teacher likes me"; "I'm generally a good student"; "That was an easy test." These attributions about learning and performance constitute an important influence on continuing motivation to learn (Weiner, 1979).

TABLE 9.1 *Examples of Attribution and the Dimensions They Comprise*

Attribution Statement	Dimensions
"I didn't study the right things."	Internal, unstable, controllable
"I forced myself to slow down and think."	Internal, unstable, controllable
"I'm just not feeling up to par today."	Internal unstable, uncontrollable
"I studied really hard."	Internal, stable, controllable
"I'm generally a good student."	Internal, stable, uncontrollable
"I'm not a good student anyway."	Internal, stable, uncontrollable
"My kids' schedule frees me to study at the same time each day."	External, stable, controllable
"Her tests are easy."	External, stable, uncontrollable
"The teacher likes me."	External, stable, uncontrollable
"That course is hard."	External, stable, uncontrollable
"It's my roommate's fault; he (she) kept me out late so I couldn't study."	External, unstable, uncontrollable
"Today is just my lucky day."	External, unstable, uncontrollable
"That was an easy test."	External, unstable, uncontrollable

"The central assumption of attribution theory…is that the search for understanding is the (or a) basic 'spring of action'" (Weiner, 1979, p. 3). In other words, people attempt to understand the causes for their successes and failures, and their attributions about these causes determine their future actions. Weiner (1985, 1986, 1992) postulated three dimensions within which most causal attributions can be categorized. These are: internal versus external, stable versus unstable, and controllable versus uncontrollable.

Internal causes of success or failure are those factors within the person, such as ability, effort, and mood. External causes are those outside the learner, such as task difficulty, the attitude of the teacher, help from other people, and so on. The stability dimension refers to how changeable a factor is over time. Ability tends to be stable, whereas mood or luck is unstable. Finally, controllability refers to the degree to which the individual has control over the causes of success or failure. You alone determine how much time you spend studying for a test, since you can set aside sufficient time and then refuse to be distracted from your appointed task. Whether you suddenly contract a stomach virus on the day of the test is beyond your control. See Table 9.1 for examples of attribution statements categorized by dimension.

It should be obvious from the examples that most factors fit along a continuum in each of the three dimensions. Ability, for instance, is internal, relatively stable, and controllable only over the long term (high achievement in a subject leads to potential for further achievement in the same subject). Help from another student, on the other hand, is external, unstable, and uncontrollable by the student experiencing learning difficulties. According to Weiner (1979, 1985, 1986, 1992), each of these dimensions presents implications for continuing motivation.

Consider the factor of ability, for example. Students tend to perceive this internal factor as uncontrollable. Those who attribute their failure to low ability, then, come to believe that "there is no response in [their] repertoire to alter the course of failure" (Graham & Barker, 1990, p. 7). As a result, a vicious cycle is instigated. Students believe they have failed because they are stupid. Since they are stupid, there is no point in trying hard or studying smarter the next time. Because they are not motivated to apply themselves on the next task, they fail again. And so it goes.

If, on the other hand, students attribute their failures to unstable or controllable causes, they are more likely to believe that they will succeed in the future. Doing poorly this time because of illness or not studying means that doing well next time is still possible. Motivation to succeed next time is likely to be enhanced when students perceive that they have the means within their control to assure goal achievement. Weiner argued, therefore, that instructors should use teaching strategies that help learners to see how learning is a function of their own efforts and effective learning strategies and not a function of low ability. This is consistent with Bandura's suggestions regarding the framing of persuasory information.

For most students, failing once is not much cause for concern. Failing repeatedly, however, causes even the most stalwart student to question his or her ability (e.g., Kelley & Michela, 1980). Moreover, indirect cues prompt failure-prone learners to ascribe their failure to low ability. Graham and Barker (1990) investigated the possibility that the offering of help might be perceived as a low-ability cue. They based their investigation on the observation that help is more likely to be offered when the need for help is perceived to be caused by uncontrollable factors. The following example is illustrative. Joan wants to borrow Mary's class notes to see what she missed when she had to leave school to go to a doctor's appointment (an uncontrollable factor). Tony wants to borrow Mary's notes, too, but he missed class because he skipped school to go to the beach (a controllable factor). Which student, Tony or Joan, would you be more likely to lend your notes to?

When help is offered by the teacher or a peer to less able students, these students are likely to infer from the offer of help that they have low ability. In testing this hypothesis, Graham and Barker (1990) demonstrated that "the targets of unsolicited help are perceived by children as less able students who are less likely than their nonhelped peers to do well in the future and to be desirable work mates" (p. 13). They concluded that some well-intentioned instructional practices (e.g., giving help) can have unexpected negative consequences for perceptions of ability.

What can we conclude, then, regarding the effect of attributions on continuing motivation? For one thing, helping learners to attribute their successes and failures to effort and effective (or ineffective) learning strategies is a procedure likely to facilitate motivation. For learners with a history of failures, however, teachers should be especially alert to cues that might further erode individuals' opinions of their abilities.

Self-Regulation

Learners who self-regulate "set goals for their learning and then attempt to monitor, regulate, and control their cognition, motivation, and behavior, guided and constrained by their goals and the contextual features of the environment" (Pintrich, 2000, p. 453). In other words, they try to manage all aspects of motivation that have been discussed so far in the chapter. Zimmerman (1994) proposed a conceptual framework for understanding academic self-regulation, shown in Table 9.2. In addition to self-goals, self-efficacy, and attributions, self-regulation also involves the use of specific strategies to control learning, monitor progress, and structure the environment in ways to support learning.

Processes of Self-Regulation

Zimmerman (2000) also suggested a three-phase cycle to describe the processes of self-regulation during learning (see Figure 9.3). According to this cycle, learners who are effective self-regulators engage first in forethought, or planning. They have "the declarative knowledge to know about specific learning strategies, the procedural knowledge to know how to implement these strategies, and the conditional/metacognitive knowledge to know the conditions and contexts when these strategies should be used" (Lapan, 2002, p. 258). With this, they combine positive self-efficacy beliefs to feel confident that they can successfully complete the learning task. So, for example, it is likely that Bill, the student in my class who became an "A" kind of guy, began to plan his schedule and study strategies after deciding to work for a higher grade on the class quizzes.

The second phase of the cycle involves volitional control over performance, wherein self-regulated learners employ a variety of strategies to manage their own learning and the environmental conditions surrounding them. They also monitor their progress toward goal attainment, making evaluative judgments about their performance, about their self-efficacy for reaching the goal, and about their personal goals in light of their achievement efforts (Bandura, 1997; see also Zimmerman & Schunk, 1989).

For example, suppose a student judges progress as satisfactory. This evaluation would probably raise the student's self-efficacy for achieving the goal and lead to continuation of whatever approach has been taken to the

TABLE 9.2 *Conceptual Analyses of the Dimensions of Academic Self-Regulation*

Scientific Questions	Psychological Dimensions	Task Conditions	Self-Regulatory Attributes	Self-Regulatory Processes
Why?	Motive	Choose to participate	Intrinsically or self-motivated	Self-goals, self-efficacy, values, attributions, etc.
How?	Method	Choose method	Planned or automatized	Strategy use, relaxation, etc.
What?	Performance outcomes	Choose performance outcomes	Self-aware of performance outcomes	Self-monitoring, self-judgment, action control, volition, etc.
Where?	Environmental (social)	Control social and physical setting	Environmentally/socially sensitive and resourceful	Environmental structuring, help seeking, etc.

Source: From B. Zimmerman, "Dimensions of Academic Self-Regulation: A Conceptual Framework for Education." In D. H. Schunk & B. J. Zimmerman (Eds.), *Self-Regulation of Learning and Performance.* Hillsdale, NJ: Lawrence Erlbaum Associates, 1994. Reprinted by permission.

task. On the other hand, if progress is deemed unsatisfactory, then two outcomes are possible. With a resilient sense of self-efficacy, the student would seek other means to achieve the goal based on the likely assumption that whatever he or she is doing now has caused the performance deficit. Alternatively, unsatisfactory progress could have a negative effect on self-efficacy, in which instance the student may change his or her own personal goals with respect to the task. Instead of striving for mastery, the student may be satisfied with something less in the belief that mastery cannot be attained.

According to Schunk and Zimmerman (1994), monitoring progress toward goal attainment is a critical component of self-regulation. It sets up what they refer to as an enactive feedback loop (Zimmerman & Schunk, 1989), composed of three strategies:

1. Observing one's performance
2. Comparing one's performance to a standard or goal
3. Reacting and responding to the perceived difference

However, Bandura (1997) views this as only one part of the self-regulatory system, the part that he refers to as discrepancy reduction. That is, people are

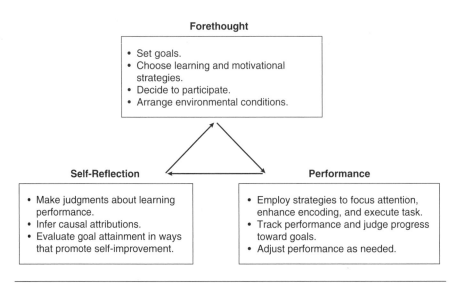

Forethought

- Set goals.
- Choose learning and motivational strategies.
- Decide to participate.
- Arrange environmental conditions.

Self-Reflection

- Make judgments about learning performance.
- Infer causal attributions.
- Evaluate goal attainment in ways that promote self-improvement.

Performance

- Employ strategies to focus attention, enhance encoding, and execute task.
- Track performance and judge progress toward goals.
- Adjust performance as needed.

FIGURE 9.3   *Three-Phase Cycle of Self-Regulation*

motivated to reduce the discrepancy they observe between their own performance (step 1) and that provided by the standard or goal (step 2). They take action (step 3) by revising their self-beliefs, changing their goals, or changing their learning tactics.

Discrepancy production, according to Bandura, is the proactive complement to the reactive discrepancy reduction component in the self-regulation system. By discrepancy production, Bandura means that learners set initial goals that they value, thus creating a state of disequilibrium. In turn, they mobilize effort in anticipation of what it will take to attain the goals and continually adjust those efforts until the desired end has been achieved. Often, once that standard has been reached, learners will set even greater challenges, thus creating new motivating discrepancies to be mastered (Bandura, 1997, p. 131).

Finally, at the end of a learning episode after performance has occurred comes the third phase of self-regulation: self-reflection. At this point, self-regulated learners evaluate their performance with an eye toward making improvements for the future. Was their performance what they expected? If not, why not? Perhaps more effective learning strategies could have been selected, or more effort could have been applied to the learning task. Self-regulated learners are likely to make causal attributions that pertain to things they can control rather than to variables such as ability or luck. They are therefore more inclined to make adaptive changes that enhance future performance (Lapan, 2002).

Developing Self-Regulation Skills

How do learners become self-regulated? According to Paris and Paris (2001), there are at least two metaphors guiding research and practice in the area of self-regulated learning, and each offers something of value to scholars and teachers alike. "One is the metaphor of acquisition, of learning new strategies and skills and applying them in school" (p. 96). In this view, teachers can teach strategies directly to learners, model good strategy use, and coach learners as to when and why strategies will be helpful to them. Modeling, in particular, is consistent with Bandura's views of self-efficacy and the observational learning processes that he proposed.

However, possessing a strategy is no guarantee that the learner will value or use it, especially when learning conditions change. As a result, critics of the so-called transmission model prefer a developmental metaphor in which students are presumed to become more self-regulated as they develop new competencies. Accordingly, they must have multiple experiences with the task conditions presented in Table 9.2 (Schunk & Zimmerman, 1994; Zimmerman, 1994). That is, learners must be given choices in and control over learning and motivation, with many opportunities for self-appraisal.

Table 9.3 provides a list of guidelines derived from both metaphors that can be used to help learners develop self-regulatory capabilities. It is important to remember, however, that developing self-regulation does not happen overnight. Rather, it is likely to be a lengthy and effortful process.

A good example of the time and effort it takes to develop self-regulatory skills can be seen in a graduate course that I teach, in which students are provided a great deal of control over what and how they learn. Students make choices about what to read in the course, what level of proficiency they want to attain, and how they will apply the concepts and ideas they are learning. To the extent possible, I also try to create a knowledge-building community in which the products of learning (i.e., students' assignments) are available for everyone in the community to read and use (e.g., Scardamalia & Bereiter, 1994).

What I have discovered in teaching this course is that even graduate students find it difficult to become self-regulated. The all-too-frequent lament is, "How am *I* supposed to know what to read? *You're* the teacher and you're not teaching me anything!" In time, along with appropriate instructional support and modeling from me (Pintrich, 1995), however, the students generally learn how to manage the learning resources and themselves to achieve their goals.

Summary

We have seen in the previous sections the influence of context and consequences on students' continuing motivation to learn. Motivation appears to be enhanced when learners' expectancies are satisfied and when they attribute their successes to their own efforts and effective learning strategies.

TABLE 9.3 *Guidelines for Facilitating the Development of Learners' Self-Regulation.*

1. Provide opportunities for learners to set their own goals and to manage the ways in which they attain those goals.
   - Learning goals are more effective than performance goals, and they should be challenging but attainable.
   - Modeling and directed reflection can help learners choose effective strategies for learning, managing their time, and controlling the context surrounding learning.

2. Provide opportunities for self-appraisal.
   - Analyzing personal styles of learning and comparing them to others can increase learners' awareness of different ways of learning.
   - Monitoring progress (what is known, what has been done, what is yet to be done or learned) can help learners adjust strategies, allocate their efforts, and revise their goals.
   - Periodic self-assessment can promote feelings of self-efficacy.

3. Create a reflective community.
   - The more opportunities and ways learners can reflect on their learning and that of others, the greater the habit of self-regulation.

Learners become increasingly self-regulated when they acquire skills to plan their learning, monitor their own progress, and evaluate the success of their efforts so as to improve their strategies in the future.

With these findings, taken together with those described in the first section, we are ready to consider an integrated model of motivational design. This attempts to answer the question, How can a teacher or instructional designer incorporate into instruction the appropriate motivational conditions for all learners?

A Model of Motivational Design

For the last 15 or so years, John M. Keller has been developing and testing an integrated model for understanding motivation and for systematically incorporating motivational concerns into instruction. He combines the variety of inputs to motivation that have already been discussed and suggests strategies for instruction that they imply. As you can see from Figure 9.4, Keller (1983, 1984) assumes that students' motives (or values), together with their expectancies (efficacy and outcome expectations), will influence the degree of attention and effort they will supply to a learning task. Although effort then contributes to performance, so, obviously, do the individual's current abilities, skills, and knowledge. Finally, both the consequences of

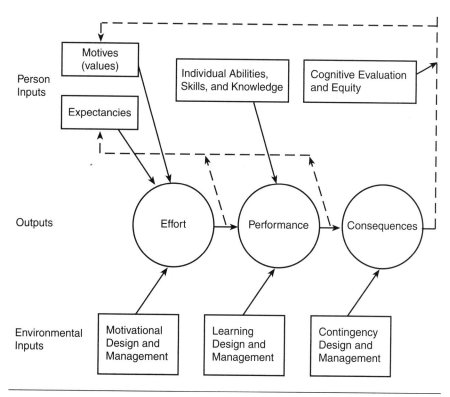

FIGURE 9.4 *A Model of Motivation, Performance, and Instructional Influence*

Source: From Keller, J. M. A model of motivational design. In *Instructional-design theories and models.* Edited by C. M. Reigeluth, 1983, Hillsdale, NJ: Lawrence Erlbaum Associates. Copyright 1983 by Lawrence Erlbaum Associates. Reprinted by permission.

achievement (or the failure to achieve) and the learner's attributions (cognitive evaluation) concerning his or her performance influence motivation in future learning episodes.

In considering the instructional implications of this model, Keller (1983) proposed four conditions for motivation that must be met to have a motivated learner. These correspond to each of the four letters in the acronym, ARCS (Keller, 1984):

A—attention
R—relevance
C—confidence
S—satisfaction

As these are described further in the following section, you will see how they integrate and build upon the sources of motivation discussed earlier in the chapter. Then, armed with a repertoire of these strategies, teachers and instructional designers may use the systematic process described by Keller (1987b) to effectively meet the motivational needs of their learners.

Strategies for Stimulating Motivation

Keller (1987a) appears to view the task of motivating learners as a sequential process. One must first gain the attention of learners and engage them in the learning activity before anything else can take place (*A*). Once involved, however, learners are known to ask the age-old question: "Why must I learn this?" Before instruction can proceed in an optimal way, then, students must believe that it is related to their personal goals and will meet their specific needs (*R*). Even with attentive learners who see personal relevance in the learning task, motivation can still flag as the activity wears on. Some, like Sean in the Workshop Worries scenario, may have fears about the subject that impede their learning it effectively. This is a problem of confidence (*C*). Others, despite their best efforts, may find their attention wandering if the pace and method of instruction never change (a problem of sustaining *A*). "Finally," Keller wrote, "comes the payoff. Or does it?" (1987a, p. 2). As we have seen earlier in the chapter, learning must result in a sense of satisfaction for students to have a continuing desire to learn (*S*).

What are ways, then, that teachers, trainers, or instructional designers can bring about the conditions necessary for motivation? Let's examine Keller's recommendations in each category.

Gaining and Sustaining Attention.   Curiosity has already been described as a strong source of motivation, but one that can be fleeting. To make the most of curiosity caused by stimulus changes, teachers can capture students' interest by using novel or unexpected approaches to instruction or injecting personal experiences and humor. Keller himself, for example, often opens a presentation with a funny story that relates in some way to the topic of his talk. Other examples include beginning a class on American literature with a dramatic reading from a book under study, showing visual tricks in a class studying perception, or including a startling picture in the pages of a textbook.

To stimulate more lasting curiosity, or what Keller (1987a) called an attitude of inquiry, instructors should employ techniques that invoke a sense of mystery and involve students in solving problems. The CTGV instructional video series mentioned earlier in the chapter offers a good example. The instructional goal of one series specifically concerns mathematical problem-solving, but it is embedded in the context of a story about a kid named Jasper Woodbury. In one episode, Jasper plans a trip downriver to buy a boat and must contend with problems like the tide of the river, inclement weather, not enough gas, and so on. As students learn to solve these problems, they become able to solve analogous ones, such as how long would it take Jasper to reach his intended destination if he could only travel 15 mph, instead of 25 mph? Curiosity in the problem solving process is maintained, however, by the narrative character of the instruction. Not only are students interested in what will happen to Jasper next, they can create their own Jasper adventures (CTGV, 1990, 1991a, 1991b).

Finally, Keller (1983, 1987a) recommended that instructors maintain students' attention by varying the instructional presentation. No matter how interested someone is in the topic of a lecture, movie, demonstration, or audio presentation, that interest will wane in the face of unending sameness. Despite my best efforts and intrinsic interest in many nature specials on television, for example, I find myself nodding off after 15 or 20 minutes of listening to the narrator's well-modulated drone. Similarly, many students will lose interest or find their attention wandering when the instruction is always the same and therefore highly predictable. As a change of pace, lecturers might consider presenting some of their material via some form of media, or alternating lecture with demonstrations, small group discussions, or whole class debates. Likewise, printed text can be varied through different type sizes or fonts or the inclusion of diagrams or pictures. Soundtracks can be made more interesting by the use of two or more narrators and by a variation in format (conversation or interview as opposed to narration).

Enhancing Relevance. "Relevance, in its most general sense, refers to those things which we perceive as instrumental in meeting needs and satisfying personal desires, including the accomplishment of personal goals" (Keller, 1987a, p. 3). What Keller seems to describe with this statement are two aspects of the relevance problem, one that is ends-oriented and one that is means-oriented. To be motivated, learners must first recognize that given instruction has personal utility, i.e., will help them achieve personal goals (or ends). Instructors can assist in this recognition by providing statements of utility along with the goals of instruction, or helping learners to define their own goals and statements of utility. The latter strategy works particularly well in advanced topics with learners who have elected to study those topics. In an advanced research seminar I taught, for example, I asked students to determine their own goals and means of assessing progress toward goal attainment. The goals they pursued and the amount of work they completed generally exceeded the expectations I would have set for them.

A particular challenge for teachers arises in situations like the one described in the Camouflage Training scenario, where students fail to find relevance in a required course with prescribed instructional goals. Sometimes, motivating these students amounts to persuasion, often with assurances that the students will eventually see the relevance of what they are learning. In the interim, Keller suggests that means-oriented strategies may be useful.

Described earlier in the chapter were the concepts of need for achievement and need for affiliation. In terms of motivation, these needs have less to do with what is taught than how something is taught. Therefore, teachers can help to motivate students by providing opportunities for matching their motives and values. These may include, for example, providing leadership opportunities, occasions for self-study or working in cooperative groups, or allowing friendly competition on individual or group projects. Rob does this when he challenges student teams to camouflage a jeep so well that he can't find it. Finding ways to actively engage students in learning can be an effective means of motivating them, irrespective of whether they yet see the relevance of the learning activities.

Finally, Keller includes familiarity as a component of relevance. As he put it, "People enjoy more about things they already believe in or are more interested in" (Keller, 1987a, p. 4). Therefore, to the extent possible, instructors should relate instruction to their learners' experiences by providing concrete examples and analogies. The more familiar something is, the more likely it is to be perceived as relevant to the learner. This recommendation should itself seem familiar. If you recall, the cognitive theories of learning (see Chapters 3 to 5) strongly emphasized the importance of a familiar and meaningful context for learning something new. It seems likely, then, that the facilitative effect of context on learning has both cognitive and affective (motivational) components.

Building Confidence. The research on self-efficacy that was reviewed earlier in the chapter established the importance of learners' confidence in their willingness to engage in learning. The question to be addressed here, then, is how to instill confidence in learners who believe they are unable to do, or fear they will fail if they attempt, a given learning task. Keller (1987a) suggested three strategies. First, instructors can create a positive expectation for success by making it clear just what is expected of students. Sometimes, fear of failure is simply fear of the unknown. Because students can be overwhelmed by a detailed discussion of performance requirements and evaluative criteria, Keller recommends progressive disclosure, or telling students what is expected of them as they are ready and able to understand the requirements. In addition, students can be shown how complex, seemingly unreachable goals are made more manageable by their being broken down into subgoals and small steps.

As we have seen from self-efficacy theory, students gain confidence in their own abilities when they actually experience success at challenging tasks. Therefore, a second strategy for building confidence is to provide success opportunities for students. This does not mean that students should never experience failure. Quite the contrary—failure experiences can be constructive, as long as (1) there is a good match between the challenge of the task and the learner's capabilities, (2) the learner's performance is self-initiated, and (3) the learner attributes failure to the poor use of strategies inherent to learning (Clifford, 1984).

Learners are also likely to gain confidence when they are given just enough assistance to perform a task that they are not quite capable of achieving on their own. If you recall from Chapter 7, Vygotsky proposed the "zone of proximal development" as that realm between what learners can achieve on their own and what they can achieve given assistance. Any learning task in this zone will be a challenge, but not an insurmountable one. Moreover, the teacher's goal concerning such tasks should be to gradually reduce his or her assistance until the learner is capable of independently performing the task.

Finally, consistent with attribution and self-regulation theory, instructors can build confidence by providing learners with a reasonable degree of control over their own learning and helping learners to recognize that learning is a direct consequence of their own efforts and effective learning strategies. Both Keller (1987a) and Clifford (1984) pointed to the importance of detailed, unambiguous feedback to students to maintain a task orientation and prompt appropriate attributions. A single score on a project or essay assignment, for example, provides little information to the student. The student, in turn, is likely to react with increased anxiety because no way has been provided to learn from his or her mistakes. A better approach would be for the instructor to conduct separate analyses and assign multiple scores for different aspects of the project or essay (e.g., organization, theme, use of resources, grammar, etc.). In this way, students can gain confidence from what they have done well and attribute poor performance to specific problems that can be corrected.

Generating Satisfaction.   Keller (1987a) again suggested three categories of strategies for generating learning satisfaction, which correspond with natural consequences, positive consequences, and equity.

Opportunities to use newly acquired skills or knowledge in meaningful ways allow for the natural consequences of learning. So, for example, an arithmetic teacher might suggest to students that they calculate their school team's statistics as a means of practicing newly acquired arithmetic skills. Or, an engineering instructor might provide students with the design specifications called for in a completed contract, and then have students compare their designs to what was actually used. Simulations of all kinds work well to furnish appropriate learning environments within which students can tackle real-world problems.

As indicated earlier in the chapter, not all skills or knowledge readily lend themselves to immediate application. Sometimes, component skills or bits of knowledge must accumulate over a long period before they become useful. Alternatively, some students may have no particular interest in the subject but are enrolled to meet some external requirement. In these situations, the use of positive consequences, such as verbal praise, incentives, or real or symbolic awards, may be effective in generating satisfaction. At the conclusion of a training workshop, for example, the sponsoring agency might award participants with certificates of achievement.

"A final and important point," wrote Keller (1987a), "is that people do not look at rewards in isolation" (p. 6). Rather, they tend to make comparisons between themselves and other people going through the learning experience with them. Satisfaction with a particular achievement might be dimmed by the observation that everyone else performed just as well or better. I can remember the first footrace I entered after having taken up running. It was eminently satisfying to actually finish the race, but even more so to finish in the middle of the pack and not last, which I had feared would happen.

Ways to handle equity, according to Keller, include making sure that learning outcomes are consistent with the expectations established at the outset of learning and maintaining consistent standards and consequences for task achievement. To revisit the running example, a colleague of mine did, in fact, finish last in his first footrace. But he derived great satisfaction from this accomplishment anyway because his only goal (and expectation) concerned running the race from start to finish at his own pace. Obviously, maintaining consistent standards throughout a course or training experience is essential for learners to feel that they have been fairly and equitably treated.

Summary.   Table 9.4 presents a summary of the components of motivation, as proposed by Keller, along with strategies within each component that can contribute to the process of motivating learners. Recent studies of the ARCS model and its application have provided some interesting findings. First-year elementary school teachers, for example, used strategies in all four categories of ARCS, but those pertaining to relevance bore the strongest positive relationship to on-task behavior (Newby, 1991). In other words, "those classrooms in which there was a higher incidence of giving reasons for the importance of a task or in which students were encouraged to relate the task to their personal experiences showed a higher rate of on-task behavior" (Newby, 1991, p. 199). On the other hand, satisfaction strategies having to do with rewards and punishments produced a negative correlation with on-task behavior.

Motivational messages based on ARCS were tested in a staff development course for professionals from the Mozambique Ministry of Education and found to positively affect motivation in the course (Visser & Keller, 1990). Likewise, the motivation of college learners increased when relevance-enhancing strategies were embedded in instruction (Means et al., 1997). Finally, suggestions have been made to use ARCS as the basis for determining the motivational needs of adult learners (Bohlin & Milheim, 1994) and to incorporate it into instructional design models (Okey & Santiago, 1991).

How particular motivational strategies might be most effectively selected and implemented is discussed in the next section of the chapter.

The Process of Motivational Design

Think back for a moment to the scenarios with which this chapter began. Suppose Sean asked whatever questions would help clarify his confusions,

TABLE 9.4 *Instructional Strategies for Stimulating Motivation as Suggested by the ARCS Model*

Component of Motivation	Corresponding Strategies
Gaining and sustaining attention	• Capture students' attention by using novel or unexpected approaches to instruction. • Stimulate lasting curiosity with problems that invoke mystery. • Maintain students' attention by varying the instructional presentation.
Enhancing relevance	• Increase the perception of utility by stating (or having the learners determine) how instruction relates to personal goals. • Provide opportunities for matching learners' motives and values with occasions for self-study, leadership, and cooperation. • Increase familiarity by building on learners' previous experiences.
Building confidence	• Create a positive expectation for success by making clear instructional goals and objectives. Alternatively, allow learners to set their own goals. • Provide opportunities for students to successfully attain challenging goals. • Provide learners with a reasonable degree of control over their own learning.
Generating satisfaction	• Create natural consequences by providing learners with opportunities to use newly acquired skills. • In the absence of natural consequences, use positive consequences, such as verbal praise, real or symbolic awards. • Ensure equity by maintaining consistent standards and matching outcomes to expectations.

and soldiers came to camouflage training interested and eager to learn these skills. Would they be a focus of attention in this chapter? Of course not. Only when there is evidence that motivation is a problem do we become concerned about how to solve it—how to motivate learners. The same holds true when it is suspected that motivation will be a problem, i.e., when learners, for whatever reasons, are expected to be uninterested, fearful, or generally disinclined to learn. The motivational design process, therefore, begins with consideration of learner characteristics, or what Keller (1987b) calls audience analysis.

Step 1: Analyze the Audience.   Who are your learners? How likely are they to be interested and ready to learn what you wish to teach? Before you can decide how to go about motivating learners, you must have some idea as to what motivational problems you are likely to face. Keller (1987b) recommended developing an audience profile using the ARCS model in order to identify any gaps in motivation. He noted as well that overmotivation can be as much a problem as undermotivation. For example, a person who claims to know it all already (i.e., is overconfident) is likely to pay little attention in class and make more mistakes as a consequence. Such a person might also prove to be a disruptive influence, diverting other students from assigned tasks.

An audience profile also helps you to determine when motivation is not a likely problem. Where learners are already motivated, it is neither necessary nor desirable to add motivational strategies to the instruction. Imagine your irritation when an instructor spends significant time telling you how valuable the course is and you already know just what you want out of it. Similarly, mediated materials (such as computer software) in which "bells and whistles" are used for motivational purposes may only annoy their users, who want to "get on with it."

Conducting an audience analysis, then, requires rating the attitudes of audience members in each of the categories of ARCS. In many cases, this will involve a "best guess" estimate based on past experience with similar learners. In some cases, however, Keller (1987a) suggested that it may be advisable to conduct interviews with members of the target population. This might be true, for example, in a situation in which one has no knowledge whatever of the learners on which to base an estimate.

In order to acquire a sense of the audience analysis process, consider the following hypothetical cases.

Case 1

A course in education is required of all persons seeking teacher certification in the state. Most of the students are upper division (junior, senior) and majoring in one of the teacher education areas of concentration. A few students come from disciplines outside education, and a few have already taken and failed the teacher certification test.

Hypothetical Analysis

Attention	Initially low. Education courses have a reputation for being low-level and boring. Also, since the course is required, students are likely to be there because they have to be, not because they want to be.

Relevance	Moderate to high. The goal of the course is to teach skills assessed by the teacher test. Therefore, most students will see the relevance of this course for meeting their certification goals.
Confidence	Variable. The education students will view this course as similar to others in which they have already been successful. They will therefore be quite confident in their ability to do well. Students from other disciplines, or students who have already failed the teacher examination, are likely to have genuine concerns about their ability to learn the skills necessary to pass the certification examination.
Satisfaction Potential	Moderate to high. As long as students find something useful in this course, something that enables them to be effective teachers and makes it likely they will pass the teacher test, they will feel satisfied.

Case 2

A literacy course is offered to farmers in an underdeveloped nation. The course is offered in the evening and populated by both men and women from the ages of 15 to 61. None of the students knows how to read.

Hypothetical Analysis

Attention	Variable. Because this is a volunteer audience, the fact that they have come at all indicates some level of attentiveness. However, since they are coming from work and are undoubtedly tired, they will require changes of pace and participatory activities to keep them attentive.
Relevance	Initially low. Participants are unlikely to view literacy as something meaningful to their lives, especially the older ones who have survived without knowing how to read.
Confidence	Initially low and probably variable. Most of the participants have probably had little, if any, formal schooling. Thus, they will be uncertain about their ability to learn to read.
Satisfaction Potential	Positive. If participants can be shown that literacy is a means for them to take control of their lives, then they will feel the effort of learning to read is worthwhile.

It should be obvious that both analyses rely upon assumptions made about the learners in each case. If different assumptions are made, or if other characteristics are known about the learners, then the resulting analyses are likely to be different as well. You may find it useful to imagine what sorts of learners would yield high or low ratings in each of the ARCS categories. For example, in what situations might learners have an especially low Satisfaction Potential but adequate ratings in the other three categories? When might they have low Confidence but high ratings in other categories? And so on.

Step 2: Define Motivational Objectives. From the audience profile, a teacher or instructional designer can determine what motivational needs exist and therefore what motivational objectives should be set. In both hypothetical cases, for example, learner attention and confidence are at levels below optimum. These are areas, then, that can be targeted for motivational design. Objectives need not be written, however, for satisfaction, since this showed high potential in both cases.

Like other types of instructional goals, motivational objectives should be written from the learner's perspective. That is, what change in learner performance or attitude is to be expected from achievement of this goal? So, for example, an objective for confidence that might be written for Case 2 is:

> Participants will indicate greater confidence in their ability to read by trying the read-aloud activities in class.

Or, an objective for attention that might be generated for Case 1 is:

> Students will indicate a higher degree of attention in class by participating in large group discussion and debate.

As you can see from these examples, the attainment of many motivational objectives can be assessed by direct observation. Most instructors, in fact, can sense whether particular motivational strategies have had the desired effect by the interactions they have with students in class. In some situations, though, self-report measures may be useful for determining whether motivational objectives have been met (Keller, 1987b). For example, participants in a technical training workshop might be asked if their confidence in applying these skills has been increased, or if they found the workshop worthwhile.

Step 3: Design a Motivational Strategy. In this step, specific motivational strategies are selected and integrated into instruction. Keller's ARCS categories serve as an obvious guide to this step, because there are strategies associated with each of the four motivational components of the model. However, these strategies are rather general in nature and must be tailored to the characteristics of the target learners and the subject matter being taught. Under attention, for example, a strategy used to stimulate an attitude of inquiry would be quite different for college students in an education course than for adult learners in a literacy class. Likewise, what tasks might be considered challenging would be quite different in the two cases.

Keller (1987a) recommended brainstorming many different ideas for accomplishing motivational objectives and then selecting those that might best fit the students, the style of the instructor, and the content and format of the instruction. Other factors, such as time and available resources, must also be considered.

Step 4: Try Out and Revise as Necessary. The final step of the motivational design process calls for the teacher or instructional designer to try out the strategies selected in the previous step. This might occur in a field trial of the instruction prior to its actual implementation, as in the formative evaluation of a course, workshop, or set of instructional materials. More likely, however, it occurs in the natural implementation of the instruction, as when a teacher meets her class and begins the school term. What is important about this step is that motivation should be thought about separately from other aspects of instruction (Kefler, 1987b). The instructor should attempt to be sensitive to what effects the motivational strategies are having, whether desired or undesired. Then, if the strategies are failing to produce intended results, they can be revised or replaced.

In some cases, revision of the motivational design is also warranted because the audience profile is faulty. In hypothetical Case 2, for example, the participants may already be aware of the important role literacy can play in their lives. If that is so, then a comment or two to confirm the relevance of the material can replace exercises or activities designed to establish relevance. Similarly, different instructional methods might be selected, or a different sequence of activities designed, for students who are found to be attentive, when low attention and interest were expected.

Summary. Table 9.5 displays a summary of the steps in the motivational design process which, together with the strategies summarized in Table 9.3, provide teachers and other designers of instruction with an effective means for enhancing motivation. Keller (1987b) also reminded us, however, to draw upon personal experiences while using his model:

> After all, we have been consumers of instruction for more years of our lives than we care to remember. We have seen many examples, and nonexamples, of motivating instruction. This personal knowledge combined with some formal knowledge of motivation and a systematic process for motivational design can be powerful tools in improving the motivational appeal of instruction. (p. 7)

TABLE 9.5 *Keller's Motivational Design Process*

Step 1: Analyze the audience and develop a motivational profile based on ARCS.

> **Example:** A—initially low
> R—moderate to high
> C—variable
> S—moderate to high

Step 2: Define motivational objectives based on the audience profile.

> **Example:** 1. Students will indicate a higher degree of attention in class by participating in group discussion and debate (**A**).
> 2. Students will exhibit greater confidence by setting and pursuing their own goals for an application project (**C**).

Step 3: Design a motivational strategy and integrate it into instruction.

> **Example:** 1. Plan debates and discussion to be interspersed with lecture. Select media to accompany lecture (**A**).
> 2. Set up the structure for a self-study project (**C**).

Step 4: Try out and revise the strategy as necessary.

> **Example:** Not enough direction given for the self-study project. Student still anxious, lacks confidence in ability to complete it on time. Therefore, provide more direction by breaking the project into more manageable subparts.

Motivation and Self-Regulation in "Kermit and the Keyboard"

There is ample evidence of both intrinsic motivation and self-regulation in the story "Kermit and the Keyboard." An unmotivated Kermit would not have decided to learn a new skill by himself. Instead, we can see highly goal-directed behavior. Kermit purchases a keyboard with particular capabilities, brings out of storage some music instruction books, buys some additional music fake books, and begins to systematically self-instruct. It is likely that he has high self-efficacy for this task, or a strong belief in his ability to learn to play the keyboard. Even though he has never played this particular instrument before, he was previously successful at learning to play clarinet and saxophone and became proficient enough to play in a symphony and dance band. Such enactive mastery experiences are the most powerful type in facilitating positive self-efficacy.

His high self-efficacy makes it likely that Kermit will persist in his efforts, even in the face of difficulty. We do see, however, evidence that failure experiences have an adverse effect on Kermit's motivation to learn to play particular songs. He forsakes those on which he continues to make many mistakes in favor of those with which he is more successful. Likewise, he stops playing sooner when he experiences continued difficulty with a particular song.

Kermit demonstrates many competencies of self-regulation. He has set a distal and general goal—learning to play the keyboard—but he appears to set more proximal and specific goals as well, such as making a list of particular songs he would like to learn to play. His goals are very much mastery oriented, making them learning goals rather than performance goals. He does not worry about how his playing compares to that of others but focuses only on what he needs to do to improve his own skills.

Kermit plans particular activities that he thinks will facilitate his learning (e.g., practicing exercises as well as working on songs, practicing at a slower tempo and working up to the recommended tempo, reading particular sections of the manual), puts those plans into action, and adjusts his plans in light of his performance. For example, when he has difficulty understanding a feature of the keyboard he wants to learn, he consults his wife or goes on-line to seek assistance. The third phase of the self-regulation cycle—self-reflection—is perhaps the hardest to detect in this story, but we might see it in Kermit's contemplation about whether to join the Sunday jam sessions. He considers whether joining the group will enable him to learn more than the approach he is taking currently.

Theory Matrix

Theory	Motivation and Self-Regulation
Prominent Theorists	A. Bandura; J. M. Keller; P. R. Pintrich; D. H. Schunk; B. Zimmerman
Learning Outcome(s)	Goal-directed behavior
	Ability to set goals, monitor progress, and adjust learning strategies to assure goal attainment
Role of the Learner	Determine areas of interest and value
	Appraise utility of learning strategies and make necessary adjustments to improve the learning process
	Calibrate learning efforts with results
Role of the Instructor	Enhance motivation with strategies that gain attention, enhance relevance, foster confidence and ensure satisfaction
	Provide opportunities for learners to set goals, determine learning methods, and self-appraise
Inputs or Preconditions to Learning	Presence and participation in a learning environment.
Process of Learning	Not specifically addressed. Modern approaches to motivation and self-regulation are consistent with a social-cognitive view of learning.

Suggested Readings

Bandura, A. (1997). *Self-efficacy: The exercise of control.* New York: W. H. Freeman and Company.

Boekaerts, M., Pintrich, P. R., & Zeidner, M. (Eds.). (2000). *Handbook of self-regulation.* New York: Academic Press.

Schunk, D. H. & Zimmerman, B. J. (Eds.). (1994). *Self-regulation of learning and performance.* Hillsdale, NJ: Erlbaum.

Weiner, B. (1992). *Human motivation: Metaphors, theories, and research.* Newbury Park, CA: Sage Publications.

Reflective Questions and Activities

1. Consider what assumptions about knowledge and knowing may underlie the conceptions of learner motivation that are discussed in this chapter. With what

epistemological tradition do they seem to be most closely associated? What evidence supports your choice?

2. At the conclusion of several other chapters (i.e., Chapters 2, 3, 5, and 8), you generated plans for facilitating learning of some difficult goal, involving yourself or other learners. Reflect back on those situations from the perspective of motivation. How much of the learning difficulty might be attributable to a lack of motivation, as opposed to lack of prerequisite skill or poor instruction? How might you now add a motivational design to your instructional plan?

3. Review your answer to Question 5 of Chapter 6, in which you discussed instructional strategies suitable for adults versus children. Add a motivational component to your instruction. What would be important to consider in motivating children versus adults?

4. Select a scenario from any previous chapter. Using the ARCS model, analyze the situation for its probable motivational characteristics. Determine a set of motivational objectives, and then suggest strategies you think would be effective for stimulating motivation. Provide a rationale for each of your decisions.

5. Describe a learning situation in which you expect to find learners with low self-efficacy. First, how would you determine that they in fact have low self-efficacy? What behaviors and attitudes would you expect these learners to exhibit? Then, generate an instructional plan that would help learners become more efficacious.

Part VII: Learning and Instruction

10

Gagné's Theory of Instruction

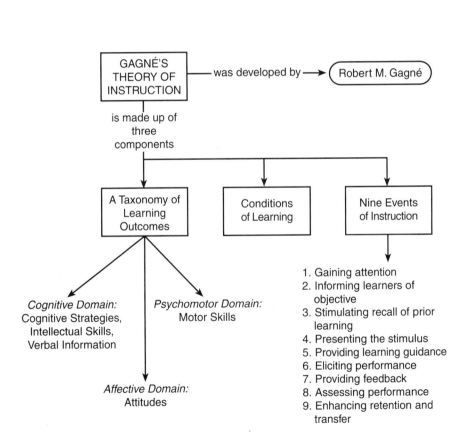

GAGNÉ'S THEORY OF INSTRUCTION — was developed by → Robert M. Gagné

is made up of three components

A Taxonomy of Learning Outcomes

Conditions of Learning

Nine Events of Instruction

Cognitive Domain:
Cognitive Strategies, Intellectual Skills, Verbal Information

Psychomotor Domain:
Motor Skills

Affective Domain:
Attitudes

1. Gaining attention
2. Informing learners of objective
3. Stimulating recall of prior learning
4. Presenting the stimulus
5. Providing learning guidance
6. Eliciting performance
7. Providing feedback
8. Assessing performance
9. Enhancing retention and transfer

Consider these scenarios.

• *Medical School*

At the University of Anywhere Medical School, instructors routinely face the problem of biomedical misconceptions among students. That is, medical students, despite exposure to appropriate information, continue to make diagnostic errors in many of the clinical cases that they study. Instructors have found that students, in their diagnoses, tend to oversimplify, overrely on general theories, and disregard unique or puzzling symptoms. How to best deal with these problems is of major concern, particularly in light of the spiraling costs of medical school education. The instructors want to know how they should revise their instruction or devise new learning experiences, so that students will avoid making so many errors.

• *A&B Agency*

Like other organizations in recent times, A&B Agency has become increasingly sensitive to issues of sexual harassment in the workplace. The

Agency Board of Directors decides that the training provided to all new employees should be expanded to include the topic of sexual harassment. Primarily, the Board wants employees to know the legal definition of sexual harassment and procedures for reporting it, whether the harassment is either personally experienced or observed in others. An implicit goal of the training, or course, is that employees will treat their co-workers with respect and refuse to engage in any form of sexual harassment, no matter how seemingly benign.

Think back for a moment to the scenarios with which the other chapters in this book began. How do the scenarios here differ from those? All of the scenarios are in some way concerned with a learning problem, which is used to illustrate the theories discussed in each chapter. But whereas the scenarios from the previous chapters described the problem from the perspective of a learner (or learners), the ones in this chapter (and the next) focus on the problem from the standpoint of an instructor or designer of instruction. For you to think about learning from the instructor's or designer's perspective is, in a sense, a goal of every chapter. After all, a major purpose for reading this book is to acquire a sufficient understanding of learning to teach effectively or to design effective instruction. But the two chapters in this section are specifically devoted to discussions on theories of instruction, rather than theories of learning.

It is important to note that several theories (or partial theories) of instruction have already been suggested in some of the other chapters, as they have derived from particular views of learning. Radical behaviorism (Chapter 2), for example, provided a foundation for performance analysis and improvement. Ausubel's meaningful reception learning (Chapter 4) served as the foundation for Reigeluth's (1983) Elaboration Theory. Notions about situated cognition (Chapter 5) led to concepts of authentic instruction and apprenticeship models of teaching. Bruner himself (Chapter 7) articulated features of an instructional theory, and his work bears significant similarity to the Inquiry Models developed by Collins and Stevens (1983), Taba (in Joyce & Weil, 1986), and Suchman (in Gunter, Estes, & Schwab, 1990). Finally, Bandura's (1986, 1997) work in self-efficacy and social learning theory and Keller's (1983) model of motivational design (Chapter 9) suggested ways to enhance students' motivation to learn.

What these theories all have in common, with the possible exception of behaviorism, is a limitation of scope. That is, each proposes instructional methods thought to provide the necessary learning conditions for a particular type of learning goal. Ausubel, for example, was largely concerned with how learners acquire bodies of information as knowledge. Bruner, along with Collins and Stevens, Taba, and Suchman, addressed himself to the attainment of concepts and inquiry skills. Keller obviously confined his attention to the engagement of students in learning. As for behaviorism, Skinner would probably have argued that its principles serve equally well for promoting any kind of learning. However, with its emphasis on observable behavior, it has not always served educators well who want to engender skills and knowledge in learners that are not easily observed.

In this chapter and the next, two theories that their proponents claim are significantly broader in scope than those mentioned earlier will be discussed. The first, Gagné's (1985) conditions for learning, underwent development and revision for twenty or more years. With behaviorist roots, it now brings together a cognitive information-processing perspective on learning with empirical findings of what good teachers do in their classrooms. Gagné's theory also serves as the basic framework for a prominent instructional design theory (Gagné, Briggs, & Wager, 1992). In contrast to Gagné's theory is the constructivist approach to instruction. Rather than a single theory, constructivism represents a collection of similar approaches which have been gaining currency in education and training. They stem from a view of learning more compatible with the ideas of Piaget, Bruner, and Vygotsky than with information processing. Since constructivism continues to develop, it remains to be seen whether a single instructional theory will emerge. At present, then, we can only examine the similarities among approaches as they collectively differ from Gagné's theory.

Before proceeding to the specific instructional theories of Gagné and constructivism, let us take a brief look at instructional theory in general.

Instructional Psychology, Instructional Theories, Instructional Models

Instructional psychology is essentially what this book is about. "Instructional psychologists...are concerned with how best to enhance learning" (Dillon & Sternberg, 1986, p. ix). Therefore, they rely on the findings of psychological and instructional research to solve instructional problems and make decisions about instructional practice (Gagné & Dick, 1983; Gagné & Rohwer, 1969; Resnick, 1981). Instructional theory results when instructional psychologists deductively derive principles of instruction from existing learning theory or inductively develop such principles from empirical studies.

Reigeluth (1983) defined **instructional theory** as *identifying methods that will best provide the conditions under which learning goals will most likely be attained.* He stated further that, for an instructional theory to be effective, it must either build on or be compatible with existing learning theory. In other words, learning theory specifies the link between what is learned and the conditions under which learning occurs. Instructional theory, as depicted in Figure 10.1, adds the component of instructional method to the existing equation. What should also be noted about instructional theory is that it involves intentional learning goals. That is, learning will occur whenever conditions are ripe, and in fact, learning goes on all the time. **Instruction,** however, refers to *the deliberate arrangement of learning conditions to promote the*

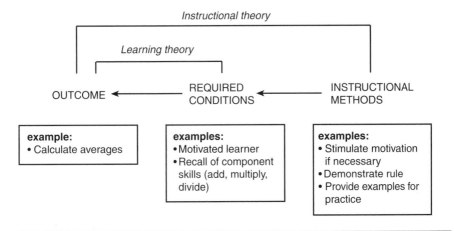

FIGURE 10.1 *The Relationship between Instructional Theory and Learning Theory*

attainment of some intended goal. Therefore, the purpose of instructional theory is to be prescriptive, to provide principles by which teachers and instructional designers can assure learning. Because prescription is probabilistic in nature, rather than deterministic, Reigeluth (1999) prefers to use the term "design-oriented". That is, design-oriented theories offer methods of instruction for different situations that increase the probability that desired learning outcomes will occur, but they do not guarantee it. The goal of any instructional theory, however, is "to attain the highest possible probability of the desired results" (Reigeluth, 1999, p. 11).

Schott and Driscoll (1997) proposed a universal instructional theory, arguing that teachers and designers must consider these four components when they develop instruction:

1. The learner
2. The learning task (including desired learning outcomes)
3. The learning environment (learning conditions and instructional methods)
4. The frame of reference (or the context in which learning is to occur)

Perhaps an example will be illustrative. Suppose a chemistry instructor is assigned to teach a section for preservice teachers of elementary education. The instructor wants students to learn not only chemistry, but also how they might teach it effectively to their students in elementary school. What learning conditions are necessary for the preservice teachers to achieve these goals? From motivation theory, we know that the students must see some value in learning chemistry, and they must have some confidence that they can both learn it themselves and teach it to others. Information-processing theory suggests that the students must know certain prerequisite information and that new information should be presented to them in a way that facilitates encoding. Finally, if situated cognition theory is considered, then it is important for students to engage in activity that is meaningful and relevant. These learning conditions all have implications for the types of learning tasks and instructional methods that are likely to be most effective.

On the basis of instructional theory, effective methods might include demonstrations, followed by providing, as practice, meaningful chemistry problems for students to solve. But even these simple methods can be implemented in various ways. The practice problems might appear in a textbook, on a computer monitor displayed in class, or embedded in a discovery scenario in which students are asked to experiment and describe what they learn from the chemical reactions that they try.

To guide an instructor's actions, then, are instructional models, or "step-by-step procedure[s] that lead to specific learning outcomes" (Gunter et al., 1990, p. 67). Such models are typically articulated as the principles of instructional theories are tested and validated. Any comprehensive instructional theory that pertains to multiple learning outcomes will provide multiple instructional models. And what models are implemented for a specific goal can depend on the context for instruction as well as the nature of the learning goal. This is similar to Reigeluth's (1999) conception of instructional-design theory, which indicates what methods of instruction to use, as well as when and how to use them in specific situations, subject to the constraints of those situations. In the case of the chemistry instructor, for example, the conduct of experiments requires certain resources and a laboratory setting that may be unavailable to the instructor.

Gagné's theory of instruction is perhaps a clearer demonstration of a comprehensive instructional theory, so let us consider it first. Then the collective approaches to constructivism will be discussed in Chapter 11.

Robert M. Gagné and the Conditions of Learning

Robert M. Gagné published the first edition of *The Conditions of Learning* in 1965 and the fourth edition in 1985. In that time, the theory evolved significantly from one that was extensively behavioral to one that is now predominantly cognitive in nature. At the end of his career, Gagné published an adaptation of *The Conditions of Learning* specifically for the job-training context (*The Conditions of Learning: Training Applications*, published in 1996 by Robert M. Gagné and Karen L. Medsker).

Much of Gagné's early experience as an instructional psychologist was spent tackling practical problems of training air force personnel. He dealt particularly with problems in determining just what skills and knowledge are required for someone to be an effective performer at a given job. Once job requirements were identified, the task then became one of determining how those requirements might best be learned by a person in training for the job.

Briggs (1980), who was a long-term collaborator of Gagné's, wrote, "I have never asked Gagné about this, but I believe that his early work in the Air Force must have been an important factor in his later derivation of his (a) taxonomy of learning outcomes, (b) concept of learning hierarchies, and (c) related concepts of instructional events and conditions of learning" (pp. 45–46). In fact, Gagné proposed a version of his learning taxonomy in an address to the APA Division of Military Psychology in 1955. Interestingly, elements of cognition were also present in his work early on, long before he came to deliberately incorporate notions of information-processing into his theory (Driscoll & Burner, in press)

As it has evolved, Gagné's theory incorporates three major components: a taxonomy of learning outcomes, specific learning conditions required for the attainment of each outcome, and the nine events of instruction. Because Gagné eventually adopted information-processing theory as a foundation for his theory, the conditions for learning include both internal events (such as previously encoded information) and external events (such as methods of elaboration to facilitate encoding). Additionally, the events of instruction refer to methods or procedures designed to facilitate the specific processes (such as encoding, retention, retrieval, etc.) thought to occur during learning.

A Taxonomy of Learning Outcomes

If you recall from Chapters 3 and 8, cognitive psychologists and neuroscientists both provided evidence supporting a distinction between declarative and procedural knowledge. Declarative knowledge refers to factual knowledge, or knowing that (e.g., "I know that Shakespeare lived in the sixteenth century"). Procedural knowledge, by contrast, refers to cognitive skills, such as knowing how (and therefore being able to demonstrate how), for example, to conjugate Latin verbs or balance a budget. Cognitive psychologists have also investigated conditional knowledge, the metacognitive knowledge that enables learners to determine when and how to apply declarative or procedural knowledge. For example, I know to look for major headings to organize my learning from textbooks.

All of these types of knowledge are undetectable in the learner purely by observation. That is, I cannot tell by looking at you whether you know when Shakespeare lived, whether you can balance a budget, or whether you pay attention to headings when you study from a textbook. Such knowledge must be inferred from some behavior that is observable. You could tell me the dates Shakespeare lived, or write down the conjugations of certain Latin verbs, or construct an outline of some text chapter.

Telling and writing are behaviors that imply another kind of knowledge. For instance, to write anything, a learner must be able to form the appropriate letters with a writing device. This type of performance is fundamentally different from declarative, procedural, or conditional knowledge in that it involves the use and movement of muscles. Generally called motor skills, these capabilities must also have a psychological component, because they do not have to be relearned with every performance. Despite long periods of nonuse, people generally do not forget completely how to ride a bicycle, shift a car, or swim the breaststroke.

In addition to cognitive and motor types of knowledge, humans appear to have the capacity for affective knowledge. Why, for example, do you listen to a certain type of music or participate in a certain sport or physical activity? Because you like it, it makes you feel good. These internal states of feeling predispose learners to engaging in some activities over others. This helps to explain why an individual who knows perfectly well what to do ("Stop when the light turns red") may choose not to do it ("I'm worried that my pay will be docked if I'm late").

In their search for ways to facilitate learning, then, instructional theorists have found it useful to distinguish the variety of capabilities humans can acquire. In doing so, they make a fundamental assumption that different capabilities require different conditions for learning. Helping someone learn to operate a piece of machinery, in other words, is assumed to demand different types of assistance than helping someone memorize lines to a play.

Benjamin Bloom, a contemporary of Gagné's, was among the first to accept the notion that humans' learned capabilities comprise three major domains: cognitive, affective, and psychomotor. Furthermore, he proposed a taxonomy of levels within the cognitive domain that is still in wide use today (Bloom et al., 1956; see Table 10.1). Extending this work, Krathwohl, Bloom, & Masia (1964) developed a taxonomy of outcomes within the affective domain (Table 10.2). Finally, Simpson (1966–1967) prepared a plan for a taxonomy of psychomotor outcomes (Table 10.3). Other taxonomies have been suggested, particularly in the cognitive and, more recently, the affective domains (see contributions to Reigeluth [1999] for examples). But Gagné remains the only instructional theorist to propose an integrated taxonomy of learning outcomes that included all three domains.

According to Gagné (1972), there are five major categories of learning outcomes: (1) verbal information, (2) intellectual skills, (3) cognitive strategies, (4) attitudes, and (5) motor skills. The five categories are also summarized in Table 10.4, along with examples of each.

Verbal Information.   **Verbal information** is Gagné's category in the cognitive domain for *declarative knowledge*. It refers to the vast bodies of organized

TABLE 10.1 *Bloom's Taxonomy of Cognitive Outcomes*

Knowledge	Remembering previously learned material, including facts, vocabulary, concepts, and principles
Comprehension	Grasping the meaning of material
Application	Using abstractions, rules, principles, ideas, and other information in concrete situations
Analysis	Breaking down material into its constituent elements or parts
Synthesis	Combining elements, pieces, or parts to form a whole or constitute a new pattern or structure
Evaluation	Making judgments about the extent to which methods or materials satisfy extant criteria

TABLE 10.2 *A Taxonomy of Affective Outcomes*

Receiving	Becoming sensitized to or willing to receive certain information
Responding	Becoming involved or doing something
Valuing	Displaying a commitment to something because of its inherent worth
Organization	Organizing a set of values and determining their relationships, including which should dominate
Characterization by value	Integrating values into a total philosophy and acting consistently in accord with that philosophy

TABLE 10.3 *Simpson's Plan for Taxonomy of Psychomotor Outcomes*

Perception	Becoming aware of stimulation and the need for action
Set	Preparing for action
Guided response	Responding with assistance from a teacher or coach
Mechanism	Responding habitually
Complex response	Resolving uncertainty and performing difficult tasks automatically
Adaption	Altering responses to fit new situations
Origination	Creating new acts or expressions

knowledge that learners acquire through formal schooling, books, television, and many other means (Gagné, 1985; Gagné & Driscoll, 1988). Verbal information is what individuals recall when playing such popular games as *Jeopardy*™ and *Trivial Pursuit*™. Examples include stating the capital city of Botswana, reciting Hamlet's famous soliloquy, and, as might be required in the scenario, Medical School, listing the symptoms typical of a heart attack.

It should be obvious by now that researchers have been interested for a long time in understanding how information is acquired and what functions it serves for the learner. Gagné's view is consistent with the views of Ausubel, information-processing theorists, and schema theorists in accepting that learners organize their knowledge in themes or schemata. These then provide the necessary foundation for acquiring related information as well as solving problems. Problem solving is not itself verbal information, but its success depends upon the learner being able to apply relevant information to the problem. For example, to assist your learning about a particular tribe in Africa, you would call to mind anything else you knew about the region in question—its geography, weather, or form of government. Likewise, to diagnose the probable cause of a particular patient's distress (an example of problem solving), a doctor would rely on his or her knowledge of symptoms associated with particular diseases.

Gagné's conception of verbal information appears to incorporate the first two levels of Bloom's taxonomy, knowledge and comprehension. Sometimes, for instance, learners memorize information without regard to its meaning. Although they may then be able to recite what was learned, they probably cannot give an adequate account of it in their own words. On the other hand, when comprehension has occurred, learners can paraphrase or otherwise explain the information that was acquired. In this case, the information no longer remains isolated in memory but becomes integrated within a larger context of related ideas. For obvious reasons, comprehension is usually considered to be a more desirable educational goal than inert, memorized knowledge.

Intellectual Skills.   A second category in the cognitive domain of Gagné's taxonomy is that referred to as intellectual skills (Gagné, 1985). **Intellectual skills** are the equivalent of *procedural knowledge* and are divided into five, hierarchically ordered subcategories. These are: discriminations, concrete concepts, defined concepts, rules, and higher-order rules.

Gagné's proposal to subdivide the intellectual skill category grew out of his work with learning hierarchies (e.g., Gagné, 1968, 1977). A **learning hierarchy** refers to *a set of component skills that must be learned before the complex skill of which they are a part can be learned* (Gagné, 1985). The hierarchy itself results from an analysis of the desired terminal skill in terms of its prerequisites. Moreover, the relationship between each skill in the hierarchy and its

TABLE 10.4   *Gagné's Taxonomy of Learning Outcomes with Examples*

Learning Outcome	Definition	Example
Verbal Information	Stating previously learned material such as facts, concepts, principles and procedures	Listing the seven major symptoms of cancer
Intellectual Skills		
Discrimination	Distinguishing objects, features, or symbols	Feeling the difference in texture between two fabrics being considered for drapery linings
Concrete concepts	Identifying classes of concrete objects, features, or events	Picking all the wrenches out of a toolbox
Defined concepts	Classifying new examples of events or ideas by their definition	Noting the armed conflict between two peoples in a country as a "civil war"
Rules	Applying a single relationship to solve a class of problems	Calculating the earned run averages (ERAs) of the Atlanta Braves
Higher order rules	Applying a new combination of rules to solve a complex problem	Generating a plan to manage a major change in a client organization
Cognitive Strategies	Employing personal ways to guide learning, thinking, acting, and feeling	Incorporating visual displays into a presentation for a client
Attitudes	Choosing personal actions based on internal states of understanding and feeling	Choosing to respond to all incoming e-mail within 24 hours
Motor Skills	Executing performances involving the use of muscles	Performing CPR on a person who has stopped breathing

immediate prerequisite is one of "necessary, whether or not sufficient." Consider the example shown in Figure 10.2.

According to the assumptions of learning hierarchies, students must already be able to distinguish triangles from other shapes (Box 2) before they

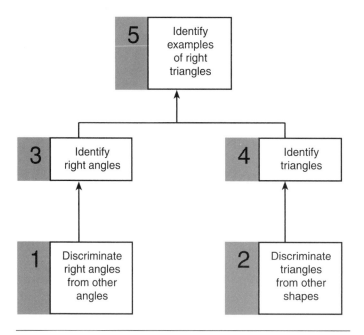

FIGURE 10.2 *A Simple Learning Hierarchy*

will be able to learn the identifying characteristics of triangles (Box 4). In other words, if they cannot see a perceptual difference between triangles and, say, squares, they will be unable to identify examples of triangles. Thus, the discrimination skill is a necessary (and sufficient) prerequisite to the identification skill. Similarly, identification of right triangles (Box 5) requires identification of triangles and right angles. These two identifications are each necessary and together sufficient for the final skill to be acquired.

Learning hierarchies provide three distinct advantages for planning instruction (Gagné & Medsker, 1996). First, they ensure that instruction is complete by identifying all the components of an intellectual skill that could be included in a lesson. Second, they enable appropriate sequencing of instruction by showing what components must be learned before others are tackled. Finally, they provide for efficient instruction by focusing on essential components rather than extraneous or "nice-to-know" topics.

Based on the types of relationships that could result from an instructional analysis, Gagné proposed the five levels of intellectual skills. Discrimination is the ability to distinguish, on the basis of perceptual characteristics, one object from another, one feature from another, one symbol from another. Discrimination is also prenomial, which means that some difference is detected without the learner being capable of naming or explaining that difference. In other words, infants can feel and respond to differences in textures of cloth without the words to express *smooth* or *rough*. Similarly, my husband can distinguish among different colors quite plainly, but apparently he never learned the same color terms as the rest of us. For instance, he can draw matching socks out of his drawer, but he is likely to call a green dress "purple" or a tan car "brown."

Humans typically acquire many gross discriminations pertaining to the environment at a very young age. Then with experience, these discriminations increase in the fineness of detail to which they refer (Gagné & Driscoll, 1988). Certain environmental circumstances also demand that finer discriminations be developed. Eskimos, for example, can distinguish many more snow conditions than the average person who lives where snow is not common. Likewise, counselors have learned to detect subtle differences in the facial expressions of their clients, microbiologists have learned to see tiny irregularities in the shape and makeup of cells, and sailors have learned to feel almost imperceptible changes in wind direction or velocity.

Once prerequisite discriminations have been acquired, concept learning can occur. According to Gagné (1985), concrete concepts are classes of objects, features, and events, distinguishable by their perceptual characteristics and identifiable by name. So, for example, young children learn such concrete concepts as colors, shapes, and letters of the alphabet. At a more advanced level, a home carpenter must learn to identify wood screws and toggle bolts, whereas a mechanic should know engine oil and brake fluid.

Many concepts, however, cannot be pointed out directly but must be identified by means of a definition. Gagné (1985) called these defined concepts and argued that for learners to have truly acquired defined concepts, they must use the definitions for classifying new instances. It is not enough, therefore, to say that "positive reinforcement means increasing the occurrence of some behavior by rewarding it." One must recognize examples such as a child speaking up in class more often following encouragement by the teacher.

Tessmer, Wilson, and Driscoll (1990) agreed with Gagné that defined concepts make up a significant part of school learning. They suggested, however, that classification of new examples is not the only desirable outcome of defined concept learning. Some defined concepts, such as perestroika or beauty, do not always yield clear or unambiguous examples. A learner's understanding of such terms might be better assessed in other ways. Tessmer et al. (1990) suggested, as alternatives to concept classification, asking learners to generate inferences or reason through some problem involving the concept in question.

Although a defined concept is arguably the simplest type of rule, rule learning typically involves the use of symbols to represent and interact with the environment in generalized ways (Gagné & Driscoll, 1988). There are rules for decoding words, for constructing grammatical sentences, for calculating averages, and for factoring equations. What is particularly important about rule learning is not whether students can verbalize, or state, the rule. Rather, it is whether they can demonstrate the rule by applying it appropriately to a class of problems, even problems that have not been encountered before.

Finally, higher-order rules represent combinations of simpler rules for the solving of complex problems. "A higher-order rule is still a rule and differs only in complexity from the simpler rules that compose it" (Gagné & Driscoll, 1988, p. 52). Higher-order rules are thought to develop when learners must apply a new combination of rules already known and used individually. This would occur, for example, when a carpet layer must determine how much carpet is required to cover an irregularly shaped room. This is a novel problem, because the carpet layer has not encountered a room with quite this shape before, but it is a solvable one using standard rules of geometry. Similarly, when a nutritionist devises meal plans for a given client, he or she applies standard rules in a unique way to meet the particular needs of that person.

Altogether, Gagné's intellectual skills incorporate reasonably well the remaining four levels of Bloom's taxonomy. Application is demonstrated in concept and rule use, whereas analysis, synthesis, and evaluation are all, to some degree, present in higher-order rule using (or problem solving). In order to determine what rules are likely to be effective for solving a given problem, the learner must analyze it, generating subproblems or taking note of important constraints. Applying some combination of rules to solve the problem represents a synthesis. Evaluation occurs when the learner monitors the success of the selected rules for effecting a solution. It also seems likely, however, that analysis, synthesis, and evaluation would also be present in the next category of Gagné's taxonomy.

Cognitive Strategies. **Cognitive strategies** consist of *numerous ways by which learners guide their own learning, thinking, acting, and feeling.* Gagné (1985) conceived of cognitive strategies as representing the executive control functions of information processing, and they compose what others have called conditional knowledge. As such, learners employ cognitive strategies to monitor their own attention, to help themselves better encode new information, and to improve their success at remembering critical information at test time. Learners may arrive at these strategies through their own trial-and-error experiences, or they may be explicitly taught strategies that have proven effective with other learners.

Developing unique as well as effective cognitive strategies is typically considered a part of learning to learn and learning to think independently. Unfortunately, a difficulty with cognitive strategies as desirable learning outcomes is that they are not particularly amenable to assessment. Frequently, because cognitive strategies are employed in the service of other learning goals, it is the attainment (or not) of those goals that is noticed. What cognitive strategies were used is often not immediately evident.

Another aspect of learning to think independently, however, is learning to think creatively, and it is creative thinking where we may detect better evidence of effective cognitive strategies. What constitutes creative thinking is certainly a matter of some debate, but most would agree that it involves originality, seeing problems in new and insightful ways, or finding a solution to what others did not recognize as a problem. Bruner (1973b) perhaps put it best when he distinguished between problem solving and problem finding. In problem solving, the learner tackles a problem defined by someone else. Moreover, the existing parameters of the problem generally constrain its solution, so that all solvers will arrive at more or less the same outcome. The carpet example described earlier illustrates this well. There are only so many ways to determine how much carpet is required, and all carpet layers (if they want to remain in business) will generate similar estimates for the same room.

By contrast, learners generate their own problems in problem finding and bring to bear upon them both previously acquired rules and their own personal ways of thinking (Gagné & Driscoll, 1988). As an example, consider the long, lamented decline in Scholastic Aptitude Test (SAT) scores that has been seen in the United States over the last 20 years. Some statisticians do not perceive this to be a problem, claiming the observed decline is merely an artifact of test construction procedures and statistical regression effects. Other educational researchers, however, perceive the decline in scores to be a symptom of some educational problem. How they define what the problem is determines what actions they take to generate solutions. As a result, many different solutions are offered to what is thought to be wrong with the American education system. These solutions, then, are the outcomes, or evidence, of cognitive strategies.

Attitudes.   Whereas verbal information, intellectual skills, and cognitive strategies are all part of the cognitive domain, attitudes are considered to be in affective domain. Gagné (1985) defined **attitudes** as *acquired internal states that influence the choice of personal action* toward some class of things, persons, or events. For example, one's attitudes toward pollution and ecology will affect the purchasing of substances in aerosol spray cans, which have been shown to have a deleterious effect on the earth's ozone layer. Likewise, choosing to save part of one's income every month reflects attitudes toward money and the future. Finally, attitude learning is likely to be involved in several ways in the A&B Agency scenario. Any employee who knows that sexual harassment is illegal and not tolerated within the Agency can still engage in such behavior. Similarly, employees who learn Agency policies regarding sexual harassment can choose not to report observed incidences.

When attitudes are organized into a consistent set, philosophy, or worldview that governs subsequent personal action, then they are typically referred to as values. According to the taxonomy of affective outcomes (cf. Krathwohl et al., 1964), we may consider Gagné's definition of attitudes to incorporate the first two levels of receiving and responding. These two levels also highlight two of the three accepted components of attitude formation: the informational component and the behavioral component. That is, information pertaining to an attitude must be known to a learner before he or she can choose to respond in a particular way. The response itself constitutes the behavioral component. The third, or emotional, component of attitude formation refers to the feelings that frequently accompany the choice of personal action. As we shall see later in the chapter, all three components are important to consider when designing instruction to teach or influence attitudes.

Finally, notice the similarity between Gagné's concept of attitude and motivation as discussed in the previous chapter. Clearly, attitudes can serve as motivating forces, and motivating learners is, to some extent, a matter of attempting to instill certain attitudes in them. Motivation, however, is probably a more transitory state than that typically associated with attitudes. For example, a student who is interested in a particular subject may be motivated to attend class regularly. Given a different class, however, the same student may choose to come irregularly, if at all. By contrast, a student with a positive attitude toward school (including obedience to its rules and regulations) is likely to attend all classes regularly, regardless of how interesting or boring they may be.

Motor Skills.   The fifth type of outcome in Gagné's taxonomy, corresponding to the psychomotor domain, is motor skills. By **motor skills,** Gagné means the *"precise, smooth and accurately timed execution of performances involving the use of muscles"* (Gagné & Driscoll, 1988, p. 59). Examples of motor skills include serving a tennis ball, executing a triple axle jump in ice skating, dribbling a basketball, and lifting a barbell with weights. These are performances all associated with sports and all continuous in nature. That is, although each skill can be roughly subdivided into component movements (e.g., a tennis serve consists of the toss, contact, and follow-through), it is intended to be performed in a single fluid motion.

Other examples of motor skills, however, are complex procedures made up of discrete subskills. For example, a dance may call for a series of discrete steps to be performed. Rounding a mark in a sailboat regatta requires raising one sail, lowering another, resetting the positions of the sails, and moving the tiller to change the direction of the boat. Taking a blood sample from a patient requires putting a cuff around the patient's arm, locating a vein, sterilizing the point of injection, and so on. These examples, along with those above, also illustrate that motor skills are generally acquired in combination with various cognitive skills. To play tennis competitively, for instance, one must know the rules of the game and play strategically, in addition to executing the shots with precision. Therefore, not only motor skills, but also intellectual skills and cognitive strategies, are involved.

As indicated previously, Gagné, like other instructional theorists, proposed his taxonomy with the assumption that different outcomes call for different learning conditions. Thus, during the design of instruction, complex learning goals like those cited above must be considered for their multiple types of outcomes and learning conditions provided that will support the attainment of all components. Just what learning conditions should be provided is the subject of the next section.

Conditions for Learning

In order to plan what learning conditions should be present in instruction, Gagné, Briggs, and Wager (1992) recommended categorizing learning goals according to the type of outcome they represent. From the standpoint of the teacher or instructional designer, this means some very careful consideration of just what ends or results are desired. It may also mean making reasonably concrete what are otherwise fuzzy, vague, or unspecified goals. For example, the goal of an instructor in the Medical School scenario might be that students "understand views associated with a patient's 'right-to-die'." What does this mean to the instructor? It probably does not suggest that students must be able to recite the arguments leading to a 1997 Supreme Court decision on a "right-to-die" case. Nor is it likely to mean that students must adopt a particular view. But to provide effective instruction, the medical school professor should decide more precisely what he or she expects of students.

There has been considerable controversy over the use and effectiveness of instructional objectives in facilitating learning. Objectives obviously spring from a behavioral tradition, because they are intended to specify the learned behavior that is desired of students (see Chapter 2). Most studies investigating their use, however, have shown either a small positive or no effect on intentional learning (i.e., that related directly to the objectives) and a deleterious effect on incidental learning (i.e., information unrelated to the objectives) (Klauer, 1984). Despite these results, objectives have gained and maintained a solid footing in education and training. Why?

To begin with, investigations on objectives can be faulted on several grounds, so that findings of no effect may not be true. First, most researchers defined objectives for the recall of information only. Second, the instruction used in the studies was typically very short, not more than a few pages. As a result, the objectives in some cases bore a one-to-one correspondence with the sentences in the experimental text. Third, objectives were frequently employed with no regard for whether students knew how to use them, and, in fact, students are likely to disregard objectives unless they are shown how objectives can help them learn. Finally, the only outcome examined by most studies was some measure of student learning. Therefore, the potential benefit of objectives for anyone other than learners (e.g., teachers or designers) remained in question.

Although objectives may indeed be of limited benefit to learners, they can be extremely useful to teachers and other designers of instruction as a plan both for instruction and for testing. A central tenet of most instructional design models (e.g., Reiser & Dick, 1996; Gagné, Briggs, & Wager, 1992) and many texts on assessment (e.g., Nitko, 2001) is that there should be congruence between instructional goals, lessons, and assessment measures. The only way to determine such congruence is from an initial statement of goals.

Once instructional goals have been categorized into types of learning outcomes, then, planning for instruction can proceed systematically. A teacher or instructional designer can determine just what unique conditions are required for learners to acquire each desired skill, knowledge, or attitude. Summarized in Table 10.5 are the external conditions that Gagné proposed as essential for learning the different varieties of outcomes. Recall that internal conditions are specified by the information-processing model and research conducted on human cognition.

Conditions for Learning Verbal Information. Assuming that verbal information is stored in vast, interrelated networks in human memory (see Chapter 3) or in schemata and mental models (see Chapter 4), how might instruction be planned to best facilitate learning of new information? To be meaningful, new information must be related in some way to what learners already know. Therefore, important internal conditions include the recall of related material. In addition, learners can process only so much information at one time because of the limitations of short-term memory.

As for external conditions, then, it is important to present information in meaningful chunks so as not to overload the learner's processing system. And for effective encoding to occur, a meaningful context must be either activated or provided. Techniques such as imagery, organizers (advance or comparative), themes, and mnemonics have proven to be effective for this purpose. Remember from Chapter 3 that whatever cues are used for encoding are also likely to be effective retrieval cues. Moreover, a greater variety of cues used during initial learning is likely to ensure better generalization of the information to appropriate but new contexts.

When planning instruction for verbal information outcomes, it is also important to remember that information is typically embedded in some larger context. Not everything a professor says in a lecture must be learned and retained in detail, for example. Similarly, textbooks, movies, computer

TABLE 10.5 *A Summary of External Conditions That Can Critically Influence Learning of the Five Major Varieties of Learning Outcomes*

Type of Learning Outcome	Critical Learning Conditions
Verbal Information	1. Draw attention to distinctive features by variations in print or speech. 2. Present information so that it can be made into chunks. 3. Provide a meaningful context for effective encoding of information. 4. Provide cues for effective recall and generalization of information.
Intellectual Skills	1. Call attention to distinctive features. 2. Stay within the limits of working memory. 3. Stimulate the recall of previously learned component skills. 4. Present verbal cues to the ordering or combination of component skills. 5. Schedule occasions for practice and spaced review. 6. Use a variety of contexts to promote transfer.
Cognitive Strategies	1. Describe or demonstrate the strategy. 2. Provide a variety of occasions for practice using the strategy. 3. Provide informative feedback as to creativity or originality of the strategy or outcome.
Attitudes	1. Establish an expectancy of success associated with the desired attitude. 2. Assure student identification with an admired human model. 3. Arrange for communication or demonstration of choice personal action. 4. Give feedback for successful performance, or allow observation of feedback in the human model.
Motor Skills	1. Present verbal or other guidance to cue the executive subroutine. 2. Arrange repeated practice. 3. Furnish immediate feedback as to the accuracy of performance. 4. Encourage the use of mental practice.

Source: From Gagné, R. M. & Driscoll, M. P. *Essentials of learning for instruction* (2nd ed.). Boston, MA: Allyn and Bacon, 1988. Reprinted with permission.

simulations, and television documentaries present tremendous amounts of information—far more than a learner is expected to remember or use. Therefore, instructional tactics should be used that direct learners' attention to significant points. These include, for example, the use of italics and boldface print in textbooks or voice inflections and gestures in a lecture. The bulleted points on a PowerPoint slide also draw attention to important information to be learned.

Conditions for Learning Intellectual Skills.   Intellectual skills are similar to verbal information in that it is easy to overload the learner in their instruction. Whereas information had to be associated with previously learned and related ideas, intellectual skills build upon previously learned component skills. Therefore, these must be recalled for learning to proceed effectively. Moreover, multiple steps to a new skill should be presented in increments and at a pace that does not strain the limitations of short-term memory. Imagine the result, for example, if a statistics professor explained a new analysis procedure rather rapidly, in highly complicated steps and without defining terms.

As with information, the learning of intellectual skills requires the learner's attention to be directed, but in this case to distinctive features of the concept or rule to be learned. For example, the three sides of triangles distinguish them from other similar shapes and so should be emphasized to the learner. Likewise, staining slides can highlight features of cells or tissues to which biologists should attend when learning to distinguish normal from abnormal conditions.

When rules require a series of steps to be performed in sequence, instruction in their use should include cues as to the appropriate order of steps. These cues can range from verbal statements listing the steps, as might occur in long division, for example, to reminders of the conceptual basis for the rule. Converting temperatures between the Fahrenheit and Celsius scales, for example, can be cued with a reminder as to which number should be larger. "You're starting with a temperature on the Celsius scale. That's the smaller number. So that must mean…" (thus prompting the rule to multiply by 9/5 and add 32).

Finally, Gagné and Driscoll (1988) pointed out the ease and speed with which intellectual skills may be initially acquired, but the apparent difficulty with their being retained and widely applied in new situations. For example, students who appeared to understand the new statistical analysis procedure when the instructor went over it in class may experience problems trying to use it on new sets of data outside of class. They may also fail to recognize instances in which the use of the procedure would be appropriate. Therefore, practice with a variety of examples and problems is an essential external condition to facilitate the internal processes of retention and transfer (or generalization).

Conditions for Learning Cognitive Strategies.   Internal conditions necessary for the acquisition of cognitive strategies include prior knowledge of the simple concepts and rules that make up highly general strategies, such as "Break the problem down into parts" (Gagné, 1985). But they may also include task-relevant concepts, rules, and information. In the case, for example, of developing a strategy to research the decline of SAT scores (a task-specific, undoubtedly complex strategy), learners must have prior research skills, know facts related to the SAT, and understand certain concepts of education.

What external conditions will facilitate the development of cognitive strategies is a matter of some debate. Certainly, many simple and task-oriented strategies are discovered by learners in their attempts to solve a problem or remember something for a test (Gagné, 1985). Other such strategies can apparently be established through demonstration or verbal instructions to the learner (Gagné & Driscoll, 1988). Teachers frequently remind learners to paraphrase, for example, when they say, 'Tell me in your own words what _____ [you fill in the blank] means," or "Don't just copy the definitions in your book; write them in your own words." More complex or difficult strategies may also require demonstration. The main idea of a textbook or lecture is not always self-evident to learners, but identification can be easily modeled by a teacher who constructs outlines of important information.

Whether strategies are taught or discovered, learners must have ample opportunities to practice them, particularly in novel situations. The Cognition and Technology Group at Vanderbilt (1991a) lamented their students' inability to generate relevant plans for solving problems, which they attributed to a curricular emphasis on memorization of facts and practice on isolated subskills. They suggested as a solution more in-context practice on complex problems. Derry and Murphy (1986) also recommended that teachers of different subjects coordinate their efforts for developing strategies useful across disciplines. They stated, for example:

> One form of coordination is through the use of a common planning model, or metastrategy, called the Four C's Learning Plan. The four C's are as follows: clarify the learning situation, come up with a plan, carry out the plan, and check your results. Thus language arts teachers explain how reading and memorization tactics fit into the four C's, while math teachers explain problem-solving, and physical education teachers explain mood control tactics using the same framework. (p. 18)

Finally, Gagné and Driscoll (1988) considered the provision of informative feedback to be as important as the setting of problem situations. Learners must have some notion as to whether their strategic efforts are effective, creative, or efficient. In some situations, it may also be desirable to explicitly encourage learners to be systematic and efficient in their use of strategy. Duffield (1990) and Atkins and Blissett (1992), in separate studies investigating what children learn from instructional software that purports to teach problem-solving strategies, showed that learners most often used trial and error, despite feedback providing clues, which could be used systematically to solve the problem at hand. In neither case, however, were learners encouraged to adopt a systematic strategy or one that would help them solve the problem quickly. Indeed, reflection of any sort concerning strategy effectiveness was generally absent and not nurtured. Yet, such reflection may well be essential to cognitive strategy learning and so should be facilitated by relevant external conditions.

Conditions for Learning Attitudes.   For any attitude to be learned and expressed, learners must already possess a variety of related concepts and information. If the attitude to be acquired is "Just say no to drugs," for instance, learners must know something about drugs and their effects. According to Gagné (1985), they must also understand the source of the attitudinal message, the situations in which drugs are likely to be encountered, and the actions likely to be involved in "just saying no." With these prerequisite internal conditions in place, attitudes may be established through a variety of external learning conditions.

Consistent with Skinner's views on the establishment of any behavior, some attitudes are likely to be acquired because they have been consistently reinforced over time. Consider, for example, the enjoyment of reading as a pastime activity. Individuals who like to read probably had parents who reinforced this activity at a young age, perhaps by reading to the child, discussing what was read, and ensuring that many interesting books were available to be read. Undoubtedly, the experience of being successful at the task also had a hand in establishing a positive attitude toward reading. As Gagné (1985) noted, repeated experiences of failure will tend to engender attitudes of dislike. Moreover, when these experiences occur in association with events that produce fear or other unpleasant feelings (as in a teacher, parent, or peers berating a person for failing), then the negative attitude that results may persist for years, changing only with great effort and difficulty.

An equally effective set of external conditions for altering or establishing attitudes can be found in human modeling (Bandura, 1969; Gagné, 1985). As we have already seen in the previous chapter, learners modified expectations of themselves and their own behavior after observing the behavior of models with whom they could identify. Because attitudes are a matter of choice, learning attitudes from models involves learning to make the same choices of action that they do. This occurs because people tend to want to "be like" those whom they respect or with whom they identify.

For modeling (or reinforcement) to be most effective in establishing attitudes, instructional conditions should (1) create an expectation in learners that they will be successful in the chosen activity, (2) provide for the activity associated with the attitude to be performed (by the model or the learner), and (3) give feedback for successful performance (Gagné & Driscoll, 1988). In the case of modeling, the latter is often communicated in a testimonial given by the model, as in a sports figure describing during a school visit the improvements in his life since getting off drugs.

Conditions for Learning Motor Skills.   Whether a particular motor skill is made up of discrete subskills (e.g., a pattern dance) or continuous part-skills (e.g., a tennis serve), it nonetheless has component skills that must be mastered separately before they can be assembled into the single, terminal performance. These, then, comprise important internal conditions for the learning of motor skills. Also an essential prerequisite, however, is recall of the executive subroutine (Fitts & Posner, 1967), or procedure that dictates the sequence of movements.

As for external conditions, Gagné, along with many motor learning theorists (e.g., Singer & Dick, 1980) incorporated the three phases Fitts and Posner (1967) proposed for motor learning. These are: (1) the early cognitive phase, in which learners attempt to understand the executive subroutine; (2) the intermediate phase, during which learners alternate practice of the subskills with practice of the total skill; and (3) the final autonomous phase, in which skill performance becomes virtually automatic. With the increased emphasis on lifelong motor development that has accompanied recent theories of motor development, Gallahue and Ozmun (1995) characterized these three phases as transition (getting the idea of how to perform the motor skill), application (developing higher levels of skill through practice), and lifelong utilization (fine-tuning of skills over a lifetime of use).

Instructional conditions corresponding to these phases require methods for cueing the subroutines (such as verbal directions or demonstrations of the skill), repeated practice, and immediate feedback to correct errors and avert the possibility of bad habits developing. Gallahue and Ozmun (1995) also recommend a simple-to-complex and general-to-specific approach during practice that will enable learners to produce increasingly refined performances.

When learners reach the autonomous phase of skill development, mental practice may be useful in helping them reach their peak for competition (Singer, 1980). World class athletes, for example, report benefits of imagining their entire performance before they take their turn to compete. It is useful to remember, however, that only perfect practice makes perfect; imperfect practice simply leads to bad habits that may become nearly impossible to break.

Summary.   The learning conditions described in this section appear to critically influence the learning of various outcomes. For this reason, Gagné and

Driscoll (1988) referred to them as the building blocks for instruction. At the least, instruction should provide for these conditions, and when multiple outcomes are desired, all types of goals with their corresponding conditions should be considered. But planning instruction also requires taking care to support, throughout a lesson or course, all of the internal processes presumed to occur during learning regardless of what is being learned. Gagné (1985) referred to these external conditions as the events of instruction.

The Nine Events of Instruction

Recall from Chapter 3 that information is presumed to undergo a series of transformations as it passes through the stages of memory. Processes thought to be responsible for these transformations include attention, pattern recognition, retrieval, rehearsal, encoding, retention, and so on. Modifying the information flow, as well as setting processing priorities, are executive control processes. Because learning takes place only when these processes are activated, the goal of instruction, according to Gagné (1985), should be to facilitate this activation. And he proposed the events of instruction to do just that.

Listed in Table 10.6 are the nine events of instruction together with the internal processes that they support. Although Gagné believed that most lessons should follow the sequence of events as shown, he recognized that this order is not absolute (Gagné & Driscoll, 1988). Moreover, the manner in which the events are implemented may vary greatly depending upon the instructional delivery system that is chosen. What a teacher will do in the classroom, for example, is likely to differ markedly from activities embedded in a computer-based tutorial. But the effects of the two types of activities, in terms of learning, should be similar if both are designed to implement the same event of instruction. This point should become clearer as the instructional events are illustrated with specific examples. Let us now turn to an examination of these events.

Event 1: Gaining Attention.   Since learning cannot occur unless the learner is in some way oriented and receptive to incoming information, gaining attention is the obvious first event that must occur in instruction. The importance of attention was also discussed in the previous chapter, where it played a prominent role in Keller's model of motivational design. Typically, gaining attention is accomplished by some sort of stimulus change, which may be repeated in various forms throughout a lesson to regain students' attention when they appear to be off-task. Examples include the teacher calling out particular students' names, using verbal signals such as "Listen up, everybody," or turning the lights on and off. In mediated instruction, gaining attention might take the form of flashing signals on the screen or the sound of beeps indicating "Look for a message on the screen."

Event 2: Informing the Learner of the Objective. We saw in the previous chapter the effect that self-expectations can have on motivation. A similar case is holding an expectancy about what one is to learn will influence subsequent processing of information related to that expectancy. If, for example, learners are aware and prepared to learn certain information, they will be more alert to any stimuli related to that goal. Expectancies are easily established by simple statements of instructional goals, references to what students will be able to do after instruction, or demonstrations of anticipated learning outcomes. It should be noted that all students, whether young or mature, will develop expectations about what they are supposed to learn in any instructional situation. When the teacher or instructional material is not explicit about learning goals (or they are in conflict with one another), students are likely to take their cues from what happens in class and what appears on tests (Driscoll et al., 1990).

Event 3: Stimulating Recall of Prior Learning. Although new learning depends to a large extent on what has been learned before, students do not

TABLE 10.6 *Gagné's Nine Events of Instruction Associated with the Internal Learning Process They Support*

Internal Process	Instructional Event	Action
Reception	1. Gaining attention	Use abrupt stimulus change.
Expectancy	2. Informing learners of the objective	Tell learners what they will be able to do after learning.
Retrieval to working memory	3. Stimulating recall of prior learning	Ask for recall of previously learned knowledge or skills.
Selective perception	4. Presenting the content	Display the content with distinctive features.
Semantic encoding	5. Providing "learning guidance"	Suggest a meaningful organization.
Responding	6. Eliciting performance	Ask learner to perform.
Reinforcement	7. Providing feedback	Give informative feedback.
Retrieval and reinforcement	8. Assessing performance	Require additional learner performance with feedback.
Retrieval and generalization	9. Enhancing retention and transfer	Provide varied practice and spaced reviews.

Source: Gagné, R. M. & Medsker, K. L. *The conditions of learning: Training applications.* Fort Worth: Harcourt Brace College Publishers, 1996. Reprinted with permission.

always call to mind and use relevant information when faced with a new learning task. This is perhaps truer of younger learners than older learners, simply because younger learners have not yet built a broad base of knowledge. However, as discussed in Chapter 5, the transfer of knowledge, i.e., the application of something previously learned to a new problem or in a new context, is difficult at any age. Therefore, to prepare learners for encoding or transfer, instructors should assist them in recalling relevant and prerequisite information.

Stimulating recall of prior learning can be as simple as reminding learners of what was studied the day before, or last week, in class. This is often observed in the quick reviews with which many teachers begin each day's activities. In some instances, however, simple reminders are not enough. It then becomes necessary to reinstate the prerequisite knowledge or skills by some practice activity (Gagné & Driscoll, 1988). An example can be seen in the following protocol, taken from Driscoll and Dick's (1991) observations of an eighth grade science teacher about halfway through an instructional unit on light and lenses.

> MLH is circulating about the classroom, helping individual kids as they ask questions. Then she goes to the board, puts up the formula—$t = d/r$ (t is time, d is distance, r is the speed of light)—and says, "Listen up, everybody. Remember how we do these problems. We're given the distance, which is what? 3.8 times 10 to the eighth meters. Right! And we know the speed of light through a vacuum. Remember, it's in your book. Yes, it's 3.0 times 10 to the eighth meters per second. So what do we do to figure out how long it will take for the light to go this far? Righhhht! That's good! Divide...." MLH goes on to give several more examples. The kids are apparently having difficulty with Question 1 under *READING CRITICALLY*. Several seem to have asked her a question about it, so she goes over the procedures again for everyone.

Considerable effort is often required for learners to transfer prior knowledge to new situations, even when they are aware that they have such relevant knowledge (Salomon & Perkins, 1989). Moreover, learners may simply find it easier to ask someone else for the answer than to figure it out for themselves. In situations in which the process of solving problems is an important goal of instruction, then, students should be prompted in ways that promote their persistence in "sticking with it."

Event 4: Presenting the Stimulus.   This event of instruction depends upon what is to be learned. If the goal of instruction is information acquisition, then the stimulus may consist of a textbook chapter, lecture, or film containing the content. If, on the other hand, the desired outcome is intellectual skill learning, then the most effective stimulus is one that prominently displays distinctive features of the concept or rule to be learned. In Driscoll and Dick's (1991) observations, for example, the concept of focus was presented by the textbook in a diagram highlighting its essential features and by the teacher using a light box, lenses, and chalk dust. In the latter case, the teacher emphasized essential features of the concept through gestures and verbal explanations as she conducted the demonstration.

Presenting the stimulus for motor skill or cognitive strategy learning consists of demonstrating the desired outcome or giving verbal directions. For attitude learning, the stimulus is a demonstration of the desired action or choice, generally by a model. For all types of outcomes, the stimulus presentation should emphasize distinctive features or essential elements of the desired outcome in order to facilitate the processes of pattern recognition and selective perception.

Event 5: Providing Learning Guidance. How or what learning guidance is provided in instruction also depends upon the desired outcome, but the primary process to be facilitated is semantic encoding. Specifically, instructional activities should promote the entry of what is to be learned into long-term memory in a meaningful way. Here is where a teacher or instructional designer should refer to the learning conditions that are critical and unique to each type of learning outcome.

How much learning guidance to provide is a separate question and one that depends upon several factors, including the ability and sophistication of the learners, the amount of time available for instruction, and the presence of multiple learning goals. Very able or sophisticated learners probably require less guidance than not so able students. For example, highly educated communications technicians who attend training to learn the latest developments in technology typically approach the situation with very focused goals. "Just tell me what I should know or where I can find the required information," they say, indicating a need for mostly stimulus presentation and little learning guidance. By contrast, third grade children having difficulty reading are likely to require considerable learning guidance.

When the process or experience of learning and problem solving is to be emphasized, instructors may find it desirable to provide minimal learning guidance of a highly directive nature. Rather, discovery learning is stressed. Hints or cues are provided, but learners are expected to figure things out for themselves without being told just what to do. Because discovery learning can also be quite time consuming, instructors generally must weigh its benefits (e.g., facilitating long-term retention and transfer) against its costs (e.g., need for extensive resources and time). Remember as well that Ausubel argued against using discovery learning for most school situations because he believed that meaningful reception learning was as cognitively active and much more efficient. Bruner, however, would be more likely to argue that, although active cognition might be possible under conditions of receiving information, it does not occur very often that way. Certainly, instructor beliefs will also play a part in the decision to use discovery learning methods.

Event 6: Eliciting Performance. Instructional Events 1 through 5 presumably assure that learning has occurred, i.e., that what was to be learned has been sufficiently encoded and stored in long-term memory. Event 6, then, enables the learners to confirm their learning—to themselves, their teachers, and others. It requires the learner to produce a performance, something that is an appropriate indicator of what was learned. Remember that learning must be inferred from behavior, so for this event, an important question to answer concerns what behavior will serve as the best index of the desired learning goal.

The intent of eliciting performance is for learners to demonstrate what they have learned without penalty. In other words, this event provides an opportunity to gauge progress, with the assumption that errors are still undergoing correction and performance is still being improved. The next event, then, provides the learners with information useful for effecting performance improvement.

Event 7: Providing Feedback. Having shown what they can do, learners should be provided informative feedback on their performance. This implies, for knowledge and skills that call for discrete answers, telling the learners whether or not their answers are correct. If incorrect, feedback should assist learners in detecting and correcting their errors.

Kulhavy and Stock (1989) developed a feedback model from their research that explains how feedback works as a function of learners' confidence in their initial responses. Consider, for example, any test you have taken recently. You get the test back and discover marked wrong a question that you were really sure you had answered correctly. What would you do? According to Kulhavy and Stock's model, you would most likely pay careful attention to what the teacher says about that item when she goes over the test. Or, you might carefully search through your notes or the textbook to determine what your mistake had been. In either case, the feedback plays an important role in your correcting the error, and you will pay close attention to it.

By contrast, when learners get test items wrong that they were most unsure about anyway, feedback plays a different role. In this case, error correction is not so much the issue as learning better what the question was intended to assess. Instead of a definite misconception, the learner has only a vague conception. Feedback, then, should consist of reteaching or extended elaboration on the knowledge or skill in question.

Obviously, not all material to be learned consists of right and wrong answers. Motor skills, for example, may be performed correctly, but inexpertly or clumsily. Feedback, then, should be aimed at showing learners how to improve their current skill. Similarly, feedback for cognitive strategy learning may inform learners as to how their performance might become more strategic or more creative.

Event 8: Assessing Performance.   Remember that learning was defined in terms of a change in behavior or performance that persists over time. In other words, a new skill must be performed dependably before most teachers will agree that it has been well learned. Therefore, after learners have had opportunities to demonstrate and refine their knowledge, it may be formally assessed. This event is typically carried out through unit or chapter tests, projects, portfolios, skill demonstrations, and so on. It also tends to be the basis on which student grades are assigned. Even with this event occurring so late in a lesson, however, Gagné and Driscoll (1988) stated that it is desirable for each correct performance to be given suitable feedback.

Event 9: Enhancing Retention and Transfer.   Although this is the last event in the series, instructional activities to enhance retention and transfer are frequently built into the instruction at a much earlier phase. It has already been suggested, for instance, that a variety of examples and contexts are critical learning conditions for learners to be able to transfer intellectual skills appropriately. These would most likely be planned during Event 5, providing learning guidance. Similarly, spaced reviews facilitate retention of intellectual and motor skills and could be planned as several iterations of Events 6 and 7, eliciting performance and providing feedback.

Attitude learning perhaps has unique requirements for retention and transfer. Many attitudes, such as that pertaining to drug use, are unlikely to be performed in the context of the original instruction. That is, it would be unethical, not to mention illegal, for a teacher to offer drugs to students in the hope that they would say no and that behavior would be appropriately reinforced. Therefore, activities should be used, such as role plays or discussions centered around scenarios and questions of "What would you do if...?". The point of these activities is to encourage students to reflect upon their own knowledge and belief systems as they are exposed to those of other people. Finally, computer-based simulations, albeit still in their infancy, are likely to prove useful in helping students to examine their own attitudes in a wide variety of situations. Simulations can show students what the consequences of their decisions can be, thus making more personal the information associated with attitudes.

Summary: Planning Instructional Events.   Does effective instruction depend upon the inclusion of all nine events of instruction? Can the same events apply to multiple learning goals at the same time? Is the teacher or instructional designer always responsible for planning the instructional

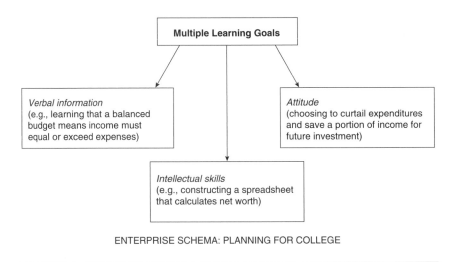

FIGURE 10.3   *Example of an Enterprise Schema for Teaching Multiple Learning Outcomes*

events? Cannot learners sometimes be held responsible for their own instruction? In answer to these questions, the choice of instructional events, and who makes that choice, should depend upon the nature of the learning situation (Gagné & Driscoll, 1988). For example, in the classroom that Driscoll et al. (1990) studied, the teacher reviewed material frequently (Events 3 and 9), perhaps because the textbook did a poor job of it. Using cooperative learning structures, however, she often relied on the students to provide each other with both learning guidance and feedback.

Complex learning situations—where it is desirable for learners to acquire multiple, related learning goals—dictate special consideration in the choice of instructional events. Gagné suggested that a larger scale activity, or enterprise, be used as a means of communicating the purpose of instruction and establishing a meaningful context within which individual learning objectives can be attained (Gagné & Merrill, 1990). When these individual learning outcomes are integrated during learning, they comprise a schema in the mind of the learner (See Figure 10.3).

Finally, "including more instructional events than are necessary is likely to lead to boredom on the part of the students. Providing fewer than are needed, however, has the serious consequence of inadequate learning, misdirected learning, or no learning at all" (Gagné & Driscoll, 1988, p. 131). Gagné and Medsker (1996) noted that many training failures occur because one or more of the nine events of instruction has been omitted. For example, either practice is not included or insufficient practice is included, with the expectation that the information from a lecture or one-way communication will be enough. As they point out, "Hearing about a new product line does not mean that salespeople can describe it to customers or use the information to determine customer needs. 'Being exposed' to the latest technologies does not ensure that engineers can apply them in their work. Yet many training programs offer no practice, too little practice, or inappropriate practice" (Gagné & Medsker, 1996, p. 151). Perhaps the best guide to planning instructional events is the students themselves.

An Application of Gagné's Instructional Theory

Throughout this chapter, we have examined the components of Gagné's instructional theory and what each implies for the design of instruction. But we have not yet seen how the theory might be applied from start to finish in the solving of a complex instructional problem. Let us reexamine the Medical School scenario and see how Gagné's theory might play out.

To begin with, we must determine what sort of learning outcome is desired. Because the details provided in the scenario are limited, assumptions will have to be made about the intent of the medical school instructors. Let us assume that the outcome of interest is something like this:

> Students will appropriately diagnose a medical problem based on the presenting symptoms of the patient.

Using Gagne's taxonomy as a guide, this outcome would probably be classified as the intellectual skill of problem solving. While that sounds simple enough, an analysis of the desired outcome would undoubtedly reveal that a considerable amount of prerequisite knowledge and skills must be acquired before medical students would be capable of mastering this desired outcome. Imagine, for example, the vast array of possible medical conditions and their attendant symptoms that any given patient might present. By the time medical students start making diagnoses, they would have learned discriminations (e.g., is the patient's temperature elevated from normal?), concepts (e.g., basal metabolic temperature), rules (e.g., how to read a thermometer or blood pressure monitor), motor skills (e.g., how to withdraw a sample of blood or insert a catheter), and verbal information (e.g., an elevated temperature is often the first sign of infection).

Once the desired outcome is determined, one would consider the conditions necessary to learn that outcome. In the case of intellectual skills, previously learned component skills must be recalled, distinctive features of the skill to be learned must be apprehended, and the skill must be practiced, preferably in a variety of contexts (refer to Table 10.5 for the conditions of learning). What might those conditions suggest in this case? Assuming that students had appropriate prerequisite skills, effective instruction should, at least, provide opportunities for students to solve a variety of medical diagnostic problems. During the problem-solving process, instructors could point out distinguishing characteristics of cases that point to one diagnosis over another, especially when symptoms are similar or present in more than one affliction. For example, elevated body temperature is a symptom caused by a variety of diseases, so it would not be the distinguishing feature that leads to a particular diagnosis.

How might the events of instruction be employed in designing instruction to teach medical diagnostic problem solving? It is particularly important at this point to consider who the students are and which events they might reasonably be expected to supply for themselves. At the risk of promoting stereotypes, it is probably safe to assume that most medical students are motivated to learn diagnostic procedures, so that their attention is readily assured. Likewise, the instructional objective of diagnosing illness is implicit in all of their training. Therefore, Events 3 through 9 are probably the most important to include in this instruction (refer to Table 10.6).

What strategies are chosen to implement the events of instruction depends at this point on a variety of factors, such as the availability of resources and the inclusion of other objectives in the instruction. For example, medical case books abound that provide descriptions of patients that could be used for diagnostic problem solving. However, when the time comes for medical students to learn how to solicit information about symptoms from patients, then it would be important for them to have contact with real patients. The enterprise of a diagnostic clinic, whether real or simulated, would also provide a meaningful context within which the desired learning outcomes could be attained.

Regardless of what instructional strategies are chosen or the form the instruction takes in the end, instructional design theorists point to the importance of formatively evaluating the instruction to make sure it is effective (Dick & Carey, 1996; Gagné, Briggs, & Wager, 1992). If it is not, then revisions would be undertaken to improve those aspects of the instruction that are not performing as desired.

Conclusion

Gagné's instructional theory is widely used in the design of instruction by instructional designers in many settings, and its continuing influence in the field of educational technology can be seen in the more than 130 times that Gagné has been cited in prominent journals in the field during the period from 1985 through 1990 (Anglin & Towers, 1992). The increasing interest in constructivism, however, has caused researchers to question theories like Gagné's and to examine whether they are compatible with the goals and assumptions of constructivist epistemology.

In a case study investigating a particular teacher's implementation of cooperative learning, for example, Flynn (1992) attempted to determine if and how Gagné's events of instruction are carried out in a cooperative learning structure. He concluded that the two approaches—cooperative learning and the events of instruction—each brought something valuable to the understanding of what went on in that classroom. More such studies are necessary, however, to determine just what is illuminated or obscured by each perspective about learning.

In the next chapter, the various approaches to constructivism are discussed, with contrasts drawn to the theory discussed in this chapter.

"Kermit and the Keyboard": How does Gagné's Instructional Theory Fit?

What might be some of the desired learning outcomes in the story "Kermit and the Keyboard" and how would they be classified according to Gagné's taxonomy? Consider the following possibilities.

Reading notes in a musical score (*intellectual skill*)

Playing a song on the keyboard at a given tempo (*motor skill*)

Choosing to practice exercises from music instruction books (*attitude*)

Playing different backgrounds and voices to create different sounds for the same songs (*cognitive strategy*)

Learning to play the keyboard is clearly a complex affair that likely involves desired outcomes across the spectrum of Gagné's taxonomy. Learning the functions of the keyboard probably involves the acquisition of verbal information as well (for example, knowing which button to push to select the voice or what number to enter to select a particular background).

Because Kermit is teaching himself, the instruction per se is not well designed in the sense of applying Gagné's theory systematically. Yet there is evidence of both appropriate conditions of learning and events of instruction. For instance, Kermit practices repeatedly (an important condition for intellectual and motor skills and a component of learning guidance). He consults the manual for specific, relevant information regarding keyboard functions he is trying to learn (presenting the stimulus and directing attention to distinctive features). He is provided direct feedback by hearing what he plays. An incorrect performance is often immediately evident, as when he plays a discordant note that violates his expectation of the way the song should sound. But in the case of the repeated mistake in rhythm that he plays in "House of the Rising Sun," you can see that sometimes feedback that is natural in a situation is not enough. Kermit would benefit from someone pointing out the error and demonstrating what the correct rhythm should be while he follows along in the music.

Why does Kermit choose to practice exercises in addition to the songs he wants to learn to play? The story does not provide enough information for us to determine how this attitude was established, but we can speculate that his early training in music played a part. It is likely that he experienced firsthand the benefits of systematic practice on part skills to help develop automaticity, and this success would have reinforced a belief that his learning would benefit now by such practice.

Theory Matrix

Theory	Gagné's Instructional Theory
Prominent Theorists	R. M. Gagné
Learning Outcome(s)	Verbal information, intellectual skills, cognitive strategies, motor skills, attitudes
Role of the Learner	Participate in instruction as a processor of information
	Depending on circumstances, may identify own learning outcomes, arrange for conditions of learning, and supply own events of instruction
Role of the Instructor or Instructional Designer	Systematically arrange conditions of learning and events of instruction based on desired learning outcomes and learner characteristics
Inputs or Preconditions to Learning	Internal and external conditions of learning that depend on the type of learning outcome
	Events of instruction that facilitate information processing
Process of Learning	Adopts the cognitive information processing model as an explanation of learning

Suggested Readings

Gagné, R. M. (1985). *The conditions of learning.* (4th ed.). New York: Holt, Rinehart & Winston.
Gagné, R. M., Briggs, L. J., and Wager, W. W. (1992). *Principles of instructional design.* (4th ed.). Fort Worth: Harcourt Brace Jovanovich.
Gagné, R. M., and Driscoll, M. P. (1988). *Essentials of learning for instruction.* (2nd ed.). Englewood Cliffs, NJ: Prentice-Hall.
Gagné, R. M., and Medsker, K. L. (1996). *The conditions of learning: Training applications.* Fort Worth: Harcourt Brace College Publishers.

Reflective Questions and Activities _____

1. Apply Gagné's taxonomy to a subject you expect to teach and generate examples in each category. Give your examples (randomly ordered) to a fellow student and ask him or her to sort the examples into the same categories. Do your categorizations agree? Discuss any disagreements. Try to reach consensus on the usefulness of Gagné's conception of learning outcomes.

2. Select a unit of instruction, such as a single topic in a course syllabus or a stand-alone, independent study module. Examine this instruction (and its accompanying materials, such as textbooks, lectures, handouts, and the like) from the perspective of Gagné's theory. What features would be considered well designed, and what features does it lack to be "good instruction"? Predict what effects this instruction is likely to have on learners. If it is possible, observe learners going through the instruction and compare its actual effects to those you predicted.

3. Rewrite one of the instructional plans you have already generated in the course of reading this book. Apply Gagné's instructional theory. Evaluate the results in terms of the probable effects on learning. What has Gagné's theory added to the plan that was lacking before?

11

Constructivism

	CONSTRUCTIVISM
Assumes knowledge is constructed ←	

Learning Goals include

- Reasoning
- Critical thinking
- Understanding and use of knowledge
- Self-regulation
- Mindful reflection

Conditions for Instruction

Methods of Instruction

1. Complex and relevant learning environments
2. Social negotiation
3. Multiple perspectives and multiple modes of learning
4. Ownership in learning
5. Self-awareness of knowledge construction

Microworlds and hypermedia designs

Collaborative learning and problem scaffolding

Goal-based scenarios and problem-based learning

Open software and course management tools

Consider these scenarios. (The scenario, Medical School, is reprinted from Chapter 10.)

• *Medical School*

At the University of Anywhere Medical School, instructors routinely face the problem of biomedical misconceptions among students. That is, medical students, despite exposure to appropriate information, continue to make diagnostic errors in many of the clinical cases that they study. Instructors have found that students, in their diagnoses, tend to oversimplify, over-rely on general theories, and disregard unique or puzzling symptoms. How to best deal with these problems is of major concern, particularly in light of the spiraling costs of medical school education. The instructors want to know how they should revise their instruction or devise new learning experiences, so that students will avoid making so many errors.

• *Olympic Games*

With the help of an instructional design student at a nearby university, Ms. Patterson designed an Internet Web site devoted to the Olympic Games. This is a topic she particularly enjoys teaching in her seventh grade classroom, especially when it's a year that the Games are actually being held. The Web site is supplemental to the activities Ms. Patterson conducts in her class.

Students can log on from school or home and explore at will. Within the Web site are links to the history of the Olympic Games, the types of games played, records set, and so on. The Web site is rich with information in graphics and text. There are also links to related Web sites; students tend to follow these when they get fascinated about some aspect of the Games. Raja, for example, was completely taken by the bobsled competition, and he researched how bobsleds were originally designed and how they are now built.

Imagine the sort of instruction that might have resulted for the Medical School scenario had we taken the application of Gagné's theory to its conclusion in the previous chapter. Although direct instruction is not a premise or a requirement of that theory, it is often the product when Gagné's theory guides the instructional design process. It is almost as if the internal organization and orderliness of the theory invites its use in a systematic and direct fashion. Such a use is also consistent with epistemic beliefs in knowledge as acquired through information processing.

Try to imagine now what instructional strategies might be proposed given a different view of learning and instruction, a view in which knowledge is assumed to be constructed rather than acquired. In this chapter, potential answers are discussed that arise from constructivist theory. As you read the chapter, you may also find it worthwhile to look back at Chapters 5, 6, and 7 to review some of the concepts that relate to or underpin constructivist theory.

Constructivism: A Contrasting Theory

"Constructivism has multiple roots in the psychology and philosophy of this century" (Perkins, 1991a, p. 20). Among those already discussed in this book are the cognitive and developmental perspectives of Piaget (see Chapter 6), the interactional and cultural emphases of Bruner and Vygotsky (see Chapter 7), and the contextual nature of learning emphasized in Chapter 5. In addition to these, constructivist researchers acknowledge the philosophies of Dewey (1933) and Goodman (1984), and the ecological psychology of Gibson (1977) as important influences on their work. Ernst von Glasersfeld (1984, 1991, 1995, 2002) has had a considerable influence on constructivist thinking in mathematics and science education, and "the work of Thomas S. Kuhn on scientific revolutions and paradigms has been a major influence on several of the constructivist sects" (Phillips, 1995, p. 6). Matthews (2003) also credits the views of Derrida and Foucault as contributors to constructivist thinking in the postmodern era.

As mentioned in Chapter 10, there is no single constructivist theory of instruction. Rather, there are researchers in fields from science education to educational psychology and instructional technology who are articulating various aspects of a constructivist theory. Moreover, constructivism is only one of the labels used to describe these efforts. Its use probably stems from Piaget's reference to his views as "constructivist" (see Chapter 6) and Bruner's conception of discovery learning as "constructionist" (see Chapter 7). Other labels include generative learning (CTGV, 1991a, 1991b; Wittrock, 1985a, 1985b), embodied cognition (Johnson, 1987; Lakoff, 1987), cognitive flexibility theory (Spiro et al., 1991, 1995), and postmodern and poststructural curricula (Hlynka, 1991; Culler, 1990). Some of the work presented in Chapter 5 under the heading of situated cognition has also been represented as constructivist (e.g., the semiotic perspective and anchored instruction). In this chapter, then, no single constructivist approach will be described. Instead, the assumptions common to the collection of approaches will be examined, together with the learning conditions and instructional methods being proposed as consistent with these assumptions.

Constructivist Assumptions About Learning

Theorists who write in the emerging constructivist tradition often contrast their ideas with the epistemological assumptions of the objectivist tradition. Objectivism is the view that knowledge of the world comes about through an individual's experience of it. As this experience grows broader and deeper, knowledge is represented in the individual's mind as an ever-closer approximation of how the world really is (see Chapter 1). In a sense, then, knowledge is thought to exist independently of learners, and learning consists of transferring that knowledge from outside to within the learner.

Both behavioral and cognitive information-processing theories of learning emerged from the objectivist tradition. Consider, for example, the emphasis on universal laws of learning that is one of the hallmarks of behaviorism. Behaviorists define desired learning goals independent of any learner and then proceed to arrange reinforcement contingencies that are presumed to be effective with any learner; only the type of reinforcer is assumed to vary according to the individual. Although information-processing theorists put mind back into the learning equation, they, too, appear to assume that knowledge is "out there" to be transferred into the learner. The computer metaphor itself suggests that knowledge is input to be processed and stored by learners.

In contrast to the objectivist view, then, constructivist theory rests on the assumption that knowledge is constructed by learners as they attempt to make sense of their experiences. Learners, therefore, are not empty vessels waiting to be filled, but rather active organisms seeking meaning. Regardless of what is being learned, constructive processes operate and learners form, elaborate, and test candidate mental structures until a satisfactory one emerges (Perkins, 1991a). Moreover, new, particularly conflicting experiences will cause perturbations in these structures, so that they must be constructed anew in order to make sense of the new information. This should sound much like the development and revision of mental models, as discussed in Chapter 4. In Chapter 6, Piaget referred to a similar process as schema accommodation, and other developmental theorists called it knowledge restructuring. Both Bruner and Vygotsky, as well, devised similar concepts to account for the changes in children's knowledge as they develop (see Chapter 7).

What constructivists argue strongly, however, is that knowledge constructions do not necessarily bear any correspondence to external reality. That is, they do not have to reflect the world as it really is to be useful and viable. This is consistent with the idealist or interpretist epistemology that was discussed in Chapter 1. Perhaps an example would help to illustrate this idea.

Recall from Chapter 6 the research revealing children's conceptions of the earth in relation to the sun. Because children's experience is that of a flat earth with the sun moving across the sky during the day, they typically believe that the earth is flat and that the sun revolves around it. In the constructivist view, they have constructed a perfectly viable model, which accounts well for their own experience. We know in this case that, for most people, this model is revised to reflect current understanding of the earth's relationship to the sun. As a pragmatist (see Chapter 1) would suggest, however, the current model will prevail for only as long as the collective experience of scientists supports it. Therefore, the model should not be assumed to reflect reality; instead, it should be construed as the best construction of humankind's experience of its world.

If no correspondence is presumed between reality and the learner's cognitive constructions of it, does this mean that all constructions are equally viable? Those subscribing to an idealist philosophy might say yes (see Chapter 1), but most constructivist theorists would say no. There must be limits to what sense learners make of their environment and their experience. Limits are imposed by human biological characteristics as well as by what is possible in reality. Moreover, learners must have some reliable and systematic way to test their observations and the sense they are making of the world around them (Matthews, 2003). As a consequence, many constructivist theorists adhere to Vygotsky's notions about the social negotiation of meaning (see Chapter 7). That is, learners test their own understandings against those of others, notably those of teachers or more advanced peers.

Constructivist Models of Memory

Although constructivists have described, often in detail, the epistemological assumptions underlying their work, they have been less clear about what models of memory arise from these assumptions. Cunningham (1988) explored the implications of Eco's rhizome metaphor. The rhizome is a tangle of tubers with no apparent beginning or end. It constantly changes shape, and every point in it appears to be connected with every other point. Break the rhizome anywhere and the only effect is that new connections will be grown. The rhizome models the unlimited potential for knowledge construction, because it has no fixed points (no nodes or basic representation units) and no particular organization (my own mental image of a rhizome resembles a plate of spaghetti; Eco [1976] also spoke of a jar full of marbles, which, when shaken, will produce a new configuration and a new set of connections among marbles).

Consider the differences in a rhizome-like structure of memory compared to the models that were discussed in Chapter 3. According to a network model of memory, knowledge of a concept such as heron, for example, would be stored in terms of a heron concept node, with various features connected by association. Propositional models suggest that the features are part and parcel of an understanding of herons, since propositions, rather than concept nodes, are stored. PDP models refer to the patterns of activation related to understanding of herons. But now think of herons and air traffic control. Shank (1988) argued that, through the method of juxtaposition, any two things may be linked, with meaningful relationships generated between them. In fact, interesting insights can occur in the juxtaposition of disparate ideas. But the relationships you have now generated between herons and air traffic control are not easily accounted for in current memory models, which do not adequately capture the dynamic nature of knowing. The rhizome metaphor, however, allows for infinite juxtaposition.

If the rhizome is limitless in possibility, and therefore indescribable at a global level, then we are forced to consider cognition at a more local level, as "transitory systems of knowledge" (Eco, 1984, p. 84). Particular slices of the rhizome reveal a person's knowledge at that time in that context, with no assumption of invariability over time or across contexts. This presumes that neither knowledge nor the ways in which we use to describe it are stable. Rather, "the rhizome concept alerts us to the constructed nature of our [environmental understanding] and the possibilities of different meaning, different truths, different worlds" (Cunningham, 1992, p. 171).

The connectionist models of memory (described in Chapters 3 and 8) appear to embody characteristics similar to the rhizome and may hold promise for constructivist theories. Bereiter (1991) argued, for example, that concepts "are much more like perceptions than they are like rule-defined categories" (p. 13), and that, in fact, it seems likely students do not learn rules at all. What they learn instead are connections, which, to satisfy constraints of experience and environment, come to resemble rule-based performance.

Finally, John R. Anderson, known for his ACT model of memory (see Chapter 3), is exploring new directions for the study of human cognition that seem increasingly compatible with the assumptions of constructivism. Rather than continue the atomistic analysis of cognitive mechanisms which characterized his earlier work, Anderson (1990) has proposed an approach to building a theory of cognition that focuses on the adaptation of human behavior in terms of achieving human goals. That is, Anderson assumes that "the cognitive system operates at all times to optimize the adaptation of the behavior of the organism" (1990, p. 28). This is similar to the view espoused by Bruner (1986), who stated that "meaning...is an enterprise that reflects human intentionality and cannot be judged for its rightness independently of it" (p. 158). Furthermore, ACT-R includes a mechanism of knowledge compilation, which is an accommodation process that involves creating new rules via analogy when a new problem is encountered that cannot be solved (Anderson, 1993). Anderson argues that this process is consistent with constructivist notions of how learning occurs, even though he adheres to an information-processing perspective, which many constructivists believe is antithetical to their approach (Anderson, Reder, & Simon, 2000). Empirical data are now being amassed that should begin to sort out various claims of constructivism and how they relate to previous approaches discussed in this book. These are reviewed as they pertain to the sections ahead.

Let us now turn to an examination of the instructional recommendations emanating from constructivism. Because any theory of instruction must deal with learning goals, conditions of learning, and instructional methods to bring about these conditions, it makes sense to consider what constructivist approaches propose in each of these categories.

Constructivist Learning Goals

Unlike the "objectivist approach...that focuses on identifying the entities, relations, and attributes that the learner must 'know'" (Duffy & Jonassen, 1991, p. 8), the constructivist approach to identifying learning goals emphasizes learning in context. Brown et al. (1989), for example, argued that knowledge that learners can usefully deploy should be developed. Moreover, this can only be done in the context of meaningful activity. It is not enough, in other words, for students to acquire concepts or routines that lie inert, never to be called upon even in the face of relevant problems to be solved. Instead, knowledge must develop and continue to change with the activity of the learner. "'Learning [is] a continuous, life-long process resulting from acting in situations" (Brown et al., 1989, p. 33).

In this statement, we see from the start how constructivist ideas have emerged from or are consistent with theories discussed in previous chapters. That knowledge develops in context is central to the notions of situated learning (see Chapter 5), Bruner's discovery learning (see Chapter 7), and the dialectics of Vygotsky's theory (see Chapter 7).

As a start to articulating what is meant by "deployable knowledge learned in context," the CTGV (1991a) defined thinking activities to be the primary goals of concern to constructivists. Specifically, they named: "the ability to write persuasive essays, engage in informal reasoning, explain how data relate to theory in scientific investigations, and formulate and solve moderately complex problems that require mathematical reasoning" (CTGV, 1991a, p. 34). Virtually agreeing with these sentiments, Perkins (1991a) declared, "The basic goals of education are deceptively simple. To mention three, education strives for the retention, understanding, and active use of knowledge and skills" (p. 18). Put another way, "knowledge does not come into its own until the learner can deploy it with understanding" (Perkins & Unger, 1999, p. 94).

Other authors have offered variations of these goals. Spiro et al. (1991) described the need for learners to acquire cognitive flexibility, whereas Culler (1990) spoke of the need to foster poststructuralist thinking, a kind of reflective criticism. The ability to solve ill-structured problems (Jonassen, 1999), acquire content knowledge in complex domains along with critical thinking and collaboration skills (Nelson, 1999), and develop personal inquiry skills (Hannafin, Land, & Oliver, 1999) are also cited as typical constructivist goals. Finally, epistemic fluency, or the ability to identify and use different ways of knowing, is among those goals thought to be fostered by constructivist pedagogy (Morrison & Collins, 1996).

If we consider this constructivist collection of goals in light of a taxonomy such as Gagné's, what would we conclude? Are the authors cited above defining educational goals that Gagné would categorize as higher-order rule-using (problem-solving) and cognitive strategies? Dick (1991) clearly thought so when he discussed, from an instructional designer's perspective, research and development efforts of the Cognition and Technology Group at Vanderbilt and others. Goals that instructional designers might define for the Medical School scenario, for example, include diagnose hypertension, and for the A&B Agency scenario, recognize sexual harassment in the workplace. These seem to be virtually no different from goals that constructivists might define for those situations. But, as we shall see, how constructivists would proceed to design instruction to meet those goals differs in fundamental ways from how someone following Gagné's theory would proceed.

Constructivists are also interested in having learners identify and pursue their own learning goals. In the scenario Olympic Games, for example, the teacher may have some specific learning objectives in mind, but she also wants to provide students with an opportunity to explore and learn something of personal interest. Without this sort of personal freedom during instruction, someone like Raja probably would not have learned so much about a subject like bobsleds. Recall from Chapter 9 that this is a condition of learning that has been found to promote self-regulation in learning. And self-regulation is clearly desirable to constructivist educators.

Dick (1991) raised a concern, however, about the lack of attention paid by constructivists to the entry behaviors of students. Not all students are as capable as Raja to pursue an independent project, and open-ended learning environments afford an opportunity to play as much as they do to learn. Dick noted,

> Designers use analytic techniques to determine what a student must know or be able to do before beginning instruction, because without these skills research shows they will not be able to learn new skills. Why are constructivists not concerned that the gap will be too great between the schema of some students and the tools and information that they are provided? (Dick, 1991, p. 43)

In Dick's view, achievement of a goal such as diagnosing hypertension must depend upon prior knowledge of hypertensive symptoms, as well as the ability to distinguish those from similar conditions that might be attributable to some other disease. An instructional analysis would reveal not only what these prior skills are that must be acquired before the end goal can be reached, but also whether students have actually acquired the identified skills. If they have not, then remediation would be prescribed before students engaged in solving problems dependent upon those skills.

In response to Dick's concerns, Perkins (1991b) acknowledged the cognitive demands that constructivist learning goals and instruction typically place on learners. Learners must deal with complex problems, and they must "play more of the task management role than in conventional instruction" (Perkins, 1991b, p. 20). According to Perkins, however, this simply implies that teachers must coach individual students who lack adequate entry skills. "It is the job of the constructivist teacher…to hold learners in their 'zone of proximal development' by providing just enough help and guidance, but not too much" (Perkins, 1991b, p. 20). Similarly, Cunningham (1992) commented that teachers must not only coach students who lack prerequisite skills, but persuade those who are unwilling or unmotivated to engage in instruction. Just how teachers can best coach unable students and coax unwilling ones remains an open question (Driscoll & Lebow, 1992).

One possible way to deal with the lack of prerequisite knowledge and skills is to identify and ameliorate gaps within the context of the desired problem solving (CTGV, 1992). In other words, a part of solving complex problems involves determining what skills or information a learner needs to know. And learners who discover that, to solve a problem at hand, they must acquire some other skill or piece of information will be more motivated to do just that. Consider, for example, your own knowledge of the word processor or other computer software that you use regularly. Chances are that you do not know all of its possible functions and routines. Chances are even greater that to learn some of those that you do not know will require learning one or two other routines first. But it is unlikely that you will take the time to learn any of these unknown routines until you encounter a need for them. Once that need is present, however, you will learn whatever prerequisites are necessary to acquire the skill that meets your needs.

The same is probably true for learners involved in solving a complex problem like those presented by the CTGV. As students determine what sub-problems must be solved in order to solve the challenge presented in an instructional video (e.g., what is the fastest way to rescue an injured eagle from a meadow to which there are no passable roads?), they discover needs for further learning (e.g., how do we determine how much fuel would be needed if an ultralight aircraft is used to fly to the meadow?). "Once these insights about need occur, then it is appropriate and beneficial to let students find environments (e.g., drill-and-practice programs) that can help them master specific types of information more efficiently" (CTGV, 1992, p. 77). Thus, the medical student who realizes, in the course of a clinical interview, that she or he cannot call to mind the symptoms of hypertension with which to compare an observed symptom will be motivated to restudy that information.

Prerequisite skills or entry learning goals, then, are not necessarily ignored by constructivists, but they are attended to largely in the context of higher-order goals. Moreover, detailed analyses of learning goals, of the sort intended to yield specific instructional objectives, are likely to be viewed by many constructivists as destroying the essence, or holistic nature, of the goal. This is because such analyses tend to result in "decontextualized" skills and knowledge where the very reason for learning them is lost or forgotten. Instead, constructivists prefer to retain their focus on higher-order goals and just make sure the necessary scaffolding is there for support when, and if, learners require it.

It seems clear from the remarks of constructivist researchers that constructivist learning goals are best met through a variety of instructional conditions that differ from any proposed by theorists like Gagné. Let us now consider what these might be.

Constructivist Conditions for Learning

If problem solving, reasoning, critical thinking, and the active and reflective use of knowledge constitute the goals of constructivist instruction, what are the learning conditions likely to bring these goals about? Again we see a variety of recommendations from the numerous researchers attempting to articulate constructivist theory. Moreover, many of these recommendations embody instructional principles that were originally derived from theories already discussed. Finally, as we shall also see, they largely emphasize the process of learning, rather than the products of learning. Collectively, these recommendations include the following:

1. *Embed learning in complex, realistic, and relevant environments.* See, for example, Duffy and Cunningham (1996), CTGV (1991a, 1992); Hannafin (1992), Honebein (1996); Honebein, Duffy, and Fishman (1993); and Lebow and Wager (1994). This condition also finds support in schema theory and mental models research (Chapter 4) as well as situated cognition (Chapter 5).

2. *Provide for social negotiation as an integral part of learning.* This learning condition is inherent in Piaget's theory (Chapter 6), Vygotsky's and Bruner's theories (Chapter 7), and situated cognition theory (Chapter 5). It also derives from the work of Cunningham (1992; Duffy & Cunningham, 1996), Honebein (1996; Honebein et al., 1993), CTGV (1990), and the Language Development and Hypermedia Group (1992a, 1992b), among others.

3. *Support multiple perspectives and the use of multiple modes of representation.* The juxtaposition of instructional content to provide for multiple perspectives is one of the central themes in Spiro's cognitive flexibility theory (Spiro et al., 1991, 1995). Providing for the use of multiple modes of representation in learning is supported by the work of researchers such as Cunningham (1992; Duffy & Cunningham, 1996), Honebein (1996), and Gardner (1983, 1985).

4. *Encourage ownership in learning.* Much of the work on self-regulated learning (Chapter 9) is consistent with this recommendation. See also Duffy and Cunningham (1996), Honebein (1996), and Lebow (1993).

5. *Nurture self-awareness of the knowledge construction process.* Cunningham (1987, 1992) called such self-awareness "reflexivity" and noted that consciously adopting different ways of constructing knowledge enables one to see what is illuminated or hidden by any particular way.

Let us examine each of these constructivist conditions in some detail.

Complex and Relevant Learning Environments. *"Students cannot be expected to learn to deal with complexity unless they have the opportunity to do so"* (CTGV, 1991a, p. 36; emphasis theirs). This bold statement undoubtedly reflects the opinions of most constructivist authors, who further believe that simplifying tasks for learners will prevent them from learning how to solve the complex problems they will face in real life. For problem-solving skills to be maximally facilitated, they argue, learners must cope with very complex situations. Remember from Chapter 5 that Schoenfeld's students believed math problems were virtually unsolvable if they could not be solved in 5 minutes or less (Schoenfeld, 1988). Experience with only simple problems can lead to such beliefs, whereas experience with more complicated and realistic problems can prevent such erroneous ideas.

What complex problems entail seems to depend largely upon the subject matter within which problem solving and reasoning are being learned. To a somewhat lesser extent, perhaps, they also depend upon the ages and characteristics of the targeted learners. The video-based learning environments that the CTGV (1990, 1991a, 1993) developed for mathematical problem solving, for example, contain problems of more than 15 interrelated steps. All of the information required to solve these problems is incorporated into each video, but the students must decide what information is relevant and how various pieces fit together. Initially used with fifth and sixth grade students, the videos have apparently been adapted successfully for use with first and second graders (CTGV, 1991b).

Learning environment complexity can also be conceived in terms of both the tools and the content of learning (Perkins, 1991a, 1991b). With respect to content, much constructivist instruction aims to debunk students' naive conceptions or misconceptions, particularly in the areas of science and mathematics. To do this, situations must make plain the inconsistencies and inadequacies of the learners' models and "challenge [them] either to construct better models or at least to ponder the merits of alternative models presented by the teacher" (Perkins, 1991b, p. 19). But what should such situations look like?

This is where the tools of a rich learning environment come in. Specifically, Perkins proposed that "construction kits" and "phenomenaria" be widely used in the classroom (1991a; see also Wilson, 1996). Construction kits enable learners to assemble "not just things, such as TinkerToys, but more abstract entities, such as commands in a program language, creatures in a simulated ecology, or equations in an environment supporting mathematical manipulations" (Perkins, 1991a, p. 19). So, for example, Legos, learning logs, and software such as *Geometric Supposer* would be considered construction kits (Wilson, 1996).

Similarly, phenomenaria enable students to observe various phenomena and to manipulate concepts and assumptions within those phenomena. The popular software series *SimCity* and *SimEarth* are good examples of phenomenaria. *SimCity* is a simulation of real-world cities that allows students to explore what it means to build and manage all the various aspects of city life. Unlike simulations that are carried out for scientific investigation or technical purposes, phenomenaria emphasize the instructional nature of simulations (Wilson, 1996).

An alternative argument for complex learning environments comes from research on how people learn to solve problems in "ill-structured domains" (Spiro et al., 1991, 1995; see also Spiro & Jehng, 1990; Jonassen, 1997, 1999). Unlike solving an algebraic problem, for example, diagnosing a medical problem depends more on heuristics than on well-formed rules. Furthermore, a doctor (unlike a mathematician) has no proven means for determining whether a diagnosis is correct. Although a prescribed treatment may appear to be successful in curing the patient, at least two other possibilities are often equally plausible. The treatment may be ineffective and the patient got better on his or her own or the treatment effectively cured the problem, but the problem was not what was originally diagnosed. Doctors must be prepared to accept either of these possibilities if additional evidence seems to warrant it.

Spiro and his colleagues documented the tendency of medical students to oversimplify the concepts and principles comprising diagnostic medicine. They argued that "instructional focus on general principles with wide scope of application across cases or examples" (Spiro et al., 1991, p. 27) was the cause. Part of the solution, therefore, should be to retain, in medical instruction, the complexity inherent in this ill-structured domain. In order to do this, cases should be studied as they really occurred, "not as stripped down 'textbook examples' that conveniently illustrate some principle" (Spiro et al., 1987, p. 181). In learning about hypertension, then, medical students might best examine multiple case histories of hypertensive patients, so that the full range of their symptoms might be illustrated.

Jonassen (1997, 1999) offered an instructional design model for developing instruction to teach problem solving in both well-structured and ill-structured domains. With respect to ill-structured problems, he recommended that a context analysis be conducted to lay out the nature of the problem domain and the constraints that might affect problems in the domain. In a domain such as medical diagnostics, for instance, an increase in malpractice suits could certainly affect doctors' use of additional tests to verify an initial diagnosis. Jonassen suggested that these kinds of constraints be introduced during instruction as students pondered case problems.

Sometimes, complex and realistic learning environments are taken to mean the same thing as authentic, or real-world, learning environments. Certainly, there is value in learners practicing their skills in an authentic performance context, as when young musicians play in an orchestra recital at their school. But they would have difficulty becoming proficient players if all their practice occurred in that context. Thus, Anderson, Reder, and Simon (2000) sounded a cautionary note about complex learning situations, echoing Jonassen's (1999) belief that a restrictive conception of authentic will result in learning environments that are authentic only in a narrow context (p. 221).

Social Negotiation.   "…learning in most settings is a communal activity, a sharing of the culture" (Bruner, 1986, p. 127). Or, to paraphrase Vygotsky and situated cognition theorists, higher mental processes in humans develop through social interaction. Because constructivists hold to these beliefs about learning and thinking, they emphasize collaboration as a critical feature in the learning environment. Collaboration is not just a matter of asking students to work together in groups or to share their individual knowledge with one another. Rather, collaboration enables insights and solutions to arise synergistically (Brown et al., 1989) that would not otherwise come about. For example, can you recall a situation in which, but for the efforts of a group, some problem would have gone unsolved? No single member of the group would have had the wherewithall to independently generate an effective solution, but the members together had the necessary knowledge.

Another important function of collaboration in learning environments is to provide a means for individuals to understand point of view other than their own. Cunningham (1992), for example, argued that dialogue in a social setting is required for students to come to understand another's view. Listening, or reading privately, is not sufficient to challenge the individual's egocentric thinking. Echoing Cunningham's view, the Language Development and Hypermedia Group (1992a, 1992b) described instruction as a matter of nurturing processes by which learners develop and defend individual perspectives while recognizing those of others. What happens in learning, then, is the transmission or sharing of cultural knowledge, i.e., how concepts in a particular culture are understood and applied by its members.

As an example, consider how medical interns can be brought together to discuss symptoms noticed in a particular case. Having taken note of different things, they may propose alternative treatments, which they must then justify to their peers. Similarly, students involved in solving a challenge such as those proposed in the CTGV's instructional videodisks may propose alternative solutions and then justify the reasoning behind their proposals. Hearing a variety of other perspectives helps learners to judge the quality of their own solutions and to learn perhaps more effective strategies for problem solving.

The communicative aspect of collaboration during learning can also have the effect of transforming all parties involved (Pea, 1994; Edelson, Pea, & Gomez, 1996). Most constructivist researchers have argued forcefully against a transmission view of communication, i.e., communication as a message sent by one person and received by another. Rather, they have conceived of communication as a representation of shared belief—participants in sociocultural communities perpetuating their culture (see Chapter 5). Pea and his colleagues, however, proposed a transformative view of communication that they believe is facilitated through constructivist conditions of learning. According to a transformative view, "The initiate in new ways of thinking and knowing in education and learning practices is transformed by the process of communication with the cultural messages of others, but so, too, is the other (whether teacher or peer) in what is learned about the unique voice and understanding of the initiate" (Pea, 1994, p. 288).

Imagine, for example, what would happen if Raja, in the scenario Olympic Games, found a Web site on the Internet for the Jamaican bobsled team, which allowed him to communicate with various members of the team. The richness of his learning about bobsledding as an Olympic sport would be tremendously enhanced. But the transformation would hold in both directions—from the team to Raja, and from Raja to the team. His unique voice and communications could have untold effects on team members' views of themselves and their sport, on the information they provide on their Web site, and so on.

According to Edelson et al. (1996), advances in technology starting with the personal computer have "assisted in broadening the form that collaboration takes to include not just discussion but the sharing of artifacts and cooperative work across time and distance" (p. 152). Moreover, the potential is there for technology to play a "revolutionary role in supporting new forms of learning conversations in educational settings" (Edelson et al., 1996, p. 152). Indeed, a whole new genre of research and application has emerged as computer-supported collaborative learning (CSCL; Koschmann, 1996).

Multiple Perspectives and Multiple Modes of Learning.   Characteristic of ill-structured content domains are cases or examples that are diverse, irregular, and complex (Spiro et al., 1991, 1995; Feltovich et al., 1996). General principles do not apply widely across cases, nor is it possible to use a single analogy or model to represent all cases or content in the domain. When learners attempt to apply, to ill-structured domains, the strategies they have used effectively for understanding well-structured domains, they make errors of oversimplification, overgeneralization, and overreliance on context-independent representations (Spiro et al., 1988).

In the biomedical domain, for example, which Spiro and his colleagues have contended is ill-structured, students who use only the metaphor of the machine to help them understand how the body functions tend to analyze cases only partially. The same is true among students who understand bodily functions only in terms of organicist metaphors. The point Spiro makes is that neither metaphor is wrong, but neither metaphor captures all aspects of body functions.

Remember the difficulties inherent in selecting pedagogical models for helping students to develop mental models of complex phenomena (see Chapter 4). Whereas mental models researchers proposed the use of one model, pointing out its limitations, or a series of models to illustrate different aspects of the phenomenon, Spiro and his colleagues advocated the use of multiple forms of models, multiple metaphors and analogies, and multiple interpretations of the same information. These are the hallmarks of Cognitive Flexibility Theory (Spiro et al., 1991, 1995; Feltovich, et al., 1996). "Revisiting the same material, at different times, in rearranged contexts, for different purposes, and from different conceptual perspectives is essential for attaining the goals of advanced knowledge acquisition" (Spiro et al., 1991, p. 28). Spiro called this multiple juxapositions of instructional content, or "criss-crossing the landscape," and suggested that hypermedia provides an excellent tool for achieving it. A rich and flexible knowledge base can be built that enables learners to systematically explore multiple models and multiple interpretations. You can see how advantageous this might be for medical students. They would be able to examine a single case from many different vantage points and see firsthand the effect of reinterpreting a particular symptom.

It is now largely accepted among contructivists that hypermedia can be effectively used to encourage students to think about ideas, theories, literary works, or whatever, from a variety of perspectives (e.g., Cunningham, 1992). In a sense, books such as this one about theories of learning are written with much the same goal in mind. Many of the same questions about learning are tackled by different theorists from different perspectives, and different metaphors for learning function to highlight different aspects of the same content. The actual juxtaposition of ideas, however, is largely in your hands as the reader. It would be unwieldy for me, as the author, to revisit content to the extent that you, as the reader, can do very easily. For this reason, perhaps, many constructivist theorists have turned to emerging technologies as the most promising means by which to implement essential learning conditions.

Finally, using multiple modes of representation can serve as a means of juxtaposition. That is, viewing the same content through different sensory modes (such as visual, auditory, or tactile) again enables different aspects of it to be seen. It is also worth noting that multiple modes of representation have now received support as an instructional strategy from cognitive information-processing theory, educational semiotics, and biological theories, as well as from constructivism.

Ownership in Learning. Arranging instruction to meet individual student needs is not an idea new to constructivism. It has been a recurring theme throughout not only this book, but also learning theory development in general. What distinguishes the constructivist perspective is the placement of the student as "the principal arbiter in making judgments as to what, when, and how learning will occur" (Hannafin, 1992). In other words, students are not passive recipients of instruction that has been designed for them. Instead, they are actively involved in determining what their own learning needs are and how those needs can best be satisfied. As Perkins (1991b) put it, "Students are not likely to become autonomous thinkers and learners if they lack an opportunity to manage their own learning" (p. 20). Thus, it is important to facilitate student ownership in learning (Duffy & Cunningham, 1996; Honebein, 1996; Hannafin, Land & Oliver, 1999).

Consider the following report of a project with elementary school students:

> In Harel and Papert's [1992] work, elementary school students who displayed a great dislike for fractions tackled the task of learning about fractions with great enthusiasm when their role was changed from students to software designers. They were asked to design a computer program in LOGO (software they were already familiar with) that would teach the basics of fractions to children one year younger than themselves. In order to do this, they first had to teach themselves what was important to know about fractions. When the project was complete, the students had learned not only about fractions, but also about software design and instructional design. (Honebein et al., 1993, p. 9)

This example is remarkably similar to one cited in an earlier chapter in which an elementary school teacher had students produce videotapes to teach their peers about topics in science. In both cases, the students have an investment in the project, making their own decisions and evaluating their own progress. The teacher is there to serve as coach and resource, sharing in the learning process rather than controlling it.

Ms. Patterson, in the Olympic Games scenario, is also facilitating student ownership by providing the Web site and encouraging students to identify and investigate topics of interest to them. A likely outcome is enhanced learning and motivation.

Whether students are prepared to take ownership and manage their own learning is a question posed by critics of contructivism. Clark (1982) reviewed research on student attitudes toward and preferences for particular instructional strategies and concluded that students are not the best judges of their own learning needs. For the most part, they preferred methods that were not well suited for facilitating their individual achievement. Many investigators of learner control in computer-based instruction have reached much the same conclusion (Steinberg, 1989). When given options, learners apparently choose the quickest route through the instruction, whether or not that route best meets their learning needs.

Two issues are raised by these findings. The first concerns whether students are capable of making effective judgments about their own learning needs and how to satisfy them, whereas the second concerns whether they are willing to do so. A tacit assumption of constructivist learning environments is that students possess whatever metacognitive skills are necessary to successfully navigate in those environments (Hannafin, 1992). If they do not, then designers of these environments should embed aids to students that will help them navigate lessons. These might include, for example, an organizing theme, various forms of help, advice, hints, or guided reflection.

Perkins (1991b) agreed that students must often be assisted in managing learning tasks and referred to the classic solution of scaffolding, or coaching, mentioned earlier. Exactly how to do this, particularly by one teacher with a number of students, is less clear and is indicated by Driscoll and Lebow (1992) as a pressing problem for constructivist researchers to solve.

As for the concern that students do not all "buy into" the notion of managing their own learning, it has already been suggested that teachers must persuade them. To do this requires that a "teacher or instructional designer approach the double agenda as such, engaging students constructively in thinking both about X [the content] and about the learning process reflectively" (Perkins, 1991b, p. 20).

Finally, perhaps one of the reasons that students have difficulty navigating a learning environment or try not to do so on their own accord is that such environments have typically been decontextualized. Without a meaningful context to guide them, learners are left to figure out "what the teacher wants" or "what will be on the test." When that happens, learning tasks become tests of endurance, something "to be gotten through." On the other hand, "tasks that are thought to be difficult when attempted in a decontextualized environment become intuitive when situated in a larger framework" (Honebein et al., 1993), that is, a more authentic context. The reasons become clear as to why information and skills should be learned, and their learning advances the students toward the achievement of some larger goal, like the production of videotapes to teach peers what they have learned.

Self-Awareness of Knowledge Construction.   Cunningham (1987, 1992; Language Development and Hypermedia Group, 1992a, 1992b) defined reflexivity as *"the ability of students to be aware of their own role in the knowledge construction process."* Awareness of one's own thinking and learning processes is a capability cognitive information-processing theorists have commonly called metacognition (see Chapter 3). Helping learners to become more aware of their thinking processes is thought by many, including Gagné, to be essential in the development of mindful, strategic behavior or cognitive strategies. Although constructivists might well agree with cognitive information-processing theorists on the definition and importance of metacognition, they mean something more by reflexivity.

With reflexivity, a critical attitude exists in learners, an attitude that prompts them to be aware of how and what structures create meaning. With this awareness comes the ability to invent and explore new structures or new interpretive contexts. In other words, when learners come to realize how a particular set of assumptions or worldview shapes their knowledge, they are free to explore what may result from an alternate set of assumptions or a different worldview.

The goal of reflexivity is partly supported by the juxtaposition of instructional content and the resulting emphasis on multiple perspectives. It is also very much related to ownership in instruction and the learner's subsequent commitment to a particular perspective.

Consider, for example, the different views of learning that are presented in this book. What do they each imply about your own learning of their assumptions and principles? From a cognitive information-processing point of view, you might be expected to treat the book as declarative knowledge to be acquired, with different schemata about the various theories constituting the result of your learning efforts. By contrast, from a constructivist point of view, you might be expected to recognize that all these theories are constructed to make sense of the phenomenon of learning. Their different assumptions lead to different pictures of learning, and consequently, of instruction. From discussion with your classmates and others, you might develop a personal view as to what theory (or theories) is the most right or useful. Or you may reject the assumptions upon which all these theories have been built in order to pose a new set of assumptions and explore a potentially new theory of learning.

It should be noted that this contrast between constructivist and information-processing theory has been drawn rather sharply to illustrate the point of reflexivity. Not everyone would agree with my distinctions, but the very debate that would be prompted by such disagreement would serve to further illuminate both positions.

Nurturing self-awareness of knowledge construction, then, is a learning condition that constructivists assert is essential to the acquisition of goals such as reasoning, understanding multiple perspectives, and committing to a particular position for beliefs that can be articulated and defended.

Summary.   Displayed as a summary in Table 11.1 are the learning goals associated with constructivism, together with the learning conditions presumed to bring about those goals. We are now ready to consider the third element in constructivist instructional theory: specific methods of instruction. Suggested methods are also presented in Table 11.1.

Constructivist Methods of Instruction

Some methods have already been suggested that are shown or likely to be effective in implementing the conditions constructivists believe are essential for learning. Others—including microworlds and hypermedia designs, collabora-

TABLE 11.1   *A Summary of Goals, Conditions of Learning, and Instructional Methods Consistent with Constructivism*

Instructional Goals	*Conditions of Learning*	*Methods of Instruction*
Reasoning	Complex, realistic and relevant environments that incorporate authentic activity	Microworlds, problem-based learning
Critical thinking		
Retention, understanding, and use	Social negotiation	Collaborative learning, Bubble Dialogue
Cognitive flexibility	Multiple perspectives and multiple modes of learning	Hypermedia
Self-regulation	Ownership in learning	Open-ended learning environments, collaborative learning, problem-based learning
Mindful reflection, epistemic flexibility	Self-awareness in knowledge construction	Bubble Dialogue, role plays, debates, collaborative learning

tive learning and problem scaffolding, goal-based scenarios and problem-based learning, and open software and course management tools—serve to implement multiple conditions simultaneously. Each merits a brief discussion. Before proceeding, however, it is important to note that there has been an explosion of activity over the last few years in the design and use of these types of learning environments. It would be impossible to describe them all in this chapter. Therefore, I have tried to give you a sense as to what they are like and urge you to look up original sources for more information. It is also important to realize that, as I write this, more project reports and descriptions of projects exist than empirical data showing their effectiveness.

Microworlds and Hypermedia Designs.   As the name implies, microworlds are small but complete subsets of real environments that promote discovery and exploration (Papert, 1981). Their design has been influenced by research on mental models (see Chapter 4) as well as theoretical developments leading to the emergence of constructivism. Microworlds have two essential characteristics that distinguish them from similar concepts, such as simulations (Rieber, 1991b; see also Rieber, 1996). That is, they embody the simplest working model of a domain or system, and they offer a point of entry that matches the learner's cognitive state. LOGO, for example, perhaps the most widely researched microworld currently in existence, permits children to explore and discover the world of computer programming by writing commands that drive a "turtle" (Papert, 1980).

In *ScienceVision*, an interactive videodisk-based microworld, students conduct scientific experiments of the sort that would generally be precluded from middle school instruction because of prohibitive expense, time requirements, or potential danger to the students (Tobin & Dawson, 1992). For example, in the study of ecology, students can investigate what it would take to convert a mining site to farmland. Through simulation, they analyze soil samples, plant and monitor various crops, and conduct cost-benefit analyses based on their findings.

Because interactive videodisk microworlds are themselves expensive to design and produce, some researchers and instructors are turning to hypermedia as a less expensive and more widely available alternative. Hypermedia designs typically run on microcomputers, which can be networked and therefore accessed by several learners at once. Design strategies include representing a vast body of information about the topic of interest, including such types of information as autobiographical data, descriptions, definitions, photographs or graphic designs, interviews or other samples of research data, and the like. For example, in the Lab Design Project (Honebein, Chen, & Brescia, 1992), graduate students investigate the sociology of a building by exploring different aspects of it that are represented in the hypermedia data base. They can call up from the data base the types of information they would actually collect if they were to do research in a real building (Honebein et al., 1993).

At the least, microworlds and hypermedia provide rich, student-centered learning environments in which authentic activity is stressed. Depending upon their use in an instructional context, they may also support conditions of social negotiation (e.g., Emihovich, 1981) and nurturance of reflexivity (Rieber, 1991a, 1991b).

Collaborative Learning and Problem Scaffolding.   Collaborative learning has already been discussed to some extent, with mention made of the extensive advances in computer-supported collaborative learning. Much of the impetus for CSCL can be attributed to an area of study known as computer support for collaborative work (or CSCW; Galegher & Kraut, 1990). A fundamental assumption of CSCW is that computers and their related technologies can "facilitate, augment, and even redefine interactions among members of a work group" (Koschmann, 1994, p. 219). Software designed to be used by groups to facilitate and manage the interaction among group members is known as groupware.

Such collaborative technologies are now finding their way into instruction to support learning of students engaged in a learning task as members of a group. CSCL applications have been designed for use within a classroom (e.g., CSILE; see Chapter 5) and to connect learners across classrooms and outside of classrooms (e.g., the Collaborative Visualization project, or CoVis; Pea, 1993a).

An advantage of collaborative technologies that are Web-based is that they can provide problem scaffolding (Hannafin et al., 1997) in the form of virtual access to knowledge experts and on-line support to make thinking visible. In this way, students can identify learning goals, conduct investigations, keep track of their progress, think about their ideas and those of others, and communicate to others within and outside the immediate learning community.

Goal-Based Scenarios and Problem-Based Learning.   The Goal-Based Scenarios (GBS) framework (Schank et al., 1993/1994, 1999; Bell, Bareiss, & Beckwith, 1993/1994; Kass et al., 1993/1994) is an example of a computer-based learning environment but with a different emphasis than the collaborative technologies. GBSs present a clear and concrete goal to be achieved (e.g., composing a piece of music, designing a car, starting a business, eradicating a disease) and provide a task environment where learners learn and practice target skills. Schank et al. (1993/1994, 1999) use the metaphor of a mission to describe GBS, in that there is a mission context (including a cover story and explicit statement of the mission) and a mission structure. The mission structure includes a focus and operations to be carried out to achieve the mission. The GBS is similar in many respects to anchored instruction (see Chapter 5), but GBS researchers claim that learners are participants in the goal scenario, rather than observers of the video-based anchored instruction.

They assume roles within the mission and essentially engage in a real-time simulation.

Problem-based learning (PBL; Duffy & Jonassen, 1992; Savery & Duffy, 1996; Nelson, 1999) has recently re-emerged as a constructivist method after a long history of use in medical education. Like other collaborative technologies, students in problem-based learning work in groups, and like GBSs, groups work to solve a "real" problem. Unlike these other approaches, however, learners may seek out a variety of resources, technological and otherwise, to help them arrive at possible solutions. The emphasis in PBL is to provide a problem-solving process that students may use systematically to identify the nature of the problem, assign tasks to be completed, reason through the problem as data and resources are gathered and consulted, arrive at a solution, and then assess the adequacy of the solution. Once the problem is concluded, the learners also reflect on their reasoning, their strategies for resource gathering, their group skills, and so forth.

Software Shells and Course Management Tools.   Software shells are largely empty of content, providing instead functions that can be readily adapted to the user's intended application. A tool known as Bubble Dialogue is an example (Language Development & Hypermedia Group, 1992a, 1992b). Through Bubble Dialogue, students create conversations among comic strip characters, including thoughts that would not be said out loud. In this way, they have the opportunity to express "personal (perhaps naïve) views of the world, to contemplate multiple perspectives in both public and private domains and to accommodate their own thinking to contrary views" (Language Development and Hypermedia Group, 1992a, p. 44).

The authors of Bubble Dialogue have found the tool useful in facilitating dialogue among grade school children about the long-standing conflict in Northern Ireland and among preservice teachers about teaching strategies. Moreover, the permanent archive created by the program facilitates later editing or reflection and supports the development of literacy.

The STAR LEGACY is another sort of software shell that is designed to support flexibly adaptive learning environments (Schwartz, Lin, Brophy, & Bransford, 1999). It makes explicit a learning cycle that embodies a problem solving process—from accepting a learning challenge, to generating ideas, to testing one's understanding, and finally to learners publishing the results of their thinking for others to consider. STAR LEGACY helps teachers and learners to see where they are and reflect on the learning process. Successive use of the legacies left by each group of students enables progressive deepening of understanding about the topics under study.

Finally, the course management tool known as Construe (Lebow et al., 1996; Gilbert & Driscoll, 1998) is a software shell that is designed to enable course instructors to mount Web-based courses with constructivist principles already designed in. For instance, an informational data base is present in the form of on-line articles that can be searched easily by author or keyword. A variety of reports provides the means for learners to publish on-line their thoughts and opinions on the articles as they read them, to describe projects in which they are engaged, and to bring new resources to the class that may benefit members. A computer conferencing system is also available so that learners can discuss articles and projects as the semester proceeds. These features together provide a public, on-line learning environment in which the artifacts produced stand as evidence of the knowledge-building within the community.

Walter Wager, one of the developers of Construe, tells interested colleagues that using Construe does not assure a constructivist learning environment (personal communication, September 1998). The software can, after all, be used to support very traditional instructional strategies. However, as one who has herself employed Construe in a graduate course, I am convinced that the use of all the software's features as an integrated system guarantees a very powerful learning environment that will yield learning outcomes consistent with constructivism.

Summary.   It is probably no accident that constructivism is gaining popularity and momentum at the same time interactive, user-friendly computer technologies are becoming widely available. The computer offers an effective means for implementing constructivist strategies that would be difficult to accomplish in other media. However, this is not to imply that other media cannot also be effectively employed within constructivist pedagogy. The discussion that is facilitated by Bubble Dialogue, for example, can also occur in well managed debates and role plays. Moreover, projects need not be situated in hypermedia data bases to provide authentic activity. However, it is likely that a variety of resources and time will be required to effectively implement most constructivist principles.

Conclusion

Constructivism has taken such a strong hold in many areas of education today that it seemed appropriate to discuss it within its own chapter, despite the fact that it is not one theory but a multitude of approaches. As these approaches develop and proliferate, it also becomes less clear as to whether constructivism is a theory or a philosophy (Lebow, 1993). As a theory, it may indeed be incommensurable with an instructional theory such as Gagné's, because the two would have been built from opposing assumptions. But as a philosophy, constructivism may be viewed as not competing with other instructional theories, but providing them with an alternative set of values that deserve serious consideration.

These values, according to Lebow (1993), form the basis for five principles which should perhaps be incorporated into any theory of instruction:

> (a) Maintain a buffer between the learner and the potentially damaging effects of instructional practices in use, (b) provide a context for learning where the needs for both autonomy and belongingness are supported, (c) embed the reasons for learning something into the learning activity itself, (d) support self-regulation through the promotion of skills and attitudes that enable the learner to assume increasing responsibility for the developmental restructuring process, and (e) strengthen the learner's tendency to engage in intentional learning processes. (pp. 4–5)

Much remains to be done to articulate constructivist theory and determine its place in the broader framework of learning and instructional theory. Theory and conjecture continue to far outstrip empirical findings. It is not difficult to understand why, when one considers how difficult it can be to implement and study constructivist pedagogy. Hickey, Moore, and Pellegrino (2001) noted that teachers did not always implement the constructivist curriculum (in this case, the Jasper series) as the developers intended. "Most teachers reported or were reported to have used 'fact sheets' to structure the problem-solving activity, and in one of the classrooms, the Jasper activity was largely reduced to having students compete with each other in answering questions on the fact sheets" (Hickey, Moore, & Pellegrino, 2001, p. 634). However, when the curriculum was implemented as intended, positive consequences for student learning were generally the result.

Constructivism is not without its critics, however. Matthews (2003) questioned the validity of the constructivist world view in light of findings reported by Chall (2000) that teacher-centered approaches were more effective than student-centered approaches for enhancing academic achievement. Likewise, Anderson, Reder, and Simon (2000) examined some of the claims of constructivism and found them to be wanting. In their opinion, constructivism offers little that is new and ignores much that is known. However, there is broad consensus on several points (Anderson, Reder, & Simon, 2000):

- Only the active learner is a successful learner.
- Learning from examples and learning by doing enable learners to achieve deep levels of understanding.
- Learning with understanding is what is desired, not rote learning.
- The social structure of the learning environment is important.

In time, research on constructivism should provide the empirical evidence needed to evaluate its claims and implications for teaching and learning.

A Constructivist Perspective on "Kermit and the Keyboard"

The story "Kermit and the Keyboard" illustrates many aspects of a constructivist learning environment. The learning goal of playing the keyboard skillfully, using a variety of backgrounds and voices to achieve a desired sound, is complex and involves use of knowledge, critical thinking, and self-regulation. The physical skill of actually playing the instrument is not well addressed by constructivist theory, but the cognitive skills associated with it are. Kermit has complete ownership over his own learning. He decides what he wants to learn and how he will go about doing it. The learning environment is certainly complex, and Kermit has a variety of information resources available to him (such as the keyboard manual, the fake books, the music instruction books, his wife, and online chat groups and web sites). When he works on a particular song and reaches a section that is difficult to play, he can resort to exercises in the music instruction books to help him develop the necessary skill. In addition, when he is ready to learn a new feature on the keyboard, he can consult the manual for relevant information and diagrams showing him how that feature functions. When understanding proves difficult, there are the on-line resources or his wife to help him overcome the problem.

Kermit epitomizes the constructivist learner in that he comes to the learning task already motivated and with enough relevant prior knowledge to be successful in his learning efforts. Interestingly, we can see the failure of this environment to support Kermit when he makes a lot of mistakes during his practice sessions. There is no systematic scaffolding as recommended by constructivist theory for when learning and performance fail. As a consequence, Kermit does not overcome his errors, nor does he persist in attempting those songs on which he makes many mistakes.

Theory Matrix

Theory	Constructivism
Prominent Theorists	D. J. Cunningham (see also Chapter 5); D. Jonassen Learning Technology Center at Vanderbilt; D. Perkins; E. von Glasersfeld (radical constructivism);
Learning Outcome(s)	Reasoning, critical thinking, understanding and use of knowledge, self-regulation, mindful reflection
Role of the Learner	Active constructor of knowledge, making meaning of the world surrounding him or her
Role of the Instructor or Instructional Designer	Provide complex and realistic learning environments that challenge learners to identify and solve problems Support learners' efforts and encourage them to reflect on the process
Inputs or Preconditions to Learning	Ill-structured problems, information and technology resources to support problem-solving; ability to be self-directed or conditions to support becoming self-directed
Process of Learning	Besides referring to structuring and restructuring knowledge and the dynamic nature of knowledge, constructivists are vague about the process of learning

Suggested Readings

Koschmann, T. (Ed.). (1996). *CSCL: Theory and practice of an emerging paradigm.* Mahweh, NJ: Lawrence Erlbaum Associates.

Steffe, L. P., & Gale, J. (Eds.). (1995). *Constructivism in education.* Hillsdale, NJ: Lawrence Erlbaum Associates.

The Journal of the Learning Sciences. (1993/1994). Special issue: Goal-based scenarios, 3(4).

The Journal of the Learning Sciences. (1993/1994). Special issue: Computer support for collaborative learning, 3(3).

Wilson, B. G. (Ed.). (1996). *Constructivist learning environments: Case studies in instructional design.* Englewood Cliffs, NJ: Educational Technology Publications.

Reflective Questions and Activities

1. Contrast the epistemologies underlying Gagné's instructional theory and constructivism, with a view toward determining their compatibility or incompati-

bility. When Kuhn (1970) described the process of scientific revolution, in which one paradigm (and corresponding epistemology) supplants another, he argued that competing paradigms are incommensurable. In other words, one could not at the same time be an objectivist and a constructivist. Review other points of view on the incommensurability thesis (see, for example, past issues of the *Educational Researcher*). Decide what your own views are on the subject and present arguments to support your case.

2. Using the unit of instruction you analyzed from the perspective of Gagné's theory, examine it again from the perspective of constructivism. What features now would be considered well designed, and what features does it lack to be good instruction? From a constructivist point of view, what effects would this instruction be likely to have on learners? Are these effects the same or different from those predicted on the basis of Gagné's theory? Explain.

3. Writing and/or using instructional objectives is something that most instructional designers and many teachers take for granted and think little about. Objectives, however, as you have seen in this book, come from a behaviorist tradition and reflect an empiricist perspective on learning. For this reason, the practice of using objectives has been criticized by constructivists. Considering the role that objectives have played in assessment, how should objectives and assessments change to be consistent with constructivism?

4. Locate and view a hypermedia microworld or learning environment. Analyze its features in terms of Gagné's instructional theory and the principles of constructivism, and compare your analyses.

5. Rewrite one of the instructional plans you have already generated in the course of reading this book, this time in terms of constructivism. Compare how this plan differs from its Gagné version, and evaluate the probable effects of the two plans on learning.

Part VIII: Epilogue

12

Toward a Personal Theory of Learning and Instruction

Throughout this book, I have tried to emphasize the nature of theories as provisional and limited in their views of learning. That is, any given learning theory accounts for only some of the data that have been amassed about learning phenomena. Moreover, each theory provides a particular picture of learning that highlights some aspects and obscures others. Because learning is such a complex matter, it is perhaps impossible to conceive of a single theory broad enough to encompass all important aspects of learning and yet still specific enough to be useful for instruction. So, like the blind men, each touching a different part of the elephant, we must evaluate each separate theory for what it illuminates about learning and for how it can guide the development of effective instruction.

Evaluating various learning theories for their validity and usefulness ultimately becomes a matter of developing a personal theory of learning and instruction. Before you began reading this book, you already possessed many intuitive theories about learning and instruction. These would have been based on your own experience of schooling and instruction, on any experiences you had as a teacher or designer of instruction, and on any previous knowledge you had acquired about learning and instruction. You may or may not, however, have given much thought to your intuitive theories or their influence on your actions in the classroom or at the design table. An experienced teacher or designer is likely to have been prompted to reflect upon his or her practices by classes that somehow went wrong or by instruction that failed to facilitate learning. But the neophyte's tacit theories have probably not been tested.

Now, however, you are in a position to construct anew your personal theory of learning, with the expectation that it should serve as an improved guide to your own instructional practices. With each chapter, you have encountered concepts and ideas that added to or challenged your previous

411

knowledge about learning and instruction. With each chapter, you have also had practice comparing, criticizing, and applying theories, and then reflecting on the results of those comparisons, criticisms, and applications. Summarized in Table 12.1 on pages 417–422 are the contents of the theory matrix that appeared in each chapter. In essence, you have conducted much the same process of theory building as any of the theorists discussed in this book, especially if you have had the opportunity to try out some of the ideas presented here. Figure 12.1 illustrates how the systematic and recursive process of theory building that was depicted in Figure 1.1 at the beginning of the book can be revised to represent your personal theory building.

Two aspects of Figure 12.1 are particularly noteworthy to discuss. First, evidence from diverse sources, many of which were discussed in this book, suggests that people are unlikely to change their beliefs unless prompted to reflect critically upon them. I hope that you have had many opportunities while reading this book to engage in that reflection, to examine your beliefs about

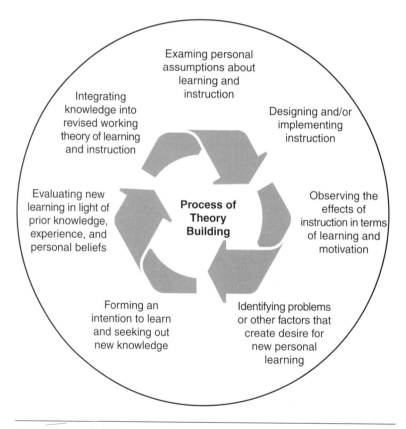

FIGURE 12.1   *Building a Personal Theory of Learning and Instruction*

learning and instruction in light of the theories you were studying. For some, this reflection may lead to significant changes in your thinking and lead you to try new strategies in your professional practice. For others, the changes in thinking caused by critical reflection may be more subtle; rather than a restructuring of beliefs, you may have experienced an expansion—broadening or deepening—of existing beliefs.

The second aspect worth noting in Figure 12.1 is the intention to learn that springs from problems experienced in your professional practice or simply a desire to maintain currency in the knowledge that informs your practice. Either way, having the intention to learn is essential to the recursive process of personal theory building.

As you think about your personal theory of learning and instruction, you may also wish to articulate it in a specific professional context. That is, most of us work with certain populations and not others. I am concerned primarily about the learning of graduate and undergraduate students. You may be concerned about the learning of adults in training programs, or the learning of children in elementary schools, or the learning of clients in a counseling practice. As a consequence, some principles and theories of learning will be more useful to you than will others. Recently, a European colleague and I proposed an approach to assist researchers and practitioners in developing instructional theories to help design instruction (Schott & Driscoll, 1997). We wanted the approach to be prescriptive, systemic, wholistic, and humane (pp. 138–139):

Prescriptive—oriented to solving problems of instruction

Systemic—focused on relations among possibilities and constraints produced in a situated instructional context

Wholistic—based on an integration of current learning theory

Humane—founded in respect for the personality of individual learners

UCIT was the result: Universal Constructive Instructional Theory.

With UCIT, our intent was to provide an approach to cover a variety of different learners, different learning environments, and different subject matters. That is the universal aspect. The constructive aspect comes from the hope that our efforts would spur others to develop and present competing approaches with the effect of revitalizing discussion of instructional theory. As noted in the beginning of the section on learning and instruction (Chapter 11), few integrated or unifying instructional theories exist, yet instruction has become ever more important in today's world. "Lifelong learning has become a necessity, [and] training at the beginning of a job is often not sufficient to prepare the worker for changing conditions in the job due to new technologies or new roles" (Schott & Driscoll, 1997, p. 136). Moreover, knowledge has become something that is possessed by the tools we use to perform our jobs.

For example, word processors keep track of spelling and grammar, notifying the writer immediately about mistakes with colored wavy underlines. Such "intelligent" technology was practically unthinkable not so very long ago.

With UCIT, then, Schott and I proposed an organized and systematic approach to devising situated instructional theories. To begin with, the subject matter or function of an instructional theory pertains to the goal of instruction, and we defined three overall goals: acquisition, storage, and use of knowledge. To make these goals happen requires a dynamic interchange among the learner, learning task, and learning environment, all within a specified frame of reference. The subject matter to be learned is embedded in the learning task and other mediators of learning, such as a teacher or an interactive multimedia program (to name two), are included in the learning environment. The frame of reference accounts for the cultural and organizational context in which instruction and learning take place. Finally, situated possibilities-constraints (SPC) systems establish the range of what is possible for the learner to learn as well as the appropriate instructional methods and media to be employed. See Figure 12.2 for a depiction of the components of UCIT.

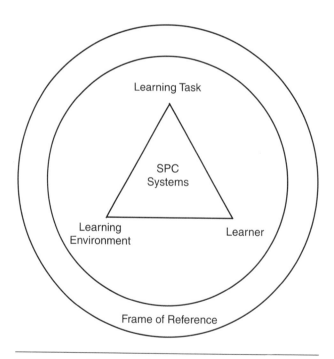

FIGURE 12.2 *Elements of a Universal Constructive Instructional Theory*

How might UCIT be used to construct a situated instructional theory? Consider the following example. In Chapter 9, I described very briefly one of the graduate courses I teach in which a goal of instruction is for students to develop self-regulated learning skills. For the most part, the learners are masters and doctoral students majoring in some aspect of education. The relevant subject matter is current research and theory on learning and instruction, especially as it represents new insights or alternatives to established views. One of the learning tasks is for students in teams to identify a topic of interest to investigate that will contribute to the overall learning goal established by the class. The learning environment includes an on-line data base of readings, software to support brainstorming, a course Web site on which students publish all their work, and the weekly meeting of the class.

Already, you should be able to see operating some of the possibilities and constraints of the SPC systems. Inability of students to use the required technology or to access the Internet would constitute constraints mitigating against the use of these tools in the instruction, despite their relevance in demonstrating application of certain learning theories. Indeed, when I first introduced e-mail as a required means of submitting assignments, I met with a great deal of opposition from students who did not own computers. Nonetheless, I believed the learning possibilities of using the technology outweighed the constraint (and inconvenience) of students having to use computers in campus labs.

The frame of reference in which my situated instructional theory is evolving includes the culture of the southeastern university and community where I work, the relatively high proportion of international students who take this course, and, in a particular semester, the enrollment of four students who took the course at a distance. These are factors over which an instructor or designer has little control, and yet they certainly influence, once again, the possibilities and constraints of the relations among learner, learning environment, and learning task. Consider, for instance, the impact on a learning task assigned to a team when one member of the team is participating from another country. Adjustments to the typical implementation of cooperative learning strategies had to be made. Likewise, the course Web site offered both possibilities and constraints to the international students—possibilities because the published work of other students provided models for improving their writing skills in English, and constraints because they were the students least likely to possess an Internet-connected computer at home. It was, however, an international student who suggested a design change to the Web site that, once effected, assisted the learning of the distance students as well. The change was to post a summary of class discussion each week on the course home page. This served to reorient the international students after classes in which they lost the thread of the discussion when it challenged their language skills. But the summary also served to inform the distance students about what happened in class and helped them to feel more a part of the community.

This dynamic interaction among the components of UCIT will, we hope, enable designers and instructors to "create learning systems that are simultaneously and adaptively sensitive to instructional decisions at the design and delivery phases of instruction" (Schott & Driscoll, 1997, p. 170). Moreover, UCIT "should be as useful for articulating a constructivist instructional model...as in articulating a more traditional...model" (p. 170). I invite you to give the process a try.

Although this is the end of the book, it is hoped that your reflective theory building has only begun. New findings in diverse fields from neuropsychology to computer-based training continually provide information for theory and practice in psychology and education. And as you gain experience, your practical knowledge will serve to temper your theoretical understandings to enable you to make instruction as good as it can be.

TABLE 12.1 Comprehensive Theory Matrix

Theory	Prominent Theorists	Learning Outcome(s)	Role of the Learner	Role of the Instructor	Inputs or Preconditions to Learning	Process of Learning
Radical Behaviorism	B. F. Skinner J. B. Watson	Observable behavior	Active in the environment, consequences that follow behavior determine whether it is repeated	Identify learning goals Determine contingencies of reinforcements Implement program of behavior change Negotiate all these with the learner's input	Environmental conditions serve as discriminative stimuli, cueing which behavior is appropriate to perform	Not addressed in this theory. All learning is assumed to be explained in terms of observable behavior and environmental events surrounding its occurrence.
Cognitive Information Processing	Many including: J. R. Anderson R. C. Atkinson A. M. Collins G. A. Miller A. Paivio M. R. Quillian R. M. Shiffrin	Declarative knowledge, procedural knowledge, memory	Attend to and process incoming information, relating it to what is already in memory	Organize information, direct attention, enhance encoding and retrieval, provide practice opportunities, and help learners monitor their learning	Sensory information in the environment	Processing information and storing it in memory (including processes of attention, pattern recognition, encoding, chunking, rehearsal, and retrieval)

(continued)

TABLE 12.1 *Comprehensive Theory Matrix* (continued)

Theory	Prominent Theorists	Learning Outcome(s)	Role of the Learner	Role of the Instructor	Inputs or Preconditions to Learning	Process of Learning
Meaningful Reception Learning	D. P. Ausubel R. E. Mayer	Organized conceptual knowledge that involves understanding	Make connections between prior knowledge and to-be-learned information that results in an elaborated cognitive structure	Make materials meaningful to the learner Activate learners' prior knowledge, and organize instruction to help them make meaningful connections to what they already know	Potentially meaningful materials, an orientation toward meaningful (as opposed to rote) learning, relevant prior knowledge	Incorporating new information into cognitive structure by attaching it to anchoring ideas through processes of subsumption, superordinate and combinatorial learning
Schema Theory and Mental Models	D. A. Norman D. E. Rumelhart J. Sweller J. van Merrienboer	Organized conceptual knowledge and mental models that can be used to interpret events and solve problems	Construct schemata and mental models Use, modify and automate schemata in solving problems.	Activate learners' existing schemata Help learners' develop and refine appropriate mental models, manage cognitive load Use thought-demanding activities to facilitate understanding	Preexisting schemata that can be modified or reconstructed by analogy to account for new knowledge Materials and problems that do not overload working memory	Accretion, tuning, and restructuring of schemata Automation of schemata

Situated Cognition	Among others: C. Bereiter A. L. Brown J. G. Greeno J. Lave J. L. Lemke M. Scardamalia E. Wenger	Ability to use the concepts and tools of a community of practice Contribute to invention of new tools and practices within the community	Participate increasingly in the activities of a community of practice	Model appropriate practices as a "senior partner" in the learning enterprise Nurture semiosis and promote reflexivity in learning Help learners value participation in a community of practice	Materials and activities of the culture or community of practice	Semiosis, or sign activity (the process of interpreting and creating signs and sign systems); legitimate peripheral participation
Genetic Epistemology	J. Piaget	Physical knowledge, logical-mathematical knowledge, social knowledge	Actively manipulate objects and ideas Experience cognitive conflict Invent and reinvent knowledge through interaction with the world and people surrounding him or her	Provide a rich learning environment that supports activity of the learner and encourages interactions with peers Ask probing questions to make children aware of conflicts and inconsistencies in their thinking	Concrete materials to manipulate, cognitive conflicts to stimulate disequilibrium	Development of cognitive structuring progresses through 4 stages involving processes of assimilation, accommodation, and equilibration Global restructuring occurs through cognitive conflict

(continued)

TABLE 12.1 *Comprehensive Theory Matrix* (continued)

Theory	*Prominent Theorists*	*Learning Outcome(s)*	*Role of the Learner*	*Role of the Instructor*	*Inputs or Preconditions to Learning*	*Process of Learning*
Interactional Theories of Cognitive Development	J. S. Bruner L. S. Vygotsky	Thinking, conceptual knowledge, ability to use the tools of one's culture, awareness of one's own thinking	Interact with the instructor, peers, and sociocultural environment to solve problems	Involve learners in a process of inquiry and problem-solving Ask medium-level questions to provoke cognitive conflict Engage learners in socially organized labor activities relevant to their culture with learning partners appropriate for the desired goals of instruction	A "well-prepared mind," culturally relevant tools, and prior knowledge	For Bruner, a progression through successively more sophisticated modes of thinking (enactive to iconic, to symbolic) For Vygotsky, mediation to apprehend tools of the culture, internalization of socially-mediated understanding to become personal knowledge For both, learning serves to pull development along

Biological Bases of Learning	L. Cosmides (evolution) M. S. Gazzaniga M. R. Rosenzweig D. L. Schacter (neuropsychology)	Thoughts, behaviors, emotions, physical changes in the brain	Interact with a hierarchy of environments	Understand the interactive relation between nature and nurture Attempt to determine what things in learning are tied to critical periods for development Provide rich, complex, and emotionally engaging learning environments and allow for practice	Maturation, different kinds of experiences	Synaptic formation and pruning; organizing and reorganizing brain structures
Motivation and Self-Regulation	A. Bandura J. M. Keller P. R. Pintrich D. H. Schunk B. Zimmerman	Goal-directed behavior Ability to set goals, monitor progress, and adjust learning strategies to assure goal attainment	Determine areas of interest and value Appraise utility of learning strategies and make necessary adjustments to improve the learning process Calibrate learning efforts with results	Enhance motivation with strategies that gain attention, enhance relevance, foster confidence and ensure satisfaction Provide opportunities for learners to set goals, determine learning methods, and self-appraise	Presence and participation in a learning environment	Not specifically addressed. Modern approaches to motivation and self-regulation are consistent with a social-cognitive view of learning.

(continued)

TABLE 12.1 *Comprehensive Theory Matrix* (continued)

Theory	*Prominent Theorists*	*Learning Outcome(s)*	*Role of the Learner*	*Role of the Instructor*	*Inputs or Preconditions to Learning*	*Process of Learning*
Gagne's Instructional Theory	R. M. Gagné	Verbal information, intellectual skills, cognitive strategies, motor skills, attitudes	Participate in instruction as processor of information Depending on circumstances, may identify own learning outcomes, arrange for conditions of learning, and supply own events of instruction	Systematically arrange conditions of learning and events of instruction based on desired learning outcomes and learner characteristics	Internal and external conditions of learning that depend on the type of learning outcome Events of instruction that facilitate information processing	Adopts the cognitive information processing model as an explanation of learning
Constructivism	D. J. Cunningham (see also Chapter 5) D. Jonassen Learning Technology Center at Vanderbilt D. Perkins E. von Glasersfeld (radical constructivism)	Reasoning, critical thinking, understanding and use of knowledge, self-regulation, mindful reflection	Active constructor of knowledge, making meaning of the world surrounding him or her	Provide complex and realistic learning environments that challenge learners to identify and solve problems Support learners' efforts and encourage them to reflect on the process	Ill-structured problems; information and technology resources to support problem-solving; ability to be self-directed or conditions to support becoming self-directed	Besides referring to structuring and restructuring knowledge and the dynamic nature of knowledge, constructivists are vague about the process of learning

References

Anderson, J. R. (1976). *Language, memory and thought.* Hillsdale, NJ: Erlbaum.

Anderson, J. R. (1983). *The architecture of cognition.* Cambridge, MA: Harvard University Press.

Anderson, J. R. (1990). *The adaptive character of thought.* Hillsdale, NJ: Erlbaum.

Anderson, J. R. (1993). *Rules of the mind.* Hillsdale, NJ: Erlbaum.

Anderson, J. R. (1996). ACT: A simple theory of complex cognition. *American Psychologist, 51,* 355–365.

Anderson, J. R., & Bower, G. H. (1973). *Human associative memory.* Washington, DC: Winston.

Anderson, J. R., Reder, L. M., & Simon, H. A. (1996). Situated learning and education. *Educational Researcher, 25,* 5–11.

Anderson, J. R., Reder, L. M., & Simon, H. A. (1997). Rejoinder: Situative versus cognitive perspectives: Form versus substance. *Educational Researcher, 26,* 18–21.

Anderson, J. R., Reder, L. M., & Simon, H. A. (2000). Applications and misapplications of cognitive psychology to mathematics education. *Texas Education Review, 1*(2), 29–49.

Anderson, R. C. (1977). The notion of schemata and the educational enterprise. In R. C. Anderson, R. J. Spiro, & W. E. Montague (Eds.), *Schooling and the acquisition of knowledge.* Hillsdale, NJ: Erlbaum.

Anderson, R. C. (1982). Allocation of attention during reading. In A. Flammer & W. Kintsch (Eds.), *Discourse processing.* Amsterdam: North Holland.

Anderson, R. C., & Ortony, A. (1975). On putting apples into bottles—A problem of polysemy. *Cognitive Psychology, 7,* 167–180.

Anderson, R. C., & Pichert, J. W. (1978). Recall of previously unrecallable information following a shift in perspective. *Journal of Verbal Learning and Verbal Behavior, 17,* 1–12.

Anderson, R. C., Spiro, R. J., & Anderson, M. C. (1978). Schemata as scaffolding for the representation of information in connected discourse. *American Educational Research Journal, 15,* 433–440.

Andre, T. (1979). Does answering higher-level questions while reading facilitate productive learning? *Review of Educational Research, 49,* 280–318.

Andre, T., & Phye, G. D. (1986). Cognition, learning, and education. In G. D. Phye & T. Andre (Eds.), *Cognitive classroom learning.* Orlando: Academic Press.

Anglin, G. J., & Towers, R. L. (1992). Reference citations in selected instructional design and technology journals, 1985–1990. *Educational Technology Research and Development, 40,* 40–46.

Armbruster, B. B. (1986). Schema theory and the design of content-area textbooks. *Educational Psychologist, 21,* 253–267.

Atkins, M., & Blissett, G. (1992, January). Interactive video and cognitive problem-solving skills. *Educational Technology, 32,* 44–54.

Atkinson, J. W. (1964). *An introduction to motivation.* Princeton, NJ: Van Nostrand.

Atkinson, R. C., & Shiffrin, R. M. (1968). Human memory. A proposed system and its control processes. In K. Spence & J. Spence (Eds.), *The psychology of learning and motivation* (Vol. 2). New York: Academic Press.

Atkinson, R. C., & Shiffrin, R. M. (1971). The control of short-term memory. *Scientific American, 225,* 82–90.

Ausubel, D. P. (1960). The use of advance organizers in the learning and retention of meaningful verbal material. *Journal of Educational Psychology, 51,* 267–272.

Ausubel, D. P. (1961). In defense of verbal learning. *Educational Theory, 11,* 15–25.

Ausubel, D. P. (1962). A subsumption theory of meaningful verbal learning. *Journal of General Psychology, 66,* 213–224.

Ausubel, D. P. (1963a). *The psychology of meaningful verbal learning.* New York: Grune & Stratton.

Ausubel, D. P. (1963b). Cognitive structure and the facilitation of meaningful verbal learning. *Journal of Teacher Education, 14,* 217–221.

Ausubel, D. P. (1965). A cognitive structure view of word and concept meaning. In R. C. Anderson & D. P. Ausubel (Eds.), *Readings in the psychology of cognition.* New York: Holt, Rinehart and Winston.

Ausubel, D. P. (1968). *Educational psychology: A cognitive view.* New York: Holt, Rinehart and Winston.

Ausubel, D. P. (1980). Schemata, cognitive structure, and advance organizers: A reply to Anderson, Spiro, and Anderson. *American Educational Research Journal, 17,* 400–404.

Ausubel, D. P., & Fitzgerald, D. (1961). The role of discriminability in meaningful verbal learning. *Journal of Educational Psychology, 52,* 266–274.

Ausubel, D. P., & Fitzgerald, D. (1962). Organizer, general background, and antecedent learning variables in sequential verbal learning. *Journal of Educational Psychology, 53,* 243–249.

Ausubel, D. P., Novak, J. D., & Hanesian, H. (1978). *Educational psychology: A cognitive view* (2nd ed.). New York: Holt, Rinehart and Winston.

Ausubel, D. P., & Youssef, M. (1963). The role of discriminability in meaningful parallel learning. *Journal of Educational Psychology, 54,* 331–336.

Ayllon, T., & Azrin, N. H. (1968). *The token economy.* New York: Appleton-Century-Crofts.

Azrin, N. H. (1967, May). Pain and aggression. *Psychology Today, 1,* 27–33.

Azrin, N. H., & Holz, W. C. (1966). Punishment. In W. A. Honig (Ed.), *Operant behavior: Areas of research and application.* New York: Appleton-Century-Crofts.

Bach-y-Rita, P. (1980). Brain plasticity as a basis for therapeutic procedures. In P. Bach-y-Rita (Ed.), *Recovery of function: Theoretical considerations for brain injury rehabilitation.* Baltimore: University Park Press.

Bach-y-Rita, P. (1982). The relationship between motor processes and cognition in tactile vision substitution. In W. Prinz & A. Sanders (Eds.), *Cognition and motor processes.* New York: Springer-Verlag.

Baillargeon, R., Kotovsky, L., & Needham, A. (1995). The acquisition of physical knowledge in infancy. In D. Sperber, D. Premack, & A. J. Premack (Eds.), *Causal cognition: A multidisciplinary debate.* Oxford: Clarendon Press.

Bandura, A. (1969). *Principles of behavior modification.* New York: Holt, Rinehart and Winston.

Bandura, A. (1977). Self-efficacy: Toward a unifying theory of behavioral change. *Psychological Review, 84,* 195–215.

Bandura, A. (1982). Self-efficacy mechanism in human agency. *American Psychologist, 37,* 122–147.

Bandura, A. (1986). *Social foundations of thought and action: A social-cognitive theory.* Englewood Cliffs, NJ: Prentice-Hall.

Bandura, A. (1997). *Self-efficacy: The exercise of control.* New York: W. H. Freeman.

Bandura, A., Ross, D., & Ross, S. A. (1961). Transmission of aggression through imitation of aggressive models. *Journal of Abnormal and Social Psychology, 63,* 575–582.

Bandura, A., Ross, D., & Ross, S. A. (1963). Imitation of film-mediated aggressive models. *Journal of Abnormal and Social Psychology, 66,* 3–11.

Barclay, J. R., Bransford, J. D., Franks J. J., McCarrell, N. S., & Nitsch, K. (1974). Comprehension and semantic flexibility. *Journal of Verbal Learning and Verbal Behavior, 13,* 471–481.

Barnes, B., & Clawson, E. U. (1975). Do advance organizers facilitate learning? Recommendations for further research based on the analysis of thirty-two studies. *Review of Educational Research, 45,* 637–659.

Barnes, C. A. (1998). Memory changes during normal aging: Neurobiological correlates. In J. Martinez & R. Kesner (Eds.), *Neurobiology of learning and memory.* San Diego: Academic Press.

Bartlett, F. C. (1932). *Remembering: A study in experimental and social psychology.* Cambridge, England: Cambridge University Press.

Bates, J. A. (1979). Extrinsic reward and intrinsic motivation: A review with implications for the classroom. *Review of Educational Research, 49,* 557–576.

Bateson, G. (1979). *Mind and nature.* New York: Dutton.

Beck, I. L. (1981). Reading problems and instructional practice. In T. G. Waller & G. E. MacKennon (Eds.), *Reading research: Advances in theory and practice* (Vol. 2). New York: Academic Press.

Beck, I. L. (1983). Developing comprehension: The impact of the directed reading lesson. In R. Anderson, R. Tierney, & J. Osborn (Eds.), *Learning to read in American schools.* Hillsdale, NJ: Erlbaum.

Beissner, K. L., Jonassen, D. H., & Grabowski, B. L. (1994). Using and selecting graphic techniques to acquire structural knowledge. *Performance Improvement Quarterly, 7,* 20–38.

Bell, A., & Forbes, R. (1997). Performance management. In R. Kaufman, S. Thiagarajan, & P. MacGillis (Eds). *The guidebook for performance improvement.* San Francisco: Pfeiffer.

Bell, B., Bareiss, R., & Beckwith, R. (1993/1994). Sickle Cell Counselor: A prototype goal-based scenario for instruction in a museum environment. *The Journal of the Learning Sciences, 3,* 347–386.

Bellezza, F. S. (1981). Mnemonic devices: Classification, characteristics, and criteria. *Review of Educational Research, 51,* 247–275.

Bellugi, U. (1967). *The acquisition of negation.* Unpublished doctoral dissertation, Harvard University.

Bereiter, C. (1991, April). Implications of connectionism for thinking about rules. *Educational Researcher, 20,* 10–16.

Bereiter, C. (1997). Situated cognition and how to overcome it. In D. Kirshner & J. A. Whitson (Eds.), *Situated cognition: Social, semiotic, and psychological perspectives.* Mahwah, NJ: Erlbaum.

Bereiter, C., & Scardamalia, M. (1996). Rethinking learning. In D. Olson & N. Torrance (Eds.), *Handbook of education and human development: New models of learning, teaching and schooling.* Cambridge, MA: Basil Blackwell.

Berlyne, D. E. (1965). *Structure and direction in thinking.* New York: Wiley.

Bernhard, J. G. (1988). *Primates in the classroom: An evolutionary perspective on children's education.* Amherst: The University of Massachusetts Press.

Bertelson, P. (1982). Lateral differences in normal man and lateralization of brain function. *International Journal of Psychology, 17,* 173–210.

Bielaczyc, K., Pirolli, P. L., & Brown, A. L. (1995). Training in self-explanation and self-regulation strategies. Investigating the effects of knowledge acquisition activities on problem solving. *Cognition and Instruction, 13,* 221–252.

Bilodeau, I. M., & Schlosberg, H. (1951). Similarity in stimulating conditions as a variable in retroactive inhibition. *Journal of Experimental Psychology, 41,* 199–204.

Bloom, B. S. (1986, February). "The hands and feet of genius." Automaticity. *Educational Leadership,* 70–77.

Bloom, B. S., Engelhart, M. D., Furst, E. J., Hill, W. H., & Krathwohl, D. R. (1956). *Taxonomy of educational objectives, handbook I: Cognitive domain.* New York: McKay.

Bohlin, R. M., & Milheim, W. D. (1994). Analyses of the instructional motivation needs of adults. *Canadian Journal of Educational Communication, 23,* 47–55.

Bornstein, R. F. (1988). Radical behaviorism, internal states, and the science of psychology: A reply to Skinner. *American Psychologist, 43,* 819–821.

Bourne, L. E., Dominowski, R. L., Loftus, E. F., & Healy, A. F. (1986). *Cognitive processes* (2nd ed.). Englewood Cliffs, NJ: Prentice-Hall.

Bousfield, W. A. (1953). The occurrence of clustering in the recall of randomly arranged associates. *Journal of General Psychology, 49,* 229–240.

Bower, G. H. (1981). Mood and memory. *American Psychologist, 36,* 129–148.

Bower, G. H., Black, J. B., & Turner, T. J. (1979). Scripts in memory for text. *Cognitive Psychology, 11,* 177–220.

Bower, G. H., & Clark, M. C. (1969). Narrative stories as mediators for serial learning. *Psychonomic Science, 14,* 181–182.

Bower, G. H., Clark, M. C., Lesgold, A. M., & Winzenz, D. (1969). Hierarchical retrieval schemes in recall of categorized word lists. *Journal of Verbal Learning and Verbal Behavior, 8,* 323–343.

Bower, G. H., & Hilgard, E. R. (1981). *Theories of learning* (5th ed.). Englewood Cliffs, NJ: Prentice-Hall.

Bower, G. H., Karlin, M. B., & Dueck, A. (1975). Comprehension and memory for pictures. *Memory and Cognition, 3,* 216–220.

Brainerd, C. S. (1978). *Piaget's theory of intelligence.* Englewood Cliffs, NJ: Prentice-Hall.

Bransford, J. D. (1979). *Human cognition: Learning, understanding, remembering*. Belmont, CA: Wadsworth.

Bransford, J. D., & Franks, J. J. (1971). The abstraction of linguistic ideas. *Cognitive Psychology, 2,* 331–350.

Bransford, J. D., & Johnson, M. K. (1972). Contextual prerequisites for understanding: Some investigations of comprehension and recall. *Journal of Verbal Learning and Verbal Behavior, 11,* 717–726.

Bransford, J. D., & Johnson, M. K. (1973). Considerations of some problems of comprehension. In W. G. Chase (Ed.), *Visual information processing*. New York: Academic Press.

Breland, K., & Breland, M. (1961). The misbehavior of organisms. *American Psychologist, 16,* 681–684.

Brewer, W. F. (1974). There is no convincing evidence for operant or classical conditioning in adult humans. In W. Weimer & D. Palermo (Eds.), *Cognition and the symbolic processes*. Hillsdale, NJ: Erlbaum.

Briggs, L. J. (1980, February). Thirty years of instructional design: One man's experience. *Educational Technology, 20,* 45–50.

Broadbent, D. E. (1957). A mechanical model for human attention and immediate memory. *Psychological Review, 64,* 205–215.

Brooks, F. B., & Donato, R. (1994). Vygotskian approaches to understanding foreign language learner discourse during communicative tasks. *Hispania, 77,* 262–274.

Brooks, L. W., & Dansereau, D. F. (1983). Effects of structural schema training and text organization on expository prose processing. *Journal of Educational Psychology, 75,* 811–820.

Brown, A. L. (1980). Metacognitive development and reading. In R. J. Spiro, B. C. Bruce, & W. F. Brewer (Eds.), *Theoretical issues in reading comprehension*. Hillsdale, NJ: Erlbaum.

Brown, A. L. (1992). Design experiments: Theoretical and methodological challenges in creating complex interventions in classroom settings. *The Journal of the Learning Sciences, 2,* 141–178.

Brown, A. L., Ash, D., Rutherford, M., Nakagawa, K., Gordon, A., & Campione, J. C. (1993). Distributed expertise in the classroom. In G. Salomon (Ed.), *Distributed cognition*. New York: Cambridge University Press.

Brown, A. L., & Ferrara, R. (1985). Diagnosing zones of proximal development. In J. V. Wertsch (Ed.), *Culture, communication, and cognition: Vygotskian perspectives*. New York: Cambridge University Press.

Brown, A. L., & Palincsar, A. S. (1982). Inducing strategic learning from texts by means of informal, self-control training. *Topics in Learning and Learning Disabilities, 2,* 1–17.

Brown, J. (1958). Some tests of the decay theory of immediate memory. *Quarterly Journal of Experimental Psychology, 10,* 12–21.

Brown, J. S., Collins, A., Duguid, P. (1989, January/February). Situated cognition and the culture of learning. *Educational Researcher, 18,* 32–42.

Bruer, J. T. (1997). Education and the brain: A bridge too far. *Educational Researcher, 26*(8), 4–16.

Bruner, J. S. (1957/1973). Going beyond the information given. Originally published in *Contemporary approaches to cognition,* and reprinted in J. M. Anglin (Ed.), *Jerome S. Bruner: Going beyond the information given*. New York: Norton.

Bruner, J. S. (1960). Readiness for learning. In J. S. Bruner, *The process of education*. Cambridge, MA: Harvard University Press.

Bruner, J. S. (1961). The act of discovery. *Harvard Educational Review, 31,* 21–32.

Bruner, J. S. (1962). Introduction. In L. S. Vygotsky, *Thought and language*. Cambridge, MA: MIT Press.

Bruner, J. S. (1964). The course of cognitive growth. *American Psychologist, 19,* 1–15.

Bruner, J. S. (1965). The growth of mind. *American Psychologist, 20,* 1007–1017.

Bruner, J. S. (1966). *Toward a theory of instruction*. Cambridge, MA: Belknap.

Bruner, J. S. (1973a). Preface. In J. S. Bruner, *The relevance of education*. New York: Norton.

Bruner, J. S. (1973b). Some elements of discovery. In J. S. Bruner, *The relevance of education*. New York: Norton.

Bruner, J. S. (1973c). Culture and cognitive growth. In J. S. Bruner, *The relevance of education*. New York: Norton.

Bruner, J. S. (1973d). Poverty and childhood. In J. S. Bruner, *The relevance of education*. New York: Norton.

Bruner, J. S. (1983). *In search of mind: Essays in autobiography*. New York: Harper & Row.

Bruner, J. S. (1985). On teaching thinking: An afterthought. In S. F. Chipman, J. W. Segal, & R. Glaser (Eds.), *Thinking and learning skills* (Vol. 2). Hillsdale, NJ: Erlbaum.

Bruner, J. S. (1986). *Actual minds, possible worlds*. Cambridge, MA: Harvard University Press.

Bruner, J. S. (1992). On searching for Bruner. *Language and Communication, 12,* 75–78.

Bruner, J. S. (1996a). *The culture of education*. Cambridge, MA: Harvard University Press.

Bruner, J. S. (1996b). What we have learned about early learning. *European Early Childhood Education Research Journal, 4,* 5–16.

Bruner, J. S. (1997). Celebrating divergence: Piaget and Vygotsky. *Human Development, 40,* 63–73.

Bruner, J. S., & Bornstein, M. H. (1989). *Interaction in human development*. Hillsdale, NJ: Erlbaum.

Bruner, J. S., Goodnow, J., & Austin, G. A. (1956). *A study of thinking*. New York: Wiley.

Bruner, J. S., Oliver, R., & Greenfield, P. M. (1966). *Studies in cognitive growth*. New York: Wiley.

Bruning, R. H., Schraw, G. J., Norby, M. M., & Ronning, R. R. (2004). *Cognitive psychology and instruction* (4th ed.). Upper Saddle River, NJ: Pearson.

Bushell, D., Wrobel, P., & Michaelis, M. (1968). Applying "group" contingencies to the classroom study behavior of pre-school children. *Journal of Applied Behavior Analysis, 1,* 55–61.

Calder, B. J., & Staw, B. M. (1975). Self-perception of intrinsic and extrinsic motivation. *Journal of Personality and Social Psychology, 31,* 599–605.

Campione, J. C., Brown, A. L., Ferrara, R. A., & Bryant, N. R. (1984). The zone of proximal development: Implications for individual differences and learning. In B. Rogoff & J. V. Wertsch (Eds.), *New Directions for Child Development*: No. 23. *Children's learning in the "zone of proximal development."* San Francisco: Jossey-Bass.

Carey, S. (1985a). *Conceptual change in childhood*. Cambridge, MA: MIT Press.

Carey, S. (1985b). Are children fundamentally different kinds of thinkers and learners than adults? In S. F. Chipman, J. W. Segal, & R. Glaser (Eds.), *Thinking and learning skills* (Vol. 2). Hillsdale, NJ: Erlbaum.

Carey, S. (1986). Cognitive science and science education. *American Psychologist, 41,* 1123–1130.

Carey, S. (1991). Knowledge acquisition: Enrichment or conceptual change? In S. Carey & R. Gelman (Eds.), *Epigenesis of mind: Studies in biology and cognition.* Hillsdale, NJ: Erlbaum.

Carey, S. (1996). Cognitive domains as modes of thought. In D. R. Olson & N. Torrance (Eds.), *Modes of thought: Explorations in culture and cognition.* New York: Cambridge University Press.

Carey, S., & Spelke, E. (1994). Domain specific knowledge and conceptual change. In L. A. Hirschfeld & S. A. Gelman (Eds.), *Mapping the mind: Domain specificity in cognition and culture.* New York: Cambridge University Press.

Carlsson, A. (1978). Antipsychotic drugs, neurotransmitters, and schizophrenia. *American Journal of Psychiatry, 135,* 164–173.

Carroll, L. (1946). *Through the looking glass* (special ed.). New York: Random House.

Case, R. (1978). Piaget and beyond: Toward a developmentally-based theory and technology of instruction. In R. Glaser (Ed.), *Advances in instructional technology,* (Vol. 1). Hillsdale, NJ: Erlbaum.

Case, R. (1980). Intellectual development: A systematic reinterpretation. In F. Farley and N. J. Gordon, (Eds.), *Psychology and education: The state of the union.* Berkeley, CA: McCutchan.

Case, R. (1984). The process of stage transition: A neo-Piagetian view. In R. J. Sternberg (Ed.), *Mechanisms of cognitive development.* New York: Freeman.

Case, R. (1992). Neo-Piagetian theories of child development. In R. J. Sternberg & C. A. Berg (Eds.), *Intellectual development.* New York: Cambridge University Press.

Case, R. (1993). Theories of learning and theories of development. *Educational Psychologist, 28,* 219–233.

Case, R. (1995). Capacity-based explanations of working memory growth: A brief history and reevaluation. In F. E. Weinert & W. Schneider (Eds.), *Memory performance and competencies: Issues in growth and development.* Mahwah, NJ: Erlbaum.

Case, R., & Okamoto, Y. (1996). The role of central conceptual structures in the development of children's thought. *Monographs of the Society for Research in Child Development, 61,* 1–265.

Chall, J. S., & Peterson, R. W. (1986). The influence of neuroscience upon educational practice. In S. L. Friedman, K. A. Klivington, & R. W. Peterson (Eds.), *The brain, cognition, and education.* Orlando: Academic Press.

Chang, F. R. (1981). *Distribution of attention within a single fixation in reading: Studies of the perceptual span.* Unpublished Doctoral dissertation, University of Oregon, Eugene.

Champagne, A. B., Klopfer, L. E., & Anderson, J. H. (1980). Factors influencing the learning of classical mechanics. *American Journal of Physics, 48,* 1074–1079.

Champagne, A. B., Klopfer, L. E., Fox, J., Scheuerman, K. (1982). Laws of motion: *Computer-simulated experiments in mechanics (the a-machine and the inclined plane).* New Rochelle, NY: Educational Materials & Equipment.

Chase, W. G., & Simon, H. A. (1973a). Perception in chess. *Cognitive Psychology, 4,* 55–81.

Chase, W. G., & Simon, H. A. (1973b). The mind's eye in chess. In W. G. Chase (Ed.), *Visual information processing.* New York: Academic Press.

Cheng, P. W., Holyoak, K. J., Nisbett, R. E., & Oliver, L. M. (1986). Pragmatic versus syntactic approaches to training deductive reasoning. *Cognitive Psychology, 18,* 293–328.

Chi, M. T. H. (1978). Knowledge structures and memory development. In R. Siegler (Ed.), *Children's thinking: What develops?* Hillsdale, NJ: Erlbaum.

Chi, M. T. H., de Leeuw, N., Chiu, M.-H., & LaVancher, C. (1994). Eliciting self-explanations improves understanding. *Cognitive Science, 18,* 439–477.

Chi, M. T. H., Glaser, R., & Rees, E. (1982). Expertise in problem solving. In R. Sternberg (Ed.), *Advances in the psychology of human intelligence.* Hillsdale, NJ: Erlbaum.

Chiesi, H. L., Spilich, G. J., Voss, J. F. (1979). Acquisition of domain-related information in relation to high and low domain knowledge. *Journal of Verbal Learning and Verbal Behavior, 18,* 257–273.

Chipman, S. F. (1986). Integrating three perspectives on learning. In S. L. Friedman, K. A. Klivington, & R. W. Peterson (Eds.), *The brain, cognition and education.* Orlando: Academic Press.

Chomsky, N. (1959). Review of Skinner's *Verbal Behavior. Language, 35,* 26–58.

Chomsky, N. (1965). *Aspects of a theory of syntax.* Cambridge, MA: MIT Press.

Chomsky, N. (1972). *Language and mind* (enlarged ed.). New York: Harcourt Brace Jovanovich.

Clancey, W. J. (1997). *Situated cognition: On human knowledge and computer representations.* New York: Cambridge University Press.

Clark, R. E. (1982). Antagonism between achievement and enjoyment in ATI studies. *Educational Psychologist, 17,* 92–101.

Clifford, M. M. (1984). Thoughts on a theory of constructive failure. *Educational Psychologist, 19,* 108–120.

Cognition and Technology Group at Vanderbilt (1990, April). Anchored instruction and its relationship to situated cognition. *Educational Researcher, 19,* 2–10.

Cognition and Technology Group at Vanderbilt. (1991a, May). Technology and the design of generative learning environments. *Educational Technology, 31,* 34–40.

Cognition and Technology Group at Vanderbilt. (1991b, September). Some thoughts about constructivism and instructional design. *Educational Technology, 31,* 16–18.

Cognition and Technology Group at Vanderbilt. (1992). The Jasper experiment: An exploration of issues in learning and instructional design. *Educational Technology Research and Development, 40,* 65–80.

Cognition and Technology Group at Vanderbilt. (1993). Anchored instruction and situated cognition revisited. *Educational Technology, 33,* 52–70.

Cognition and Technology Group at Vanderbilt. (1994). The relationship between situated cognition and anchored instruction. *Educational Technology, 34,* 28–32.

Cohen, N. (1984). Preserved learning capacity in amnesia: Evidence for multiple memory systems. In L. R. Squire & N. Butters (Eds.), *Neuropsychology of memory.* New York: Guilford Press.

Cohen, N., & Squire, L. R. (1981). Preserved learning and retention of pattern-analyzing skill in amnesia. *Science, 210,* 207–210.

Cole, M., & Bruner, J. S. (1971). Cultural differences and inferences about psychological processes. *American Psychologist, 26,* 867–876.

Cole, M., & Scribner, S. (1978). Introduction. In L. S. Vygotsky, *Mind in society.* Cambridge, MA: Harvard University Press.

Collins, A. (1990). Reformulating testing to measure learning and thinking. In N. Frederiksen, R. Glaser, A. Lesgold, & M. G. Shafto (Eds.), *Diagnostic monitoring of skill and knowledge acquisition.* Hillsdale, NJ: Erlbaum.

Collins, A. M., & Quillian, M. R. (1969). Retrieval time from semantic memory. *Journal of Verbal Learning and Verbal Behavior, 8,* 240–247.

Collins, A., & Stevens, A. L. (1982). Goals and strategies of effective teachers. In R. Glaser (Ed.), *Advances in instructional psychology* (Vol. 2). Hillsdale, NJ: Erlbaum.

Collins, A., & Stevens, A. L. (1983). A cognitive theory in inquiry teaching. In C. M. Reigeluth (Ed.), *Instructional-design theories and models.* Hillsdale, NJ: Erlbaum.

Collins, A., Warnock, E. H., & Passafiume, J. J. (1975). Analysis and synthesis of tutorial dialogues. In G. H. Bower (Ed.), *The psychology of learning and motivation* (Vol. 9). New York: Academic Press.

Collins, P. H. (1990). *Black feminist thought: Knowledge, consciousness, and the politics of empowerment.* Boston: Unwin Hyman.

Cooper, G., & Sweller, J. (1987). The effects of schema acquisition and rule automation on mathematical problem-solving transfer. *Journal of Educational Psychology, 79,* 347–362.

Corte, H. E., Wolf, M. E., & Locke, B. J. (1971). A comparison of procedures for eliminating self-injurious behavior of retarded adolescents. *Journal of Applied Behavior Analysis, 4,* 201–214.

Cosmides, L. (1989). The logic of social exchange: Has natural selection shaped how we reason? *Cognition, 31,* 187–276.

Cosmides, L., & Tooby, J. (1989). Evolutionary psychology and the generation of culture, Part II: Case study: A computational theory of social exchange. *Ethology and Sociobiology, 10,* 51–98.

Cosmides, L., & Tooby, J. (1994). Beyond intuition and instinct blindness: Toward an evolutionarily rigorous cognitive science. *Cognition, 50,* 41–77.

Cosmides, L., & Tooby, J. (1995). From evolution to adaptations to behavior: Toward an integrated evolutionary psychology. In R. Wong (Ed.), *Biological perspectives on motivated activities.* Norwood, NJ: Ablex.

Cosmides, L., Tooby, J., & Barkow, J. H. (1992). Introduction: Evolutionary psychology and conceptual integration. In J. H. Barkow, L. Cosmides, & J. Tooby (Eds.), *The adapted mind: Evolutionary psychology and the generation of culture.* New York: Oxford University Press.

Crawford, C. B. (1993). The future of sociobiology: Counting babies or studying proximate mechanisms? *Trends in Ecology and Evolution, 8,* 183–186.

Crawford, C. B., & Anderson, J. L. (1989). Sociobiology: An environmentalist discipline? *American Psychologist, 44,* 1449–1459.

Cromer, R. F. (1981). Reconceptualizing language acquisition and cognitive development. In R. L. Scheifelbusch & D. D. Bricker (Eds.), *Early language: Acquisition and intervention.* Baltimore: University Park Press.

Crowder, N. A. (1960). Automatic tutoring by intrinsic programming. In A. A. Lumsdaine & R. Glaser (Eds.), *Teaching machines and programmed learning.* Washington, DC: National Education Association.

Crutcher, K. A. (1991). Anatomical correlates of neuronal plasticity. In J. L. Martinez, Jr. & R. P. Kesner (Eds.), *Learning and memory: A biological view* (2nd ed.). San Diego: Academic Press.

Culler, J. (1990, April). *Fostering post-structuralist thinking.* Paper presented at the Annual Meeting of the American Educational Research Association, Boston.

Cunningham, D. J. (1987). Outline of an education semiotic. *American Journal of Semiotics, 5,* 201–216.

Cunningham, D. J. (1988, April). *Abduction and affordance: A semiotic view of cognition.* Paper presented at the Annual Meeting of the American Educational Research Association, New Orleans.

Cunningham, D. J. (1992). Beyond educational psychology: Steps toward an educational semiotic. *Educational Psychology Review, 4,* 165–194.

D'Andrade, R. (1995). *The development of cognitive anthropology.* Cambridge: Cambridge University Press.

Damarin, S. K. (1993). Schooling and situated knowledge: Travel or tourism? *Educational Technology, 33,* 27–32.

Damasio, A. R., Damasio, H., & Chang Chui, H. (1980). Neglect following damage to frontal lobe or basal ganglia. *Neuropsychologia, 18,* 123–132.

Dansereau, D. F., Collins, K. W., McDonald, B. A., Holley, C. D., Garland, J. C., Dickhoff, G., & Evans, S. H. (1979). Development and evaluation of a learning strategy program. *Journal of Educational Psychology, 71,* 64–73.

Darwin, C. J., Turvey, M. T., & Crowder, R. G. (1972). The auditory analogue of the Sperling partial report procedure: Evidence for brief auditory storage. *Cognitive Psychology, 3,* 225–267.

Dasen, P. R. (1972). Cross-cultural Piagetian research: A summary. *Journal of Cross-Cultural Psychology, 3,* 23–39. Reprinted in J. Berry & P. Dasen (Eds.). (1974). *Culture and cognition: Readings in cross-cultural psychology.* London: Methuen.

Dean, P. J., Dean, M. R., & Rebalsky, R. M. (1996). Employee perceptions of workplace factors that will most improve their performance. *Performance Improvement Quarterly, 9,* 75–89.

De Bono, E. (1985). The CORT thinking program. In J. W. Segal, S. F. Chipman, & R. Glaser (Eds.), *Thinking and learning skills: Relating instruction to basic research* (Vol. 1). Hillsdale, NJ: Erlbaum.

Deci, E. L. (1975). *Intrinsic motivation.* New York: Plenum Press.

Derry, S. J., & Murphy, D. A. (1986). Designing systems that train learning ability: From theory to practice. *Review of Educational Research, 56,* 1–39.

Derry, S. J., Hawkes, L. W., & Tsai, C-J. (1987). A theory for remediating problem-solving skills for older children and adults. *Educational Psychologist, 22,* 55–87.

Dewey, J. (1933). *How we think: Restatement of the relation of reflective thinking to the educative process.* Boston: Heath.

Dewey, J. (1958). *Experience and nature.* New York: Dover. (Original work published 1929.)

Dewey, J. (1896). The reflex arc concept in psychology. *Psychological Review, 3,* 357–370.

Dewsbury, D. A. (1991). "Psychobiology." *American Psychologist, 46,* 198–205.

Dick, W. (1991, May). An instructional designer's view of constructivism. *Educational Technology, 31,* 31–44.

Dick, W., & Carey, L. (1996). *The systematic design of instruction* (4th ed.). New York: Harper Collins.

Dillon, R. F., & Sternberg, R. J. (1986). *Cognition and instruction*. Orlando: Academic Press.

diSessa, A. A. (1982). Unlearning Aristotelian physics: A study of knowledge-based learning. *Cognitive Science, 6*, 37–75.

Domjon, M. (1980). Ingestional aversion learning: Unique and general processes. *Advances in the study of behavior* (Vol. 11). New York: Academic Press.

Donaldson, M. (1978). *Children's minds*. New York: Norton.

Donato, R. (1994). Collective scaffolding in second language learning. In J. Lantoff & G. Appel (Eds.), *Vygotskian approaches to second language acquisition*. Norwood, NJ: Ablex.

Donegan, N. H., & Thompson, R. F. (1991). The search for the engram. In J. L. Martinez, Jr., & R. P. Kesner (Eds.), *Learning and memory: A biological view* (2nd ed.). San Diego: Academic Press.

Dooling, D. J., & Lachman, R. (1971). Effects of comprehension on retention of prose. *Journal of Experimental Psychology, 88*, 216–222.

Driscoll, M. P. (1984, Winter). Alternative paradigms for research in instructional systems. *Journal of Instructional Development, 7*, 2–5.

Driscoll, M. P. (1985). Measures of cognitive structure: Do they assess learning at the level of comprehension? *Contemporary Educational Psychology, 10*, 38–51.

Driscoll, M. P., & Burner, K. (in press). The cognitive revolution and instructional design. In J. M. Royer (Ed.), *The impact of the cognitive revolution on educational psychology:* Information Age Publishing.

Driscoll, M. P., & Dick, W. (1991). What do textbooks contribute to learning? Unpublished raw data.

Driscoll, M. P., & Lebow, D. (1992). Making it happen: Possibilities and pitfalls of Cunningham's educational semiotic. *Educational Psychology Review, 4*, 211–221.

Driscoll, M. P., & Rowley, K. (1997). Semiotics: Toward learning-centered instructional design. In C. R. Dills & A. J. Romiszowski (Eds.), *Instructional development paradigms*. Englewood Cliffs, NJ: Educational Technology Publications.

Driscoll, M. P., & Tessmer, M. (1985, February). The rational set generator: A method for creating concept examples for teaching and testing. *Educational Technology, 25*, 29–32.

Driscoll, M. P., Dick, W., Johnson, M., & Flynn, J. (1990, April). *Textbooks in schools: What part do they play in effective instruction?* Paper presented at the Annual Meeting of the American Educational Research Association, Boston.

Duckworth, E. (1964). Piaget rediscovered. In R. E. Ripple & V. N. Rockcastle (Eds.), *Piaget rediscovered*. Ithaca, NY: Cornell University Press.

Duell, O. K. (1986). Metacognitive skills. In G. D. Phye & T. Andre (Eds.), *Cognitive classroom learning*. Orlando: Academic Press.

Duffield, J. A. (1990, April). *Problem-solving software: What does it teach?* Paper presented at the Annual Meeting of the American Educational Research Association, Boston.

Duffy, F. H., Burchfield, J. L., & Lombroso, C. T. (1979). Brain electrical activity mapping (BEAM): A method of extending the clinical utility of EEG and evoked potential data. *Annals of Neurology, 5*, 309–321.

Duffy, F. H., Denckla, M. B., Bartels, P. H., & Sandini, G. (1980). Dyslexia: Regional differences in brain electrical activity by topographic mapping. *Annals of Neurology, 7,* 412–420.

Duffy, F. H., Denckla, M. B., Bartels, P. H., Sandini, G., & Kiessling, L. D. (1980). Dyslexia: Automated diagnosis by computerized classification of brain electrical activity. *Annals of Neurology, 7,* 421–428.

Duffy, T. M., & Cunningham, D. J. (1996). Constructivism: Implications for the design and delivery of instruction. In D. H. Jonassen (Ed.), *Handbook of research for educational communications and technology.* New York: Macmillan.

Duffy T. M., & Jonassen, D. H. (1991, May). Constructivism: New implications for instructional technology? *Educational Technology, 31,* 7–12.

Duffy, T. M., & Jonassen, D. H. (Eds.). (1992). *Constructivism and the technology of instruction: A conversation.* Hillsdale, NJ: Erlbaum.

Dweck, C. S. (1986). Motivational processes affecting learning. *American Psychologist, 41,* 1040–1048.

Dweck, C. S., & Elliott, E. S. (1983). Achievement motivation. In P. H. Mussen (Gen. Ed.) & E. M. Hetherington (Vol. Ed.), *Handbook of child psychology: Vol. IV. Social and personality development* (pp. 643–691). New York: Wiley.

Dweck, C. S., & Leggett, E. L. (1988). A social-cognitive approach to motivation and personality. *Psychological Review, 95,* 256–273.

Ebbinghaus, H. (1885). *Memory: A contribution to experimental psychology.* (H. A. Ruger & C. Bussenius, trans.). (1913). New York: Columbia University, Teacher's College Press.

Eco, U. (1976). *A theory of semiotics.* Bloomington: Indiana University Press.

Eco, U. (1984). *Semiotics and the philosophy of language.* London: Macmillan Press.

Edelson, D. C., Pea, R. D., & Gomez, L. (1996). Constructivism in the collaboratory. In B. G. Wilson (Ed.), *Constructivist learning environments: Case studies in instructional design.* Englewood Cliffs, NJ: Educational Technology Publications.

Eick, C. J., Ware, F. N., & Williams, P. G. (2003). Coteaching in a science methods course: A situated learning model of becoming a teacher. *Journal of Teacher Education, 54*(1), 74–85.

Elliott, E. S., & Dweck, C. S. (1988). Goals: An approach to motivation and achievement. *Journal of Personality and Social Psychology, 54,* 5–12.

Ellis, S., & Rogoff, B. (1982). The strategies and efficacy of child versus adult teachers. *Child Development, 43,* 730–735.

Emihovich, C. E. (1981, May–December). Social interaction in two integrated kindergartens. *Integrated Education, 19,* 72–78.

Epstein, H. T. (1990). Stages in human mental growth. *Journal of Educational Psychology, 82,* 876–880.

Estes, W. K. (1972). Reinforcement in human behavior. *American Scientist, 60,* 723–729.

Estes, W. K. (1988). Toward a framework for combining connectionist and symbol-processing models. *Journal of Memory and Language, 27,* 196–212.

Evertson, C. M., Emmer, E. T., Clements, B. S., & Worsham, M. E. (1994). *Classroom management for elementary teachers* (3rd ed.). Boston: Allyn and Bacon.

Feldman, H., Goldin-Meadow, S., & Gleitman, L. (1978). Beyond Herodotus: The creation of language by linguistically deprived deaf children. In A. Lock (Ed.), *Action, symbol and gesture: The emergence of language.* New York: Academic Press.

Feltovich, P. J., Spiro, R. J., Coulson, R. L., & Feltovich, J. (1996). Collaboration within and among minds: Mastering complexity, individually, and in groups. In T. Koschmann (Ed.), *CSCL: Theory and practice of an emerging paradigm*. Mahwah, NJ: Erlbaum.

Ferster, C. B., & Skinner, B. F. (1957). *Schedules of reinforcement*. Englewood Cliffs, NJ: Prentice-Hall.

Feuerstein, R., Rand, Y., Hoffman, M. B., & Miller, R. (1980). *Instrumental enrichment: An intervention program for cognitive modifiability*. Baltimore: University Park Press.

Fitts, P. M., & Posner, M. I. (1967). *Human performance*. Belmont, CA: Brooks/Cole.

Flavell, J. H. (1979). Metacognition and cognitive monitoring: A new area of cognitive developmental inquiry. *American Psychologist, 34*, 906–911.

Flavell, J. H. (1984). Discussion. In R. J. Sternberg (Ed.), *Mechanisms of cognitive development*. New York: Freeman.

Flavell, J. H. (1985). *Cognitive development*. Englewood Cliffs, NJ: Prentice-Hall.

Flynn, J. L. (1992, October). Cooperative learning and Gagné's events of instruction: A syncretic view. *Educational Technology, 32*, 53–60.

Forman, E. A. (1987). Learning through peer interaction: A Vygotskian perspective. *The Genetic Epistemologist, 15*, 6–15.

Fowler, A. (1986). Down's syndrome language: Syntax and morphology. In D. Cicchetti & M. Beeghley (Eds.), *Down's Syndrome: The developmental perspective*. New York: Cambridge University Press.

Friedl, A. E. (1991). *Teaching science to children: An integrated approach*. New York: McGraw-Hill.

Friedman, S. L., & Cocking, R. R. (1986). Instructional influences on cognition and on the brain. In S. L. Friedman, K. A. Klivington, & R. W. Peterson (Eds.), *The brain, cognition and education*. Orlando: Academic Press.

Fry, P. S. (1992). A consideration of cognitive factors in the learning and education of older adults. *International Review of Education, 38*, 303–325.

Fuson, K. C., & Willis, G. B. (1989). Second graders' use of schematic drawings in solving addition and subtraction problems. *Journal of Educational Psychology, 81*, 514–520.

Gagné, E. D. (1985). *The cognitive psychology of school learning*. Boston: Little, Brown.

Gagné, R. M. (1968). Learning hierarchies. *Educational Psychologist, 6*, 1–9.

Gagné, R. M. (1972). Domains of learning. *Interchange, 3*, 1–8.

Gagné, R. M. (1977). Task analysis. In L. J. Briggs (Ed.), *Instructional design: Principles and application*. Englewood Cliffs, NJ: Educational Technology Publications.

Gagné, R. M. (1983). Some issues in the psychology of mathematics instruction. *Journal of Research in Mathematics Education, 14*, 7–18.

Gagné, R. M. (1985). *The conditions of learning* (4th ed.). New York: Holt, Rinehart & Winston.

Gagné, R. M., Briggs, L. J., & Wager, W. (1992). *Principles of instructional design* (4th ed.). Fort Worth: Harcourt Brace Jovanovich.

Gagné, R. M., & Dick, W. (1983). Instructional psychology. *Annual Review of Psychology, 34*, 261–295.

Gagné, R. M., & Driscoll, M. P. (1988). *Essentials of learning for instruction* (2nd ed.). Englewood Cliffs, NJ: Prentice-Hall.

Gagné, R. M., & Glaser, R. (1987). Foundations in learning research. In R. M. Gagné (Ed.), *Instructional technology: Foundations*. Hillsdale, NJ: Erlbaum.

Gagné, R. M., & Medsker, K. L. (1996). *The conditions of learning: Training applications*. Fort Worth: Harcourt Brace College.

Gagné, R. M., & Merrill, M. D. (1990). Integrative goals for instructional design. *Educational Technology Research and Development, 38*, 23–30.

Gagné, R. M., & Rohwer, W. D., Jr. (1969). Instructional psychology. *Annual Review of Psychology, 20*, 381–418.

Galegher, J., & Kraut, R. E. (1990). Technology for intellectual teamwork: Perspectives on research and design. In J. Galegher, R. Kraut, & C. Egido (Eds.), *Intellectual teamwork: Social and technological foundations of cooperative work*. Hillsdale, NJ: Erlbaum.

Gallahue, D. L., & Ozmun, J. C. (1995). *Understanding motor development* (3rd ed). Madison, WI: WCB Brown & Benchmark Publishers.

Garcia, J., Brett, L. P., & Rusiniak, K. W. (1989). Limits of Darwinian conditioning. In S. B. Klein & R. R. Mowrer (Eds.), *Contemporary learning theories: Instrumental conditioning theory and the impact of biological constraints on learning*. Hillsdale, NJ: Erlbaum.

Garcia, J., Clark, J., & Hankins, W. (1973). Natural responses to schedule rewards. In P. Bateson & P. Klopfer (Eds.), *Perspectives in ethology*. New York: Plenum Press.

Garcia, J., & Koelling, P. A. (1966). Relation of cue to consequence in avoidance learning. *Psychonomic Science, 4*, 123–124.

Gardner, H. (1982). Giftedness: A biological perspective. In D. Feldman (Ed.), *Developmental approaches to giftedness and creativity: New directions for child development*. San Francisco: Jossey Bass.

Gardner, H. (1983). *Frames of mind: The theory of multiple intelligences*. New York: Basic Books.

Gardner, H. (1985). *The mind's new science*. New York: Basic Books.

Gardner, H. (1986). Notes on cognitive development: Recent trends, new directions. In S. L. Friedman, K. A. Klivington, & R. W. Peterson (Eds.), *The brain, cognition, and education*. Orlando: Academic Press.

Gazzaniga, M. S. (1984). Advances in cognitive neurosciences: The problem of information storage in the human brain. In G. Lynch, J. L. McGaugh, & N. M. Weinberger (Eds.), *Neurobiology of learning and memory*. New York: The Guilford Press.

Gazzaniga, M. S. (1995). On neural circuits and cognition. *Neural Computation, 7*, 1–12.

Gazzaniga, M. S., Eliassen, J. C., Nisenson, L., Wessinger, C. M., Fendrich, R., & Baynes, K. (1996). Collaboration between the hemispheres of a callosotomy patient: Emerging right hemisphere speech and the left hemisphere interpreter. *Brain, 119*, 1255–1262.

Gelman, R. (1972). The nature and development of early number concepts. In H. Reese (Ed.), *Advances in child development and behavior* (Vol. 7). New York: Academic Press.

Gelman, R. (1978). Cognitive development. In M. R. Rosenzweig & L. W. Porter (Eds.), *Annual Review of Psychology* (Vol. 29). Palo Alto, CA: Annual Reviews, Inc.

Gelman, R. (1983). Recent trends in cognitive development. In G. Scherrer & A. M. Robers (Eds.), *The G. Stanley Hall Lecture Series* (Vol. 3). Washington, DC: American Psychological Association.

Gelman, R., & Baillargeon, R. (1983). A review of some Piagetian concepts. In P. Mussen (Ed.), *Manual of child psychology* (4th ed.). *Vol.: 3. Cognitive development* (J. H. Flavell & E. M. Markman, Eds.). New York: Wiley.

Gentner, D. (1982). Why nouns are learned before verbs: Linguistic relativity vs. natural partitioning. In S. Kuczaj (Ed.), *Language development: Language, culture, and cognition*. Hillsdale, NJ: Erlbaum.

Gershberg, F. B., & Shimamura, A. P. (1998). The neuropsychology of human learning and memory. In J. Martinez & R. Kesner (Eds.), *Neurobiology of learning and memory*. San Diego: Academic Press.

Gibson, J. J. (1966). *The senses considered as perceptual systems*. Boston: Houghton Mifflin.

Gibson, J. J. (1977). The theory of affordance. In R. Shaw & J. Bransford (Eds.), *Perceiving, acting, and knowing*. Hillsdale, NJ: Erlbaum.

Gibson, J. J. (1986). *An ecological approach to visual perception*. Hillsdale, NJ: Erlbaum. (Original work published 1979.)

Gilbert, N. J., & Driscoll, M. P. (1998, April). *Collaborative knowledge-building environments: A case study*. Paper presented at the Annual Meeting of American Educational Research Association, San Diego.

Glachan, M., & Light, P. (1982). Peer interaction and learning: Can two ways make a right? In G. Butterworth & P. Light (Eds.), *Social cognition: Studies of the development of understanding*. Brighton: Harvester Press.

Gladwin, T. (1970). *East is a big bird*. Cambridge, MA: Harvard University Press.

Glaser, R. (1984). Education and thinking: The role of knowledge. *American Psychologist, 39*, 93–104.

Gleason, J. B. (1973). Code switching in children's language. In T. E. Moore (Ed.), *Cognitive development and the acquisition of language*. New York: Academic Press.

Gleitman, L. (1986). Biological preprogramming for language learning? In S. L. Friedman, K. A. Klivington, & R. W. Peterson (Eds.), *The brain, cognition and education*. Orlando: Academic Press.

Glynn, S. M., & Divesta, F. J. (1977). Outline and hierarchical organization as aids for study and retrieval. *Journal of Educational Psychology, 69*, 9–14.

Glynn, S. M., & Divesta, F. J. (1979). Control of prose processing via instructional and typographical cues. *Journal of Educational Psychology, 71*, 595–603.

Goldenberg, C. N. (1992). The limits of expectations: A case for case knowledge about teacher expectancy effects. *American Educational Research Journal, 29*, 517–544.

Goldman-Rakic, P. S. (1986). Setting the stage: Neural development before birth. In S. L. Friedman, K. A. Klivington, & R. W. Peterson (Eds.), *The brain, cognition and education*. Orlando: Academic Press.

Good, T. L. (1987). Two decades of research on teacher expectations: Findings and future directions. *Journal of Teacher Education, 38*, 32–47.

Good, T. L., & Brophy, J. E. (1984). *Looking in classrooms*. New York: Harper & Row.

Goodman, N. (1984). *Of mind and other matters*. Cambridge, MA: Harvard University Press.

Goodwin, B. (1985). Constructional biology. In G. Butterworth, J. Rutkowska, & M. Scaife (Eds.), *Evolution and developmental psychology*. Great Britain: The Harvester Press Limited.

Goodwin, D. W., Powell, B., Bremer, D., Hoine H., & Stern, J. (1969). Alcohol and recall: State-dependent effects in man. *Science, 163*, 1358.

Grabe, M. (1986). Attentional processes in education. In G. D. Phye & T. Andre (Eds.), *Cognitive classroom learning.* Orlando: Academic Press.

Graham, S., & Barker, G. P. (1990). The down side of help: An attributional-developmental analysis of helping behavior as a low-ability cue. *Journal of Educational Psychology, 82,* 7–14.

Graham, S., & Golen, S. (1991). Motivational influences on cognition: Task involvement, ego involvement, and depth of information processing. *Journal of Educational Psychology, 83,* 187–196.

Greenfield, P. M. (1984). A theory of the teacher in the learning activities of everyday life. In B. Rogoff & J. Lave (Eds.), *Everyday cognition.* Cambridge, MA: Harvard University Press.

Greeno, J. (1980). Trends in the theory of knowledge for problem solving. In D. Tuma & F. Reif (Eds.), *Problem solving and education: Issues in teaching and research.* Hillsdale, NJ: Erlbaum.

Greeno, J. G. (1997). *Response:* On claims that answer the wrong questions. *Educational Researcher, 26,* 5–17.

Gruber, H. E., & Vonèche, J. J. (1977). *The essential Piaget.* New York: Basic Books, Inc., Publishers.

Gruber, H. E., & Vonèche, J. J. (1995). *The essential Piaget.* Northvale, NJ: Jason Arons.

Gunter, M. A., Estes, T. H., & Schwab, J. H. (1990). *Instruction: A models approach.* Boston: Allyn & Bacon.

Guthrie, E. R. (1933). Association as a function of the time interval. *Psychological Review, 37,* 412–428.

Hannafin, M. J. (1992). Emerging technologies, ISD, and learning environments: Critical perspectives. *Educational Technology Research and Development, 40,* 49–64.

Hannafin, M. J., Hannafin, K. M., Land, S. M., & Oliver, K. (1997). Grounded practice and the design of constructivist learning environments. *Educational Technology Research & Development, 45,* 101–117.

Hannafin, M., Land, S., & Oliver, K. (1999). Open learning environments: Foundations, methods, and models. In C. M. Reigeluth (Ed.), *Instructional-design theories and models.* Mahwah, NJ: Lawrence Erlbaum Associates, Publishers.

Hansen, J. C., & Hillyard, S. A. (1980). Endogenous brain potentials associated with selective auditory attention. *Electroencephalography and Clinical Neuropsychology, 49,* 277–290.

Harding, S. (1986). *The science question in feminism.* Ithaca, NY: Cornell University Press.

Harding, S. (1991). *Whose science? Whose knowledge?* Ithaca, NY: Cornell University Press.

Harris, F. R., Wolf, M. M., & Baer, D. M. (1967). Effects of adult social reinforcement on child behavior. In S. W. Bijou & D. M. Baer (Eds.), *Child development: Readings in experimental analysis.* New York: Appleton-Century-Crofts.

Harris, R. J., Schoen, L. M., & Lee, D. J. (1986). Culture-based distortion in memory for stories. In J. L. Armagost (Ed.), *Papers from the 1985 Mid-America Linguistics Conference.* Manhattan: Kansas State University Department of Speech.

Hartley, J., & Davies, I. K. (1976). Pre-instructional strategies: The role of pretests, behavioral objectives, overviews, and advance organizers. *Review of Educational Research, 46,* 239–265.

Hartsock, N. (1983). The feminist standpoint: Developing the ground for a specifically feminist historical materialism. In S. Harding & M. Hintikka (Eds.), *Discovering reality: Feminist perspectives on epistemology, metaphysics, methodology, and philosophy of science.* Dordrecht, Holland: D. Reidel.

Heminway, J. (Producer, Director, and Author) & Tegriti, A. (Author). (1984). *The brain: Learning and memory.* WNET New York: Education Broadcasting.

Hergenhahn, B. R., & Olson, M. H. (1997). *An introduction to theories of learning.* (5th ed.). Upper Saddle River, NJ: Prentice-Hall.

Herrnstein, R. J., & Boring, E. G. (1965). *A sourcebook in the history of psychology.* Cambridge, MA: Harvard University Press.

Higbee, K. L. (1979). Recent research on visual mnemonics. Historical roots and educational fruits. *Review of Educational Research, 49,* 611–630.

Hickey, D. T., Moore, A. L., & Pellegrino, J. W. (2001). The motivational and academic consequences of elementary mathematics environments: Do constructivist innovations and reforms make a difference? *American Educational Research Journal, 38*(3), 611–652.

Hlynka, D. (1991, June). Postmodern excursions into educational technology. *Educational Technology, 31,* 27–30.

Holland, J., & Skinner, B. F. (1961). *The analysis of behavior.* New York: McGraw-Hill.

Holtzman, J. D., & Gazzaniga, M. S. (1982). Dual task interaction due exclusively to limits in processing resources. *Science, 218,* 1325–1327.

Honebein, P. C. (1996). Seven goals for the design of constructivist learning environments. In B. G. Wilson (Ed.), *Constructivist learning environments: Case studies in instructional design.* Englewood Cliffs, NJ: Educational Technology Publications.

Honebein, P. C., Duffy, T. M., & Fishman, B. J. (1993). Constructivism and the design of authentic learning environments: Context and authentic activities for learning. In T. M. Duffy, J. Lowyck, & D. Jonassen (Eds.), *Designing environments for constructive learning.* Hillsdale, NJ: Erlbaum.

Honebein, P. C., Chen, P., & Brescia, W. (1992). Hypermedia and sociology: A simulation for developing research skills. *Liberal Arts Computing, 1,* 9–15.

Houser, N., & Kloesel, C. (1992). *The essential Peirce: Selected philosophical writings* (Vol. I). Bloomington: Indiana University Press.

Hubel, D., & Wiesel, T. (1962). Receptive fields, binocular interaction, and functional architecture in the cat's visual cortex. *Journal of Physiology, 160,* 106–154.

Hudspeth, W. J., & Pribham, K. H. (1990). Stages of brain and cognitive maturation. *Journal of Educational Psychology, 82,* 881–884.

Inhelder, B., & Piaget, J. (1958). *The growth of logical thinking.* New York: Basic Books.

Inhelder, B., & Piaget, J. (1964). *The early growth of logic in the child: Classification and seriation.* London: Routledge.

Inhelder, B., Sinclair, H., & Bovet, M. (1974). *Learning and the development of cognition.* Cambridge, MA: Harvard University Press.

Jackson, N. C., & Mathews, R. M. (1995). Using public feedback to increase contributions to a multipurpose senior center. *Journal of Applied Behavior Analysis, 28,* 449–455.

Jacoby, L. L., Levy, B. A., & Steinbach, K. (1992). Episodic transfer and automaticity: Integration of data-driven and conceptually-driven processing in reading. *Journal of Experimental Psychology: Learning, Memory and Cognition, 18,* 15–24.

Jenkins, J. J. (1974). Remember that old theory of memory? Well, forget it! *American Psychologist, 11*, 785–795.

Jih, H. J., & Reeves, T. C. (1992). Mental models: A research focus for interactive learning systems. *Educational Technology Research and Development, 40*, 1042–1629.

John-Steiner, V., & Souberman, E. (1978). Afterword. In L. S. Vygotsky, *Mind in society.* Cambridge, MA: Harvard University Press.

Johnson, K. R., & Perkins, M. R. (1976). *Mastery workbook for educational psychology.* Dubuque, IA: Kendall-Hunt.

Johnson, M. J. (1987). *The body in the mind: The bodily basis of meaning.* Chicago: University of Chicago Press.

Johnson, M. K., & Chalfonte, B. L. (1994). Binding complex memories: The role of reactivation and the hippocampus. In D. L. Schacter & E. Tulving (Eds.), *Memory systems 1994.* Cambridge, MA: MIT Press.

Johnson, R. T., Johnson, D. W., & Stanne, M. B. (1985). Effects of cooperative, competitive, and individualistic goal structures on computer-assisted instruction. *Journal of Educational Psychology, 77*, 668–677.

Johnson-Laird, P. N. (1983). *Mental models.* Cambridge, MA: Harvard University Press.

Jonassen, D. H. (1997). Instructional design models for well-structured and ill-structured problem-solving learning outcomes. *Educational Technology Research & Development, 45*, 65–94.

Jonassen, D. (1999). Designing constructivist learning environments. In C. M. Reigeluth (Ed.), *Instructional-design theories and models.* Mahwah, NJ: Erlbaum.

Jonassen, D. H., Beissner, K., & Yacci, M. (1993). *Structural knowledge: Techniques for representing, conveying, and acquiring structural knowledge.* Hillsdale, NJ: Erlbaum.

Jones, B. H. (1988). Learning computer systems by analogy: Mental models research. *International Journal of Instructional Media, 15*, 59–65.

Joyce, B., & Weil, M. (1986). *Models of teaching* (3rd ed.). Englewood Cliffs, NJ: Prentice-Hall.

Kahneman, D. (1973). *Attention and effort.* Englewood Cliffs, NJ: Prentice-Hall.

Kantor, J. R. (1945). *Psychology and logic* (Vol. 1). Bloomington, IN: Principia.

Kaplan, B. (1967). Meditations on genesis. *Human Development, 10*, 65–87.

Kass, A., Burke, R., Blevis, E., & Williamson, M. (1993/1994). Constructing learning environments for complex social skills. *The Journal of the Learning Sciences, 3*, 387–428.

Kaufman, R., Thiagarajan, S., & MacGillis, P. (Eds.). (1997). *The guidebook for performance improvement.* San Francisco: Pfeiffer.

Keller, F. S. (1968). "Goodbye, teacher…" *Journal of Applied Behavior Analysis, 1*, 79–89.

Keller, J. M. (1983). Motivational design of instruction. In C. M. Reigeluth (Ed.), *Instructional-design theories and models.* Hillsdale, NJ: Erlbaum.

Keller, J. M. (1984). Use of the ARCS model of motivation in teacher training. In K. E. Shaw (Ed.), *Aspects of educational technology XVII. Staff development and career updating.* New York: Nichols.

Keller, J. M. (1987a, October). Strategies for stimulating the motivation to learn. *Performance and Instruction Journal*, 1–7.

Keller, J. M. (1987b, November/December). The systematic process of motivational design. *Performance and Instruction Journal*, 1–8.

Kelley, H. H., & Michela, J. (1980). Attribution theory and research. In M. Rosenzweig & L. Porter (Eds.), *Annual Review of Psychology* (Vol. 31, pp. 457–501). Palo Alto, CA: Annual Reviews.

Kesner, R. P. (1998). Neurobiological views of memory. In J. Martinez & R. Kesner (Eds.), *Neurobiology of learning and memory*. San Diego: Academic Press.

Kessen, W. (1984). Introduction: The end of the age of development. In R. J. Sternberg (Ed.), *Mechanisms of cognitive development*. New York: Freeman.

Kiewra, K. A. (1985). Investigating notetaking and review: A depth of processing alternative. *Educational Psychologist, 20,* 23–32.

Kiewra, K. A., DuBois, N. F., Christian, D., McShane, A., Meyerhoffer, M., & Roskelley, D. (1991). Note-taking functions and techniques. *Journal of Educational Psychology, 83,* 240–245.

Kiewra, K. A., & Frank, B. M. (1988). Encoding and external-storage effects of personal lecture notes, skeletal notes and detailed notes for field independent and field dependent learners. *Journal of Educational Research, 81,* 142–148.

Kimble, G. A. (1994). A new formula for behaviorism. *Psychological Review, 101,* 254–258.

Kingstone, A., Enns, J. T., Mangun, G. R., & Gazzaniga, M. S. (1995). Guided visual search is a left-hemisphere process in split-brain patients. *Psychological Science, 6,* 118–121.

Kintsch, W. (1974). *The representation of meaning in memory*. Hillsdale, NJ: Erlbaum.

Kintsch, W. (1976). Memory for prose. In C. N. Cofer (Ed.), *The structure of human memory*. San Francisco: Freeman.

Kintsch, W. (1977). *Memory and cognition* (2nd ed.). New York: Wiley.

Kintsch, W., & van Dijk, T. (1978). Toward a model of text comprehension and production. *Psychological Review, 85,* 363–394.

Kirschner, P. A. (2002). Cognitive load theory: implications of cognitive load theory on the design of learning. *Learning and Instruction, 12,* 1–10.

Kirshner, D., & Whitson, J. A. (1997). Editor's introduction. In D. Kirshner & J. A. Whitson (Eds.), *Situated cognition: Social, semiotic, and psychological perspectives*. Mahwah, NJ: Erlbaum.

Klahr, D. (1984). Transition processes in quantitative development. In R. J. Sternberg (Ed.), *Mechanisms of cognitive development*. New York: Freeman.

Klahr, D. (1995). *Computational models of cognitive development: The state of the art*. In T. J. Simon and G. S. Halford (Eds.), *Developing cognitive competence*. Hillsdale, NJ: Erlbaum.

Klahr, D., & Wallace, J. G. (1973). The role of quantification operators in the development of conservation of quantity. *Cognitive Psychology, 4,* 301–327.

Klahr, D., & Wallace, J. G., (1976). *Cognitive development: An information-processing view*. Hillsdale, NJ: Erlbaum.

Klatzky, R. L. (1980). *Human memory* (2nd ed.). New York: Freeman.

Klauer, K. J. (1984). Intentional and incidental learning with instructional texts: A meta-analysis for 1970–1980. *American Educational Research Journal, 21,* 323–340.

Kohler, W. (1917). On the insight of apes. (Trans. E. G. Boring) In R. J. Herrnstein & E. G. Boring (Eds.), *A sourcebook in the history of psychology*. Cambridge, MA: Harvard University Press, 1961.

Kohler, W. (1925). *The mentality of apes*. London: Routledge & Kegan Paul.

Koschmann, T. (1994). Toward a theory of computer support for collaborative learning. *The Journal of the Learning Sciences, 3,* 219–225.

Koschmann, T. (1996). *CSCL: Theory and practice of an emerging paradigm.* Mahwah, NJ: Erlbaum.

Kosslyn, S. M. (1980). *Image and mind.* Cambridge, MA: Harvard University Press.

Kozminsky, E. (1977). Altering comprehension: The effect of biasing titles on text comprehension. *Memory and Cognition, 5,* 482–490.

Krathwohl, D. R., Bloom, B. S., & Masia, B. B. (1964). *Taxonomy of educational objectives, handbook II: Affective domain.* New York: McKay.

Kuhn, D. J., & Novak, J. D. (1971). A study of cognitive subsumption in the life sciences. *Science Education, 55,* 309–320.

Kuhn, T. S. (1970). *The structure of scientific revolutions* (2nd ed.). Chicago: University of Chicago Press.

Kulhavy, R. W., & Stock, W. A. (1989). Feedback in written instruction: The place of response certitude. *Educational Psychology Review, 1,* 279–308.

Kulhavy, R. W., & Swenson, I. (1975). Imagery instructions and the comprehension of text. *British Journal of Education Psychology, 45,* 47–51.

Kulik, J. A., Kulik, C. C., & Cohen, P. A. (1979). A meta-analysis of outcome studies of Keller's Personalized System of Instruction. *American Psychologist, 34,* 307–318.

LaBerge, D., & Samuels, S. J. (1974). Toward a theory of automatic information processing in reading. *Cognitive Psychology, 6,* 293–323.

Ladavas, E., Del Pesce, M., Mangun, G. R., & Gazzaniga, M. S. (1994). Variations in attentional bias of the disconnected cerebral hemispheres. *Cognitive Neuropsychology, 11,* 57–74.

Lakoff, G. (1987). *Women, fire and dangerous things: What categories reveal about the mind.* Chicago: University of Chicago Press.

Language Development and Hypermedia Group. (1992a, February). "Open" software design: A case study. *Educational Technology, 32,* 43–55.

Language Development and Hypermedia Group. (1992b). Bubble dialogue: A new tool for instruction and assessment. *Educational Technology Research and Development, 40,* 59–67.

Languis, M. L., Bireley, M., & Williamson, T. (1990, April). *Brain mapping assessment of information processing patterns in gifted/learning disabled students.* Paper presented at the Annual Meeting of the American Educational Research Association, Boston.

Languis, M. L., Miller, D., & Bertoline, G. (1990, April). *Spatial visualization skill: Topographic brain mapping assessment; Influence of cognitive intervention.* Paper presented at the Annual Meeting of the American Educational Research Association, Boston.

Lapan, R. T. (2002). Empowering students to become self-regulated learners. *Professional School Counseling, 5*(4), 257–265.

Larken, J. H., McDermott, J., Simon, D. P., & Simon, H. A. (1980). Models of competence in solving physics problems. *Cognitive Science, 4,* 317–345.

Lashley, K. S. (1929). *Brain mechanisms and intelligence.* Chicago: University of Chicago Press.

Lashley, K. S., & Franz, S. I. (1917). The effects of cerebral destruction upon habit-formation and retention in the albino rat. *Psychobiology,* 71–139.

Lave, J. (1988). *Cognition in practice: Mind, mathematics and culture in everyday life.* New York: Cambridge University Press.

Lave, J. (1990/1997). The culture of acquisition and the practice of understanding. Reprinted in D. Kirshner & J. A. Whitson (Eds.), *Situated cognition: Social, semiotic, and psychological perspectives.* Mahwah, NJ: Erlbaum.

Lave, J., & Wenger, E. (1991). *Situated learning: Legitimate peripheral participation.* New York: Cambridge University Press.

Lave, J., Murtaugh, M., & de la Rocha, O. (1984). The dialectic of arithmetic in grocery shopping. In B. Rogoff & J. Lave (Eds.), *Everyday cognition.* Cambridge, MA: Harvard University Press.

Leahey, T. H., & Harris, R. J. (1997). *Learning and cognition.* (4th ed.). Upper Saddle River, NJ: Prentice-Hall.

Lebow, D. (1993). Constructivist values for instructional systems design: Five principles toward a new mindset. *Educational Technology Research & Development, 41,* 4–16.

Lebow, D., & Wager, W. W. (1994). Authentic activity as a model for appropriate learning activity: Implications for emerging instructional technologies. *Canadian Journal of Educational Communication, 23,* 231–244.

Lebow, D. G., Wager, W. W., Marks, P., & Gilbert, N.J. (1996, June). *Construe: Software for collaborative learning over the World Wide Web.* Paper presented at the AECT/FSU Conference on Distance Learning, Tallahassee, FL.

Lemke, J. L. (1988). Genres, semantics, and classroom education. *Linguistics and Education, 1,* 81–99.

Lemke, J. L. (1997). Cognition, context, and learning: A social semiotic process. In D. Kirshner & J. A. Whitson (Eds.), *Situated cognition: Social, semiotic, and psychological perspectives.* Mahwah, NJ: Erlbaum.

Lenneberg, E. H. (1964). A biological perspective of language. In E. H. Lenneberg (Ed.), *New directions in the study of language.* Cambridge, MA: MIT Press.

Lenneberg, E. H. (1967). *Biological foundations of language.* New York: Wiley.

Leontiev, A. N. (1981). The problem of activity in psychology. In J. V. Wertsch (Ed.), *The concept of activity in Soviet psychology.* Armonk, NY: Sharpe.

Leslie, A. (1994). ToMM, ToBy, and Agency: Core architecture and domain specificity. In L. A. Hirschfield & S. A. Gelman (Eds.), *Mapping the mind: Domain specificity in cognition and culture.* New York: Cambridge University Press.

Levin, J. R. (1983). Pictorial strategies for school learning: Practical illustrations. In M. Pressley & J. R. Levin (Eds.), *Cognitive strategy research: Educational applications.* New York: Springer-Verlag.

Levin, J. R., & Kaplan, S. A. (1972). Imaginal facilitation of paired-associate learning: A limited generalization? *Journal of Educational Psychology, 63,* 429–432.

Levin, J. R., & Pressley, M. (Eds.). (1986). Learning strategies (Special issue). *Educational Psychologist, 21* (1 & 2).

Lewin, K. (1936). *Principles of topological psychology.* New York: McGraw-Hill.

Lewin, K. (1946). Behavior and development as a function of the total situation. In L. Carmichael (Ed.), *Manual of child psychology.* New York: Wiley.

Lewis, A. B. (1989). Training students to represent arithmetic word problems. *Journal of Educational Psychology, 81,* 521–531.

Lewis, E. L., Stern, J. L., & Linn, M. C. (1993, January). The effect of computer simulations on introductory thermodynamics understanding. *Educational Technology*, 45–58.

Light, L. L., & Berger, D. E. (1976). Are there long-term "literal copies" of visually presented worlds? *Journal of Experimental Psychology: Human Learning and Memory, 2*, 654–662.

Lin, X., Bransford, J. D., Hmelo, C. E., Kantor, R. J., Hickey, D. T., Secules, T., Petrosino, A. J., Goldman, S. R., and the Cognition and Technology Group at Vanderbilt. (1996). Instructional design and development of learning communities: An invitation to a dialogue. In B. G. Wilson (Ed.), *Constructivist learning environments: Case studies in instructional design*. Englewood Cliffs, NJ: Educational Technology Publications.

Litchfield, B. C., Driscoll, M. P., & Dempsey, J. V. (1990). Presentation sequence and example difficulty: Their effect on concept and rule learning in computer-based instruction. *Journal of Computer-Based Instruction, 17*, 35–40.

Locke, E. A., Shaw, K. N., Saari, L. M., & Latham, G. P. (1981). Goal setting and task performance: 1969–1980. *Psychological Bulletin, 90*, 125–152.

Loftus, E. F. (1979). *Eyewitness testimony.* Cambridge, MA: Harvard University Press.

Loftus, E. F., & Palmer, J. C. (1974). Reconstruction of automobile destruction: An example of the interaction between language and memory. *Journal of Verbal Learning and Verbal Behavior, 13*, 585–589.

Lohordo, V. M., & Droungas, A. (1989). Selective associations and adaptive specializations: Taste aversions and phobias. In S. B. Klein & R. R. Mowrer (Eds.), *Contemporary learning theories: Instrumental conditioning theory and the impact of biological constraints on learning*. Hillsdale, NJ: Erlbaum.

Luck, S. J., Hillyard, S. A., Mangun, G. R., & Gazzaniga, M. S. (1994). Independent attentional scanning in the separated hemispheres of split-brain patients. *Journal of Cognitive Neuroscience, 6*, 84–91.

Ludwig, P. J., & Maehr, M. L. (1967). Changes in self-concepts in stated behavioral preferences. *Child Development, 38*, 453–469.

Lutkehaus, N. C., & Greenfield, P. M. (2003). From *The Process of Education* to *The Culture of Education:* An intellectual biography of Jerome Bruner's contributions to education. In B. J. Zimmerman & D. H. Schunk (Eds.), *Educational psychology: A century of contributions*. Mahwah, NJ: Erlbaum.

Mager, R. F. (1962). *Preparing instructional objectives.* Belmont, CA: Fearon.

Malcolm, N. (1964). Behaviorism as a philosophy of psychology. In T. W. Wann (Ed.), *Behaviorism and phenomenology*. Chicago: University of Chicago Press.

Malone, T. (1981). Toward a theory of intrinsically motivating instruction. *Cognitive Science, 4*, 333–369.

Mandler, J. M., Johnson, N. S., & DeForest, M. (1976, April). *A structural analysis of stories and their recall: From "once upon a time" to "happily ever after."* Center for Human Information Processing Technical Report.

Mannes, S. M., & Kintsch, W. (1987). Knowledge organization and text organization. *Cognition and Instruction, 4*, 91–115.

Margolin, D. (1978). The hyperkinetic child syndrome and brain monoamines: Pharmacology and therapeutic implications. *Journal of Clinical Psychiatry, 39*, 130–140.

Margolis, M. (1987). *Patterns, thinking, and cognition: A theory of judgment.* Chicago: The University of Chicago Press.

Martinez, J. L., & Kesner, R. P. (1991). *Learning and memory: A biological view* (2nd ed.). San Diego: Academic Press.

Martinez, J., & Kesner, R. (Eds). (1998). *Neurobiology of learning and memory.* San Diego: Academic Press.

Matthews, W. J. (2003). Constructivism in the classroom: Epistemology, history, and empirical evidence. *Teacher Education Quarterly, 3*(Summer), 51–64.

Matlin, M. (1983). *Cognition.* New York: Holt, Rinehart & Winston.

Mayer, R. E. (1977). The sequencing of instruction and the concept of assimilation-to-schema. *Instructional Science, 6,* 369–388.

Mayer, R. E. (1979). Can advance organizers influence meaningful learning? *Review of Educational Research, 49,* 371–383.

Mayer, R. E. (2003). *Learning and Instruction.* Upper Saddle River, NJ: Pearson.

Mayer, R. E., & Gallini, J. K. (1990). When is an illustration worth ten thousand words? *Journal of Educational Psychology, 82,* 715–726.

McCall, R. B. (1990). The neuroscience of education: More research is needed before application. *Journal of Educational Psychology, 82,* 885–888.

McClelland, D., Atkinson, J. W., Clark, R. W., & Lowell, E. L. (1953). *The achievement motive.* New York: Appleton-Century-Crofts.

McClelland, J. L. (1988). Connectionist models and psychological evidence. *Journal of Memory and Language, 27,* 107–123.

McClelland, J. L. (1994). The organization of memory: A parallel distributed processing perspective. *Revue Neurologique, 150,* 570–579.

McClelland, J. L. (1995). A connectionist perspective on knowledge and development. In T. J. Simon & G. S. Halford (Eds.), *Developing cognitive competence: New approaches to process modeling.* Hillsdale, NJ: Erlbaum, Inc.

McClelland, J. L., Rumelhart, D. E., & the PDP Research Group. (1986). *Parallel distributed processing: Explorations in the microstructure of cognition* (Vol. II). Cambridge, MA: Bradford Books.

McCloskey, M., Caramazza, A., & Green, B. (1980). Curvilinear motion in the absence of external forces: Naive beliefs about the motion of objects. *Science, 210,* 1139–1141.

McGeoch, J. A. (1932). Forgetting and the law of disuse. *Psychological Review, 39,* 352–370.

McLellan, H. (1993). Situated learning in focus: Introduction to Special Issue. *Educational Technology, 33,* 5–9.

McLellan, H. (1994). Situated learning: Continuing the conversation. *Educational Technology, 34,* 7–8.

Mead, G. H. (1934). *Mind, self, and society from the standpoint of a social behaviorist* (C. W. Morris, Ed.). Chicago: University of Chicago Press.

Means, T. B. et al. (1997). Enhancing relevance: Embedded ARCS strategies vs. purpose. *Educational Technology Research & Development, 45,* 5–17.

Meece, J. L. (1994). The role of motivation in self-regulated learning. In D. H. Schunk & B. J. Zimmerman (Eds.), *Self-regulation of learning and performance.* Hillsdale, NJ: Erlbaum.

Merrill, M. D. (1983). Component display theory. In C. M. Reigeluth (Ed.), *Instructional-design theories and models.* Hillsdale, NJ: Erlbaum.

Miller, G. A. (1956). The magical number, seven, plus or minus two: Some limits on our capacity for processing information. In G. A. Miller (1967). *Psychological Review, 63,* 81–97.

Miller, G. A. (1967). *The psychology of communication.* Baltimore, MD: Penguin Books.

Miller, G. A. (1981). *Language and speech.* San Francisco: Freeman.

Minsky, M. (1975). A framework for representing knowledge. In P. H. Winston (Ed.), *The psychology of computer vision.* New York: McGraw-Hill.

Mishkin, M., Malamut, B., & Bachevalier, J. (1984). Memories and habits: Two neural systems. In G. Lynch, J. L. McGaugh, & N. M. Weinberger (Eds.), *Neurobiology of learning and memory.* New York: The Guilford Press.

Mishkin, M., & Petri, H. L. (1984). Memories and habits: Some implications for the analysis of learning and retention. In N. Butters & L. R. Squire (Eds.), *Neuropsychology of memory.* New York: The Guilford Press.

Morrison, D., & Collins, A. (1996). Epistemic fluency and constructivist learning environments. In B. G. Wilson (Ed.), *Constructivist learning environments: Case studies in instructional design.* Englewood Cliffs, NJ: Educational Technology Publications.

Mowrer, R. R., & Klein, S. B. (1989). A contrast between traditional and contemporary learning theory. In S. B. Klein & R. R. Mowrer (Eds.), *Contemporary learning theories: Instrumental conditioning theory and the impact of biological constraints on learning.* Hillsdale, NJ: Erlbaum.

Mulligan, J., Oglesby, S., & Perkins, M. R. (1980). *The status of on-site rehabilitation in private proprietary homes for adults: Issues, problems, and recommendations regarding program standards, guidelines, and training.* Report prepared for the Office of Mental Health, Albany, NY.

Myers, L. J. (1988). *Understanding an Afrocentric world view: Introduction to an optimal psychology.* Dubuque, IA: Kendall-Hunt.

National Research Council. (2000). *How people learn: Brain, mind, experience, and school.* Washington, D.C.: National Academy Press.

Nelson, L. M. (1999). Collaborative problem solving. In C. M. Reigeluth (Ed.), *Instructional-design theories and models.* Mahwah, NJ: Erlbaum.

Newby, T. J. (1991). Classroom motivation strategies of first-year teachers. *Journal of Educational Psychology, 83,* 195–200.

Newell, A., & Simon, H. A. (1972). *Human problem solving.* Englewood Cliffs, NJ: Prentice-Hall.

Newell, A., Simon, H. A., & Shaw, J. C. (1958). Elements of a theory of human problem solving. *Psychological Review, 65,* 151–166.

Newport, E. L., Gleitman, H., Gleitman, L. R. (1977). Mother I'd rather do it myself: Some effects and noneffects of maternal speech style. In C. E. Snow & C. A. Ferguson (Eds.), *Talking to children: Language input and acquisition.* New York: Cambridge University Press.

Nitko, A. J. (2001). *Educational assessment of students* (3rd ed.). Upper Saddle River, NJ: Merrill.

Norman, D. A. (1982). *Learning and memory.* San Francisco: Freeman.

Norman, D. A. (1983). Some observations on mental models. In D. Gentner & A. L. Stevens (Eds.), *Mental models.* Hillsdale, NJ: Erlbaum.

Norman, D. A., Gentner, D. R., & Stevens, A. L. (1976). Comments on learning schemata and memory representation. In D. Klahr (Ed.), *Cognition and instruction.* Hillsdale, NJ: Erlbaum.

Oakeshott, M. J. (1992). *Rationalism in politics, and other essays.* New York: Basic Books.

Okey, J. R., & Santiago, R. S. (1991). Integrating instructional design and motivational design. *Performance Improvement Quarterly, 4,* 11–21.

Oppenheimer, R. (1956). Analogy in science. *American Psychologist, 11,* 127–135.

Ormrod, J. E. (1990). *Human learning: Theories, principles, and educational applications.* Columbus, OH: Merrill.

Ormrod, J. E. (2004). *Human learning* (4th ed.). Upper Saddle River, NJ: Pearson.

Paas, F. G. W. C., Renkl, A., & Sweller, J. (2003). Cognitive load theory and instructional design: Recent developments. *Educational Psychologist, 38*(1), 1–4.

Paivio, A. (1971). *Imagery and verbal processes.* New York: Holt, Rinehart & Winston.

Paivio, A. (1986). *Mental representation: A dual-coding approach.* New York: Oxford University Press.

Paivio, A. (1991). Dual coding theory: Retrospect and current status. *Canadian Journal of Psychology, 45,* 255–287.

Paivio, A., Yuille, J. C., & Rogers, T. B. (1969). Noun imagery and meaningfulness in free and serial recall. *Journal of Experimental Psychology, 79,* 509–514.

Palincsar, A. S. (1986). The role of dialogue in scaffolded instruction. *Educational Psychologist, 21,* 73–98.

Palincsar, A. S. (1989). Debating the solution: A rejoinder to Palincsar and Wineburg. *Educational Researcher, 18,* 5–7.

Palincsar, A. S., & Brown, A. L. (1984). Reciprocal teaching of comprehension-fostering and monitoring activities. *Cognition and Instruction, 1,* 117–175.

Papert, S. (1980). *Mindstorms: Children, computers, and powerful ideas.* New York: Basic Books.

Papert, S. (1981). Computer-based microworlds as incubators for powerful ideas. In R. Taylor (Ed.), *The computer in the school: Tutor, tool, tutee.* New York: Teacher's College Press.

Paris, S. G., & Paris, A. H. (2001). Classroom applications of research on self-regulated learning. *Educational Psychologist, 36*(2), 89–101.

Pea, R. D. (1993a). The collaborative visualization project. *Communications of the ACM, 36,* 60–63.

Pea, R. D. (1993b). Practices of distributed intelligence and designs for education. In G. Salomon (Ed.), *Distributed cognition.* New York: Cambridge University Press.

Pea, R. D. (1994). Seeing what we build together: Distributed multimedia learning environments for transformative communications. *Journal of the Learning Sciences, 3,* 285–299.

Peirce, C. S. (1955). *Philosophical writings of Peirce.* J. Buchler (Ed.). New York: Dover.

Peper, R. J., & Mayer, R. E. (1978). Notetaking as a generative activity. *Journal of Educational Psychology, 70,* 514–522.

Perfetti, C. A., & Curtis, M. E. (1986). Reading. In R. F. Dillon & R. J. Sternberg (Eds.), *Cognition and instruction.* Orlando: Academic Press.

Perkins, D. N. (1991a, May). Technology meets constructivism: Do they make a marriage? *Educational Technology, 31,* 18–23.

Perkins, D. N. (1991b, September). What constructivism demands of the learner. *Educational Technology, 31,* 19–21.

Perkins, D. N., & Unger, C. (1999). Teaching and learning for understanding. In C. M. Reigeluth (Ed.), *Instructional-design theories and models.* Mahwah, NJ: Erlbaum.

Perner, J. (1991). *Understanding the representational mind.* Cambridge, MA: MIT Press.

Peterson, L. R., & Peterson, M. (1959). Short-term retention of individual items. *Journal of Experimental Psychology, 58,* 193–198.

Peterson, P. L., Carpenter, T., & Fennema, E. (1989). Teachers' knowledge of students' knowledge in mathematics problem solving: Correlational and case analyses. *Journal of Educational Psychology, 81,* 558–569.

Phillips, D. C. (1983, September/October). After the wake: Post-positivistic educational thought. *Educational Researcher, 12,* 4–12.

Phillips, D. C. (1995). The good, the bad, and the ugly: The many faces of constructivism. *Educational Researcher, 24,* 5–12.

Phye, G. D., & Andre, T. (Eds.). (1986). Cognitive classroom learning. Orlando: Academic Press.

Piaget, J. (1951). *Play, dreams, and imitation in childhood.* New York: Norton.

Piaget, J. (1969). *Science of education and the psychology of the child.* New York: Viking.

Piaget, J., & Inhelder, B. (1967). *The child's conception of space.* New York: Norton.

Piaget, J., & Inhelder, B. (1969). *The psychology of the child.* New York: Basic Books.

Pichert, J. W., & Anderson, R. C. (1977). Taking different perspectives on a story. *Journal of Educational Psychology, 69,* 309–315.

Picton, T. W., Stuss, D. T., & Marshall, K. C. (1986). Attention and the brain. In S. L. Friedman, K. A. Klivington, & R. W. Peterson (Eds.), *The brain, cognition and education.* Orlando: Academic Press.

Pine, K. J., & Messer, D. J. (2000). The effect of explaining another's actions on children's implicit theories of balance. *Cognition and Instruction, 18,* 35–51.

Pintrich, P. R. (1995). Understanding self-regulated learning. *New Directions for Teaching and Learning, 63,* 3–12.

Pintrich, P. R. (2000). The role of goal orientation in self-regulated learning. In M. Boekaerts & P. R. Pintrich & M. Zeidner (Eds.), *Handbook of self-regulation* (pp. 452–502). New York: Academic Press.

Posner, G. J., Strike, K. A., Hewson, P. W., & Gertzog, W. A. (1982). Accommodation of a scientific conception: Toward a theory of conceptual change. *Science Education, 66,* 211–227.

Posner, M. I. (1984). Selective attention and the storage of information. In G. Lynch, J. L. McGaugh, & N. M. Weinberger (Eds.), *Neurobiology of learning and memory.* New York: The Guilford Press.

Posner, M. I., & Friedrich, F. J. (1986). Attention and the control of cognition. In S. L. Friedman, K. A. Klivington, & R. W. Peterson (Eds.), *The brain, cognition and education.* Orlando: Academic Press.

Prawatt, R. S. (1989). Promoting access to knowledge strategy and disposition in students. *Review of Educational Research, 59,* 1–41.

Premack, D. (1959). Toward empirical behavior laws: I. Positive reinforcement. *Psychological Review, 66,* 219–233.

Pressey, S. L. (1926). A simple apparatus which gives tests and scores—and teaches. *School and Society, 23,* 373–376.

Pressey, S. L. (1927). A machine for automatic teaching of drill material. *School and Society, 25,* 549–552.

Pressey, S. L. (1964). Autoinstruction: Perspectives, problems, potentials. In E. R. Hilgard (Ed.), *Theories of learning and instruction.* Chicago: National Society for the Study of Education and University of Chicago Press.

Pressley, M., Borkowski, J. G., & O'Sullivan, J. R. (1984). Memory strategy instruction is made of this: Metamemory and durable strategy use. *Educational Psychologist, 19,* 94–107.

Pressley, M., & Levin, J. R. (1983). *Cognitive strategy research: Educational applications.* New York: Springer-Verlag.

Price, E. A., & Driscoll, M. P. (1997). An inquiry into the spontaneous transfer of problem-solving skill. *Contemporary Educational Psychology, 22,* 472–494.

Pylyshyn, Z. W. (1973). What the mind's eye tells the mind's brain: A critique of mental imagery. *Psychological Bulletin, 80,* 1–24.

Radziszewska, B., & Rogoff, B. (1988). The influence of collaboration with parents versus peers in learning to plan. *Developmental Psychology, 24,* 840–848.

Rayner, K., Well, A. D., & Pollatsek, A. (1980). Asymmetry of the effective visual field in reading. *Perception and Psychophysics, 27,* 537–544.

Reeves, T. C., & Okey, J. R. (1996). Alternative assessments for constructivist learning environments. In B. G. Wilson (Ed.), *Constructivist learning environments: Case studies in instructional design.* Englewood Cliffs, NJ: Educational Technology Publications.

Reigeluth, C. M. (1979). In search of a better way to organize instruction: The elaboration theory. *Journal of Instructional Development, 2,* 8–15.

Reigeluth, C. M. (1983). Instructional design: What is it and why is it? In C. M. Reigeluth (Ed.), *Instructional-design theories and models.* Hillsdale, NJ: Erlbaum.

Reigeluth, C. M., & Stein, F. (1983). The elaboration theory of instruction. In C. M. Reigeluth (Ed.), *Instructional-design theories and models.* Hillsdale, NJ: Erlbaum.

Reigeluth, C. M. (1999). *Instructional-design theories and models.* (Vol. II). Mahwah: Erlbaum.

Reigeluth, C. M. (1999). What is instructional-design theory and how is it changing? In C. M. Reigeluth (Ed.), *Instructional-design theories and models* (Vol. II, pp. 5–29). Mahwah: Erlbaum.

Reiser, R. A., & Dick, W. (1996). *Instructional planning: A guide for teachers.* Boston: Allyn & Bacon.

Reiser, R. A., Driscoll, M. P., & Vergara, A. (1987). The effects of ascending, descending, and fixed criteria on student performance and attitude in a mastery-oriented course. *Educational Communications and Technology Journal, 35,* 195–202.

Resnick, L. B. (1981). Instructional psychology. *Annual Review of Psychology, 32,* 659–704.

Reynolds, G. S. (1968). *A primer of operant conditioning.* Glenview, IL: Scott-Foresman.

Rice, G. E., & Meyer, B. J. F. (1985). Reading behavior and prose recall performance of young and older adults with high and average verbal ability. *Educational Gerontology, 11,* 57–72.

Rieber, L. P. (1991a). Animation, incidental learning, and continuing motivation. *Journal of Educational Psychology, 83,* 318–328.

Rieber, L. P. (1991b, February). *Computer-based microworlds: A bridge between constructivism and direct instruction.* Paper presented at the Annual Meeting of the Association of Educational Communications and Technology, Orlando.

Rieber, L. P. (1996). Seriously considering play: Designing interactive learning environments based on the blending of microworlds, simulations, and games. *Educational Technology Research & Development, 44*, 43–58.

Roediger, H. L., III (1980). Memory of metaphors in cognitive psychology. *Memory and Cognition, 8*, 231–246.

Rogoff, B. (1984). Introduction: Thinking and learning in social context. In B. Rogoff & J. Lave (Eds.), *Everyday cognition.* Cambridge, MA: Harvard University Press.

Rosch, E. H. (1973). Natural categories. *Cognitive Psychology, 4*, 328–350.

Rosch, E. H. (1975). Cognitive representations of semantic categories. *Journal of Experimental Psychology: General, 104*, 192–233.

Rose, M. (1999). "Our hands will know": The development of tactile diagnostic skill—Teaching, learning, and situated cognition. *Anthropology & Education Quarterly, 30*(2), 133–160.

Rosenthal, R., & Jacobson, L. (1968). *Pygmalion in the classroom: Teacher expectation and pupils' intellectual development.* New York: Holt, Rinehart & Winston.

Rosenzweig, M. R. (1984). Experience, memory, and the brain. *American Psychologist, 39*, 365–376.

Rosenzweig, M. R. (1986). Multiple models of memory. In S. L. Friedman, K. A. Klivington, & R. W. Peterson (Eds.), *The brain, cognition and education.* Orlando: Academic Press.

Rosenzweig, M. R. (1998). Historical perspectives on the development of the biology of learning and memory. In J. Martinez & R. Kesner (Eds.), *Neurobiology of learning and memory.* San Diego: Academic Press.

Roth, K. T., Anderson, C. W., & Smith, E. L. (1986, February). *Curriculum materials, teacher talk, and student learning: Case studies in fifth-grade science teaching.* East Lansing: Michigan State University, The Institute for Research on Teaching.

Rotter, J. B. (1966). Generalized expectancies for internal versus external control of reinforcements. *Psychological Monographs, 80*, 1–28.

Royer, J. M. (1990). The sentence verification technique: A new direction in the assessment of reading comprehension. In S. Legg & J. Algina (Eds.), *Cognitive assessment of language and math outcomes. Advances in discourse processes* (Vol. 36). Norwood, NJ: Ablex.

Royer, J. M. (1996). The assessment of levels of domain expertise while reading. *Cognition and Instruction, 14*, 373–408.

Royer, J. M., & Cable, G. W. (1975). Facilitated learning in connected discourse. *Journal of Educational Psychology, 67*, 116–123.

Royer, J. M., Lynch, D. J., Hambleton, R. K., & Bulgareli, C. (1984). Using the sentence verification technique to assess the comprehension of technical text as a function of subject matter expertise. *American Educational Research Journal, 21*, 839–869.

Royer, J. M., & Perkins, M. R. (1977). Facilitative transfer in prose learning over an extended time period. *Journal of Reading Behavior, 9*, 185–188.

Royer, J. M., Perkins, M. R., & Konold, C. E. (1978). Evidence for a selective storage mechanism in prose learning. *Journal of Educational Psychology, 70*, 457–462.

Rumelhart, D. E. (1975). Notes on a schema for stories. In D. G. Bobrow & A. M. Collins (Eds.), *Representation and understanding: Studies in cognitive science.* New York: Academic Press.

Rumelhart, D. E. (1980). Schemata: The building blocks of cognition. In R. J. Spiro, B. C. Bruce, & W. F. Brewer (Eds.), *Theoretical issues in reading comprehension.* Hillsdale, NJ: Erlbaum.

Rumelhart, D. E. (1995). Brain style computation: Learning and generalization. In S. F. Zornetzer, J. L. Davis, C. Lau, & T. McKenna (Eds.), An introduction to neural and electronic networks (2nd ed.). *Neural networks: Foundations to applications.* San Diego: Academic Press.

Rumelhart, D. E., & Norman, D. A. (1978). Accretion, tuning, and restructuring: Three modes of learning. In J. W. Cotton & R. L. Klatzky (Eds.), *Semantic factors in cognition.* Hillsdale, NJ: Erlbaum.

Rumelhart, D. E., & Norman, D. A. (1981). Analogical processes in learning. In J. R. Anderson (Ed.), *Cognitive skills and their acquisition.* Hillsdale, NJ: Erlbaum.

Russell, J. (1982). Cognitive conflict, transmission, and justification: Conservation attainment through dyadic interaction. *Journal of Genetic Psychology, 140,* 287–297.

Sagan, C. (1977). *The dragons of Eden: Speculations on the evolution of human intelligence.* New York: Ballantine Books.

Salomon, G., & Perkins, D. N. (1987). Transfer of cognitive skills from programming: When and how? *Journal of Educational Computing Research, 3,* 149–169.

Sarter, M., Berntson, G. G., & Cacioppo, J. T. (1996). Brain imaging and cognitive neurosciences: Toward strong inference in attributing function to structure. *American Psychologist, 51,* 13–21.

Savery, J. R., & Duffy, T. M. (1996). Problem-based learning: An instructional model and its constructivist framework. In B. G. Wilson (Ed.), *Constructivist learning environments: Case studies in instructional design.* Englewood Cliffs, NJ: Educational Technology Publications.

Sawyer, R. J., Craham, S., & Harris, K. R. (1992). Direct teaching, strategy instruction, and strategy instruction with explicit self-regulation: Effects on the composition skills and self-efficacy of students with learning disabilities. *Journal of Educational Research, 84,* 340–352.

Saxe, G. B. (1977). A developmental analysis of notational counting. *Child Development, 48,* 1512–1520.

Saxe, G. B. (1982). Developing forms of arithmetical thought among Oksapmin of Papua, New Guinea. *Developmental Psychology, 18,* 583–594.

Saxe, G. B. (1990). *Culture and cognitive development: Studies in mathematical understanding.* Hillsdale, NJ: Erlbaum.

Scaife, M. (1985). The implications of a structuralist biology for developmental psychology. In G. Butterworth, J. Rutkowska, & M. Scaife (Eds.), *Evolution and developmental psychology.* Great Britain: The Harvester Press.

Scardamalia, M., & Bereiter, C. (1994). Computer support for knowledge-building communities. *Journal of the Learning Sciences, 3,* 265–283.

Scardamalia, M., & Bereiter, C. (1996). Adaptation and understanding: A case for new cultures of schooling. In S. Vosniadou, E. deCorte, R. Glaser, & H. Mandl (Eds.), *International perspectives on the design of technology-supported learning environments.* Mahwah, NJ: Erlbaum.

Scardamalia, M., Bereiter, C., McLean, R. S., Swallow, J., & Woodruff, E. (1989). Computer supported intentional learning environments. *Journal of Educational Computing Research, 5,* 51–68.

Schacter, D. L. (1992). Understanding implicit memory: A cognitive neuroscience approach. *American Psychologist, 47,* 559–569.

Schacter, D. L., & Tulving, E. (Eds.). (1994). *Memory systems 1994.* Cambridge, MA: MIT Press.

Schank, R. C., & Abelson, R. P. (1975). Scripts, plans, and knowledge. *Advance Papers of the Fourth International Joint Conference on Artificial Intelligence.* Tbilisi, Georgia, USSR.

Schank, R. C., & Abelson, R. P. (1977). *Scripts, plans, goals, and understanding.* Hillsdale, NJ: Erlbaum.

Schank, R. C., Berman, T., & Macpherson, K. A. (1999). Learning by doing. In C. M. Reigeluth (Ed..), *Instructional-design theories and models.* Mahwah, NJ: Erlbaum.

Schank, R. C., Fano, A., Bell, B., & Jona, M. (1993/1994). The design of goal-based scenarios. *Journal of the Learning Sciences, 3,* 305–346.

Schoenfeld, A. H. (1985). *Mathematical problem solving.* New York: Academic Press.

Schoenfeld, A. H. (1988). When good teaching leads to bad results: The disasters of "well-taught" mathematics courses. *Educational Psychologist, 23,* 145–166.

Schoenfeld, W. N. (1993). The necessity of "behaviorism." *Educational Technology,* Special Issue: Behaviorism Today, *33,* 5–7.

Schommer, M. (1994). Synthesizing epistemological belief research: Tentative understandings and provocative confusions. *Educational Psychology Review, 6,* 293–319.

Schooler, L. J., & Anderson, J. R. (1997). The role of process in the rational analysis of memory. *Cognitive Psychology, 32,* 219–250.

Schott, F., & Driscoll, M. P. (1997). On the architectonics of instructional theory. In R. Tennyson & F. Schott (Eds.), *Instructional design: International perspectives,* (Vol. 1). Hillsdale, NJ: Erlbaum.

Schunk, D. H. (1987). Peer models and children's behavioral change. *Review of Educational Research, 57,* 149–174.

Schunk, D. H. (1990). Introduction to the special section on motivation and efficacy. *Journal of Educational Psychology, 82,* 3–6.

Schunk, D. H. (2004). *Learning theories: An educational perspective* (4th ed.). Upper Saddle River, NJ: Pearson.

Schunk, D. H., & Gaa, J. P. (1981). Goal-setting influence on learning and self-evaluation. *Journal of Classroom Interaction, 16,* 38–44.

Schunk, D. H., & Hanson, A. R. (1985). Peer models: Influence on children's self-efficacy and achievement. *Journal of Educational Psychology, 77,* 313–322.

Schunk, D. H., & Zimmerman, B. J. (1994). *Self-regulation in education: Retrospect and prospect.* In D. H. Schunk & B. J. Zimmerman (Eds.), *Self-regulation of learning and performance.* Hillsdale, NJ: Erlbaum.

Schwartz, D. L., Lin, Z., Brophy, S., & Bransford, J. D. (1999). Toward the development of flexibly adaptive instructional designs. In C. M. Reigeluth (Ed.), *Instructional-design theories and models.* Mahwah, NJ: Erlbaum.

Scribner, S. (1984). Studying working intelligence. In B. Rogoff & J. Lave (Eds.), *Everyday cognition.* Cambridge, MA: Harvard University Press.

Segal, J. W., Chipman, S. F., & Glaser, R. (1985). *Thinking and learning skills: Relating instruction to research* (Vol. 1). Hillsdale, NJ: Erlbaum.

Seligman, M. E. P., & Maier, S. F. (1967). Failure to escape traumatic shock. *Journal of Experimental Psychology, 74,* 1–9.

Sen, A., & Posner, M. I. (1979). The effect of unattended visual and auditory words on cross modal naming. *Bulletin of the Psychonomic Society, 13,* 405–408.

Shank, G. (1988). Three into two will go: juxtapositional strategies for empirical research in semiotics. In J. Deely (Ed.), *Semiotics 1987.* New York: University Press of America.

Shank, G. (1990). Qualitative vs. quantitative research: A semiotic non-problem. In T. Prewitt, J. Deely, & K. Haworth (Eds.), *Semiotics: 1989* (pp. 264–270). Washington, D.C.: University Press of America.

Shank, G. (1992). Educational semiotic: Threat or menace? *Educational Psychology Review, 4,* 195–209.

Shepard, R. N. (1978). The mental image. *American Psychologist, 33,* 125–137.

Shiffrin, R. M., & Schneider, W. (1977). Controlled and automatic human information processing. II. Perceptual learning, automatic attending, and a general theory. *Psychological Review, 84,* 127–190.

Shulman, L. S. (1988). Disciplines of inquiry in education: An overview. In R. M. Jaeger (Ed.), *Complementary methods for research in education.* Washington, DC: American Educational Research Association.

Siegler, R. S. (1983). Five generalizations about cognitive development. *American Psychologist, 38,* 263–277.

Siegler, R. S. (1984). Mechanisms of cognitive growth: Variation and selection. In R. J. Sternberg (Ed.), *Mechanisms of cognitive development.* New York: Freeman.

Siegler, R. S. (1986). *Children's thinking.* Englewood Cliffs, NJ: Prentice-Hall.

Siegler, R. S. (1995). How does change occur: A microgenetic study of number conservation. *Cognitive Psychology, 28,* 225–273.

Siegler, R. S. (1996). *Emerging minds: The process of change in children's thinking.* New York: Oxford University Press.

Siegler, R. S., & Klahr, D. (1982). What do children learn? The relationship between existing knowledge and the acquisition of new knowledge. In R. Glaser (Ed.), *Advances in instructional psychology.* Hillsdale, NJ: Erlbaum.

Siegler, R. S., & Richards, D. (1982). The development of intelligence. In R. J. Sternberg (Ed.), *Handbook of human intelligence.* Cambridge, England: Cambridge University Press.

Siegler, R. S., & Svetina, M. (2002). A microgenetic/cross-sectional study of matrix completion: comparing short-term and long-term change. *Child Development, 73*(13), 793–810.

Simon, H. (1986). The role of attention in cognition. In S. L. Friedman, K. A. Klivington, & R. W. Peterson (Eds.), *The brain, cognition and education.* Orlando: Academic Press.

Simon, T. J., & Klahr, D. (1995). A computational theory of children's learning about number conservation. In T. J. Simon & G. S. Halford (Eds.), *Developing cognitive competence.* Hillsdale, NJ: Erlbaum.

Simpson, E. J. (1966–67). The classification of educational objectives, psychomotor domain. *Illinois Teacher of Home Economics, 10,* 110–144.

Singer, R. N. (1980). *Motor learning and human performance* (3rd ed.). New York: Macmillan.

Singer, R. N., & Dick, W. (1980). *Teaching physical education* (2nd ed.). Boston: Houghton Mifflin.

Skinner, B. F. (1938). *The behavior of organisms: An experimental analysis.* Englewood Cliffs, NJ: Prentice-Hall.

Skinner, B. F. (1948). Surperstition in the pigeon. *Journal of Experimental Psychology, 38,* 168–172.

Skinner, B. F. (1950). Are theories of learning necessary? *Psychological Review, 57,* 193–216.

Skinner, B. F. (1957). *Verbal behavior.* Englewood Cliffs, NJ: Prentice-Hall.

Skinner, B. F. (1958). Reinforcement today. *American Psychologist, 13,* 94–99.

Skinner, B. F. (1969). *Contingencies of reinforcement.* Englewood Cliffs, NJ: Prentice-Hall.

Skinner, B. F. (1974). *About behaviorism.* New York: Knopf.

Skinner, B. F. (1987). Whatever happened to psychology as the science of behavior? *American Psychologist, 42,* 780–786.

Skinner, B. F., & Krakower, S. (1968). *Handwriting with write and see.* Chicago: Lyons & Carnahan.

Slavin, R. E. (1991, February). Synthesis of research on cooperative learning. *Educational Leadership, 48,* 71–77.

Smith, E. E., Shoben, E. J., & Rips, L. J. (1974). Structure and process in semantic memory: A featural model for semantic decision. *Psychological Review, 81,* 214–241.

Snowman, J. (1986). Learning tactics and strategies. In G. D. Phye & T. Andre (Eds.), *Cognitive classroom learning.* Orlando: Academic Press.

Solnick, J. V., Rincover, A., & Peterson, C. R. (1977). Some determinants of the reinforcing and punishing effects of timeout. *Journal of Applied Behavior Analysis, 10,* 415–424.

Spence, I., & Hively, W. (1993). What makes Chris practice? *Educational Technology,* Special Issue: *Behaviorism Today, 33,* 15–20.

Sperber, D. (1994). The modularity of thought and the epidemiology of representations. In L. A. Hirschfeld & S. A. Gelman (Eds.), *Mapping the mind: Domain specificity in cognition and culture.* New York: Cambridge University Press.

Sperling, G. (1960). The information available in brief visual presentations. *Psychological Monographs, 74* (Whole No. 498).

Spielberger, C. D. (Ed.). (1966). *Anxiety and behavior.* New York: Academic Press.

Spilich, G. J., Vesonder, G. T., Chiesi, H. L., & Voss, J. F. (1979). Text processing of domain-related information for individuals with high and low domain knowledge. *Journal of Verbal Learning and Verbal Behavior, 18,* 275–290.

Spiro, R. J. (1977). Remembering information from text: Theoretical and empirical issues concerning the "State of Schema" reconstruction hypothesis. In R. C. Anderson, R. J. Spiro, & W. E. Montague (Eds.), *Schooling and the acquisition of knowledge.* Hillsdale, NJ: Erlbaum.

Spiro, R. J., Coulson, R. L., Feltovich, P. J., & Anderson, D. K. (1988). Cognitive flexibility theory: Advanced knowledge acquisition in ill-structured domains. In *Tenth Annual Conference of the Cognitive Science Society.* Hillsdale, NJ: Erlbaum.

Spiro, R. J., Feltovich, P. J., Jacobson, M. J., & Coulson, R. L. (1991, May). Cognitive flexibility, constructivism, and hypertext: Random access instruction for advanced knowledge acquisition in ill-structured domains. *Educational Technology, 31,* 24–33.

Spiro, R. J., Feltovich, P. J., Jacobson, M. J., & Coulson, R. L. (1995). Cognitive flexibility, constructivism, and hypertext: Random access instruction for advanced knowledge acquisition in ill-structured domains. In L. P. Steffe & J. Gale (Eds.), *Constructivism in instruction*. Hillsdale, NJ: Erlbaum.

Spiro, R. J., & Jehng, J. C. (1990). Cognitive flexibility and hypertext: Theory and technology for the nonlinear and multidimensional traversal of complex subject matter. In D. Nix & R. J. Spiro (Eds.), *Cognition, education and multimedia*. Hillsdale, NJ: Erlbaum.

Spiro, R. J., Vispoel, W., Schmitz, J., Samarapungavan, A., & Boerger, A. (1987). Knowledge acquisition for application: Cognitive flexibility and transfer in complex content domains. In B. C. Britton (Ed.), *Executive control process*. Hillsdale, NJ: Erlbaum.

Squire, L. R. (1983). The hippocampus and the neuropsychology of memory. In W. Seifert (Ed.), *Neurobiology of the hippocampus*. New York: Academic Press.

Squire, L. R. (1986). Memory and the brain. In S. L. Friedman, K. A. Klivington, & R. W. Peterson (Eds.), *The brain, cognition and education*. Orlando: Academic Press.

Squire, L. R. (1994). Declarative and nondeclarative memory: Multiple brain systems supporting learning and memory. In D. L. Schacter & E. Tulving (Eds.), *Memory systems 1994*. Cambridge, MA: MIT Press.

Squire, L. R., & Knowlton, B. J. (1995). Memory, hippocampus, and brain systems. In M. S. Gazzaniga (Ed.), *The cognitive neurosciences*. Cambridge, MA: MIT Press.

Stamm, J. S., & Kreder, S. V. (1979). Minimal brain dysfunction: Psychological and neurophysiological disorders in hyperkinetic children. In M. Gazzaniga (Ed.), *Handbook of behavioral neurobiology. Vol. 2: Neuropsychology*. New York. Plenum Press.

Steinberg, E. (1989). Cognition and learner control: A literature review, 1977–1988. *Journal of Computer-Based Instruction, 16*, 117–121.

Steinmetz, S. K. (1977). *The cycle of violence*. New York: Praeger.

Sternberg, R. J. (1984a). Preface. *Mechanisms of cognitive development*. New York: Freeman.

Sternberg, R. J. (1984b). Mechanisms of cognitive development: A componential approach. In R. J. Sternberg (Ed.), *Mechanisms of cognitive development*. New York: Freeman.

Sternberg, R. J. (1985). *Beyond IQ: A triarchic theory of human intelligence*. New York: Cambridge University Press.

Sternberg, R. J., & Davidson, J. E. (1983). Insight in the gifted. *Educational Psychologist, 18*, 52–58.

Sternberg, R. J. (1997). *The triarchic theory of intelligence*. New York: The Guilford Press.

Stevens, A. L., & Collins, A. (1980). Multiple conceptual models of a complex system. In R. Snow, P. Federico, & W. Montague (Eds.), *Aptitude, learning and instruction: Cognitive process analysis*. Hillsdale, NJ: Erlbaum.

Stolovitch, H. D., & Keeps, E. J. (Eds.). (1992). *Handbook of human performance technology*. San Francisco: Jossey-Bass.

Strauss, M. A., Gelles, R. J., & Steinmetz, S. K. (1980). *Behind closed doors: Violence in the American family*. Garden City, NY: Doubleday.

Streibel, M. J. (1993). Queries about computer education and situated critical pedagogy. *Educational Technology, 33*, 22–26.

Streibel, M. J. (1994). Misattributions about situated learning. *Educational Technology, 34*, 14–16.

Suchman, L. (1987). *Plans and situated actions: The problem of human-machine communication*. Cambridge: Cambridge University Press.

Sui, P. K. (1986). Understanding Chinese prose: Effects of number of ideas, metaphor, and advance organizers on comprehension. *Journal of Educational Psychology, 78,* 417–423.

Sulin, R. A., & Dooling, D. J. (1974). Intrusion of a thematic idea in retention of prose. *Journal of Experimental Psychology, 103,* 255–262.

Sulzer, B., & Mayer, G. R. (1972). *Behavior modification procedures for school personnel.* Hinsdale, IL: Dryden Press.

Sussman, D. M. (1981). PSI: Variations on a theme. In S. W. Bijou & R. Ruiz (Eds.), *Behavior modification: Contributions to education.* Hillsdale, NJ: Erlbaum.

Sweller, J., Mawer, R. F., & Ward, M. R. (1983). Development of expertise in mathematical problem solving. *Journal of Experimental Psychology: General, 112,* 639–661.

Sweller, J. (1989). Cognitive technology: Some procedures for facilitating learning and problem solving in mathematics and science. *Journal of Educational Psychology, 81,* 457–466.

Sweller, J., van Merrienboer, J. J. G., & Paas, F. G. W. C. (1998). Cognitive architecture and instructional design. *Educational Psychology Review, 10*(3), 251–296.

Symons, D. (1992). On the use and misuse of Darwinism in the study of social behavior. In J. H. Barkow, L. Cosmides, & J. Tooby (Eds.), *The adapted mind: Evolutionary psychology and the generation of culture.* New York: Oxford University Press.

Tennyson, R. D., & Cocchiarella, M. J. (1986). An empirically based instructional design theory for teaching concepts. *Review of Educational Research, 56,* 40–71.

Terrace, H. (1963a). Discrimination learning with and without errors. *Journal of Experimental Analysis of Behavior, 6,* 1–27.

Terrace, H. (1963b). Errorless transfer of a discrimination across two continua. *Journal of Experimental Analysis of Behavior, 6,* 223–232.

Tessmer, M., & Driscoll, M. P. (1986). Effects of a diagrammatic display of concept definitions on classification performance. *Educational Communications and Technology Journal, 34,* 195–205.

Tessmer, M., Wilson, B., & Driscoll, M. (1990). A new model of concept teaching and learning. *Educational Technology Research and Development, 38,* 45–54.

Thomson, D. M., & Tulving, E. (1970). Associative encoding and retrieval: Weak and strong cues. *Journal of Experimental Psychology, 86,* 255–262.

Thompson, R. F. (1994). Behaviorism and neuroscience. *Psychological Review, 101,* 259–265.

Thorndike, E. L. (1913). *Educational psychology. Vol. II. The psychology of learning.* New York: Teachers College, Columbia University.

Timberlake, W., & Lucas, G. A. (1989). Behavior systems and learning: From misbehavior to general principles. In S. B. Klein & R. R. Mowrer (Eds.), *Contemporary learning theories: Instrumental conditioning theory and the impact of biological constraints on learning.* Hillsdale, NJ: Erlbaum.

Tobias, S. (1976). Achievement-treatment interaction. *Review of Educational Research, 46,* 61–74.

Tobin, K., & Dawson, G. (1992). Constraints to curriculum reform: Teachers and the myths of schooling. *Educational Technology Research and Development, 40,* 81–92.

Tolman, E. C. (1948). Cognitive maps in rats and men. *Psychological Review, 55,* 189–208.

Tooby, J., & Cosmides, L. (1989). Evolutionary psychology and the generation of culture, Part I: Theoretical considerations. *Ethology and Sociobiology, 10,* 29–49.

Tooby, J., & Cosmides, L. (1992). The psychological foundations of culture. In J. H. Barkow, L. Cosmides, & J. Tooby (Eds.), *The adapted mind: Evolutionary psychology and the generation of culture.* New York: Oxford University Press.

Torello, M. W., & Duffy, F. H. (1985). Using brain electrical activity mapping to diagnose learning disabilities. *Theory into Practice, 25,* 95–99.

Torgeson, J. K. (1977). The role of nonspecific factors in the task performance of learning disabled children: A theoretical assessment. *Journal of Learning Disabilities, 10,* 27–34.

Treisman, A. M. (1960). Contextual cues in selective listening. *Quarterly Journal of Experimental Psychology, 12,* 242–248.

Tripp, S. D. (1993). Theories, traditions, and situated learning. *Educational Technology, 33,* 71–77.

Tudge, J., & Rogoff, B. (1989). Peer influences on cognitive development: Piagetian and Vygotskian perspectives. In M. H. Bornstein & J. S. Bruner (Eds.), *Interaction in human development.* Hillsdale, NJ: Erlbaum.

Tudge, J., & Scrimsher, S. (2003). Lev S. Vygotsky on education: A cultural-historical, interpersonal, and individual approach to development. In B. J. Zimmerman & D. H. Schunk (Eds.), *Educational psychology: A century of contributions.* Mahwah, NJ: Erlbaum.

Tulving, E. (1962). Subjective organization in free recall of "unrelated" words. *Psychological Review, 69,* 344–354.

Tulving, E. (1972). Episodic and semantic memory. In E. Tulving & W. Donaldson (Eds.), *Organization and memory.* New York: Academic Press.

Tulving, E., & Thomson, D. M. (1973). Encoding specificity and retrieval processes in episodic memory. *Psychological Review, 80,* 352–373.

Turvey, M. T., & Shaw, R. E. (1995). Toward an ecological physics and a physical psychology. In R. L. Solso & D. W. Massaro (Eds.), *The science of the mind.* New York: Oxford University Press.

Vaccarino, F. J., Schiff, B. B., & Glickman, S. E. (1989). Biological view of reinforcement. In S. B. Klein & R. R. Mowrer (Eds.), *Contemporary learning theories: Instrumental conditioning theory and the impact of biological constraints on learning.* Hillsdale, NJ: Erlbaum.

van Dijk, T. A., & Kintsch, W. (1983). *Strategies of discourse comprehension.* New York: Academic Press.

Varnhagen, C. K., & Goldman, S. R. (1986). Improving comprehension: Causal relations instruction for learning handicapped learners. *The Reading Teacher, 39,* 896–904.

Vera, A. H., & Simon, H. A. (1993). Situated action: A symbolic interpretation. *Cognitive Science, 17,* 7–48.

Visser, J., & Keller, J. M. (1990). The clinical use of motivational messages: An inquiry into the validity of the ARCS model of motivational design. *Instructional Science, 19,* 467–500.

von Glasersfeld, E. (1984). An introduction to radical constructivism. In P. Watzlaw-ick (Ed.), *The invented reality*. New York: Norton.

von Glasersfeld, E. (Ed.) (1991). *Radical constructivism in mathematics education*. Dordrecht, The Netherlands: Kluwer.

von Glasersfeld, E. (1995). A constructivist approach to teaching. In L. P. Steffe & J. Gale (Eds.), *Constructivism in instruction*. Hillsdale, NJ: Erlbaum.

von Glasersfeld, E. (Ed.) (2002). *Radical constructivism in mathematics education*. New York: Kluwer.

Vosniadou, S. (1988, April). *Knowledge restructuring and science education*. Paper presented at the Annual Meeting of the American Educational Research Association, New Orleans, LA.

Vosniadou, S., & Brewer, W. F. (1987). Theories of knowledge restructuring in development. *Review of Educational Research, 57,* 51–67.

Vosniadou, S. (1992). Mental models of the earth: A study of conceptual change in childhood. *Cognitive Psychology, 24,* 535–585.

Vygotsky, L. S. (1934/1987). *The collected works of L. S. Vygotsky*. R. W. Rieber & A. Carton (Eds.). New York: Plenum Press.

Vygotsky, L. S. (1962). *Thought and language*. Cambridge, MA: MIT Press.

Vygotsky, L. S. (1978). *Mind in society*. Cambridge, MA: Harvard University Press.

Vygotsky, L. S. (1981). The genesis of higher mental functions. In J. V. Wertsch (Ed.), *The concept of activity in Soviet psychology*. Armonk, NY: Sharpe.

Wadsworth, B. J. (1978). *Piaget for the classroom teacher*. New York: Longman.

Wadsworth, B. J. (1996). *Piaget's theory of cognitive and affective development* (5th ed.). White Plains, NY: Longman.

Wager, W. W., & Driscoll, M. P. (1999). *Seeking indicators of transformation*. Paper presented at the Annual Meeting of the Association for Educational Communications and Technology, Houston, TX.

Walkerdine, V. (1997). Redefining the subject in situated cognition theory. In D. Kirshner & J. A. Whitson (Eds.), *Situated cognition: Social, semiotic, and psychological perspectives*. Mahwah, NJ: Erlbaum.

Walters, G. C., & Grusec, J. E. (1977). *Punishment*. San Francisco: Freeman.

Wang, M. C., & Palincsar, A. S. (1989). Teaching students to assume an active role in their learning. In M. C. Reynolds (Ed.), *Knowledge base for the beginning teacher*. New York: Pergamon Press for the American Association of Colleges for Teacher Education.

Wason, P. (1968). Reasoning about a rule. *Quarterly Journal of Experimental Psychology, 20,* 273–281.

Wason, P., & Shapiro, D. (1971). Natural and contrived experience in a reasoning problem. *Quarterly Journal of Experimental Psychology, 23,* 63–71.

Watson, J. B. (1913). Psychology as the behaviorist views it. *Psychological Review, 20,* 158–177.

Watson, J. B., & Rayner, R. (1920). Conditioned emotional reactions. *Journal of Experimental Psychology, 3,* 1–14.

Weiner, B. (1979). A theory of motivation for some classroom experiences. *Journal of Educational Psychology, 71,* 3–25.

Weiner, B. (1985). An attributional theory of achievement motivation and emotion. *Psychological Review, 92,* 548–573.

Weiner, B. (1986). *An attributional theory of motivation and emotion.* New York: Springer-Verlag.

Weiner, B. (1990). History of motivational research in education. *Journal of Educational Psychology, 82,* 616–622.

Weiner, B. (1992). *Human motivation: Metaphors, theories, and research.* Newbury Park, CA: Sage.

Weiner, H. (1969). Controlling human fixed-interval performance. *Journal of Experimental Analysis of Behavior, 12,* 349–373.

Weinstein, C. E. (1982). A metacurriculum for remediating learning strategy deficits in academically unprepared students. In L. Noel & R. Levitz (Eds.), *How to succeed with academically unprepared students.* Iowa City, IA: American College Testing Service.

Wenger, E. (1998). *Communities of practice: Learning, meaning, and identity.* New York: Cambridge University Press.

Werner, H. (1957). The concept of development from a comparative and organismic point of view. In D. Harris (Ed.), *The concept of development.* Minneapolis: The University of Minnesota Press.

Wertheimer, M. (1959). *Productive thinking.* New York: Harper & Row.

Wertsch, J. V. (1984). The zone of proximal development: Some conceptual issues. In B. Rogoff & J. V. Wertsch (Eds.), *New directions for child development.* No. 23: *Children's learning in the "zone of proximal development."* San Francisco: Jossey-Bass.

Wertsch, J. V. (1985). *Vygotsky and the social formation of mind.* Cambridge, MA: Harvard University Press.

Wertsch, J. V. (1998). *Mind as action.* New York: Oxford University Press.

Wertsch, J. V., & Sohmer, R. (1995). Vygotsky on learning and development. *Human Development, 38,* 332–337.

Wertsch, J. V., & Tulviste, P. (1992). L. S. Vygotsky and contemporary developmental psychology. *Developmental Psychology, 28,* 548–557.

Wertsch, J. V., del Rio, P., & Alvarez, A. (Eds.). (1995). *Sociocultural studies of mind.* New York: Cambridge University Press.

West, C. K., Farmer, J. A., & Wolff, P. M. (1991). *Instructional design: Implications from cognitive science.* Englewood Cliffs, NJ: Prentice-Hall.

West, L. H. T., & Fensham, P. J. (1976). Prior knowledge or advance organizers as effective variables in chemical learning. *Journal of Research in Science Teaching, 13,* 297–306.

White, N. M., & Salinas, J. A. (1998). Pharmacological approaches to the study of learning and memory. In J. Martinez & R. Kesner (Eds.), *Neurobiology of learning and memory.* San Diego: Academic Press.

White, R. W. (1959). Motivation reconsidered: The concept of competence. *Psychological Review, 66,* 297–333.

Whitson, J. A. (1997). Cognition as a semiosic process: From situated mediation to critical reflective transcendence. In D. Kirshner & J. A. Whitson (Eds.), *Situated cognition: Social, semiotic, and psychological perspectives.* Mahwah, NJ: Erlbaum.

Wilson, B. G. (1996). What is a constructivist learning environment? In B. G. Wilson (Ed.), *Constructivist learning environments: Case studies in instructional design.* Englewood Cliffs, NJ: Educational Technology Publications.

Wilson, E. O. (1998). *Consilience: The unity of knowledge.* NY: Knopf.

Wineburg, S. S. (1989, May). Remembrance of theories past. *Educational Researcher, 18,* 7–10.

Wittrock, M. C. (1985a). Teaching learners generative strategies for enhancing reading comprehension. *Theory into Practice, 24,* 123–126.

Wittrock, M. C. (1985b). The generative learning model and its implications for science education. *Studies in Science Education, 12,* 59–87.

Wolf, M. M., Risley, T. R., & Mees, H. L. (1964). Application of operant conditioning procedures to the behavior problems of an autistic child. *Behavior Research and Therapy, 1,* 305–312.

Wolpe, J. (1958). *Psychotherapy by reciprocal inhibition.* Stanford, CA: Stanford University Press.

Wolpe, J. (1969). *The practice of behavior therapy.* Oxford: Pergamon Press.

Wood, D., Bruner, J. S., & Ross, G. (1976). The role of tutoring in problem solving. *Journal of Child Psychology and Psychiatry, 17,* 89–100.

Yuille, J. C., & Cutshall, J. L. (1986). A case study of eyewitness memory of a crime. *Journal of Applied Psychology, 71,* 291–301.

Zigon, J. (1997). Rewards and performance incentives. In R. Kaufman, S. Thiagarajan, & P. MacGillis. (Eds.), *The guidebook for performance improvement.* San Francisco: Pfeiffer.

Zimmerman, B. (1994). Dimensions of academic self-regulation: A conceptual framework for education. In D. H. Schunk & B. J. Zimmerman (Eds.), *Self-regulation of learning and performance.* Hillsdale, NJ: Erlbaum.

Zimmerman, B., & Schunk, D. (1989). *Self-regulated learning and academic achievement: Theory, research, and practice.* New York: Springer-Verlag.

Zimmerman, B. J. (1989). A social cognitive view of self-regulated academic learning. *Journal of Educational Psychology, 81,* 329–339.

Index